The Routledge Handbook of Multimodal Analysis

Multimodality is an innovative approach to representation, communication and interaction which looks beyond language to investigate the multitude of ways we communicate: through images, sound and music to gestures, body posture and the use of space.

The Routledge Handbook of Multimodal Analysis, Second Edition provides a comprehensive 'research tool kit' for multimodal analysis, with thirty-four chapters written by leading figures in the field on a wide range of theoretical and methodological issues. This new edition includes twelve new chapters on theoretical and methodological developments, and multimodal research on digitally mediated texts and interaction.

The *Handbook* includes chapters on key themes within multimodality such as technology, culture, notions of identity, social justice and power, and macro issues such as literacy policy. Taking a broad look at multimodality, the contributors engage with how a variety of other theoretical approaches have looked at multimodal communication and representation, including visual studies, anthropology, conversation analysis, socio-cultural theory, sociolinguistics, new literacy studies, multimodal corpora studies, critical discourse, semiotics and eye-tracking.

Detailed multimodal analysis case studies are also included, along with an extensive updated glossary of key terms, to support those new to multimodality and to allow those already engaged in multimodal research to explore the fundamentals further.

The Routledge Handbook of Multimodal Analysis is essential reading for undergraduate and post-graduate students as well as researchers involved in the study of multimodal communication.

Carey Jewitt is Professor of Technology and Learning at University College London, Institute of Education.

Related titles

The Routledge Handbook of English Language Teaching
Edited by Graham Hall

The Routledge Handbook of Language Learning and Technology
Edited by Fiona Farr and Liam Murray

The Routledge Handbook of Language and Identity
Edited by Siân Preece

The Routledge Handbook of English for Academic Purposes
Edited by Ken Hyland and Philip Shaw

The Routledge Handbook of Language and Digital Communication
Edited by Tereza Spilioti

The Routledge Handbook of Literacy Studies
Edited by Kate Pahl

The Routledge Handbook of Interpreting
Edited by Renée Jourdenais

The Routledge Handbook of Hispanic Applied Linguistics
Edited by Manel Lacorte

The Routledge Handbook of Educational Linguistics
Edited by Martha Bigelow and Johanna Ennser-Kananen

The Routledge Handbook of Forensic Linguistics
Edited by Malcolm Coulthard and Alison Johnson

The Routledge Handbook of Corpus Linguistics
Edited by Anne O'Keeffe and Mike McCarthy

The Routledge Handbook of World Englishes
Edited by Andy Kirkpatrick

The Routledge Handbook of Applied Linguistics
Edited by James Simpson

The Routledge Handbook of Discourse Analysis
Edited by James Paul Gee and Michael Handford

The Routledge Handbook of Second Language Acquisition
Edited by Susan Gass and Alison Mackey

The Routledge Handbook of Language and Intercultural Communication
Edited by Jane Jackson

The Routledge Handbook of Language Testing
Edited by Glenn Fulcher and Fred Davidson

The Routledge Handbook of Multilingualism
Edited by Marilyn Martin-Jones, Adrian Blackledge and Angela Creese

The Routledge Handbook of Translation Studies
Edited by Carmen Millán-Varela and Francesca Bartrina

The Routledge Handbook of Language and Health Communication
Edited by Heidi E. Hamilton and Wen-ying Sylvia Chou

The Routledge Handbook of Language and Professional Communication
Edited by Stephen Bremner and Vijay Bhatia

The Routledge Handbook of Multimodal Analysis

Second Edition

Edited by
Carey Jewitt

LONDON AND NEW YORK

First published in paperback 2017

First published 2014
by Routledge
2 Park Square, Milton Park, Abingdon, Oxon OX14 4RN

and by Routledge
711 Third Avenue, New York, NY 10017

Routledge is an imprint of the Taylor & Francis Group, an informa business

British Library Cataloguing in Publication Data
A catalogue record for this book is available from the British Library

Library of Congress Cataloging in Publication Data
The Routledge handbook of multimodal analysis/Edited by
Carey Jewitt.—Second Edition.
pages cm
Includes bibliographical references.
1. Modality (Linguistics)—Handbooks, manuals, etc.
2. Communication. 3. Semiotics. 4. Symbolism. I. Jewitt, Carey.
II. Title: Handbook of multimodal analysis.
P99.4.M6R68 2014
302.2'2—dc23
2013017667

ISBN: 978-0-415-51974-8 (hbk)
ISBN: 978-1-138-24519-8 (pbk)

Typeset in Bembo
by Book Now Ltd, London

Dedication

To Gunther Kress

Contents

Illustrations

Figures

Plates

Tables

Contributors

Editor

Carey Jewitt is a Reader in Education and Technology at the London Knowledge Lab and Research Director of the IoE Centre for Multimodal Research at the Institute of Education, University of London. Her research is involved in developing visual and multimodal method and theory and investigates the relationships between representation, technologies and pedagogy. Carey is a founding editor of the journal *Visual Communication*, with Theo Van Leeuwen and her books include: *Technology, Literacy, Learning: A Multimodality Approach* (2008, Routledge); *English in Urban Classrooms* (2005, Routledge) with Gunther Kress and colleagues; *Multimodal Literacy* edited with Gunter Kress (2003, Peter Lang); *Rhetorics of the Science Classroom: A Multimodal Approach* (2001, Continuum) with Gunther Kress and colleagues, and *A Handbook of Visual Analysis* edited with Theo Van Leeuwen (2001, Sage).

Contributors

Arlene Archer is the director of the Writing Centre at the University of Cape Town, South Africa. She teaches in Applied Language Studies, Higher Education Studies, Film and Media. Her research employs a social semiotic perspective to re-look at key concerns and concepts of an 'academic literacies' approach to teaching and research. It also draws on popular culture and multimodal pedagogies to enable student access to Higher Education. She has published in journals such as *Language and Education, Visual Communication, Teaching in Higher Education, English in Education, Social Dynamics* and *British Journal of Educational Technology*.

John A. Bateman is Professor of Applied Linguistics at Bremen University and leads a faculty research group on transmedial textuality. He has been researching issues of meaning-making employing diverse semiotic modalities since the mid-1990s. After working on the automatic generation of mixed-mode page-based documents, he began in the early 2000s to apply linguistically inspired methodologies to both static and dynamic multimodal artefacts (e.g. narrative film) and to address the semiotic foundations of multimodality. Books in the area include: *Multimodality and Genre: A Foundation for the Systematic Analysis of Multimodal Documents* (2008), *Multimodal Film Analysis: How Films Mean* (with Karl-Heinrich Schmidt, 2011) and the forthcoming textbook *Text and Image: A Critical Introduction to the Visual/Verbal Divide* (due 2014).

Jeff Bezemer is a Senior Research Fellow and Co-Director of the Centre for Multimodal Research at the Institute of Education, University of London. He is interested in reframing communication, learning and identity from a multimodal perspective, using ethnographic, semiotic and interactional theories and methods. He has (co-) directed funded research methods training programmes and funded research projects on multilingualism in schools, representation in textbooks, clinical communication, surgical education and online patient forums. He has published widely in a range of different journals and books, addressing substantive issues (social inequality, patient-safety), issues in multimodality (gesture, visual design, digital technologies) and methodological issues (multimodal transcription and video-analysis). For more details please visit jeffbezemer.wordpress.com.

Anders Björkvall is Associate Professor in Scandinavian Languages at the Department of Swedish Language and Multilingualism, Stockholm University. Anders currently co-ordinates a research project on 'one-to-one' computing and young people's multimodal literacies. His recent publications include 'Multimodality' in *Handbook of Pragmatics* (2012), 'The materiality of discourses and the semiotics of materials: A social perspective on the meaning potentials of written texts and furniture' in *Semiotica* (2011, with Anna-Malin Karlsson) and 'Young children's exploration of semiotic resources during unofficial computer activities in the classroom' in *Journal of Early Childhood Literacy* (2010, with Charlotte Engblom). Anders has also published a Swedish handbook of multimodal analysis (*Den visuella texten: Multimodal analys i praktiken*, 2009), introducing a social semiotic approach to multimodality to a Scandinavian audience.

Andrew Burn is Professor of Media Education at the Institute of Education, University of London. He has researched and published work on many aspects of the media arts, including young people's production of digital media such as computer games, digital video and animation. He has research interests in the multimodal nature of the moving image and computer games. His recent research projects include studies of children's playground games (with the British Library), of young people's videogames of Shakespeare (with the Globe Theatre) and of young people's machinima-making (with the British Film Institute). His most recent books are *Making New Media: Creative Production and Digital Literacies* (New York: Peter Lang); and *Media Literacy in Schools: Practice, Production, Progression* (London: Paul Chapman).

Lilie Chouliaraki is Professor in the Department of Media and Communications, London School of Economics. She is the author of Discourse in Late Modernity (with N. Fairclough, EUP, 2000), The Spectatorship of Suffering (Sage, 2006) and The Ironic Spectator. Solidarity in the Age of Post-humanitarianism (Polity, 2012) as well as numerous publications in the fields of media ethics, journalism, humanitarian communication, discourse theory and analysis.

Chris Cléirigh has been a Research Fellow at the University of New England and is currently a Research Fellow and Research Associate at the University of Sydney. His most recent publication is: Thomson, E.A., Cléirigh, C., Head, L. and Muir, P. (2008) 'Gardeners' Talk: A linguistic study of relationships between environmental attitudes, beliefs and practices', in *Linguistics and the Human Sciences*, Vol. 2.3, Equinox: London.

Marissa K. L. E is a Teaching Fellow at the Centre for English Language Communication at the National University of Singapore. Her research interests include systemic functional linguistics, multimodal discourse analysis and their applications in analyzing the constitution, perpetuation and evolution of ideologies and culture as manifested in traditional and emergent forms of media communication. She has worked on inter-disciplinary projects at the Multimodal Analysis Lab at the National University of Singapore involving the application of mathematical modeling techniques to the analysis of multimodal data and the development of interactive and collaborative software for multimodal analysis for research and educational purposes. Her publications reflect this synthesis of digital and traditional humanities in various areas such as climate science news, institutional business news, corporate advertisements and education.

Rosie Flewitt is a Senior Lecturer in Early Years and Primary Education at the Institute of Education, London, and a member of the London Knowledge Lab. Her research interests include communication and literacy in home and educational settings, with a focus on ethnographic and multimodal methodologies. Recent research includes an evaluation of Vivian Gussin Paley's Helicopter Technique for storytelling and story acting in early education (Esmée Fairbairn), the multimodal potential of the iPad for early literacy learning (Open University) and Multimodal Literacies in the Early Years (ESRC), exploring the range of literacy skills and practices that 3- and 4-year-old children develop as they engage with diverse printed and electronic texts.

Regine Hampel is a Senior Lecturer in Modern Languages at the Open University and Associate Dean (Research and Scholarship) in the Faculty for Education and Language Studies. Her research focuses on the impact of using digital media for language learning and teaching. She is particularly interested in the affordances of new technologies, task design, learner interaction and collaboration, online literacies, and teacher training. Her publications include the book *Online Communication in Language Learning and Teaching*. She is co-editor of *System: An International Journal of Educational Technology and Applied Linguistics*.

Mirjam Hauck is a Senior Lecturer in German and the Associate Head of the Department of Languages at the Open University/UK. For over a decade she has been involved in investigations of virtual spaces for the learning of languages and culture. In her current research and publications she explores the role of digital literacy in globally networked learning where synchronous and asynchronous online tools are used to bring together students from different parts of the world for the development of collaborative project work and intercultural exchange. Her particular focus in this context is the interdependence between multimodal communicative competence and intercultural communicative competence in online (language) learning and teaching environments.

Christian Heath is Professor in the Department of Management, King's College London and is co-director of the Work, Interaction and Technology Research Centre. He has held positions at the Universities of Nottingham, Manchester, Konstanz, Trento and Trondheim and the Xerox Research Laboratories. He specializes in fine-grained video-based studies of social interaction in organizational settings and is currently undertaking research in areas that include surgery, auctions, command and control, and museums and galleries. Projects are funded by the research councils (ESRC, EPSRC, AHRC), the EU IST programmes and the NSF. His publications include numerous journal articles and eight books including most recently *The Dynamics of Auction: Social Interaction and the Sale of Fine Art and Antiques* (Cambridge) and *Video in Qualitative Research: Analysing Social Interaction in Everyday Life* (with Hindmarsh and Luff Sage). He is co-editor of the monograph series Learning in Doing (Cambridge).

Jana Holsanova is Associate Professor in Cognitive Science and Senior Researcher in Linnaeus environment 'Cognition, Communication, and Learning' at Lund University, Sweden. Her research focuses on language, images, cognition and visual communication. Jana uses eye movement measurement to study image perception, the interplay between language and images, the role of images for learning, visual thinking (mental images), and interaction with various media. Her books include *Discourse, Vision and Cognition* (2008), *Myths and Facts About Reading. On the Interplay Between Language and Pictures in Various Media* (2010) and *Methodologies for Multimodal Research* (2012, Special issue of *Visual Communication*, Sage). Jana is Chair elect of the Visual communication division, International Communication Association and Chairman of the Swedish Braille Authority at the Swedish Agency for Accessible Media.

David Howes is Professor of Anthropology at Concordia University, Montreal and the Director of the Centre for Sensory Studies. He is the co-author of *Ways of Sensing: Understanding the Senses in Society* (2013, with Constance Classen), author of *Sensual Relations: Engaging the Senses in Culture and Social Theory* (2003), and editor of *The Varieties of Sensory Experience* (1991), *Cross-Cultural Consumption* (1996) and *Empire of the Senses* (2005), among other works. He has carried out field research on the cultural life of the senses in Argentina, Arizona, and Papua New Guinea. His other research interests revolve around medical anthropology, psychological anthropology, legal sociology, and cross-cultural jurisprudence.

Jonas Ivarsson is Professor in the Department of Education, Communication and Learning, and, Research Dean at the Faculty of Education, University of Gothenburg. He has a background in cognitive science and communication studies, with a PhD in educational science. His general research interests concern the role of representational technologies in the preservation, transmission and development of specialized knowledge and competence. Ivarsson has studied work carried out in the areas of science education, radiology, and architecture.

Adam Jaworski is Professor at the School of English and Associate Dean (Research) at the Faculty of Arts, The University of Hong Kong. His research interests include discourses of mobility and globalization, nonverbal communication, and affordances of speech and writing in the visual arts. He co-edits the book series *Oxford Studies in Sociolinguistics* (Oxford University Press, with Nikolas Coupland).

Rodney H. Jones is Associate Head of the Department of English at City University of Hong Kong. For more than twenty years he has been involved in the study of discourse and the various methods of discourse analysis to contexts as diverse as sexual health, drug abuse, computer mediated communication, professional writing and extreme sports. He has taken a major role in the development of the theory and methods of mediated discourse analysis.

John S. Knox is a Lecturer in the Department of Linguistics, Macquarie University, Sydney, Australia. His research interests include multimodality, media discourse, language in education, and systemic functional theory. He has published research in journals such as *Visual Communication*, *Social Semiotics*, *Discourse and Communication*, and *Distance Education*.

Gunther Kress is Professor of Semiotics and Education at the Institute of Education. His interests are in meaning-making and communication in contemporary environments. He has two aims: one to use any insights gained to develop an apt theory of learning – and apt forms of valuation; and, at the same time, to continue work in developing a social semiotic theory of multimodal communication. Some of his books are *Social Semiotics* (1988); *Before Writing: Rethinking the Paths to Literacy* (1996); *Reading Images: The Grammar of Graphic Design* (1996/2006); *Multimodal Discourse: The Modes and Media of Contemporary Communication* (2001); *Literacy in the New Media Age* (2003); *Multimodality: A Social Semiotic Approach to Contemporary Communication* (2010).

Lesley Lancaster is a Senior Lecturer at Manchester Metropolitan University. She currently teaches applied linguistics at undergraduate, postgraduate, and doctoral levels. Her current research interests are in how very young children understand symbolic forms and systems, in embodied meaning, and in the development of multimodal systems of description and analysis. She has recently been involved in the Communicating Matters 3-5 (DFES), and Grammaticization of Early Mark Making (ESRC) projects. She has contributed articles to the *Journal of Early Childhood Literacy*, and to a number of publications including *Multimodal Literacy* and *The Handbook of Early Childhood Literacy*.

Kevin M. Leander is Associate Professor in Language, Literacy, and Culture at Vanderbilt University. Leander's special areas of interest include literacy and geography, practice theories of identity, digital literacies, classroom interaction, and multimodality. Leander has published articles in *Cognition and Instruction*, *Research in the Teaching of English*, *Ethos*, *Reading Research Quarterly*, *Discourse Processes*, *Journal of Literacy Research*, and other venues. With Margaret Sheehy, he has co-edited the book *Spatializing Literacy Research and Practice*, published by Peter Lang. Leander's recent research projects include *Wired Up*, an examination of how immigrants use new media practices (with Sandra Ponzanesi and Mariette de Haan), spatial design and learning environments with Rogers Hall and Embodied Math, a multi-institutional project on how embodied activities in social spaces at different scales function in the learning of maths.

Jay Lemke is Senior Research Scientist in the Laboratory of Comparative Human Cognition (LCHC) and adjunct full Professor of Communication at the University of California, San Diego. He was formerly Professor in the School of Education at the University of Michigan, affiliated with the Ph.D. programs in Science Education, Learning Technology, and Literacy Language and Culture, and Professor and Executive Officer of the Ph.D. Program in Urban Education at the Graduate Center of the City University of New York, where he is Professor Emeritus. Jay is the author of *Talking Science: Language, Learning, and Values* and *Textual Politics: Discourse and Social Dynamics* as well as of over 100 other scholarly publications in the fields of discourse linguistics, multimedia semiotics, social theory, and science and literacy education. His current research focus is on the integration of feeling and meaning in multimedia activity systems and Design Research.

Jonas Linderoth is an associate professor at the Departement of Education, Communication and Learning, University of Gothenburg. He has a background as artist and art teacher. Most of his research concerns games and gaming as cultural practices. Jonas is the author of several articles for journals such as *Journal of gaming and virtual worlds* and to *DIGRA* (*Transactions of the Digital Games Research Association*). He is also a contributor to the volume *Sports Videogames* published by Routledge. Currently most of his work concerns issues about game perception from an ecological perspective.

Paul Luff is Professor of Organizations and Technology at the Department of Management, King's College London. His research involves the detailed analysis of work and interaction and drawing upon video recordings of everyday human conduct. With his colleagues in the Work, Interaction and Technology Research Centre, he has undertaken studies in a diverse variety of settings including control rooms, news and broadcasting, healthcare, museums, galleries and science centres and within design, architecture and construction. Over the past few years, Paul Luff has been particularly concerned with the use of apparently mundane objects, specifically paper documents, and how these support what are often very complex work practices. This research, and related studies, has been reported in numerous articles in the fields of CSCW, HCI, Requirements Engineering, Studies of work practices and ubiquitous and mobile systems. Paul Luff is co-author with Christian Heath of Technology in Action, published by Cambridge University Press.

David Machin is Professor of Media and Communication Studies at Örebro University. He has published eight books, including *Introduction to Multimodal Analysis* (2007), *Global Media Discourse* (2007), *Analysing Popular Music* (2010), *The Language of Crime and Deviance* (2012) and *The Language of War Monuments* (2013), a number of edited collections and over sixty journal articles and book chapters mainly around topics relating to linguistic analysis of media and institutional texts and also around systematic analyses of both visual design and sound as communication. He is Co-Editor of the journal *Social Semiotics*.

Diane Mavers is a Visiting Research Associate at the Institute of Education, University of London. Taking a social semiotic approach, her research investigates a variety of ways in which early years and primary children interpret and produce meaning in the everyday classroom: how what they draw and write, and say and do, relates to pedagogic interactions around curricular entities, learning materials and digital technologies. More recent projects have investigated communication around a class visualizer (a digital display technology). Use of video for recording the detail of what goes on and for fine-grained analysis has led to an interest in methods of transcribing the multimodality of social interaction. Diane's academic journal articles include contributions to the *Journal of Early Childhood Literacy*. Her book *Children's Drawing and Writing: The Remarkable in the Unremarkable* was published by Routledge (New York) in 2011.

Denise Newfield is an Associate Professor in English and Education at the University of the Witwatersrand, South Africa. She applies multimodal social semiotics to her work in teacher education; literature, language and literacy pedagogy and curriculum; and popular culture. Her research focuses on the transformative role multimodal pedagogies can play in classrooms, especially those of disadvantage, and during times of political transition. Her PhD study (University of London) is called 'Transmodal semiosis in classrooms'. She has published in the fields of English education, visual literacy, multiliteracies and multimodality. She co-edited a special edition of *English Studies in Africa*, entitled 'English Education in Africa' (2006), which contains her award-winning article, 'Mobilising and modalising poetry in a Soweto classroom'. Amongst her recent articles are 'Multimodality, social justice and becoming a really South African democracy' and 'Multimodality and children's participation in classrooms'. She is currently co-editing a book on multimodality in South African education.

Sigrid Norris is Director of the Multimodal Research Centre in the School of Communication Studies at Auckland University of Technology in New Zealand. Sigrid is the author of *Identity in (Inter)action: Introducing Multimodal (Inter)action Analysis* and *Analyzing Multimodal Interaction: A Methodological Framework*, the editor of *Multimodality and Practice: Investigating Theory-in-Practice-through-Method* and co-editor of *Discourse in Action: Introducing Mediated Discourse Analysis*. She is also the editor of the journal *Multimodal Communication*. Sigrid's main research interests are the theoretical and methodological development of multimodal (inter)action analysis and multimodal identity production.

Kay L. O'Halloran is Associate Professor in the School of Education at Curtin University in Perth, Western Australia. She was founding Director of the Multimodal Analysis Lab and Deputy Director of the Interactive & Digital Media Institute at the National University of Singapore. Her areas of research include multimodal analysis, social semiotics, mathematics discourse, and the development of interactive digital media technologies and mathematical and scientific visualization techniques for multimodal and socio-cultural analytics. She was Principal Investigator for large research projects in these areas in the Multimodal Analysis Lab at the National University of Singapore and has published widely in these fields. She is expanding this research at Curtin University.

Kate Pahl is a Reader in Literacies in Education at the University of Sheffield. She is the author, with Jennifer Rowsell, of *Artifactual Literacies: Every Object Tells a Story* (2010) and *Literacy and Education: Understanding the New Literacy Studies in The Classroom*, 2nd Edition (2012). She is particularly interested in collaborative ethnographic research in community contexts with a focus on the cultural making of civic engagement. She works in partnership with community organizations, artists, museums and cultural services with an interest in the co-production of research. She directs the Ed D in Literacy and Language at the University of Sheffield and teaches on the MA in Working with Communities, and is Deputy Director of the Research Exchange, promoting engaged and collaborative research with local communities.

Karola Pitsch received her PhD in Linguistics from Bielefeld University, Germany (2006). She has held since positions as postdoctoral researcher in EU-projects at King's College London, UK (2005-2008) and the Research Institute for Cognition and Robotics, Bielefeld University (2008-2011). In 2011, Karola became a Dilthey Fellow (Volkswagen Foundation) and Principal Investigator of projects within the Centre of Excellence 'Cognitive Interaction Technology' and the CRC 673 'Alignment in Communication'. Since 2012, she has headed the research group 'Interactional Linguistics & Human-Robot-Interaction' at Bielefeld University. Karola's research focuses on multimodal communication and linguistics in everyday, professional and technologically mediated settings. She investigates the practices by which coparticipants coordinate and organize their courses of actions and the linguistic and embodied resources they deploy to do so. She also draws on Conversation Analysis to inform – in interdisciplinary collaboration – the modelling and evaluation of human–robot/agent interaction.

Jennifer Rowsell is Professor and Canada Research Chair in Multiliteracies at Brock University's Faculty of Education where she directs the Centre for Multiliteracies. She has co-written and written several books in the areas of New Literacy Studies, multimodality, ecological research, and multiliteracies. Her current research interests include children's digital and immersive worlds; adopting and applying multimodal epistemologies with adolescents and teenagers; and ecological work in communities examining everyday literacy practices. She is the author of *Working with Multimodality: Learning in a Digital Age* (Routledge).

Roger Säljö is professor of psychology of education at the University of Gothenburg. Previously he has been professor of communication research at the University of Linköping, and he has held visiting professorships at Utrecht, University of California San Diego, Oslo, Göttingen and other universities. His research interests concern learning, interaction and development in a socio-cultural perspective. Recently he has worked with issues of how learning and development are contingent on the uses of representational (and other) technologies. He is also the director of The Linnaeus Centre for Research on Learning, Interaction and Mediated Communication in Contemporary Society (LinCS), which is a centre of excellence funded by the Swedish Research Council. Recent publications include 'Literacy, digital literacy and epistemic practices: The co-evolution of hybrid minds and external memory systems', *Nordic Journal of Digital Literacy* (2012) and 'Analysing and preventing school failure: Exploring the role of multi-professionality in pupil health team meetings', *International Journal of Educational Research* (with E. Hjörne, 2013).

Ron Scollon was a linguistic anthropologist whose professional work engaged with issues of world concern – food in the world system, dialogue among local communities and global resource development stakeholders, and local security in environments of resource development and war.

Suzie Wong Scollon is a linguistic anthropologist with degrees in psychology and linguistics who has focused on locating the macrosociological perspectives of political scientists and economists in the micro-interaction of human bodies with objects in the physical environment on various timescales.

Maree Stenglin is an Honorary Associate of the University of Sydney and the University of Technology Sydney. Her research interests include multimodality, social semiotics and literacy. Her doctoral thesis, *Packaging Curiosities: Towards a Grammar of three-dimensional space*, developed a metafunctionally diversified theory of 3D space. In the past 10 years, she has applied the space grammar to the analysis of art and history exhibitions in a wide range of cultural institutions as well as homes, restaurants and a winery. She is currently extending the theoretical tools of Binding and Bonding to the analysis of hospital birth spaces for women.

Hartmut Stöckl is full professor of English and Applied Linguistics at Salzburg University, Austria. His main research areas are in semiotics, text linguistics/stylistics, pragmatics and multimodal communication. A recurrent theme surfacing in most of his work is a concern with a pluralistic theory of the multimodal text and effective analytical methods for uncovering its structures and styles. He is particularly interested in the linkage of language and image in modern media, typography and an aesthetic appreciation of advertising. His latest edited volumes are: *Bildlinguistik* (2011, Erich Schmidt), *Medientheorien und Multimodalität* (2011, Herbert von Halem), and *Werbung – Keine Kunst!?* (2012, Winter). He is currently editing the handbook *Sprache im multimodalen Kontext* (2014, de Gruyter) in the 21-volume series *Sprachwissen*.

Brian Street is Professor Emeritus of Language in Education at King's College, London University and Visiting Professor of Education in the Graduate School of Education, University of Pennsylvania. He has a commitment to linking ethnographic-style research on the cultural dimension of language and literacy with contemporary practice in education and in development. Over the past 25 years he has undertaken anthropological field research and been consultant to projects in these fields in countries of both the North and South (e.g. Nepal, S. Africa, India, USA, UK). Recent publications include: Street, B And Lefstein, A 2007 *Literacy: An Advanced Resource Book*, Routledge: London; and Heath, S.B. and Street, B. 2008 *On Ethnography: Approaches to Language and Literacy Research*, National Conference on Research in Language and Literacy, Teachers College Columbia.

Sabine Tan lectures in the Department of English Language & Literature at the National University of Singapore and the Singapore Institute of Management University in Singapore. Her research interests include multimodal discourse analysis, social semiotics, and visual communication. She is particularly interested in the application of multidisciplinary perspectives within social semiotic theory to the analysis of institutional discourses involving traditional and new media, such as business news mediated on the internet, corporate advertisements in print and television, corporate web-pages, and other emergent multimodal discourse genres. As a member of the research team at the Multimodal Analysis Lab at the National University of Singapore she participated in inter-disciplinary projects involving the development of interactive and collaborative software for multimodal analysis for research and educational purposes.

Crispin Thurlow is Professor (Language and Communication) in the School of Interdisciplinary Arts & Sciences, University of Washington, Bothell, USA. His research examines how language and other semiotic modes work to produce social difference/inequality in two key domains of contemporary life: the new media and global mobilities. His books include *Tourism Discourse* (Palgrave), written with Adam Jaworski, and the edited collection *Digital Discourse* (Oxford).

Len Unsworth is Professor in Education at Griffith University, Brisbane, Australia. His books include *Literacy Learning and Teaching* (Macmillan, 1993), *Researching Language in Schools and Communities* (Continuum, 2000), *Teaching Multiliteracies Across the Curriculum* (Open University Press, 2001), *E-literature for Children and Classroom Literacy Learning* (Routledge, 2006) (with Angela Thomas, Alyson Simpson and Jenny Asha), *Teaching Children's Literature with Information and Communication Technologies* (McGraw-Hill/Open University Press 2005), *New Literacies and the English Curriculum: Multimodal Perspectives* (Continuum, 2008), *Multimodal Semiotics* (Continuum, 2008) and *Reading Visual Narratives* (Equinox, 2012).

Theo Van Leeuwen is Professor of Media and Communication and Dean of the Faculty of Arts and Social Sciences at the University of Technology, Sydney. He has published widely in the areas of critical discourse analysis, multimodality and visual communication. His books include *Reading Images – The Grammar of Visual Design* (with Gunther Kress); *Speech, Music, Sound*; *Multimodal Discourse – The Modes and Media of Contemporary Communication* (with Gunther Kress); *Introducing Social Semiotics*; *Global Media Discourse* (with David Machin); and *Discourse and Practice – New Tools for Critical Discourse Analysis*. His latest book is *The Language of Colour*. With Carey Jewitt, he is a founding editor of the journal *Visual Communication*.

Lalitha M. Vasudevan is Associate Professor of Technology and Education at Teachers College, Columbia University in the Communication, Computing, and Technology in Education Program. She engages participatory, ethnographic, and multimodal methodologies to study how youth craft stories, represent themselves, and enact ways of knowing through their engagement with literacies, technologies, and media. Lalitha has written articles and co-edited two volumes related to these areas of interest: *Arts, Media, and Justice: Multimodal Explorations with Youth* (2013) and *Media, Learning, and Sites of Possibility* (2008).

Tore West is currently associate professor at Stockholm University, Sweden. His research focuses on video-recorded classroom interaction with an interest in multimodal analysis of educational communication, assessment practices, knowledge representations, and designs for learning, primarily in the context of music education. Publications include 'Didactic interaction design' in the Swedish anthology *Design för lärande* (2010), 'Music education as text' in '*Nordic Research in Music Education* (2008), 'Multi-layered analysis of teacher-student interactions' in *Pedagogies* (2007), 'Theoretical and methodological perspectives on designing video studies of interaction' in *International Journal of Qualitative Methods* (2005), as well as a number of articles on interaction and learning in music education. Current research includes studies of representations and assessment of knowledge across school subjects, assessment in higher arts education, factors influencing highly trained musicians to choose a teaching career, and open educational resources for school teachers.

Acknowledgements

This book builds on the research collaborations and many conversations that have had with colleagues since I joined the Institute of Education at the University of London in 1997. I would like to thank Gunther Kress, my mentor, colleague and friend for his insightful comments and conversations over the years, as well my colleagues at the Institute of Education, especially those associated with the Centre for Multimodal Research. In particular I would like to thank Jeff Bezemer and Sara Price. More specifically, Chapters 1 and 2 benefited significantly from ongoing discussion with David Machin, Jeff Bezemer, Kay O'Halloran and Gunther Kress, and the thoughtful comments on early drafts of these chapters by Theo Van Leeuwen and Sigrid Norris.

In addition, I would like to acknowledge the colleagues beyond the Institute who I have enjoyed an collaborations with over the years, in particular Theo Van Leeuwen, David Machin, Denise Newfield, Arlene Archer, Ben Rampton, Ron Scollon, Philip Scott, Staffan Selander, Pippa Stein, Brian Street and Teal Triggs. I would especially like to acknowledge the significance of Pippa Stein's work for multimodal research; Pippa sadly died in 2008. I had the pleasure of working with Pippa on the Three Continents Project; she was an inspiration to work with as well as great fun and full of generosity. I would also like to acknowledge the importance of Ron Scollon's work for multimodality. Ron, who sadly died in 2009, was among many things co-editor of the journal *Visual Communication* and was an intelligent and thoughtful colleague.

I would like to thank Anna Waring for her administrative support on this publication. Finally I would like to thank the following people and organizations for granting permission to reproduce the following figures in this handbook: Equinox Publishing Ltd (Figure 3.3, Transcription of an advertisement (Baldry and Thibault, 2006 Appendix I, I, © 2006); Sage Publications (Figure 3.4, Transcription of multiparty interaction (Norris, 2006, p. 405, copyright © 2006) and Figure 3.5, Drawings integrated into an extensive transcript of speech (Goodwin, 2007 63, copyright © 2007 by Sage); Heinemann Publications (Figure 4.1, Digestive system: originally a double-page image (pp. 90-91), Salters GCSE Science Y11, Science Education Group (2002); Bodelian Library, Oxford University (Figure 8.1(a), *The Method of Fluxions and Infinite Series* (Newton, 1736: 51); Dover Publications, New York (Figure 8.1(b). *La Geómetrié* (Descartes, 1954 [1637]: 236–237); The John Rylands University

Library, University of Manchester, Figure 8.1(c), *Mathematische Schriften: Band IV* (Leibniz, 1859: 358) and Figure 8.1(d), *Mathematische Schriften: Band I* (Leibniz, 1849); Elibron Classics: Adamant Media Corporation (Figure 8.2(a)–(b) *Philosophiæ Naturalis Principia Mathematica* (Newton, 1739); Fridae.com (Figures 9.2-9.4, A personal profile on the popular Hong Kong gay website Fridae.com); Scholastic Australia (Figure 12.2, Life cycle of a cicada (Bird & Short, 1998 p. 29); Pearson Education Australia (Figure 12.3, Making switches (Bartholomew, 2003, p. 10), Harcourt Publishers; Figure 12.4, A Greek water clock (Chapman, 1996), Harcourt Publishers; Bridget Somekh, Project Director of the Grid Club evaluation for permission to publish the mind maps produced as part of the Grid Club research (Figures 32.1–5); and Ella Dreyfus for permission to reproduce the images in Figures 31.1–4.

Introduction

Handbook rationale, scope and structure

There is increasing interest among academics, professionals and students in the role of image, gesture, gaze, posture, the use of space in representation and communication – in other words, multimodality. These modes are understood as intimately connected, enmeshed through the complexity of interaction, representation and communication. Comments on the multimodal character of communication, texts and media are increasingly commonplace across a range of disciplines (e.g. anthropology, education, design, linguistics, media and culture studies, musicology, sociology). But what does it actually mean to call a text, practice, or indeed anything else, multimodal or to approach communication from a multimodal perspective? And how might one take a multimodal perspective to research, what might that actually involve? Perhaps most importantly, why might a researcher want to look in this way at a phenomenon, and what might the benefits of doing so be? These are the questions that this handbook sets out to address.

This chapter introduces the term multimodality, and situates it in broader context of social and technological change in contemporary society. That communication is multimodal is not *new* – people have always used image and non-verbal forms to communicate – however, the use of technologies certainly enables modes to be configured, be circulate, and get recycled in different ways. Nonetheless, this chapter asks, why is it that multimodality of such significance now? Can we talk of a turn to the multimodal? The scope and structure of the handbook is also outlined in this introductory chapter. But first, what is multimodality?

What is multimodality?

Put simply, multimodality approaches representation, communication and interaction as something more than language. Kress and Van Leeuwen define multimodality as, 'The use of several semiotic modes in the design of a semiotic product or event' (2001: 20). The starting point for multimodality is to extend the social interpretation of language and its meanings to the whole range of representational and communicational modes or semiotic resources for making meaning with employed in a culture – such as image, writing, gesture, gaze, speech, posture.

Multimodality starts from the position that all modes, like speech and writing, consist of sets of semiotic resources (semiotic resource refers to resources that people draw on and configure in specific moments and places to represent events and relations). From this perspective the modes and semiotic resources a person chooses (or are permitted) to use shape communication and meaning. Treating the choice of mode as significant and looking beyond language a multimodal perspective rejects the traditional almost habitual conjunction of language and communication, for instance with respect to learning or identity formation.

It could be argued that, strictly speaking, multimodality refers to a field of application rather than a theory, although the on-going development of theories that account for the multimodal is an imperative to support high-quality research. Comparison with Green and Bloome's commentary on ethnography is useful here. They make a distinction between 'doing' an ethnography, taking an ethnographic perspective, and using ethnographic research tools (Green and Bloome, 1997: 183). A similar scale of differentiation can be made to describe the different degrees of engagement with multimodality and to make sense of what is seen to count as multimodal.

A variety of disciplines and theoretical perspectives can be used to explore different aspects of the multimodal landscape. Psychological theories can be applied to look at how people perceive different modes or to understand the impact of one mode over another on memory for example. Sociological and anthropological theories and interests could be applied to examine how communities use multimodal conventions to mark and maintain identities. Indeed, as the chapters in Part III of this volume indicate, an interest in multimodal communication informs the study of language (Chapter 14), visual studies (Chapter 15), New Literacy Studies (Chapter 16), corpora studies (Chapter 17), conversation analysis (Chapter 22) and anthropology (Chapter 23). Similarly, multimodality has been in conversation with and influenced by research concepts and theories from linguistics, interactional sociology, semiotics (Chapter 19), art history, cultural studies, and new media studies (Chapter 27) among others. The term multimodality is, however, strongly linked with three perspectives on representation and communication, social semiotics, discourse analysis (Chapter 18), and interactional analysis (Chapter 2). These three perspectives are best described as placing emphasis on different aspects of multimodality rather than being wholly distinct methodological theories of the multimodal. They share many theoretical assumptions and key conceptual terms (discussed in Chapter 1). However, each has a particular historical trajectory, which has led to variation, the foregrounding of distinctive sets of interests, as well as different notions of data and ways of collecting and handling data (see Chapter 2).

Multimodality is sometimes misunderstood as an attempt to 'side-line' language. Scollon and Scollon in Chapter 14 argue strongly against this, and examine how multimodal perspectives have been influenced in significant ways by the study of language and vice versa. A key aspect of multimodality is indeed the analysis of language, but language as it is nestled and embedded within a wider semiotic frame. This offers new ways to explore and understand language, and its place in a multimodal communicational landscape. That said, multimodal research looks beyond language to explore a wide range of modes and communicational contexts. The chapters in this volume examine multimodal discourses, as realized by modes (including written and spoken language) in a variety of contexts, including workplaces, the home, the museum exhibition, and online environments, realized across a range of genres (e.g. student drawings, mathematical documents, educational websites) and technologies.

Increasing interest in multimodality, witnessed in the explosion of multimodal studies, raises a question that is addressed in the next section: 'why now?'

Why now?

This interest in multimodality across many disciplines has emerged against a backdrop of considerable social change in contemporary global, fluid and networked society (Bauman, 1998; Castells, 2001). This is typified by changing relationships to truth and authority – in which knowledge is no longer certain or stable, and there is an expansion in knowledge production as a domain of the elite to the masses. Society can also be described as having new requirements and access to information and knowledge; reconfiguration, changing roles, and possibilities for people's identity formation; and connections across local/national and global/international boundaries. Intimately connected with these changes but not driving them is the development of technologies of visual representational and the changing communicational possibilities that these make available for mediated interaction.

These new social conditions have had a significant impact on the communicational landscape of the twenty-first century. A key aspect of this is how image, action, sound and multimodal ensembles feature in this landscape and people's daily lives. The terrain of communication is changing in profound ways and these changes extend across elements of everyday life, even if these changes are occurring to different degrees and at uneven rates (Luke and Carrington, 2002). Multimodality is gaining pace as a research approach, as speech and writing no longer appear adequate in understanding representation and communication in a variety of fields and the need to understand the complex ways in which speech and writing interact with 'non-verbal' modes can no longer be avoided.

The next section turns to commentaries on the place of visual communication in contemporary society to explore the notion of a turn to the multimodal across a wide variety of disciplines.

A turn to the multimodal?

Much has been written about the particular dominance of the visual in contemporary society. Indeed it has been argued that the modern world has become a visual phenomenon that conflates looking, seeing and knowing (Jenks, 1995) – a kind of 'vision machine' created through new visualizing technologies in which people are all caught (Virilio, 1994). Mitchell (2002, 2005a), a leading figure in visual studies, has, however, asked if this characterization of the world as newly visual is true. In *What do Pictures Want?* (Mitchell, 2005b) taking a historical view he argues that the visual turn is not new – recalling the illuminated manuscripts of medieval times, the complex iconographic paintings of the past and so on. Many other areas of life also have a long and intimate relationship with the visual. The visual has always played a role in school English, for example, including specially illustrated editions of novels and poetry such as Dickens and Milton, picture books, graphic novels, comic strips and manga, as well as film, television and computer games (Burn and Dixon, 2005: 1). Mitchell argues that the visual or pictorial turn can be more usefully understood as a repeated narrative that marks 'specific moments when a new medium, a technical invention, or a cultural practice erupts in symptoms of panic or euphoria (usually both) about the visual' (Mitchell, 2002: 173).

Understanding the visual turn as a commentary on new ways of making images and the marking of a historical turning point is also significant and productive for multimodality. It is especially useful in three ways.

First, it refuses to confine visuality and multimodality to the modern era and in doing so it connects the contemporary with the past. Multimodal perspectives connect with, and are influenced by the pioneering work of early anthropology, sociology and some forms of linguistics, notably, the pioneering work of Bateson, Birdwhistell, Hall, Goffman and Pike on the Natural History of the Interview study. This heralded another moment (in the 1950s) that recognized the need to understand language in relation to non-linguistic modes of communication – particularly gesture, space, gaze and posture (discussed in this volume by Scollon and Scollon in Chapter 14). This enables patterns and narratives of the use of modes to be seen over time and for connections to be made with respect to practices across different technologies. Taking a social, historical and cultural stance is particularly useful in decoupling multimodality and new technologies. New technologies do play a central role in how modes are made available, configured and accessed (Jewitt, 2006; Jones, Chapter 9 this volume; Burn, Chapter 27 this volume). The texts that circulated in the world and interactions between people have always been multimodal, although the ways in which texts were modally realized, and the forms of interaction, as well as the extent to which research could observe and record it, have been extended by digital technologies.

Second, understanding multimodality as a commentary on new ways of making meaning and marking a historical turning point, acknowledges that to live in *any* culture is to live in a multimodal culture and therefore it extends discussion of multimodality beyond western societies – that is there is no monomodal culture.

Third, understanding the visual or multimodal *turn* as an account or repeated narrative connected with new media technology and cultural practice moves away from the (easy) construction of binary models of history that centre on a turning point and 'declare a single great divide between the age of literacy (for instance) and the age of visuality' (Mitchell, 2003: 173) and other common dichotomies (e.g. page and screen). These three points, when combined, demand that attention is paid to the specificity of how modes are configured and elaborated in different historical, social, cultural contexts. This moves the debates on representation and communication away from questions about the extent to which image and other non-linguistic modes dominate word or vice versa, instead sharpening the focus on *how* the visual and other modes are configured and put to work for the purposes of society – and how (as well as why) this might be redesigned.

The twenty-first century can be viewed as a historical moment when technology aids the production and circulation of visual and multimodal communication at an 'unimagined level' (Jay, 2002: 88). The use of technology can literally transform what can be seen and by whom it can be seen: for example, making phenomena newly visible, and contributing to the construction of phenomena. However, this volume calls for a better understanding of how images, gesture, gaze and other modal forms are used within particular situations (workplaces, advertising, the school and so on) as part of broader social and cultural work. This is not to deny that technologies have transformed the ways in which image and other non-linguistic modes circulate and are mobilized by people in powerful ways.

It is this multimodal representational and communicational landscape that this book is designed to help the reader to navigate.

The scope and structure of this book

On the one hand, this handbook is a response to increasing interest in multimodal research. On the other, it speaks to the need to further develop the field of multimodality, its theoretical tools and methodological tools and processes. The chapters in this book are organized into four parts, each of which is briefly introduced here.

The focus of Part I is theoretical and methodological tools for multimodal analysis. Multimodality is a relatively new approach to research. One consequence of this is that some theoretical and methodological tools and procedures remain unsettled, others need further development, while some are yet to become firmly established. Undertaking research that looks beyond language across a variety of contexts and concerns can be rather overwhelming.

The chapters in this part attend to the need to clarify terms and concepts in multimodal theory and method. These chapters synthesize the key literature to date with in-depth exploration and illustrative analysis to provide the basis of a 'research tool kit' for multimodal analysis. Carey Jewitt introduces multimodality, its theoretical assumptions and key concepts in Chapter 1 and explores different approaches to multimodality in Chapter 2. What are multimodal data and transcription, is the question posed in Chapter 3, by Rosemary Flewitt and colleagues. The chapter identifies the challenges and considerations to be accounted for in multimodal data collection and transcription, offers examples of different transcription methods, and discusses the losses and gains of these procedures. The concept of mode is essential to multimodality, and in Chapter 4 Gunther Kress investigates this often taken for granted concept and asks 'what is mode?'. Using a range of examples of contemporary textbooks and online educational resources he addresses matters such as the 'logics' of modes, the relationship of mode, representation and knowledge and the notion of epistemological commitment. Theo Van Leeuwen discusses materiality and its expressive potential in contemporary communication drawing on examples of the human voice, instrumental timbres, typographic and calligraphic letterforms and colour, in Chapter 5. Chapter 6, by Sigrid Norris, focuses on the relationships between modes, and the concept of modal density and modal intensity to investigate the complexity through which an action is constructed. This part of the handbook closes with Chapter 7 by Denise Newfield, with a discussion of how semiotic meanings shift when the modal form changes in representation and communication with a focus on the process of modal transformation, transduction, and the transmodal moment.

Multimodal research, in all its varieties, is strongly underpinned by social and cultural theories of representation and communication, and the link between representation and communication and the social, cultural and historical conditions of societies is fundamental. Social, cultural and historical factors influence and mediate how modes are taken up and used for practices of meaning making and the conventions that stabilize around these practices. The chapters in Part II of the handbook, 'Key themes for multimodality', illustrate this, through a focus on time scales, technology, culture, notions of power and identity and macro issues such as literacy policy. Kay O'Halloran focuses on the historical changes in the semiotic landscape of mathematics – from calculation to computation – in Chapter 8. This chapter explores the complex relationship between social and technological change in the context of mathematics. Jones, in Chapter 9, examines technology as a site of display and its impact on multimodal communication. In particular he explores how technology has affected the ways people use their bodies as a communicative resource in social interaction through the study of internet use of gay men. In Chapter 10, Kevin Leander and Lalitha Vasudevan approach the theme of culture and multimodality through the lens of technology. They take the emergent practices with mobile (cell) phones as an illustration of the relationship between multimodality and culture and ask how practice appears to hybridize modalities. Lemke, in Chapter 11, explores meaning effects across multiple timescales, using the illustrative example of the computer and video games, and considers what happens when games, films, books, and other media and merchandise are linked in *transmedia* franchises, where meaning effects are integrated by consumers across multiple media, on even longer timescales. Literacy is a key factor for multimodal research, and this is taken up in Chapter 12 by Len Unsworth and Chris Cléirigh who examine the significance of images and image–text relations in the construction of interpretive possibilities in informational and fictional material for children as an increasingly important dimension of reading comprehension development. This part of the book concludes with a discussion of power, social justice and multimodal pedagogies in Chapter 13 in which Arlene Archer explores some of the links between multimodal pedagogies and social justice, looking at examples from South African educational contexts. In doing so she identifies some of the challenges and opportunities of using multimodal approaches to pedagogy in local and global contexts of diversity.

Part III, 'Multimodality across different theoretical perspectives', takes a broad look a multimodality and engages with how a variety of other theoretical approaches have looked at multimodal communication and representation. How multimodality describes visual communication and the way it characterizes seeing are issues that have been the basis of much philosophical and methodological discussion for many years, and across a range of academic disciplines. Multimodality has to a large extent emerged from linguistic theories, and several of the chapters in this part challenge the basic premise of building on a model of language to understand the visual.

Part III opens with Chapter 14 from Ron and Suzie Wong Scollon, which takes what they term as a 'retrospective and prospective view' on mutltimodality and language and visit early work by socio–linguistics which attempted to move beyond language and account for the 'non-verbal'. David Machin reminds us in Chapter 15 that visual studies has been looking at visual communication for many years, and he draws on this work to critique multimodal approaches in an endeavour to develop multimodality. Brian Street, Kate Pahl and Jennifer Rowsell, Chapter 16, provide the reader with an account of what research looks like that sits within the intersection of the New Literacy Studies and multimodality and outlines specific studies that work across these two fields. John Bateman, in Chapter 17, sets out a multimodal corpora approach moving away from a focus a small-scale qualitative approach to multimodality, to critique and empirically validate multimodal concepts and to explore the potential boundaries of multimodal theory. In Chapter 18, Lilie Chouliaraki explores the potential of bringing together discourse analysis and multimodality for the analysis of the visual and linguistic properties of media discourses. Hartmut Stöckl, in Chapter 19, shows the potential of semiotics for multimodality and outlines the points of departure and connection between semiotics and multimodality and the central concepts from semiotics that can travel into multimodal research. In Chapter 20, Jana Holsanova gives an overview of the different ways in which eye-tracking methodology can be used in research on multimodality and presents a new perspective that focuses on the reception of multimodality and emphasizes how multimodal messages are perceived by the users. In Chapter 21 Jonas Ivarsson, Jonas Linderoth and Roger Säljö provide a socio-cultural approach theory of mind and mediated action to multimodality. Their focus is on how representations serve as resources for communicating and meaning-making, in ways that are essential to all human practices including perception, remembering and thinking and other psychological activities. Luff, Heath and Pitsch, Chapter 22, bring a conversation analysis and ethnomethodological approach to work-based studies together with multimodal analyses of everyday organizational activities, revealing the ways in which those activities are contingently accomplished through social interaction. Part III closes with David Howes, Chapter 23, on anthropology and multimodality: the conjugation of the senses, which proposes a cross-cultural multi-modal theory of sense perception born out of the fusion of cognitive science and sensory anthropology.

The methodological questions raised by multimodality and the focus of chapters in Part I of the handbook are addressed throughout the volume, and provide a focus for the detailed multimodal analysis provided in Part IV, 'Multimodal case studies', such as the collection and management of multimodal data and transcription. In Chapter 24, Anders Björkvall describes the dimensions of tables as products and three-dimensional objects as mode. A number of semiotic resources of tables are discussed – shape, size, finish, colour, and how functional values are realized by differences in the size and elevation of the table top as well as interpersonal aspects of tables is discussed. In Chapter 25, Bezemer analyses the use of gesture in the professional activities of health-care professionals in operating theatres. Taking surgical activity as an exemplar of all kinds of 'operations' in everyday and professional life he explores gesture in an environment where speech is the occasional accompaniment of gesture.

Jaworski and Thurlow turn to the modes of gaze and gesture, in Chapter 26, as well as the camera as an object, all of which they demonstrate are central modes in tourists' social interaction with and construction of place and identities. In Chapter 27, Burn proposes a multimodal theory of the moving image, named the kineikonic mode: kineikonic results from a combination of the Greek words for 'to move' (*kinein*) and 'image' (*eikon*) (Burn and Parker, 2003a, b) which emphasizes the interplay of all the modes which contribute to the moving image. The semantic patterns arising from the integration of language, images and audio resources in multimodal texts is the focus of Chapter 28, what O'Halloran refers to as multimodal analytics. The chapter reports on research which aims to address these issues through a multimodal digital semiotics approach involving the development of interactive software with functionalities and facilities for systematic multimodal analysis of text, images and videos. Keeping attention on moving image, film and video, for a third chapter, Van Leeuwen shifts attention to the role of colour as a code, mode and modality in Chapter 29. Chapter 30 turns to the mode of sound and music, where West offers an analysis of interaction as a combination of music, speech, and gesture (including gaze, body movement, positioning in the room, use of artefacts, etc.) within an educational setting. The communicative functions of space is the focus of Stenglin's case study in Chapter 31 that focuses on the analysis of an exhibition in a Sydney gallery. The analysis considers how space is designed to evoke powerful visceral responses from visitors. Children's use of the modal resources of writing and image is discussed by Mavers in Chapter 32. She shows how analysing image in the multimodal ensemble is framed by the affordances of drawing and the benefits of examining different 'levels' of text in a multimodal ensemble. Finally, in Chapter 33, Knox examines the modal resources of website structure, page design and layout in the reporting of news in online newspapers.

These four parts are designed to orientate the reader but there are many connections across the chapters within the volume. Throughout the handbook, each chapter is supplemented by suggestions for further reading (collated for chapters in Part I), and a comprehensive glossary of key terms is provided. The handbook provides a comprehensive research 'toolkit' and case study examples of multimodal analysis to support those who are new to multimodal research, as well as those who are already undertaking multimodal research but want to explore the fundamentals further and to engage with different perspectives within multimodality. Chapter 34 concludes the handbook with a look forward and asks 'What next for multimodality?'.

Gunther Kress and Theo Van Leeuwen, in the preface to their book *Multimodal Discourse: The Modes and Media of Contemporary Communication* (2001), wrote that their intention was to 'start a discussion, to open up the question of multimodality, not to close it'. This second edition of *The Routledge Handbook of Multimodal Analysis* sets out to build on their work and to continue the conversation.

Theoretical and methodological tools for multimodal analysis

Introduction to Part I

Looking beyond language raises many questions for research. What does it involve? How can I tell if something is a mode? What do I need to attend to? What modes should I focus on? What data should I collect? What do I need to know about the person who is communicating and their situation? How can I transcribe multimodal data? What kinds of questions can I ask using a multimodal approach? How can I analyse the relationships between modes? How can I investigate the distribution of meaning across modes? What are the benefits and limitations of attending to all modes?

The seven chapters in this part address these and many other questions about multimodal theory and method. Each chapter provides an in-depth exploration of a specific aspect of multimodal research, discusses relevant theoretical issues, and introduces methodological tools and procedures to support the process of multimodal analysis. Taken as a whole, this part provides a 'research toolkit' for multimodal analysis, underpinned by an overview of the key literature and research, and illustrative analysis where appropriate.

Multimodality is a widely used term and one that is frequently used interchangeably with multimedia or multisensory. It is used to refer to events, objects, practices and processes (e.g. multimodal teaching), as well as intelligence and ways of communicating. In Chapter 1, Carey Jewitt introduces multimodality, discusses how it is defined and understood, and outlines the theoretical assumptions that underpin this approach. The chapter provides a brief overview of the scope of multimodal research and highlights some of the key studies and authors in this field. Having sketched the terrain of multimodal research, the chapter elaborates on seven core concepts for multimodality. These concepts are mode, materiality, modal affordance, meaning potential or metafunction, and intersemiotic or intermodal relationships, discourse and genre. The chapter provides a set of working definitions for these key concepts and elaborates on their origins and development within multimodal research. The nuances in how each of these concepts is articulated in different approaches to multimodality is also discussed. Multimodality has much to offer research but like all perspectives it has limitations, and these are briefly discussed in the chapter. The concepts introduced in the chapter are taken up, put into action and expanded upon across other chapters within the handbook.

Multimodality has been developed in conversation with different historical influences and research interests to realize interconnected but distinctive approaches to multimodal research. In Chapter 2, Carey Jewitt argues that multimodality can be understood as a theory, a perspective or a field of enquiry or a methodological application. She explores how mode and semiotic resource are articulated across different approaches to multimodality and teases out what this means for the kinds of data and questions each might address. The chapter focuses on three perspectives within multimodality: social semiotic multimodal analysis, a systemic functional approach (multimodal discourse analysis), and multimodal interactional analysis. The particular accent each of these approaches gives to multimodality is explored. Multimodality is a feature within other disciplines, and the chapter closes with a brief introduction to some of the theoretical approaches that have taken an interest in multimodality; this theme is the focus of the chapters in Part III. Having sketched the scope, purpose and variation of multimodal research, Chapter 3 turns to more practical questions concerning multimodal research. The need to develop practices of multimodal transcription and systematic multimodal analytical processes for working with video data is high on the multimodal research agenda. Multimodal transcription is at a relatively early stage of development with a range of procedures in use and few established conventions. Multimodal concordancing has developed alongside the question of how to transcribe and handle multimodal data (Baldry and Thibault, 2006). The work of Kress and colleagues (Kress *et al.*, 2001, 2004) has examined the use of video, transcription and processes of analysis that examine a range of modes, and their relationships. In *Technology, Literacy and Learning: A Multimodal Approach* (2008a), Jewitt suggests that transcription can be used to focus analytical attention on different planes of activity, for example the plane of the computer screen and the plane of classroom interaction. Norris, in her book *Analyzing Multimodal Interaction* (2004a) provides a practical introduction to transcription and multimodal analysis that relies on digital stills, and there are a range of computer applications that enable researchers to link video data, transcripts and analytical annotation.

In Chapter 3, Rosemary Flewitt and colleagues address the question, what are multimodal data and transcription? The chapter identifies the challenges and considerations to be accounted for in multimodal data collection and transcription. It offers a variety of models for multimodal transcription and highlights the issues for consideration when undertaking this complex work. Each transcription method is discussed in terms of the losses and gains of the procedure. Theoretical work across disciplines and unprecedented developments in the area of information and related technologies have led to significant changes in what is now accepted as analysable data and present significant challenges to researchers. The chapter considers whether there are limits to what might be included as multimodal data per se, or what it is possible to describe and transcribe. Some of the more intractable problems that might be associated with the transcription and analysis of multimodal data are highlighted in the chapter.

Mode is a fundamental concept within multimodality; Chapter 1 offers a working definition of mode and outlines its importance. Gunther Kress, in Chapter 4, investigates mode as an often taken-for-granted concept and asks 'what is mode?'. Mode is a socially shaped and culturally given resource for making meaning. From this perspective, image, writing, layout, music, gesture, speech, moving image and soundtrack are examples of modes used in representation and communication. Phenomena which are the product of social and cultural work have meaning in the environment, so that furniture, clothing and food also 'have' meaning. If their primary function is not that of representation and communication, however, there is a question for Kress as to whether they should be considered as modes.

Using a range of examples of contemporary textbooks and online educational resources, Kress explores the question of what is a mode and, in the process, he addresses matters such as the 'logics' of modes, the relationships between mode, representation and knowledge, and the notion of epistemological commitment.

There is considerable debate about the role of materiality in multimodal research, revolving around the relationships between the physical or natural and the social or cultural shaping of meaning. In Chapter 5, Theo Van Leeuwen is concerned with materiality and its expressive potential in contemporary communication. Culture and nature, meaning and materiality have, he states, often been opposed to each other, and in this chapter Van Leeuwen argues strongly for their 'inextricable connection'. He offers an account of the semiotics of voice quality and meaning and uses this account to demonstrate that while on the one hand 'there is nothing natural about the way meaning is assigned to voice quality' rather that this is historically and culturally shaped, on the other hand, voice quality is 'grounded in something that is natural', that is, the human body. This debate is key to the question of what it is that multimodal research needs to attend to and more broadly to issues of meaning.

The interaction of semiotic modes is a major theme within multimodality, and how to theorize and investigate the relationships between modes is a central task for multimodal research. The need to rethink the relationship between modes, for example, the interaction between image and writing in a text, is at the heart of much multimodal research. One of the starting points for multimodality is that there is in principle equity between all modes. That writing and image, for example, can be of equal importance, this is not to say that they are always equal in every communicative event, sometimes writing is dominant, other times image is and each is often attending to distinct communicative work. Understanding the relationships between modes demands new tools for analysing modal relations, and this is the focus of Sigrid Norris in Chapter 6. She introduces concepts for thinking about these relationships, namely modal density. The concept of modal density, a recent development by Norris, refers to the modal intensity and or complexity through which an action is constructed. Modal density (intensity and complexity) is a conceptual tool for separating out the modes as analytical units. Norris demonstrates this concept through an illustrative example of interaction in a store. In the chapter she sets out a way of thinking about the relationships between modes in terms of a scale of low to high intensity and contributes to the theorization of the relationship across and between modes.

In Chapter 7, Newfield discusses and operationalizes concepts pertaining to the representation and communication of meaning through processes of modal transfer – transformation, transduction, chains of semiosis and the transmodal moment. These are concepts used in the field of multimodality to describe and explain the process of making meaning through the construction of signs. A feature of the human condition, semiosis is ceaseless and ongoing (Kress and Van Leeuwen, 2001), whether the agent of semiosis is conscious of it or not. It develops an analytical approach to tracking semiotic shift in chains of semiosis. Using these concepts enables a description of what happens semiotically in the 'translation' of meaning, theme and topic across modes, a process that involves multiple semiotic changes in both form and content.

Multimodality is a relatively new approach to research and some aspects of it remain theoretically and methodologically contested. Added to the challenge of the development of multimodality as a field of research, multimodal representations and practices are themselves in a constant state of change. What is counted as a mode is highly contingent and continues to expand as new modes enter the communicational landscape. In addition, the intersemiotic relations between modes are remade by

13

the social and technological demands and possibilities of the contemporary world, in which relations between image and word, action and sound are emerging in new and hybrid genres. In short, multimodality is complex. The chapters in this part provide theoretical and methodological research tools to support looking at this complexity that focus on the principles and assumptions of multimodality. This focus allows the research tools provided in these chapters to be flexible enough to be useful in a changing environment, and strong enough to offer a theoretical anchor and methodological steer through this sometimes stormy landscape.

An introduction to multimodality

Carey Jewitt

This chapter introduces the theoretical assumptions of multimodality, describes its scope, and elaborates on seven core concepts for multimodality: mode, materiality, modal affordance, meaning potential or metafunction, intersemiotic or intermodal relationships, discourse and genre, which inform the handbook chapters.

Theoretical assumptions that underpin multimodality

Multimodality describes approaches that understand communication and representation to be more than about language, and which attend to the full range of communicational forms people use – image, gesture, gaze, posture, and so on – and the relationships between these.

Four interconnected theoretical assumptions underpin multimodality as it is broadly conceived. These are briefly introduced and discussed below.

The first assumption underlying multimodality is that language is part of a multimodal ensemble. This weaves across all the chapters in the volume and different perspectives on multimodality. Language is widely taken to be the most significant mode of communication; this is particularly so in contexts of learning and teaching. Multimodality, however, proceeds on the assumption that representation and communication always draw on a multiplicity of modes, all of which have the potential to contribute equally to meaning. The basic assumption that runs through multimodality is that meanings are made, distributed, received, interpreted and remade in interpretation through many representational and communicative modes – not just through language – whether as speech or as writing. As Norris asserts: "'all interactions are multimodal" and multimodality "steps away from the notion that language always plays the central role in interaction, without denying that it often does'" (Norris, 2004a: 3).

Gaze, gesture and posture, for instance, tend to be considered a support to speech; reinforcing or otherwise modifying speech but not providing communication in its own right, and image is often thought to be in a supportive relation to writing. Multimodal research across a range of social settings casts doubt on this assumption. In the classroom or the workplace, for instance, it is entirely common practice for people to use demonstrations and gestures (e.g. Chapters 6, 22, 25 and 26), images and models (e.g. Chapters 4, 7, 15 17. 18,

32 and 33) to explain phenomena, or to set and engage in tasks that require a response using visual or other non-linguistic means.

As the chapters in this volume demonstrate, multimodal research provides tools for analysing and describing the full repertoire of meaning-making resources which people use to communicate and represent (e.g. students and teachers bring to the classroom) and how these are 'organized' to make meaning. From a multimodal perspective, language is therefore only ever one mode nestled among a multimodal ensemble of modes. Others have looked before at 'non-verbal' modes; however, multimodality differs in that it does not take language as its starting point or as providing a prototypical model of all modes of communication (i.e. where language provides the conceptual tools, framework and processes for understanding all forms of communication). That is, as Scollon and Scollon argue in Chapter 14, multimodality offers a new perspective and methods for understanding language and 'is not a simple rephrasing of nonverbal communication'.

The second assumption central to multimodal research is that each mode in a multimodal ensemble is understood as realizing different communicative work. Multimodality assumes that all modes have, like language, been shaped through their cultural, historical and social uses to realize social functions. Multimodality takes all communicational acts to be constituted of and through the social. Image and other non-linguistic modes take on specific roles in a specific context and moment in time. These roles are not fixed but articulated and situated. For example, a key finding of Kress *et al.*'s (2001) in-depth study of London school science classrooms was that how teachers' choice and use of different modes of representation led to radically different constructions of the scientific and natural world in the classroom. For example representation of a cell in the science classroom as an image or through writing, in colour or black and white, or as 3D model or an animated sequence on a CD-ROM or webpage makes available and foregrounds different aspects of the concept of cell. Each of these representational forms makes different demands on the learner. There was also evidence that different modes have differential potential effects for learning, the shaping of learner identities and how learners create reading pathways through texts. The choice of mode, then, is a central aspect of the epistemological shaping of knowledge and ideological design. What can be done and thought with image, writing, or through action differs in ways that are significant for learning. In this regard, the longstanding focus on language as the principal, if not sole medium of instruction, can at best offer a very partial view of the work of communicating in the classroom and beyond. In the examples discussed in this volume the resources of gesture (e.g. Chapters 25 and 26), for instance the spatial extent of a *gesture*; the intonational range of *voice*; the direction and length of a *gaze* are all understood as part of the resources for making meaning.

This connects with the third assumption underpinning multimodality – that people orchestrate meaning through their selection and configuration of modes. Thus the interaction between modes is significant for meaning-making. While multimodal communication is not in and of itself new, Ventola *et al.* (2004: 1) have suggested that:

> The various possibilities of combining communication modes in the 'new' media, like the computer and the Internet, have forced scholars to think about the particular characteristics of these modes and the way they semiotically function and combine in the modern discourse worlds.

The meanings in any mode are always interwoven with the meanings made with those of all other modes co-present and 'co-operating' in the communicative event. The interaction between modes is itself a part of the production of meaning – a point this chapter returns to.

Finally, multimodality is built on the assumption that the meanings of signs fashioned from multimodal semiotic resources are, like speech, social. That is, they are shaped by the norms and rules operating at the moment of sign-making, influenced by the motivations and interests of sign-maker in a specific social context. That is, sign-makers select, adapt and refashion meanings through the process of reading/interpretation of the sign. These effect and shape the sign that is made.

Before introducing the central concepts of multimodality, the next section sets out to indicate something of the scope of multimodality, and where appropriate, chapters in this volume are introduced to point the reader in the direction of a fuller discussion.

The scope of multimodality

This section gives a sense of what multimodal research can do and what it is good for, rather than providing an exhaustive account of the literature on multimodal research. It indicates the potential of multimodal research to describe semiotic resources for meaning-making and inter-semiotic relations, to develop research tools, and its successful application across a range of topics or contexts including technology-mediated interaction, questions of knowledge, pedagogic practices and literacy, as well as the production of identity. This brief introduction is supported by the analysis and discussion across the chapters in this volume, which include key references and suggested readings to support readers who want to investigate a specific aspect of multimodality in more depth.

Describing semiotic resources

Multimodality can be used to build inventories of the semiotic resources (that is, the actions, materials and artefacts people communicate with) that modes make available to people in particular places and times (what is meant by mode is discussed in detail later in this chapter and by Gunther Kress in Chapter 4 and Theo Van Leeuwen in Chapter 5). The work by O'Toole (1994) and Kress and Van Leeuwen (1996, 2006) has contributed to mapping the semiotic resources of art and visual images. Detailed studies have also been undertaken to describe the semiotic resources, organizing principles, and cultural references of many other modes. These include the semiotic modes of colour (Kress and Van Leeuwen, 2002; Van Leeuwen, 2010), gesture and movement (Kress et al., 2001, 2004; Martinec, 2000; Bezemer, Chapter 25 this volume; Bezemer et al., 2011; Mondada, 2011), gaze (Lancaster, 2001; Bezemer, 2008), voice and music (Van Leeuwen, 1999; West, 2007, Chapter 30 this volume) and space (O'Toole, 2004; Stenglin, 2009, Chapter 31 this volume; Van Leeuwen, 2005a), to name a few.

Numerous studies have been conducted that set out to understand how semiotic resources are used to articulate discourses across a variety of contexts. The semiotic resources, functions and systems of multiple modes have been described with respect to buildings and rooms, for instance how the design of a child's bedroom connects with notions of gender identity (Kress and Van Leeuwen, 2001), how framing – disconnection and connection of elements – is realized through the use of spatial rhyme or contrast, segregation or separation of elements in school and office buildings (Van Leeuwen, 2005a), the analysis of ranks and metafunctional systems in the Sydney Opera House to understand its meanings (O'Toole, 2004), as well as the design and experience of museum exhibitions (e.g. Ravelli, 2005; Diamantopoulou, 2008; Stenglin, Chapter 31 this volume). Multimodal studies have focused on how the resources of image and writing as well as other modes are organized on the page or screen of textbooks, websites and other digital learning resources (e.g. Unsworth, 2001; Kress and Bezemer, 2008; Jones, 2005, Chapter 9 this volume; Guo, 2004; Lim Fei, 2004; Norris, 2012; O'Halloran and Smith, 2011) as well as films, adverts and other new media texts (e.g. O'Halloran, 2004a, Chapter 8 this volume; Burn and Parker, 2003; Burn, 2009, Chapter 27 this volume; Baldry, 2004) and other multimodal texts. As this brief review suggests, the scope of resources that multimodal research engages with is wide-ranging.

Chapters 24–33, which form Part IV of this handbook, provide case study analysis of modes, and are briefly introduced here.

The dimensions of tables as products and three-dimensional objects as mode is described by Björkvall in Chapter 24, who draws out the relation between practical function and symbolic meaning potential of such objects. Bezemer focuses in on the semiotic resources of gesture as a mode in the context of surgical operations in Chapter 25. Jaworski and Thurlow in Chapter 26 investigate how gaze and gesture and the camera as an object are central modes in tourists' social interaction with and construction of place and identities. The next three chapters take film and video as their research focus. Burn in Chapter 27 discusses the mode of moving image that he names the 'kineikonic mode'. The semantic patterns and multimodal relationships within complex multimodal texts such as film are the focus of O'Halloran in Chapter 28, while Van Leeuwen uses film and video to explore colour as a mode in Chapter 29. In Chapter 30, West offers an analysis of interaction as a combination of speech, gesture (including gaze, body movement, positioning in the room, use of artefacts, etc.) and music within the specific educational setting. The communicative functions of space are the focus of Stenglin's case study in Chapter 31 on the analysis of a gallery exhibition. The use of the modal resources of writing and image is discussed by Mavers in Chapter 32 in her analysis of children's multimodal mapping as one instance of image in the multimodal ensemble. Finally, Knox focuses on the semiotic resources and functions of structure and layout in online newspaper texts.

Some multimodal studies use a style of diagramming called *system networks* to map the metafunctional meaning potentials of modes (e.g. Kress and Van Leeuwen, 1996; Van Leeuwen, 1999). Several authors in this book make explicit use of the metafunctions and system networks (see Van Leeuwen, Chapter 5, Björkvall, Chapter 24; Stenglin, Chapter 31; Knox, Chapter 33), although how the metafunctions feature within multimodal analysis varies. Within systemic functional approaches to multimodality the metafunctions and the development of corresponding system networks are used to map the potentials for making meaning as a system, while within the social semiotic approach to multimodality, the metafunctions are generally used as a conceptual tool to describe and explore the semiotic resources and meaning potential that people use to make meaning rather than to map the system itself.

Investigating intersemiotic relations

The relationships across and between modes in multimodal texts and interaction are a central area of multimodal research. Substantial theoretical descriptions of the dynamics of interaction between image and language have been offered, for example, by the early work of Kress and Van Leeuwen (1996) and Lemke's work on science textbooks (1998b) and work by Bezemer and Kress (2008). Bezemer and Kress examine contemporary curriculum materials to investigate the learning gains and losses of different multimodal ensembles. This work draws on a corpus of learning resources for secondary school in science, mathematics and English from the 1930s, the 1980s and from the first decade of the twenty-first century, as well as digitally represented and online learning resources from the year 2000 onward. The project provides a social semiotic account of the changes to the design of learning resources and of their epistemological and social/pedagogic significance and shows that image and layout are increasingly meshed in the construction of content. O'Halloran has also examined intersemiotic relations between language, images and mathematical symbolism in mathematics texts (2005, Chapter 8 this volume) and mathematics classrooms (2000). Research on the multimodal resources of digital screen-based texts also supports this finding: in complex multimodal texts, the boundaries between modes blur and mesh in new configurations (Chapters 20, 27, 8, 29, 33 and 34).

Research by Martinec and Salway (2005) examines the relationship between image and text. They draw on systemic functional grammar to classify the relations between image and text in terms of the dependency relations between image and word (equal or unequal) and the nature of the semantic linkage between elements. They classify these relations as elaboration, extension, or enhancement. *Elaboration* refers to a relation where one clause restates or clarifies another; in *extension* one clause adds information to another; and in *enhancement* one clause provides information such as how, when, where or why in relation to the other clause. Martinec and Salway have identified examples of these three kinds of linkages between images and text segments and offer a semantic system of image–text relations. Martinec and Van Leeuwen's (2008) study of intersemiotic relations in new media texts suggests that the relations between image and text are potentially remade through their reconfiguration in digital media, although these relations are not (yet) fully established or stable.

How people draw on different modes when they communicate has also been the subject of studies within multimodality. Bourne and Jewitt (2003), for example, analysed how a teacher's orchestration of modes in a classroom drew together the semiotic and social resources of texts and students to create a gendered debate. Shifting the focus from teachers to students, Flewitt's (2006) multimodal study of preschool classroom interaction demonstrates the strong link between the communicative demands of a context (in this case home and preschool playgroup) and the modes in use. Focusing on all modes of communication (speech, gesture, movement, gaze and so on) she is able to scrutinize young children's multifunctional uses of different modalities as 'intentional, socially organized activity in the construction of meaning' and to argue against 'pathologizing the absence of talk' (Flewitt, 2006: 47). These studies show the potential of multimodal research to offer a different account of classroom communication by locating the analysis of speech in the broader context of children's total multimodal resources.

The theorization of intersemiotic resources is a key aspect of multimodality. One associated concept is multimodal cohesion (Van Leeuwen, 2005a; Adami, 2010); this explores how different semiotic resources are integrated to form multimodal texts and communicative events via rhythm, composition, information linking, and dialogue.

Many of the chapters in this volume are concerned with the interaction of semiotic modes. Norris in Chapter 6 introduces two concepts for thinking about these relationships, namely *modal density* and *modal intensity*. Newfield in Chapter 7 outlines the concepts of transformation, transduction and the transmodal moment as tools for analysing the interaction of modes across texts. Unsworth and Cléirigh discuss image text relations in Chapter 12 and critically engage with early work emphasizing the distinctively different semiotic affordances of image and language and propose a semiotic framework designed to address the synergistic nature of image–language interaction in meaning construction. Approaching intersemiotic relations from a different starting point in Chapter 8, O'Halloran takes a historical view of the semiotic landscape in mathematics, with a particular focus on mathematical symbolic notation.

Multimodality and technology

The multimodal facilities of digital technologies enable image, sound and movement to enter the communicational landscape in new and significant ways. The facilities and features of multimodal configurations can impact on design and text production and interpretative practices.

Multimodal research has been conducted on the technologization of practices and communication and interaction more generally (e.g. Marsh, 2005; Alvermann, 2001; Leander, 2007; Unsworth *et al.*, 2005; Lankshear and Knobel, 2003; Cope and Kalantis, 2000). Much of this work explores and theorizes the nature of image and writing relations in narratives, relationships between book- and computer-based versions of texts, and the role of on-line communities of various kinds in the critique, as well as the interpretation and generation of new forms of multimodal and digital narratives and literacy practices. This work often describes new forms of literacy in an attempt to remap the territory of communication in a contemporary context and the kinds of practices that help move across it, such as blogging and culture jamming (Lankshear and Knobel, 2003; Sefton-Green and Sinker, 2000). Recent studies suggest that conventional print literacy pedagogy proceeds independently of the everyday multimodal social and communicative worlds of many children (e.g. Marsh, 2006). Marsh's studies (2006), for example, investigate young children's (age 2.5 to 4 years) mediascapes to identify the complex multimodal communicative practices that they are engaged with in the home. Her focus is on understanding the functions that these digital media expressions have in maintaining the social relations of the family, accessing knowledge, self-expression, and the development of literacy skills. She documents how migrant students reappropriate and use media designs in creative play, family life and home/school transitions.

The visual character of writing comes to the fore on screen, for instance, to function as objects of literacy in fundamentally different ways than it does on the page (Jewitt, 2002, 2005). Jewitt's (2002) case study on the transformation from printed novel to novel as CD-ROM, for example, suggests that the visual character of writing on screen, combined with the dominance of image, serves to restructure texts, and fragment forms of writing. A modularization that can be seen across many contexts as information is reorganized across the screen, and elsewhere, to produce information in bite-size chunks regardless of media and mode. Another potential resource of digital technologies is the mode of hypertext which embeds writing, image (and other modes) into web-like patterns and layers of information and genres that make meaning-making a process of navigation and choice, and create new resources (and demands) on meaning-making (Luke, 2003; Lemke, 2002b; Zammit and Callow, 1998; Zammit and Downes, 2002).

Technology and its impact on multimodal representation and interaction is a theme that runs across this handbook, and which is foregrounded in several of its chapters.

In Chapter 8, for example, O'Halloran examines the impact of the printing press and computer technology on the semiotic landscape of mathematics. Rodney Jones in Chapter 9 investigates technology as a site of display and its impact on multimodal communication. In particular he explores how technology has affected the ways people use their bodies as a communicative resource in social interaction through the analysis of how gay men use an internet website to create displays of their bodies. Kevin Leander and Lalitha Vasudevan approach the theme of culture and multimodality through the lens of mobile and video technology in Chapter 10. In Chapter 11, Lemke explores issues of how technologies produce meaning effects across multiple timescales, using the illustrative example of the computer and video games and transmedia franchises, which are typically experienced over times as long as 50 hours over periods of weeks or months, while in Chapters 27, 28, 29 and 33 the modal configurations of digital technologies are a focus of investigation in the context of film, games and online news.

Knowledge, pedagogy and literacy

When first made by the New London Group (1996) (Courtney Cazden, James Gee, Gunther Kress, Allan Luke and others) the call to understand knowledge and pedagogy as multimodal was radical. A key design element of a future pedagogy was heralded as 'designs for other modes of meaning' (New London Group, 1996). In part this call was a response to the social and cultural reshaping of the communicational landscape (related to globalization, new technologies, and new demands for work). The conclusion that reading this 'new' multimedia, multimodal landscape for its linguistic meanings alone is not enough was inevitable. This work spawned a strand of educational research and pedagogic models within which multimodality (broadly conceived) is a key factor (Cope and Kalantzis, 2000).

A special issue of *Linguistics and Education* on multimodality was one of the first publications to provide tools for educational researchers wanting to undertake multimodal research (Lemke, 1998c). From early 2000 there has been an explosion of interest in multimodality within research and this perspective has been actively taken up by educational researchers leading to substantial work that looks at multimodal meaning-making across a wide range of sites. Substantial multimodal research has been undertaken in pre-school and early years contexts, with a focus on meaning multimodal making practices (e.g. Bearne and Kress, 2001; Kress, 1997a; Kenner, 2004; Mavers, 2003; Pahl, 1999; Lancaster, 2001; Marsh, 2006). Science education has proven to be a productive site for multimodal investigations into the construction of knowledge across a range of resources (e.g. Kress *et al.*, 2001; Reis *et al.*, 2007), as has mathematics education (O'Halloran, 2000, 2005), music education (West, 2007) and school English and Media education (Goodwyn, 2005; Kress *et al.*, 2005; Burn and Durran, 2007). Multimodal studies in Higher Education have also examined pedagogic strategies and learning (Archer, 2008).

Taken as a whole, these multimodal studies show that significant pedagogic work is realized through a range of modes. The Multimodal Production of School English project (Kress *et al.*, 2004) showed that this holds true even in a curriculum context such as English where talk and writing dominate the classroom. The complex ways in which image, gesture, gaze, interaction with objects, body posture, writing and speech interact in the classroom production of school subject knowledge. It highlighted how students and teachers co-produce notions of ability, resistance and identity in the classroom through their multimodal interaction. The project also analysed how classroom displays, space, furniture and artefacts were designed to realize versions of English. This research showed that the work of interpreting school English is beyond language and requires the ability to make sense of a range of modes and the relationships between them. It also highlighted the complex multimodal identity work that students are engaged with in the classroom.

Gunther Kress, in Chapter 4, explores how modes shape knowledge and practices and the role of layout in the social and ontological consequences of the designed multimodal classification of information. The need to rethink what it means to learn and to be literate is a thread that runs through much multimodal research. This raises numerous research questions in relation to learning, including how representations impact on thinking and learning, as well as what literacy is and could be in a multimodal and multilingual communicational landscape and how to study it. These issues are picked up across the handbook, and are central to the arguments of Newfield (Chapter 7) and Archer (Chapter 13) that explore literacy, knowledge and pedagogic power through a multimodal lens, as well as Chapter 16 by Street, Pahl and Rowsell, who explore the potential of merging of New Literacy Studies with multimodality.

Identity practices

How identities are articulated through multimodal means is an area that has attracted some attention within multimodal research. Norris (2004a) has explored this by examining how people shift modes, and modal awareness to manage multiple identity roles in interaction (e.g. a mother engaging with their child, in the context of another interaction). Bezemer and Kress (2008) explore how pupil identities are negotiated in the classroom through the use of gaze, and orientation to texts and teachers. Jones (Chapter 9 this volume) explores how sexual identities are performed and managed through the display and withholding of representations of the body. Much of the work on what might broadly be called literacy practices from a multimodal perspective is also concerned with the production of identities (e.g. Pahl and Pollard, 2008; Stein, 2003, 2008; Stein and Mamabolo, 2005). For example, Stein (2008) explores how students in South African educational contexts express complex narratives of identities and culture through multimodal texts, highlighting the links between representational means, the production of identities, and social justice. Her work explores how multimodal pedagogy can reconnect linguistically disenfranchised learners – through the use of performance, semiotic artefacts, visual representation and so on. In the Olifantsvlei fresh stories project, Stein (2003) undertook a literacy project over six months with teachers and students of grades one and two at a Johannesburg primary school which serves children of unemployed and migrant families living in informal settlements. She worked with multimodal literacy practices and pedagogy through a systematic use of different semiotic modes in order to develop forms of learning beyond language. The project explored the relations between creativity, multimodal pedagogy, representation and learning. Student case studies involved observation and interviews, students' use of two-dimensional drawings, writing, three-dimensional figures, spoken dialogues, multimodal play and performance to create narratives of identity and culture. The focus was on the representation of doll and child figures and their symbolic meanings. Stein describes the children's transformation and recontextualization of culturally and historically situated practices of these representations. Stein argues that multimodal pedagogy enables the assertion of student identity, cultural practices and community to enter the school context in ways that are significant for literacy and teaching.

Identity is another theme that weaves its way across several chapters in this book, some more strongly than others. For instance, how young men interact with mobile technologies in the performitivity of their identities is a theme in Chapter 10 by Leander and Vausdevan. Lemke, in Chapter 11, who argues that how people experience and make sense of multimedia is strongly related to their identities, values and desires. Taking a different starting point for thinking about identity, Björkvall touches on the table as a marker of identity in Chapter 24, while Jaworski and Thurlow explore gesture and gaze as part of the identity practices of tourists in Chapter 26, and Burn develops them in different ways through his discussion of games and film in Chapter 27.

The following section discusses seven core concepts for multimodality: mode, materiality, modal affordance, meaning potential or metafunction, intersemiotic or intermodal relationships, genre and discourse. The nuances and differences in emphasis between the approaches to multimodality are discussed in Chapter 2, but it is worth noting here that these concepts are not given the same import or attention within each approach.

Core concepts for multimodal analysis

The following core concepts are in a state of change and fluidity, and are continuously taken up and shaped in different ways by different approaches to multimodal research. The descriptions that follow are therefore intended to provide the reader with useful (working) definitions.

Mode

Within social semiotics, a mode, its organizing principles and resources, is understood as an outcome of the cultural shaping of a material. The resources come to display regularities through the ways in which people use them. In other words in a specific context (time and place) modes are shaped by the daily social interaction of people. It is these that multimodal analysts call *modes*. Kress (Chapter 4 this volume) sets out the central issues of the category of mode, as seen from a social semiotic multimodal perspective. The chapter includes discussion of the 'logics' of modes; issues of mode, representation and knowledge; sign and mode, including the notion of modal choice and epistemological commitment; as well as the notion of sign, genre and discourse.

O'Halloran and O'Toole have a slightly different conception of 'semiotic resource' and 'mode' does not feature in the same way as for Kress and Van Leeuwen. From this perspective (and following from Halliday (1978), *Language as Social Semiotic*) language, mathematical symbolism and images, for example, are understood as semiotic resources rather than modes. Semiotic resources consist of systems of meaning that realize different functions, and therefore, meaning becomes a matter of choice from the systems of meaning from different semiotic resource, and how these choices integrate in multimodal phenomena. From this starting point, Language can be realized through written text (a visual mode) and spoken language (an oral mode). As O'Halloran argues in Chapter 8, the meanings of modern mathematical symbolism, for example, change when developed in the written mode as opposed to when it is realized in the oral mode.

Multimodal interactional analysis focuses on action and therefore does not have the same focus on mode, although all actions are understood as 'mediated by the systems of representation that they draw on' (Norris, 2004a: 12–13). However, the focus is on the situated interplay between modes at a given moment in social interaction (see Chapter 6).

The regular pattern of using a set of resources has traditionally been called 'grammar'. Machin has questioned the possibility and usefulness of applying a linguistic term such as 'grammar' to image and other modes (Chapter 15 this volume, and Machin, 2007). However, a general principle is that in order for something to 'be a mode' there needs to be a shared cultural sense of a set of resources and how these can be organized to realize meaning. A number of detailed studies on specific modes have helped to describe these semiotic resources, material affordances, organizing principles, and cultural references (e.g. the work on images by O'Toole (1994) and Kress and Van Leeuwen (1996) set out to map the semiotic resources of image). The chapters within this volume examine a variety of modal resources and their use including space, gesture, gaze, body posture and movement, sound, voice and music, image, mathematical symbolism, written and spoken language, and three-dimensional objects such as tables; as well as examining how these modal choices and configurations vary across a range of social settings and media.

The purpose of multimodal investigations is to understand the principles of use and modal resources available in a multimodal representation (a multimodal text) or the situated communicative moment, rather than to seek to establish a universal inventory for a mode. What is considered a mode and interaction between modes is inextricably shaped and construed by social, cultural and historical factors. These factors influence and mediate how modes are taken up and used for meaning-making and the production of modal conventions. People draw upon the available modal resources to make meaning in specific contexts. Consequently, any given mode is contingent upon fluid and dynamic resources of meaning, rather than static skill replication and use. It is in this way that modes are constantly transformed by their users in response to the communicative needs of communities, institutions and societies: new modes are created, and existing modes are transformed.

The influences of timescales, technologies and sites of display, history and culture are central to the idea of mode, issues that inform many of the chapters; in particular, see O'Halloran (Chapter 8). The resources of modes and the functions they are used to realize are also shaped in important ways by changing facilities of technologies, itself a part of the social landscape (see Jones, Chapter 9; Leander and Vausdevan, Chapter 10; Lemke, Chapter 11; Chouliaraki, Chapter 18; Knox, Chapter 33).

Semiotic resource

Semiotic resource is central to multimodality, although it features slightly differently within particular approaches. Kress and Van Leeuwen suggest semiotic resource can be thought of as the connection between representational resources and what people do with them. Van Leeuwen describes semiotic resource as follows:

> Semiotic resources are the actions, materials and artifacts we use for communicative purposes, whether produced physiologically – for example, with our vocal apparatus, the muscles we use to make facial expressions and gestures – or technologically – for example, with pen and ink, or computer hardware and software – together with the ways in which these resources can be organized. Semiotic resources have a meaning potential, based on their past uses, and a set of affordances based on their possible uses, and these will be actualized in concrete social contexts where their use is subject to some form of semiotic regime.
>
> (Van Leeuwen, 2005a: 285)

As indicated earlier, O'Toole (1994) and O'Halloran (2005) view semiotic resources (language, image, etc.) as systems of meaning that people have at their disposal. People make choices across different semiotic resources simultaneously and these combine in multimodal phenomena.

The emphasis on rules within social semiotics is on rules as socially made and changeable through social interaction (Van Leeuwen, 2005a). This stands in contrast to traditional semiotic understanding of rules (or codes) as fixed and resistant to modification (Saussure, 1974; Barthes, 1977c). Traditional semiotics sees language and other semiotic systems as a code or sets of rules for connecting signs and meanings. This means that once two or more people have understood the same code they can connect the same meanings to the same sounds or graphic patterns and understand each other. This suggests that the semiotic system is simply 'there'. It can be used but it cannot be changed in any way. The sign is viewed as a pre-existing conjunction of a signifier and signified, an element in a code, to be understood and used. This view of semiotic systems places people in a passive role to the production of meaning and establishes language and other semiotic systems as entirely stable.

The concept of semiotic resource offers a different starting point for thinking about semiotic systems and the role of the sign-maker in the process of making meaning. In this perspective, signs are a product of a social process of sign-making. A person (sign-maker) 'chooses' a semiotic resource from an available system of resources. They bring together a semiotic resource (a signifier) with the meaning (the signified) that they want to express. In other words, people express meanings through their selection from the semiotic resources that are available to them in a particular moment: meaning is choice from a system. But this choice is always socially located and regulated, both with respect to what resources are made available to who, and the discourses that regulate and shape how modes are used by people. There are various kinds of normative discourses for how we use semiotic resources – sometimes more, sometimes less binding, and of different kinds, but nonetheless they do provide 'rules' for their use. Discourses of gender, social class, race, generation, institutional norms and other articulations of power shape and regulate people's use of semiotic resources. These are not 'codes' in the sense that they cannot be changed and that they 'are simply there' – but they are social rules (Van Leeuwen, 2005a).

In addition to mapping the semiotic resources available to people to make meaning with, multimodality can *also* contribute to the development of new ways of using semiotic resources. Focusing (through historical analysis) on how semiotic resources come to be as they are multimodality can ask why they are as they are. This is a powerful way of enabling people to see *how* it is a 'reality' comes to be represented and offering the potential to *imagine* it differently and to *redesign* it. This shifts the primary focus from descriptive accounts to connect more explicitly with macro social, political and cultural concerns within design.

Metafunctions

The turn to social explanations within linguistics, for instance in the work of McDerrmot, Hymes and Halliday to name a few shifted attention onto how language is shaped by how people use it – the social functions that the resources of language are put to. This turn to the social provides the context for the linguist Michael Halliday's (1978) theorization of the social functions of language as realizing three *metafunctions*.

People, Halliday theorized, construct representations of 'what goes on in the world' and their experience of the world through the *ideational* resources of a mode. (*Ideational* meaning is also referred to as presentational meaning, and sometimes called experiential meaning or logical meaning.) In language this may be achieved in a number of ways, including the words chosen to represent people, places and things in the world; or the creation of different kinds of relationships between these 'participants' by positioning them as active, passive or reactive. Social relations between the person who makes a sign, the person who engages with it, and the thing that is represented are also realized in a sign. These relations are constituted and enacted by the *interpersonal* resources of a mode (sometimes referred to as 'orientational' meaning). These meanings need to be organized into texts and this draws on the *textual* resources of a mode (sometimes called organizational meaning). Language provides many different resources for realizing the cohesion and structure of a text. Halliday's work explores how these three kinds of meaning potentials are 'held by' the grammar and elements of language.

Multimodal approaches take up the concept of the metafunctions and apply them to *all* modal (semiotic) resources (that is the metafunctions are viewed as a higher order of meaning rather than specific to language). Another way of thinking about the metafunctions is as meaning potential that is 'what can be meant' or 'what can be done' with a particular set of modal (semiotic) resources. Jewitt (2006), for example, employed the metafunctions to analyse the how technology mediated learning influences the shapes of curriculum knowledge in the classroom with respect to image, gaze, gesture, writing, speech and so on. The ideational metafunction enabled questions to be asked on how the multimodal computer applications in use presented 'the world': what was included and excluded and how what was displayed shaped curriculum knowledge. Using the interpersonal metafunction made it possible to explore how learners were positioned to knowledge through the design of the multimodal applications they used. The textual metafunction provided a tool with which to get at how the arrangement of multimodal elements on screen organized the text.

Modal affordance, meaning potential and materiality

The term *affordances* is contested and continuously debated within multimodal research. It has particular emphasis and currency in social semiotic approaches to multimodality. It originated in the work on cognitive perception of Gibson (1977). It was later taken up by Norman in relation to design (1988, 1990). Norman's view of affordance considers the material and social aspects of design. Van Leeuwen uses affordance following Gibson and uses the term 'meaning potential' to refer to the material and the cultural aspects of modes. Taking a slightly different emphasis, *modal affordance*, is used by Kress (1993) to refer to what it is possible to express and represent easily with a mode. He positions affordance as a complex concept connected to both the material *and* the cultural, and the social historical use of a mode (each of which is intimately connected), while Jewitt argues that neither Gibson nor Norman's notion of affordance can adequately acknowledge how tools (conceptual and material objects) are shaped by people's use of them in specific social situations (Jewitt, 2008a).

In other words, the affordance in Kress's terms, or the meaning potential of a mode for Van Leeuwen, is shaped by how a mode has been used, what it has been repeatedly used to mean and do, and the social conventions that inform its use in context. Where a mode 'comes from', its history of cultural work, its provenance, becomes a part of its *affordance* or *meaning potential*. It thus follows, that image, in the form of graphic marks on a two-dimensional surface (i.e. its material) as well as how it has been socially shaped through its use, combine to offer different meaning potentials for the expression and representation of meaning than speech in the form of sounds over time and space.

The particular semiotic resources of a mode (or the particular systems of semiotic resources, from the perspective of O'Toole and O'Halloran) have come to be shaped through these different histories and so has people's use of them. Each mode (as it is realized in a particular social context) possesses a specific logic and provides different communicational and representational potentials, referred to as modal logic. The sounds of speech for instance usually happen across time, and this sequence in time shapes what can be done with (speech) sounds. The logic of sequence in time is unavoidable for speech: one sound is uttered after another, one word after another, one syntactic and textual element after another. This sequence becomes an affordance or meaning potential: it produces the possibilities for putting things first or last, or somewhere else in a sequence. The mode of speech is therefore strongly governed by the logic of time. In contrast, (still) images are more strongly governed by the logic of space and simultaneity. Like all governing principles they do not hold in all contexts and are realized through the complex interaction of the social as material and vice versa – in this sense the material constitutes the social and vice versa.

The connection between culture and nature, meaning and materiality is the focus of Chapter 5 by Theo Van Leeuwen who argues for 'their inextricable connection' through an account of the semiotics of voice quality and is a theme taken up across many of the chapters in this handbook.

The repeated use of modes to represent and communicate particular meanings in specific social contexts has resulted in the specialization of modes. From this perspective not every mode is equally 'useable' for a particular task. Some things can be signified in an image as well as through talk, while some others can only be realized in an image and others only in talk. This introduces the importance of the concept of intersemiotic relations, also referred to as intermodal relations, or multimodal ensembles.

Intersemiotic relationships

Modal affordance or meaning potential raises the question of what image is 'best' for and what words, and other modes and their arrangements are 'best' for in a particular context (Lanham,

2001). When several modes are involved in a communicative event (e.g. a text, a website, a spoken interchange) all of the modes combine to represent a message's meaning (e.g. Kress *et al.*, 2001, 2004). The meaning of any message is, however, distributed across all of these modes and not necessarily evenly. The different aspects of meaning are carried in different ways by each of the modes in the ensemble. Any one mode in that ensemble is carrying a part of the message only: each mode is therefore partial in relation to the whole of the meaning and speech and writing are no exception (Jewitt and Kress, 2002). Multimodal research attends to the interplay between modes to look at the specific work of each mode and how each mode interacts with and contributes to the others in the multimodal ensemble. At times the meaning realized by two modes can be 'aligned', at other times they may be complementary and at other times each mode may be used to refer to distinct aspects of meaning and be contradictory, or in tension (Lemke, 1998a). As Lemke has stated (2002: 303):

> No [written] text is an image. No text or visual representation means in all and only the same ways that text can mean. It is this essential incommensurability that enables genuine new meanings to be made from the combinations of modalities.

The relationships between modes as they are orchestrated in interactions (and texts) may realize tensions between the aspects of meaning in a text. This kind of tension can itself be meaningful and a means for encouraging reflection and critique. The structure of a text and hyperlinks realizes connections and disconnections between screens. These contribute to the expansion of meaning relations between elements. The question of what to attend to, what to 'make meaningful' is a significant aspect of the work of making meaning. In other words, the task of what to attend to and to select as salient to the task at hand is amplified by a multimodal focus.

As mentioned earlier, the question of how modes interact is dealt with by authors throughout this volume, in particular by Norris (Chapter 6), Jones (Chapter 9), Unsworth and Cléirigh (Chapter 12), Stöckl (Chapter 19), Jaworski and Thurlow (Chapter 26), Burn (Chapter 27), O'Halloran (Chapter 28) and Knox (Chapter 33).

Multimodal discourse

Multimodal discourse is a term used by many of the authors throughout this handbook and one that is fully engaged with by Chouliaraki in Chapter 18 on critical discourse analysis and multimodality. It is an important yet contested term rooted in different disciplines and used in a variety of ways. In a narrow sense, discourse can be understood as language in use – everyday ways of talking – what James Gee in his book *Social Linguistics and Literacies: Ideology in Discourses* (1996) refers to as 'little d' discourse. In a broader sense it can be used to refer to a system of language use and other meaning-making practices (e.g. behaviour, dress and customary practices/habits) that form ways of talking about social reality – what Gee refers to as 'big D' Discourse. For example the Discourse of traffic regulation, commercial Discourse, medical Discourse, or legal Discourse. In socio-linguistics, discourse tends to be used to refer to extended stretches of speech or writing and to draw attention to the uses and organization of language in its social context. In sociology and philosophy, the writings of Foucault have been particularly important, bringing into focus not only the social origins but also the social effects of power that discourse has on social practices. Critical discourse analysis (CDA) is usually associated with the work of Chouliaraki and Fairclough, which provides a method of analysing texts to complement

Foucault's theories and concepts, as well as offering examples for the study of media discourse, policy discourse and interactional discourse.

Discourse is an important term for multimodality, and many working in this area are concerned with understanding the use and effects of discourse through the uses of modes and their arrangement in modal ensembles. The assumption is that all multimodal texts, artefacts and communicative events are always discursively shaped, and that all modes, in different ways, offer means for the expression of discourses. From this perspective, different discourses may be brought into play modally and, therefore, the choice of modes may itself be used analytically to indicate the presence of different discourses in specific texts.

As increasingly media are multimedia forms that occupy multimodal spaces it is perhaps not surprising that CDA has strong links with multimodality, notably in the work of Chouliaraki. In her edited collection *Self-Mediation: New Media, Citizenship and Civil Selves* (2012), she looks into the multimodality of new media discourses, such as convergence journalism and social networking sites, so as to explore how these discourses blur the boundaries between private and public selves and change the ways in which we understand and enact practices of citizenship.

Multimodal genre

The term 'genre' originates from literary studies and has been extended to describe the regular patterns of semiotic choices in multimodal communicative objects and events that are particular to specific communities and cultures. John Bateman (Chapter 17) has led research in this area, notably his book *Multimodality and Genre* (2008) with a focus on extending genre to the formally specified and technical usage within functional linguistics to provide a theoretical mechanism that is both predictive and explanatory to support the interpretation of genre as a socially significant activity. He describes a multimodal genre as 'a temporarily stabilized, conventionalized and structured bundle of adopted solutions to a socially recognized and for that genre distinctive communicative task among a community of users' (Bateman, 2008: 227). Genre is intimately tied to the modes made available by a medium, the social context and communicative purpose. Multimodal genres are, according to Bateman,

> constituted by collections of rhetorical strategies deploying the semiotic modes provided by the medium within which the communication is being enacted. These strategies may vary in their form of realization over time and (co)operate (i) in order to achieve the genre's socio-communicative goals and (ii) in order to support the genre's recognition (i.e. over-coded expressions that indicate that the genre is being enacted).
>
> (2008: 224)

From this perspective, genre is a means to understand the link between social context and a meaning system.

Bateman analyses page-based and filmic multimodal texts that combine modes in layouts that are becoming ever more sophisticated. The interpretation and effective use of these texts present serious challenges for document design and document interpretation. Bateman's work is also significant in that it documents how genres change over time and why this forms an essential part of document production and analysis. John Knox (Chapter 33) is another scholar who has made a significant contribution to understanding multimodal genre in theorizing and empirically researching the changing genres of online newspapers. His work outlines a genre-specific visual grammar for online newspaper home pages is emerging in response to the demands of the new medium and historical and social trends in news reporting (Knox, 2007).

The concepts introduced above are common across multimodal research in this volume. There are, however, important nuances and differences in emphasis with the field of multimodality and these are the focus of the next chapter.

The limitations of multimodal research

Although multimodal research has much to offer, it also has limitations that need to be considered and understood.

A criticism sometimes made of multimodality is that it can seem rather impressionistic in its analysis. How do you know that this gesture means this or this image means that? In part this is an issue of the linguistic heritage of multimodality, that is, how do you get from linguistics to all modes. In part it is the view of semiotic resources as contextual, fluid and flexible – which makes the task of building 'stable analytical inventories' of multimodal semiotic resources complex. It is perhaps useful to note that this problem exists for speech or writing. The principles for establishing the 'security' of a meaning or a category are the same for multimodality as for linguistics (or philosophy or fine art). It is resolved by linking the meanings people make (whatever the mode) to context and social function. Increasingly, multimodal research looks across a range of data (combining textual/video analysis with interviews for example) and towards participant involvement to explore analytical meanings as one response to this potential problem.

Linked with the above problem of interpretation is the criticism that multimodality is a kind of 'linguistic imperialism' that imports and imposes linguistic terms on everything. But these critics overlook the fact that much of the work on multimodality has its origins in a particular strand of linguistics: namely, the social semiotic theory of communication first proposed by Halliday (1978). The social component of this perspective on language sets it apart from narrower concerns with syntactic structures, language and mind and language universals that have long dominated the discipline. This view of communication can be applied (in different ways) to all modes, to gesture and image no less and no more than to speech and writing.

Description is theoretically grounded and contributes to theory building. There is a need to ask questions of and through detailed description. For instance, to ask what kind of discourses are being articulated in a context and why, what is the social function of the representations being described. For example, to ask how the multimodal design of the English classroom shapes what school English is, what texts are included in English and how does this shape what it might mean to be student in that classroom and so on. This analytical focus is important to show how discourses are articulated in a context so that they can be made explicit, shared or challenged and redesigned. Multimodal research is problematic if it offers endless detailed descriptions and fails to make clear the broad questions it seeks to answer.

Multimodal analysis is an intensive research process in relation to both time and labour. Multimodal research can be applied to take a detailed look at 'big' issues and questions through specific instances. Nonetheless the scale of multimodal research *can* restrict the potential of multimodality to comment beyond the specific to the general. The development of multimodal corpora may help to overcome some of these limitations, as might the potential to combine multimodal analysis with quantitative analysis in innovative ways.

One purpose of this handbook is to engage with these limitations, to clarify what multimodality can and cannot do, and to explore the ways in which multimodality can be brought into productive conversation with other theoretical approaches to further develop this approach and its methodological tools (see Part III).

Summary

This chapter has provided an introduction the theoretical assumptions that underpin multi-modal research. In response to the question of whether multimodality can truly be considered a theory or whether it is more appropriate to view it as a method, this chapter has suggested that the comparison with Green and Bloome's (1997) commentary on ethnography, as theory, as perspective, or as method, is useful and that these different degrees of engagement with multimodality help to make sense of what is seen to count as multimodal. The chapter has provided a set of working definitions for the key concepts that inform approaches to multimodality, elaborating on the origins and development of these concepts over the past decade and begun to explore some of the nuances and differences across approaches most strongly associated with multimodality: social semiotics, discourse analysis, and interactional analysis. Having sketched the terrain of multimodality as a research field, the next chapter focuses on these three approaches to examine the variation between them, each of which informs the work in this volume.

2

Different approaches to multimodality

Carey Jewitt

Introduction

Chapter 1 discussed how the term multimodality is used, the main assumptions that underlie this approach, and the core concepts that inform multimodal analysis. It focused on the theoretical and methodological connections across different perspectives on multimodality and the interests that bind them: the fine-grained analysis, the need to understand the details of texts and interactions, the focus on meaning-making as social and semiotic, the interest in the place of language within a multimodal ensemble, and the demand to broaden conceptions of communication beyond language. The shared interests, and to some extent the shared histories of different approaches to multimodality, make multimodal approaches distinct from other takes on communication and meaning-making. For instance, multimodality is distinct from cognitive psychological approaches that focus more explicitly on the internal, notions of mind, and cognitive processes. (However, there may well be considerable potential for productive research working across semiotic and cognitive approaches.)

This chapter turns now to investigate the differences between particular approaches to multimodality. This chapter focuses on the three main perspectives within multimodality: social semiotic multimodal analysis, a systemic functional approach (multimodal discourse analysis), and multimodal interactional analysis. It explores how features such as mode and semiotic resource are articulated across these different perspectives and teases out what this means for the kinds of data and questions each perspective might address. As argued in the previous chapter, multimodality can be understood as a theory, a perspective, or a field of enquiry or methodological application. The chapter closes with a brief introduction to some of the disciplines and theoretical approaches that are in conversation with multimodality as discussed in the chapters in Part III of the handbook.

Three approaches within multimodality

The different approaches to multimodality can be roughly categorized into three main approaches: a social semiotic approach to multimodal analysis associated originally with the work of Kress and Van Leeuwen (e.g. Kress and Van Leeuwen, 2001; Van Leeuwen, 2005a); a systemic functional grammar (SFG) multimodal approach to discourse analysis (associated with O'Toole, Baldry and Thibault, and O'Halloran (e.g. O'Halloran, 2004b, 2005, 2011); and multimodal interactional analysis (linked initially with the work of Scollon and Scollon and that of Norris (e.g. Scollon and Scollon, 2003; Norris, 2004a, 2012)). The following section summarizes these three primary perspectives and gives a sense of the particular accent each brings to multimodality.

The differences between these three approaches stem from the historical influences and directions that have shaped them, as well as the degree of emphasis each gives to context, the internal relations within modes or modal systems (e.g. level and rank), and the agentive work of the sign-maker. How each of these three perspectives configures these factors is both constituted by and constitutes the kind of research that is typically undertaken – in other words, how each has evolved to attend to particular aspects of multimodality and, to some extent, to specific sites of research. As with any mapping of a complex terrain the boundaries drawn may sometimes prove to be too crude. In addition, any boundary will be contested and remade. Nonetheless boundaries and definitions can provide useful opportunities to cross and transgress, to rethink and to collaborate across – it is with this in mind that the boundaries between these perspectives are drawn here.

Social semiotic multimodality

Halliday's theories of social semiotics and systemic functional grammar provided the initial starting point for social semiotic multimodal analysis (Kress and Van Leeuwen, 2001; Van Leeuwen, 2005a). In *Language as Social Semiotic* (1978) Halliday argued for the need to socially situate language and to understand texts as complex signs. Signs, for Halliday, are a material instantiation of the three types of social meaning/functions introduced earlier in Chapter 1 (i.e. the *ideational*, *interpersonal* and *textual metafunctions*). Kress and Van Leeuwen in their book *Reading Images* (1996/2006) indicated how these meaning functions are realized visually, through concepts such as composition, modality and framing. They offered a framework to describe the semiotic resources of images and analyse how these resources can be configured to design interpersonal meaning, to present the world in specific ways, and to realize coherence. *Reading Images* demonstrated and generated a series of semiotic network systems that show the semiotic resources of image in play and how discourses are articulated visually through the design of these resources. Together they set out to describe available choices and visual semiotic resources as having meaning potentials and to show how choices of visual semiotic resources can be used to communicate ideologies and discourses.

Kress and Van Leeuwen's work on visual communication opened the door for multimodality and laid the groundwork for extending and adapting social semiotics across a range of modes (Kress et al., 2001, 2004; Kress and Van Leeuwen, 2001; Kress, 2003b, 2010a; Van Leeuwen, 1999, 2005d). As this social semiotic approach to multimodality evolved there was a growing emphasis on how the context of communication and the sign-maker shaped signs and meaning. Kress (and differently so, Van Leeuwen, who maintains a stronger relationship to SFG) moved towards a more flexible notion of grammar, with a focus on people's situated choice of resources rather than emphasizing the system of available resources. The SFG model, while still considered relevant in many respects, was re-evaluated and a looser reading of Halliday was adopted. Alongside this loosening, Kress and Van Leeuwen, and others working from this perspective, looked elsewhere for resources to assist the analysis of multimodal resources and to further explore the situated character of meaning-making.

Multimodality, as developed by Kress and Van Leeuwen and associates, expanded the realm of reference to draw on interactional socio-linguists, particularly the work of Goffman, Bateson and Hall. They also looked to other approaches offering insight into non-linguistic modes such as film theory, art history and iconography and musicology. Less explicit but still significant influences include the work of sociologists Foucault, Bernstein and Bourdieu and work within visual communication on perception and cognition. This approach to multimodality goes beyond the traditional linguistic foundations of multimodality.

A primary focus of social semiotic multimodal analysis is on mapping how modal resources are used by people in a given community/social context, in other words sign-making as a social process. The emphasis is on the sign-maker and their situated use of modal resources. This foregrounds the question of what choices people make (from the resources available to them) and the non-arbitrary and motivated character of the relationship between language and social context. There is therefore a strong emphasis on the notion of context within social semiotic multimodal analysis. The context shapes the resources available for meaning-making and how these are selected and designed.

From this perspective analytical interest in the modal system (its resources and principles) is strongly located in (and regulated through) the social and cultural. When making signs, people bring together and connect the available form that is most apt to express the meaning they want to express at a given moment. Signs, modes and meaning-making are treated as relatively fluid, dynamic and open systems intimately connected to the social context of use. There is less focus on the development of general modal networks and systems, and the notion of level and rank is given little emphasis. Research within this approach is concerned with the resources of modes, gesture or image for example, but this concern centres on mapping resources through detailed observational accounts of these modes as they are realized in a given social context. In Kress and Bezemer's analysis of school textbooks for example, the analytical dimensions of layout or image are generated from the analysis of the texts themselves rather than from a predefined system. In other words modal systems are studied in context, with a focus on how they are used and this use is socially and culturally contextualized. The semiotic resources of a mode are understood as constantly in a process of change both at the level of cultural regulation of semiotic resources (rather than a strict prescriptive grammar) and the elements for meaning-making. This opens up new possibilities for semiotic resources to come into the 'modal stock' of meaning-making potentials.

Kress introduced a strong emphasis on the social character of text in his work with Hodge (Hodge and Kress, 1988) and developed the concept of the motivated sign (Kress, 1993). This served to foreground the agency of the sign-maker and the process of sign-making. In *Before Writing* (Kress, 1997a) Kress offers a detailed account of the materiality and processes of young children's engagement with texts, and how they interpret, transform and redesign the semiotic resources and signs available to them.

From this perspective, signs (e.g. talk, gestures, and textual artefacts) are analysed as material residues of a sign-maker's interests. The analytical focus is on understanding their interpretative and design patterns and the broader discourses, histories and social factors that shape that. In a sense then, the text is seen as a window onto its maker. Viewing signs as motivated and constantly being remade raises the question of what motivates a person's choice of one semiotic resource over another. Kress developed the idea of *interest* in response to this question:

'Interest' is the articulation and realisation of an individual's relation to an object or event, acting out of that social complex at a particular moment, in the context of an interaction with other constitutive factors of the situation which are considered as relevant by the individual.

(Kress, 1993: 174)

33

Interest connects a person's choice of one resource over another with the social context of sign production. The modal resources that are available to the person are a part of that context. So whereas in some perspectives on meaning the focus is on the *modal system*, here the focus is on the process of meaning-making. In this way the relationship between a *signifier* and a *signified* is seen as a trace of the characteristics of the person who made the sign and what they want to represent. From this perspective the sign is a product of the complex interaction of the sign-maker's 'physiological, psychological, emotional, cultural, and social origins' (Kress, 1997: 11). It is the sign-maker's 'interest' that motivates their selection of semiotic resources – their decision of what it is criterial to represent.

Van Leeuwen's analytical focus is on rules and normative discourses (discussed in Chapter 1 with relation to semiotic resource). This offers a different emphasis on the agency of the sign-maker. In comparison to Kress's notion of interest, Van Leeuwen's focus on the social production and articulation of meaning gives less emphasis to the individual and the contingent and places more emphasis on the communal and the social. Jewitt (2008b) argues for the need to understand the social beyond its articulation through the individual sign-maker and attempts to bring together multimodality and activity theory to realize this. Across these positions nonetheless a primary analytical focus of a social semiotic perspective on multimodal analysis is how these meaning potentials are selected and orchestrated to make meaning by people in particular contexts to realize specific social meaning. In this sense social semiotic multimodality places the work of the sign-maker at its centre.

Broadly speaking, the authors within this volume whose work could be described as being situated within this approach to multimodality include Gunther Kress (Chapter 4), Denise Newfield (Chapter 7), Arlene Archer (Chapter 13), Carey Jewitt (Chapters 1 and 2), David Machin (Chapter 15), Jeff Bezemer (Chapter 25), Andrew Burn (Chapter 27), Diane Mavers (Chapter 32), and Theo Van Leeuwen (Chapters 5 and 29), although each differs in some respect from the other.

Multimodal discourse analysis

Halliday's social systemic functional grammar (SFG) (Halliday, 1985) provided the foundation and remains the central theoretical framework for what O'Halloran has called multimodal discourse analysis (MDA) and systemic functional multimodal discourse analysis (SF-MDA). The name clearly foregrounds 'discourse'. A concern with 'discourse' also runs through the work of Hodge and Kress in *Social Semiotics* (1988), and Kress and Van Leeuwen in *Multimodal Discourse* (2001). However, the word 'discourse' is used with a wide range of meanings, ranging from a sociologically oriented approach (Foucault) to a more linguistic one. So theoretically, methodologically and analytically the word 'discourse' is used to describe different approaches. O'Halloran's multimodal discourse analysis approaches 'discourse' at the micro-textual level. In the social semiotics of Hodge and Kress, and Kress and Van Leeuwen, 'discourse' names macropolitical and social/institutional interests. As Kress and Van Leeuwen (2001: 4) state: 'Discourses are socially constructed knowledges of (some aspect of reality) … developed in specific social contexts, in ways which are appropriate to the interests of social actors in these contexts … .'

This perspective on multimodality builds on O'Toole's application of SFG to examine art images in his book *The Language of Displayed Art* (1994). O'Toole offers a framework for the analysis of paintings using a constituent structure approach with ranks including picture, figure and member. He documents the systems of meaning (e.g. resources such as vertical lines, direction of gaze) for the realization of the syntax of the metafunctions – representational (i.e. ideational), modal (i.e. interpersonal) and compositional (i.e. textual). This approach to visual analysis has been extended across a range of dimensions of art and taken forward by O'Halloran (2004b, 2005, 2011) to describe the grammatical systems that constitute the meaning potential of semiotic resources and the metafunctions as providing a 'common platform for conceptualizing semiotic resources and for analysing the ways semiotic choices integrate in objects and events' (Chapter 8 this volume). This approach has been used by O'Halloran to examine the integration of mathematical symbolism, images and mathematical symbolism in mathematics texts (O'Halloran, 2005), mathematical classroom discourse (2000) and visual semiosis in film through the application of 'a metafunctionally organized rank constituent structure with ranks film plot, sequences, scene, mise-en-scene and frame' (2004a: 114). (The benefits of breaking images down into these ranks is questioned and critiqued by Machin in Chapter 15 this volume.)

This perspective on multimodality emphasizes the *metafunctional systems* underlying semiotic resources and the integration of system choices in multimodal phenomena, while multimodality as developed by Kress and Van Leeuwen (discussed in the previous section) has emphasized the *social semiotic*. The MDA approach is to develop a theoretical framework for describing the metafunctional-based systems for each semiotic resource and the intersemiotic mechanisms through which semiotic choices combine in multimodal discourse and use the theoretical framework to analyse multimodal phenomena. This approach involves a focus on both system and system in use. This interest in the system and meaning as choice from a system has meant that Halliday's social semiotic theory, and concepts from SFG have provided fundamental starting points for O'Halloran and others. For example, SFG concepts and categories (e.g. rank, clause, phase) and the concept of stratification where semiotic systems are modelled according to the expression plane (e.g. phonology, graphology and typography for language), content plane (grammar and discourse semantics) and context plane (context of situation, i.e. register, and context of culture, i.e. genre, and ideology) are used to support the development of systems for semiotic resources beyond language and the integration of semiotic choices in multimodal artefacts and events. The analytical focus is on accounting for, and describing the semiotic instantiation of these – how a system achieves this focus, how the metafunctions are realized through the systems of meaning which constitute the meaning potential of semiotic resources, and how system choices integrate in multimodal phenomena to create meaning in the context of the situation and the context of culture.

The systemic functional linguistic emphasis is clear in O'Toole's analysis of the Sydney Opera House, for example:

> Like a clause in language, a building incorporates Types of Process and their Participants; its specific functions are modified in terms of material, size, colour and texture; and its component elements are organized taxonomically like lexical items in the vocabulary of our language.
>
> (O'Toole, 2004: 15)

This approach foregrounds syntax-level rank-scale (a hierarchical organization of elements) as one of its starting points differentiating between the options available at lower ranks in relation to those available at higher ranks. In his analysis of the Sydney Opera House, elements are ranked from the smallest rank, that is, the rank of Element, for instance the one million roof tiles, lamps and windows, moving up to rank of room, the rank of floor and the rank of building. This interest in rank is seen in the work of Baldry (2004: 84) working within what he calls the 'Systemic functional tradition of multimodality'. He argues for the 'need to show how meaning is built up as a series of functional units – typically sub-phases, phases, but also potentially macrophases, minigenres and genres'. His analysis of a car advert focuses on its phasal and metafunctional organization in order to show the values that are associated with the advert and to provide a systematic description. The intention is the specification of the system that makes up the grammar of a semiotic resource (such as architecture) in order to understand the social and political choices someone has made. This approach is more clearly aligned with the Halliday's social semiotic theory and has engaged less with other theories of the visual or non-linguistic forms.

Multimodal discourse analysis, as it is associated with O'Halloran, is concerned with the development of focused systemic grammars – often in the form of system networks – which map the semiotic resources available. In this way, semiotic resources are seen as systems of meaning which change over time. It takes a systematic focus to semiotic resources as sets of sets of metafunctionally orientated systems. The aim is to produce a metatheory capable of theorizing semiotic resources, their functionality and meaning potential, and their integration in multimodal phenomena that are interpreted in the context of situation and culture. The ultimate task of this perspective is the development of a comprehensive multimodal social semiotic theory for the articulation of meaning in multisemiotic and multimodal artefacts and events that constitute culture. The descriptions of language and other semiotic systems are conceptualized at a level of abstraction most directly relevant in some respects to social meaning-making in general. The emphasis is placed on understanding and describing semiotic resources and principles of their systems of meaning in order to understand how people use these resources in social contexts for specific purposes. In addition to understanding and examining social semiotic resources as systems of meaning, the focus is on exploring the system in use and the social contexts that it is embedded in. Thus the multimodal phenomenon, not the sign-maker, is the focus of this perspective on multimodality.

Authors within this volume whose work falls broadly speaking within this approach to multimodality include Kay O'Halloran (Chapter 8 and 28), Len Unsworth and Chris Cléirigh (Chapter 12), and Maree Stenglin (Chapter 31), and John Knox (Chapter 33).

Multimodal interactional analysis

In their book *Discourses in Place* (2003) Scollon and Scollon combined interactional sociolinguistics, intercultural communication and multimodal semiotics to explore how the physical and material characteristics of language as it is situated in the world give meaning to people's actions. Interactional socio-linguistics, particularly the work of the Scollons on mediated discourse, but also Goffman, Gumperz and Tannen, provided one of the foundations for the development of the third key perspective on multimodality included in this volume, that is, multimodal interactional analysis (Norris, 2004a; R. Jones, 2005; Norris and Jones, 2005). The other influences on this approach are provided by work by Kress and Van Leeuwen on multimodality (2001) discussed earlier and the data collection possibilities enabled by digital technology. More specifically, this way of looking has emerged from the ethnographic study of the everyday identity construction, in which identity was constructed on multiple levels in multiple modes.

Given the historical influences on multimodal interactional analysis it is not surprising that this perspective places considerable emphasis on the notion of context and situated interaction. The focus is on the action taken by a social actor with or through multimodal mediational means, that is, how a variety of modes are brought into and constitutive of social interaction, identities and relations, with a particular interest in habitus and embodiment (see Norris and Jones, Chapters 6 and 9 this volume). The work of the actor is, therefore, everything, as it is through their interaction that social occasions are instantiated. As Norris (2004a: 4) explains, 'Multimodal Interactional Analysts set out to understand and describe what is going on in a given interaction. We analyse what individuals express and react to in specific situations, in which the ongoing interaction is always co-constructed.' This perspective shifts attention from representation and communication (the focus of Kress, Van Leeuwen and O'Halloran) to inter- action. However, Norris defines communication as interaction:

> Communicating is interaction if one person conveys a message and another person perceives it. The modes utilized for interacting do not create a communicative moment as an interaction, but rather the process of doing something to or for or with people allows us to understand a communicative moment as an interaction.
>
> (2004a: 149)

Here, multimodality expands the focus of interaction, moving away from interaction as lin- guistic to explore how people employ gesture, gaze, posture, movement, space and objects to mediate interaction in a given context.

An important consequence of the focus on interaction is that the modal system is no longer a primary concern. Modes are understood as made and constituted through interaction and action, and thus there is no notion of a modal system outside of interaction – mode, sign-maker, and context are too intimately connected to tear apart: 'Social actors always co-construct their actions from the environment and/or from the other social actors so that we can never extricate a social actor's actions from the environment and/or from the other social actors involved' (Norris, Chapter 6 this volume).

It is possible to talk about the affordances and constraints of different media in a general way outside of a specific context, but from this perspective this is of little use as it is not possible to generalize in relation to how affordances and constraints are altered as people mix them in specific social actions (see Norris and Jones, Chapters 6 and 9 this volume).

The semiotic system is the primary problem space and focus for O'Halloran's multimodal discourse analysis; and for Kress and Van Leeuwen and social semiotic approaches, the rules, regularities and patterns that lie in modal systems of representation and communication in use are key. However, for Norris and multimodal interactional analysis, the focus is on 'the rules and regularities that come about while social actors use systems of representation' (Norris, Chapter 6 this volume). As she expands in 2004,

> a communicative mode is never a bounded or static unit, but always and only a heuristic unit. The term 'heuristic' highlights the plainly explanatory function, and also accentuates the constant tension and contradiction between the system of representation and the realtime interaction among social actors. … Individuals in interaction draw on systems of representation while at the same time constructing, adopting, and changing those systems through their actions. In turn, all actions that individuals perform are mediated by the system of representation that they draw on.
>
> (Norris, 2004a: 12-13)

From this perspective, as Norris states, 'modes never exist without social actors utilizing them in some way' (Chapter 6 this volume). Multimodal interactional analysis is therefore concerned with the situated interplay between modes at a given moment in social interaction, but as Jones (Chapter 9 this volume) states, 'we cannot presume that a modal configuration at one point in time utilized by one social actor is translatable to the same modal configuration at a different point in time utilized by the same or another social actor'. This serves to shift the emphasis from mapping the modal resources used in a general sense to understanding modes in action, and the hierarchical and non-hierarchical structures that can be found among the modes used in specific social interactions.

Within this volume the authors whose work could be broadly situated within this approach are Rodney Jones (Chapter 9) and Sigrid Norris (Chapter 6), and those associated with it include Ron Scollon and Suzie Scollon (Chapter 14).

Comparison of perspectives

Table 2.1 is intended as a useful tool for thinking about the differences between these three main approaches: differences that distinguish the accents each brings to multimodality. However, it is crudely drawn and also presents something to argue with and explore, and is not a definitive classification. The columns are intended to be read as aspects of the moment of sign-making that are in a constant dialogue with one another: the normative rules and discourses that circulate across a context, the sign-maker and the system are all balanced in the micro-system of the moment of sign-making.

Each of the perspectives enables a researcher to ask different kinds of questions of an event, to the extent that they may select different kinds of events to examine. They each will emphasize distinct aspects of an event, and in turn will require different types of data, and provide a different analytical route through it. An example may help to illustrate this point, and for the purpose of this argument I use Bezemer and Kress's Loss and Gains research project (2008) as an illustrative example. The project is on how the design of learning resources (i.e. educational textbooks and digital resources) shapes knowledge (discussed by Kress in Chapter 4). The dataset includes a sample of textbooks and other learning resources from across the time span of 1930 to 2000.

Bezemer and Kress (2008) approach these texts from a social semiotic perspective; they treat the design of learning resources as a material instantiation of social conditions and the representation of knowledge. The starting point and questions from a social semiotic perspective are how have the relationships between image and writing changed over the past 70 years, and what are the epistemological effects of these changes? The project emphasizes the ways in which processes of design have changed across this period and how these relate to shifts in the social organization of education and the changing demands placed on it. The texts are analysed for patterns and changes in designers' use of resources (such as layout) within changing historical (including curriculum) contexts. In other words the text is foregrounded as the semiotic work of the designer, and the primary concern with the investigation is the kinds of choices she/he made within the contextual constraints of the curriculum, the pedagogy as the social relations in the classroom and the technologies of printing/digital design, the discourses realized and the potential effects on learning.

A researcher within multimodal discourse analysis tackling a similar dataset would perhaps focus on building an inventory of the semiotic potentials available to designers across these texts, mapping the choices available and those which are taken. The primary interest and research questions would be in understanding and making an inventory of the system, the resources, principles and rules, the levels and ranks within systems according to a stratal model which includes the expression plane, content plane and context plane. In order to do this the analytical focus would be more firmly on the texts rather than the curriculum and social, historical context outside of the actual texts.

Table 2.1 A comparison of historical influences and the theoretical emphasis of three multimodality perspectives

Perspective	Historical influences	Emphasis on the moment of situated sign-making (Context)	Emphasis on system	Emphasis on sign-maker
Social semiotic multimodal analysis	Marx and Soviet psychology (Bakhtin, Voloshinov) Social semiotics (Halliday) Semiotics (i.e. Barthes) Interactional sociology (e.g. Goffman, Hall, Bateson) Art history Iconography Discourse (Foucault and Bernstien) SFG (choice from system)	Medium to high: articulated through the interest at the moment of sign-making as these are balanced with the normative discourses that act upon it	Medium: as a resource with regularity and dynamic character	High: the interest of the sign-maker
Multimodal discourse analysis	Systemic functional grammar (Halliday, O'Toole)	Medium–high (following Halliday view that meaning is contextual)	High: the system as a set of choices, levels and organizational principles	Low
Multimodal interactional analysis	Interactional sociology (e.g. Goffman) Interactional socio-linguistics (e.g. Tannen, Gumperz) Mediated discourse analysis (Scollons) Multimodality (Kress and Van Leeuwen)	High: articulated through the interest in the moment of (inter)action	Low	High: the interest in the social actor performing an action; however, agency itself is not taken-for-grated: the actor may communicate without intention as well

The different interests and analytical focus of multimodal interactional analysis would probably lead it to start from a quite different place than Kress and Bezemer. The focus on texts as analytical objects separated from their use would be rejected because within this perspective the meaning of the texts could only be usefully understood by investigating these, and their material constraints and affordances, as they feature in and mediate face-to-face social interaction. (For Bezemer and Kress, the focus is on the textually mediated interaction between the designer and the learner.) Similarly, the historical aspect of the project would not enter the analytical concerns of this approach – as how such texts featured in distant interactions would not be recoverable as data and would therefore be outside of the analytical tools and focus of this approach. This would lead to a very different set of data, research questions and focus, perhaps starting with an ethnographic study of the interaction of designers in producing these kinds of learning resources, or observations of how these resources are taken up and used through the interaction of teachers and learners within a specific context.

This touches on the broader issue of what is multimodal data and how can it be collected and transcribed. This issue is addressed across all the chapters in this volume, especially through the exemplar analyses that are provided in each chapter. This illustrates the diversity in multimodal data, and approaches to handling, transcribing and analysing data. It is also tackled head-on by Flewitt and colleagues in Chapter 3. They consider how theoretical work across a range of disciplines combined with technological developments has changed both what is accepted as data and processes of data collection, transcription and analysis. This expansion and rethinking of data raises new challenges for research, including what it is possible to describe and transcribe. Flewitt and colleagues discuss these issues with regard to common and current concerns regarding the transcription, description and analysis of multimodal data.

Each of the different 'takes' on multimodality described in this section is valid and useful; however, each offers a particular starting point and pathway into multimodal research. The question of which perspective is 'best', just like the question of which mode is 'best', is dependent on the interests of a researcher and what it is that they want to investigate. Other disciplines and related approaches also acknowledge the multimodal character of communication, representation and interaction.

In addition to the differences across perspectives that might be described as within multimodal research, there is considerable interest in multimodality from a variety of disciplines.

Multimodality in conversation with other approaches

Multimodal research has made a distinctive contribution within the field of linguistics and education; however, it would be wrong to claim that those working within multimodal research are the first to look beyond language. The multimodal character of communication, representation and interaction has been acknowledged by many disciplines for some time, including sociointeractional linguistics, anthropology, psychology, media and cultural studies, and sociology. That meaning is made in many modes is nothing new to many, especially those in design, art and art history, visual studies, architecture, synaesthesia, and multisensorial design. Indeed, to some extent multimodality has looked to many of these disciplines for theoretical concepts and research tools to support it.

The ways in which multimodality has been engaged with across different theoretical perspectives is the focus of Part III of this volume. These chapters explore how a variety of methods and theoretical approaches can be used to think about different aspects of the multimodal landscape.

Multimodality has to a large extent emerged from linguistic theories, and in Chapter 14 Scollon and Scollon explore the need for multimodality to move away from a focus in which language is at the theoretical centre. They argue that studies such as *The Natural History of the Interview (NHI)*, while innovative and significant for multimodality, relied too much on language to provide the principles of analysis, a reliance that was supported by the belief that 'linguistics held the key which would unlock the structural, patterned truth of what had until then seemed to be highly elusive and subjective human experience'. Indeed Scollon and Scollon cite the failure to recognize that this was not the case, as the 'fatal assumption' of the NHI project.

The very way multimodality describes visual communication and the way it characterizes seeing are issues that have been the basis of much philosophical and methodological discussion for at least half a century across a range of academic disciplines, perhaps most notably art and visual studies. Machin, in Chapter 15, explores how visual studies has engaged with some of the concerns that underlie multimodality at the same time as constructively challenging some of the basic premises of using a model of language and grammar to understand the visual. By engaging with these different perspectives the volume hopes to clarify what a multimodal perspective can offer, and the benefits of engaging with other theoretical perspectives.

Multimodality has been taken up by many working within New Literacy Studies and there is now considerable connection between these two perspectives within literacy studies. Many studies have used a multimodal approach to investigate children's literacy practices and text-making (e.g. Pahl, 1999; Kenner, 2004; Lancaster, 2001; Ormerod and Ivanic, 2002; Jewitt, 2006). In Chapter 16, Street, Pahl and Rowsell address the different epistemological framings of New Literacy Studies and the multimodal tradition; one rooted in an ethnographic perspective and the other more focused on social semiotics and systemic function linguistics. They explore how New Literacy Studies can inform research from a multimodal perspective and vice versa. The chapter describes a number of research projects that combine these approaches and argues that 'Multimodality and New Literacy Studies, when brought together, serve to fill out a larger more nuanced picture of social positioning and group practices, texts, contexts, space, and time'.

Multimodality has also been taken up and extended by those working within corpus studies. In Chapter 17 John Bateman sees this extension as increasingly important to empirically evaluate the hypotheses and theories of multimodal meaning-making. This move beyond illustrative cases helps to establish the degree to which the concepts of multimodality can explain uses of multimodality more generally. The chapter engages with how multimodal corpora can be used to critique and empirically validate multimodal concepts and to explore the potential boundaries of multimodal theory. In doing so Bateman shows how the scale of multimodality as a method can be extended, and the importance of empirically interrogating theory towards theoretical development and robustness.

Critical discourse analysis and multimodality have something of a shared history. In Chapter 18 Lilie Chouliaraki explores the potential of a framework that brings these two theoretical lenses together for the analysis of media discourse. Such a framework can, she argues, take into account how media texts are embedded in both technological artefacts and social relationships. Chouliaraki applies a multimodal discourse analysis onto media texts in order to study their visual and linguistic properties including camera/visual, graphic/pictorial or aural/linguistic. This framework enables the critical concerns on the ethical and political role of television and other media in the contemporary media landscape as a 'global village' to be addressed.

Hartmut Stöckl argues in Chapter 19 that semiotics and multimodality are connected via conceptual and methodological origins and interests. He argues that, 'multimodality studies are in need of a semiotic underpinning' as it treats all signifying and communicative phenomena in the same way and that similarly 'any semiotic venture presupposes a multimodal conception of signs, texts and communication from the start'. From this starting point the chapter outlines the points of departure and connection between semiotics and multimodality and the central concepts from semiotics that can travel into multimodal research.

How to apply eye-tracking methodology in multimodal research is the topic of Chapter 20, by Jana Holsanova. It gives an overview of different ways in which eye-tracking methodology can be used in research on multimodality. Various application areas associated with the use of eye-tracking methodology are summarized and the potentials and limitations of this methodology are listed. The chapter presents a new perspective that focuses on the reception of multimodality and emphasizes how multimodal messages are perceived by the users. The perspective is described in relation to three main production-oriented perspectives within multimodality: social semiotic multimodal analysis, a systemic functional approach and multimodal interactional analysis (each of which were introduced in this chapter). Holsanova argues and illustrates that eye-tracking measurements, in combination with verbal protocols, interviews, comprehension tests and questionnaires, are a suitable method for studying reception of multimodality. The chapter provides examples from eye-tracking studies focusing on the integration of various modes to demonstrate the use of these methods.

In Chapter 21, Ivarsson, Linderoth and Säljö analyse ideas of multimodality within the framework of a socio-cultural theory of mind and mediated action. According to this perspective, meaning-making through words, images, sounds, and forms of mediation is not a 'private' affair of subjectively imposing values, knowledge or motives on one's 'own' perceptions. Nor is it a matter of unpacking or interpreting universal and culturally given meanings of an 'objective' world. Rather, meaning-making is seen as emerging from interpretative practices in social activities in which participants relate what they see and hear to the *socio-historical resources*, for instance by way of canons of representation, as well as to the *situated resources* they have available and which may be negotiated in the face-to-face interaction.

Against that backdrop, Luff, Heath and Pitsch demonstrate in Chapter 22 how workplace studies, an approach that draws on ethnomethodology and conversation analysis, and ethnography looks beyond word. They show how this approach focuses on 'the situated character of practical action to address the ways in which particular actions and sequences of action contingently arise within the emergent or ongoing accomplishment of workplace activities'. Their focus is primarily the contributions of others, of co-participants, within the 'moment by moment, concerted and interactional accomplishment of particular actions and activities' and 'the practices and reasoning in and through which people produce particular actions and make sense of the actions of others'. They set out to discover and describe these practices, and explain how participants orient to and rely upon these practices.

Multimodality is intimately tied to the senses and perception, although the study of sense perception has traditionally fallen to psychologists. Psychology has tended to investigate perception on a one-sense-at-a-time basis. In Chapter 23 on anthropology and multimodality, David Howes suggests that this approach is problematic:

> Recent research in cognitive neuroscience and in sensory anthropology has shown this serial approach to be misguided, the latter by pointing to the myriad ways in which the senses are conjugated (discriminated and combined) differently in different cultures, the former by revealing how the processing of information in one modality is continually modulated by concurrent activity in other modalities.

He proposes instead a 'cross-cultural multi-modal theory of sense perception born out of the fusion of cognitive science and sensory anthropology'. The chapter draws on a series of case studies in the cultural life of the senses from Melanesia, and North and South America to illustrate the main tenets of his theoretical approach.

The ways in which the multimodal character of representation, communication and interaction has been taken up within different disciplines and approaches is examined in the chapters outlined above. The benefits and challenges of combining multimodal approaches to research with other theoretical and methodological approaches are also explored.

Summary

This chapter has shown how features such as mode and semiotic resource are articulated differently across the three perspectives most strongly associated with multimodality: social semiotic multimodal analysis, a systemic functional approach (multimodal discourse analysis), and multimodal interactional analysis. These issues are further taken up and explored across the chapters in this volume.

It has also given a brief introduction to the ways in which multimodality is in conversation with a range of disciplines and used in combination with other theoretical concepts and approaches. This is the focus of Part III of this volume.

Overall, this chapter has provided a snapshot of the contemporary landscape of multimodality, its current forms, historical influences, connections and divergences. Mapping multimodality, the complexity and variety of multimodality, in this way aims to provide a guide across this terrain rather than offering a monolithic and unified history of multimodal research.

3

What are multimodal data and transcription?

*Rosie Flewitt, Regine Hampel, Mirjam Hauck and
Lesley Lancaster*

This chapter opens with a discussion of what is meant by 'multimodal data' and 'multimodal text', and reflects on theoretical approaches to multimodal communication that derive from social semiotics. It then discusses how technological developments have changed the tools for data collection and analysis, and have created new contexts for study. Finally, the chapter focuses on a selection of different transcription techniques which provide a sense of the choice-making processes involved in multimodal data analysis and representation.

What are multimodal data?

The recent paradigm shift in research into the communication of meaning, as discussed in Chapters 1 and 2, has major theoretical and practical implications for what are now accepted as analysable data, and for the analytic tools required to describe and interpret these data. It is theory that drives their choice and selection, and advances in thinking in any field of enquiry are likely to be followed by a parallel review of what constitutes evidence. Moreover, there is an essential relationship between this evidence and the methodological tools used to capture, describe and analyse it. The diversity of multimodal data presents particular challenges, requiring descriptive and analytic tools that can both accommodate their variability and reflect their complexity. Transcription however, still relies largely on the use of written script. As a result, the debate continues about whether techniques based on written language are a sufficient and acceptable way to mediate multimodal meanings, or whether multimodal data require a reconceptualisation of the approaches used to describe them.

Past times

Within mainstream linguistic theory the written sentence was the generally accepted unit of analysis well into the twentieth century. Chomsky's exclusive concern with the 'ideal speaker-listener' (Chomsky, 1965: 3), for example, followed a mentalist tradition in which sentences were intuited from the mind of the researcher, written down, and then analysed.

The examination of data independently of their social context was sufficient for the purpose of analysis within the theoretical constraints of generative grammar, with its focus on the universal mental properties of grammar. However, for those whose theoretical interests lay with language as socially situated, such constraints on the collection and analysis of data were inappropriate. Today, discourse analysis has become an extensive, cross-disciplinary field (Blommaert, 2005; Van Dijk, 1985, 2012), with a common interest in collecting data that show language used in the course of social interactions (Schiffrin, 1994). The expansion of the field since the 1970s has paralleled developments in technology where audio and video recording devices have become increasingly accessible and sophisticated, allowing researchers to record interactions in informal as well as formal settings, and to transcribe them in ways that take close account of social context.

Despite these developments, writing and speech have remained predominant in research accounts within the social sciences. Linguistic data on their own, however, provide only partial evidence. Whilst discourse analysis has extended the boundaries of research into human communication, it tends to describe other modalities in terms of their relation to language, rather than as distinct communicative modes in their own right. Intonation, facial expression, gestures and vocalisations are often described as 'para' or 'extra'-linguistic features (Cruttenden, 1997; Trask, 1993; Bloome *et al.*, 2005) and are rarely incorporated in transcriptions. Particular problems are presented to discourse and multimodal analysts alike by the materiality of texts and objects at the centre of interactions, by the representation of spatial relationships and temporal organisation, and by the complex interrelation between different communicative modes. Non-linguistic elements are never semiotically innocent however, and provide data whose significance is frequently lost in translation, or reduced to the status of 'context'. In this way processes are divided from outcomes, and form from meaning. Multimodal approaches attempt to redress the balance and to achieve more unified and comprehensive descriptions, although the variation between different kinds of transcripts shows that there is no single way of doing this (see 'What is multimodal transcription?').

More recent developments

It is not our intention to devalue the immense strides that discourse analysis has made in extending our understanding of human interaction, nor to underestimate the extent of the work accomplished by generations of linguists. Rather, we aim to highlight the enormity of the task of attempting to arrive at 'a common terminology for all semiotic modes' (Kress and Van Leeuwen, 2001), that would allow researchers across disciplines to describe and interpret data in diverse modalities at equivalent levels of detail and theoretical rigour. Moreover, the question of what is meant by 'multimodal data' is not straightforward. Whilst the meaning-making opportunities provided by an explosion of new technologies have generated ideal climate for the reappraisal of theories about the representation and communication of meaning, some fundamental things have not changed: we still use our bodies when we use the internet, and we still need to read written text and interpret images. In other words, we remain as reliant on the same bodily and symbolic resources as ever, even if there are qualitative differences in how we use them, and in the social and technological settings in which this takes place. Nevertheless the development of new media has radically changed the communicative landscape for researchers, including the way we take account of more traditional resources. Multimodal data derive as much from reappraising familiar modes of making meaning as from description and analysis of the new. Decisions about what constitute data continue to reflect the practical and theoretical interests of investigators, and multimodality provides a fluidity and diversity in approaches to data collection and analysis with considerable cross-disciplinary relevance.

Multimodality and text

The fluid approach of multimodality to data collection and analysis also extends to the ways in which we understand the meaning of 'text'. A unimodal view might be that text involves written language, and contains a singular message. Whilst the singularity of the meaning of written text has long been challenged (Belsey, 1980), the idea that it is writing per se that is the unique or privileged source of meaning is more persistent. Kress and Van Leeuwen's (2001: 24) description of the multimodality of text diverges significantly from such a view:

> We want to insist from the beginning that the semiotic instances in which we are interested – the texts – include the everyday practices of 'ordinary' humans as much as the articulations of discourses in more conventionally text-like objects such as magazines, TV programmes, and so on. We will refer to these [as] 'practically lived texts'.

Not only does this definition include 'conventionally text-like objects' that are dominated by images rather than by writing, and 'moving' rather than 'still' text, it also includes day-to-day lived events (Lancaster, 2011). Such a theoretical stance extends the range and complexity of the textual landscape considerably, and pushes textual boundaries to incorporate features and manipulation of the processes of production, as well as material outcomes. From this perspective, for example, all writing involves the production of situated, multimodal texts. This provides the researcher with potentially far richer and more complex data sets from which to work. For instance, Ormerod and Ivanic's (2002) corpus study of project writing by schoolchildren shows that the decision-making processes of the writers can be traced by examining scanned images of early drafts, and material features of the original documents. Kress and Van Leeuwen (1996) show that writing is also subject to constraints of design when it shares signification with other visual modes, for example in advertising and information texts. Machin (2007) looks at the semiotic potential of typefaces in newspapers and other printed matter, and suggests that this is integral rather than incidental to the meaning. On the internet, writing is invariably an essential part of texts, along with still and moving images, and often accompanied by sound. Digital communication also allows writing to be used interactively through, for example, email, internet forums, and texting, providing textual data that show users in the process of continuously designing and shaping how, as well as what, they communicate (Mavers, 2007). In this way, written language is also taking over some of the functions of spoken language (Hampel, in press).

In spite of the richness of multimodal data, and the possibilities that they offer for extending the understanding of human meaning-making activity, it is important to bear in mind the need for the common terminology and rigour of description referred to by Kress and Van Leeuwen (2001). Arriving at levels of description that parallel those already achieved for language is a complex task. This involves the description and interpretation of data both inter-modally and intra-modally: describing the ways in which different modes interact together in different circumstances, and in different combinations but also describing how individual modes are constituted, and the differential function of their constituents in different sites of representational activity.

Body and meaning

Johnson (1987) points out that human reality is shaped by patterns of bodily movement. As we have said, from a multimodal perspective, embodied, representational activity includes language, rather than is language; the ways in which we direct our gaze, use facial expressions, gesture, move, stand, and manipulate things are an integral part of communicative activity. Without the familiarity of these recurring patterns of physical activity, our experience would be chaotic and incomprehensible. We are conscious of the world, and act on it through the medium of the body (Merleau-Ponty, 1945). This includes sensory activity: the affect and the semiotic impact of seeing, hearing, smelling, tasting, touching and feeling. Gray (2004) points out that we rarely experience a conscious event isolated to just one sense; rather we are aware of an integrated 'multimodal scene'. Yet, in terms of using this as data, a number of practical and theoretical challenges arise. There is the difficulty of unpicking and interpreting data: identifying the modes involved, understanding how they operate, and assessing the contribution that both inter- and intra-modal activity make to the meaning of the 'scene'. There are also difficulties in 'recording' and interpreting sensory modes such as smell, taste, certain sounds, and feelings of pain and pleasure and of accurately taking account of the materiality of any objects involved. Furthermore, there are epistemological and analytical tensions between multimodal approaches to the senses that derive from social semiotics, and approaches that derive from anthropologically informed sensory ethnographic methodologies (Pink, 2011).

In spite of these difficulties, work that takes into account diverse modes of communication has been developing for many years across a number of disciplines and fields of enquiry. McNeill (1992), for example, has described the variety of gestures used by people concurrently with speech. Gesture and spoken language are seen as 'different sides of a single underlying mental process', with gesture providing visible evidence of the 'operations of the mind', and having distinct forms with differential functions. Alibali *et al.* (1997) also consider gestural data as evidence of thinking, arguing that the gestures of children doing mathematical calculations provide evidence of cognition that is distinct from that provided by their speech. Kress *et al.* (2001) look at how gestures are used as part of a complex ensemble of communicative modes associated with teaching and learning in the science classroom, and a similar position is taken by Heath and Luff (2007), looking at how auctioneers deploy complex ensembles of talk, gesture and bodily communication in the course of their work, with each mode displaying essential and distinct characteristics of operation. Similarly, Bezemer *et al.* (2011) observe how surgeons and nurses use talk and bodily conduct to request, provide and apply surgical instruments, making the social interaction between surgeons and nurses analytically inseparable from the 'technical' demands of their work. Gesture also operates as an independent and fully articulated mode in the sign languages of the hearing-impaired (Sutton-Spence and Woll, 1999; Capone and McGregor, 2004). In cognitive neuroscience, Alač and Hutchins (2004) have analysed the interaction of semiotic resources, such as gesture, language, and material structure, within social environments as a means of examining actions that constitute thinking.

Investigations of gaze in its social context include the work of Kendon (1967), Streek (1993) and Erickson (2004), identifying its different meaning-making functions during social interactions. Lancaster (2001) looked at the differential functions of gaze in mediating young children's interpretation of graphic text, and Bourne and Jewitt (2003) have examined its role in learning in the secondary English classroom. There has also been extensive work exploring the role of gaze in the development of children's language and communication, providing significant evidence for theories of language learning that highlight the importance of 'shared attention' between infants and adults (Tomasello, 2003). Another rapidly growing field is the exploration of gaze in CMC-based second language acquisition. Using eye tracking technology Smith (2010), for example, investigates the effectiveness of implicit corrective feedback in a text-based synchronous CMC learning environment.

Bodily and sensory modes have been considered as data in social situations where affective issues like trust and fear are central: the ways in which certain kinds of gaze and body position facilitate trust between therapist and clients (Roten *et al.*, 2000), and, by contrast, the ways in which innocent and comforting touching of children by adults can become the basis for moral panic (Piper and Stronach, 2008).

These examples of some of the ways in which gesture and gaze have been analysed are instances of interpreting communication in terms of Kress and Van Leeuwen's 'practically lived texts'. However, bodily activity can also be formalised and presented as scripted performance in art forms like dance and mime, where movements of the body and gestures have primacy over other modes, and are used to communicate narrative, affective and aesthetic meanings (Royce, 1984; Álvarez *et al.*, 2010). Facial expression, colour, music, and costume are important signifiers in performance, with seemingly 'negative' signifiers such as stillness and silence being used deliberately and systematically to carry meaning, becoming examinable and analysable data. Bodily activity is also used to 'perform' distinct meanings in less predictable ways by young children engaged in sign-making activity, where a sign might be represented partially graphically, and partly by means of a physical 'enactment' of aspects of the meaning (Flewitt, 2005; Lancaster and Roberts, 2007; Vygotsky, 1978).

Materiality and material settings

Finally, there is the relatively recent development of the inclusion of the physical and material setting of communicative and representative activity within the description of 'lived texts', facilitated through digital cameras and imaging techniques. Norris (2004a, b) for example, examines the ways in which we use space, the arrangement of furniture, and the role of other material objects within our interactions, and Dicks *et al.* (2006) have examined how exhibits in a museum communicate their meanings through location, arrangement, and materiality. With a focus on the materiality of everyday objects, Pahl and Rowsell (2010) discuss how artefacts constitute the daily, sensory world in which we live, and are infused with personal, social and historical meanings.

The impact of technology

In addition to investigating face to face interaction, one of the main challenges for multimodal research is to adopt a critical stance to the impact of new technologies on communication, and to make explicit how different modes work together to create meanings in different media, both in technologically mediated worlds and in research representations of those worlds.

Technology and multimodal data collection

In addition to creating new communicative contexts for study, new technologies have transformed the tools that are available for data collection, such as digital photography, video film, graphics and discreet audio recording devices. These in turn create new kinds of research texts that force a reconsideration of taken-for-granted methods of categorising, ordering, displaying and disseminating the outcomes of social research. Whilst video recordings have been a feature of social research for many decades (see Erickson, 2011), the now compact size and affordability of video-recording devices, including mobile phones, have proliferated their use. Banks (2007) proposes that visual images may reveal sociological insights that are not accessible by other means, and Flewitt (2006, 2011) discusses how video recordings produce rich data for ethnographic studies, but only capture a partial view of the social worlds they are being used to observe. Visual data are just one methodological tool among many, and ethnographic researchers remain reliant on supplementary methods, such as interviews, documentation and field notes, that give insights beyond the limited focal range of a video lens. The combination of 'new' and more traditional tools for data collection creates a dynamic constellation of resources, where meanings are produced through the inter-relationships between and within the data sets, permitting the researcher literally and metaphorically to 'zoom in' on fine grained detail and to pan out to gain a broader, socially and culturally situated perspective.

Technology, multimodal data storage and presentation

In addition to new technological tools for data collection, a range of data analysis resources have now become widely available and affordable. These include Computer Assisted Qualitative Data Analysis Software (CAQDAS) packages that offer the potential for systematic storage and analysis of complex multimedia data, such as Atlas.ti, Elan (http://www.lat-mpi.eu/tools/elan/elan-description), HyperRESEARCH, MAXqda, NVivo, QUALRUS and Transana (see http://caqdas.soc.surrey.ac.uk for more details of different CAQDAS). These offer efficient, systematic frameworks for the organisation, coding, searching and retrieval of data, for the creation of visual analytic networks and for building portfolios of linked multimedia data clips, which can be accessed in just one or two clicks. Although the underlying logic of data coding in CAQDAS is essentially the same as in manual techniques, their structure is inherently biased towards coding and this can tend to shape the processes and outcomes of data analysis (see Mavrikis and Geraniou, 2011). Some coding schemes are hierarchical, and most impose a linear, time-oriented format on transcripts, presenting tensions for multimodal studies that require spatially-oriented representation (see also Coffey *et al.*, 1996). Whilst CAQDAS may help qualitative researchers to manage multimedia data sets, and facilitate new forms of transcription, they do not perform the fine craft of interpretation and analysis, and do not replace researchers' knowledge and skills (Van der Putten, 2010).

An intrinsic element of technology is its transient, changing nature, and new technological innovations to support multimedia data are constantly emerging. For example, at the National Centre for e-Social Science (NCeSS), a multimodal corpus tool has been developed which allows for the analysis of relationships between linguistic features, proxemic movements and gesture in naturally occurring communication contexts (Adolphs *et al.*, 2011). Inter-disciplinary projects such as this offer exciting possibilities for the future of multimodal research, but also raise fundamental questions about the value and potential structural bias of new technological tools for analysis that emerge in an atheoretical framework.

Although new tools for data collection and analysis may offer the methodological benefits of accuracy, efficiency and systematicity, they are not 'innocent' and must be used critically and reflectively. Lomax and Casey (1998) discuss the uniquely distorting effect of the video camera on the researched phenomenon, and, in relation to her anthropological work on sensory experience, Pink (2007) articulates the theoretical and methodological basis for how 'walking with video' can act as a catalyst for creating ethnographic understandings of other people's experiences. As with all methodologies, whether using traditional or new technologies, researchers must ensure that the media chosen for data collection and dissemination do not become the research message.

What is multimodal transcription?

Traditionally, the term 'transcription' has referred to the process of turning audio-recorded data into examinable written text without too much consideration of the consequences of this transformation from one modality to another. More recently, however, researchers have started to examine the wider implications of data representation and to reflect critically on alternative ways of transforming interactions, objects and processes into examinable written, visual and/ or multimodal texts.

What is transcribed depends on the research context and on what the researcher is trying to find out, but all transcriptions must be recognised as reduced versions of observed reality, where some details are prioritised and others are left out. As Ochs (1979) argues, 'transcription is theory: the mode of data presentation not only reflects subjectively established research aims, but also inevitably directs research findings'. Bucholtz (2000) underscores the strategic aspect of transcription referring to it as a political act which involves scholars who have a particular interest in talk. For example, conversation analysts will view data differently to sociolinguists, who place more value on the ideological implications of language use, whereas archaeologists may use more visual methods for data analysis, such as categorising specimens of dirt according to the Munsell colour chart.

The purpose of research

In all research endeavours, there is therefore a challenging balance to strike between the accurate notation of events, clear description for the research 'reader', and a transcription format that reflects the purpose of the research *and* does justice to the type of data collected. The transcription and analysis of a static text such as a newspaper or textbook page will be different from that of the more dynamic text of a television advertisement or a classroom setting. With reference to the transcription of advertisements, Baldry and Thibault (2006: 30) suggest that 'multimodal transcriptions are ultimately based on the assumption that a transcription will help us understand the relationship between a specific instance of a genre, for example a text, and the genre's typical features'. When transcribing situated, social activity the purpose of analysis is likely to be different, relating more to how participants make meaning in naturally occurring interactions, where information about the setting, manipulation of objects, body language, etc. may need to be integral to transcription. For further discussion of how treating 'texts' as divorced from the social situations in which they are made can be problematic, see Kress (2011) and Flewitt (2011).

Units of analysis

In dynamic texts, units of transcription are usually measured as turns of speech, but it is questionable whether this convention is useful for multimodal analysis. As soon as multiple modes are included, the notion of speech turns becomes problematic as other modes contribute meanings to exchanges during the silences between spoken turns. One alternative is to link measurement to the visual mode and use visual frames as units, or use time as a unit of measurement. In their transcription of TV advertisements, Baldry and Thibault (2006) use the temporal unit of one second; in static texts, Jewitt and Kress (2003a) use rhetorical frames and in their transcriptions of video footage. Heath *et al.* (2010) use 'actions' as analytic units (for further discussion, see Bezemer and Mavers, 2011). Furthermore, there are macro and micro approaches to transcription. Macro-transcription (of a page, for example) helps to reveal the relationships between primary objects, while in micro-analysis the researcher treats the page 'as a composite of clusters and looks at their composition, including a characterisation of the relationships existing *within* these objects' (Baldry and Thibault, 2006: 27).

Yet the critical issue – namely the representation of the complex simultaneity of different modes and their different structure and materiality – has not been resolved in transcription, nor have satisfactory ways as yet been found to combine the spatial, the visual and the temporal within one system in ways that take account of the perceptual difficulties that inevitably arise when attempting a simultaneous reading.

What is transcribed?

As mentioned in the first section, the traditional approach to the transcription of oral communication has been to focus on spoken language and on transcribing speech only, for example, spoken *verbal* language, including temporal information such as timings, pauses, overlapping and contiguous utterances. Depending on their particular discipline and research aims, some researchers have included features such as speech delivery/intonation (emphasis, long/short vowels, volume, and aspirations), laughter and other sounds that the speaker makes, sounds in the immediate environment, and gaze. For this traditional way of transcribing, Jefferson's conventions (see Sacks *et al.*, 1974) are still considered an acceptable model despite the fact that these features are subordinated to language, and context is viewed as secondary to spoken/written discourse. Such transcription is used in discourse analysis (e.g. of classroom interaction, see Coulthard, 1977) or conversation analysis. Yet, as mentioned above, there has been a change in perception over the past years as to what discourse is:

> Discourse analysts have long been aware of the dialogicality between naturally occurring language and context. Although context has traditionally been viewed as encompassing everything that surrounds a strip of talk, more recently some concurrent actions have become part of the analyzed aspects. The center of analysis, however, remained spoken language within focused interaction.
>
> (Norris, 2004b: 101)

Gradually, 'context' has been gaining ground, and the contribution of different modalities to meaning-making has been acknowledged. Norris (2004a) includes proxemics, posture, gesture, head movement, gaze, music, print and layout in her work, categorising each according to their characteristics. Yet, it is not sufficient to analyse different modes in isolation, as modes interconnect to make meaning and form larger patterns of discourse that need to be considered as units (Baldry and Thibault, 2006).

So meaning is seen as *multiplicative* rather than additive (Baldry and Thibault, 2006; Lemke, 1998), highlighting the fact that '[m]ultimodal texts are *composite* products of the combined effects of all the resources used to create and interpret them' (Baldry and Thibault, 2006: 18). In this 'orchestration of meaning' (Kress *et al.*, 2001), the overall result is more than the sum of its different parts. Transcription is thus tasked with 'seek[ing] to reveal the *multimodal basis* of a text's meaning in a *systematic* rather than an *ad hoc* way' (Baldry and Thibault, 2006: 21).

Most recently, researchers have gone even further, questioning the distinction between text and context, and turning the focus 'to the *actions* that are being taken with these tools – whether they be trees, computer components or written texts' (Jones and Norris, 2005: 4-5). This 'mediated discourse analysis' prioritises action over discourse: 'The first question it asks is, "What is/are the action/s that is/are being taken here?" and only after answering this question does it go on to ask, "What is the role of discourse in this/those action/s?"' (Scollon, 2001: 9).

Agreeing to include the complexity of multiple modes in the analysis leads to inevitable consequences for transcription, and to questions regarding how far researchers should take transcription, how to identify and represent the constituents of modes, how productive macro analysis is and what micro analysis may contribute to a particular research endeavour. Although the answers to these questions depend on the research aims and theoretical underpinnings, researchers must also take into account the paradox, whereby the perceptual difficulties for the audience of 'reading' genuinely multimodal transcription might outweigh the advantage of its descriptive 'purity'.

Transcription as transduction

The act of transcribing any data involves a process of 'transduction' from one mode to another: transforming the energy of observed action and the situated complexity of spoken language to a differently dynamic, written descriptive or diagrammatic account, or still photograph of a moment of action. Transcription therefore involves more than a process of 'translation', as the act of moving from one mode into another mode changes the material structure and dynamism of how meanings are expressed. For example, if transcribing with Jefferson's conventions, a pause in speech becomes one or two dots between two brackets (.), or if transcribing video-recorded data, an action may be reduced to a written verbal description or to a still frame which captures a microsecond of the embodied movement. In both these cases, the dynamic of the situated speech or action is converted into a slower-paced format, and during the process of transduction, researchers are able to see their data differently. This can help with the analysis – Newfield (Chapter 7 this volume), for example, refers to how 'transmodal moments' may be seen as critical and imaginative semiotic spaces which are conducive to reflection and exploration at a time of the closing down of thought.

How is the transcription presented?

Given the growing tendency to include multiple modes in the analysis of diverse texts, there is corresponding diversity in the semiotic resources used to represent data. Conventionally, research data are presented in written form, that is, one or several modes are 'transducted' into the verbal mode. If, however, the aim in the analysis is not to priori-tise spoken (or written) language, researchers need to ask themselves how they can transcribe

Part	Date	Time	Film clip	Participants			
1	2/5/2004	00:00:05 - 00:19:52	ARC Project 020504.avi	Students 1–5, native-speaker (NS) informants 1 and 2, researchers (Uschi, Mirjam)			
turn id	start time	actor	audio	text chat	vote	other tools	comments
	00:18:18	Mirjam	können das mal alle bestätigen ob sie diese konzept map sehen - bitte? - (v29) (v30) (1) (v31) (v32) (1) (v33;34)				Mirjam wants everyone to confirm that they can see the concept map.
vote29		NS informant 1			yes		
vote30		Student 1			yes		
vote31		Uschi			yes		
vote32		Student 2			yes		
vote33		Student 3			no		Student 3 replies no.
vote34		NS informant 2			yes		
audio97	00:18:27	Uschi	ja ich sehe sogar zwei - woll soll soll (ich) lieber nur eine eine aufmachen? (1)				
audio98	00:18:33	Mirjam	ja und zwar das kann man folgendermaßen korrigieren - in dem - [student 4] jetzt den gather (1) knopf drückt und dann kommen wir alle automatisch zu [student 4] (7)				
audio99	00:18:51	Mirjam	(gar langsam)>				
audio100	00:18:51	Student 4	<und wenn ich jetzt zum beispiel (1,5) (l12) auf eh - (remove) drücke auf der recht in den rechten oben ecke kann ich denn das also die konzept map (entitled) eins - schließen (3)				
line-up12		Mirjam					
audio101	00:19:07	Mirjam	könntest du das bitte [mal machen?]				
audio102	00:19:08	Student 4	[(wer will das)] machen (3)				
audio103	00:19:12	Mirjam	langsam noch eine frage [student 3] [student 3] können - kannst du (ot2) sehen? kannst du die konzep map (1) ah (jetzt) hat einer alles zugemacht - ok – [student 4] bitte noch mal von vorne (6) (ot3)				Mirjam picks up on vote33
other tools 2		Student 4?				the concept map is closed again	
other tools 3		?				the concept map is opened	
audio104	00:19:28	Student 4	Ehm - ja also - also super jetzt hats jemand aufgemacht ((giggles)) gut (2) (l13) (2) (t13)				
line-up13		Mirjam					
text13		Student 1		Bitte sehr			

Figure 3.1 Transcription of synchronous online interaction in an audio conferencing environment.

Source: Hampel and Hauck, 2006.

in accessible, 'readable' ways. In an attempt to overcome the limitations presented by the sequential organisation of data and to represent simultaneous multimodal phenomena, matrices with columns have been used by an increasing number of researchers to add a spatial dimension, as shown in Figure 3.1.

In Figure 3.1 researchers have re-presented the interaction in a German language tutorial that took place in an internet-based audio-graphic conferencing environment, *Lyceum*. This tool provides multiple synchronous audio channels as well as synchronous text chat and several shared graphical interfaces (see also Hampel and Hauck, 2006). The transcription incorporates the temporal sequence of the tutorial (columns) while also describing spatial elements (rows). The interrelation between the modes has been given more prominence by concentrating less on detailed audio transcription and more on the diversity of modalities used by participants. However, the modality used for transcription is still written language and the layout favours the verbal element by placing it towards the left hand side. As Thibault (2000: 318) asserts, the layout of a matrix may create a false impression within Western traditions of visual literacy, where being placed on the left is doubly privileged with both temporal and logical priority.

The transcription in Figure 3.2 describes the communicative modes used by a 30–month-old boy, as he makes an inventory of friends and family members attending a party, in collaboration with his father. The micro-analytic time frame used in this transcription replicates the speed of transition from one event segment to the next, reflecting the overall dynamic of the activity. The transcribers have used 'gaze' as the anchor mode, initially because it enabled the researchers to track the process and movement of the child's interpretation and construction of textual meaning. It was also a relatively stable mode, with changes of gaze direction generally marking the longer time-frame of movement from one

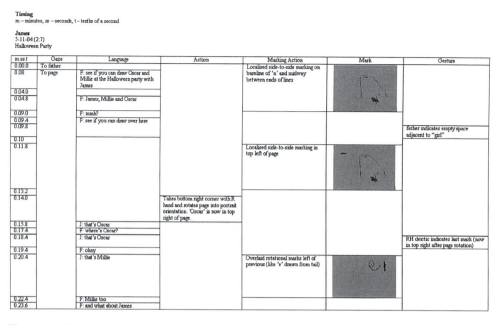

Timing
m – minutes, ss – seconds, t – tenths of a second

James
5-11-04 (2:7)
Halloween Party

m.ss.t	Gaze	Language	Action	Marking Action	Mark	Gesture
0.00.0	To father			Localised side-to-side marking on baseline of 'n' and midway between ends of lines		
0.08	To page	F: see if you can draw Oscar and Millie at the Halloween party with James				
0.04.0						
0.04.8		F: James, Millie and Oscar				
0.09.0		F: mmh?				
0.09.4		F: see if you can draw over here				
0.09.8						father indicates empty space adjacent to "girl"
0.10						
0.11.8				Localised side-to-side marking in top left of page		
0.13.2						
0.14.0			Takes bottom right corner with R hand and rotates page into portrait orientation. 'Oscar' is now in top right of page.			
0.15.8		J: that's Oscar				
0.17.4		F: where's Oscar?				
0.18.4		J: that's Oscar				RH deictic indicates last mark (now in top right after page rotation)
0.19.4		F: okay				
0.20.4		J: that's Millie		Overlaid rotational marks left of previous (like 'e' drawn from tail)		
0.22.4		F: Millie too				
0.23.6		F: and what about James				

Figure 3.2 Transcription of a section of an episode of naturally occurring interaction between adult and child around the construction of a text.

Source: Lancaster and Roberts, 2007.

complete event to the next, and thereby facilitating the transcription process. These transcription formats in turn formed data sets which provided the basis for further interpretation of young children's graphic activity. They were invariably 'read' alongside re-viewings of the corresponding videos, and despite the perceptual difficulties of attending to static and moving data simultaneously, the researchers concluded that there would have been considerable advantage in embedding both kinds of data into the transcripts from the outset, so that episodes could be read more speedily and accurately.

Adopting a similar framework, Baldry and Thibault (2006) use matrices with stills inserted in the first column, emphasising the visual element to their analyses of TV advertisements (see Figure 3.3). This micro-analytical approach uses time (in seconds), visual frame (one still per second), visual image (notational glosses on the frame), kinesic action (use of body movements), soundtrack (including language, music and other sounds) and metafunctional interpretation (textual, experiential/ideational and interpersonal meaning). Nevertheless, the transcript turns the continuous visual sequence (which in reality are 15 frames per second) into a list of individual frames (one per second) chosen by the researchers, and the elements that occur simultaneously are displayed in a linear order (from left to right).

Domingo (2011) also uses matrices in her analysis of features of design in music video to show how young people's social identities are present in the digital products they make and circulate. Arguing that the layering of moving images and sounds in digital video design can provide social and cultural insights, Domingo discusses the challenges of representing recorded speech, digital stills, music, gestures, etc. in isolation from one another. With a focus on six modes in music video (landscape, gestures, language, visual effects, sound effects, colour) and the interrelations among these modes, Domingo uses colour in a multimodal transcription matrix to accommodate the simultaneous and co-dependent nature

Appendix I: Multimodal Transcription of the *Westpac* advertisement (T= time in seconds)					
T **C.1**	**VISUAL FRAME** *Column 2*	**VISUAL IMAGE** *Column 3*	**KINESIC ACTION** *Column 4*	**SOUNDTRACK** *Column 5*	**METAFUNCTIONAL INTERPRETATION PHASES AND SUBPHASES** *Column 6*
1	Shot 1	CP: stationary HP: frontal VP: median D: VLS VC: sheep, eucalyptus tree, utility van, sheep dog VS: progressive magnification of form of herdsman (1-10) CO: naturalistic	[Herdsman starts walking from car towards viewer; sheep dog goes to left; Herdsman starts rolling up left sleeve] Tempo: M	[○silence]	PHASE 1ₐ
2			Herdsman bends down and twice slaps thighs to recall dog to his side Tempo: M	{RG} [♪]Solo keyboard (pp, TWO CHORDS ^ [○sheep]: S1 Volume: p Tempo: S	EXP: Actor; action (Herdsman walks towards viewer)
3			(^ Dog returns to herdsman). Herdsman starts rolling up right sleeve Tempo: M		INT: Viewer positioned as belonging to depicted world and its shared values;
4			[Herdsman stands upright; Starts rolling up left sleeve]^ [dog returns to his side; resumes walking] Tempo: M	{RG} [♪]Drum (p):1 [♪ ♀ chorus]; (*) roll Volume: pp Tempo: S	Imperative mood of chorus: exhortation to act addressed to viewer; minor dyadic exchange;
5			[Herdsman continues rolling up left sleeve; dog runs ahead]. Tempo: M		Herdsman/dog; low volume, slow tempo of music: intimate communion

Figure 3.3 Transcription of an advertisement.

Source: Baldry and Thibault, 2006: Appendix I, I, © Equinox Publishing Ltd 2006.

of the modes (see Plate 3.1). Here, for example, sound effects are represented in orange and visual effects in purple, and the corresponding graphic display incorporates both these colours to indicate the inseparability of the two modes.

Giving the visual even more prominence, Norris (2004a) employs sequences of stills with spoken language, overlaid in a typeface that represents the dynamism of speech and intonation, to convey the complexity of interaction. She turns her focus on analysing the interplay between proxemics, gesture, gaze, head movements and language (when it is present), as shown in Figure 3.4. Using the notion of mediated action, her transcripts are an attempt to unpick the different modes used to perform a particular action or actions.

Goodwin (2001) suggests that '[i]n many cases different stages of analysis and presentation will require multiple transcriptions. There is a recursive interplay between analysis and methods of description' (p. 161). In his research on how stories are organised as multiparty interactive fields, where not only the talk of the speaker, but also the stance and embodied actions of hearers play a crucial role, Goodwin presents his data in carefully designed combinations of representational modes. As can be seen in Figure 3.5, these include short extracts of audio transcript aligned with line drawings, analytic and contextual details (in italic script), and timed pauses to indicate the temporally unfolding nature of participation. When analysing how utterances and stories emerge through processes of interaction in which both speakers and hearers of various types play a crucial role, Goodwin has also used video stills with superimposed arrows to emphasise the role of gaze.

Other forms of transcription result directly from technological advancements. In computer-mediated communication it is common practice for users to have access to system logs ranging from simple chat logs to recordings of entire videoconferencing sessions. Thus an application

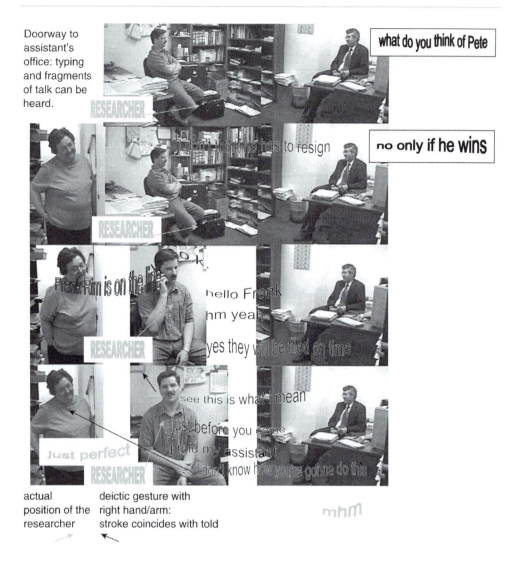

Figure 3.4 caption labels: Doorway to assistant's office: typing and fragments of talk can be heard. / what do you think of Pete / no only if he wins / actual position of the researcher / deictic gesture with right hand/arm: stroke coincides with told

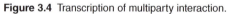

Figure 3.4 Transcription of multiparty interaction.

Source: Norris, 2006: 405, copyright © 2006 by Sage, reprinted by permission of Sage.

such as *Flashmeeting* (which offers video and audio conferencing, text chat, an onscreen white-board and file upload/download features; more information available at http://flashmeeting.open.ac.uk/home.html) includes automatic 'time-stamped' recordings. In addition, the application provides logs and visualisations of the online 'events', where participant activity is logged within the programme, including spoken language, written language, images, communication icons such as emoticons, and time. The visualisations (which use a different colour for each mode/tool) show who does what at what point in time and for how long. Figure 3.6 shows the communication of eight participants in a 59-minute session.

In contrast to the reductive form of data representation in Figure 3.6, Jewitt and Kress (2003a: 280) use 'thick descriptive' accounts to present the richness of video data, mixing images with

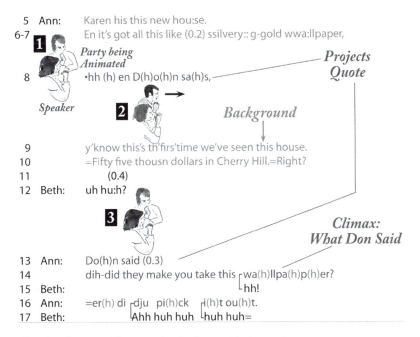

5 Ann: Karen his this new hou:se.
6-7   En it's got all this like (0.2) ssilvery:: g-gold wwa:llpaper,

            *Party being
            Animated*

            *Projects
            Quote*

8   ·hh (h) en D(h)o(h)n sa(h)s,

            Speaker

            Background

9   y'know this's th'firs'time we've seen this house.
10   =Fifty five thousn dollars in Cherry Hill.=Right?
11   (0.4)
12 Beth: uh hu:h?

            *Climax:
            What Don Said*

13 Ann: Do(h)n said (0.3)
14   dih-did they make you take this ⌜wa(h)llpa(h)p(h)er?
15 Beth: ⌞hh!
16 Ann: =er(h) di ⌜dju pi(h)ck ⌜i(h)t ou(h)t.
17 Beth: ⌞Ahh huh huh ⌞huh huh=

Figure 3.5 Drawings integrated into an extensive transcript of speech.

Source: Goodwin, 2007: 63, copyright © 2007 by Sage, reprinted by permission of Sage.

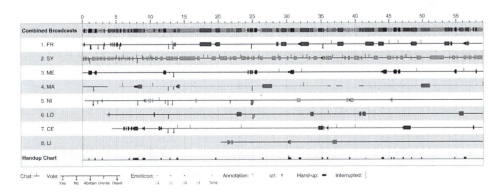

Figure 3.6 Visualisation of 60-minute videoconferencing session, showing use of broadcasting tool (speech), chat and other tools.

Source: Hampel and Hauck, 2006.

verbal transcriptions of speech and verbal descriptions of action to re-present eye-movement; gaze and direction of gaze; facial expression; hand and arm movement/configurations; the use of the whole body to make gestures; body posture; the position of people in the room and their use of space; the location and context of the action (e.g. the semiotics of architecture); the semiotic objects of action; and speech.

This approach highlights yet again that it is the research interests that determine the choice of transcription. While providing the research 'reader' with a high level of detail, complex transcriptions are, however, not only extremely time consuming but present undoubtedly a new challenge to those analysing multimodal data. Furthermore, they pose significant disadvantages for research dissemination, where the dominant media are still printed, written or visual formats. Consequently, they need to be transformed yet again for presentational purposes of publication.

The future for transcription

Although multimodal approaches to transcription and representation attempt to capture something of the complexity of communication, they remain necessarily reduced accounts of lived events. However, if digital devices are used in the processes of data collection, analysis and dissemination, then new forms of representation, and richer interpretations become possible. For example, if research findings are disseminated electronically, then sound or video clips can be made accessible, or hyperlinks can be created that permit readers to navigate their own way through research write-ups, from final reports back to data extracts and vice versa (Dicks *et al.*, 2005). This more open and iterative style of presentation allows 'readers' of research texts (whether written, visual or linked to raw sound or video data extracts) to reflect on sections of data from their own perspectives, thus creating new opportunities for a more critical analysis of the researcher's interpretations. Readers can thus, in a sense, 'become authors of their own reading; they are not simply the passive recipients of a determinate textual form' (Coffey *et al.*, 1996: 8.4). One example of a hypertext authoring tool is Storyspace, which has been used successfully for creating hyperlinks between media by Coffey *et al.* (see Coffey *et al.*, 2008 for an online example). Although hyperlinking per se is not a particularly new idea, it can certainly help to overcome some of the issues of spatiality and linearity discussed here, and the development of effective hypertext, and hypermedia systems is a growing field of research (Jacobson and Azevedo, 2008).

Summary

This chapter has considered how theoretical work across disciplines, and unprecedented developments in the area of information and communication technologies have led to significant changes in what is now accepted as analysable research data. For researchers interested in approaching these data from a multimodal perspective the diverse modes and means used for the representation of meaning in the twenty-first century constitute a significant challenge that will continue to evolve as communication technologies develop. The comparatively recent paradigm shift away from a focus on 'monomodality' (Kress and van Leeuwen, 2001: 1) and towards an interest in analysing how different modes interact together in a 'multimodal ensemble' (Kress *et al.*, 2001) reflects the changing nature of communication in an age of digitisation and mobile devices. Yet multimodality has always been an important feature of human communication. One of the main tasks for multimodal research is to adopt a systematic, critical stance to how modes are used in face-to-face, printed and online communication, and to make explicit how different modes work together to create meanings in different media and in different social contexts.

The authors have considered what multimodal data are, how such data can be represented, and how limitations are imposed by what can be transcribed and disseminated at this point in time. Drawing on findings from across a number of disciplines and research fields, including applied linguistics, visual ethnography, symbolic representation and computer mediated communication we have highlighted common concerns regarding the transcription, description and analysis of multimodal texts.

The complexity of multimodal data sets requires descriptive and analytic tools that can accommodate their variability and reflect their diversity. With the examples provided the authors have demonstrated some of this diversity and identified communalities and divergences in current approaches to multimodal data transcription and analysis. With the use of new technologies changing apace, both in everyday life and in the realm of research, the potential for new forms of data and for new transcription and dissemination formats is assured. However, the usefulness of any new formats will always pivot on the rigour and systematicity of their application, and on their relevance to theoretical conceptualisations of social phenomena.

4

What is mode?

Gunther Kress

Introduction

Mode is a socially shaped and culturally given resource for making meaning. *Image, writing, layout, music, gesture, speech, moving image, soundtrack* are examples of modes used in representation and communication. Phenomena which are the product of social and cultural work have meaning in their environments, so that furniture, clothing, food also 'have' meaning. As their primary function is not that of representation and communication, there is a question whether they should be considered as modes – even though they can be used to make meaning and to communicate.

Within broad areas of the Humanities, the Social Sciences, the Arts, in Education, in short wherever meaning is *the* issue, the concepts of *mode* and *multimodality* are rapidly gaining significance. However, multimodality as such is not a theory even though it is often used as if it were. The term maps a domain of inquiry. In its use in various disciplines and professions – in medicine for instance, in anthropology (Goodwin, 2006), in psychology (Ainsworth, 2008) – theories from those disciplines are brought to multimodal issues in the respective field of work. As a consequence, 'multimodality' is embedded in distinct approaches and shaped by them. The approach taken here is that of a socially founded semiotic theory (Hodge and Kress, 1974, 1979, 1988; Halliday, 1978; Kress, 1996, 2003; Kress and Van Leeuwen, 1996/2006, 2001; Van Leeuwen, 2005a) within a broad frame of an interest in power, representation and communication.

The introduction of the concepts of mode and multimodality produces a challenge to hitherto settled notions of language. After all, if all modes are used to make meaning, it poses the question whether they are merely a kind of duplication of meanings already made in speech or writing – maybe as 'illustration' or 'ornamentation' – or whether they are distinct, 'full' meanings. If the latter, then language has to be seen in a new light: no longer as dominant and central, as fully capable of expressing all meanings, but as one means among others for making meaning, each of them specific. It is the route taken in social semiotic approaches to multimodal representation.

Modes, materiality and affordance

Modes offer different potentials for making meaning; these have a fundamental effect on choices of mode in specific instances of communication. *Writing* (in English culture as in others) has *words, clauses, sentences*, organized in grammar and syntax. It has graphic resources such as *font, size, bolding, spacing*. To *frame* its units, it has syntactic, textual and social-semiotic resources (e.g. *sentence, paragraph, genre*). These frames are realized through a variety of (graphic) resources: punctuation marks; spacing between words and around paragraphs; increasingly, *layout* is used to produce 'blocks' of writing, at times in different colours, on surfaces such as pages or screens. These resources have specific forms in different cultures, leaving aside the fundamental issue of differences of script-systems. That makes it problematic to speak of 'writing' as such; it seems preferable to say writing in this culture or that. What applies to the mode of writing in this respect applies to all modes.

Speech shares certain aspects of *lexis, syntax* and *grammar* with writing. Sound, the material of speech, is, however, entirely different from the (graphic) material of writing. Sound is received via the physiology of hearing; the graphic material of writing via the physiology of sight. Sound offers resources such as (variation in) energy – loudness or softness – used to produce *stress* as *accent*; and through alternations of stress as *rhythm*, the rhythmic organization of speech. *Pitch* and *pitch variation* – the variations of the frequency of oscillation of the 'vocal' chords – produce *tone* in tone–languages such as Mandarin or Igbo and *intonation* in languages such as English. Speech has *vowel quality, length* and *silence* as *pauses*. Speech uses sound for the framing of its units. In English for instance, the contours of intonation form *intonation units*, which frame semiotic entities, *information units*. The material features of (higher or lower levels of) pitch are used to mark *given* and *new* information in information units (Halliday, 1967–68). If I say 'It was **last** Saturday he came' ('not the Saturday two weeks ago') with high intonation on **last** and falling away, the informational meaning is different to 'It was last **Saturday** he came' ('not last Sunday').

These larger intonational frames produce chunkings of meaning similar to paragraphs in writing and yet also distinct in their potentials for meaning. Sound happens in time and that allows the voice to sustain a sound, to 'stretch' it as a resource for meaning – as in the lengthening of vowels and the reduplication of consonants: 'Aaaalbert, come here', 'yummmmie', 'pssssst'. Writing uses graphic means – **bolding**, size, s p a c i n g – to achieve effects which are semiotically similar and yet distinct in their specific meanings to those produced by sound in speech. They are distinct means in specific modes which belong to one, more general semiotic category, 'emphasis'. Bolding in writing and loudness in speech are means of producing emphasis.

Mode as cultural resource: materiality, semiotic logics and social action

In a social semiotic approach to mode, equal emphasis is placed on the material 'stuff' of mode and on the work of culture over often long periods with that material. Social action and affordances of material (Gibson, 1986) together produce semiotic resources which are the product of the potentials inherent in the material, of a society's selection from these potentials and of social shaping over time of the features which are selected. Hence the resources of a mode, say gesture, image, speech, writing, are both similar to and different from culture to culture in their potentials for representation. As a semiotic resource, the modes of gesture or speech in one culture are therefore not identical to gesture or speech in another, even across closely related cultures such as English, French or German. The French shrug of the shoulder has no real equivalent in German or English cultures; and the same is true for differences in rhythm, intonation, pace, vocalic quality and the signs made with these.

Yet there are commonalities. Speech happens in time; one sound, one word, one sentence follows another, so that *sequence in time* is a fundamental organizing principle and a major means for making meaning in this mode. This is common to all cultures. Image, by contrast, is 'displayed' in a (usually) framed *space* on a surface. Its elements are *simultaneously* present; the arrangement of elements in relation to each other in that space is a major means for making meaning. While time and the *sequence of elements* in time provide the 'semiotic logic' of speech (or dance, gesture, moving image), space and the *relation of the simultaneously present elements* in that space provide the underlying 'semiotic logic' of (still) image (or sculpture, layout). The 'logics' of time and space offer distinct potentials for making meaning.

Some modes, *gesture* or *moving image* for instance, combine the logics of time and space. Gesture is realized as a sequence in time of the movement of arms, hands, head and facial features, as well as of their simultaneous display against the stable *spatial* frame of the upper part of the torso. In (older versions of) moving image the logic of sequence in time is realized by a succession of frames of images, each of which is itself organized by the logic of space and simultaneity.

Alphabetic writing is a border category in this respect: it is spatially displayed, yet it 'leans on' speech in its logic of sequence in time, which is 'mimicked' in writing by the spatial sequence of elements on the *line* on which writing is displayed. This spatial display of writing gives rise to the sense that it works in some ways at least like an image. However, while the relations of elements of an image can usually be 'read' in an order shaped by the interest of the 'viewer', the reading of writing is governed by *linearity* and *directionality* – left to right or right to left – and by the ordering of syntax. Unlike image, writing is not, dominantly and finally, organized by the logic of space; as readers we are bound by the orderings of syntax and the directionality of the line. In alphabetic cultures, speech and writing share – even though in significantly different ways – features of syntax and lexis; with that go the distinctly different material potentials for meaning of sound and of graphic 'stuff', both also socially shaped.

Looked at in this way, the differences between speech and writing may be as or more significant than the similarities. This makes it surprising that speech and writing are subsumed under one label, 'language'. From a social semiotic perspective, the shared label obscures their distinctness as modes with related yet importantly distinct affordances.

The resources of the mode of image differ from those of either speech or writing. Image does not 'have' sounds organized as phonology, nor words, nor the syntax and grammar of either speech or writing; and none of their other entities/units. There is no point searching images for syllables, morphemes, words, phrases, clauses, sentences, paragraphs or any other language-based entity. Still image is based on the logic of space: it uses the affordances of a (framed) space: whether page or canvas, a piece of wall or a T-shirt. Meaning is made by the arrangement of entities in the framed space; by the *kinds* of relations between the depicted entities; as well as by size, colour, line and shape. Where writing or speech have words, image has 'depictions'. It uses basic visual entities – *circles, squares, lines, triangles*. Words are spoken or written; images are 'displayed'; the 'site of display' is a semiotic entity characteristic of image(-like) communication.

The differing affordances of modes enable specific semiotic work drawing on these affordances. These are constantly reshaped along the lines of the social requirements expressed in that work by those who make meanings. Whatever is not a social need is not elaborated in modes. As a consequence, not all the potentials inherent in the *materiality* of a mode are used to become affordances of that mode in a particular culture. All this ensures a tight link of social practice and meanings with modal affordance. Nor are the affordances used in one culture used for the same or similar purposes in another. My mention of pitch is an example. In tone-languages pitch is used – among other things – for lexical purposes: with the same syllabic (or multisyllabic) form, difference in pitch – 'tone' – produces different words. In English, pitch-movement is used predominantly for grammatical purposes, for forming questions or statements; as well as for the expression of affect. In English, pitch is used for lexical purposes too, but in a lesser way: try saying 'yes' to mean 'are you really sure?' or 'maybe' or to express sceptical, half-agreement. These variants use the same syllable – 'yes'; in fact they are different words.

Cultures select 'materials' – sound, clay, movement of (parts of) the body, wood, stone, gaze – which appear useful or necessary for meaning-work to be done. In communities of humans who are speech-impaired, the affordances of bodily movement – the positioning and the movement of limbs, of facial expression – are developed into a fully articulated mode, as *signing* (see also Sacks, 1989). In communities where speech is available, a narrow selection of these affordances is used as gesture, differently from society to society. Societies select differently, constantly reshaping the cultural/semiotic resources of mode.

The focus on materiality marks two decisive moves: one is away from abstractions such as 'language', 'the linguistic system' or 'grammar', towards specificity, the materiality of modes developed in social uses. The other is linking modes as means for representation with the body-liness of humans: through the physiology of sound and hearing, of sight and seeing, of touch and feeling, of taste and tasting, a recognition that humans make meaning through all these means and a realization that these means of engaging with the world are linked and make meaning jointly. That brings the possibility of recognizing meaning as embodied and provides a means of getting beyond separations in abstractions such as mind and body, affect and cognition.

The 'reach' of modes

Humans engage with the world and each other through socially made and culturally specific resources, in ways that arise out of their interests. This leads to the well-enough understood problems of *translation*: in one culture, certain cultural domains are well supplied with syntactic and lexical resources, others are poorly supplied; or a domain may be entirely missing in a culture. Compared to the world that might be named or depicted, every culture provides *partial* means for naming or depiction only. The 'semiotic reach' of modes – what can be expressed readily or at all by image, speech, gesture, writing, dance, gaze, music – is always specific and partial in any one culture, though differently specific and partial. This partiality of naming, depiction, 'signing' or of any modal 'labelling' is a feature of all cultures and all modes: there are always gaps. Areas in the centre of social attention are well supplied with semiotic resources; others less so; and what is not attended to in a society is not named or depicted at all.

Societies have modal preferences: this mode used for these purposes in this society, that other mode for those other purposes. Over several centuries now, 'western' societies have preferred writing to image for most areas of public communication. At other times *oratory* was most prized in western history; as it still is in many societies. Hence there is differential 'density' of semiotic entities, whether of 'names' or of means of relating entities to each other, even within one society. The material affordances of modes play into this: the 'sweep' of a gesture is infinitely variable in its expressive potential; gesture affords infinitely gradable signifiers. A gesture is transient – once made, no trace remains of it. Gesture may therefore be a preferred mode in certain social domains, as in the community of amateur fishermen.

63

As a consequence, the 'reach' of modes varies from culture to culture. What is done by speech in one culture may be done by gesture in another; what may be well done through image in one culture may be better done in three-dimensional forms in another; and so on. We cannot assume that translations from one mode to the 'same' mode in another culture can draw on the same resources. In other words, the implicit assumption that 'languages' (and now modes) can deal broadly with the same domains in different cultures – even if differently – is likely to be unfounded. It may be that a meaning expressed by gesture in this culture has to be *spoken* in that other culture; what may be handled by image here, may need to be *written* there. That may be the case among groups in one society. In other words, the assumption that what is represented in speech in Culture A will also be represented by speech in Culture B (with different lexis, syntax, genres) may be quite unfounded.

What *is* a mode?

The former certainties about 'language' had acted as a barrier to posing questions such as: 'What other means for making meaning are there?' and 'What are they like?' The issue of affordance could not arise when 'language' seemed all there was and was seen as fully sufficient for all of human representation. Turned around, these could have become unsettling questions such as 'What, actually, is language like?' 'What can it do and what can it not do?' *Affordance* – the potentials and limitations of material drawn into semiosis as mode – applies to all modes and 'language' is no exception. The idea of limitations of language, of its *partiality*, is new. Now that issue is firmly on the agenda. 'Language', which had been seen as a full means of expression, as the foundation of rationality, as sufficient for all that could be spoken and written, thought, felt and dreamt (Eco, 1976), is now seen as a partial means in relation to these.

From this perspective, profound questions pose themselves, the 'reach' of mode being one of these. I have alluded to two others: 'If "language" is a mode, then what are its potentials and what are its limitations?' and 'What semiotic resources are included in that mode?' These are questions that apply to all modes.

The moment we ask the question, the wide diversity of phenomena assembled under the term 'language' becomes apparent. 'What (kinds of) features make up writing or speech?' and 'What integrating principles might provide coherence to these features?' These questions now need answers. With speech we can ask: 'What does pitch have in common with lexis?', 'What connects energy – loudness and softness – with syntax?', 'What links tonal variation with morphology?', 'What does pace share with vocalic and consonantal features?' These are entirely disparate kinds of phenomena collected together under the label 'speech'. Writing is no different: 'What does font have in common with lexis?' or 'What connects orthography with syntax?' Joining these under the label either of speech or of writing shows one problem. Unifying speech with writing – with their different materiality; the distinct logics of time and space, of sequence and simultaneity – exposes the implausibility of a mode called 'language'.

From a multimodal perspective it becomes difficult to see what principles of coherence might unify them. As a consequence, I take speech and writing to be distinct modes.

To treat speech and writing (let alone language) as modes is to accept that modes consist of bundles of (highly diverse) features. Further questions might follow: 'What is *in* and what is *outside* a mode?' and 'Why?' These, however, are questions about social practices and histories; about what has been considered essential, important, salient in a society and in its valuations. They do not get to the core about criteria for the status of mode. To do that we might for instance undertake a full inventory of a mode from that perspective, look at it both comparatively across cultures or in the context of all other modes in its culture; as in my sketch of features assembled 'in' speech and writing.

There are some simple means of starting that task: take my example of saying 'yes' to mean 'are you really sure?' It shows one meaning-potential of speech. How could this meaning be realized in writing (or in gesture or in image)? The answers would tell us about the different potentials of each: speech providing infinite variability of (not just attitudinal) meanings through sound, which writing could not emulate, easily or at all. Colour (-saturation) is a resource with similar variability in image; as might the pace or sweep of a gesture.

Two other answers to the question 'What is a mode?' are essential. One emphasizes the *social* in social semiotics; the other emphasizes the *formal requirements* of a social semiotic theory of communication. The first can be briefly stated: socially, a mode is what a community takes to be a mode and demonstrates that in its practices; it is a matter for a community and its representational needs. I might say image is a mode; a photographer is appalled by such a crude classification: for her or him photography is a mode; a painter might feel similarly about painting; both with plausible reasons. A socially oriented approach says that if there is a community which uses the resources of font, layout and colour with discernable regularity, consistency and shared assumptions about their meaning-potentials, then yes, font, etc. are modes for that group.

There is, to some extent, a generational gap here: this answer seems improper to those socialized when authority decided what was and what wasn't 'a language'. The contemporary approach departs from that tradition, which might be characterized as 'A language is a language. Full stop'. While the new approach reduces certainty, it seems closer to how communities – professional, generational, geographical – actually do treat the matter. Given such social divergence, it is unsurprising that there is no straightforward answer to questions such as 'Are font, layout and colour modes?'

Take colour as another instance. All societies have a strong sense of the meanings of colour, even though most of their members could not articulate what these meanings are. Yet the meaning of 'the little black dress' is understood: it is *little* – with meanings about gender and the erotic – and it is *black* – with meanings about power and the erotic. 'Power-dressing' has its colour-schemes, whether for men's suits, shirts and ties or for women's skirts, shirts and shoes. The meanings of font, colour and layout are culturally made, socially agreed and socially and culturally specific.

Formally, a social semiotic theory of communication has specific requirements for mode. While with the socially oriented approach, shared understandings and practices are in focus, formally, the focus is on communicational requirements. In a social semiotic theory any communicational resource has to fulfil three functions: to be able to represent what 'goes on' in the world – states, actions, events: the *ideational function*; to represent the social relations of those engaged in communication: the *interpersonal function*; and to represent both these as message-entities – texts – coherent internally and with their environment: the *textual function*. If music or colour or layout meet these requirements, they are modes; if they do not, then not.

This provides a 'test' for the status of mode: whether and how a semiotic resource meets these criteria in instances of use.

As a test I ask: 'is layout a mode?' Consider Figure 4.1, from a science textbook for 13-14-year-olds, published in 2005.

The questions are: 'Can layout represent what "goes on" in the world – states, actions, events?' 'Can layout represent social relations of those engaged in communication?' and 'Can layout represent these meanings as texts which are internally coherent and which cohere with their environment?' My answer to all three – to jump ahead a bit – is 'yes', layout meets the criteria. So on that basis, it is a mode.

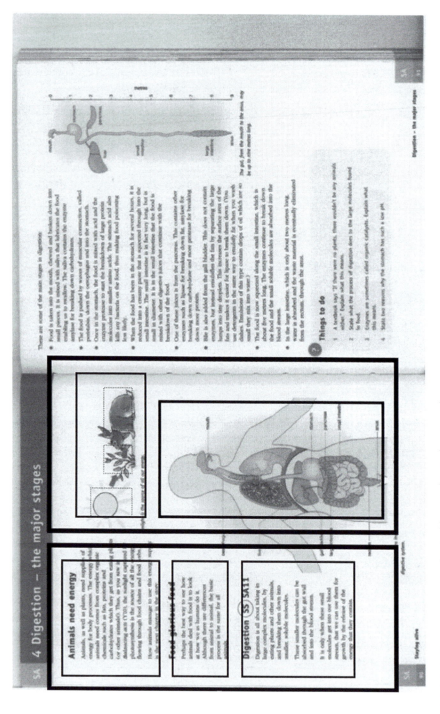

Figure 4.1 Digestive system: original a double-page image (pp. 90–91).

Key: heavy line – entities at level 1; lighter line – entities at level 2; dotted line – entities at level 3

Source: Salters GCSE Science Y11, Science Education Group (2002) published by Heinemann.

For the textual function I can ask 'Are there texts which are *incoherent* internally and which *do not cohere with their environment?*' This text appears in a science lesson; in a school year for which it was designed – for a group of 13-14-year-olds; it has a place in a curricular sequence; it functions aptly in its environment. Clearly, it coheres with its environment; it is not difficult to imagine any number of environments in which it would be incoherent. As far as internal coherence is concerned, I can ask: 'Will changes in the "arrangement" of the elements which make up this text, produce a different text?' 'Will they produce incoherence?' or 'Will changes make no difference at all?' If changes make no difference, then there is nothing to say as far as the textual function is concerned: it does not apply. Layout would have failed the mode test.

In Figure 4.2, the column of writing and that of image – elements at level 1 – are interchanged in position: the image column is now on the left and the column of writing is on the right. In my reading, this produces a text which is coherent, although information is now differently distributed. If left position indicates 'What is assumed to be shared/*given*' and right position 'What is assumed to be not shared/*new*', then the two pages have different meanings. In the original it is assumed that the starting point in learning about digestion is stuff about nutrients, processes of photosynthesis, enzymes, etc. – the biochemistry of nutrition and digestion. That is given, assumed as known and shared. The new is information about the structure of the digestive system. In Figure 4.1, the distribution of information is the other way around. These two distributions of information suggest different assumptions about the audience. The change of elements at level 1 retains coherence, each with distinct meaning.

We could interchange elements at level 3 across the two columns, as in Figure 4.3. Now the sun no longer shines on the plant but on the nether regions of the human digestive system; an element from the column of writing sits in the image column. The text/page is incoherent.

The formal technique of *commutation*, borrowed from structuralist linguistics, can be used to test for the ideational function. It allows me to ask 'What changes in meaning are produced if I substitute this element for that in the text I am concerned with?'

To apply this test I need to know what the elements are, at various levels. In Figure 4.1, the immediately obvious elements

at level 1, the largest level, are the *column of writing* and the *column of image*.

at level 2, the column of writing consists of three 'blocks', each with a heading. The image column consists of two images, the one at the bottom much larger than the one at the top.

at level 3, the top-most block of writing consists of two segments and the bottom-most block of three. The top-most image consists of three elements: the left-most, the central and the right-most, with arrows connecting the left-most element to the central element and it, in turn connected to the right-most. The lower image shows – at level 3 – a division of a pale pink background to indicate the torso and green, blue and red to indicate the digestive organs.

This description identifies the elements/entities sufficiently to show different arrangements at the various levels. Using this description with the first criterion – 'can layout represent what "goes on" in the world – states, actions, events?' – in the top image (level 3) of the image column, we can swap the left-most element (the sun) with the right-most (the rabbit). One arrow now points from the rabbit's back to the small plant; the arrow emanating from the plant points at the sun. The result is incongruous, though some bizarre meaning could be made of it.

The semiotic effects are clear: with some of these changes neither the page-as-text nor the two level 1 elements any longer cohere (Figure 4.3). There was coherence before; now there is not.

SA 4 Digestion – the major stages

Animals need energy

Animals, as well as plants, need supplies of energy for body processes. The energy which animals need comes from complex organic chemicals such as fats, proteins and carbohydrates which they get from eating plants (or other animals). Thus, as you saw in *Balancing acts* (Y10), the sunlight captured by photosynthesis is the source of all the energy flowing through food chains and food webs.

How animals manage to use this energy supply is the next chapter in the story.

Sunlight is the source of all our energy.

Food glorious food

Perhaps the best way to see how animals deal with food is to look at how we as humans do it. Although there are differences from animal to animal, the basic process is the same for all animals.

Digestion SS SA11

Digestion is all about taking in large complex molecules, by eating plants and other animals, and breaking them down into smaller, soluble molecules.

These smaller molecules can be absorbed through the gut wall and into the blood stream.

It is only when these small molecules get into our blood stream, that we can use them for growth by the release of the energy that they contain.

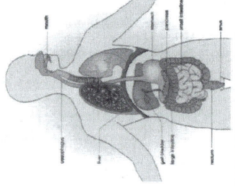

The main organs involved in digestion are shown here. This is called the digestive system.

These are some of the main stages in digestion:

● Food is taken into the mouth, chewed and broken down into small pieces. It is mixed with saliva that lubricates the food enabling us to swallow. The saliva contains the enzyme amylase for breaking down carbohydrates.

● The food is pushed by waves of muscular contraction, called peristalsis, down the oesophagus and into the stomach.

● Once in the stomach, the food is mixed with acid and the enzyme protease to start the breakdown of large protein molecules into smaller amino acids. The stomach acid also kills any bacteria on the food, thus making food poisoning less likely.

● When the food has been in the stomach for several hours, it is reduced into a creamy paste that is squeezed through into the small intestine. The small intestine is in fact very long, but is small in diameter. It is in the small intestine that the food is mixed with other digestive juices that continue with the breakdown of the food.

● One of these juices is from the pancreas. This contains other enzymes such as lipase for breaking down fat, amylase for breaking down carbohydrate and more protease for breaking down more protein.

● Bile is also added from the gall bladder. This does not contain enzymes, but instead emulsifies the fats by separating the large lumps into tiny droplets. This increases the surface area of the fats and makes it easier for lipase to break them down. (You use detergent in the same way to emulsify fat when you wash dishes. Emulsions of this type contain drops of oil which are so small they mix into water.)

● The food is now squeezed along the small intestine, which is about five metres long. The enzymes continue to break down the food and the small soluble molecules are absorbed into the blood stream.

● In the large intestine, which is only about two metres long, water is absorbed and the waste material is eventually eliminated from the rectum, through the anus.

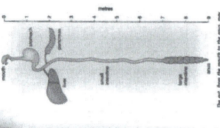

metres

The gut, from the mouth to the anus, may be up to nine metres long.

 **Things to do**

1. A textbook says "If there were no plants, there wouldn't be any animals either." Explain what this means.

2. State what the process of digestion does to the large molecules found in food.

3. Enzymes are sometimes called organic catalysts. Explain what this means.

4. State two reasons why the stomach has such a low pH.

Figure 4.2 Digestive system: columns of image and writing reversed.

SA 4 Digestion – the major stages

Animals need energy

Animals, as well as plants, need supplies of energy for body processes. The energy which animals need comes from complex organic chemicals such as fats, proteins and carbohydrates which they get from eating plants (or other animals). Thus, as you saw in *Balancing acts* (Y10), the sunlight captured by photosynthesis is the source of all the energy flowing through food chains and food webs.

How animals manage to use this energy supply is the next chapter in the story.

These smaller molecules can be absorbed through the gut wall and into the blood stream.

Sunlight is the source of all our energy.

Food glorious food

Perhaps the best way to see how animals deal with food is to look at how we as humans do it. Although there are differences from animal to animal, the basic process is the same for all animals.

Digestion SS SA11

Digestion is all about taking in large complex molecules, by eating plants and other animals, and breaking them down into smaller, soluble molecules.

It is only when these small molecules get into our blood stream, that we can use them for growth by the release of the energy that they contain.

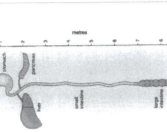

The main organs involved in digestion are shown here. This is called the digestive system.

Staying alive

These are some of the main stages in digestion:

- Food is taken into the mouth, chewed and broken down into small pieces. It is mixed with saliva that lubricates the food enabling us to swallow. The saliva contains the enzyme amylase for breaking down carbohydrates.

- The food is pushed by waves of muscular contraction, called peristalsis, down the oesophagus and into the stomach.

- Once in the stomach, the food is mixed with acid and the enzyme protease to start the breakdown of large protein molecules into smaller amino acids. The stomach acid also kills any bacteria on the food, thus making food poisoning less likely.

- When the food has been in the stomach for several hours, it is reduced into a creamy paste that is squeezed through into the small intestine. The small intestine is in fact very long, but is small in diameter. It is in the small intestine that the food is mixed with other digestive juices that continue with the breakdown of the food.

- One of these juices is from the pancreas. This contains other enzymes such as lipase for breaking down fat, amylase for breaking down carbohydrate and more protease for breaking down more protein.

- Bile is also added from the gall bladder. This does not contain enzymes, but instead emulsifies the fats by separating the large lumps into tiny droplets. This increases the surface area of the fats and makes it easier for lipase to break them down. (You use detergents in the same way to emulsify fat when you wash dishes. Emulsions of this type contain drops of oil which are so small they mix into water.)

- The food is now squeezed along the small intestine, which is about five metres long. The enzymes continue to break down the food and the small soluble molecules are absorbed into the blood stream.

- In the large intestine, which is only about two metres long, water is absorbed and the waste material is eventually eliminated from the rectum, through the anus.

The gut, from the mouth to the anus, may be up to nine metres long.

Things to do

1 A textbook says "If there were no plants, there wouldn't be any animals either." Explain what this means.

2 State what the process of digestion does to the large molecules found in food.

3 Enzymes are sometimes called organic catalysts. Explain what this means.

4 State two reasons why the stomach has such a low pH.

Figure 4.3 Digestive system: '(intra)textual incoherence'.

In these changes the ideational function – meanings about states, actions and events in the world – is involved. Taking the example – just described – of changes in arrangement of the level 2 element *sun-arrow-plant-arrow-rabbit* in the image column, the original has a broadly (causal) meaning of 'sun affects a plant, which a rabbit is eating'. If we rearrange the positions of rabbit and sun, the new version has nothing like that meaning. Semiotically, the rearrangement has changed a relation of *causation* to one of *connection* or *relation*. However, it could be said that this is dealing with image, rather than settling the question about layout as mode.

So then the interpersonal function: does layout enable us to represent meanings about the social relations between those engaged in communication? In Figure 4.2, the order of the two columns has been inverted. Following Kress and Van Leeuwen (1996/2006), the horizontal, left–right ordering of elements is meaningful. The assumption is that cultures have specific, if often implicit, 'semiotic orientations'. In this example, the taken-for-granted reading direction ('where we start from and where we go to') is from left to right; this ordering has the general meaning of left-most element as socially shared – 'given' – that is, information assumed to be *known* by the addressee; and of right-most element as not socially shared, not known to the addressee, that is, information regarded as *new* to the addressee, not shared by the social group.

This classification of information has social and ontological consequences: knowledge of a particular kind, as socially significant characteristics, is ascribed to the audience, correctly or not, and social interaction proceeds on that basis. The organization of information through layout as given and new information realizes (and can be used to project) particular ontological and social arrangements in the world of this interaction. This shapes the communicational relations of the participants and in that way it affects their social relation. That meets the theoretical requirement of the interpersonal function.

Modes have different affordances; speech and writing 'name'; image 'depicts'; gestures lend emphasis and sketch out themes and topics. Layout does not 'name' as words do or 'depict' as (elements in) images do; it organizes information. It indicates aspects of the social 'status' of representations – as 'given' or 'new'; through that layout categorizes and orients participants as 'part of my group or not'; and epistemologically as 'aware of specific knowledge or not'; ontologically, it indicates the social status of knowledge.

Layout 'orients' viewers/readers to meanings such as 'centrality' or 'marginality', 'given' or 'new', 'prior' and 'later', 'real' and 'ideal'. These are states of affairs in the world, different to and yet as significant in their way as 'naming', 'relating', 'depicting'. According to layout the status of mode means rethinking the scope of the ideational function, in line with the affordances of this mode. That is a consequence of a multimodal approach; or, we might say, of taking meaning seriously.

Meaning, mode, text: 'fixing' and 'framing'

Multimodality offers the possibility of choice of modes to make meaning material, to *realize* meaning. Depending on the media involved, on what is to be communicated and on the salient characteristics of the audience there are choices to be made: do you wish to realize the meaning that you wish to make and communicate as *image* or as *gesture*, as a *moving image* or as *speech*, or as ensembles of these? This possibility, a requirement actually, shows what has always happened – and was understood before – but had not really become focal, namely that meaning 'exists' only when it is made material – 'materialized' or 'realized' – in a specific mode or modes as a multimodal ensemble. Given the specific affordances of modes, the choice of modes has social, epistemological and ontological consequences.

The relation of meaning and mode presents itself in three ways. First, as a social/rhetorical issue, a matter jointly of affordances of the modes and of the rhetorical assumptions of the environment of communication: Which modes are apt given the rhetorical task to be achieved? Who is the audience? What is to be communicated to that audience by what technological means? Second, given the different 'takes' on the world implicit in modes, it presents itself as an ontological issue: do I want to present 'blood-circulation' through an abstract set of categories and their relation; or do I want to represent it in terms of, say, a temporal sequence? That question will be explored in the example below. Third, it appears in the issue of 'multimodal ensembles', as a question of style, aesthetics, and the politics of the situation, deciding which modes are to be selected and in what 'arrangements'. That is the subject of a different chapter.

In a social semiotic approach to meaning, the process of semiosis – of meaning-*making* – is seen as always social, whether 'externally' – between social actors – or 'internally', and as ceaselessly on-going. Most of this semiotic action is an 'inner action'; it never 'sees the light of day', so to speak. That is, the meanings which all of us make ceaselessly, as a constant internal flow, constantly changes meanings yet is never visible or apparent. It is only when this ceaseless 'inner' flow is 'interrupted', momentarily, by some need for 'uttering' a meaning, with social and individual design, then this meaning has to be appear in material form. At this point – borrowing a metaphor from older forms of photography, where a chemical substance placed on a film was the means of 'fixing' light and thereby fixing that which was the subject of the photograph – the question becomes: 'In what modes should my meaning be "fixed"?' (Kress, 1997b). Just as different chemical coatings provided different means of 'capturing' the world, with differing effects – most noticeably the difference between black-and-white and colour photography – so now the choice of modes provides means of 'fixing meaning': maybe as sequentially organized; or as a classification; or as causally; or as spatial relations. 'Modal fixing' is used in that sense. *Speech* and its affordances provide one distinctive 'fixing' of the world; *image* another; gesture yet another still; so does colour. And nearly always, and inevitably, meaning is 'fixed' in an ensemble of modes in line with a rhetor's wishes and the designer's actions. In the examples in Figures 4.4 and 4.5, the topic of blood-circulation is *fixed*, in one instance, in *writing* (in the genre of 'diary') and in the next instance in *image* (in the genre of 'concept map').

In Figure 4.4, the temporal/sequential organization of the genre of 'diary' fits well with the affordances of *speech* as actions and events in temporal sequence. Mode (of speech) and genre (of diary) make an ideal ensemble; and that is clearly there in the evidence: 'I left the heart; I had to come ...; (I had to) squeeze through ...; the heart beat got stronger; I left the heart.' The affordances of both mode and genre are used to shape the topic ontologically: the scientific 'entities' are arranged like beads on a string: the top right chamber of the heart; the right atrium; the right ventricle; the lungs; the capillaries.

The two concept maps, Figure 4.5, were each produced by two students jointly, in class. Many of the same scientific 'entities' appear here, though this time organized through the affordances of *image*: in the use of *space* and of *spatial relations* of simultaneously present entities. This produces a different meaning: not as *sequence* but as *hierarchy*.

It matters which mode is used to 'fix' meaning. Scientific conceptions, as much as 'common sense', are shaped by that choice. Once particular means of 'fixing meaning' have become habituated in mode and in genre – for instance, in formal accounts of events in *writing* and in *report* – it is likely that the world as represented through the combined affordances of mode and of genre will come to seem like this 'naturally'. *Modal fixing* provides the fundamental epistemological and ontological basis for representation and communication. Modal fixing combines with social *framings*, such as those of genre, for instance, to produce a meaning in which the social order is doubly present: once through the selection of the socially shaped material category of mode, and once through the framing representations of social relations in genre.

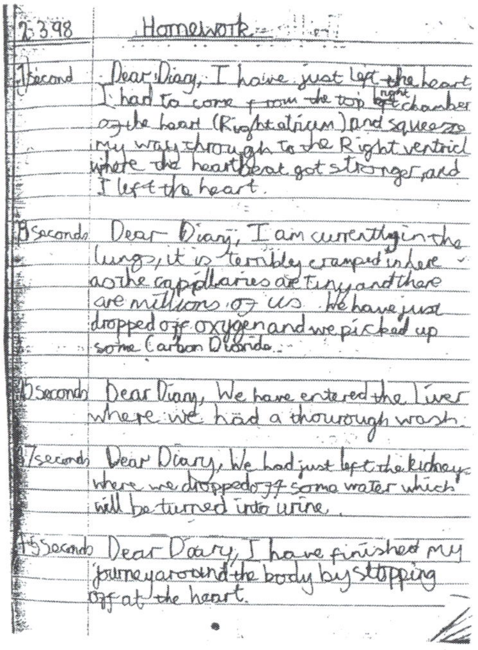

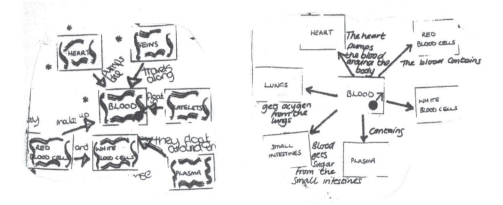

[handwritten diary entry:]

2.3.98   Homework

1 second   Dear Diary, I have just left the heart. I had to come from the top right chamber of the heart (Right atrium) and squeeze my way through to the Right ventricl where the heartbeat got stronger and I left the heart.

3 seconds   Dear Diary, I am currently in the lungs, it is terribly cramped in here as the capillaries are tiny and there are millions of us. We have just dropped off oxygen and we picked up some Carbon Dioxide.

10 seconds   Dear Diary, We have entered the liver where we had a thourough wash.

13 seconds   Dear Diary, We had just left the kidneys where we dropped off some water which will be turned into urine.

15 seconds   Dear Diary, I have finished my journey around the body by stopping off at the heart.

Figure 4.4 Blood-circulation: diary.

'Fixing' (in modes) and 'framing' through a variety of socially constructed semiotic devices are always present in a (complex) sign/message. If 'fixing' attempts to convey the sense 'this is what this phenomenon is like', then 'frame' is oriented more to the meaning-maker's perspective: 'this is what the world looks/is like from where I am located'. 'Frames' may be material, and they may be 'immaterial', as in the category of genre. Both are the result of social practices over long time. When painters or film directors want to get a sense of what should be represented, they form a rectangle with thumb and fingers of both hands and look at the world through that makeshift frame. They move that frame around until what is in the frame conforms

Figure 4.5 Blood-circulation: concept maps.

to what they have imagined or have wanted to see. Less evidently, a frame is constructed at the same time attempting to 'capture' social relations between participants, a 'frame' of genre.

The frame has two effects: it separates and it unites. What is in the frame now appears as separated from what is outside the frame; and everything that is inside the frame now forms a unity, in some way. Everything in the frame belongs together: or at least, a requirement appears that everything in the frame should be seen together. In a social semiotic perspective, 'frame' names the semiotic resource which are available to produce this dual effect: to separate an entity from other entities; and to provide unity and coherence to what is framed, the elements inside the frame. Semiotically, the frame is essential to make meaning: without the frame we do not know what is to be put into relation with what; what is to be put together with what; and where the boundaries to interpretation are. Frames and means of framing are essential to all meaning-making, in all modes (Goffman, 1986; Bateson, 2000). We might say: Without 'frame', no meaning.

From a multimodal perspective, the issue of 'frame' is significant because the material forms of frames depend on the material affordances of the material of the mode. To put it very concretely, the affordances of sound also become the affordances of possible frames. At that point the social (semiotic) reappears in the form of what kinds of frames a particular society regards as significant, and how the materiality of the mode is used to produce these. As before: at one level there is commonality: frames are essential; in one society, the kinds of frames that are regarded as essential will apply to all modes. At the level of a particular mode, the realization of frames – their strength, for instance – will depend on the material affordances of the modes.

Images have frames. Often these are borders of some material kind; wooden or plastic frames; blank space as frame; a band of distinct colour; some material shaped to mark a discontinuity between what is within the frame and what is outside; a discontinuity of frame and that which is framed and of frame and that which is outside the frame. The ornateness or simplicity of the frame suggests the value of what is framed.

In *writing*, there are frames for units such as *texts*; they tend to have significant frames – of free space, of strong lines, etc., depending of what kind of text in what kind of medium. *Paragraphs* within texts have frames, to mark them as discrete and significant; the kinds of frames used differ from society/culture to society/culture, though the principle will carry across cultures. *Sentences* within paragraphs have as frames (in most anglo-phone cultures) a capital initial letter and a full stop. And there are frames for *clauses* and *phrases* within sentences. A common term for some of the (graphic/syntactic) means for framing in writing is *punctuation*: comma, full stop, semicolon, colon, dash. The elements within the framed entity have 'unity', coherence. Whatever definition of the larger element – sentence, paragraph – we might use, the implication is that what is 'in' the frame of the sentence or of the paragraph belongs there; is to be read together; forms a unity of one kind.

Each mode has its specific means for framing. It is a matter for a semiotic theory to provide general, over-arching categories, applicable to all modes and to articulate labels for specific modes. In the images of Figures 4.1–4.3, *colour* is used as a resource for framing within the image of the digestive system: the de-saturated pinkish background for the body (which is not the focus) and the saturated blues for the organs, which are the focus. This is a very different resource to that of spatial 'gap' or temporal 'pause', or of a distinct graphic mark such as a 'comma'. Inevitably, framing devices are more elaborated for modes which have received much semiotic attention over long periods. There is much room for individual innovation. I recall a (then regional, later national) BBC newsreader who, having read the evening news, invariably concluded the event with the tiniest of nods, eyes firmly shut, lips pressed together: a very clear *gestural* full stop indeed.

Frames and framing devices are signifiers and as such have meaning potential; the meaning of a band of white space is different to that of a bold line; the meaning of a comma is different to that of a semicolon or a colon. As *signifiers*, framing devices are resources for making signs. The entities framed by a colon are different to those framed by a semicolon or those framed by a full stop. The meaning of framing devices – white space, colour bands, silence, punctuation marks – is a semiotic issue; it defines what kinds of intra-textual entities there can be. Punctuation marks may seem entirely conventional, yet the *signs* made with them are specific, made for this occasion with culturally given resources. If I chose to frame an image with a wavy line or segment my writing with a comma, I have made a sign different to what it would have been had I framed it with a straight line, a semicolon or a full stop.

Frames *hold together* and they *segment*. Frames make demands of hearers, viewers, readers to attend to the entities within the frame as connected, as having unity and coherence. Frames are used to do semiotic work and frames demand semiotic work. At the same time frames separate what is 'in' from what is 'out'; and the hearer, viewer, reader is asked to regard what is outside the frame as different from what is inside; and, if to be connected, then differently connected.

What has been *fixed* modally has to be *framed* modally. Jointly, the two processes establish the foundations of meaning in each instance of meaning-making.

Conclusion

Given the emphasis on affordances of the materiality, on the different 'logics' of modes, on the social work performed with the different materials chosen by a culture for the work of representation, it is clear that a theory or labels produced specifically for one mode can not deal with all the different potentials of all modes used in any one culture. At one level of generality, all modes and hence their functions, and therefore their categories, are produced in one culture. At that level there is a commonality. At the 'lowest' level, the level of a specific mode in its use and application the uses and characteristics are likely to differ, given the material affordances, and the kinds of social shaping done with a mode So two kinds of labels are needed: labels apt for the detail of specific modes and labels for the functions and purposes common to, shared by all modes.

Instances of such common semiotic functions across all modes are, e.g. 'separation' and 'unifying' by framing; 'emphasis'/'bringing to attention' by intensity; 'giving prominence' by foregrounding/highlighting; 'indicating connection' by kinds of linking, etc. and each mode will need to play its role in relation to the (Hallidayan) meta-functions mentioned earlier. While modes differ materially, and in the amount and length of social-historical work that has been expended in their shaping, I assume that all rely in some way on material resources to allow the indication of *levels of energy* (high or low intensity); of means for *marking emphasis*; for *foregrounding/highlighting*. With light and colour this can appear as saturation or de-saturation; with sound, high energy leads to loudness, whether in speech or music or soundtrack; or it may lead to the distinction of strong and weak consonants in speech; in graphic representation, in framing, it can be shown as strong thick lines or faint dotted lines; in writing it may lead to the use of bolding; to the use of an exclamation mark rather than a full stop; in clothing to the use of tough or soft fabrics – denim versus cotton; and so on.

The objection is frequently made that 'yes, maybe there is something in this, but '"in the end" we rely on language'. There are communities which cannot and do not rely on 'language' (or they may use writing but cannot use speech) and yet they have undeniably highly developed, sophisticated and subtly articulated communicational resources: I am thinking of communities of speech-impaired people and *signing*. The fact that dominant, mainstream society has called these semiotic resources 'languages' – sign-languages – is a consequence of histories of power and the mis-recognition due to power. Signing is a complex resource founded on the logics of space and time jointly, on simultaneity and sequentiality, with other elements beyond those of gesture. My assumption – I am speaking as an entire outsider – is that signing is different to either speech or writing in its materiality and in its social histories. Here I permit myself a value judgement: signing, having the logics of both time and space is a richer semiotic resource than one relying on one or other of the two logics alone. These are communities which do not, 'in the end', rely on language. They have developed the potentials of one set of communicational resources such that it does all that these communities need from that resource. Of course, these communities rely on the use of many modes other than those of signing.

Acknowledgement

This chapter draws on an ongoing research project, 'Gains and Losses: Changes in Representation, Knowledge and Pedagogy in Learning Resources' (2007–09).

5

Parametric systems

The case of voice quality

Theo Van Leeuwen

Introduction

Culture and nature, meaning and materiality, have often been opposed to each other. In this chapter I try to argue for their inextricable connection. I offer an account of the semiotics of voice quality, of the kinds of meanings that may be conveyed by different voice qualities and the way these meanings are conveyed, and of the voices of iconic actors like Lauren Bacall, Marilyn Monroe and Marlon Brando, who have modelled what can be meant with voice quality. I will, on the one hand, try to show that there is nothing natural about the way meaning is assigned to voice quality. In different historical and cultural contexts, voice quality may play different roles and occupy a more or less prominent space in the semiotic landscape. On the other hand, I will also try to show that voice quality is ultimately grounded in something that *is* natural, the human body, the human vocal apparatus, an instrument built, not by human hand, but by nature.

I will also try to show that there are different kinds of semiotic systems. In systemic-functional accounts of multimodality, a single model, that of the 'system network' has generally been used. Here I will argue that, yes, there are, on the one hand, semiotic practices which can be described as system networks, or 'modes', as Kress and I called them in our book *Multimodal Discourse* (2001), but on the other hand, practices that are better described as parametric systems, systems which articulate meaning directly in or with the material characteristics of the signifier, or 'media', as we called them in *Multimodal Discourse*.

In short, I will, in this chapter, interweave the systematic-analytical and the cultural-historical aspect of multimodality, and I hope I will succeed in modelling how this can be done.

Voice quality

In the 1960s and 1970s, voice quality was not seen as a linguistic or semiotic resource. David Crystal, in his *Prosodic Systems and Intonation in English* (1969), saw voice quality as a more or less arbitrary mark of individual or social identity, and described it in purely formal articulatory and acoustic terms. On the one hand, voice quality was individual, 'that relatively permanent, non-institutionalized, idiosyncratic, background voice-quality which accompanies a person when he speaks and is the main source of our ability to recognize personal identity vocally' (1969: 98). On the other hand, he did recognize that there were 'voice stereotypes', mostly aspects of dialect, as recognized in Firth's often quoted remark that it is 'part of the meaning of an American to sound like one' (Firth, 1957: 22).

In the same period, Pittenger and Danehy, in *The First Five Minutes* (1960), had seen the meaning of voice quality as indexical or 'symptomatic', providing clues about a speaker's body build, age, health, possible state of intoxication, etc. Somewhat later, John Laver (1979: 1) *did* describe voice quality as 'an audible index of [the speaker's] identity, personality and mood' and did discuss examples of regional, foreign and social 'accents', such as Trudgill's work (1974) on the distinct voice quality of Norwich working-class speakers. But he did so only in the introduction to his book. The book itself focused, again, on the purely formal, articulatory and acoustic description of the *components* of voice quality, and Laver did his best to remove any trace of meaning, any 'impressionistic and holistic labels', from his terminology.

Clearly, at this time, voice quality was not yet seen as a semiotic resource in its own right. It was a kind of individual and social fingerprint, an indelible mark of speakers' individual and social identities.

In roughly the same period, *cultural* theorists also discussed voice quality and, although they wrote in a very different style, what they said was not so different. In 'The grain of the voice', Roland Barthes (1977a: 179ff) distinguished between two aspects of the voice in singing. There were on the one hand 'the features which belong to the structure of the language being sung, the rules of the genre, the coded form of the composer's idiolect, the style of the interpretation: in short, everything in the performance which is in the service of communication, representation, expression' and there was, on the other hand, 'the grain of the voice', the 'materiality of the body speaking its mother tongue', 'something which is directly brought to your ears in one and the same movement from deep down in the activities, the muscles, the membranes, the cartilages'. The grain of the voice, he argued, is the unique quality of the singer's or speaker's voice which escapes the semiotic and the social, and provides an ineffable kind of *aesthetic* quality. Kaja Silverman, a film theorist writing about the voice, similarly called the voice 'the site of perhaps the most radical of all subjective divisions – the division between meaning and materiality' (1988: 44).

It is true that the voice is the embodiment of language, and that it fundamentally involves those 'cavities, muscles, membranes and cartilages'. But I do not think it is true that this is opposed to 'communication, representation, expression', and I do not think there is a radical and unbridgeable divide between materiality and meaning. On the contrary, as I will try to show, the voice and its meanings can ultimately only be understood on the basis of our bodily experience, and vocal semiosis can ultimately only be explained by paying close attention to the physicalities of articulation.

Speech is material and experiential as well as semiotic and social. In speech, the somatic and the semiotic intertwine.

Metaphor and meaning

My own account of voice quality (Van Leeuwen, 1999), builds directly on the body of phonetic and linguistic work I have just described. It was – and still is – a rich body of work, providing many good ideas for identifying and describing the components of voice quality, and of sound quality generally. But I did try to add something to it. I did try to *semioticize* it, to theorize how voice quality can be used to make meaning, and what kinds of meanings it can make. As I will discuss more fully later, this was needed, not because I discovered something that had always been there and that no-one had noticed before. It was needed because the semiotic landscape itself had changed. It was a necessary response to the semioticization of materiality, which, at that time, was rapidly becoming a key semiotic resource for the expression of individual and corporate identity, and a key feature of the semiotic landscape of today's global, corporate culture.

My point of departure for semioticizing voice quality was the metaphor theory of Lakoff and Johnson (1980), and more precisely their argument that we understand metaphors on the basis of our *concrete* experiences: 'No metaphor can ever be comprehended or even adequately represented independently of its experiential basis' (Lakoff and Johnson, 1980: 19).

For Lakoff and Johnson, this included physical, bodily experience, such as walking upright, or, for instance, tensing the voice, a component of voice quality that is mentioned throughout the literature, e.g. in Trudgill's description of the voice set of working-class speakers from Norwich. When the vocal muscles are tensed, the voice becomes higher, sharper and brighter, because in their tensed state, the walls of the throat dampen the sound less, just as is the case with the difference, say, between the sound of walking in a tiled corridor or a heavily carpeted room. It is a very physical, very material thing. It bridges materiality and meaning. The resulting sound not only *is* tense, it also *means* 'tense'. We can recognize tension in our own voice and in the voice of others, and we know from experience *when* our voice is likely to become tense, for instance when we are nervous, or anxious, or intimidated, or threatened – or excited. This complex of experiential knowledge can then be exploited as a meaning potential. It can map out *what kinds of things* might be communicated by vocal tension – in this case certain states of mind, whether temporary and fleeting ones, or mindsets that have become the more or less permanent habitus of an individual or a group.

Meaning potentials – metaphor potentials – of this kind are very broad. But context can narrow them – the other, concurrent features which make up a voice quality, for instance, have metaphor potentials of their own (e.g. loudness and pitch range) and the broader situational and socio-cultural context also contributes. In my book *Speech, Music, Sound* (Van Leeuwen (1999) I used a quote from Alan Lomax, who, in the 1960s, conducted a large research project on singing styles across the world, which remains a goldmine of information for anyone interested in the semiotics of sound. Lomax's comment is about the high degree of tension in the preferred female singing styles of cultures with quite severe sexual repression of women (Lomax, 1968: 194):

> It is as if one of the assignments of the favoured singer is to act out the level of sexual tension which the customs of the society establish as normal. The content of this message may be painful and anxiety-producing, but the effect upon the culture member may be stimulating, erotic and pleasurable, since the song reminds of familiar sexual emotions and experiences.

So here vocal tension signifies a specific kind of female identity which female singers model in a specific social and cultural context.

Looking at things this way, the materiality of the voice is not opposed to the semiotic and the social. There is no divide between materiality and meaning. On the contrary, knowledge of, and attention to, the 'cavities, muscles, membranes and cartilages' is a fundamental resource for semiosis, for making meaning with voice quality.

Tension is of course not the only resource for vocal meaning. Voice qualities have a *range* of components, and combine a *range* of vocal features, each one deriving from a particular, specific articulatory gesture. They are high or low *and* soft or loud *and* tense or lax and so on, and all these features are capable of fine gradation: there are many different pitch registers and many degrees of loudness and tension. Meaning derives from all of these features, in their specific combinations or degrees. And as a result, very complex articulations of meaning and identity become possible. I will discuss a few of these, indicating also how they have contributed to the development of semiotic resources for expressing identity with voice quality in twentieth century acting, singing, and public speech.

Pitch range

Our experience of pitch range tells us two things: men's voices are, on average, lower than those of women and children, and smaller resonating chambers (e.g. violins) produce higher sounds than larger resonating chambers (e.g. double basses). But people can modify the pitch range they use, whether intentionally or by force of ingrained habit, and this can inflect the expression of gender identities through pitch. Men use the higher regions of their pitch range to assert themselves and to dominate – only the very highest regions (e.g. the counter-tenor) can become ambiguous in gender terms. Women tend to use the lower end of their pitch range to be assertive. But, as it is difficult to be low and loud at the same time, women face a dilemma. They can speak low (which is assertive) and soft (which is intimate), which results in 'assertive intimacy' and can invoke the 'dangerous woman' stereotype that has been the staple fare of so many Hollywood stories, or they can speak high ('belittling' themselves) and loud (being assertive), resulting in 'assertive femininity', which can be considered 'shrill', lacking in 'feminine modesty'. In other words, women are caught between a rock and a hard place. In both cases dominant norms of public, assertive (and 'masculine') gender identity are at odds with dominant norms of private, intimate (and 'feminine') gender identity.

Women's voices with iconic status in popular culture have enshrined such meanings in public consciousness. Marilyn Monroe used a high, yet breathy voice, combining 'feminine' vulnerability and seductiveness. Lauren Bacall used a sensuous, low voice. In her autobiography she recalls how Howard Hawks conceived of her character for *To Have and Have Not* (1944) as 'a *masculine* approach – insolent. Give as good as she got, no capitulation, no helplessness' (Bacall, 1979: 87). To this end Hawks not only invented 'the look' – a quizzical look upwards with the head slightly bowed, suggesting feminine deference as well as insolence – but also told her to work on her voice, to 'practice shouting, keeping the register low' (ibid.: 92).

In other words, gestures and voice qualities of this kind were quite deliberately produced and distributed, to then become a resource for the expression of gender identities and roles the world over, a model for the millions.

Loudness

Our experience tells us that loudness indexes social distance, both literally and figuratively. As Edward Hall has shown (1964, 1966), at 'close range' our voice will be a soft whisper, whether for reasons of intimacy or conspiracy. At somewhat greater distance, it will no longer be a whisper, but still low enough not to be overheard by strangers. Further still, the loudness of the voice will signal that we are no longer speaking about personal matters, and no longer care about being overheard. Beyond that lies public speech, where we speak to a larger group rather than to a single person or small group.

Before amplification, there was a direct relation between voice level and social distance. Voice level would signify actual relationships, along the lines suggested by Hall. Amplification has changed that. A soft, breathy whisper can now be heard by a crowd, and the screaming of rock singers can be played at a comfortable background level. Level now constructs *imaginary* relations, whether in acting, in singing, or in public speech. But, at least for the moment, we still understand it on the basis of, and by reference to, our everyday experience.

These meanings were, again, pioneered in twentieth-century popular-culture singing, acting and public speech. In singing, the 'crooning' style of Bing Crosby pioneered an 'intimate, personal relationship with fans suited for domestic listeners' (Frith, 1988: 19). When the movies acquired soundtracks, actors had to wean themselves away from the projected voices of 1930s box-office plays and adopt more intimate, close-up styles. At the same time, politicians began to take note and replace oratory with conversational speech, as in President Roosevelt's 1930s 'fireside chats', which addressed listeners in 'calm, measured statements …as though he were actually sitting on the front porch or in the parlour with them' (Barnouw, 1968: 8), and radio speakers, too, learned to adopt a low-key conversational manner (Cardiff, 1981), so as to 'sound like the listener's best friend' (Leitner, 1980). In short, the public and the private began to intermix, undoing the nineteenth-century separation between the individual and the social, the public and the private voice, and creating space for the production of other kinds of meaning with vocal style.

Rough, smooth and breathy voices

In rough voices we can hear other things beside the tone of the voice itself – hoarseness, harshness, rasp. The opposite of the rough voice is the clean, smooth, 'well-oiled' voice from which all noisiness is eliminated. Again, the meaning of roughness lies in what it *is*: rough. Our experience tells us that roughness comes from wear and tear, whether as a result of smoking and drinking, hardship and adversity, or old age. In Van Leeuwen (1999: 131), I describe the rough voice as the 'vocal equivalent of the weatherbeaten face, the roughly plastered wall, the faded jeans, the battered leather jacket' and the smooth voice as 'the vocal equivalent of unblemished young skin, polished surfaces, designer plastic, immaculate tuxedos'. How such metaphors are valued depends on the context. In Western classical music, perception and polish is highly valued, for instance, and in African-American music, roughness.

In the breathy voice, another sound mixes in with the tone of the voice itself – breath. Its metaphor potential derives from our experience of what can make our voice breathy – exertion of some kind, or excitement, sexual arousal. Breathiness is often combined with a soft voice, suggesting intimacy, for instance in commercials, where advertisers use it to give their message a sensual, erotic appeal. Singers use it for the same reason.

Articulation

'Frontal' vowels are articulated with the tongue in the front of the mouth (e.g. the [i] of *heed*), back vowels with the tongue in the back of the mouth (e.g. the [a] of *hard*). This has often been commented on in relation to sound symbolism. In many languages words meaning 'close' use frontal vowels and words meaning 'far' back vowels, e.g. *near* and *far* in English, *hier* ('here') and *daar* ('there') in Dutch, *ici* and *là-bas* in French, *hier* and *dort* in German. But frontality and its opposite can also be overall speech characteristics, expressing a quality of being 'up front', 'confronting', or of 'holding back', 'not coming out with it'. Trudgill's description of Norwich working-class speech, for instance, included 'frontal and lowered articulation'.

The same can be said for 'aperture'. Some vowels are pronounced with the mouth comparatively closed and the oral cavity therefore comparatively small, others with the mouth comparatively open and the oral cavity therefore larger. The [i] of *heed* and the [u] of *hood* are less open, for instance, than the [a] of *hard*. This, too, has mostly been discussed in relation to sound symbolism. Words with an 'open' [a] have been said to be 'heavy, big and round', for instance, and words with the [i] 'small, light and pointed' (Brown and Hildum, 1956). But aperture can also become an overall feature of vocal style, expressing the *idea* of openness or closed-ness. Vocal settings of this kind are often used in puppetry and animation. In *Star Wars – The Phantom Menace* (George Lucas, 2000), for instance, the treacherous Viceroy of Naboo, a character with an inscrutable fish-like physiognomy, not only has a vaguely Chinese accent, but also speaks with a stiff jaw and an almost closed mouth, using a breathy, hollow-sounding 'faucalized' voice.

Resonance

The musicologist Shepherd (1991) has discussed the voices of different kinds of rock singers. 'Hard rock' voices are rough, loud and high. Their timbre reminds one of shouting, or even screaming. Resonance is produced almost entirely in the throat and the mouth. According to Shepherd this 'reproduces tension and experiential repression as males engage with the public world' (1991: 167).

In a female rock singing style which Shepherd describes as the style of 'woman as emotional nurturer', the voice is soft and warm, relatively low and with an open throat. It uses the resonating chambers of the chest, says Shepherd, so that the voice literally comes from the region of the heart or the breast. Softer male singers such as Paul McCartney tend to use the head as resonator and therefore sound 'lighter and thinner':

> The typical sound of the woman-as-sex-object involves a similar comparison. The softer, warmer, hollower tones of the woman singer as emotional nurturer become closed off with a certain edge, a certain vocal sheen that is quite different from the male-appropriated, hard core timbre typical of 'cock' rock. Tones such as that produced by Shirley Bassey in 'Big Spender', for instance, are essentially head tones, and it could in this sense be argued that the transition from woman the nurturer to woman the sex object represents a shift, physiologically coded, from the 'feminine heart' to the 'masculine head'.
>
> (Shepherd, 1991: 167–68)

Shepherd's discussion reminds us that voice qualities, in speech as in singing, are always a *combination* of features – 'soft' *and* 'warm' *and* 'hollow' *and* 'low' *and* 'open' *and* 'coming from the heart or breast', and that meanings such as 'woman-as-nurturer' result from the way in which these features are combined. The famous voice of Marlon Brando in *The Godfather* (1972) is another example. It is a comparatively high voice, and we have seen that men tend to use high voices to dominate. It is also hoarse and rough, signalling the Godfather's harsh and unforgiving side. And it is articulated with a stiff jaw and an almost closed mouth, suggesting an unwillingness to 'give' that keeps us guessing as to what he might be keeping from us. Yet it is also soft and breathy, at times almost a whisper, making the Godfather's menacing presence disturbingly intimate and attractive.

There is no space here to discuss all the parameters of voice quality in detail (see Van Leeuwen, 1999: 125ff for further detail), but I hope I have been able to demonstrate how the innovative semiotic potential of the experiential metaphor can change 'meaningless' characteristics into a semiotic resource, and how, in the course of the twentieth century, actors, singers and public speakers have exploited this in the creation of a new semiotic resource for the expression of new kinds of identity.

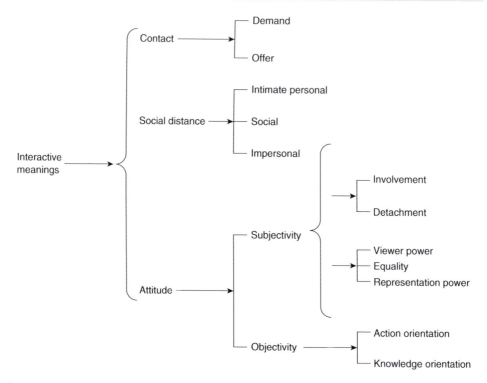

Figure 5.1 System network for the expression of 'attitude' in images.

Source: Kress and Van Leeuwen, 1996: 154.

Parametric systems

In our work on visual communication Gunther Kress and I had used 'system networks', taxonomic diagrams that lay out the semiotic choices available in a given domain (Kress and Van Leeuwen, 1996). The network in Figure 5.1 is an example. Focusing just on the lower part of the diagram, it says, essentially, that an image can express two kinds of attitude towards what is represented, subjective and objective attitudes. An image-maker will have to choose between the two, creating either a 'subjective' or an 'objective' image. The former will use perspective, to create a subjective 'angle', the latter will be front on or top down, 'flattening' the representation. Each choice leads to further, more 'delicate' choices. The curly bracket suggests, not an 'either/or' but a 'both/and' choice. A subjective image will have both a horizontal angle, expressing either involvement ('frontal') or detachment ('profile'), or something in between, and a vertical angle, expressing either viewer power (looking down on what is represented) or representation power (looking up to what is represented), or something in between, and so on.

System networks can therefore include both binary and simultaneous choices. But the idea of a taxonomically organized paradigm of choices, distinguished from each other in terms of single, crucial functional-semantic features, remains fundamental in system networks, and hence in the organization of semiotic modes that are based on this principle. And the problem was that, in the case of voice quality, I found *only* simultaneous choices, as shown in Figure 5.2, and, as the double-headed arrows indicate, these choices are not binary, not 'either/or', but graded choices, a range of intermediate positions between 'maximally low' and 'maximally high', or 'maximally loud' and 'maximally soft'.

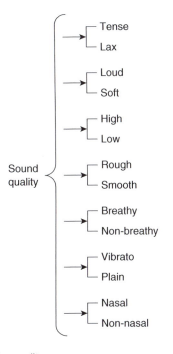

Figure 5.2 System network for voice quality.

Source: Van Leeuwen, 1999: 151.

At the time I presented this network without further comment. But eventually I had to come to the conclusion that systems like voice quality, if they can indeed be called 'systems', are organized, not taxonomically, but parametrically, through a set of parameters which *all* have to *always* be chosen, but to different degrees. In subsequent work I developed other parametric systems, for instance colour (Kress and Van Leeuwen, 2002), and typography (Van Leeuwen, 2006). All these semiotic resources had one thing in common. They had previously been described as non-systematic and usually also non-semiotic, or, as for instance in the case of colour, as *physically* systematic, but in ways that were entirely unrelated to the unsystematically organized 'psychological' meanings that were also ascribed to them. But now these resources were clearly drawn back into the semiotic circle again.

While the linguistic inspiration for our work on images had largely come from Halliday's lexicogrammar, in our work on colour, Kress and I sought inspiration in phonology, and argued that actual colours, voice qualities and so on are complexes of distinctive features in just the way that Jakobson and Halle (1956) had described phonemes, not as unitary atoms, [p]'s, [b]'s etc., but as complexes of features such as 'voiced/voiceless', 'strident/mellow', 'tense/lax' etc. But unlike Jakobson and Halle, we saw such 'phonological' features, not as merely distinctive, not as merely facilitating lexicogrammatically realized meanings, but as adding another layer of meaning themselves. In other words, phonology, or, as we had termed it (Kress and Van Leeuwen, 2001), the stratum of *production*, also creates meaning.

But not necessarily the same kind of meaning. It became increasingly obvious that parametric systems were used, especially, for creating textual meanings and identity meanings. Textually, voice quality, colour and typography can be used to 'frame' the different parts of a text, and at the same time provide them with a different identity. In the song 'Bubble Pop Electric', for instance, singer Gwen Stefani uses a low, husky voice when she addresses her boyfriend ('Drive in movie. Drive in, move me') and a higher, tenser voice with a somewhat artificial, 'electric' sheen, evoking a 1950s teenage culture of 'penny loafers and poodle skirts', for the refrain, where she repeats the words 'Bubble Pop Electric'. As for identity, I have already given an example of the complex identities that can be created with voice quality in describing Marlon Brando's both menacing and sensuously attractive voice in *The Godfather*, and quoted John Shepherd's account of the identities projected by different singers.

The social voice

So far I have sketched a 'physiologically coded' semiotics of the voice, to use John Shepherd's term – a semiotics in which the voice is what it means and means what it is, and in which meaning is made with the body, and understood on the basis of bodily experience. As I have described in greater detail elsewhere (Van Leeuwen, 2005b: 26ff), such experiential semiotics come to the fore in times of semiotic change, and the twentieth century, with its new communication technologies, has certainly been a period of such change. For a time voices had been disciplined towards uniform and institutionalized standards of educated propriety, and actors and singers had been schooled in singular aesthetic ideals, although this had of course never meant complete uniformity. On the contrary, it had allowed for subtle forms of individuality and distinction, more or less in the same way that the cut of apparently almost identical grey business suits can signal subtle degrees of sartorial elegance and finesse. Then amplification came along and allowed actors and singers to develop their own, immediately recognizable voices. In the course of less than a century, voices such as those of Lauren Bacall, Marilyn Monroe, Jimmy Stewart, Marlon Brando and others built a new semiotic resource, a new language of the voice, as did the singing voices of Ray Charles, Bob Dylan, Nina Simone, and Astrid Gilberto, to name just a few.

Dialects and accents took part in this opening-up of vocal semiotic resources. In the era of semiotic uniformity, they had signalled more-or-less permanent, stable social identities (origin, class etc.), and often stigmatized speakers. To upper-middle-class city dwellers, country dialects were backward, working-class dialects inferior, and foreign accents either suspect or funny. Dialects and accents carried the kind of connotations which Barthes (1973) had called 'myths' and referred to with terms such as 'Italian-ness', to indicate that they condensed into a single, diffuse concept everything the *bourgeoisie* 'knew' about Italians as well as the value judgments they attached to it. Much of this still lingers. The story of *Pygmalion* is still understood. Yet much has changed. In the early 1930s MGM still worried about Greta Garbo's accent, yet her voice was to become another key icon in the new semiotics of voices. Soon Hollywood scriptwriters would recommend the use of accents and dialects. As one authoritative Hollywood manual of scriptwriting stated: 'Dialect … is as revelatory as make-up, as picturesque as costume, as characteristic as gestures, as identifiable as physical disabilities, and as dramatically effective as facial expressions' (Herman, 1952: 198).

Amongst other things, the author of this manual recommended 'the dropped "h" in cockney, the "d" and "t" substitutes for "th" in German, together with the dropped final "g" in Afro-American English, as in "fightin" and "doin" '(ibid.: 200). Such dialects and accents would soon be familiar to movie audiences the world over, their meanings as easily understood as those of the clichés of classical Hollywood musical scores. Public speech, for instance on radio, also became much more varied. Even on the BBC, where not long ago only 'the Queen's English' had been permitted, a wide variety of accents and dialects can now be heard, and not only in 'vox pops'.

Once dialects, accents and vocal styles are no longer seen as a kind of fingerprint, an indelible social marker, they lose their ties with a specific place or social group, and develop into a medium of expression. Speaking 'broad Australian', for instance, is no longer a matter of destiny, indexing the milieu in which you happen to be born, but a choice as to how much to associate yourself with the 'Aussie' lifestyle and values, and something which can be switched on and off at will. 'Cool' young people everywhere pick up token elements of the speech of Afro-American rappers, but not necessarily all the time and everywhere. The same goes for the singing styles of singers like Madonna and Gwen Stefani, or for movie actors. As Michel Chion (1999: 173) has noted, actors no longer project a single persona with their voice, but adjust their voice quality to the role or the scene they are playing:

> There is timbre, the way of creating a voice that is hoarser, more metallic, more full-throated, more sonorous, or less harmonically rich. Compare two roughly contemporaneous Dustin Hoffman movies. In Barry Levinson's *Rain Man*, he has a metallic and nasal voice and in Stephen Frears' *Hero* it is coarser. If you listen to both films without the picture, it is quite difficult to identify both voices as coming from the same actor.

Marlon Brando's hoarse whisper is now part of the repertoire of many American actors, to be deployed whenever a sense of brooding, yet sensuously attractive menace is required. The same applies to the way singers like Madonna and Gwen Stefani draw on a wide range of recognizable singing styles. Voice quality no longer indexes individual character or social destiny. As Michael Chion has argued in relation to the voice of movie actors:

> The voice is ceasing to be identified with a specific face. It appears much less stable, identified. This general realization that the voice is radically other than the body that adopts it (or that it adopts) for the duration of a film seems to me to be one of the most significant phenomena in the recent development of the cinema, television, and audiovisual media in general.
>
> (Chion, 1999: 174)

The voice ceases to be 'the body speaking its mother tongue' here. The period of semiotic change I have described is drawing to an end, and the repertoire is stabilizing, at least for the moment. Although the meanings of this voice repertoire still derive from bodily experience, this is less foregrounded now. Voices begin to be understood on the basis of cultural connotation, on the basis of 'where they come from', of familiarity with the movie roles and songs in which they have been used, for instance. Another, socially and culturally coded, semiotic regime takes over from the physiologically coded regime that gave birth to it.

As speech synthesis technology develops, this new language of the voice may well harden into the kind of bony-structured binary code that digital technology requires. Under the pressure of technology, parametric systems, with their subtly graded expressive potentials, may yet evolve into binary systems. Sound engineers can already enhance recorded voices, turning up the tension a little, or adding a touch of synthetic breathiness. Nevertheless, it is always possible to go back to the source, always possible to reconnect with the physicalities of voice production, and to explore the many possible voices and the many possible meanings that have not yet entered into the mainstream of cultural production.

6

Modal density and modal configurations

Multimodal actions

Sigrid Norris

Introduction

Social actors often are involved in more than one higher-level action. For example, a father watches his toddler (a higher-level action) and converses with a client on the phone (a higher-level action). A business woman has her child playing in the office and engages in computer-mediated interactions with colleagues. A student is sending a text message (SMS) at a bus stop while conversing in person with a fellow student. Examples of simultaneous engagements in higher-level actions are abundant; a way to study them, however, is still in its infancy. In this chapter, I would like to discuss two notions which help in the analysis of higher-level actions.

The first notion is called "modal density" (Norris, 2004a) and refers to the modal intensity and/or the modal complexity through which a higher-level action is constructed. This concept enables the researcher to investigate simultaneous higher-level action construction: the student sending the SMS, for example, utilizes high modal density, involving the modes of object handling, gaze, and language, paying much attention to the SMS; while she uses medium modal density, utilizing modes such as posture, proxemics, gaze, language, gesture, layout and so on, simultaneously paying a bit less attention to conversing with a fellow student at the bus stop. Modal density is always linked to the multiple actions that a social actor performs and to the (heuristic) consciousness of the actor, which means the amount of attention paid, or the amount of awareness given by the social actor who performs the actions. Modal density can therefore not be dislodged from an individual's phenomenal conscious mind *and* the individuals' phenomenal actions.

The second notion is called "modal configuration" (Norris, 2005) and refers to the hierarchical, equal, or connected relationships among the modes that are at play in a given moment of a higher-level action. This concept enables the researcher to investigate the hierarchical positioning of various modes within a higher-level action and to compare these to other higher-level actions: When a father watches his toddler, gaze takes on a hierarchically higher position than language, while at other times when the father conveys a certain limitation to the child, language takes on a hierarchically higher position than gaze. Modal configuration is a concept that investigates how modes in interaction are structured in relation to one another.

Both concepts, modal density and modal configuration, are clearly linked to the actions that social actors take. It is important to note the difference between modal density and "semiotic resources" and between modal configuration and "semiotic meaning potential": a semiotic resource, according to Halliday (1978: 192) is a "resource for making meanings". Modal density, in contrast, is the intensity and/or complexity through which a higher-level action is constructed, which allows us to determine the level of attention paid to and/or the awareness of that higher-level action performed. Van Leeuwen (2005a: 4) explains the concept of semiotic meaning potential as "Almost everything we do or make can be done or made in different ways and therefore allows, at least in principle, the articulation of different social and cultural meanings". Modal configuration, in contrast, investigates the hierarchical and/or equal and/or connected orderings of modes utilized by social actors within a higher-level action. While all four concepts, modal density, modal configuration, semiotic resources and semiotic meaning potential, allow us to study multimodality, it is noteworthy that the concepts of modal density and modal configuration differ significantly from the other two concepts, but also differ from each other. In the following paragraphs, I discuss modal density and modal configuration in detail, but first it is necessary to define the following terms: interaction, communicative mode or mode of communication, mediated action, higher-level action, lower-level action, frozen action, modal density and level of attention, and modal configuration.

Terminology

In this section, I will define the necessary terminology by linking terms to the relevant literature.

Interaction

The term interaction as it is used in multimodal interaction analysis refers to any action that a social actor performs in which the actor communicates a message. Such a message can be co-constructed intentionally or given off unintentionally. Thus, an action is a social action if it is communicated. Many of the actions that social actors perform are out of their awareness. Many of the messages that social actors gather are also out of their awareness. This, however, does not mean that the social actions that are being communicated out of awareness are less important than those that social actors intentionally and full of awareness communicate.

The use of the term interaction in this framework grows out of three intertwined theoretical directions: first, the direction of interactional socio-linguistics, which has its origin in anthropology (Gumperz, 1982); second, the direction of sociology (Goffman, 1963, 1974); and third, the direction of mediated discourse analysis (Scollon, 1998a, 2001). Gumperz's work is primarily concerned with language and culture; Goffman's work delineates self and society; while Scollon's work broadens language to communication and combines the anthropological with the sociological interest, exploring communication, culture, self and society.

Communicative mode

Communicative modes or modes of communication, as used in this chapter, are systems of representation or semiotic systems with rules and regularities attached to them. Here, the term of medium, as Kress and Van Leeuwen (2001) use it, is taken for granted, when speaking of the term communicative mode. Kress and Van Leeuwen (2001: 22) state:

Media are the material resources used in the production of semiotic products and events, including both the tools and materials used (e.g. the musical instrument and air; the chisel and the block of wood). They usually are specifically produced for this purpose, not only in culture (ink, paint, cameras, computers), but also in nature (our vocal apparatus) ... Only eventually, as the particular medium gains in social importance, will more abstract modes of regulation ("grammars") develop, and the medium will become a mode.

Because I am interested in investigating social interaction and, since my focus of study and unit of analysis is the mediated action (Wertsch, 1991; Scollon, 1998a, 2001), I view both, media and mode, as meditational means or cultural tools (I will use the terms mediational means and cultural tools interchangeably). Thus, both the musical instrument and the air are mediational means; both the chisel and the wooden block are cultural tools; all culturally produced tools such as ink, paint, cameras, or computers, and also the language we use are mediational means; and all tools produced in nature such as our vocal apparatus, our hands/arms, or faces, are cultural tools.

All mediational means (all media and all modes) carry affordances and constraints. Each mode of communication (a mediational means or cultural tool) has to be accessed via media (or, in this view, other mediational means). In other words, if we speak of gesture as a communicative mode, a social actor necessarily needs to utilise the mediational means (or in Kress and Van Leeuwen's terms, the medium) of hand and/or arm in order to utilize, produce and reproduce the communicative mode of gesture (itself a mediational means).

Here then, I do not distinguish between medium and mode, but use communicative mode as the term that encompasses both aspects, taking for granted the fact that several mediational means are at play. Further, I am not concerned here with the closer distinction between a medium without rules and regularities and a mode as a medium with rules and regularities. In the view taken up here, there appear to be always rules and regularities in the "use" of communicative modes, whereby the rules and regularities may lie in the "use" rather than the "medium" or "mode" itself. Thus, while the notion of "rules and regularities attached to a mode" is carried over from Kress and Van Leeuwen's (2001) postulation, the essential idea behind the notion is slightly different: Kress and Van Leeuwen's focus is on the rules and regularities that can be found in systems of representation in use, while my focus is on the rules and regularities that come about while social actors use systems of representation (see also Norris, 2004a).

Thus, the focus here is always the action taken by a social actor *while* acting with or through mediational means (Wertsch, 1991; Scollon, 1998a, 2001); and communicative modes are mediational means that the social actors utilize, draw on and co-construct usually in some rule-governed and regularized fashion. The use of communicative modes is the use of mediational means that situate a social actor's actions in time and place. In other words: social actors always co-construct their actions with the environment and/or with other social actors so that we can never extricate a social actor's actions from the environment and/or from the other social actors involved.

Mediated action

The mediated action is a notion that was developed by the Russian psychologists Vygotsky, Leont'ev, and Luria in the 1920s and 1930s, when developing a general cultural-historical conceptual system that is based on a set of basic principles, called activity theory. One of the main principles is tool mediation, and others are hierarchical structure of activity, continuous development, object-orientedness, the concepts of internalisation/externalisation, and a focus on practice. This set of basic principles was then used to derive more specific theories, one of which was mediated discourse analysis (Scollon, 1998a, 2001). In mediated discourse analysis, as in activity theory, we find an emphasis on social actors and on the interaction between social actors and between social actors and their environment. This emphasis elucidates the primary role of mediation in both theories.

Multimodal interaction analysis (Norris, 2004a) is a branch of mediated discourse analysis, advancing it in the direction of multimodal use in interaction.

When using the mediated action as our unit of analysis, the action can neither be analysed without analysing the social actor(s) who is(are) performing the action, nor can it be analysed without the mediational means that the social actor(s) draws on when performing the action. Thus, the point of view is: actions are performed by social actors who are acting with or through cultural tools (Wertsch, 1991).

Actions can be defined in various ways and on first sight it may appear to be too vague a concept to be useful as a unit of analysis. However, when looking at the concept more closely, you will find that each action has a beginning and an end, no matter which level of action you are investigating: a family dinner starts at some point and ends at another point; a conversation starts at some point and ends at another point; a topic starts at some point and ends at another point; and a gesture starts at some point and ends at another point. No matter which level of action you are investigating, you always want to delineate the action by finding the starting and the ending points. Once you start investigating starting and ending points, you will discover that there often are many layers of actions, which coincides with activity theory's postulation of a hierarchical structure of activity. These layers are here termed various layers of higher-level actions, lower-level actions, and frozen actions (Norris, 2004).

Higher-level actions

A conversation is a higher-level action; a family dinner is a higher-level action; a business meeting is a higher-level action; and so is a music lesson. Some higher-level actions are embedded within another higher-level action, for example a conversation may be embedded within a family dinner. This notion of embeddedness of higher-level actions is also not unlike the notion of framing (Goffman, 1974).

The higher the level of higher-level action, the more complex it usually is. For example, taking the action of studying as an undergraduate student: the action has a beginning and an ending point; there are also many other higher-level actions embedded within this level of higher-level action from taking classes and learning about specific subjects to meeting new people and making friends, or eating lunches and taking showers. Some of these actions are distinct in time and space, while others may overlap. Some of these actions are consecutive, while others are simultaneous. It may appear that it is impossible to distinguish, yet, when you tease out the actions that are being performed, you can always find a starting and an ending point for the action, giving you an analysable unit.

When thinking of undergraduate studies as a high level of higher-level action, we can easily see that this action is made up of many other levels of higher-level action, and that, simultaneously, this high higher-level action is constructing the various higher-level actions. Thus, there is always construction of actions from the smaller to the larger and *concurrently* from the larger to the smaller actions.

Lower-level actions

A conversation is (co)constructed via many chains of lower-level actions such as via many utterances (chains of lower-level actions that utilize the mode of spoken language through and with the media of vocal folds, air, lips and teeth); via many gestures (chains of lower-level actions that utilize the mode of gesture through and with the media of hands, arms and fingers); and via many postural shifts (chains of lower-level actions that utilize the mode of posture through and with the media of the torso, the shoulders, the hips and legs). A lower-level action is taken to be a smallest meaning unit (Norris, 2004a), in which a social actor draws upon a communicative mode such as gesture, posture, spoken language or layout, and constructs meaning.

When a social actor performs a lower-level action, the social actor draws on a meaning system that has been learned throughout the social actor's life, while, at the very same time, the social actor establishes, modifies and develops the very meaning system that is being drawn upon. Meaning system, as used here, therefore is the real-time, non-reified use of a communicative mode which also includes the utilized media as discussed under the heading "communicative mode" above. Thus, in this framework, we explore meaning systems by investigating social actors while constructing meaning. Of course, meaning is not only constructed through actions, but also through objects in the world. Since objects also entail actions, or, at least are assigned actions by social actors, I call them frozen actions.

Frozen actions

Buildings, furniture, and paintings on a wall may all be involved during a conversation. The objects, of course, had to be built, placed and hung by social actors, leaving a trace of just these actions. Thus, these actions that were performed by social actors at the prior moment are frozen in time. These frozen actions can, and often do, play a role in the actions that people take. For example, we often find that individuals ask about the architecture, the origin of furniture or the theme of paintings on a wall when conversing with others.

Frozen actions are often manifestations of higher-level actions that are made up of an abundance of lower-level actions, but are also manifestations of lower-level actions. What this means is that when a conversation takes place in somebody's dining room and the conversation turns to a painting that hangs on a wall: the painting entails the higher-level action of having been acquired by somebody, the higher-level action of having been placed on the wall, or the higher-level action of having been painted by somebody. Now, we can also surmise that the actual painting shows some of the lower-level actions of the artist. Brush strokes for, example, leave traces, and it is these lower-level actions that are entailed in the painting.

Density and modal density

Density is a term borrowed from physics, where density is mass per unit volume, which is the ratio of the amount of matter in an object compared to its volume (density = mass/volume). Thus, the density of a piece of lead is higher than the density of a piece of cork of the same size. Analogously, the amalgamation of various metals has greater density than a ball of paper. Modal density is viewed in a similar sense, where, instead of chemical substance, we think of communicative modes at play in interaction.

Modal density can either come about through modal intensity (comparative to the piece of lead above) or through modal complexity (comparative to the amalgam above). Speaking in interactional terms, the mode of language takes on high modal intensity when two social actors engage in a phone conversation. Here, the phone conversation builds the higher-level action, which is (co)constructed through high modal density. Similarly, a dinner-time conversation is (co)constructed through high modal density by the participants because of the complexly intertwined multiple modes that the social actors utilize. At a dinner table, the social actors intricately intertwine the modes of spoken language, gesture, posture, gaze, with object handling and lay-out. As noted above, the media used to access, produce, change and reproduce the various modes of communication are viewed as a necessary given when speaking of modal use, as modal use cannot be achieved without a use of multiple mediational means. As I have discussed earlier,

> The intensity, weight, or importance of specific modes in interaction are determined by the situation, the social actors, and other social and environmental factors involved. There-fore, the weight of any specific mode changes from one interaction to the next, and may change within an interaction.
>
> (Norris, 2004a: 79)

We can determine these fluctuations in use when investigating real interactions taking place in time and space. When investigating the complexities of multimodal interaction, it is useful to realize that social actors act on a variety of levels of attention. We often find that social actors are engaged in a range of social actions to variant degrees of attention/awareness. When heuristically viewing these levels of attention as a foreground–background continuum, we can find the simi-larities to sound and music or to paintings and films. Schaffer (1977), for example, illustrates the notion of a foreground–background continuum in sound scapes, and Van Leeuwen (1999) explicates the same concept in music and language; we speak of foreground and background in photography, in paintings, in multimedia computing and many other environments.

Modal density, higher-level actions and levels of attention

Every time social actors perform higher-level actions, they are paying some level of attention to the action. It is argued here, that the higher the modal density that a social actor utilizes in order to construct the higher-level action, the more attention the social actor pays to the action. In other words, if a father watches his toddler while conversing with a client on the phone, the father can either pay more attention to his toddler or pay more attention to the client. While the level of attention may shift from toddler to client and back again, both interactions – the interac-tion of the father with his toddler and the interaction of the father with his client – are being attended to by the father throughout. When investigating modal density, we can determine which interaction the father is phenomenally focused upon and which interaction the father pays less phenomenal attention to at any given moment.

Modal density for various simultaneous higher-level actions may be produced through the use of one and the same communicative modes and/or through the use of different communicative modes. Teasing out which modes are used for which action appears to be more difficult than it really is. When analysing a higher-level action, the analyst wants to determine the importance of modes in relation to the action performed. Thus, the questions that need to be asked are: What is/are the action(s)? What does the social actor do while performing the action(s)? Which modes are absolutely necessary so that the social actor can perform the action(s)? Which modes are not as necessary, but are still used in a particular way in order to perform the action(s) as the social actor does? Which modes are irrelevant to the higher-level action(s) being analysed?

Higher-level actions are then hierarchically placed on a modal density foreground–background continuum which heuristically illustrates the attention/awareness levels that the social actor phenomenally places on the specific actions that the social actor performs at a certain time in a certain location (Norris, 2004a).

Modal configuration

Each higher-level or frozen action is made up of several modes at play. Lower-level actions, however, are constructed through a social actor's use of "one mode", whereby the term mode is cumbersome and the notion of countability is incorrect. A mode, as discussed above, is a mediational means or a cultural tool, which is made up of mode and multiple media (in Kress and Van Leeuwen's sense). A mode is not easily definable as one, and the same mode can either be viewed as one mode (i.e. hand/arm gesture) and simultaneously be divided into many modes (i.e. iconic gestures, beat gestures or metaphoric gestures); but the ostensible "one mode" of gesture can also be combined with other modes such as posture, head movement and the like, and be termed "gesture".

Again, when thinking of modal configurations, I do not differentiate between modes and medium. Modes, as discussed above, are viewed in the sense of pragmatics and always take the stance that modes are used by social actors. Thus, in this sense, modes never exist without social actors utilizing them in some way. Even if a researcher analyses a website, the researcher is actually using the embedded modes of the webpage. Further, the modes have been embedded by other social actors, as the social actors who constructed the web page have used computer programs and other cultural tools. Here, also, it is essential to note that computer programs do not work without a social actor using them. Taking this notion a bit further, we can then say that, while computer programs are programmed by social actors to, for example, pick colour palettes, a programmer had to program the software to make such self-choosing selections within a program possible. When now investigating a webpage, we can investigate how a social actor uses the modes by interacting with/through the program in some way.

When I speak of modal configurations, I delve into a deeper analytical perspective, never, however, taking the above tension between social actors acting with/through cultural tools for granted. This tension is always important, making each moment specific, and disallowing the researcher to reinterpret this theoretical notion as a reified framework.

Thus, while we can investigate the interplay among modes at a given moment in (inter) action, we cannot presume that a modal configuration at one point in time utilized by one social actor is translatable to the same modal configuration at a different point in time utilized by the same or another social actor. Modal configurations change and meanings of modal configurations change. What we can say about modal configurations at a given point in time, however, concerns the hierarchical and non-hierarchical structures that can be found among the modes used. Thus, the notion of modal configuration allows us to understand the interplay of communicative modes as they are structured in relation to one another within a higher-level action that a social actor performs.

The notion of modal configuration grows out of the notion of modal density and both concepts relate directly. When thinking of the questions we ask to discover a higher-level action's modal density, we can then extend the answers that we obtained in order to gain insight into modal configurations.

Exploration of the concepts: modal density and modal configurations

In the following paragraphs I shall explore the concepts of modal density and modal configuration by looking at one and the same example. In this example, a woman, whom I call Sandra, is in the middle of a move. She is sitting on the floor of her living room and is

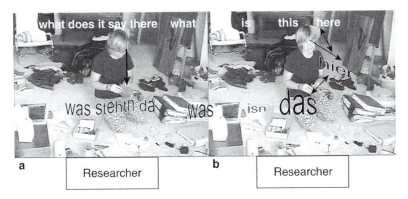

Figure 6.1 Higher-level action of assembling DSL; simultaneous higher-level action of interacting with the researcher.

assembling her Internet (DSL) connection. Sandra has been working, sitting in this position for some time. Loud hard- rock-type music is playing in the background, and all of Sandra's movements, performed with her hands/arms, shoulders and head are performed rhythmically. The researcher is sitting across from Sandra at a desk, filming Sandra with a video camera placed next to her.

Here we see that Sandra interacting with her environment and with the researcher present: actions performed at a specific time and place.

At this moment, Sandra is trying to read the small writing on a label of one of the parts that she is working with. Sandra says "was stehtn da, was isn das hier" (translation: what does it say there what is this here). In Figure 6.1a, we see how Sandra is looking at the label, pointing with her left index finger, while speaking the words "was stehtn da" (what does it say there). Then, she raises her voice a bit and rephrases the utterance, saying "was isn das hier" (what is this here). As she says "das" (this), Sandra lifts her left index finger and performs a beat. As her pointer has moved back to the label, Sandra raises her head and performs a beat with the head ending in a gaze directional shift. When looking at the continuity of the clip, she holds this new gaze direction for 6 seconds and then changes her complete position before ending the task for a while.

In the following paragraphs, I will focus in particular on Figure 6.1a, but will briefly refer to Figure 6.1b as well.

Modal density

In order to arrive at modal density, we need to answer the questions that I suggested above. The first and primary question is: What are the actions? The first and most obvious action is the higher-level action of Sandra assembling the DSL by using a number of communicative modes. The second action is less obvious. This is the action of Sandra interacting with the researcher by using a number of communicative modes. For both actions, we thus have a social actor performing an action with and/or through the use of multiple mediational means or communicative modes.

The next question is: What does the social actor do while performing the actions? Sandra, who had placed the necessary parts in a specific reachable place, is holding a part. She reads the label by sitting in a certain position directed towards the researcher and the camera, holding her head in a specific way. She speaks and listens to music.

Now, we will look at the two higher-level actions that Sandra performs – the assembling of the DSL and her interaction with the researcher – as separate actions.

Assembling the DSL

Here, we want to ask: Which modes are absolutely necessary for the social actor to perform this action? In order for Sandra to assemble the DSL, she needs to have the part(s) in a reachable place (modes: object handling, layout). Sandra further has to read the label (modes: gaze, print, head movement).

Next, we will want to ask: Which modes are not as necessary, but are still used in a particular way in order to perform the action as the social actor does? When looking at Figure 6.1, we see that Sandra is sitting in a particular way and that her body is directed in a certain direction (mode: posture). When thinking of the meaning potential, we can determine that she does not have to sit in this way, nor does she have to sit in this direction in order to assemble the DSL. Further, Sandra's spoken discourse is not necessary for her to perform the action of assembling the DSL.

One could suggest that she is thinking out loud, using spoken language and gesture to structure her thoughts, and that this may be useful to her, but it cannot be viewed as absolutely necessary to the action of assembling the DSL, as she is not using the mode of spoken language to talk herself through the action, but rather is using it to comment upon the action. These modes are therefore not as important as the mode of object handling nor even as essential as the printed label that Sandra is reading.

With this, we come to the last question that we have to ask: Which modes are irrelevant to this higher-level action? While Sandra is listening to the music, and the music is certainly rhythmically structuring her lower-level actions, we can argue that Sandra could perform the action just as well without the music.

Interacting with the researcher

For this higher-level action, we start out with the same first question as above: Which modes are absolutely necessary for the social actor to perform this action? In order for Sandra to interact with the researcher, she has to take up a position that allows for the interaction to develop. She does this by utilizing the space in a way that allows her to take up an open posture with her body facing the researcher (modes: layout, posture).

Next, we ask: Which modes are not as necessary, but are still used in a particular way in order to perform the action as the social actor does? When Sandra thinks out loud, we can argue that she is at least in part speaking with the researcher. Her gesture, the pointed index finger on the label (and the later beat) is linked to Sandra's spoken utterance. The researcher can clearly understand Sandra's utterance because of her pointed index finger (modes: spoken language, gesture). Further, both, Sandra and the researcher are sharing the listening to the music, the music thus building part of this interaction (mode: music).

Then, we want to ask: Which modes are irrelevant to this higher-level action? Since the researcher is not engaged with the assembly of the DSL, Sandra's holding the part and reading the label are not relevant to her mid-grounded higher-level action of interacting with the researcher (modes: object handling, print, gaze, head movement).

As soon as we have answered these questions, we can draw modal density circles and place the higher-level actions on a foreground–background continuum as illustrated in Figure 6.2.

Thus, modal density allows us to determine the relational phenomenal attention/awareness levels that a social actor utilizes in order to perform simultaneous actions. Modal density is

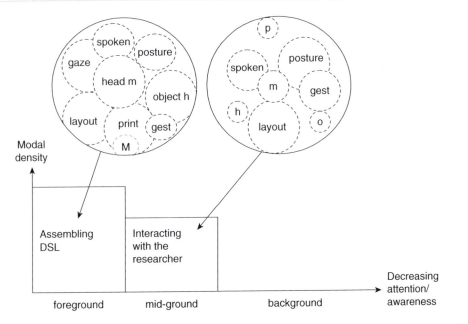

Figure 6.2 Sandra's foregrounded and mid-grounded higher-level actions constructed simultaneously with the same modes but a differing modal density.

always directly linked to the higher-level actions that a social actor performs with and/or through multiple communicative modes. This is a heuristic concept to allow a researcher to tease out various simultaneous actions performed by one and the same social actor. Modal density, the higher-level action(s) performed, and the phenomenal attention/awareness level(s) of a social actor, cannot be dislodged as they build a unity.

Modal configuration

In order to determine the modal configurations, we take a closer look at the questions and answers that we have asked for modal density. Here, we again look at the two higher-level actions that Sandra performs – the assembling of the DSL and her interaction with the researcher – as separate actions.

Assembling the DSL

In order to arrive at modal density we had asked: Which modes are absolutely necessary for the social actor to perform this action? The answer was: object handling, layout, gaze, print, head movement.

When now taking this thought further, we need to ask if any one of these modes is more important for Sandra than any other of these modes (Figure 6.3). When thinking about this, we can say that it is not possible to perform the action of assembling the DSL if Sandra does not have the parts. The mode of object handling is therefore the most important mode present. Certainly, the parts have to be in some reachable location for Sandra and thus, layout falls hierarchically right below object handling. Now, Sandra is reading the label on one of the parts by utilizing head movement, gaze, and the mode of print. It is impossible for her to read the label without looking at it, while the exact way she holds her head is not as important. While gaze

95

Most important
to least
important

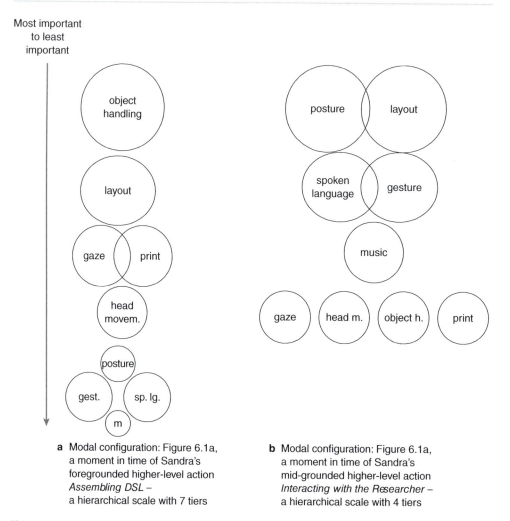

a Modal configuration: Figure 6.1a,
a moment in time of Sandra's
foregrounded higher-level action
Assembling DSL –
a hierarchical scale with 7 tiers

b Modal configuration: Figure 6.1a,
a moment in time of Sandra's
mid-grounded higher-level action
Interacting with the Researcher –
a hierarchical scale with 4 tiers

Figure 6.3 Modal configurations for two simultaneously performed higher-level actions.

and print are fully interlinked and one mode cannot be used by the social actor without the other, Sandra could glance at the label without lowering her head to the extent she does. Here, gaze and print build a mode aggregate, which is hierarchically positioned just below the mode of layout. The mode of head movement, on the other hand, is not linked, and is hierarchically positioned just below the gaze–print aggregate.

For modal density we next asked: Which modes are not as necessary, but are still used in a particular way in order to perform the action as the social actor does? The answer was: posture, spoken discourse, gesture. With this, we can now determine that the modes of posture, gesture and spoken language are located below the mode of head movement on a hierarchical scale. But what are the relations of these three modes to one another? Sandra speaks and points simultaneously. However, we can imagine that Sandra could have only pointed or that she could have only spoken the words she spoke. One mode could have been used without the other in the higher-level action of assembling the DSL. Thus, these two modes do not build an aggregate in this action. While they are used simultaneously, each one could have been used by itself, and neither mode is more important than the other. When thinking about Sandra's posture, we can determine that her posture could have been very different without having had a large impact upon the action of assembling the DSL. Her posture, it can be argued, is less important than the gesture and the spoken words. Both modes, the modes of gesture and spoken language, even though possibly peripherally, move Sandra through the process of the action, while the way she is sitting has little impact upon the action itself. Thus, we can now say that the modes of gesture and spoken language are equally positioned just below the mode of head movement, and that the mode of posture is positioned below gesture and spoken language on this hierarchical scale.

Then, lastly we asked for modal density: Which modes are irrelevant to the higher-level action in focus? The answer was: music. In this sense, we can now place the mode of music on the lowest position of the hierarchical scale of communicative modes.

Interacting with the researcher

In order to arrive at modal density we first asked: Which modes are absolutely necessary for the social actor to perform this action? The answer was: layout and posture, and we can see that Sandra utilizes the modes of layout and posture as the hierarchically superior mode aggregate in the interaction with the researcher.

The next question for modal density was: Which modes are not as necessary, but are still used in a particular way in order to perform the action as the social actor does? The answer was: spoken language and gesture, and music. With this, we can now place the modes of spoken language and gesture as another aggregate in the second position on our hierarchical scale, right under the layout–posture aggregate. To this action, which is co-constructed with the researcher, the mode of music takes on importance, since both social actors involved in the co-construction of this action are sharing the mode of music. Therefore, we can place the mode of music underneath the spoken language–gesture aggregate.

The final question for modal density was: Which modes are irrelevant to this higher-level action? The answer was: object handling, print, gaze, head movement. Therefore, the modes of object handling, print, gaze and head movement are all of an equal value for this higher-level action and they all reside on the lowest position on the scale.

Thus, the concept of modal configuration allows us to determine the relational hierarchical and/or equivalent levels of communicative modes to one another within a higher-level action. Modal configuration, thus, is always directly linked to the higher-level action that a social actor performs at a specific moment in time. It is a heuristic concept, building on modal density, to allow a researcher to tease out mode aggregates and hierarchical structures among the modes present. Modal configuration, modal density and the higher-level action(s) performed by a social actor can therefore never be dislodged, as they again build a unity.

Discussion

In this framework, communicative modes are always directly linked to the actions that social actors perform at a particular time and in a particular location. Communicative modes are never viewed as tangible and existing in and by themselves, focusing the analyst upon specific actions. This emphasis upon specific actions appears to make generalizations impossible. Certainly, no action is performed in the very same way by the same or a different social actor; and the question of the bigger picture remains: What does this mean for research in interaction? On the one hand, the discussed concepts illustrate some of the complexities of interaction that have so far not been investigated. To date, we can generalize by saying that, often, social actors are simultaneously engaged in several higher-level actions. We can further say that modal configurations between higher-level actions and even within higher-level actions fluctuate from one moment to the next. However, the most important generalization according to my findings is that there are no predetermined modal hierarchies and no one mode takes on precedence over all other modes at all times.

However, far from being perfect, this brief chapter does not allow for a full investigation into the concepts, and I am afraid that the concepts, as illustrated here, may even appear flat. Because of space available, I found myself forced to explain the concepts by only investigating one social actor, and not showing the co-constructed aspect of the actions performed by Sandra, leaving out the actions of the researcher. In a perfect analysis, all social actors' higher-level actions should be analysed side-by-side to illustrate the co-construction and the intertwined character of actions as they are being performed together or separately.

Conclusion

In this chapter, I discussed the concepts of modal density and modal configuration. I illustrated that the notions of modal density and modal configuration are always and only linked to the actions that a social actor performs in a particular place at a particular time by using communicative modes (or a variety of mediational means).

In the above data analysis, I illustrated that one and the same social actor may be involved in simultaneous higher-level actions, drawing on the same communicative modes. However, because modes and their meaning are directly related to the actions being taken, the underlying structures among the modes differ for each higher-level action. While the first higher-level action is constructed through a hierarchical scale of communicative modes with seven tiers (Figure 6.3a), the second higher-level action is constructed via a hierarchical scale with only four tiers (Figure 6.3b). On one hand we find a gaze–print aggregate, and we find that the modes of gesture and spoken language reside on the same tier (tier 6) without, however, building an aggregate, in the first higher-level action (Figure 6.3a). For the simultaneously co-constructed higher-level action of Sandra interacting with the researcher on the other hand, we find that the modes posture and layout and also the modes spoken language and gesture each build an aggregate and that these aggregates are located on the first and second tier respectively (Figure 6.3b).

Thus, it is important to note that not only modal density differs when we investigate a social actor's performance of higher-level actions, but that modes are also structured differently to one another, resulting in a different modal configuration because of the different meanings that are being constructed.

Further development

Multimodal interaction analysis is, as all other directions of multimodal discourse analysis, still in its infancy. Taking these concepts and investigating them further by looking at various interactions will undoubtedly result in new developments for the field of multimodality. But one possibly particularly fruitful development appears to be the linkage of the concepts discussed here to the concept of semiotic resources and semiotic meaning potential.

Summary

This chapter discusses the two concepts called "modal density" and "modal configuration". Both concepts are always linked to the actions social actors take, locating them in time and space. We arrive at modal density by investigating the simultaneous actions that social actors take in the world; and we arrive at modal configuration by closely looking at modal density. The chapter illustrates that both modal density and modal configuration differs for each higher-level action taken.

7

Transformation, transduction and the transmodal moment

Denise Newfield

This chapter discusses and operationalises concepts pertaining to the representation and communication of meaning through processes of modal transfer – 'transformation' (Kress, 2000a), 'transduction' (Kress, 2000a, 2010a), 'chains of semiosis' (Kress, 2000c; Stein, 2003, 2008) and 'the transmodal moment' (Newfield, 2009; Newfield and Maungedzo, 2006). It develops an analytical approach to tracking semiotic shift in chains of semiosis. Using these concepts enables a description of what happens semiotically in the 'translation' of meaning, theme and topic across modes, a process that involves multiple semiotic changes in both form and content.

Processes of cross-modal mobility, of trans-semiotic mutation and generativity are of interest to studies of multimodality across a range of different domains and disciplines such as the media, the arts, the field of representation and communication, semiotics, anthropology, architecture, psychology and education. The idea has been categorised in different ways according to the focus of interest. Architect Lindsay Bremner argues that her study into the ever-changing, evasive city of Johannesburg is 'nomadic', undertaken and represented through movement and the connections between writing, photography, pedagogy, architecture and city-making (2010). Clingman considers the ongoing metamorphoses and mutations in the work of artist William Kentridge (both across different art forms and within individual texts at the micro-level) as the central creative principle in his work which he calls 'the art of transformation' (2011). 'Transformations' in its plural form is the term used by Pahl to describe children's meaning-making in nursery education (1999). Finnegan, writing as an anthropologist, describes the varied, complex and constantly shifting, performed textualities of communities as 'serial transformations' (2002: 179–200). In media education, Semali calls the cross-modal process 'transmediation' (2002), a term used also by Sanders in a recent book on integrating literacy, the arts and multimodality in English curricula (2010: 110). Iedema advances the term 'resemiotization', to be used as a tool in multimodal discourse analysis for tracing processes of semiotic translation in relation to larger socio-historical processes and issues of institutional power (2003). 'Transmedia' is widely used to name the phenomenon of the circulation and convergence of content across a range of media platforms (Jenkins, 2006a), while the term 'transmedia traversals' is used by Lemke to convey a

sense of a 'dynamic semiotic cycle in which users interpret what is being displayed to them across many media'(2007). Writing of synaesthetic semiotic activity as 'entirely usual' rather than pathological, Kress uses the term 'transduction' (2000a: 159). However, the term 'trans-modal' is currently used by a number of scholars. For example, Cytowic, writing in the field of psychology, uses the term 'transmodal' in a study of synaesthesia: 'Relevant to synesthesia, what are called transmodal modules (meaning not pertaining to any single sense) … con-struct multisensory representations of the world' (2002: 17). Pennycook uses 'transmodal' to describe the varied articulations of hiphop culture in lyrics, music, bodily action and cloth-ing (2007) and the urban semiotics of graffiti (2010). Goodwin and Alim (2010) show how young girls construct identities of self and other through 'transmodal stylisations'. The term 'trans-modal translation' has been applied to subtitles in the field of cinema studies (Transla-tion Directory, article 2184). In their evaluation of digital literacy, Wyatt-Smith and Kimber (2009) use the concept of a 'transmodal operation' to describe how digital meaning-makers move between and across modes and technological platforms to create texts and 'transmodal facility' to describe the ability to do so. This chapter uses the term 'transmodal' to categorise semiotic movement across modes as an external, material practice. This seems an apt term, since if multimodality refers to the existence and interaction of multiple modes as resources for meaning-making, 'transmodality' refers to a particular process, the shifting of modes – or 'multi-modes' (Kress, 2000b: 183), a term signalling that modes tend to occur simultane-ously, even where one mode is dominant and has greater 'intensity' (Norris, 2004a) than the others.

Key concepts

'Transformation', 'transduction', 'chains of semiosis' and 'the transmodal moment' are con-cepts used in the field of multimodality to describe and explain semiosis, the process of making meaning through the construction of signs. A feature of the human condition, semiosis is ceaseless and ongoing (Kress and Van Leeuwen, 2001), whether the agent of semiosis is conscious of it or not. Developing a new theory of semiosis adequate to the facts of the changed communicational landscape and the facts of individual, always situated, meaning-making has been a central project of multimodal social semiotics (Hodge and Kress, 1988; Kress, 1997a, 2000a, 2000b, 2000c, 2010a; Kress *et al.*, 2001; Kress and Van Leeuwen, 1996, 2001; Jewitt and Kress, 2003b).

Transformation

Transformation is a foundational principle of Kress's work in social semiotics. It highlights the creative, agentive action of *sign-making*, which is based on the selection of apt, available resources to represent and communicate the sign-maker's interest. The term 'transformation' foregrounds the challenge by social semiotic theory to dominant theories of language as use of a 'stable (and largely autonomous) system of elements, categories and rules of combination'. Rather, the makers of messages 'stretch, change, adapt, and modify all of the elements used, all the time, and thereby change the whole set of representational resources with its internal relations' (Kress, 2000a: 155). Social semiotics conceptualises semiosis as a process of selecting semiotic resources, which have been shaped in specific contexts through cultural practice, and then transforming them to approximate the maker's interest and accord with the demands of

a particular situation. Kress's epigrammatic statement of what is required in an adequate theory of semiosis proposes that meaning-making be theorised as a transformation of available semiotic resources: 'An adequate theory of semiosis will be founded on a recognition of the "interested action" of socially located, culturally and historically formed individuals, as the remakers, the transformers and the re-shapers of the representational resources available to them' (Kress, 2000a: 155).

Kress's theory foregrounds the sign-makers themselves and the agentive realisation of their 'interest' through transformative semiotic action rather than through *use* of a pre-existing system. Semiosis is considered to be 'action', a term evoking a sense of activity, performance and the use of force or energy. This action is 'interested' since it is directed towards realisation of specific representational and communicative needs, desires and intentions of the sign-maker. Always complex, interested action is 'shaped individually and socially, over time and in the immediacy of the moment' (MODE, 2012), that is, it is situated, and shaped, in personal, social, cultural, historical and semiotic contexts.

Available representational resources are the modes and materials available for sign-making, as well as the genres and discourses that have been shaped by culture as semiotic material. The term 'mode' refers to forms, types or 'channels' (Kress, 2010a; MODE, 2012) of representation and communication that have been culturally and socially shaped as resources for meaning-making. Although the concept of mode continues to be under debate, examples of modes may be said to be 'writing and image on the page, … moving image and sound on the screen, and speech, gesture, gaze and posture in embodied action' (MODE, 2012).

In this way, sign-makers design new forms and meanings by transforming those available to them in their environment. They select what seems 'apt' using the modes and materials that are 'to hand' (Kress, 1997a) and reshape and remake them. In so doing, they 'design' their meanings, choosing, or being compelled to use – as permitted or dictated by context – particular modes and materials. But even in a relatively restricted context, 'design' signals choice, 'a deliberateness', a motivation and intention about the way in which meaning is represented (Kress and Van Leeuwen, 2001: 45).

It must be mentioned that in addition to the general semiotic principle of transformation, Kress uses the term 'transformation' in a more restricted and specific sense as well. In this restricted sense, 'transformation' refers to the process of re-ordering the elements or entities in a text or artefact in the same mode, whether from one genre to another, or from one language to another (Kress, 2010a: 124–30).

Transduction

A key feature of Kress's theorisation revolves around semiotic resources which expand far beyond the linguistic to include multiple modes as resources for representation and communication. There are two kinds of interaction between modes: the orchestration of modes within multimodal ensembles where different modes combine in different ways to form a message (Kress, 2000b, 2010a), and the way in which different resources are used at different times, sometimes in a process of semiosis that is either ongoing or interrupted but that stays with a topic, issue or experience, representing it through a range of different modes at different times (Kress, 2000b, 2010a). For Kress, this pertains not only to the level of text but also to that of cognitive processing. As he states in his chapter, 'Design and Transformation' (Kress, 2000a), semiosis is a synaesthetic process, a process in which meaning is commonly

made through processes of movement between and across modes. In formulating his 'new theory of semiosis', he states that:

> A new theory of semiosis will need to acknowledge and account for the processes of synaesthesia, the transduction of meaning from one semiotic mode to another semiotic mode, an activity constantly performed by the brain. In other words, a theory of semiosis which incorporates the facts of multimodality also needs to be a theory in which synaesthesia is seen as an entirely usual and productive process, essential equally for the understanding of semiosis in a multimodal landscape as for the possibilities of real innovation, rather than, as too often now, as a pathology to be remedied.
>
> (Kress, 2000a: 159)

While everywhere apparent in the communicational landscape, synaesthetic semiotic activity has been largely ignored in institutionalised education, aside from in particular subjects such as science and biology, where drawings and models are routinely used. Official assessment practices in other subjects tend to remain monomodal, privileging the written word over other forms of knowledge representation and literacy. While the synaesthetic element of semiosis is pertinent both to the contemporary communications landscape with its proliferation of textual forms and to other domains, as previously mentioned, this chapter focuses on the educational domain. Specifically, it focuses on students' meaning-making processes, on the ways in which students draw meaning across different modes (or multi-modes), on how meaning is modified, enriched, complexified or diminished along the way, and what this means for learning.

An area of slippage in Kress's use of the term 'transduction' concerns that of internal semiosis (meanings made in the brain) versus external semiosis (meanings made in signs or texts). Whereas the extract above refers to synaesthetic activity 'performed in the brain', Kress's more recent formulations define transduction as a process of translation in which meaning-material is moved from one mode to another (Kress, 2010a; MODE, 2012). The term 'transmodal' avoids this ambivalence, pointing clearly to meanings which are manifested externally in material form, as well as being derived from the concept of 'mode' at the heart of multimodality.

The transmodal moment

'The transmodal moment' (Newfield, 2009) is a concept that can be used in the examination of processes of transmodal translation in chains of semiosis (Kress, 2000c; Stein, 2003, 2008; MODE, 2012), or, of what has been called 'transmodal semiosis' (Newfield, 2009). A transmodal semiotic chain is a chain of sign- or text-making in which meaning is materialised in a range of differently modalised texts that are linked in theme or topic either closely or more distantly. Since meaning-making is ongoing and continuous rather than limited to one moment in time (Kress and Van Leeuwen, 2001), a transmodal semiotic chain is made up of links in different modes, which 'punctuate' the process of semiosis. These 'punctuations' (Kress, 2000c) are points of relative stasis and stability in ongoing, transmodal processes of meaning-making. The concept of the transmodal moment focuses attention on the relational aspect of the transmodal chain, on the way in which a modal shift impacts on meaning and on the way in which the links are connected or discontinuous with one another.

The transmodal moment is the moment of modal shift between texts realised in different modes in a chain of semiosis. It refers to the external manifestation of semiotic consciousness,

the realisation of an idea in a new or different mode from that in which an idea was originally encountered, what might be called the 'translation' of that idea into a new or different mode. Examining what happens in the transmodal moment enables insight into the way modal shifts bring about shifts in materiality, medium, genre as well as meaning, orientation, disposition, subjectivity, identity and affect. It can also indicate how modes relate to, and call up, the semiotic practices of different communities at different historical periods. The 'moment' of re-articulation and redesigning of meaning in differently modalised signs stands for processes which may be of shorter or longer duration; in other words, the term 'moment' is a metaphor. 'The transmodal moment' is not simple but involves a maze of semiotic decisions and interventions.

The method: operationalising the concepts

In order to demonstrate how this works, two instances of transmodal semiosis, selected as representative from many others in a larger project, are analysed. The instances derive from literacy, language and literature classrooms in South Africa where teachers have introduced a measure of semiotic freedom in relation to learning and its representation. Transmodal semiosis will be tracked by a comparative examination of texts in a transmodal sequence (Text A > Text B > Text C, etc.). The texts will be described in as much detail as the chapter allows in order to demonstrate how meaning is changed, reshaped, developed, expanded, limited and modified across the sequence of transmodalisations. The concept of 'the transmodal moment' brings into focus the way different modes encourage or enable different interests to be realised, providing different perspectives on a topic.

The Janus-faced nature of the transmodal moment, a moment 'between' texts in different modes, a moment of crossing-over, requires a *relational* method in which an eye is kept on both the *prior* texts and the *subsequent* transmodalisations. The analyst should examine the meaning-makers' semiotic starting point – the prior or source text(s) – and compare it to other texts in the transmodal semiotic journey, acknowledging that this seeming linear movement may be complicated by multifarious inputs (conscious and unconscious, deliberately sought and coincidental) along the way.

Drawing on the social semiotic approach of Kress, Jewitt and their colleagues (Jewitt and Kress, 2003b; Kress, 1997a, 2000a, 2010a; Kress and Van Leeuwen, 1996, 2001; Kress *et al.*, 2001), the comparative analysis should be focused on mode, medium, materiality, site of display and genre, taking into account the historical nature and provenance of signs and modes. Qualities of modal realisation – such as colour, shape, texture, detail, grain of voice, bodily movement, and so on – need to be taken into account, where they are relevant to the modal nature of the text under examination. This in itself is no simple task, since the range of texts and modal orchestrations may be vast and complex, deviating from the forms examined in the epic works on the grammar of visual design (Kress and Van Leeuwen, 1996), and the language of visual arts (O'Toole, 1994). The analyst may be forced to grapple with unexpected and ever-developing combinations of modes, both in the digital and non-digital semiotic worlds. The situated nature of semiosis will necessitate an ever-vigilant approach to the multiple layers of context – social, cultural, historical, institutional and semiotic.

Ethnographic approaches can be used to provide additional dimensions to analysis of the transmodal moment, since familiarity with context through observation, interviews and discussion, over some time, arguably allows for a 'dense, layered account, drawing on the understandings of participants, of meaning-making processes and practices' (MODE, 2012; Pahl and Rowsell, 2006). This bringing together of social semiotic analysis with ethnographic approaches is useful in tracking processes of semiosis across time. On the other hand, thinking about the transmodal

moment – as a microcosm of the transmodal semiotic process – can reveal insights into the ongoing, heuristic and exploratory process of semiosis.

The instances

Since transmodal semiosis, like all semiosis, is situated, it is crucial to contextualise the instances of this chapter. As previously mentioned, they are situated in South African classrooms. They are complex examples of transmodal meaning-making by adolescent and adult students who are exploring new intellectual ideas. Historically speaking, the examples span a period in South Africa's transition – still under way – which brought about a radical change in South Africa's social, cultural and political make-up. They are 'low tech' examples, in which students used the resources that were available. The first example analyses a single pair of texts; the second, a transmodal chain consisting of multiple textual links. In both, a text in print gives rise to complex multimodal ensembles.

Kim's artefact: transmodalising theory

The first instance is that of a preservice teacher's initial encounter with recently published material on literacy pedagogy. Kim was a preservice English teacher studying for her teaching diploma at the University of the Witwatersrand, Johannesburg, in 1997. The material she was asked to consider was an article on literacy and literacy education in the late twentieth century, 'A pedagogy of Multiliteracies: designing social futures' (New London Group, 1996), at the time a ground-breaking article, which was introduced to the class. Founded on premises of semiotic multiplicity in the contemporary communications landscape and on cultural and linguistic diversity in classrooms, the article advocates 'a pedagogy of Multiliteracies' rather than one dedicated to the singular, autonomous, monocultural conceptualisations of literacy prevalent in mainstream language classrooms. In keeping with the article's premises, the students were asked to read and summarise the article at home, or, to provide an alternative, transmodal response to it:

> What should English teachers teach in South Africa today, and how should they teach it? Here is a recently published article on literacy education. It begins by explaining the concept of multiliteracies and then goes on to pedagogical matters. Read it carefully at home. Then, produce your interpretation of it in whatever form you like – as a written summary, or in any other form you like, as a drawing, model or anything else. Bring it to class in three weeks' time.

Kim was the only class member who produced an artefact in a mode other than the verbal. Most members of the class produced summaries of the article. When asked, they said that they were used to writing summaries of articles rather than responding to them in other modes, so a transmodal response would add another level of difficulty to their understanding of an article that they found difficult in itself.

A relational examination of the two texts in the transmodal sequence enables the analyst to understand the role of the transmodal moment in the reshaping, deepening and modification of meaning that took place.

Text A is an academic article written by group of literacy and education scholars and published in an educational journal. It comprises 28 pages of print, which includes one diagram and four boxes to summarise key theoretical points. The article's title appears in upper case; its sub-sections

and sub-headings are printed in lower-case bold or italics. In terms of content, the article begins with an introduction concerning the role of education for the future lives of students, the role of pedagogy in building learning conditions that lead to 'full and equitable social participation' and role of literacy pedagogy in fulfilling this mission (New London Group, 2000: 9). The article challenges traditional literacy pedagogy for being restricted to 'formalised, monolingual, monocultural and rule-governed forms of language' (ibid.: 9). Instead, it proposes a pedagogy of Multiliteracies that is founded upon the nature of the communications and cultural landscapes of the present: multiplicity of text and media forms, and diversity of cultures. This is followed by sections on working lives, public lives and personal lives; on a greatly broadened outline of what students need to learn to be literate – which includes a range of different systems – the linguistic, visual, audio, gestural, spatial and multimodal – and by a four-part outline of a pedagogy to support the conception of Multiliteracies that has been sketched in the first half of the article.

Text B is the artefact produced by Kim to provide her interpretation of the article. The artefact consists of three pieces of A4-size cardboard, on which matchboxes and paper cutouts have been glued (Figure 7.1). The cardboard 'pages' follow sequentially, like the pages of a book. The first page introduces the concept 'Multiliteracies' through a large blue 'M' in the central panel, on which words pertaining to the concept – such as, 'multifarious', 'medley', 'multiculturalism' and

Figure 7.1 Kim's artefact, first 'page' (A4-size cardboard, ink, matchboxes, paper cut-outs).

'mode' – are written. Below the 'M' is a simple collage of tiny figures jumping out of a box, which is captioned 'Out of the box' and 'The way the world is moving'.

Eight matchboxes form a column of multicoloured texts to the right and left of the 'page'. Each matchbox cover has been redesigned as a miniature collage of images and words cut out from magazines and newspapers. These are a visual response to themes introduced in the article. On the next 'page', a handwritten narrative invites reader-viewers to go on a Multiliteracies journey. While the discourse of the images and brief captions or epigrams that form the collages is a reworking of popular media, the discourse of the verbal text is informal and colloquial, unlike the original article. It is both explanatory and personal, using the second-person direct appeal to reader-viewers who are addressed as 'you', or using 'our' in an inclusive chatty way; as well as asking a series of simple questions to involve the reader-viewer.

The caption 'out of the box' is revealed to be not only a contemporary idiom connoting unorthodox, original thinking; it also sums up quite literally an 'out of the box' exercise in which the reader-viewer must engage – taking the small folded notes out of the matchboxes. These display the results of a research study Kim undertook in relation to a premise in the article, namely, that contemporary urban environments are multilingual. In order to test the validity of this assumption, Kim spent three weeks listening to the languages spoken around her on the University campus

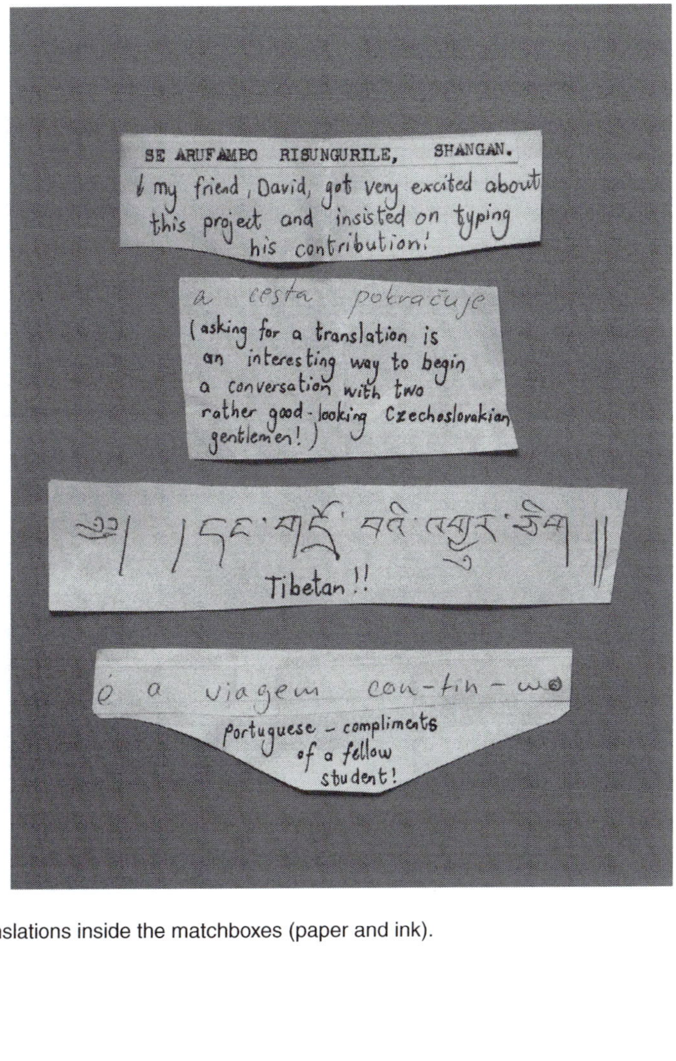

Figure 7.2 Translations inside the matchboxes (paper and ink).

and in the precinct of the African Market in Rosebank, Johannesburg. She introduced herself to speakers of languages other than English and asked them to translate the phrase, 'the journey continues', into their home languages. More than thirty different translations are found inside the matchboxes, in languages as diverse as isiZulu, isiXhosa, Sepedi, Mandarin, Tibetan, Gujerati, Italian, Greek, Portuguese, French, Ethiopian, Hebrew, German and so on (Figure 7.2).

The artefact orchestrates affect across the different modes, indicating Kim's enthusiasm for the Multiliteracies project. This is seen in her use of bright colours – blue, yellow, red, green – on the matchbox covers, as frames for the headings and questions and for the final quotation as well as in her use of exclamation marks and the welcoming discourse: 'The multiliteracies journey has an unlimited capacity! Everyone brings a uniqueness to this adventure, so everyone is welcome.' The final quotation from Picasso makes explicit Kim's interest in the aesthetic: 'Every child is an artist. The problem is how to remain an artist when he grows up.' Kim herself has clearly made aesthetic choices in designing her artefact, echoing the colours of the new South African flag and invoking a sense of the 'rainbow nation' myth prevalent at the time.

While the genre of the first text is clear (an academic article), the genre of the second is not: it is a unique, relatively unconstrained, multimodal ensemble composed of different generic and material elements – a particular orchestration of collage, discussion, questions, quotations and translations which forms Kim's transmodal response to a pedagogic task based upon the source article.

Thebuwa: transmodalising poetry and identity

The second example is of a more complex transmodal chain. The students in the second example – secondary school students in Soweto – are simultaneously exploring the genre of poetry and their own identities as young people living in post-apartheid South Africa. The setting of this example is a poorly resourced school attended by black students in post-apartheid South Africa, at a time when a unitary, equity-based educational policy has officially supplanted the previous, hierarchical, discriminatory system of Bantu education but when its legacies remain everywhere apparent. English is not the mother tongue of either students or teachers; instead it is their third, fourth or fifth language. The transmodal semiotic journey, undertaken by the class as a whole, concerns more than a sequence of two texts, as in the case of Kim's artefact; it is an ongoing sequence of texts with multiple transmodal links.

Robert's Grade 10 English class was made up of 55 mostly disaffected students, who frequently played truant, did not engage with the texts prescribed for study in class, and who resisted speaking or writing English, either out of embarrassment or out of political resistance to the use of the former oppressor's language. Robert was particularly concerned about the teaching of literature, an area of the curriculum where he is making no headway. Students did not engage with the novel they were studying (*Maru* by African writer, Bessie Head); they did not read the text, and many did not even possess copies of the text. They said he should write characters' names on the board and dictate to them what the book was about. They had little faith in schooling, stating that 'it is the criminals who cruise the streets in posh cars, while the educated are unemployed'. Robert was in a state of 'desperation'. He enrolled for a master's course in English education, and having encountered the notion of multimodality, he decided, apprehensively, to experiment with a transmodal approach to the teaching of poetry.

To his surprise, the students began to respond – at first, out of curiosity and some scepticism, and then, with enthusiasm – reading, listening to and composing poems. After two months, they produced a collective multimodal artefact, a 3.0 m × 2.8 m cloth made up of individual panels of maps, emblems, doll-like figures, photographs and praise poems in indigenous languages which they had written down and poems in English which they had composed (Plate 7.1). They named their cloth 'Thebuwa' – a coinage from three of the home languages of the students which means 'To speak' – in order to signal their journey of transformation from silence to speech.

The artefact is a complex 'punctuation' or 'moment of fixing' in the students' transmodal semiotic chain, produced as a collective assemblage of a number of previous texts. A number of 'transmodal moments' were experienced in the journey towards its production. The outcome was not preplanned, the result of an organised, logical and linear programme; rather, it developed in a dynamic, fluid and freewheeling way, in response to student reaction, performance and desire as they moved across modes.

The following schematic outline indicates the texts encountered and produced in the transmodal chain, their design elements such as the primary mode of realisation, the language, materiality, medium, site of display and genre, and what teacher or students did with the texts. Between each link in the chain is a transmodal moment of modal redesigning.

- Text A: Two poems from *Poetry Quest*, an anthology produced for second language learners in 1987, 'The Beggar' by R. Tong and 'The flattered flying fish' by E.V. Rieu

These were read out by the teacher and then discussed by students in small groups in photocopied form.

Identity: students of English as an additional language.

[*Transmodal moment*]

- Text B: Drawings and stories in response to the poems

Students wrote handwritten narratives on lined A4 sheets of paper torn out of exercise books, with blue ballpoint pens or lead pencils.

Alternatively, they made interpretative drawings on sheets of paper with pencil and, in a few cases, with pencil crayons.

[*Transmodal moment*]

- Text C: Praise poems in vernacular (e.g. isiZulu, Sepedi, Xitsonga)

These were performed in class by individuals to one another. Some students had written down their praise poems first, in order to remember them, while many had not and recited them.

Clan identity; identity as a speaker of a particular language.

[*Transmodal moment*]

- Text D: Students wrote translations of the praise poems into English on sheets of paper.

[*Transmodal moment*]

- Text E: Maps on cloth

Students drew, coloured in or painted maps of 'the new South Africa', with its revised geopolitical cartography (nine regions, as opposed to the four provinces of apartheid South Africa), on individual panels of cloth. These were sourced from their homes, and in some cases, from recycled material such as old maize bags. National and regional borders were embroidered in silk, cotton or wool, as were clan or family emblems.

National identity.

[*Transmodal moment*]

- Text F: Praise poems on cloth panels

Students inked the praise poems with their English translations onto the cloths, a demanding manual task.

[*Transmodal moment*]

- Text G: Poems in English, composed by the students

The poems were performed by individual class members to the class as a whole, and on occasions, performed impromptu, on the spot, in the manner of some hiphop artists. Students made use of the resources of voice, facial expression, gesture and bodily movement, and on a few occasions, music, to emphasise aspects of the poems. The class hooted or applauded in the manner of an audience.

Identity: young, modern Sowetan.

[*Transmodal moment*]

- Text H: The composite cloth, Thebuwa

The individual cloth panels were sewn together by a member of the class and named Thebuwa. The English poems were placed in recycled envelopes around the large central panel onto which four ethnic figures are attached. Photographs of the student makers, taken for the purpose by Thando, were affixed to the individual panels. Gold-coloured safety pins were used to decorate the cloth as a whole (in the manner of Xhosa cloths) and to link the English poems to their authors.

Group identity: members of a particular school, who were greeting the world through their 'ambassador, Thebuwa'.

[*Transmodal moment*]

- Text I: *Thebuwa* anthology

The student poems were collected, supplemented by additional poems composed by the class, and compiled by an editorial team into an anthology, *Thebuwa, Poems from Ndofaya* (Newfield and Maungedzo, 2005). This was for most class members the culminating text in the chain of transmodal semiosis, although a few students continued to write poetry over the next few years, some even to the present day.

Identity: members of a local and global community of poets.

Discussion

The discussion focuses on the nature and operations of the transmodal moment in the textual chains presented above. These are summarised under seven sub-headings.

Modal redesigning and transformation of meaning

Like all moments of articulation, the transmodal moment is one of transformation; however, the shift in mode makes it, semiotically speaking, a moment of radical change, in which the shift in mode impacts on other elements as well – materiality, site of display, medium and genre. Change of mode thus implies and determines a host of other formal changes. This occurs because different modes have different affordances and constraints, different epistemological logics and commitments; and also because modes have been shaped in particular ways in particular cultural contexts. Using certain modes catapulted the students' meanings into a new domain, style, discourse and aesthetic. In the shift from a page to a cloth, students were drawing on and displaying African semiotic forms and practices, specifically, minceka cloths and the practice of embroidery. In the shift from canonical English poems in print to praise poems in the vernacular, and then to the performance of their own poems in English, the schoolchildren were expanding their concept of poetry to include traditional oral poetry and contemporary spoken word. The modal shift enabled integration of these forms into the curriculum.

Liminality and border-crossing

The transmodal moment is a moment of cross–over and liminality. However, it is more than a simple crossing of semiotic borders; it is a semiotic relocation where the past travels with you and the future brings both losses and opportunities. The transmodal moment may thus be seen as an in-between, intermezzo and interstice, as a 'liminal' space (Turner, 1982). It is a moment of *un-becoming* and *re-becoming*. Sign-making in the transmodal moment brushes up against, refers back to and transforms prior signs, texts and practices, and in this way becomes an active link in the semiotic chain. The concept of the transmodal moment highlights processes of migratory meaning-making, erasures and alterations, assisting in the exploration of dialogues, oscillations and interactions across and between different ideas, meanings and experiences. Kim migrates from print to multimodality, erasing those parts of the article she is not interested in to focus on what most impresses her and what her transmodal choices allow or facilitate.

Temporality and spatiality of the transmodal moment

The transmodal moment is more than temporal. It consists of and combines time and space. It is both a moment in a temporal process of reshaping meaning and a zone in which multiple intersections, appropriations and improvisations, or new and different entanglements, occur. It is a zone of varied newly available resources – each with its own histories and contexts of use – affording multiple semiotic possibilities. Depending on the context, it can have a strong sense of direction, or, on the other hand, be 'rhizomatic' in character (Deleuze and Guattari, 1988), that is, giving rise to new semiotic shoots sprouting unpredictably in unexpected places, which then give rise to further shoots, which are both divergent and linked. The transmodal Thebuwa journey was characterised by unexpected excrescences and growth. Its outcomes were not preplanned by either the teacher or the students. Put in the language of an earlier time and a different discipline, the transmodal moments in the instances of this chapter are 'creative', 'combinatorial' and 'recombinatorial' (Vygotsky, 2004[1930]).

Concreteness and embodiment of the transmodal moment

The transmodal moment, though an abstract concept, refers to processes that are real and concrete. It encapsulates the *material* process of meaning-making, and is concerned with what meaning-makers *do*. It is a moment in the world of sign-makers, perceived through their eyes and ears, and made and remade through their hands and voices. It points to how they transform academic articles into matchboxes and poems into cloths. It involves bodily as well as cognitive action.

111

Agency and subjectivity

While mode shapes meaning, the *agency* of the sign-maker is apparent in the modal choices made, even as contextual features such as power relations, ideology, culture and history – as well as the material resources available – inflect its use. Sign-makers make decisions about representation, about communication to others, and about textual organisation. Both the examples above show students taking 'the [road] less traveled … And that has made all the difference' (Robert Frost, 'The Road Not Taken').

The transmodal moment is also a moment of transformation of *subjectivity*. Social semiotics holds that every sign is newly made in an always new context of making and that every time a sign is made, the inner resources of the sign-maker are augmented, leading to a change in subjectivity, no matter how infinitesimal. The two examples show significant changes. Kim gained a new perspective on literacy and language which she implemented in her practice; the Soweto class began to see themselves as meaning-makers, poets and artists, as the questionnaires, discussions and self-reflections demonstrated. Their expressive output, once negligible, became prolific, and their negative disposition towards the English language and its poetry was turned around. The transmodal journey led Thando to say, 'I'm madly in love with poetry'; Sunboy to write, 'My deep passion is … with the gift of language to express that which my opposers are preventing'; and Phillipine to discover, having composed in a number of different modes, that writing can be cathartic and pleasurable, that paper can be a friend, a lover and a confidante:

> In its ears I whisper my sorrow, secrets and desires
>
> Because when I need someone to talk to
>
> It's always there and it does hear'
>
> ('Paper and I', Newfield and Maungedzo, 2005: 15)

Transmodal moment and history

The examples above show that the transmodal moment occurs and is embedded in social time, in history. Transmodal semiosis is shaped by the conditions of production, including those determined by power relations, audience and material that is 'to hand'. Broader social and political circumstances have an impact. The students transmodalised the prior or source texts according to their 'interest' within particular social, cultural, historical and semiotic contexts. Kim's encounter with a pluralised conception of literacy is experienced with the wonder, enthusiasm and hope that 'the new South Africa' brought for a young woman on the threshold of her career, perhaps seduced by the myth of 'the rainbow nation'. For the Soweto students, transmodal semiotic practice in the classroom offered opportunities to make use of, and redesign, their home languages and semiotic practices in the representation of self, ethnicity and newly acquired nationality.

Transmodal moment and learning

Although it must be acknowledged that a number of contingent factors contributed to the deep and rich learning that arose from the transmodal journey in the above examples, teachers, students and researchers were all empowered by it. The Soweto teacher, Robert, expressed himself in these words:

I started at the station of Reluctance, passed through Uncertainty, and reached Agency....
[The transmodal journey] helped me as an educator, it gave me the courage to climb the
high walls and winding hills in search of myself and my learners.

Sonnyboy, one of his students, said: 'I think this was the most precious thing I have ever done
in my life ... . It's like I was fortified in knowledge and understanding'. For Sonnyboy and
others in the class, the transmodal moment led to the deepening, enriching, modification,
supplementation and complexification of understanding around poetry and self in 'the new
South Africa'.

Conclusion

This chapter has provided an overview of concepts pertaining to transmodal semiosis –
transformation, transduction, chains of semiosis and the transmodal moment – and has shown
the relationship among them. It has operationalised the concepts and defined the features of the
transmodal moment through an examination of two instances of transmodal designing in South
African classrooms. Based on principles of semiotic mobility and mutation, on the shifting and
expanding of perspectives, transmodal pedagogic activity harmonised with the urgent calls for
transformation being heard everywhere in 'the new South Africa'. Semiotic and political transformation were thus in alignment. There was a fruitfulness, a synergy, in their coupling. Tracking
the transmodal chains of students enables this to be seen.

Acknowledgements

This chapter remembers and pays tribute to the work of Pippa Stein, multimodal analyst par
excellence, whose passing leaves a gap. I am grateful to students and teachers whose transmodal
projects inspire this chapter, especially to Kim Wiggell and Robert Maungedzo.

Part I: Further reading

Jewitt, C. (2008) *Technology, Literacy and Learning: A Multimodal Approach*, London: RoutledgeFalmer.

Kress, G. (2010) *Multimodality. A Social Semiotic Approach to Communication*, London: RoutledgeFalmer.

Kress, G. and Van Leeuwen, T. (1996) *Reading Images: The Grammar of Visual Design*, London: Routledge.

Kress, G. and Van Leeuwen, T. (2001) *Multimodal Discourse: The Modes and Media of Contemporary Communication*, London: Arnold.

Norris, S. (2004) *Analyzing Multimodal Interaction*, London: Routledge.

Norris, S. (2012) *Multimodality in Practice: Investigating Theory-in-Practice Through Methodoglogy*, London: Routledge.

O'Halloran, K. (ed.) (2004) *Multimodal Discourse Analysis*, London: Continuum.

O'Halloran, K. and Smith, B. A. (eds) (2011) *Multimodal Studies: Exploring Issues and Domains*, London: Routledge.

Scollon, R. (2001) *Mediated Discourse: The Nexus of Practice*, London: Routledge.

Stein, P. (2008) *Multimodal Pedagogies in Diverse Classroom: Representation, Rights and Resources*, London: Routledge.

Van Leeuwen, T. (1999) *Speech, Music, Sound*, London: Macmillan.

Van Leeuwen, T. (2005) *Introducing Social Semiotics*, London: Routledge.

Part II

Key themes for multimodality

Introduction to Part II

Several recurring themes weave across the chapters in this handbook. Technology and multimodality is one such theme which addresses how digital technology enables new ways of looking at interaction, and how the use of technology can transform how researchers collect, transcribe and record events and practices. The situated character of meaning-making, choice of mode and use of modal resources in communication and representation, and the ways these change over time and with respect to culture is another theme taken up across the handbook. The intimate connection between the availability of modes, context and identity within social interaction is another key theme. For instance, the modal resources available to a teacher in a classroom are markedly different from those available to their students, differences that constrain and enable their practices, relationship to knowledge and identities.

The chapters in this part draw attention to six significant themes that mediate multimodality. These are history and timescales, the facilities of technology and their usage, social and culture factors, identity, and literacy, and power and social justice.

Multimodal research examines how people make meaning through their selection of the most apt semiotic resources from the range of modes that are available to them in a particular place in a specific moment in time. This serves to emphasize the importance of time and history as a factor in the process of meaning-making: the ways in which modes are socially shaped, the social meaning of semiotic resources, the availability of semiotic resources, and who has access to semiotic resources changes over time. For example, during the Renaissance period, the high cost of particular pigment ingredients made some colours more expensive than others. The value of specific colours led to their rarity, and association with the depiction of persons or object of status or significance. Ultramarine blue is a brilliant deep-blue pigment obtained from grinding the rock lapis lazuli and it was one of the most costly pigments during the High Renaissance. It was reserved to depict the major figures in paintings and during that period it became synonymous with depictions of the Virgin Mary and Christ. This colour is now synthetically produced and widely available; however, it has retained its religious value and significance for some people in some contexts.

The ways in which people use modes and how modes feature in the communicational and representational landscape is strongly linked to the use of technologies. Changes in the use and social history of technologies, the manual tools, mechanical tools, and laser and digital technologies have each affected how people engage in meaning-making, although the effects of each have been transformative in varying and uneven ways. As Mäkitalo *et al.* (2009) demonstrate in their study of the art and skill of Swedish engraving practices, technological change is not a simple matter of progression from manual to digital tools. Changes in technologies are, as their study shows, interconnected with changes in the identity of a sign-maker (i.e. the engraver as craft person, artist, machinist or graphic designer), the status and circulation of products (e.g. high-status individual art object, or mass reproduction), the practices and the character of the process of making, the labour involved and its division, and the community of practice that the sign-maker belongs to.

The use of technology and its historical development is a factor for multimodal research discussed by O'Halloran in Chapter 8. She examines the development of mathematical notation and maps the impact of technology on the semiotic landscape of mathematics. The chapter takes a historical view of the semiotic landscape in mathematics, with a particular focus on mathematical symbolic notation. This reveals how mathematical symbolism, language and visual images evolved to work together to fulfil specific functions in contexts shaped by social and scientific semiotic technologies. The development of mathematical notation from prehistory to modern times, and the impact of the printing press and computer technology on the semiotic landscape of mathematics are explored in this chapter. The chapter foregrounds some key innovations with regards to semiotic resources, semiotic choices and accompanying semiotic technologies. O'Halloran argues that 'understanding the semiotic basis of mathematics and the social and scientific dimensions shaping its existence leads to greater understanding of the power of semiosis to (literally) restructure the world, with a view to future possibilities' .

Jones in Chapter 9 examines technology and its effect on multimodal communication. In particular he explores how technology has affected the ways people use their bodies as a communicative resource in online social interaction. The chapter goes beyond assessing the affordances and constraints of different 'sites of display' to investigate how users make meaning, focusing on the impact of sites of display on social identities and social practices. By way of illustration, these principles are applied to an analysis of how gay men use an Internet dating website to create displays of their bodies. The analysis shows how new technologies enable new configurations of 'embeddedness' among sites of display, thereby creating new kinds of social situations and social relationships. Throughout his analysis, Jones draws on and builds upon Goffman's notion of 'display', as well as other insights from microsociololgy, ethnomethodology and mediated discourse analysis.

The analysis that Jones presents shows the complexity of how culture shapes people's use of technology, and how when new technologies are brought into existing practices their use transforms (to varying degrees) those practices. This serves to foreground the significance of the social and cultural as factors in multimodal research. How modes feature in communication is shaped by culture with respect to cultural acceptance regarding how modes are usually used; what can and cannot be said in a culture, what is taboo, will shape how other modes such as gaze and gesture feature in communication. In research on the multimodal production of School English, for example, we observed a young woman discussing Marvel's poem *To His Coy Mistress* (Kress *et al.*, 2004). She performed (and maintained) the cultural norm of femininity (not knowing or talking about sex) by falling silent and gesturing when she referred to words to describe sex and sexual desire and the boy she was working with would interject and say the word (i.e. 'horny' , or 'have sex') on her behalf (thus enabling him to perform his masculinity). Multimodal research can be used to reflect on culture and cultural discourses, including the hidden or silent discourses within a context (such as the English classroom, or a workplace).

Leander and Vasudevan approach the theme of culture and multimodality through the lens of technology in Chapter 10. They take the emergence of cell phone novels as an illustration of the relationship between multimodality, technology and culture. They show how this relatively new practice 'appears to hybridize various modalities, including speech and writing, imaging and writing, and, in the case of the emoticon, gesture and imaging'. Through their analysis they demonstrate how cell phone novels bring to life various forms of mobility, including embodied movements, the movements of 'novel bits' to a website and cell phones and so on.

Identity is a key factor within multimodal research, in terms of how identities are realized through multimodal performitivity and multimodal accounts of oneself. The way in which people represent themselves in physical and virtual encounters is articulated through a wide range of modes. For instance, the ways in which a person uses their voice (e.g. faltering, stuttering or high-pitched), their gestures, their use of gaze (e.g. steady or erratic), their body posture (e.g. jerking, shifting or still) are read in many situations as signs that indicate their comfort or unease, honesty and reliability or lack of both, or their engagement and intelligence. Often these signs are read in a context where little depends on the interpretation but frequently the sense that is made of these signs is of great significance, such as in a job interview or a court trial. Jarworski and Thurlow address the multimodal production of identity in Chapter 26, with an analysis of tourists' use of gaze and gesture.

In Chapter 11, Lemke approaches technology, culture and identity with a focus on time, not in terms of history but shorter timescales of experience. He explores issues of how technologies produce meaning effects across multiple timescales, using the illustrative example of the computer and video games which are typically experienced over times as long as 50 hours over periods of weeks or months. He considers what happens when games, films, books and other media and merchandise are linked in transmedia franchises, where meaning effects are integrated by consumers across multiple media, on even longer timescales. Lemke argues that we need to extend the usual repertory of analytical tools for critical multimedia analysis from those which look at single works to those which look across transmedia clusters, and from those which focus on the formal features of the media themselves to ones which place the experience of media within a political economy and a cultural ecology of identities, markets and values.

How the selection and use of modes reshape practice is a key factor within multimodal research. The following chapter focuses on the relationship between image and writing and examines how the practices of literacy are shaped by this relationship with respect to reading and school science textbooks. Unsworth and Cléirigh, in Chapter 12, outline early work emphasizing the distinctively different semiotic affordances of image and language and their specialized function in contributing different aspects of overall meaning in texts. They propose a semiotic framework designed to address the synergistic nature of image–language interaction in meaning construction. The framework is illustrated with reference to science books for primary-school children and an exemplar analysis accounting for children's difficulties in comprehending a science text in a reading comprehension test. They draw out the implications of the work for pedagogy involving reading to learn and for further research on explicating the role of image–language interaction in reconceptualizing literacy in multimodal terms are also briefly noted.

How power shapes and is shaped by the distribution of, access to, and use of modes is a key concern for multimodality. Multimodality provides a framework for examining the material instantiation of power relations asking questions such as who has access to particular modes, and how does the uneven distribution of modes articulate power. This part of the handbook concludes with Chapter 13 by Arlene Archer, on power, social justice and multimodal pedagogies. The chapter explores some of the links between multimodal pedagogies and social justice, looking at examples from South African educational contexts. The chapter helps to identify some of the challenges and opportunities of using multimodal approaches to pedagogy in local and global contexts of diversity. It helps to explore the potential of multimodality in contexts where there are differentials in terms of access to economic and educational resources and how these are realized materially and semiotically. The chapter focuses on the ways in which multimodal pedagogy can facilitate recognition of a range of student resources, whilst at the same time enabling access to dominant forms. This includes access to the discourses and knowledges of official curricula and formal methods of assessment, as well as creating dispositions towards meaning-making in individual and social worlds outside the classroom. Archer argues that formal education often closes down access to a range of semiotic resources and that multimodal pedagogies could potentially recover 'recognition' of these. This notion of recognition is becoming a key one within multimodal work both within contexts of learning but also in relation to exploring marginalized and diverse practices.

These six chapters provide an in-depth analysis of the themes presented above and demonstrate their significance for multimodal research.

8

Historical changes in the semiotic landscape

From calculation to computation

Kay L. O'Halloran

Introduction

The aim of this chapter is to undertake a historical view of the semiotic landscape in mathematics, with a particular focus on mathematical symbolic notation. A historical approach reveals how mathematical symbolism, language and visual images evolved to work together to fulfil specific functions in contexts shaped by social and scientific semiotic technologies. The development of mathematical notation from prehistory to modern times, and the impact of the printing press and computer technology on the semiotic landscape of mathematics are explored in this chapter. A comprehensive investigation cannot be undertaken, but some key innovations with regards to semiotic resources, semiotic choices and accompanying semiotic technologies are investigated. Understanding the semiotic basis of mathematics and the social and scientific dimensions shaping its existence leads to greater understanding of the power of semiosis to (literally) restructure the world, with a view to future possibilities.

The semiotic landscape and semiotic technologies

The semiotic landscape consists of objects and events which together constitute the phenomenon which we call culture. Semiotic resources, such as language, images, three-dimensional objects, gesture, clothing, music, sound and space, materialise and integrate across modalities which are visual, auditory and somatic (haptic, olfactory and gustatory). Therefore, the semiotic landscape consists of objects and events which are:

(a) 'Monosemiotic' involving one semiotic resource such as language, image or mathematical symbolic notation (e.g. a linguistic text) or 'multisemiotic' involving two or more semiotic resources (e.g. a mathematics text constructed using natural language, an image such as a graph or diagram, and mathematical symbolic statements);

(b) 'Monomodal' involving one modality (e.g. written mathematical text which has a visual modality), and 'multimodal' involving two or more modalities (e.g. concrete mathematical activities with visual, auditory and somatic modalities).

This definition distinguishes between semiotic resources and the modalities of their materialisation, rather than subsuming the two dimensions of semiosis under the term 'multimodal'.[1] This is an important distinction for the purposes of this chapter which is concerned with the semiotic landscape in mathematics because it permits shifts across semiotic resources *and* modalities to be mapped; e.g. from concrete activities using material objects (visual, auditory and somatic) to abstract symbolic forms (visual). Such mappings reveal how the semiotic landscape in mathematics evolved historically, from concrete counting activities to modern-day abstract mathematics.

From the social semiotic perspective adopted in this chapter, the meanings of objects and events are not fixed, but rather the meanings arise within the situational and cultural context in which the object appears or the event takes place, according to cultural conventions which are largely recognised by members of a group or community (e.g. Halliday, 1978; Hodge and Kress 1988; Van Leeuwen, 2005). Moreover, objects and events have a recursive re-contextualising relationship with each other as they materialise, appear and reappear, or otherwise permanently disappear, depending on the nature of their substance and the record of their existence. As part of this recontextualisation process, objects and events may be 'resemioticised' (Iedema, 2001b), by using a different semiotic resource (e.g. word problems expressed as mathematical symbolic equations), a different modality (e.g. spoken language transcribed into written language) or combinations of both (the photograph of an event). The resemioticisation process in mathematics where concrete activities were resemioticised into abstract written symbolic forms led to semantic expansions beyond that possible in the material world.

The semiotic landscape, the aggregate of semiotic choices materialising as objects and events which are recontextualised and resemioticised across different place and time scales, result in evolving but discernable patterns of semiosis called genres (Christie and Martin, 1997; Martin, 1993, 1997). Today, established genres such as perspective paintings, photography, film and television are refashioned in new digital media genres such as digital photography, computer games, and virtual reality. The refashioning process in new media, which Bolter and Grusin (2000) call 'remediation', brings to the forefront the significance of *technology* in the shaping of the semiotic landscape (e.g. Jewitt, 2002, 2006; Kress, 2003), a theme explored in this chapter.

Technology encompasses the multiple ways through which a culture provides the material basis of its existence. There are two basic forms:

(a) *Scientific technology*: the tools and crafts most typically produced in science, applied mathematics and engineering. Scientific technologies include technical products and instruments produced in civil and electrical engineering, medicine, biotechnology, military research and nuclear research, for example, and data-processing technologies such as computer hardware and software.

(b) *Organisational technology*: the organisations and institutions which shape products and events. Organisational technologies include universities, government bodies, corporations and research institutes which regulate and monitor products, collective goals and performances, actions and events.

Together, scientific and organisational technologies are *semiotic technologies* through which material objects are made, events take place, and the social and physical environment is controlled. Semiotic technologies work together to shape and orchestrate the semiotic landscape in social, situational and cultural contexts. In turn, social, situational and cultural contexts shape the semiotic technologies which are developed, a fact demonstrated by the impact of the First and Second World Wars on technological innovation. In what follows, semiotic resources, semiotic choices and semiotic technologies are investigated in relation to the semiotic landscape in mathematics.

Semiotic landscape in mathematics

The history of mathematical symbolic notation has attracted much attention (see Cajori, 1952, 1974) including studies which adopt a social semiotic perspective (e.g. Lemke, 1998; O'Halloran, 2005; Rotman, 1987, 1988, 2000). In particular, Cajori's (1974) account of the history of mathematical notation in elementary and higher mathematics from the Babylonians and the Greeks in antiquity to the present is unparalleled in terms of comprehensiveness. Cajori (1974) pays close attention to the rise in popularity of mathematical symbols, the rivalry and competition encountered, and their resulting spread and eventual decline. Similarly, Ifrah (2000, 2001) gives a comprehensive chronological account of mathematical number systems and computation, from the earliest representations through to the present.

In this chapter some key semiotic developments are discussed. For example, the introduction of zero in the Hindu–Arabic number systems, which led to positional notation and the formulation of arithmetical algorithms, is investigated. The impact of the printing press in the 1450s in Europe, which led to the generalisation of the arithmetical algorithms and the subsequent development of modern algebra, is explored. The visual images in early printed mathematical texts and the importance of the intersemiotic relations established between the three semiotic resources (i.e. symbolism, images and language) are discussed. Lastly, the impact of the data-processing power of modern computers on the semiotic landscape is investigated.

A theory capable of conceptualising multisemiotic–multimodal phenomena is required for the investigation of the semiotic landscape. Therefore, Michael Halliday's (1978, 1994 [1985]; Halliday and Matthiessen, 2004) social semiotic theory is reviewed before examining the historical evolution of the semiotic landscape in mathematics. Comprehensive descriptions of Halliday's systemic functional theory are found elsewhere (e.g. Eggins, 2005; Halliday, 2004; Halliday and Matthiessen, 1999; Martin and Rose, 2007).

Systemic functional approach to the semiotic landscape

Social semiosis is seen to be multifunctional from the perspective of Michael Halliday's (1994 [1985]; Halliday and Matthiessen, 2004) systemic functional theory. That is, semiotic choices simultaneously realise four metafunctions: (a) *experiential meaning*: to construct experience of the world; (b) *logical meaning*: to make logical connections in that world; (c) *interpersonal meaning*: to enact social relations; and (d) *textual meaning*: to organise and orchestrate semiotic choices. Halliday categorises the four metafunctions as ideational (experiential and logical meaning), interpersonal and textual dimensions of meaning.

Halliday (1994 [1985]; Halliday and Matthiessen, 2004) explains that semiotic resources must possess organisational properties through which the four metafunctions are realised. The organisational properties are conceptualised as abstract grammatical systems from which semiotic choices are made, according to their desired functionality in specific social contexts. Halliday (1994 [1985]; Halliday and Matthiessen, 2004) contains a comprehensive description of the grammatical systems of the English language through which the four metafunctions are realised. Halliday's systemic functional grammar constitutes one of the most comprehensive accounts of the grammar of the English language.

Halliday's systemic functional theory has been extended to displayed art (O'Toole, 1994), images and visual design (Kress and Van Leeuwen, 1996), mathematical symbolism and images (O'Halloran, 2005), action and gesture (Martinec, 2000, 2004) and music and sound (Van Leeuwen, 1999). Furthermore, Halliday's systemic functional theory has provided a platform for

125

analysing how semiotic resources integrate and make meaning in objects and events (e.g. Baldry and Thibault, 2006; Kress and Van Leeuwen, 2001; O'Halloran, 2004, 2007; Royce and Bowcher, 2006; Unsworth, 2001; Van Leeuwen, 1985, 2005; Ventola *et al.*, 2004).

Halliday's systemic functional approach to the semiotic landscape is concerned with theorising and analysing semiotic resources (in this case, mathematical symbolic notation, visual images and language) and the materialisation and integration of semiotic choices across modalities (visual, auditory and somatic). More precisely, systemic functional theory is concerned with describing the grammatical systems which constitute the meaning potential of semiotic resources, and analysing and interpreting the realities arising from the integration of semiotic choices in objects and events. Therefore, Halliday's systemic functional theory offers a well-informed approach to multisemiotic–multimodal phenomena because the metafunctional principle provides a common platform for conceptualising semiotic resources and for analysing the ways semiotic choices integrate in objects and events. A systemic functional analysis transcends the boundaries of a discursive description through the analysis of the actual choices which are made against the backdrop of other possible choices which could have been made.

In what follows, key developments in the functionality of the semiotic choices and semiotic resources in the evolution of the semiotic landscape in mathematics are discussed in relation to the accompanying semiotic technologies. Detailed systemic functional analyses of mathematical texts are found elsewhere (e.g. see O'Halloran, 1999, 2005, 2007).

Prehistory to printing press: numerical notation, images and writing

Connecting the concrete to the abstract: the semiotic impact of zero

The earliest surviving examples of semiotic representations of action and thought are inscribed on permanent materials like stone, shells and bone, and so tracing the historical development of semiotic objects, events and technologies is difficult when many events were recorded on perishable materials such as sand, skins, leaves and wood. Nonetheless, we can catch glimpses of the semiotic developments of mathematical symbolic notation, language and visual imagery, and semiotic technologies from prehistoric tools for scratching, painting and drawing to the printing press which eventually led to the scientific revolution in the sixteenth and seventeenth centuries in Europe.

Early prehistoric graphic symbols dating from 35,000 BC consist of notches cut at regular intervals into pieces of stone or bone, and these semiotic artefacts may have been forerunners of tallies and notched sticks which later recorded important data and events in Australia, pre-colonial America, Africa, Europe and China (e.g. Ifrah, 2001; Sassoon and Gaur, 1997). These are the oldest representations of numbers, but their exact purpose is not known (Ifrah, 2001). Early prehistoric emblematic symbols are geometric in nature, such as circles, loops, triangles, rectangles, spirals, zigzag lines, lines, dots and so forth (Sassoon and Gaur, 1997: 13). These early representations, incised or painted using one or more fingers or sticks dipped into paint, coincide with the use of colouring materials such as ochre and manganese and the appearance of jewellery (Sassoon and Gaur, 1997). Human figures and animals painted on rock appear around 30,000–20,000 BC, and large frescoes, like the ones found in Altamira in Spain with narrative pictures of hunters, dancers and warfare, appear around 10,000–8,000 BC.

Clay tokens of various sizes and shapes (e.g. cones, discs, spheres, small balls, rods and tetrahedral shapes) with engravings (e.g. parallel lines, crosses and other motifs) and carved figurines (e.g. animal heads) appear in the Middle East from the ninth to the sixth millennium BC. Ifrah

(2001) explains that their elements may be parts of some system, or they may be intermediate stages between a systematic symbolic expression and its formal expression in a spoken language. However, Ifrah (2001) states that people in the Middle East in the ninth to the second millennium BC calculated using cones, spheres, rods and other clay objects which stood for different units of magnitude. From the fourth millennium BC onwards, more elaborated forms of symbolic notation were found which gave rise to written counts and graphical forms.

Ifrah (2001) surmises that, over time, people developed techniques for expressing numerical quantities based on body parts and the manipulation of objects such as pebbles and clay tokens, and presumably these methods were expressed in articulated speech and gesture. The shift from the concrete to part-abstract was introduced with the shift from parts of the body to concrete objects such as notched bones and clay tokens, and from there, the shift from the concrete object itself to the numerical symbols inscribed on the tokens. Therefore, the trend was away from multimodal numerical systems (oral, visual and somatic) which utilised multiple semiotic resources (body parts, language, gesture, concrete objects and symbols) towards monosemiotic (i.e. symbolic) and monomodal (i.e. visually inscribed) numerical systems. The proliferation of numerical symbols led to counters with scales of magnitude, resulting in the concept of the base of a number system (i.e. the number of single digit numerals in the system). Base 10 has most commonly been used throughout history because we have ten fingers, even though it is not the best choice for arithmetic (having only two factors apart from 1 and itself, unlike 12) or for mathematicians (it is not a prime number, unlike 11) (Ifrah, 2001).

Multimodal arithmetic calculation, however, continued in antiquity with concrete devices which included coloured strings, abacuses traced in wax and sand, and abacuses made from wood, stone and metal. The abstractions embedded in the calculations were semioticised using different number systems developed by the Babylonians, Egyptians, Syrians, Hebrews, Greeks, Romans, Maya and Chinese and Japanese, including Peruvian and North American knotting (Cajori, 1974). The number systems were additive (i.e. written versions of ancient methods of counting with objects based on an additive principle) and hybrid types (i.e. transcriptions of oral number systems with varying degrees of organisation involving mixed multiplicative and additive principles) (Ifrah, 2001). The number systems were functional in a narrow sense, to express the abstractions embedded in the arithmetic calculations in the simplest way possible. In this way, their primary functionality was directed towards representing experiential and logical meaning.

Ifrah (2001) explains that arithmetical calculation finally connected with written numerical notation in the middle ages in the fourth to the sixth century AD when Indian arithmeticians developed positional numerical notation and discovered zero, upon which the system depends. The Indian positional numerical notation possessed a new grammatical system for encoding meaning which did not exist in the older additive and hybrid number systems; i.e. the value of the number depends on its position in the written visual representation of that number (01, 02, 03, ... 09, 10). The symbol for zero needs to exist for the positional notation system to work as a written semiotic calculating device, even though the entity zero does not exist in the material world. Thus the introduction of zero in the Indian positional number system was a critical semiotic development, one which shifted the multimodal world of abacus calculation (i.e. concrete activities with visual, auditory and somatic modalities) to the monomodal written world of symbolic notation (i.e. the visual modality of the page). Calculations could be undertaken, recorded and circulated in written form using the Indian positional number system, rather than using the abacus to perform the arithmetical operations, a procedure which left no permanent semiotic record of the operations which were performed.

Advancing the abstract: the printing press and capitalism

The positional decimal notation entered the Middle East at the end of the eighth century AD, but the Hindu–Arabic sign for zero was only introduced to Europe in the twelfth century AD. Prior to this, Europeans performed numerical calculations using an abacus of Roman origins with columns and counters marked using Arab numerals 1–9, Greek alphabetic numerals from α to θ or Roman numerals I to IX. The introduction of zero caused much controversy and hostility in medieval Europe between the 'abacists' who counted with counters and 'prisoners of a system seamed with ancient number systems such as the Roman numerals and the Greek alphabetic numerals' (Ifrah, 2001: 23) and the 'algorists' who used the Hindu–Arabic number system (e.g. Ifrah, 2001; Rotman, 1987; Swetz, 1987).

The invention of Gutenburg's printing press in the 1450s secured the place of the Hindu–Arabic positional decimal number system and the algorists' method of computation in Europe. The printing press favoured the written numerical algorithms formulated using the Hindu–Arabic number system rather than the multimodal computational methods undertaken using the abacus which were difficult to record in printed form. Therefore, despite initial opposition, the Hindu–Arabic decimal number system became established in Europe in the twelfth to fifteenth centuries where it evolved into its present form.

The introduction of the printing press coincided with new organisational technologies arising from capitalism, trade and commerce (Swetz, 1987). Capitalism demanded efficient arithmetical methods and records, and consequently, the first known printed scientific book to be printed in Europe is the *Treviso Arithmetic*, published in Treviso, Italy in 1478. The book is an early example of the Hindu–Arabic numeral system and it contained computational algorithms developed by the algorists (Swetz, 1987). Therefore, Gutenburg's printing press advanced arithmetic in a fundamental way because it resulted in widespread circulation of standardised mathematical texts which permitted the close study and subsequent development of arithmetical algorithms. These algorithms led to the establishment of generalised results and modern algebra. Therefore, the printing press contributed to the scientific revolution which used algebraic analytical methods to derive results (Eisenstein, 1979; O'Halloran, 2005; Swetz, 1987).

The preceding discussion highlights the significance of semiotic choices (e.g. introduction of zero), the grammar of semiotic resources (e.g. Hindu–Arabic positional number system) and semiotic technologies (e.g. the printing press and the organisational technologies of capitalism) on the development of arithmetic, which led to modern algebra. However, before examining further semiotic shifts in mathematics which contributed to the scientific revolution, we will examine more closely how the development of mathematical symbolic notation expanded meaning potential beyond that possible with language. In what follows, the unique functionality of mathematical notation as a semiotic resource is examined.

Arithmetical symbolic notation: beyond the semantics of language

Ifrah (2001) explains that the writing of words and numbers have common historic parallels. First, the recording of spoken language and numbers profoundly changed human life because 'each system granted direct access to the world of ideas and thoughts across space and time. By encapsulating thought, and by inspiring it in others, the writing down of thought imposed on it both discipline and organization' (Ifrah, 2001: 3). In other words, the semiotic construal of thought in written form permitted the study of ideas and the hierarchical development of knowledge. Second, the alphabet and numerical digits have a finite number of elements which are used to write every word and number respectively, apart from simple cases where, for example, letters are used for numerals. Third, Ifrah (2001) explains each written number system evolved in a similar manner to the verbal writing system which it developed with. Thus, written language and numerical notation both reflected the spoken language and cultural traditions of the time and the influence of the technologies and materials used for writing.

However, written language and numerical notation differ in one major respect, and that is their relation to spoken discourse:

> For something to be called writing, its signs must be related to a spoken language; it must reflect a conscious effort to represent speech…. By contrast, numerical notation needs no correspondence with spoken numbers. The mental process of counting is not linked to any particular act of speech …
>
> (Ifrah, 2001: 4)

Ifrah (2001) raises a key point which helps to explain how mathematics evolved to create a world view which extended beyond that possible with language. That is, mathematical symbolic notation is *a written modality* (i.e. the visual modality of the page) which is not tied to a spoken form (i.e. auditory modality). Arising from language, however, mathematical symbolic notation was free to exploit existing linguistic grammatical systems while simultaneously developing new grammatical systems which operated in the visual modality of the written form, an option not open to language which necessarily had to remain multimodal (i.e. auditory and visual). The written form of mathematical notation meant that the most effective forms of textual organisation could be developed where form, for example, had a direct relationship to meaning (e.g. place value in the Hindu–Arabic number system). Other grammatical strategies developed for mathematical symbolic notation include special symbols, rules for the order of arithmetical operations (e.g. multiplication and division before addition and subtraction, an order which could be disrupted by brackets and other forms of aggregation), spatial notation (e.g. subscripts and superscripts) and the visual layout of symbolic statements on the page. Written language does not possess the same grammatical strategies for encoding meaning as found in mathematical notation.

In addition, mathematical symbolism notation has a specific functionality, unlike natural language which traverses a broader semantic terrain with multiple functional demands. That is, mathematical notation was originally designed to abstract the context-based concrete activities of adding, multiplying, subtracting and dividing (involving visual, auditory and somatic modalities) into the written world of numerical calculation (visual modality) in a precise and efficient manner. Therefore, numerical notation evolved to include grammatical options which permit unambiguous encoding of experiential and logical meaning to capture the abstractions embedded in the numerical calculations. From there, algebra developed to encode the relations between abstract entities. Most typically, instructions about how to undertake the calculations were encoded using language.

The semiotic technologies of the printing press and capitalism led to standardised mathematical notation and the wider study of mathematics texts, leading to the development of further abstractions in mathematics for the purposes of economics, navigation and warfare. Mathematical symbolic notation continued to develop as semiotic resource with new grammatical systems based on the principles of economy and clarity of expression which permitted its use as an effective tool for logical reasoning. One historical factor enabling the semiotic resource to expand its meaning potential occurred when the semantics of mathematical symbolic notation became directly linked to geometrical lines, curves and shapes. This significant development in the semiotic landscape of mathematics is explored below.

129

Printing press to scientific revolution: intersemiotic relations in mathematics

Modern algebraic symbolic notation developed in three stages: 'rhetorical algebra' which involved linguistic descriptions and solutions to problems with some mathematical symbols; 'syncopated algebra' where frequently used quantities and operations were symbolised; and 'symbolic algebra' where mathematical operations were undertaken using mathematical symbolism (Joseph, 1991). The evolutionary basis of mathematical symbolism explains how it can be seamlessly integrated with natural language, having evolved from it, yet at the same time it possesses its own specific grammatical systems and symbols which utilise, for example, special symbols for mathematical processes and entities, spatial notation and spatial layout afforded by the visual modality. Mathematical symbolic notation took written language as its base, and developed further systems for encoding experiential and logical meaning efficiently and unambiguously; the product of its specific functionality aimed to fulfil particular goals, encoded as algorithms.

Descartes (1683, 1954 [1637]) discovered that algebraic equations could be used to describe geometric lines, curves and shapes. The linking of mathematical symbolic description to geometrical figures meant that geometrical problems could be solved using algebraic means, aided by the visual geometrical representation of the problem. Babbage (1827: 330) stresses that the power of algebraic notation for solving geometrical problems arises from its conciseness and economy of expression:

> The assumption of lines and figures to represent quantity and magnitude, was the method employed by the ancient geometers to present to the eye some picture by which the course of their reasonings might be traced: it was however necessary to fill up this outline by a tedious description, which in some instances even of no particular difficulty became nearly unintelligible, simply from its extreme length: the invention of algebra almost entirely removed this inconvenience.
>
> (Babbage, 1827: 330, cited Cajori, 1952: 331)

The intersemiotic connection between geometrical figures and algebraic description contributed to the development of advanced mathematics, including analytical geometry and calculus. The grammar of mathematical symbolism continued to develop to fulfil specific functionalities, in particular, reasoning about the relations between abstract entities, and it became the semiotic tool for the derivation of the solution to problems. Figures 8.1(a)–(c) demonstrate how Descartes, Newton and Leibniz employed algebraic analytical means to derive solutions to problems. For example, Descartes (1637) uses algebra to derive results in *La Géométrie* in Figure 8.1(b) and Newton (1736: 51) uses the same technique to develop the 'method of fluxions' (i.e. differential calculus) in Figure 8.1(a). Similarly, Liebniz (1859: 358) uses algebra as a tool for reasoning in 8.1(c).

Mathematical images developed in accordance with mathematical symbolic notation, where the experiential and logical relations between abstract geometrical entities became the object of concern. The context of problems so vividly portrayed in earlier mathematical images where human actors are portrayed undertaking some activity like shooting an arrow or firing a cannon (e.g. Galileo, 1638; Reisch, 1535; Tartaglia, 1537) disappeared as the geometrical lines, curves and shapes which accompanied the algebraic descriptions became the focus of attention (O'Halloran, 2005). This trend is evident in Figures 8.1(a) and (d) where Newton's calculus and Liebniz's (1859: 358) *Mathematische Schriften* contain abstract geometrical figures which lack material context.

19. Thus suppofing $xz = yy$, 'twill be $\dot{x}z + \dot{z}x = 2y\dot{y}$; and for $\dot{z}$ writing $\frac{x \times C t}{B t}$, there will arife $\dot{x}z + \frac{xx \times C t}{B t} = 2y\dot{y}$. Therefore $z + \frac{x \times C t}{B t} : 2y :: BD : DT$.

20. Ex. 6. Let AC be a Circle, or any other known Curve, whofe Tangent is Ct, and let AD be any other Curve whofe Tangent DT is to be drawn, and let it be defin'd by affuming AB = to the Arch AC; and (CE, BD being Ordinates to AB in a given Angle,) let the Relation of BD to CE or AE be expref'd by any Equation.

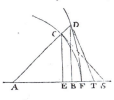

21. Therefore call AB or AC = x, BD = y, AE = z, and CE = v. And it is plain that $\dot{v}$, $\dot{x}$, and $\dot{z}$, the Fluxions of CE, AC, and AE, are to each other as CE, Ct, and Et. Therefore $\dot{x} \times \frac{CE}{Ct} = \dot{v}$, and $\dot{x} \times \frac{Et}{Ct} = \dot{z}$.

22. Now let any Equation be given to define the Curve AD, as $y = z$. Then $\dot{y} = \dot{z}$; and therefore Et : Ct :: ($\dot{y} : \dot{x}$ ::) BD : BT.

23. Or let the Equation be $y = z + v - x$, and it will be $\dot{y} = (\dot{v} + \dot{z} - \dot{x} =) \dot{x} \times \frac{CE + Et - Ct}{Ct}$. And therefore CE + E$t$ — Ct : Ct :: ($\dot{y} : \dot{x}$ ::) BD : BT.

24. Or finally, let the Equation be $ayy = v^3$, and it will be $2a y \dot{y} = (3vv^2 =) 3xv^2 \times \frac{CE}{Ct}$. So that $3v^2 \times CE : 2ay \times Ct ::$ BD : BT.

25. Ex. 7. Let FC be a Circle, which is touched by CS in C; and let FD be a Curve, which is defined by affuming any Relation of the Ordinate DB to the Arch FC, which is intercepted by DA drawn to the Center. Then letting fall CE, the Ordinate in the Circle, call AC or AF = 1, AB = x, DB = y, AE = z, CE = v, CF = t; and it will be $\dot{t}z = (\dot{t} \times \frac{CE}{CS} =)$ $\dot{v}$, and $-\dot{t}v = (\dot{t} \times \frac{-ES}{CS} =) \dot{z}$. Here I put $\dot{z}$ negatively, becaufe AE is diminifh'd while EC is increafed. And befides AE : EC :: AB :

Figure 8.1a *The Method of Fluxions and Infinite Series.*

Source: Newton 1736: 50.

The study of geometrical problems using the principles of algebra meant that mathematical symbolic notation received much attention, and attempts were made to standardise the notation, a procedure which necessarily took into account the limitations of the printing press (Cajori, 1952). The increasing sophistication of printed mathematical notation and the accompanying geometrical figures is evident in Leibniz's (1849, 1859) *Mathematische Schriften*, displayed in Figures 8.1(c)–(d), which may be compared to Descartes' and Newton's early printed works in 8.1(a)–(b). The modern translation of Descartes' (1954 [1637]) algebraic notation in the facsimile of the first edition *La Géométrie* (1637) in Figure 8.1(b) demonstrates how mathematical notation has since evolved to a spatially organised condensed form where the symbolism is separate from the linguistic text, allowing the reader to focus on important symbolic description of relations. The textual layout of the linguistic, symbolic and visual elements aids reasoning in mathematics.

GEOMETRY

Taking this from the square of IC there remains the square of CM, or

$$\frac{t^2}{4n^2u}-\frac{s}{n^2}-\frac{p\sqrt{u}}{n^2}+\frac{2my}{n^2}-y^2,$$

and this is equal to the square of GH, previously found. This may be written

$$\frac{-n^2y^4+2my^3-p\sqrt{u}\,y^2-sy^2+\frac{t^2}{4u}y^2}{n^2y^2}.$$

Now, putting

$$\frac{t}{\sqrt{u}}y^4+qy^4-\frac{1}{4}p^2y^4$$

for n^2y^4, and

$$ry^3+2\sqrt{u}\,y^3+\frac{pt}{2\sqrt{u}}y^3$$

for $2my^3$, and multiplying both members by n^2y^2, we have

$$y^6-py^5+\left(\frac{1}{4}p^2-\frac{t}{\sqrt{u}}\right)y^4+\left(2\sqrt{u}+\frac{pt}{2\sqrt{u}}\right)y^3+\left(\frac{t^2}{4u}-p\sqrt{u}\right)y^2-ty+u$$

equals

$$\left(\frac{1}{4}p^2-q-\frac{t}{\sqrt{u}}\right)y^4+\left(r+2\sqrt{u}+\frac{pt}{2\sqrt{u}}\right)y^3+\left(\frac{t^2}{4u}-s-p\sqrt{u}\right)y^2,$$

or

$$y^6-py^5+qy^4-ry^3+sy^2-ty+u=0,$$

whence it appears that the lines CG, NR, QO, etc., are the roots of this equation.

If then it be desired to find four mean proportionals between the lines a and b, if we let x be the first, the equation is $x^5-a^4b=0$ or $x^6-a^4bx=0$. Let $y-a=x$, and we get

$$y^6-6ay^5+15a^2y^4-20a^3y^3+15a^4y^2-(6a^5+a^4b)y+a^6+a^5b=0.$$

Therefore, we must take AB $=3a$, and BK, the latus rectum of the

236

LIVRE TROISIESME. 411

de IC, il reſte $\frac{tt}{4nnv}--\frac{s}{nn}--\frac{pVv}{nn}+\frac{2my}{nn}--yy$.
pour le quarré de CM, qui eſt eſgal au quarré de GH deſia trouué. Oubien en faiſant que cete ſomme ſoit diuiſée comme l'autre par $nnyy$, on a

$$\frac{--nny^4+2my^3--p\sqrt{v}\,yy--syy+\frac{tt}{4v}yy}{nnyy}.$$ Puis

remettant $\frac{t}{\sqrt{v}}y^4+qy^4--\frac{1}{4}ppy^4$, pour nny^4; &
$ry^3+2\sqrt{v}\,y^3+\frac{pt}{2\sqrt{v}}y^3$, pour $2my^3$: & multipliant l'vne & l'autre ſomme par $nnyy$, on a

$$y^6--py^5\left.\begin{matrix}--\frac{t}{\sqrt{v}}\\+\frac{1}{4}pp\end{matrix}\right\}y^4\left.\begin{matrix}+2\sqrt{v}\\+\frac{pt}{2\sqrt{v}}\end{matrix}\right\}y^3\left.\begin{matrix}--p\sqrt{v}\\+\frac{tt}{4v}\end{matrix}\right\}yy--ty+v$$

eſgal à

$$\left.\begin{matrix}--\frac{t}{\sqrt{v}}\\--q\\+\frac{1}{4}pp\end{matrix}\right\}y^4\left.\begin{matrix}+r\\+2\sqrt{v}\\+\frac{pt}{2\sqrt{v}}\end{matrix}\right\}y^3\left.\begin{matrix}--p\sqrt{v}\\--s\\+\frac{tt}{4v}\end{matrix}\right\}yy$$

C'eſt a dire qu'on a,

$$y^6--py^5+qy^4--ry^3+syy--ty+v\infty 0.$$

D'où il paroiſt que les lignes CG, NR, QO, & ſemblables ſont les racines de cete Equation, qui eſt ce qu'il falloit demonſtrer.

Ainſi donc ſi on veut trouuer quatre moyennes proportionelles entre les lignes a & b, ayant poſé x pour la premiere, l'Equation eſt $x^5****--a^4b\infty 0$ oubien $x^6****--a^4bx*\infty 0$. Et faiſant $y--a\infty x$ il vient
$y^6--6ay^5+15aay^4--20a^3y^3+15a^4yy\left.\begin{matrix}--6a^5\\--a^4b\end{matrix}\right\}y\begin{matrix}+a^6\\+a^5b\end{matrix}\infty 0.$
C'eſt pourquoy il faut prendre $3a$ pour la ligne AB, &
$\frac{\sqrt{6a^3+aab}}{\sqrt{aa+ab}}+6aa$ pour BK, ou le coſté droit de la Pa-

Fff 2 rabole

237

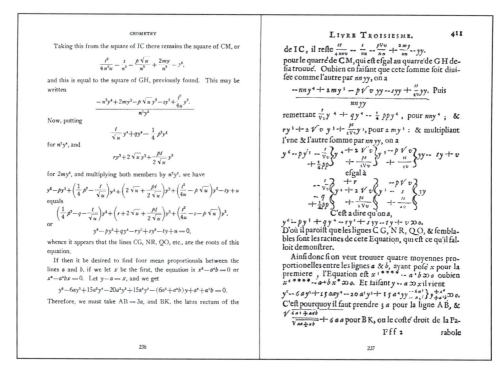

Figure 8.1b *La Géométrie.*

Source: Descartes, 1954 [1637]: 236–237.

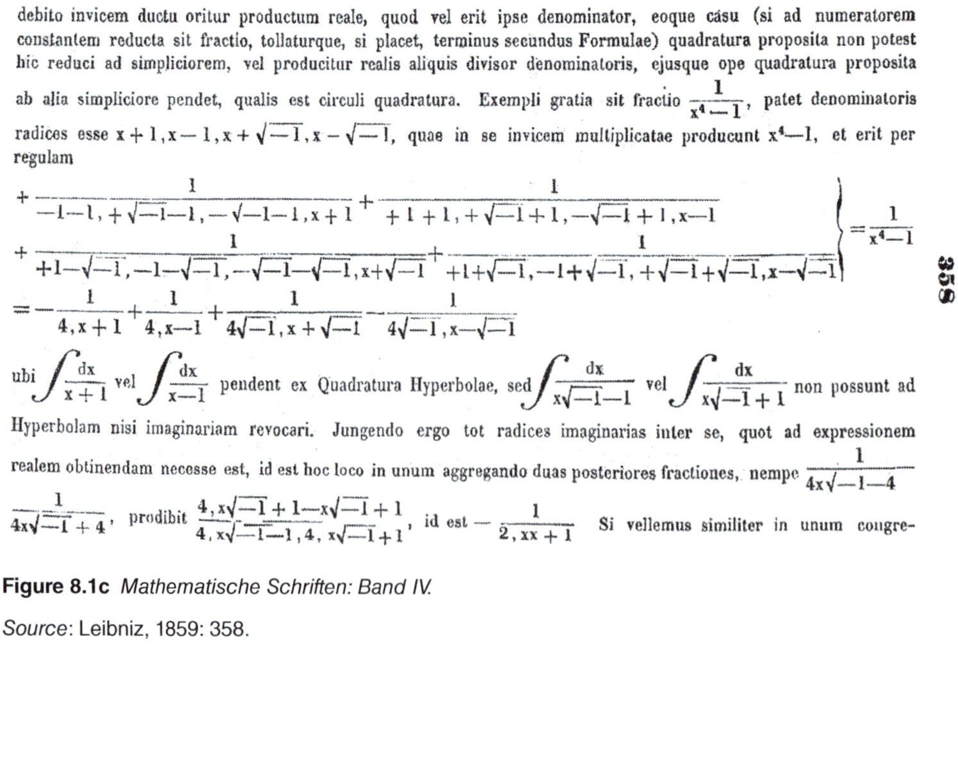

debito invicem ductu oritur productum reale, quod vel erit ipse denominator, eoque casu (si ad numeratorem constantem reducta sit fractio, tollaturque, si placet, terminus secundus Formulae) quadratura proposita non potest hic reduci ad simpliciorem, vel producitur realis aliquis divisor denominatoris, ejusque ope quadratura proposita ab alia simpliciore pendet, qualis est circuli quadratura. Exempli gratia sit fractio $\frac{1}{x^4-1}$, patet denominatoris radices esse $x+1, x-1, x+\sqrt{-1}, x-\sqrt{-1}$, quae in se invicem multiplicatae producunt x^4-1, et erit per regulam

$$\left.\begin{matrix}+\frac{1}{-1-1,+\sqrt{-1}-1,-\sqrt{-1}-1,x+1}+\frac{1}{+1+1,+\sqrt{-1}+1,-\sqrt{-1}+1,x-1}\\+\frac{1}{+1-\sqrt{-1},-1-\sqrt{-1},-\sqrt{-1}-\sqrt{-1},x+\sqrt{-1}}+\frac{1}{+1+\sqrt{-1},-1+\sqrt{-1},+\sqrt{-1}+\sqrt{-1},x-\sqrt{-1}}\end{matrix}\right\}=\frac{1}{x^4-1}$$

$$=-\frac{1}{4,x+1}+\frac{1}{4,x-1}+\frac{1}{4\sqrt{-1},x+\sqrt{-1}}-\frac{1}{4\sqrt{-1},x-\sqrt{-1}}$$

ubi $\int\frac{dx}{x+1}$ vel $\int\frac{dx}{x-1}$ pendent ex Quadratura Hyperbolae, sed $\int\frac{dx}{x\sqrt{-1}-1}$ vel $\int\frac{dx}{x\sqrt{-1}+1}$ non possunt ad Hyperbolam nisi imaginariam revocari. Jungendo ergo tot radices imaginarias inter se, quot ad expressionem realem obtinendam necesse est, id est hoc loco in unum aggregando duas posteriores fractiones, nempe $\frac{1}{4x\sqrt{-1}-4}$ $\frac{1}{4x\sqrt{-1}+4}$, prodibit $\frac{4,x\sqrt{-1}+1-x\sqrt{-1}+1}{4,x\sqrt{-1}-1,4,x\sqrt{-1}+1}$, id est $-\frac{1}{2,xx+1}$ Si vellemus similiter in unum congre-

358

Figure 8.1c *Mathematische Schriften: Band IV.*

Source: Leibniz, 1859: 358.

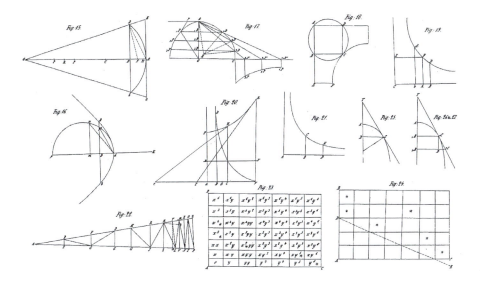

Figure 8.1d *Mathematische Schriften: Band I.*

Source: Leibniz, 1849: insert.

DE MOTU
CORPO-
RUM.

PROPOSITIO LXXXIII. PROBLEMA XLII.

Invenire vim quâ corpufculum in centro fphæræ locatum ad ejus fegmentum quodcunque attrahitur.

Si *P* corpus in centro fphæræ, & *RBSD* fegmentum ejus plano *RDS* & fuperficie fphæricâ *RBS* contentum. Superficie fphæricâ *EFG* centro *P* defcriptâ fecetur *DB* in *F*, ac diftinguatur fegmentum in partes *BREFGS*, *FEDG*. Sit autem fuperficies illa non purè mathematica, fed phyfica, profunditatem habens quam minimam. Nominetur ifta profunditas *O*, & erit hæc fuperficies (per (γ) demonftrata *Archimedis*) ut $PF \times DF \times O$. Ponamus præterea vires attractivas particularum fphæræ effe reciprocè ut diftantiarum dignitas illa, cujus index eft *n*; & vis, quâ fuperficies *EFG* trahit corpus *P*, erit (per prop. LXXIX.) ut $\dfrac{DEq \times O}{PF^{n}}$, id

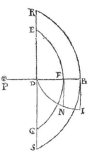

(z) eft, ut $\dfrac{2\,DF \times O}{PF^{n-1}} - \dfrac{DFq \times O}{PF^{n}}$.

Huic proportionale fit perpendiculum *FN* ductum in *O*; & (a) area curvilinea *BDI*, quam ordinatim applicata *FN* in

(γ) * *Per demonftrata Archimedis.* Nam (515) ekmentum fuperficiei E F G, eft ut P F ducta in elementum lineæ D F, adeoque ob datam P F, refpectu fuperficiei totius E F G, fuperficies illa (165.) erit ut P F × D F, & proinde lamina ex hâc fuperficie & profunditate O; genita erit ut P F × D F × O
    (2) * Id eft &c. Nam (per prop. 13. Lib. 6. Elem.) D E² = 2 P F — D F × D F = 2 P F × D F — D F². Quarè $\dfrac{DE^{2} \times O}{PF^{n}}$

$= \dfrac{2\,DF \times O}{PF^{n-1}} - \dfrac{DF^{2} \times O}{PF^{n}}$

(a) 537. * *Et area curvilinea &c.* Si fegmentum R B S D R, in laminas innumeras profunditatis evanefcentis O divifum inteligatur, & capiatur femper perpendiculum F N, vi fingularum laminarum proportionale, manifeftum eft (per Lem. 4.) fummam elementorum F N × O, feu aream curvilineam D N I B, proportionalem fore fummæ virium. Sit igitur P D = a, P F

Figure 8.2a

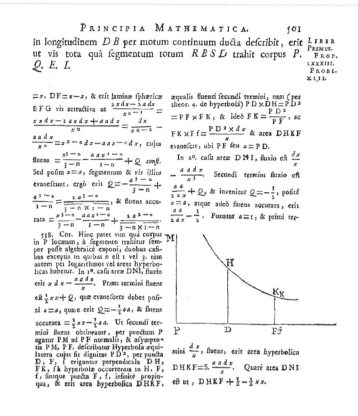

Figure 8.2a, b *Philosophiæ Naturalis Principia Mathematica.*
Source: Newton, 1739.

The mathematical rewriting of the world which took place during the scientific revolution depended on the semiotic tools of mathematical symbolism, geometrical figures and language. While Newton (1739) describes the motion of bodies in the *Principia* using geometric arguments rather than calculus, the underlying dependence on the algebraic analytical method is clear in the explanatory footnotes which accompany Newton's geometrical formulations in Figures 8.2(a)–(b).

Newton (1643–1727) and Leibniz (1646–1716) developed calculus independently, but Leibniz's notation is the one in use today. Cajori (1952) explains that Leibniz's choices of symbolic notation were the result of patient effort and experimentation over nearly one third of a century. Liebniz's decisions were

> guided in part by the principle of economy, according to which there should be not be unnecessary duplication of symbols.… He urged the avoidance of signs so closely resembling each other as to give rise to doubt or confusion. He came to realise the fundamental importance of adopting symbolisms which could be set up in a line like ordinary type, without need of widening the spaces between lines to make room for symbols with sprawling parts.
>
> (Cajori, 1952: 184)

Liebniz's dedication to finding the optimal notation meant he developed many symbols which retain their place in mathematics today.

In addition, Leibniz developed the earliest calculating machine capable of carrying out the four fundamental arithmetic operations by mechanical means, and he discovered the binary system, the foundation of virtually all modern computer architectures (Ifrah, 2001). In the last section of this paper, we consider the impact of computers on the semiotic landscape in mathematics and beyond.

From calculation to computation

It has often been stated that the computer revolution will do for man's mind what the industrial revolution did for man's muscle'

(Pirow, 1988, abstract)

A historical view of the evolution of the semiotic landscape in mathematics provides a frame for examining the impact of computer technology on the growth and expansion of mathematical knowledge. Modern computers are the product of a long and complex synthesis arising from multiple needs and initiatives, dating back to the difficulties and pitfalls of human arithmetic calculations. Ifrah (2001: 237–240) describes the contexts, structural limitations, scientific developments and the technologies leading to the modern electronic binary computer. Historically, the types of calculating devices preceding the modern computer include mechanical, analogue, mechanographical and analytical devices (Ifrah, 2001: 99). Modern computers, however, depend on symbolic logic and stored programs, unlike older analytical calculators which had external programs. The technology in modern computers arose from sequential automated techniques and the programmable machines developed to serve the needs of the Second World War and twentieth century scientific progress. The computer as a semiotic technology which shapes nearly every aspect of modern life is examined in more detail below.

The modern computer is defined as 'a functioning device that performs computations without the intervention of people while it is in progress. More specifically, a computer has also been defined as a machine that can perform calculations, sort data, file away information, edit and otherwise manipulate (process) facts' (Cortada, 1987: 85). The computer is characterised by 'its *universal application* in the field of calculation, thanks to its distinctive programmability which results in the programming instructions being registered in the internal memory and being treated in the same way as the data' (Ifrah, 2001: 363). In other words, computers can execute a wide variety of tasks through programs which contain algorithms encoded as a series of elementary operations which are automatically carried out at great speed. Computers process data and through this process, basic research is transformed into practical applications, principles come to light, and new contexts in the semiotic landscape are created. Therefore, computers are general-purpose automatic data-processing machines which are capable of translating quite different realities beyond those very specialised ones in the field of mathematics. The shift from calculation to computation has meant a move from the semiotic landscape of mathematics to the semiotic landscape of contemporary life.

Computers have a universal scope for organising, processing and transforming data through abstract symbolic logic. Computers receive multisemiotic–multimodal input (i.e. multiple semiotic resources such as language, images, sound and gesture combine across auditory, visual and haptic modalities) through a range of devices (e.g. keyboard, mouse, touch pads, pointing

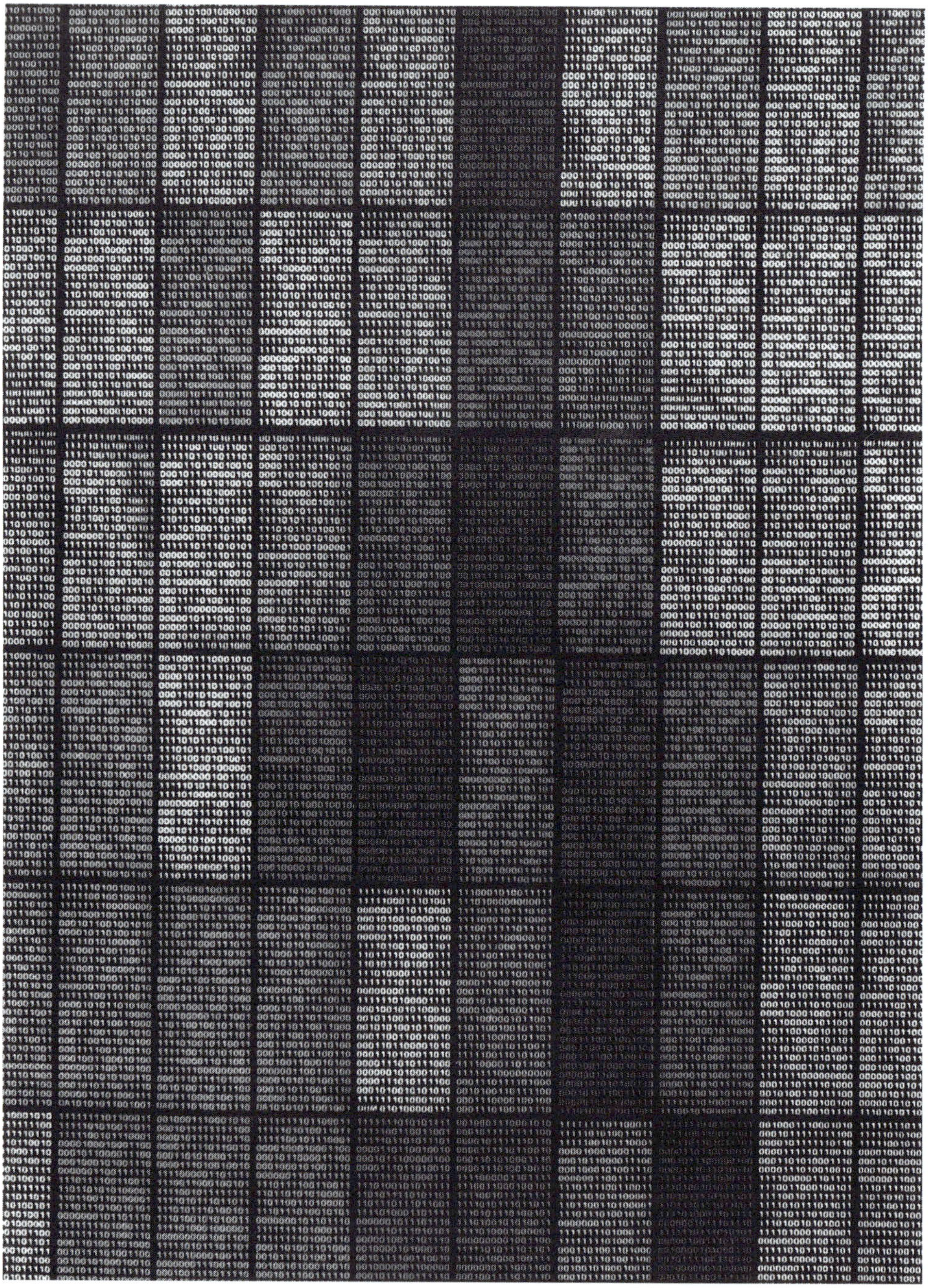

Figure 8.3 Beethoven's Fifth Symphony coded in binary.

sticks, joysticks, pen input, touch screen, digitaliser, graphics tablet scanner, microphone, electronic whiteboard, video cards and audio cards). The data is represented by symbols which are expressible in numerical code. Computers manipulate the symbols, 'effecting various operations on *character chains* (words, phrases, numbers, etc.)' (Ifrah, 2001: 305). The results are given via multisemiotic–multimodal output devices (e.g. monitors, printers, audio cards, plotters, LCD projection panels, computer facsimile (fax) and speakers).

The computer achieves its remarkable functionality for data processing through the computer chip, 'a small piece of semiconductive material through which electricity can pass from one section to another according to predetermined plans' (Cortada, 1987: 57). The chip is 'an integrated circuit of electronics without wires' because data is stored and transmitted 'on' and 'off' rather than with a variable number of states (Cortada, 1987: 57). The chip houses the electrical circuits and the programs with the algorithms, plus the data used by the computer. Chips store information in Leibniz's binary code; for example, the first few notes of Beethoven's Fifth Symphony are coded in binary in Figure 8.3.

Computers are semiotic technologies which expand the semiotic landscape in new ways. Language, number and abstract symbolism intersemiotically integrate in computer programs in complex ways which extend beyond traditional mathematical printed texts. Furthermore, the programming languages used by programmers are converted into lower-level machine code which is not decipherable by humans (Cortada, 1987: 307). In addition, computers perform multiple operations at speeds which extend beyond the limits of human capabilities. Through their unrivalled ability to process data, computers can, for example, simulate complex phenomena like weather patterns and climate change through computer models constructed through algorithms which ascribe attributes to elements of the system (e.g. temperature density, humidity, velocity and so forth) and describe the dynamical laws governing the system. The computer executes the algorithms repetitively and updates the representation of the system, thereby simulating the real physical system. Statistical methods can be used to extract features of the system and the influence of various parameters. Computer simulation is used in many contexts, ranging from physical and abstract systems to simulations of technology for performance optimisation, engineering safety and testing, and education and training. Simulation reveals the effects of alternative conditions and courses of action. Ifrah (2001: 108) explains, 'this kind of "abstract experimentation" could never be achieved with real physical systems'.

However, computers can only function according to the collection of programs which are introduced into them; i.e. *the software*. 'A formal definition of software would include programs, rules, any procedures, and documentation related to the operation of a computer. In practice, the term refers to the program written to instruct a computer what to do' (Cortada, 1987: 347). Software includes application software for end users (e.g. word processors, internet browsers and spreadsheets), system software which interfaces with the computer hardware so software applications can run (e.g. operating systems) and middleware which integrates software applications across networks (e.g. web servers and application servers). Therefore, software is the semiotic technology which shapes multimodal–multisemiotic input, the processing of the symbolic data, and the nature of the multimodal–multisemiotic output. Computers don't think or reason, they are 'work-horse[s] from which not the smallest spark of genius is to be expected' (Ifrah, 2001: 368).

Computers play a complementary role to the software programmers who write the programs and in doing so they provide physical capacities, speed and reliability. However, the software programmers have the power to conjure illusions.

This conjuring involves thinking of a series of steps in a procedure which itself can require from hundreds to ten of thousands of instructions. When written out, without mistakes and in the right order, these arcane instructions can make the computer into everyone's dream machine.

(Palfreman and Swade, 1991: 124)

However, the 'dream machine' is shaped by the hardware designers and the software programmers who provide the semiotic tools to shape the dreams which are subsequently produced.

The physical world is governed by laws whose properties can be captured (in part) by abstract symbolic notation. However, having achieved abstraction, those laws are used to act on the world. 'Precisely because humans have learned to transmute the objects of physical reality into simple objects of abstract thought, so they have been able to accomplish all the spectacular progress characteristic of humankind' (Ifrah, 2001: 101). Computer technology transmutes multimodal–multisemiotic phenomena into abstract symbols, operates on those symbols, and transmutes the results as transformed multimodal–multisemiotic output. The new realities created by computers are the promise of the future, but we need to understand the semiotic technologies and processes which create those realities. The sciences, the social sciences and the humanities need to meet on common ground to understand the computer as a semiotic technology which offers much promise for an expanded semiotic landscape, perhaps beyond the limits of the scientific revolution, which rewrote the world in mathematical terms (only).

The historical view of the semiotic landscape in mathematics reveals how mathematical knowledge evolves and materialises as multimodal and multisemiotic objects, activities and events constructed using semiotic resources which are shaped by social and scientific technologies. Judging from the state-of-the art in mathematics and the sciences at the present time, multimodal analysts from the social sciences appear to have much to gain by understanding and utilising the expanded meaning potential afforded by computer technology to further multimodal analysis theory and practice.

Note

1 The distinction between 'semiotic resource' (e.g. language, image, mathematical symbolism) and 'modality' (visual, auditory and somatic) provides a useful framework for examining the shifts between concrete mathematical activities and the abstract semiotic construal of mathematical knowledge. However, making this distinction is not a common practice in multimodal studies; for example, see concept of 'mode' in Bateman (2011).

Further reading

Bateman, J. (2008) *Multimodality and Genre: A Foundation for the Systematic Analysis of Multimodal Documents*, Hampshire: Palgrave Macmillan.

Bateman, J. (2011) 'The Decomposability of Semiotic Modes.' In K. L. O'Halloran and B. A. Smith eds. *Multimodal Studies: Exploring Issues and Domains*, London, Routledge: pp. 17–38.

Lemke, J. L. (2003) 'Mathematics in the middle: Measure, picture, gesture, sign, and word.' In M. Anderson, A. Sáenz-Ludlow, S. Zellweger and V. V. Cifarelli eds. *Educational Perspectives on Mathematics as Semiosis: From Thinking to Interpreting to Knowing*, Ottawa: Legas: pp. 215–234.

O'Halloran, K. L. (2005) *Mathematical Discourse: Language, Symbolism and Visual Images*, London: Continuum.

O'Toole, M. (1994) *The Language of Displayed Art*, London: Leicester University Press.

9

Technology and sites of display

Rodney H. Jones

Introduction

In her book, *Technology, Literacy and Learning* (2006), Carey Jewitt discusses the difference between the page and the screen as two distinct 'sites of display'. In these different sites, she observes, different modes take on different kinds of functions and different kinds of social meanings. The dynamic and ephemeral nature of print on the screen makes available different functionalities and different meaning potentials, and exists in different relationships to other modes than the permanent and linear print in a book. Jewitt's observations come chiefly from secondary school English classrooms in which she collected data on the different ways students learn with different media like computer games and novels on CD-ROM. But 'sites of display' constitute more than just the material media through which information is displayed. Sites of display are *social occasions* in which particular configurations of modes and media converge in a particular time and space in order to make particular social actions possible.

A 'site of display' consists of more that just what is displayed. It is an interaction between the display and those who use it. It is essentially what Scollon (1998) calls 'a watch' – a configuration of social actors in which one social unit (person or group) provides a *spectacle* for another social unit (person or group) to watch. 'The spectacle together with its watchers', says Scollon (283), 'constitutes "a watch"'. Examples include not just books and computer screens, but also exhibition halls, television and cinema screens, live 'platform events' (Goffman, 1983; S. Scollon, 2003) like lectures, ceremonies and beauty pageants, boxing rings, roadside billboards, shop windows and singles bars.

The problem with examining sites of display outside of the context of their use by 'watchers' to perform particular social practices is that what people can do with different sites of display alters radically in different contexts: a television set in an electronics shop, for example, is functionally different from a television set in a family's living room, embedded in different social practices, different 'interaction orders' (Goffman, 1983), and different material circumstances, and making different kinds of social identities available to watchers. While one might be able to talk about the 'affordances' and 'constraints' (Kress and Van Leeuwen, 2001) of different media in a rather general way outside of their social context of their use, one can never know how these 'affordances' and 'constraints' alter as people strategically mix media and modes in performing concrete social actions.

Figure 9.1 An example of a site of display – a noticeboard in a park in China where the daily newspaper is hung every morning and passers-by stop to peruse it.

Figure 9.1 is an example of a site of display – a notice board in a park in China where the daily newspaper is hung every morning and passers-by stop to peruse it. The closer one analyzes this situation, however, the more difficult it is to pin down what the site of display actually is: the newspaper itself would be considered a site of display if someone were holding it in his or her hands, but hung on a notice board it becomes part of a larger site of display – a notice board, with a new set of affordances and constraints. The situation becomes even more complex when such activities are used, as they sometimes are in parks in China, as a front for gay men to meet possible sexual partners (Jones 2002). In such cases, the site of display of the notice board becomes a tool through which participants engage in a different kind of 'watch' – one in which the spectacle is not the newspaper, but other 'readers'. The display of the newspaper, in other words, makes possible the creation of the display of 'reading the newspaper', which in turn makes possible other more surreptitious displays. For the analyst, as for the casual observer, the main interaction may appear to be that between the 'readers' and the news posted on the board. For participants, however, the information displayed on the notice board might be largely irrelevant.

The point of this example is to illustrate a number of principles about sites of display, which I will proceed to develop in the remainder of this chapter. The first is that sites of display are always embedded in or overlap with other sites of display, and very often what can be *done* with a site of display depends very much on this phenomenon of *embeddedness*. A newspaper on someone's breakfast table, for example, cannot be used in the same way it can when it is hanging on a notice board in a Chinese park. It is in part this situatedness of sites of display that creates opportunities for 'watchers' to use them in strategic ways.

The second principle is that sites of display are always used to take real-time social actions in the context of particular social practices, and to some degree it is the configuration of modes made available in a site of display that defines or constitutes the social practices that can be carried out with it, practices like teaching secondary school English, watching television with your family, and 'cruising' for sex partners in a public park. Social practices and sites of display, then, exist in a symbiotic relationship, with sites of display amplifying and constraining social practices and social practices affecting the kinds of functionalities that sites of display develop.

Just as sites of display help to organize social practices, they also work to organize the social relationships between and among those using them. First and foremost they help construct relationships between those who have created the spectacle and those who consume it. The relationship between the author of a book and a reader, for example, is generally more distant and anonymous than that between the authors and the readers of a weblog (on which readers are able to post comments and themselves take on the role of authors). But sites of display also help to organize relationships among 'watchers'. They allow, for example, the people who use them to claim certain kinds of interactional rights and social territory: people reading a newspaper and (increasingly) a computer screen in a coffee shop can claim very different rights – such as the right to exclusive viewing of the spectacle and the right to non-interference by others (Scollon, 1998) – than can people reading a newspaper on a public notice board or students operating computers in the kinds of English classrooms studied by Jewitt.

Finally, following from the previous points, is the notion that sites of display are inherently 'ideological' – that they help to construct social realities in which certain kinds of social practices and social identities are possible and others are not. Sites of display embedded in particular social contexts help to produce and reproduce certain sets of expectations about meaning among users which Blommaert (2005) calls *orders of indexicality* – stratified, ordered patterns of indexical values attached to semiotic signs. Different combinations of modes embedded in different social contexts result in different kinds of meanings being assigned to gestures, utterances and other social actions. Being seen reading a newspaper in a coffee shop, for example, is unlikely to leave one open to assumptions of sexual availability the way reading a newspaper posted on a notice board in certain parks in China would.

Technology and sites of display

Much has been written on how computers and other new media have altered the ways we display information and consume these displays. Most of this work comes from the field of literacy studies, and so focuses on comparing the computer screen with the printed page. One of the main differences these scholars observe between 'page' and 'screen', for example, is that information on computer screens tends to rely more on visual images and less on text (Kress, 2003b; Kress and Van Leeuwen, 2001). They also note the degree in which the screen allows the user to control and interact with the display as opposed to static text on the page, forming their own reading paths through hypertext and availing themselves of increasing opportunities to respond to the text on the screen. The interactivity of computer-based displays calls into question traditional notions of authorship as well as traditional notions of textuality itself: freed from the physical medium that conveys it, text becomes more of a dynamic process and less of a static artifact (Kress, 2003b). Finally, they note how the technology of the screen allows for the integration of multiple modes including text, images, animations, video, voice, music and sound effects, making the production of texts less a matter of 'writing' and more a matter of 'design' (Kress and Van Leeuwen, 2001).

This last observation points to one of the most important features of the screen as a site of display: its unique ability to embed and create links between different sites of display. Movie and television screens, maps, books, webcam broadcasts, advertising banners, game boards, playing fields and a host of other sites of display are regularly embedded into the display of the screen. In fact, the new configurations of *embeddedness* made possible by the screen reveal the limitations of an approach that focuses on comparing it to the printed page, an approach which is largely based on the assumption that we do the same kinds of things with computers that we do with books, when the fact is, when we use computers we spend only part of our time doing 'bookish' things like reading and searching for information, and much more of our time engaged in activities which would be more fruitfully compared to those that involve cinema screens, boxing rings, shopping malls and singles bars.

Displaying the body

In this chapter I will discuss the effects of technology on sites of display by focusing on a particular kind of display: the display of the human body. How, I will be asking, does the computer screen change the way people display their bodies and the kinds of social actions that can be taken with those displays. In particular I will be focusing on how the screen affects the display of the body in the context of a social practice not far removed from the one that takes place in the Chinese parks described above, the practice of looking for a sexual partner. New communication technologies, however, make available to participants in this activity modes of interaction, social identities and social practices that are very different from those available to the 'newspaper readers' in the public parks described above.

The mediated display of the human body goes back as far as the earliest cave paintings, but the communicative potential for such displays has altered drastically over time with the development of new technologies of representation and new sites of display. Kress and Van Leeuwen (1996), for example, observe that it was not until the fifteenth century that subjects of portraits began to look directly at the viewer, an innovation which dramatically affected the potential for the body to display information in the context of a painting by creating a sense of reciprocity between the viewer and the person depicted. The fifteenth and sixteenth centuries also saw the development of the practice of combining portraiture with written text, as in the sixteenth- century Italian convention of including mottos or slogans (called *imprese*) in paintings to enhance the role of the bodily display as an expression of the character or biography of the person portrayed. The seventeenth and eighteenth centuries brought other important innovations, such as the increased popularity of miniatures – portraits that could be held in the hand or placed inside lockets, affording to bodily displays a portability they had previously not had and giving them the status of personal possessions which could be reserved for private viewing. Another important innovation of the eighteenth century was the development of pastel portraiture which allowed artists to render bodily displays in a way that made them seem much more lifelike. West (2004: 60) comments that 'because they rendered the person both lifelike and seemingly touchable', pastel portraits began to take on an 'an erotic or fetishistic quality'. In fact, in the eighteenth and nineteenth centuries, such portraits were frequently used for purposes in many ways similar to the ways they are used in the website I will analyze below, in marriage negotiations between well-to-do families in cases where potential spouses lived a great distance from each other. Just as with the posting of snapshots on internet dating websites, these exchanges of portraits chiefly served the purpose of validating the physical attractiveness of the sitter.

Of course, the affordances offered by bodily representations, especially for such documentary or verification functions, changed dramatically with the development of photography, which allowed for representations even more lifelike and accurate than those achieved through pastels. Just as important as the increased accuracy of photographic displays, however, was the increased 'reproducibility' of them that photography made possible, and the social consequences of the rise of what Benjamin (1936) calls 'the age of mechanical reproduction'. This development also brought about changes in other traditional sites of display in which photographs could now be embedded, such as newspapers and police reports.

Another dramatic change came about when photographic equipment became widely and cheaply available, and people could produce representations of their own and others' bodies on a regular basis to later display in wallets, photo albums and, more recently, on webpages. Finally, the rise of computers and the internet further increased individuals' potential to create and control bodily displays, to reproduce them, alter them (using applications such as Photoshop), to combine them with other modes, to make them more immediate and interactive, and to disseminate them at an unprecedented speed to an unprecedented number of people, both acquaintances and strangers.

Bodily displays have taken on different kinds of social functions over the years and become implicated in a number of distinct social practices. They have functioned as works of art, as representations of the biography or the character of individuals, as documents verifying the identity or characteristics of an individual, as expressions of the relationship between the person portrayed and one or more of the viewers, and as a substitute or proxy for the absent body of that person (West, 2004). Different technologies and the sites of display associated with them give users different potential for realizing these different kinds of social functions and in carrying out different kinds of social practices. Different media impose upon the body different affordances and constraints as to what can be displayed and how, and different media come with different resources for users to control and modulate the kind of information the body 'gives' and the kind of information that it 'gives off'.

New media and bodily display: the case of Fridae.com

The website I will be analyzing represents a recent shift in the way the internet is used as a site of display from a focus on information to a focus on interaction. Known as 'Web 2.0', this shift is exemplified by the rise of interactive sites such as online communities, weblogs, social networking sites, social bookmarking sites, video sharing sites and wikis. Prototypical Web 2.0 sites include Wikipedia, Facebook, del.icio.us, Skype, dodgeball and Adsense. Such sites of display are constituted by their participants creating displays for one another, and commenting upon one another's displays. They operate according to a kind of 'attention economy' (Goldhaber, 1997; Lanham, 1994; Lankshear and Knobel, 2002) in which users attempt to attract the attention of other users and then display that attention as part of their own displays. The more people use a particular site the more its 'value' as a site of display increases, thus attracting even more people to use it, a phenomenon known as the 'network effect' (Economides, 1995).

All of these sites, however, are not the same in terms of the kinds of functions, features and modal configurations that they offer. Since sites of display develop around social practices and define the contours of such practices, the kinds of affordances and constraints they develop depends to a large degree on the demands of the social practice for which they are used.

Figure 9.2 depicts a personal profile on the popular gay website, Fridae.com, a web portal originating in Hong Kong and catering primarily to gay men and lesbians in Asia. The site contains gay-related news and information on travel, entertainment, health and advocacy, but its most popular feature is its 'personals' section where users can post their profiles and search through the profiles others have posted using a variety of search options and then interacting with the authors of these profiles in a variety of ways. These profiles nearly always contain depictions of the author's body in the form of photographs and textual descriptions. The features of the site allow users to strategically embed bodily displays within the context of other displays (including the displays of other people's bodies) to produce displays that

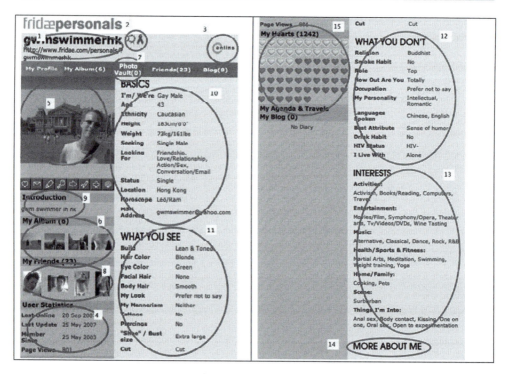

Figure 9.2 A personal profile on the popular Hong Kong gay website Fridae.com.

are dynamic and interactive, and to control and modulate the access different users have to different parts of their display. These new affordances, I will argue, give rise to new social norms and new ways of organizing relationships that are impossible in other sites of display associated with similar social practices such as gay bars, saunas, the classified sections of some publications and notice boards in Chinese parks.

The site of display created by this website's interface makes possible a multimodal display of the body involving icons, written text and photographs, in which the body is semiotized and resemiotized (Iedema, 2001b) as it interacts with these different modes and these different modes interact with one another. Below I will consider the various features of this display.

Username

The first decision a displayer on Fridae.com must make when he or she applies for a profile is what screen name to choose. As with screen names on MSN Messenger (Lou, 2005) and elsewhere, these names often contain a wealth of information in the form of socially recognized identity cues. In the example here, the name gwmswimmerhk (1) indicates that the author is a gay, Caucasian man who lives in Hong Kong and enjoys swimming. Extracting this information, however, to a large degree depends on readers understanding the 'shorthand' used by this particular discourse community (for example, abbreviations such as gwm for 'gay white man') as well as the 'orders of indexicality' for particular terms ('swimmer', for example, indexes not just participation in a particular sport but also a particular lifestyle and body type).

This label, then, often draws on information available in other places (visual and textual) in the profile (information about race, appearance, interests, etc.) and *resemiotizes* (Iedema, 2001b) it into an identity label.

Icons

The icons next to the name give further information about the author and reveal more about the orders of indexicality within which users negotiate identity. Some signs on the site give information about the author's identity. Others give information about the site of display itself and the way the author and others are interacting with or have interacted with it.

An example of the latter type of sign is the circular icon to the left of the username which shows the author's membership status, specifically whether or not the author has purchased 'perks' which allow him or her to access certain kinds of information on the profiles of others. This icon, then, is important in informing the reader of the ways in which he or she will be able to interact with the author.

A similar function is performed by the green circle to the far right (3) which indicates whether or not the user is on-line. Further information on the author's on-line habits appear in the lower left-hand corner (4) where information is given regarding when the author was last on-line, when they joined the service, when they last updated their profile and how many people have viewed their profile. This last piece of information is an example, more of which will be discussed below, of how, by interacting with the profile, in fact, simply by viewing it, 'watchers' alter the spectacle which they are watching.

Next to the circular icon is an icon of a red ribbon, which indicates whether or not the author practices (or rather, professes to practice) 'safe sex'.

The 'red-ribbon' symbol is familiar icon, the indexicality of which is easily interpretable by competent members of this discourse community. Its meaning goes beyond its association with certain concrete actions (such as using a condom), indexing a certain kind of 'gay man' and certain kinds of ideological assumptions about what it means to be a 'responsible' member of this community.

Pictures

Perhaps the most important ingredient in this site of display is the author's 'main picture' which appears near the top of the profile underneath the user's name and above the profile menu (5). In fact, it is this display which, at least initially, is likely to be the main focus of viewers, and all of the other displays available at this site somehow refer to it or depend on it; it is unlikely that viewers who are neither interested in nor attracted to this display will go on to engage with other parts of the site like the written text. This particular bodily display is just one of several that the author can make available in his or her 'album', the contents of which is displayed as thumbnail images underneath the main picture.

The semiotics and function of such pictures are complex. Like conventional portraiture, these displays are multifunctional, operating as aesthetic objects, as representations of individuals' characters or histories, as documents of identity or of particular physical traits, and as communicative gestures in the ongoing interaction among users (R. Jones, 2005). Their most important function, however, is to attract the attention of other users. As a participant in a study by Brown and his colleagues (2005) investigating a similar website put it, 'your picture is your bait'. Therefore, the kinds of features displayers choose to include in these pictures provide a good indication of the kinds of visual signs that index desirability in this particular community: certain kinds of poses, gestures and facial expressions, certain kinds of clothing (or lack thereof), certain kinds of places, certain kinds of activities, and certain kinds of bodily parts displayed in certain ways.

One important aspect of these bodily displays is that they are always *situated* within some kind of environmental and/or behavioral context – they are 'frozen actions' which portray not just social actors but also the particular place and time where the photographs were taken and the particular activities social actors were involved in. This contextual information is sometimes as important as the bodily display itself in communicating desirability. Particularly popular, for instance, are pictures taken at famous tourist destinations or in natural settings like beaches and mountains. One reason for this, of course, is that situations like visits to the beach or to foreign locales are typically occasions when one has one's picture taken, and so such photos are often those most available to authors searching for images to insert into this site. Such images, however, can also index affiliation to certain places or cultures, a certain adventurous spirit, as well as a certain economic status which makes such visits possible. Sometimes photos are taken in the company of others – friends, family members, partners – which also communicates particular character traits or social relationships indexed by the people in whose company one is photographed.

In this regard, such images are examples of 'social portraiture' (Goffman, 1979) – meant to communicate something about the 'type of person' the author is and, in doing so, to rehearse community norms about what 'type of person' is considered desirable and the kinds of 'body idiom' (Goffman, 1963) which index attractiveness in this community.

Some of the images authors include, of course, are not chosen from old snapshots but rather taken especially for use on this site. This is particularly true for images which display parts of the body not normally revealed in vacation snapshots or for images posted by authors who are concerned about revealing their identities on-line. Such images often consist of disembodied bodily parts (torsos, genitals), or of images in which the author's face has been somehow obscured by sunglasses, for example, or special photo-editing techniques. These photos are also often taken by the authors themselves sometimes using mirrors. Such photos highlight another function of bodily display on this website – its documentary function. Like images of scientific specimens, these pictures function to create a document of the specimen's physical characteristics. Thus it is common for authors to choose pictures which display their bodies in different poses, from different angles, or wearing different kinds of clothing, so as to highlight various physical features, rather in the same way police reports contain photographs of crime suspects taken from different angles.

While such photographic displays of body parts document certain features of the author's body meticulously, they also can strategically conceal other parts, most typically the author's face. It is precisely the documentary nature of such images that makes some people reluctant to 'document' their identities in the pictures they post.

The purpose of these images, then, is not just to display information, but also to conceal it, either to protect the identity or modesty of the author or to create an air of mystery or suspense (Figure 9.3).

Authors can also post images which are not publicly available in their 'albums' but rather stored in their 'photo vault' (7) and available for viewing only to those to whom the author has provided a virtual 'key'. Such images are generally more revealing (authors might include close-ups of their face, for example, or pictures of their genitals). Although 'requesting a key' involves only clicking an icon on the toolbar, it usually requires some kind of interactional history; most users will not comply with requests coming from people they have not exchanged messages with.

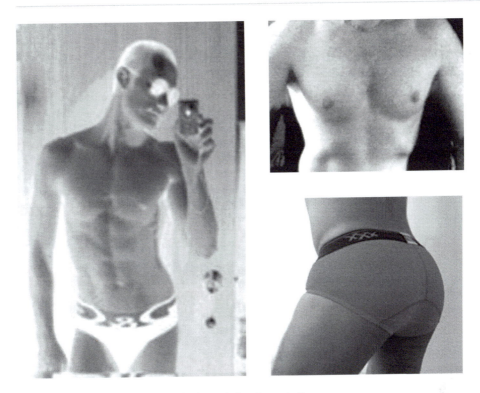

Figure 9.3 The display parts of the body posted on the website.

The images that the author posts of him or herself are not the only images available in the profile; below the thumbnail images of the author's 'album' is another row of thumbnails consisting of the images of other members of the network who have agreed to be identified as the author's 'friends'. Being someone's friend simply involves sending them an automated request to include them on one's friends list which the receiver can either approve or deny. Beyond this, 'friends' may have no other contact whatsoever. Thus, the inclusion of 'friends' in the profile is not so much a matter of friendship in a conventional sense, but more a matter of display – as with other bodily displays, bodies take on certain meanings based on the other bodies they are displayed with. In this case, one's 'friends' list expresses information not so much about one's real social relationships as about ones 'ideal' social relationships – the kinds of people one finds desirable. By inviting others to be one's 'friend', or by accepting their invitations, the displays of others become strategic ingredients in one's own display.

Text

Along with these images, authors also create a textual display of their bodies following the parameters made available at this site, and it is from these parameters that the kinds of social categories, values and orders of indexicality that govern this particular discourse community are most clearly revealed. This textual display is divided into several parts, all of which involve certain constraints upon the nature of the messages that can be included and all creating a particular kind of relationship between text and images. First, underneath the main photo, the author can include a short 'introduction'. Authors choose to use this space for a variety of functions, including providing descriptions of personal attributes (personality, profession) not evident from one's photo, providing information about the kind of interaction or the kind of person one is seeking, engaging in greetings or other phatic communication, providing slogans or mottos, and even talking about one's travel plans. Unlike one's username, one can alter the contents on one's 'Introduction' to fit one's mood or circumstances. Thus, like the MSN screen names studied by Lou (2005), these introductions are not static *sign vehicles, but rather constitute sign activities*, performances in an ongoing conversation the author engages in with other members of the community.

In addition to the introduction, the profile includes a long 'resume' of facts and figures about the author divided into four parts: 'Basics' (10), 'What you See' (11), 'What you Don't' (12), and 'Interests' (13). The information given here serves to supplement, amplify, anchor and constrain the information 'given off' by the images one includes, just as the images serve to verify claims made in the textual part of the profile. The most important thing about this information, however, is the way it anchors and constrains the kinds of selves which this site of display makes possible. Unlike the 'Introduction' discussed above, authors do not have the freedom to include any information they want in this section, but rather are limited to a fixed set of categories upon which to comment and a fixed set of identity labels to choose within these categories. The categories and the choices within them are a reflection of the 'orders of indexicality' of this community, the kinds of allowable, recognizable selves that make it up, and the values and expectations that have grown up around the social practice for which the site is used. By including ethnicity, height, weight and age under the heading 'Basics', for example, the site reinforces a view of the self based on certain aspects of physical appearance (rather than other traits like intelligence, wealth, kinship ties, religion) and reflects and facilitates the social goals associated with the site. This emphasis is also seen in other domains where gay men meet to seek sexual partners such as chat rooms, where such information (specifically age, height and weight), commonly referred to as one's 'stats', is usually exchanged at the outset of interactions (R. Jones, 2005).

The choices that appear under each category constrain users in terms of the kinds of traits they can claim: for 'build', for instance, one can be 'average', 'chubby', 'curvy', 'large/solid', 'lean/toned', 'muscular', 'overweight', 'slim' or 'voluptuous'. Descriptors for 'look' include 'alternative', 'casual', 'drag', 'formal', 'leather', 'military' and 'punk'. These pre-determined identity labels do not only serve to describe physical and personality traits, but also provide a taxonomy of recognizable social 'types' in this community. This taxonomy of social types functions as both framework through which authors describe themselves and though which they interact with and interpret the displays of others, using the identity cues provided, for instance, as a means to search through and filter potential friends and partners.

What is 'displayed' at this site, then, is not just the individual body but the community's norms about what kind of bodies one can have and what kind of values and expectations about behavior go with these bodies, including what kinds of social resources these bodies are expected to have at their disposal.

Interactivity

What is perhaps most important about this site of display from the point of view of users, and what distinguishes it from similar genres rendered through old media (such as newspaper or magazine personal advertisements – Jones, 2000) is the degree of interactivity the site affords, providing multiple ways for 'watchers' not just to interact with the author of the profile, but to interact with the profile itself in ways that alter the display. These various forms of interaction are managed though a toolbar which appears underneath the main picture in every profile (Figure 9.4). The most direct way for a watcher to interact with the display is to send a verbal

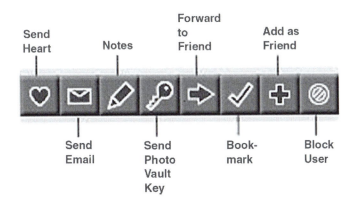

Figure 9.4 The 'hearts' toolbar of Fridae.com.

message to the author, not so different from replying by letter to a personal ad in the newspaper (only faster). Other ways more particular to this medium include inviting them to be 'friends', granting them access to one's 'photo vault' or requesting access to theirs, 'bookmarking' them, forwarding their profiles to other people, attaching notes to their profile, and 'sending hearts'.

Far and away the most popular form of interaction on this site is the practice of 'sending hearts'. In order to send a user a 'heart', one simply clicks the heart icon in the toolbar of the target's profile. Users are regularly alerted as to who has sent them hearts with a list that includes thumbnails of senders' pictures and links to their profiles. In physical practices of 'cruising', gay men rely heavily on a language of gestures and gazes (Jones, 2002), usually avoiding verbal interaction until a certain degree of interest has been negotiated non-verbally. In asynchronous virtual environments such as this, these real-time, interactive bodily displays are unavailable. In many ways, forms of interaction such as 'sending hearts', 'inviting friends' and making one's private photos available, serve the same purpose, allowing users to avoid making the commitment to verbal interaction involved in sending a message. This function is hinted at in the site's introduction, which says:

> Shy? Don't be. Fridae Personals is one of the friendliest personals sites around. "Send a heart" is a quick and friendly way of saying "I like you, wanna chat?"

Like 'inviting friends', however, 'sending a heart' is not just an expression of interest. It is also an action which alters the display of the person to whom the heart is sent – the hearts one has received appear as tiny heart icons underneath one's picture (Figure 9.2, 15) along with a tally of the total. As stated above, the chief social goal of users of this site is to attract the attention of others. The ability the site offers to 'freeze' (Norris, 2004) the acts of attention one has received and to quantify them underlies the 'economy of attention' which dominates this practice. One of the main ways one attracts attention is to display the amount of attention one has already attracted.

Consequently, the motivation for sending hearts is not always to explicitly express interest in the target. More often than not it is to try to attract others to reciprocate, increasing the number of hearts that appear on one's own profile. Many users I interviewed send and receive hundreds of hearts a day using a function that automatically sends hearts to those who have sent them to the user. A kind of 'code of reciprocity' (R. Jones, 2005) governs the exchange of hearts. As one user put it, 'I've stopped getting so excited when people send me hearts. Most people just send hearts to whoever sends hearts to them. That's how you get more hearts'.

Conclusion: the body on-line

While the kinds of social actions users can take with this site of display in many ways echo the kinds of actions involved in more physical acts of seduction, at the same time, they also constitute new forms of social action and new ways of organizing the practice of 'cruising' which exploit the affordances of the medium.

How does the screen alter the ways men can display their bodies for the purpose of attracting sexual partners, and, in so doing, alter the practice of attracting sexual partners itself? How is the body 'different' on the screen than it is in the context of other sites of display? I propose that on the screen the body changes in three key ways: it becomes more *discursive*, more *negotiated* and more *reflexive*, and these changes in the way the body is displayed have implications for the social practice these men are performing and the social identities available to them in this practice.

What I mean by the term 'discursive' is that one of the key features of this technology is that it allows users to use graphic displays of the body in ways that we normally use written or spoken text. Features of the site that allow users to be more selective in their display than they could be in other circumstances (like bars and saunas) both in terms of what is displayed and in terms of who sees it, and features which allow them to alter the 'permissions' other users have to different parts of their display over time create more incremental displays of the body which exploit the temporal orientation towards communication usually associated with text (R. Jones, 2005; Kress and Van Leeuwen, 1996). Used strategically – this process of incrementally 'showing/concealing' is central to the nature of the social practice participants are engaging in – this practice is essentially a discursive striptease (R. Jones, 2005). This temporal orientation of the display gives to it the status of the 'yet to be' – each image offered holding out the promise of what is to come – whether it be a more revealing image or a face-to-face meeting. It could be argued that it is this characteristic of 'unfinished business' that makes these images so engaging for viewers. These bodily displays never stand still but, rather, take their meaning from an infinite stream of future engagements wherein new desires and fascinations can be produced.

When I say that the body on-line is more 'negotiated', I am referring to how the same tools through which users manage incremental displays of their bodies over time also open up more aspects of embodiment itself to choice and to negotiation between spectacle and watcher. One of the main features of this negotiation is the ability of users to materially alter the displays of others by, for example, 'sending hearts' or requesting various 'permissions'. In this regard, such sites reflect the development of new kinds of 'economies of interaction', economies in which 'attention' is the primary currency. As people increasingly live their lives in the spaces of these technological sites of display, they must master new ways of getting and giving attention and of documenting and displaying the attention they have received from others. The 'economies of interaction' that develop at these sites of display have fundamentally altered the ways we organize social interaction and the ways we interpret and value the displays of others.

Finally, what I mean when I say that the on-line body becomes more 'reflexive' refers to the fact that on sites such as these users fashion displays of their own bodies, which they can then monitor by taking on the role of spectator. The body is fashioned as a reflexive looking-glass, with agents constantly turning back upon their embodiment, acting upon, maintaining it and modifying it in various ways. As Hayles (1999: xiii) puts it, 'the overlay between … enacted and represented bodies becomes … a contingent production, mediated by a technology that has become so entwined with the production of identity that it can no longer meaningfully be separated from the human subject'.

The understanding of 'sites of display' which I have attempted to advance in this chapter goes beyond technological approaches which focus on material modes and media to see display as a form of social interaction. From this perspective, sites of display not only affect the kinds of meanings that we can make, but also the kinds of social actions we can perform and the kinds of social identities we can enact. In this regard, sites of display are sites of social and cultural reproduction at which we develop and rehearse community norms about what it means to be a displayer and what it means to be a watcher.

Suggested reading

Cranny-Francis, A. (2005) *Multimedia Texts and Contexts*, London: Sage.

Jewitt, C. (2006) *Technology, Literacy and Learning: A Multimodal Approach*, London: Routledge.

Kress, G. (2003b) *Literacy in the New Media Age*, New York: Routledge.

Kress, G. and T. Van Leeuwen (2001) *Multimodal Discourse: The Modes and Media of Contemporary Communication*, London: Edward Arnold.

Snyder, I. (1997) *From Page to Screen: Taking Literacy into the Electronic Age*, London: Routledge.

10

Multimodality and mobile culture

Kevin M. Leander and Lalitha M. Vasudevan

Introduction

While commuting by train to her part-time job and in her free moments, Rin, a high-school senior, texted a story of tragic love between two high-school friends on a mobile (cell) phone and uploaded pieces of this story to a website for aspiring authors. Her story-in-progress was read on cell phones by thousands of others and ranked highly. Approximately two years later (2006), this story, now the novel *If You*, was converted into a hardcover book, selling 400,000 copies in 2007 and ranking as the fifth-best-selling novel in Japan (Onishi, 2008).

Cell-phone novelists like Rin tend to use thin descriptions and fragmented paragraphs, relying heavily on dialogue. Writers sometimes convey feelings and tone with (image-based) emoticons. The influence of visual media is also evident on the genre in another respect: critics argue that the genre has been heavily influenced by the comic book (Onishi, 2008).

The emergence of cell-phone novels provides a vivid illustration of the relationship between multimodality and culture investigated in this chapter. The new practice appears to hybridize various modalities, including speech and writing, imaging and writing, and, in the case of the emoticon, gesture and imaging. Additionally, we might remark on the new genre as an expression of familiar Japanese cultural practices, including a propensity toward technology and texting, the expansive tradition of manga, or even the practice of minimalist description in some Japanese prose and poetry. Presently, however, we focus rather on how the illustration brings to life various forms of mobility: Rin's embodied movements across a cityscape; the movements of novel bits to a website and out again to tens of thousands of cell phones; global flows of discourses of tragic love; Rin's thumbs beating out rhythms on her keypad; the production and distribution of a hardback novel; the mobilization of information on cell-phone novels to a reporter for the *The New York Times*; our own use of this information for this chapter, and our own subsequent texting about our chapter writing. This illustration, and hundreds like it, prompt us to insert the term "mobility" between the terms "multimodality" and "culture".

How do we understand multimodality on the move, and culture(s) on the move? How might we unmoor multimodality, in the first instance, from a focus on the page (the multimodal text-as-object) and in the second instance from a focus on the "event" (the multimodal performance-fixed-as-text) to follow or trace multimodal relations as they flow and stretch across people's movements in virtual and embodied contexts? In analyzing social spaces of multimodality, how do we avoid the old problem of "taming the spatial into the textual, into representation" (Massey, 2005)? That is, in analyzing multimodality and culture on the move, how do we mobilize our own approaches to reimagine things (modes, texts, cultural artifacts) as processes?

Toward addressing these questions, in this chapter we work in two complementary directions. First, heuristically, we examine our key three-way relation in two parts, first considering culture and mobility, and then turning to multimodality and mobility. Our approach to culture will be to focus on problems of identity (or identification), as work in this area provides meaningful access into broader considerations of contemporary cultural movement. Our second move in the chapter will be to examine key examples from our own research that illustrate possibilities and conundrums for analyzing multimodality and culture as mobile social practices.

Culture and mobility

In contemporary anthropology and cultural studies it has become somewhat commonplace to think of culture as mobile rather than as fixed and easily defined with a specific locale. The image of the remote village and its exotic, isolated culture has been replaced or at least modified by the image of islanders wearing tee-shirts sporting risqué slogans in English that they do not understand (Besnier, 1995); commercial products, people, capital and media circulate at increasing speeds and with greater ease, forming unpredictable blends. Through these mobilities, identity and culture are being reconceived as traveling rather than isomorphically fixed in place (Clifford, 1992), as translocal or "glocal" rather than local (Appadurai, 1996; Yeager, 1996; Kraidy, 1999). A number of theorists (e.g., Castells *et al.*, 2007; Gupta and Ferguson, 1992) have argued, however, that in contemporary, postmodern mobilities, space and place are not irrelevant, but rather that spaces and spatial practices are fundamentally changing. These changes include the ways in which spaces have become "reterritorialized" (Gupta and Ferguson, 1992) such that our experiences of space or space–time are reordered, multiple, non-sequential, and simultaneous.

The social practices of reterritorialization would appear to be critically important for interpreting the production of identity among the "space of flows" (Castells, 2000) that is played out in a world of places (McDowell, 1997). In contrast to a "situated" view of identity, in which identities differ according to the construction of social situations, and in contrast to an abstract view of stable identities, a practice theory of identity (Bourdieu, 1977; Holland *et al.*, 1998; Holland and Lave, 2001) can trace the ways in which social spaces are knit, patched, cut up, laminated, and folded together – the practices of producing and relating more or less distant localities and temporalities.

A problem with thinking through identity and social space is that space is often metaphorically constructed as an inert and empty "container" or "field", a "coordinate system of discrete and mutually exclusive locations" (Smith and Katz, 1993). Naturalized, absolutist conceptions of space productively hide the consequences of space from us. Critiques of such an inert view of social space are given by theorists such as Lefebvre (1991) and Soja (1989), who consider how power is co-produced with space (or space–time). Operating from what we take to be a usefully abstract level of theorization, Massey (2005) describes three propositions for the study of space (assumed as "social space"): (1) space is a "product of interrelations", or constituted through interactions; (2) space brings to the fore the existence of multiplicity or "contemporaneous plurality"; and (3) space is always under construction, or "always in the process of being made" (p. 9). In approaching identity as produced through multimodal social practice, we take these propositions of space-as-process (spatialization as verb) as immanently useful for our approach to multimodality as social practice (e.g., "multimodalization").

Multimodality and mobility

In recent years, we have witnessed not only the rapid growth of new kinds of multimodal texts but also of new kinds of communicative practices as everyday technologies become increasingly mobile and enabled with multimodal capabilities. Mobility affects daily multi-modal engagements – being in possession of a device with the ability to capture audio may initiate the recording of otherwise undocumented moments or inspire spontaneous spoken performances primarily for the purposes of digital archiving. The layered and multiple qual-ities of new texts is readily evident in various media spaces – profiles on social networking sites, user-designed cell-phone ring tones, and YouTube video productions, to name just a few. Each is reflective of how not only are content and text format changing but so, too, are the practices of cultural production through which texts are produced, interpreted, and shared.

New technologies and new media are helping to shape new multimodal social practices that are quickly becoming part of the commonsense fabric of everyday life. For instance, it is currently very common for people to organize social encounters with mobile phones while they are walking or driving, a practice some term "rendezvousing" (Castells *et al.*, 2007). In such practices, people are interpreting and producing their (multimodal) built environments, physical paths, voice or text messages, and perhaps Internet or geographic information system (GIS) information from cell phones. At the same time, while mobile phones afford such mobility, it is critically important not to mistake such technical affordances with actual human practices. The actual uses of mobile phones and other technologies are often highly unpredictable from an "affordance" perspective; technological (and multimodal) forms and social practices are co-constituted (Ito *et al.*, 2005). For instance, in the case of the mobile phone it appears that users in at least some countries are increasingly calling from fixed places (e.g., home or work) (Fortunati, 2005), such that mobile phone use and physical mobility cannot be easily correlated. Further complicating the picture, mobile phones are increasingly offering more forms of global connection through Internet services, supporting possibilities for ubiquitous virtual mobility (Castells *et al.*, 2007).

Multimodality offers a framework for understanding culture and cultural production by attending to the modes and modalities that are engaged at any given moment or within a particular artifact or text. Such a focus implies multiple layers of social practice, for which Kress and Van Leeuwen (2001) suggest a framework that relates four domains or "strada": discourse, design, production, and distribution. In this perspective, everything from creating highly original architectural plans to faithfully recording a musical concert participates in the production of meaning. Semiotic practices relate, organize and separate these strada in different ways; the point is not to pigeonhole particular practices in different strada, but rather to consider how different forms of articulation construct social relations through semiotic practices. Moreover, as new semiotic practices emerge (e.g., downloading music), we would expect to see new forms of articulation and therefore further stratification and emergent forms of social organization.

As Hull and Nelson (2005: 225) suggest, "multimodality can afford not just a new way to make meaning, but a different kind of meaning". These "different kind(s) of meanings" are amplified in the current social context when mobility has become a hallmark of newly developing technologies.

Newly popular communicative forms, such as mobile text messaging and video blogging, promote the hybridization of modes and illustrate the movement of texts across space and time. Additionally, as multimodality occurs within mobile spaces, the production of texts involves multiple actors. Such a participatory culture (Jenkins, 2006) is reflective of the affordances of mobile means of production that allow for emergent forms of participatory composition and culture making.

For instance, a deejay accesses multiple sources of music to produce something new – a cacophonous clash of sounds, a mellifluous union of beats and melody, or a purposeful juxta-position of particular phrases from well-known speeches (Gustavson, 2008). Gil, a youth whose turntablism Gustavson (2008: 96) explores, was engaged in "the act of sampling ... [which] was not simply [an act] of indiscriminately dropping the needle. ... [H]e knew [the speeches] inside and out". Ito (2003) describes similar remixing practices surrounding the *Yugioh* comic series, wherein the semiotic marker is interpreted, repackaged, and distributed across media for mul-tiple purposes, and through the participation of multiple publics. Simply put, remixing helps "cultural bits move around more easily" (Manovich, 2005), and technologies, with their port-ability and constant culture transmission, function as "representations of existing cultural forms and media" (Voithofer, 2005: 8).

The affordances of mobile technologies are generative of mobile, multimodal cultural pro-ductions. While each modal affordance "invariably depend(s) on how the mode and the mean-ings expressed through it exist in interdiscursive relationships with other co-present modes and meanings" (R. Jones, 2005: 70), the ability to *move with* modalities presents yet another dimen-sion of modal affordance. We are therefore concerned with not only *how* multimodality occurs and shapes cultural production, but also *when* and *where*. In other terms, we seek to consider the multimodal production of culture as characterized by changing dynamics of space and time, dynamics that are changing the meanings and effects of cultural production and distribution. Mobility, our third term introduced into the dialectic of multimodality and culture, signals for us not just "movement" but an attention to the particulars of how modes are spatially and tem-porally organized in changing productions of culture.

Illustrations of spatial relations among modes in cultural practice

Consider, for example, the everyday (yet recently developing) activities of using a global positioning system (GPS) device while driving. We might say that the GPS representation is "situated" at a particular point in space and time, and we might focus on the immediate surround of the semiotic and material environment in order to understand the representa-tion as multimodal practice or a multimodal text. From this local, place-based perspective, our interpretation of the text or practice might focus on the inter-relations of semiotic resources, including modes. Alternatively, we might step "outward" from this particular locale to consider how our focal event is shot through with discourses, texts, modes and practices that stream into and out of it from elsewhere (Scollon and Scollon, 2003). In this case, mul-tiple satellites carry the technical load of this streaming activity, but we might also consider how multinational corporations, programmers' choices of landscape and city features to include or leave out, and historical decisions about map scale and other elements function as discourses that shape the multimodal texts on the screen; the GPS display is a node in a network of multiple social activities and relations (Kostogriz, 2006). We discuss this shift from a situated perspective to a networked perspective (Leander and Lovvorn, 2006) in our first extended illustration below. This illustration traces how popular cultural texts with broad or relatively global circulations are localized in specific interactions, and how these global–local connections serve in the production of identity artifacts. We are particularly concerned with how two interactants (in this case, youths instant messaging (IMing) one another) use print in relation to images in what we consider to be "localizing moves" (Brandt and Clinton, 2002). We discuss how the meanings and effects of widely circulating images, for identity work, are stitched together through print exchanges. This illustration highlights that what we mean by appropriation or personalization of culture for practices of identity work is often achieved through multimodal engagement and hybridization.

However, in the case of identity and multimodality, we might complicate the relations of place and space still further. While the networked perspective unbrackets the situation or locale, showing how this assumed boundary is permeable, the GPS device itself, and its dynamic sets of streaming representations (the roadway, the landscape), is itself constantly on the move, continually "resituated" in relation to an ever-changing material and semiotic surround. (Of course, it is precisely the ability of the device to be resituated that gives it everyday value in the first place – very few would buy a GPS device that came with a floor anchor kit.) This case and many others like it make evident how being in space is not merely to be situated somewhere, but to participate in "distinct cultural-semiotic activities anchored to, and mediated by, particular material objects and textual representations of one's situationality" (Kostogriz, 2006). In addition to unbracketing the situation through a net-worked perspective, we describe such cases through a multispatial perspective. Multiple and dynamic spatiality allows us to consider how social spaces cannot be defined as static products, but are always in the process of being made; space in this sense is "the dimension of multiple trajectories" or a "simultaneity of stories-so-far" (Massey, 2005). Our second illustration, for instance, draws on a case of online gaming to consider how positions within the world and perspectives on the world are not merely "givens", but are rather worked out as achievements between social spaces. In particular, practices and identities are worked out across embodied and represented (e.g., mapped) social spaces, each with their own modal affordances, perspectives, and represented scales of social life. In our third illustration, we look more deeply at the relations among multiple social spaces by considering how new media productions of identity travel, with mobile production technologies, across the lived scenes of social life. In this case, a youth moving various geographic and social spaces casts and recasts his identity with new media productions, productions that rewrite and modally reconfigure his experiences of the everyday. Moreover, in these multimodal recastings of identity, the youth also positions himself as a storyteller, producer, and director of his own identities.

Localization of global texts: identity artifact production (remixing) and distribution

People use artifacts of all sorts in the cultural production of identities, including artifacts of different modalities. In this illustration we are concerned with how social practices of the production and distribution of (popular) cultural texts function as practices of social identi-fication. Here, we examine how a series of images and print exchanges in an instant message session distribute and, as a form of identity production, remix images and words. The follow-ing interaction is between Sophia ("Joellover"), a 13-year-old adolescent and fan of the punk band Good Charlotte, and her online friend "BenjiTrippin". While Sophia was involved in a number of online activities related to Good Charlotte fandom, including building a fan web-site (Leander and Frank, 2006), the following illustration particularly highlights how social spaces of identification are dynamically produced, interactionally, by (re)distributing broadly circulating cultural texts and remixing them across modalities.

At the outset of the IM session, after writing, "hey", BenjiTrippin (hereafter, "BT") sent a picture, without any accompanying written text. The picture was of one of the Good Charlotte band members licking the microphone. BT then sent two more pictures, of Joel and Benji (twin-brother members of Good Charlotte), adding quick comments of appreciation and sexual innuendo. Sophia, using a screen name that suggested her close relationship to Joel, then inquired, "Where did you get these?" and commented, "Awwww". BT replied that she couldn't remember which websites the images came from, and Sophia responded with a black-and-white drawing of a woman from what appeared to be the 1920s. Overlaying the picture was the expression, "How to be gangsta", with a numbered list of steps accompanying it. To this, BT IMed a picture of Joel in a room with candles, along with another suggestive comment. Sophia replied, "haha yup" and "very sex god".

The "image dialogue" briefly summarized above illustrates the importance of images as a communicative medium. If we record the type of texts transmitted between BT and Sophia over most of this exchange, we have the following pattern (I = image, V = verbal, I/V = image/verbal hybrid): V–I–V–I–I–V–V–I/V–I–V–V–V–I–V–V–V–I–I–V–I–I–V–I–I–V–I–V–V–I/V–I–V/V–I–I–V–V–I–I–I–V–V–V–I–V–I–I–I–V–I–I/V–I–I/V–V–V–I/V. In this sequence, 29 of 53 texts are either images or image/verbal hybrids. There was not a regular pattern, say, of verbal commentary on every image, as images were sometimes offered three or four in sequence. However, the image dialogue, once underway, did seem to be structured with an expectation of trading images for mutual pleasure – that the unspoken rules for participating involved offering up one's "own" images.

There was not a regularly patterned sense in this image dialogue that a verbal comment needed to follow each picture either from the sender or receiver; while this happened on some occasions it did not on others and pictures simply followed each other in sequence. At the same time, there did appear to be a social pattern that the two took rotating positions on being the primary image sender and BT first and then Sophia, and that the dialogue was pre-packaged with the expectation of an affective response. For example, after receiving the first three photographs from BT, Sophia responded first with a question about the distribution of the images ("where did you get these?") and secondly an evaluation ("awwww"). After BT noted that she couldn't recall her source, Sophia evaluated once again ("awwww, these are cute").

Interpreted as isolated texts, any of the images exchanged might be simply seen as a passed-along copy of a production created elsewhere. Yet, considered in the rapid flow of the interaction, the meanings and effects of the images were multimodally configured with the linguistic responses around them in a form of identity work. While emphasizing just how much of this interaction was carried out through the exchange of images, we also stress how these image meanings and effects are already hybridized with linguistic texts in the flow of interaction. Most of the talk involved brief affective evaluations of the images (e.g., "awwww"), which primarily constructed the image sharing session as one of mutual affective agreement and affinity building. Additionally, by lacing the interaction with romantic and sexual innuendo the two girls appropriated the image/words as resources for constituting identifications with individual band members and the entire band.

In the midst of this interaction, Sophia sent BT a picture of Joel holding a microphone and apparently leaning over to kiss a puppy that was sitting on top of (band member) Benji's shoulder (Figure 10.1). Immediately after the picture loaded up in the IM session, a layer loaded over it with the words "wish i was" in white bubble letters (Figure 10.2). (Note: "In that pic", and "i made that" refer to a second ongoing thread of the interaction.) The "wish i was" covered over the top part of the photo, making visible only the trunk of Joel's body and his arms, and masking the puppy. BT responded to the mix of the photo and words with "wish i was what?" to which Sophia responded "lulu". Shortly following, Sophia clarified, "lulu is the puppy on Benji". This writing of a caption, laminated over the photo, is clearly a more technically complex multimodal relation than it would have been

Figure 10.1 Picture sent by Sophia of Joel holding a microphone and apparently leaning over to kiss a puppy that was sitting on top of (band member) Benji's shoulder.

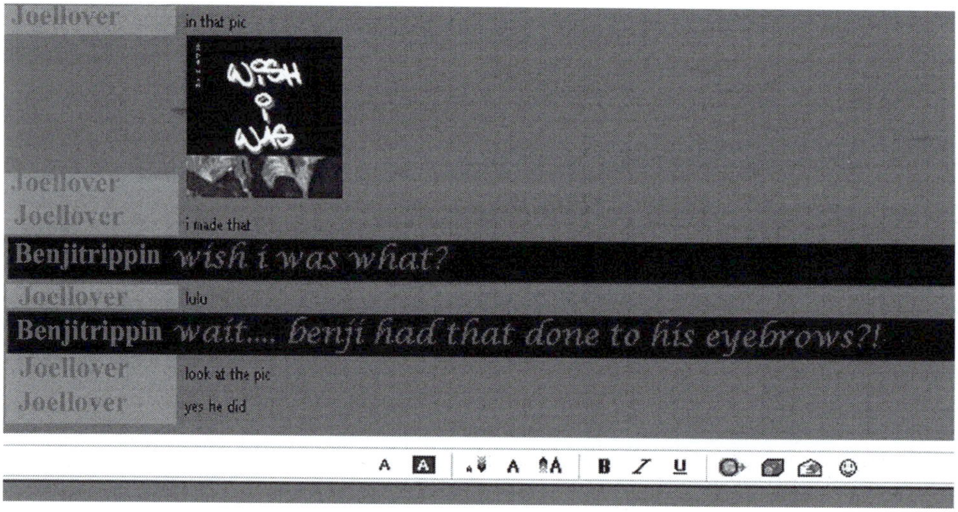

Figure 10.2 The layer loaded with the words "wish i was" in white bubble letters.

for Sophia to simply IM "wish I was Lulu" following sending the unaltered photo (Figure 10.1). Her deliberate hybridization in this case appears to index an even more deliberate attempt to appropriate and personalize the photo – to materially position herself within it by pasting her own words in the visual field of Joel's gaze.

Positionality and multiple social spaces: navigating identities with maps and (virtual) bodies

Maps have a long history of establishing cultural norms and perspectives, of providing a sense of the boundedness or openness of national and regional identities, and of serving to create the distant or exotic Other (Said, 1985). Maps are contested cultural artifacts, as is evidenced, for example, in the creation and interpretation of maps representing national and global forms of identification (Schulten, 2001). As maps become increasingly ubiquitous, dynamic, and digitally mediated, contemporary life complicates and exacerbates the role of maps in everyday thinking (Liben, 2003; National Research Council, 2006). Location-aware technologies (e.g., GPS handheld devices) are becoming embedded into a host of everyday uses (e.g, driving automobiles); television newscasts increasingly rely on GIS-enabled software to "move us into the action", and elementary-school students are trained to see the world from 3,000 feet overhead on Google Earth. One recent survey in the United States indicated that consumers favor GPS on mobile phones even above Internet access (Campbell, 2007). While there is speculation about how these new technologies and practices are changing the way we understand the world (Uttal, 2000), there is little research in this area. What do these new practices suggest concerning mobility and mulimodality?

In the following illustration we consider how mapped (represented) and embodied spaces are coordinated and circulate in relation to one another in one form of everyday cultural activity – online gaming. While online games and their virtual experiences of embodiment may be thought of as distinctive forms of multimodal practice, we suggest rather that they are merely one means of highlighting how individuals, with and without avatars, are relating multiple embodied and represented social spaces in everyday life. In this regard, our current analytic challenge is extending beyond the analysis of different perspectives or positions of the viewer with respect to the same image (Kress and Van Leeuwen, 1996) and instead involves the articulation of multiple embodied and represented spaces, often created at radically different scales.

Brian, a 13-year-old youth, expressed that his exploration of territory in the online game *Star Wars Galaxies* (LucasArts and Sony Online Entertainment, 2003) was motivated by his desire to find a location for a virtual house he wanted to have built. Although Brian was very experienced with role-player games, during this first episode of playing *SWG*, he seemed somewhat disoriented in navigating the vast terrain of the game. Drawing upon heterogeneous space–time representations, Brian's eventual successful and strategic navigation of Naboo (a planet) was a result of frequent and rapid circulations across the territory and readily available maps of Naboo. Such maps, which could be scaled at different levels, were directly pasted over Brian's embodied (avatar) perspective of the world (Figure 10.3).

Thus, as he explored Naboo, Brian continually switched between two primary perspectives: an overhead map, on the one hand, and that of his avatar's body traversing Naboo's landscape, on the other. As he began his exploration, Brian related that the map did not provide him an adequate understanding about the islands on the planet, so he needed to also be on them, to experience them in a (virtually) embodied manner, which included finding out who the "creatures" and enemies were on the planet. In the first 19 minutes of his journey, Brian circulated between a hypermediated (global) (Figure 10.3) and a transparent immediate (local) (Figure 10.4) perspective 20 times, sometimes looking at the map for nearly a minute, while other times just briefly checking something on it. This perspective switching on *SWG* is called "cycling", and is accomplished with a single keystroke.

In addition to cycling between global and local spaces, Brian also used the computer cursor as a surrogate "body", passing it over the surface of the (global) map to consider distances and relations between various locations. His hand-mouse-cursor-map tracings enabled him to dynamically engage with the map and not merely observe it a distance, hybridizing Brian's map reading and embodied activity. Further, Brian would dynamically zoom in on a particular area of the map, shaping and scaling the map to more directly correspond to his embodied positions.

159

Figure 10.3 A readily available map of Naboo which could be scaled at different levels, and directly pasted over Brian's embodied (avatar) perspective of the world.

Figure 10.4 A transparent immediate or local perspective on the map.

An even more important example of map/embodied territory hybridity – the near complete blending of two social spaces – was Brian's use of "waypoints" in navigating. From the perspective of the map, waypoints appear as triangular flags that are set by the player on the map as desired destinations, in this example marking three specific islands (Figure 10.3). In reading the map, then, Brian could compare his current location (evident as a stylized X just above the rightmost way-point) with his desired future locations indicated by the waypoints (Figure 10.3). More importantly, from the perspective of embodied play, waypoints are translated as dynamic arrows that appear in the embodied space on the screen, at about head-height with respect to the character, and tell the player which direction to move the avatar in, such as depicted in this hunting scene (Figure 10.4). The directional arrows function as a type of built-in compass for the virtual body, while Brian's ability to create and destroy waypoints on the map records his history and future goals in space–time. Once set, the waypoint is a form of hybridity or "small crossing" (Berg, 1997) with big effects. This form of mobility or crossing from (virtual) embodied space to representational (mapped) space is just another expression of a similar relation between Brian's own material body and his (repre-sented) avatar, where the avatar is another small yet significant crossing for multimodal analysis. In the interpretation of identity practices, questions of location and position thus become meaningful through the articulation not only of multiple modalities but also of multimodal spaces.

Mobile technologies, mobile production practices, and meaning-making in an urban landscape

Cultural narratives such as the "digital divide" and the "literacy crisis" undergird many of the policies governing institutions that urban youth negotiate, and engage the identities of urban youth as problematic and in need of remediation. The multimodal production of cultural arti-facts and texts that result from urban youths' engagement with mobile technologies affords new possibilities for how youth might be "read" and "written". Web 2.0 technologies and platforms combine with mobile technologies to facilitate new cultural practices of self-portraiture, identification, and global communication. In the following case, we focus on one youth's practices of identification as he traverses multiple spaces within urban institutions and cityscapes. We explore how his use of one particular multimodal, mobile technology, produces and transforms his cultural practices of identity-making.

Joey is a 19-year-old man who spent several years being disciplined by schools and jails, and ultimately stopped going to high school before enrolling in an Alternative to Incarceration Program (ATIP) for six months. It was here that his budding explorations into media production and tech-nology explorations flourished, both formally – while he was an intern at a media design company, and while enrolled in a digital media class – and informally – through his experimentation with personal technologies such as his cell phone and his PlayStation portable (PSP), a handheld, mobile gaming technology. Through these experiences, he had developed strong facility with video editing programs such as iMovie and Final Cut Pro, and the audio editing programs Garage Band and ProTools. His media production and distribution practices resonate with the growing youth media movement (e.g., Soep, 2006), as evidenced by the rapidly expanding independent, youth, and DIY media distribution outlets (e.g., ListenUp!, Street Level Youth Media, Youth Radio).

Joey's growing multimedia savvy was evident in the ways he used his PSP for documentary pur-poses, using the camera attachment that he had bought "from some guy on the street". Joey's fingers flicked and clicked rapidly for several seconds as he navigated through layers of menus and options; his actions resembled gaming maneuvers, and his use of them, while he engaged in visual documen-tation and distribution, further blurred the boundaries between his consumer and producer identities in relation to this technology. The image, video, and audio files Joey created underwent constant manipulation as he sought out and explored various editing programs to install and use on his PSP, and the editing functionalities they afforded. Likewise, the constant availability of these media production features, in the form of a modified (and modifiable) handheld gaming console inspired the documentation and subsequent cultural text production that would not have occurred otherwise. Consider the following textual chain of production, in which a spontaneous use of the camera attachment on his PSP led Joey to compose a series of new texts.

Among Joey's favorite subjects to document were his friends, with whom he spent time hanging out as well as developing his media production skills. One series of video clips showed him and his two friends taking turns in front of the camera lens, engaged in various dance-like movements. In one clip, Joey is dancing at the center of the screen and one friend stands behind him and laughs in response to Joey's antics. In other clips, a second friend performs his own series of dance moves in front of the camera. His face is intense and focused as he leaps and contorts his body across the lobby. A screening of these clips led to a discussion of the other new PSP camera features with which Joey had been experimenting, such as a PSP-based image-editing program, with which he had manipulated a series of images and videos using the effects program, many of which depict him or his friends in a variety of settings across the city. He used one of these manipulated images as a screen saver for his PSP.

The images and video clips Joey created, as well as the new documentary and editing processes that these artifacts initiated, traveled beyond the 480 × 272 pixel high-resolution screen of his PSP. Using flash memory cards and USB cables, Joey uploaded these texts to his Myspace profile, one space of many where he regularly changes his display photo, display name, and status in order to actively and multimodally recast how he desires to be read by his audience. Joey uploaded some of the self-portraits and portraits of friends to a computer workstation at a local university where he is a part of a research project. Many of the multimodal texts that Joey used for subsequent multimedia narratives originated with his use of the PSP camera attachment: a love letter "written" using iMovie, a reflection on his experience with the US National Guard, and a story of his educational journey that included steps he was taking to enroll at a four-year college. Each of these narratives brought together digital photos, popular music, and musical tracks created using sound editing programs, all of which Joey had downloaded onto his PSP. By producing texts that initiate interactions and ways of being for which the script has not yet been solidified in the broader social conscience, Joey helps to complicate the cultural narratives about and urban youth technology practices, and urban youth identities more broadly.

Thus, seemingly isolated clicks of a handheld gaming console signify a much larger narrative about the use of mobile technologies in creating cultural texts that resist and rescript existing narratives. Like Joey, young people growing up in our cities are having their daily cultural practices transformed with the growing availability of mobile technologies with documentary capabilities. Cell phones that take pictures and video and play games, mp3 players that record audio, and gaming devices that double as communication devices and cameras influence who and how young people are across multiple spaces. Joey's use of the PSP reveals the movement that mobile technologies afford for the cultural production of identity across multiple space–times. Joey's identity is made and remade through each of his modal engagements with the PSP and the subsequent artifacts that result (Figure 10.5); his identity-making is spatialized across modalities and locations, and his identity work is reflected in the texts he produces and new practices in which he engages. His practices of documentation, design, and distribution originate with his handheld video game console, which has been repurposed through his use and the device's affordances. Likewise, Joey's engagement with the PSP allows him to be a documenter, designer, and distributor.

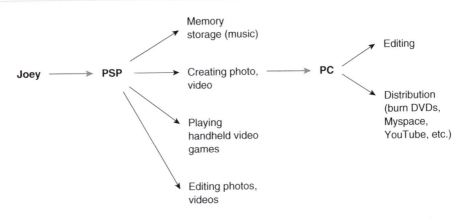

Figure 10.5 A diagrammatic representation of Joey's modal engagements with the PSP and the subsequent artifacts that result.

Discussion

In our introduction to this chapter we argued for an expansive study of multimodality and culture that moved beyond the text or "page" as the object of analysis, and beyond the spatio-temporally bracketed performance, to considering how multimodal texts and practices are mobile and constituted across social spaces. We have argued, more or less implicitly, that such an approach to multimodality resonates with current approaches to the study of identity. However, even as Lewis (2008) argues in her review of identity research in literacy, each approach or "wave" of theory has its own limitations and possibilities. For example, others (Rowsell and Pahl, 2007) have used social practice theories of identity, and especially the work of Bourdieu (1977, 1990) to consider how identities become "sedimented" into multimodal texts, over time, which then contribute to constituting the habitus (which in turn structures social practices and texts). The emphasis in this work on the co-articulation of social structure with individual history offers a lens from which to consider social reproduction, and, importantly, how texts function materially and multimodally to constitute identities over time. Temporally speaking, such an approach favors the historical accumulation of the person; relations of power and text flow "backward" in time, as it were, toward the (re)constitution of the individual and the (re)accumulation of social practice. Conversely, we have attempted to push the flow of power and text forward in time, opening up qualities of social space to "freedom, dislocation, and surprise" (Massey, 2005). Such an approach is also open to critiques of underestimating the forces of history or becoming naively optimistic concerning the possibilities of individuals in social and cultural worlds. We take from such critiques the need to continue to work out method, the notion that every theoretical position (e.g., toward history or the future) is itself a constitution of social space, and therefore ideological, and finally, the importance of continuing to apply new methods to new forms of social life, such that any theory of multimodality and culture will conceive of culture as ever-changing.

In order to study culture as living and dynamic, we have argued for a conception of social space that does not mistake social space with frozen activity or with the "flattening out of all relations in the moment" (Massey, 2005). For, ultimately, such approaches to interpreting culture as frozen representations rather than living spaces – tempting because they neatly bracket social practices – fail to capture the development of identities as a form of historical becoming, or modes as processes that are being worked out relationally. In this sense, the processes of multimodalization can be conceived as social processes of positive heterogeneity, processes that do not hold still for long, and must be considered, with long sideways glances, while on the move.

Summary

In this chapter, we have argued for unmooring or "unbracketing" current approaches to multimodality in two ways. First, our illustrations and discussion have emphasized the rapid circulation and remixing of texts of all types; Kress and Van Leeuwen's (2001) discussion of the significance of the "distribution" strada for multimodality seems increasingly relevant as mobile technologies and practices proliferate. With respect to practices of identity, we posit an examination of not only of multimedia blends, but also of the networks and nodes through which such blends are fashioned, and of processes such as "localization" that describe particular uses of globally circulating resources. Second, pushing still further away from a focus on the static page or screen, we have unbracketed the multimodal event to consider how people producing and interpreting multimedia texts are increasingly unlike academics, seated behind computer screens in office buildings. Rather, digital flows of multimedia are interpreted in the stream of moving bodies, technologies, landscapes, and events. In these cases, multimedia distribution itself is not a separate "strada" from interpretation or production; rather, distribution-like flows actively and dynamically shape mobile media use.

Further reading

Appadurai, A. (1996) *Modernity at Large: Cultural Dimensions of Globalization*, Minneapolis, MN: University of Minnesota Press.
(Now "classic" text globalization that provides a powerful means of thinking of different "flows" through the development of theory and intriguing illustrations.)
Hill, M.L. and Vasudevan, L. (eds.) (2008) *Media, Learning, and Sites of Possibility*, New York: Peter Lang.
(This volume provides new insights into the relationships between youth, pedagogy, and media, and surveys a variety of learning environments, methodological approaches, and forms of media engagement.)
Jenkins, H. (2006b) *Confronting the Challenges of Participatory Culture: Media Education for the 21st Century*, Chicago, IL: The MacArthur Foundation.
(A report that highlights the emerging participatory culture among media-savvy youth. In doing so, the report shifts the focus away from questions of technological access toward explorations of participation across digital spaces.)
Leander, K. and Sheehy, M. (eds.) (2004) *Spatializing Literacy Research and Practice*, New York: Peter Lang.
(An edited collection of empirical and theoretical work that considers how spatial theory from different traditions can be productively used to reconceptualize texts and textual practices.)
Maira, S. and Soep, E. (eds.) (2004) *Youthscapes: The Popular, the National, the Global*, Philadelphia: University of Pennsylvania Press.
(A collection of essays that investigates theories of globalization, nationalism, and citizenship by focusing on the experiences of youth and tracing youths' movements across myriad spaces within increasingly global forces.)

11

Multimodality, identity, and time

Jay Lemke

Introduction

In this chapter we will explore first the most basic issues of how media produce meaning effects across multiple timescales, and how to analyze these processes. We will consider the case of computer and video games, the most advanced forms of consumer multimedia, which are typically experienced over times as long as fifty or more hours in-game, and over periods of weeks or months. We will then consider what happens when games, films, books, and other media and merchandise are linked in *transmedia* franchises, where meaning effects are integrated by consumers across multiple media, on even longer timescales. Finally, I will identify some conceptual tools for analyzing the ways in which identity development depends on both media and peer communities organized around media, which shape our selection and experience of them, over shorter to longer timescales.

In reviewing these perspectives, I will argue that we need to extend the usual repertory of analytical tools for critical multimedia analysis from those which look at single works to those which look across transmedia clusters, and from those which focus on the formal features of the media themselves, to ones which place the experience of media within a political economy and a cultural ecology of identities, markets, and values. Throughout, we will consider how an experiential, and more generally a phenomenological, approach to multimodal analysis is a necessary (and too often neglected) complement to our much better-developed semiotic approaches.

Multimodality and time

Our semiotic traditions for the analysis of multimedia (by which I mean here multimodal media) are primarily formal. We seek to identify the formal features presented by a work that are salient for the reader/viewer/listener/user (hereafter user) in the construal of a more specific and definite meaning (which may be called the interpretation or the meaning-text) from a less definite 'meaning potential', i.e. the range of possible meanings offered by those formal features (collectively, the object-text). We then typically look for co-determinants of the meaning-text: co-texts, intertexts, situation-dependent typical meanings and patterns (e.g. genres, registers, deictic referents), and culturally typical meaning patterns of all sorts (indexical meanings, cultural narratives, stylistic trends, etc.). Attention to intertexts and culture takes us then to biographical histories of users (what intertexts we have encountered, what interpretive dispositions we have formed) and to the cultural norms and conventions for the production, interpretation, and institutional use of works of a given type, as well as the cultural classification of recognized types.

In such a model, meaning-making is essentially selective contextualization (Lemke, 1990b, 1995). Which contexts, intertexts, and cultural patterns co-determine the construal of meaning and when (i.e. under what circumstances or conditions)? In the last 20 years or so we have taken our models for the analysis of linguistic text (Halliday, 1994; Martin, 1992), abstracted the relevant semiotic principles (Lemke, 1998b), and applied them to other media such as images, architecture, and music (Kress and Van Leeuwen, 1996; O'Toole, 1994; Van Leeuwen, 1999). In the course of doing so, we have recognized that all texts or works, because they are material artifacts, are always already multimodal (Kress and Van Leeuwen, 2001). You cannot make a material sign-vehicle that can only be construed according to one semiotic system. Writing is as much a visual semiotic as a linguistic one; speech encodes non-linguistic (and so-called paralinguistic) information about bodies, social origins, and emotional states as well as linguistically coded meanings. Face-to-face communication is a tightly coupled mix of gesture, posture, movement, and speech. A painting that contains no words nevertheless gets interpreted in part through our categories of verbal semantics, and so do gestures and postures, insofar as they are salient and significant for us.

Phenomenologically, however, in relation to our actual experience with media, we ought to question whether the division of meaning-making into language, gesture, drawing, action, etc. is not mostly artificial, an artifact of the idealizations we make in analyzing the semiotic potential of different aspects or moments of what are in fact more nearly seamless and unitary phenomena. Semiotically, we can attempt to recoup what is lost with such (analytically useful) separations by looking at how these different aspects of meaning-making interact or integrate with one another. When we analyze a political cartoon, we may only laugh, only get the point, when we see both the image and the caption. It is their joint meaning, our joint construal of meaning according to two semiotic codes (one mostly visual, one mostly linguistic) which produces the actual meaning-as-experienced.

I review this tradition, to which I have myself contributed and which I use regularly, in order to move on from it here somewhat. A phenomenological perspective, which I believe necessarily complements a semiotic one, reminds us of the importance of time, pacing, feeling, affect, and embodiment, all of which are matters that can be construed semiotically, but which seem to elude being completely accounted for in formal, categorial terms. Phenomenology asks us to set aside categorizations which have become naturalized for us through history and culture and attempt to recoup the experiential feelings and nominally subjective (though not necessarily merely individual) aspects of what it means to act and be in time and with the world. Variations on this philosophical project have been described by Husserl, Heidegger, Merleau-Ponty, Bergson, and more recently in relation to media analysis by Deleuze (1983, 1989). It is perhaps best known in discourse theory through the work of the Conversation Analysis (CA) school (e.g. Schegloff, 2006), which has a multimodal extension in Goodwin (2002).

I have proposed elsewhere that semiotics itself is somewhat deficient (at least as we use it today, though perhaps not in Peirce's original conception, which is more general than Saussure's *semiologie*) insofar as we analyze meaning as dependent on *valeur*, on values assigned to construing a sign as being of one type *vs.* another type (e.g. singular *vs.* plural, present *vs.* past, /a/ *vs.* /o/, first person *vs.* second person, declarative *vs.* interrogative, etc.). There *are* other kinds of meaning: the continuous variation in spatial distribution that gives rise to irregular, verbally mostly indescribable shapes (irregular curves, cloud-shapes); the mathematics of the real (i.e. infinite decimal) numbers; indeed all meanings-by-degree as opposed to meanings-by-kind. Natural science and much early mathematics arose in the effort to create a semiotics of continuous variation. Both signifiers and signifieds may be either categorial (discrete, digital) or metric (continuous, analogue).

This is an important perspective for the analysis of multimodality. Every verbal color-term is either one or another discrete element in a finite system, but every actual color belongs to a continuum (several continua in fact) of hue, saturation, and intensity (at least). Color terms can mimic with iterations (e.g. greenish blue-green) what is basically not a discrete system of meaningful differences at all: between any two colors, there are an infinity of variations, each differing by as little as one wishes from the next. Between any two shapes, likewise. So also for degrees of light and dark, or for textures. So what happens when discrete linguistic text meets continuous visual imagery? Quite a bit, which I will not elaborate on here, but see Lemke (1998b, 2002a).

I raise these phenomenological issues as a way into some other dimensions of multimodality, beyond even the metric meanings-by-degree of the visual semiotic system. Other phenomenological qualia of multimedia as experienced works – time and pacing, space and place, affect and emotion, felt movement and participatory action – are also at least potentially, and often actually, metrically meaningful-by-degree, and so never reducible to their nearest verbal descriptions, nor consequently analyzable simply by the techniques we have developed for categorial semiotic analysis.

Let me focus this project more exactly by raising some questions about time and multimodal media. Does it matter to the experience of a text in what order we read it? Our categorial model here can give us an answer: yes, because there will be different experienced syntagms. But does it also matter how fast or how slow we read it? Does it matter how many hours or days we spend over the course of reading it, putting it aside and picking it up again? Does it matter how many times we read it? Does it matter to what the text means to us that we had to decipher it, or translate it, or struggle to understand it, and that this took a very long time? Or alternatively that we breezed through it with scarcely any perceived effort at understanding it? Similar issues are raised by Roland Barthes concerning 'readerly' *vs.* 'writerly' texts, and more generally in his phenomenological projects regarding *jouissance* and the 'grain of the voice' (Barthes, 1977a).

Consider the difference between reading a short text (a page or two) *vs.* a very long one (thousands of pages). Consider the difference between savoring a lyric poem one word or phrase at a time, read over and over again, *vs.* a quick first read-through. Both total time and pacing matter. Think about the political cartoon again. How often do we return to it? How long do we linger over it? Do we linger more over its caption text or over its drawn image? How does the relative pacing and duration of our encounter(s) with each of these components matter to our experience of the text and its ultimate meaning for us?

Take the case of the sound-film, where the film is projected outside our control and we encounter the images and the sounds in synchronization. Our attention may shift from one channel to the other, and repeated viewings may allow us to accumulate other attentional trajectories of viewing/hearing this film, but all such experiences are different from having the film on a VCR or DVD player and being able to play and replay segments, to speed up and slow down while viewing, to rewind and fast-forward. We gain the capacity to play with time. These technologies form a different medium with different affordances, and temporality shifts from a feature mainly in the control of the producers of the work to one jointly in their control and in ours. Our experience and the meanings we make over time with a work depend critically on the temporal dimensions of our experience of the work (cf. Deleuze, 1989).

Natural science, which has much more practice with such issues, has long ago found that even while time is essentially a continuum, most material processes, including our human physiological processes, effectively segment it into ranges known by the mathematical phrase 'orders of magnitude'. Each multiple of factors of ten and experiences and processes with characteristic times (durations, cycles of repetition, typical periods of constancy punctuated by radical change) of milliseconds *vs.* seconds *vs.* hours *vs.* weeks, etc. operate somewhat independently of one another (because energy or information does not get efficiently transmitted between processes that run relatively very fast compared to those that run relatively much more slowly). This leads to the useful notion of *timescales*. A process or an experience that takes minutes is very different from one that takes hours, or from one that takes weeks, or years, etc. This concept of relatively independent timescales in turn problematizes the ways in which humans do in fact integrate or cumulate meaning, experience, or identity across vastly different timescales (Lemke, 2000).

Doing so is in some sense not-natural; that is, it is far more characteristic of cultural processes to have things we do now in a relatively short period of time (move a stone) depend on much longer processes that started far in the past (building a cathedral). Our characteristic way of mediating across timescales is with semiotic artifacts (the architectural drawings and building plans for the cathedral). *In some very basic sense the use or function of every media work is not just to link a producer and a user, but to link across the timescales of production, circulation, and use.* It matters to the meanings made and the experiences had with media works what these timescales are and how they are connected or integrated (or not).

Meanings are made across time, across space, in and through matter. Experience is experience in and through time, in place and across space, in a body and in interaction with other bodies. Media-use links us into networks (Latour, 1987, 1999) that reach across processes on different timescales and normally also across places and between bodies.

Let me end this introductory discussion by considering some of the typical timescales of media use. (We might extend this also for media production and circulation.) It takes about one-half to one hour to watch an average television program, two hours to watch a commercial film, significantly longer (at least several hours) to read a typical novel. Reading the novel is usually spread out over days, maybe weeks. Not so with viewing the program or the film (even with a DVD). A typical computer game takes 20–50 hours to play through, much longer than most novels (except perhaps those serialized among many volumes). Online role-playing games have an indefinite duration for experience, hundreds or thousands of hours spread over months or years. A television series can extend itself across programs, viewed weekly, for years. Novels can be reread over a lifetime, and so now can television programs and films be viewed again over an indefinite period of time. Games can be replayed, which normally does not produce the same object-text, much less the same experience. Gameplay in online persistent worlds can be recorded and replayed *ad libitum*.

I think these examples are sufficient to raise many questions about what constitutes a 'single' multimedia work, and about how to define the timescales of use (there are several, even for a 'single work'). The new medium of computer gameplay, in which players create narratives in dialogue with both a computer program and often also with other players, raises further questions about just what our unit of analysis should be (Raessens and Goldstein, 2005). I would propose that it is the experiential, meaning-construing trajectory of the user (player) that matters to phenomenological meaning, well beyond the basic semiotic meaning potentials of the object-text (or 'work') produced by the game program's authors or developers. Generalizing from this most obvious case, I believe this experiential perspective is a reasonable one for all media.

Traversals and timescales

The notion of a user-trajectory through a work comes from the theory of hypertext, in which there are alternate possible reading pathways through the 'pages' (lexias) produced by an author (Landow, 1997). It has the advantage, in relation to all media, that it reminds us that the meaning made in experiencing a work is extended in time and is specific to the user, and not to the work alone. In a hypertext, users jump via links from one page to another. In viewing a film, our attention may wander or highlight as salient for us some, but never all, of the possible perceptions of each moment. And with DVD, we can move at will around in the work 'non-sequentially'. Indeed this is quite common when we are using the work for the *n*-th time. Likewise with a book, and for non-narrative works, we may do this even on first use.

There is perhaps a small distinction worth noting here between reading a book in its normal serial order, constructing an experience trajectory that may not notice everything we might construe from the same object-text on future readings *vs.* the case of viewing a sound-film, where often so much is happening so quickly that it is not really possible, much less normal, to attend to all the signs being presented. That is not the case with books. We can always read every word easily if we wish (unless we have the very different experience of feeling rushed by outside pressures as we read), but we cannot do so with rich, dynamic media like sound-film or complex, fast-paced computer games.

We may refer to a story in a print text as 'fast paced' relative to texts that present new events less quickly in terms of the usual rate of reading, in time, or by the count of the number of words presented before they tell of a new event or changing scene, but this is again quite different from the sense of pacing, of feeling rushed or under the pressure of time in a game, or even in a film, where the flow of events is not under our control in real time, as it is with a printed text. (For comparison, imagine a scrolling text which speeds up to an uncomfortable rate or slows down.)

In rich media we are deploying our attention as potentially salient information passes into and out of our sphere of attention, or in the trajectory metaphor, as we pass through those semiotic spaces where such information (the signs of a presented- or object-text) are available to us. We may carve out our trajectory at our own pace, or we may feel the need to keep pace with a dynamic medium.

But we are not always dealing with what is unproblematically a single medium. Simultaneous or co-presented media (image and caption in the political cartoon; film and accompanying soundtrack; sound-film with synchronized subtitle captioning) tend to count as single multi-modal genres. When the media are experienced sequentially, however, say viewing a painting and then reading the artist's account of it when we pass into the next gallery, they tend to count as separate 'texts'. We usually invoke some criteria of the intentionality of the producers regarding whether different media are 'meant' to be encountered together (serially) or not, but this is contrary to the approach we are taking here, where it is the user's experienced trajectory, not the producer's product, that provides the grounds for what is to be analyzed. (The latter enters as a condition and enabler of the former.)

In fact it is now increasingly the case that mutually relevant multimodal intertexts are experienced in a variety of different sequences by different users, across a variety of quite different media, in ways that cannot be controlled by producers, who may in fact be separate individuals or groups for the different intertextual works, and in only occasional communication with one another. There is no putative guiding intelligence across all the works aiming to coordinate them in the same way we might imagine for a composite work (say a painting and an artist's statement, or a multimedia work that presents alternately text and video). This now common new situation is the case for 'transmedia franchises' (Jenkins, 2006).

Transmedia franchises may be seen as an evolution from classic cases of semiotic re-mediation, where a work in one medium is 'adapted' into another: books to films, plays to films, films to books, books to graphic novels, books or films to games. But the transmedia franchise is much more than this. It is a complex of books, and films, and websites, and games, and a wide variety of merchandise (from clothing to toys to candy), all of which elaborate in some way on a fictional world and its characters, ethos, and mythos. The transmedia franchises for *Harry Potter* and the *Lord of the Rings* evolved from rather traditional novels; *Star Wars* from the films; *Star Trek* from a television series; Pokemon, *Yu-gi-Oh!*, and *Naruto* from manga to anime to all the rest. These franchises comprise several to dozens or even hundreds of books, often illustrated; multiple films, videos, DVDs; multiple games; and the websites which advertise and comment on them, and thousands of items of merchandise of every possible sort.

From the *Harry Potter* franchise you can read the books, see the movies, buy books about the movies, visit websites about the books, play several computer/video games, and even buy Harry's magic wand or eat the candy featured in the books and films. Who is Harry Potter for a given user? How is the sense of who he is, of who we may be identifying with, formed from the cover art and illustrations of the books (different across many international editions and translations), the descriptive passages of the texts, the impersonation by an actor in the films, the opinions about Harry voiced on the websites, the Harry we see and the Harry we become or enact in the games, or the Harry who carries the wand, eats the candy, etc.?

Our encounter with these media is not simply a trajectory through a single coherent work. It is a *traversal* across the boundaries between works, media, genres, sites, institutional contexts, activities, etc. (Lemke, 2005). And along such a traversal we are construing and cumulating across timescales *transmedia meaning effects* which do not occur within single works, or between intertexts in the same medium, or indeed within the scope of any theory of meaning-making or multimodal analysis that exists today.

Transmedia meaning effects may be based around our sense of and potential identification with a character, but also around a sense of place (Hogwarts Castle), a sense of action (wielding a magic wand), and a sense of bodily experience (playing the aerial soccer, Quidditch, of Harry's world). The textual descriptions of Quidditch combine with the computer-game immersive, interactive experience of playing Quidditch, and with the sensory experience of watching a wide-screen movie shot or animation to interpret and express this experience in the films.

Games and chronotopes

I will return to transmedia franchises and meaning effects, but I want to elaborate a bit more on the phenomenological analysis of computer games as examples of multimodal systems.

I am not calling them 'works' now for the reasons already described. Video or computer games today (specialist researchers use the term *digital games*) are a new and important medium (Raessens and Goldstein, 2005). They represent without doubt the frontier of multimedia, far in advance of film technologically, semiotically, and phenomenologically, however much they may still lag artistically. In this medium, typically a player controls a representation of him/herself on a screen, showing a visually realistic three-dimensional scene, and may act through this 'avatar' to perform almost anything that might be done in such a scene in the real world, and a great many things that could not (or not safely). In many cases one scene is seamlessly joined to the next, allowing the player to move from room to room indoors, and from hill to valley outdoors. You can run, jump, duck, fly, and teleport. You can open doors and chests, drive cars, ride horses, talk to other players in real time or to simulations of animated characters. You are normally given tasks to do or goals to achieve, but you often do not need to do them and can make your own way in this artificial world.

Of course things will befall you, triggered by where you are and what you have done in the past (and also by who you are as a character type in the game). Every action you take evokes a response from the computer program, and often also from other players in the game, and these responses are displayed as events in the realistic 3D world. In the course of gameplay, you will read printed texts, view and interpret static images of a wide variety of genres, experience in many cases video scenes that have been pre-rendered and are triggered by some pattern of action, and hear music and sound-effects. You can destroy virtual objects in the gameworld and watch them disintegrate quasi-realistically. You can deploy the laws of normal physics, or alternative physics, to roll objects down hills, set off chain reactions of explosions, or use one object to move another in ways unforeseen by the program designers.

You live in these gameworlds in something very much like real phenomenological time. In part you control the pace of events, and in part external events force you to keep pace with them. Games of different genres have different 'chronotopes' in the sense of Bakhtin (1981). There are typical temporal rhythms of action and movement from place to place. In the popular role-playing game (RPG) genre, you and your party of friends and allies build up your resources and strength at a relatively slow pace and moving over long distances, then encounter a powerful adversary in a very fast-paced but localized engagement, then hang around that place to recover any valuables, and then move on to the first part of the cycle again. There are different chronotopes for real-time strategy games (RTSs), or first-person shooter games (FPSs). All involve alternations of slower and faster-paced action, coordinated with movements between specific types of places.

A player's traversal here crosses boundaries of media and genres in the sense of internal semiotic representations in the game (texts, images, videos, mini-games) and boundaries between places or sites, though it is more like a trajectory through a single work than like the true traversal across works, media, and institutional contexts and activities for transmedia.

Interactive, immersive gameplay is a strongly embodied experience. Reading a book, we might squirm or feel anxiety; viewing a film, we might feel fear or cry or scream; playing a state-of-the-art digital game, however, you not only do all these things, but you have active experiences of exerting effort, racing against the clock, taking leisurely strolls, devising and executing short-term and long-term plans, and much more. It seems that it is easier to fool the human brain than we once thought, if you combine action that produces results with multimedia simulation of experiencing those results.

A phenomenological perspective on reading or film-viewing (or music-listening) has always been relevant to understanding the experience of meaning-making in these media, but digital games foreground and amplify its importance because the presented texts in digital games (i.e. what is in your eye and in your ear at each next moment) depend critically on user actions, which in turn depend critically on user feelings, on the experienced response to the last moment of presented stimuli, far more than in the case of traditional reading or viewing or listening. If I feel pressured by time and pacing, if I feel fear or apprehension, I will act differently, the game program will respond differently, and my trajectory of experience will be different along with the meanings and feelings I construe/experience. Multimodality itself, the combination of the semiotics of language, image, video/animation,

171

sound effects, music, and action, makes this new medium feel immersive. When the medium is not just interactive, but cumulatively responsive to user actions, not just in one moment, but over longer timescales as well, the sense of immersion is greatly enhanced, and with it the need for phenomenological modes of analysis for gameplay.

Transmedia franchises: media, identification, and peer networks

In seeking to understand how to analyze transmedia meaning effects in terms of the phenomenological experience of user traversals, we need to identify some of the principles of engagement with the media of the franchise complex that can ground cumulation and integration of meanings and feelings across media and timescales. I have already mentioned one key principle: identification. Why do users desire to engage with more and more media in the *Harry Potter*, *Star Wars*, or *Naruto* franchise? Why read your tenth or fifteenth *Star Wars* spin-off novel, often of mediocre quality? Why buy Harry Potter's wand in replica, or Darth Maul's light sabre? Why wait eagerly for the twenty-fourth manga installment of *Naruto* (the story of a Japanese boy-ninja possessed by a fox-demon spirit)? The answer in large part is because of identification: users identify with a character, or more generally with the ethos, the spirit, the mythos, the 'feel' of an entire franchise world.

Identification is a key aspect of what we might call second-wave identity theory. The earlier theories began from prior psychological theories of personality and ego-identity and rebelled against the notion of a unitary, integrated coherent identity. Perhaps that is a goal if your ego-identity is radically fragmented in ways that are upsetting to your life, but for most of us, fragmentation is functional. We are different selves in different roles and relationships and settings. We produce a conventionalized 'core' identity insofar as we are taught to do so or expected to do so, but in reality we don't pay much attention to the contradictions between our different selves. We ignore them, thereby gaining the kind of social and psychological flexibility needed to survive in a complex and contradictory world. The second-wave of identity theory, influenced more by critical feminism and queer theory than by postmodernism as such, rejected the reification of 'an identity' or 'identities' altogether, in favor of a more processual notion of 'performing identities' in the sense of the actions we take to enact or perform our various public and private selves (Butler, 1990). In this model there is far more agency for us to strategically blend and cobble together the identity of the moment, balancing bricolage with habitus (Caldas-Coulthard and Iedema, 2007).

But how do we acquire our sense of how to perform the useful identity of the moment? How do we assemble our toolkit of identity-performing practices? What are the elements of these practices and where do they come from? How is it that we each have unique repertoires of such practices and yet collectively share in common systems of them? The answer to this is *identification*: at many points in our lives we adopt identities, or the elements of performing them, from the common culture. We identify with real persons, of course, but also with fictional and idealized identities. More than this, we specifically identify with the elements or building blocks of identities: what foods we like, what clothes we wear, how we wear our hair, how we walk and talk, how we want our bodies to look and feel, what objects we want to be surrounded by, etc. We often identify today, especially in our earlier years, with elements from popular culture and peer culture. We identify with a particular brand of shoes, a particular fictional character or world, a particular opinion about adults or school, a particular music group or kind of music. In various settings, when it suits us, we mobilize these identifications to perform the identities we wish to project and have recognized or ratified by others.

That much is identification regarded sociologically or functionally. Semiotically, identification positions us among sets of somewhat mutually exclusive choices. Indexically, each identification marks us by the conventions of a community as more masculine or feminine, more cool or geeky, more straight or queer, more conforming or transgressive, more middle or more working class, more raver or more goth. In fact, a prime dimension of power in society today is the power to assign hierarchical statuses to various identifications: super-premium vodka brands *vs.* cheap beer, Armani *vs.* Marks and Spencer or H&M, opera *vs.* rap music, etc., not just for the sake of profit in the division of the market, but for the sake of privilege in the division of society.

But what is identification phenomenologically? The classic psychoanalytic theories define identification in terms of desire, either a desire that binds us to the desired object, or a reversal of desire that binds us to its opposite. We want the objects we identify with, we want to be them, to be them so completely as never to be separated from them because so long as we exist, they remain ours. We feel good when we are identifying with and participating in the franchise world: watching the movie, playing the game, acting out the character, speaking the discourse, making the moves. We feel better insofar as we have more elements of the repertoire, and insofar as we are more successful in mobilizing them in identity performances that are ratified by peers and others. Sociologically, again, this is cultural capital that is mobilized to increase social capital. Phenomenologically, it is the feeling we get when we are our chosen self, when we feel the power – especially important perhaps when we are young and not confident of our power – to identify with what we wish to identify with, and to perform identities we wish to perform.

Such identities, or clusters of identifications, grow and develop. In the work of James Gee, developing out of new approaches to defining multimedia literacy and its interaction with identity, we find both a useful discussion of the various kinds of identity we may perform or have ascribed to us by others (Gee, 2001) and detailed first-person accounts of how performance identities can develop and feel when playing a video game (Gee, 2007).

Many of the clearest examples of identification in multimedia and particularly in gameplay come from commercially well-developed franchises for younger users. But equally we might consider franchises with an older target demographic, like *World of Warcraft* or *America's Army*. The latter is a franchise started by the US Army as a recruiting tool, a game spin-off from its military combat training simulations. It offers the opportunity to identify as a good soldier, to identify with the US combat doctrine (principles of combat warfare), to identify with the United States as a dominant world-power in relation to swarthy and keffiya'd peoples everywhere. Many millions of young men have participated in this opportunity for identification, and no doubt some have continued their traversals among high-tech weaponry and idealized camaraderie and self-sacrifice by enlisting to fight in the US army. Harry Potter's wand or Luke Skywalker's light sabre are available in replica online, but the genuine combat weaponry realistically simulated in *America's Army* and other games of this class can most readily be obtained by enlisting.

In these cases, as for *Harry Potter, Star Wars,* or *Naruto,* users' interpretations and identifications, and indeed, I believe, a good part of their phenomenological experience along their traversals through the franchise, are mediated by something more than just the designs of the franchise producers. In the work of Constance Steinkuehler, as in that of Jenkins and many others, we see that they are also mediated by participation in fan/user communities: online peer social networks that provide additional cultural and social capital to fuel users' identifications (Jenkins, 2006; Raessens and Goldstein, 2005; Steinkuehler and Williams, 2006). For every franchise there are fan communities: websites, discussion forums, and large databases of useful and merely copious information about the books, games, films, and merchandise. Not only do these fan-produced and fan-maintained online communities ferret out and disseminate information, and sponsor discussions, they also lobby the producers for the desires of the community, and they produce collateral media in the world of the franchise mythos.

This last function is of great importance, I believe. User-fans, who range from novices to experts on the franchise world, write 'fan fiction', produce fan-made videos, create fan-made art. Some of this is entirely original except for the identities of the characters and other elements of the fictional world, and some of it is a montage of elements copied directly from the original media (e.g. photo-montage from film posters online, video-montage of shots from digital versions of the films). User communities act as if (and in my opinion represent valid evidence that) many commercial fictional worlds have crossed over from the domain of proprietary ownership into the domain of folk culture. Legally, the franchise owners or claimants sometimes tolerate these activities and sometimes try to control or stop them (always unsuccessfully). There are more than a quarter-million fan-authored short stories and novels set in the *Harry Potter* mythos available online. There are at least dozens if not hundreds of *Star Wars* fan-produced videos, one a fully acted 45-minute additional episode to the canonical film sequence, complete with special effects.

When users encounter transmedia franchises today, the fan-community websites are as natural and integral a part of the traversal route as the officially sanctioned franchise websites and media. The fan-produced media are becoming additions to the transmedia complex that go beyond and in general now outnumber the franchised media as such. To the extent that users encounter interpretations and expressions in this extended transmedia complex (franchise media plus fan-made media), the cumulative meanings, feelings, and sense of characters, settings, events, etc. cannot help but be influenced by the fan-made media. Some fan-media tries to remain as consistent as possible with the authorized media of the franchise, but inevitably it extends events, enlists characters in new situations and relationships, etc. Some fan-media deliberately or incidentally violates factual or conventional aspects of the official franchise. Best-known are the so-called 'slash' fan-fiction stories and videos, in which romantic relationships are constructed between franchise characters A and B (denoted A/B). These are often between two male characters, and are written by female fans. This is a very common genre across almost all popular culture media franchises (television, movies, games, etc.). It shows in a particularly strong way how fan-made media can potentially alter identifications with elements of franchise media.

Even apart from slash fiction of this kind, another popular genre is simply to set a video montage to unrelated popular music, synchronizing image content and lyrics, as well as the timing of musical rhythms/phrases and visual cuts (as long ago proposed and practiced by Eisenstein and Prokofiev, following the lead of Walt Disney). These 'music videos' can also readily recontextualize interpretations and identifications with the primary franchise content through the powerful effects, sometimes humorous, sometimes satirical, sometimes poignant, of popular music, which already has indexical and emotional meanings for many in the user community. This is another excellent example of how multimodal analysis needs to take into account affectivity and the experiential qualities of multiple modalities, here co-presented.

Summary

Semiotic and phenomenological analyses are key complementary approaches to the study of multimedia as experienced in real time. They are, however, often thought to be insufficiently critical in the strong sense of failing to make connections to macro-social models of political economy. Semiotic models can fail to recognize that key contexts for media analysis include those of their production, often for profit or to benefit an interest or ideology, and circulation (e.g. limited by cost or directed by marketing to particular users). It is, however, possible to develop a political economy of transmedia signs (Lemke, in press) and this is an important task for the future.

It has long been a commonplace of critical media analysis (Williamson, 1978) that advertising media sell not just products and services but lifestyles and ideologies. Today we can say that they sell identities: identities which imply dispositions to buy some kinds of products and services rather than others. Global producers market identities. So when we analyze transmedia franchises, we need to be aware not just of the identities they are selling and the dispositions they appeal to, but also of the larger identity markets to which these belong. Who is this game, movie, book *not* directed to? *Why* do some social groups identify with this franchise, while others may detest it?

Media mediate not just among us as we play with our identities, but also between us and the interests of large-scale producers. Into this traditional balance now come more and more the effects of peer social networks that mediate our engagements with media. Research on multimedia in the future needs to focus attention and theory-development on rich instances of consumer re-mediation of identity markets and to attend to the longer-term inseparability of meaning relations and power relations.

Further reading

From among the key works I have already cited, I would recommend that the interested reader first consult the discussion of identity in Gee (2001) and the accounts of multimodality as a dynamic and experiential phenomenon in computer games in Gee (2007) and Raessens and Goldstein (2005). For an overview of multimodal meaning-making along traversals, see Lemke (2002b); and for a compendium of recent research on multimodality, including discussions of the wider social and political dimensions, Baldry and Montagna (in press).

Among my own recent work of particular relevance are Lemke (2012) which discusses recent multimedia analysis specifically in the context of the evolution of linguistic discourse analysis and Lemke (2013), which develops further some of the themes above regarding the experiential-phenomenological aspects, particularly affective ones, in multimedia.

12

Multimodality and reading

The construction of meaning through image–text interaction

Len Unsworth and Chris Cléirigh

Introduction

The reconceptualization of literacy and literacy pedagogy has been increasingly advocated as a research imperative in view of the increasingly multimodal nature of paper and digital media texts (Chandler-Olcott and Mahar, 2003; Hull and Nelson, 2005; Kamil *et al.*, 2000; Lemke, 2006; Leu *et al.*, 2004; Richards, 2001). Many see image–text relations as central to such a reconceptualization (Andrews, 2004; Bolter, 1998; Boulter, 1999; Dresang, 1999; Jewitt, 2002, 2006; Jewitt and Kress, 2003b; Kress, 2003b; Luke, 2003; New London Group, 2000). Although a good deal of recent work addresses the ways in which images construct meanings, very little has specifically addressed the intersemiotic semantic relationships *between* images and language to show how the visual and verbal modes interact to construct the integrated meanings of multimodal texts (Martinec and Salway, 2005; Royce, 2007). While some descriptive accounts have emerged such as McCloud's (1994) explication of image–language interaction in graphic novels, and educational work on science textbooks (Roth *et al.*, 2005), research within systemic functional semiotics has provided a systematic account of a "semantic system of image–text relations that would map out how images and text interact" (Martinec and Salway, 2005: 341). Nevertheless, the development of a generalized semiotic system describing the semantics of the co-articulation of image and language remains in its infancy (Kress, 2001; Lemke, 2006; Macken-Horarik, 2003; Unsworth, 2008). Advancing understanding of how images and language interact to construct meaning seems crucial in seeking to reconceptualize literacy and literacy pedagogy from a multimodal perspective. The discussion in this chapter seeks to contribute to this kind of advancement.

Different research traditions in education have addressed image–text relations in reading comprehension but have not sought to explicate how images and language interact to construct meaning. For example, Mayer (2008) investigated a number of features of the deployment of images and language in short multimedia science explanations to determine the principles of such deployment that led to the most efficient comprehension. The resulting guidelines for learning materials included: the coherence principle (excising extraneous words, sounds and pictures); the signalling principle (highlighting essential material); and the spatial contiguity principle (placing corresponding words and pictures near each other). In other studies where the role of images in meaning making were addressed, such as the study of Brazilian school science textbooks by Roth and colleagues (2005), the image–text relations, remote from any linguistic or visual semiotic theory, were ambiguous and/or referred to relations among caption text and main text rather than between image and caption or main text (Unsworth, 2006a). Due to space constraints, this chapter focuses on the contributions of more semiotically oriented studies whose theoretical bases are more apposite to explicating the semantic nature of image–language interaction. This work mainly derives from the systemic functional linguistic (SFL) work of Michael Halliday (Halliday and Matthiessen, 2004).

Within this focus we limit our discussion to the construction of ideational or representational meaning, leaving aside issues of compositional meaning concerning layout and prominence, and issues of interactive meaning concerned with pseudo interpersonal relations between readers/viewers and the represented participants and objects in images and language. We briefly critique systemic functional semiotic approaches to describing the ideational semantics of image–language interaction, and then outline early work emphasizing the distinctively different semiotic affordances of image and language effecting their specialized function in contributing different aspects of overall meaning in texts. From this perspective we go on to propose a semiotic framework designed to address the synergistic nature of image–language interaction in meaning construction. We illustrate this framework with reference to science books for primary school children and then demonstrate the efficacy of the framework in accounting for children's difficulties in comprehending a science text in a state-wide mandatory reading comprehension test in Australia. In conclusion we note limitations of the present work in terms of the limited field of primary school science, the confining of the study to ideational meaning, and to static and pictorial images and also in terms of the range of semantic relations encompassed in the framework. Implications of the work for pedagogy involving reading to learn and for further research on explicating the role of image–language interaction in reconceptualizing literacy in multimodal terms are also briefly noted.

Describing how images and text interact in making meaning

A focus on representational/ideational meaning

Since our work focuses on representational or ideational meaning, only studies dealing with this dimension of image–language relations are included here. Although some related work has addressed moving images (Baldry and Thibault, 2006) we will deal only with studies involving static images and language in paper or digital media. We will also emphasize studies of science texts, although we note the pioneering work of Gill (2002) on "ideational concurrence" of image and language in picturebooks, and the ongoing work of O'Halloran (1999, 2000, 2003a, 2003b), who developed a system for analyzing mathematical formalism derived from O'Toole's (1994) semiotics of images, and based on Halliday's (1994) grammar, further developed the concept of semiotic metaphor to account for the nature of transformations from language to mathematical symbolism.

Describing cohesive relations between elements of images and text

Royce (1998, 2002, 2007) has taken the concept of "cohesive ties" (Halliday and Hasan, 1976; Martin, 1992) among content words distributed across texts and applied this to links between words and image segments. He mapped relations of repetition, synonymy, antonymy, meronymy, hyponymy and collocation between visual and verbal message elements in an advertisement (1998) and in a later extended article (2007) in the *Economist* magazine, and also in a high school science text book (2002). Most of the cohesive ties involved repetition, meronymy or collocation, but the meronymy and collocation indicate that the visual and verbal modes provide much more than a duplication of meanings. "Crossmodal" cohesive links were also described by Lemke (2002) to indicate the role of these image–text relations on science websites. He indicated that interpreting the contribution of the image component depended on these intermodal ties since the construction of meaning from the image necessitated integrating information from the caption texts. While these studies indicated extensive interdependence between images and text, we sought to explicate further the ideational nature of that interdependence.

Modelling image–text relations on clause types and conjunction

Martinec and Salway (2005) have taken Halliday's descriptions of the types of relations between clauses within a sentence (Halliday, 1985, 1994; Halliday and Matthiessen, 2004), and applied them to relations between language and image. There are two aspects to this. One is the notion of dependency – which are the independent clauses and which are subordinate clauses? Martinec and Salway have attempted to adapt this to describing the relative status of image and language segments as equal or unequal, and if equal whether independent or complementary, and if unequal whether the image is dependent on the language or whether the language is dependent on the image. However, there are a number of inconsistencies inherent in the status systems they propose, which are highlighted in their own data analyses, that appear to make this aspect of their proposal very difficult to work with (Unsworth and Cléirigh, 2009). But more broadly, it can be asked: what value is there in determining whether language and image are of equal or unequal status? How does it further our understanding of how language and image collaborate in the creation of a unified, coherent text? More promising, in this regard, as Martinec and Salway (2005) demonstrate, is the deployment of the second aspect of Halliday's system of interclausal relations – this is the nature of the semantic linkage between clauses.

The semantic linkages can expand the meaning of a clause in three ways. In *elaboration* one clause restates or clarifies another, in *extension* one clause adds information to another, and in *enhancement* one clause provides information such as how, when, where or why in relation to the other clause. Martinec and Salway have identified examples of these three kinds of linkages between images and text segments. However, in our view, in simply extrapolating from this aspect of clausal relations to image–text relations their account does not sufficiently attend to the reciprocity of the different affordances of image and text. This can be seen in their discussion of an image which represents people in a disaster setting with several representations of dead bodies on the floor. The caption says "Police believe a short circuit set fire to the hall's thatch roof". Martinec and Salway say that "Here the image enhances the text. The dead bodies lying on the floor are the result of *a short circuit set fire to the hall's thatch roof*" (2005: 351). What they don't pick up on is that the text also enhances the image. The text provides the reason for the image figures. In the account of our work in the subsequent sections, we build on this strand of the theorizing discussed by Martinec and Salway and also in the work of Matthiessen (2007), augmenting it with the notion of intermodal (mutual) identification.

Functional specialization of image and language in science texts

In studies of science texts, Kress (1997b, 2000a, 2003a, 2003b) and Lemke (1998b) explicated what they call the "functional specialization" of language and image. According to this the resources of language are most apposite to the representation of sequential relations and the making of categorical distinctions, while the resources of images are most apposite to the representation of spatial relations and for formulating "… degree, quantity, gradation, continuous change, continuous co-variation, non-integer ratios, varying pro- portionality, complex topological relations of relative nearness or connectedness, or non- linear relationships and dynamical emergence…" (Lemke, 1998b: 87). Lemke provides a detailed discussion of the meaning- making resources of a scientific article that includes diagram and text, although this is not a fully articulated framework of intersemiotic rela- tions that would explicate the kinds of linkages between images and language.

Kress (1997b, 2000a, 2003a, 2003b) has exemplified the functional specialization principle. His analysis of a textbook page dealing with "electronics" shows that:

> The language is about events: relatively simple sentences (one or two clauses), which are about actions – what had been done; what is to be done; what might happen if… The diagrams represent the core information of this bit of the curriculum: what a circuit consists of, and in what relation its components stand to each other.
>
> (Kress, 2000b: 197)

While the accounts provided by Kress in a number of papers do not develop a system of intersemiotic relations, Bezemer and Kress (2008) have discussed the contributions of image and text to meaning-making in terms of what they called *epistemological commitment*. They define this as an "unavoidable affordance" and provide as an example the fact that in the visual mode the artist or designer is obliged to show the distance between two characters (and other spatial relativities) which are not obligatory in a verbal description of the scene. They go on to note that: "Every mode imposes/demands such commitments as a matter of course, though each set of commitments is different" (Bezemer and Kress, 2008: 176). This means that a visual and verbal depiction of the same thing can be thought of as two different semiotic representations of the same phenomenon, so there is a simultaneous semiotic relationship of identity and dif- ferentiation. This insight is integral to the modelling of image–text relations we are proposing, and is not sufficiently addressed in existing models.

Rethinking intermodal construction of representational meaning

Reasoning towards a synergistic model of image–text relations

We know that no image or visual representation means in all and only the same ways that some text can mean (Lemke, 2002: 303–304). Some aspects of this essential incommensurability have been noted in relation to the functional specialization principle and the concept of epistemo- logical commitment. Lemke goes on to note that it is this essential incommensurability that enables new meanings to be made from combinations of modalities in texts. So, although the meaning-making affordances of image and text are very different, they interact synergistically in the construction of meaning. The challenge is how to model the nature of this synergy while preserving the notion of the distinct affordances of the different modes.

As distinct from simply applying existing linguistic descriptions to image–text interaction, we have used one aspect of systemic functional grammar as a heuristic to reason about the nature of the image–language synergy. This grammatical concept is *relational grammatical identification*. It most commonly occurs with the verb "to be" or "to have" where one par- ticipant in the clause is *identified* with another. For example, if we say "Gregory is the bald one" this indicates that in this particular context Gregory is the only bald person and hence

Who is the bald one?			*Who is Gregory?*		
Gregory	is	the bald one	Gregory	is	the bald one
Identifier		Identified	Identified		Identifier

he is uniquely identified. But in this context Gregory and "the bald one" refer to the same entity, hence either Gregory can be used to identify "the bald one" or "the bald one" can be used to identify Gregory:

In this relationship of unique identification both participants in the clause are the same person. But the clause is not tautologous, so there must be a difference between the separate representations of the participants. Halliday and Matthiessen (2004) refer to this difference as one of "expression" and "content". They use the term Token for the lower "expression" and Value for the more abstract "content". So if we say "Angelika is the School Captain" we are identifying Angelika by assigning her to a Value. Angelika is the Token (expression) and "the School Captain" is the Value (content). But all such identifying clauses can "face both ways" with either the Token (expression) as Identifier, identifying the Value (content) as Identified or the Value (content) as Identifier identifying the Token (expression) as Identified. If we go back to "Gregory is the bald one", the lower "expression" is "the bald one", so "the bald one" is the Token and the higher (content) Value is Gregory. But as shown above, either Gregory (Value) can identify who "the bald one" is, or "the bald one" (Token) can identify which one is Gregory. We refer to this kind of grammatical identification as *intensive* identification.

This concept of mutual identification is central to our theorizing of image–language relations, but to provide the complete basis for our modelling of image–text relations, we need to point out two more types of identifying clauses in English. The second type involves possession, but again we are fundamentally concerned with the relationship of identity between two participants. So, if we say "Anna has a harp" we are simply putting Anna into a class of people who have harps, so this is not an identifying clause. However, if we say "The harp is Anna's", then both "Anna's" and "the harp" refer to that which Anna possesses, and the relationship is one of identity. Here "The harp" is Token and "Anna's" is Value. We will refer to this kind of identification as *possessive*. In our discussion of image–language relations, we will suggest that this kind of identification involving possession enables us to account for the ways in which images of entities can show elements (not realized verbally) that are *possessed* by the linguistically realized entities. So this deals with images augmenting verbal information.

The third type of identifying clause occurs when the relationship between two entities is such that one entity is being identified by a *circumstantial* feature of time or place or manner etc., for example, "Tomorrow is the twelfth" or "the best way to get there is by train", or "this situation is apparently caused by anomalous low temperatures". In all cases what is being related on either side of the verb "is" in each clause is essentially the same thing. We will refer to this kind of identification as *circumstantial*. In these cases "the Token can be quite varied in grammatical class – a nominal group, an adverbial group, a prepositional phrase or an embedded clause, whereas the Value is often a nominal group with the name of a class of circumstance as Thing" (Halliday and Matthiessen, 2004: 242). However, the Token is always the "expression" form at the lower level of abstraction, so in "her act was followed by applause", the Token is "applause", and in "The way to get there is by train" the Token is "by train". Similarly in our account of image–language relations the image is always the Token – the lower "expression" form, whereas the language is the more abstract "content" form – the Value.

Intermodal relations as (mutual) identification

Introducing intermodal identification

The grammatical concept of *identification* can be used to model the bimodal synergy of pictorial images and language (i.e. to model the image–language relations that jointly construct experiential or representational meaning). An image form, as the lower order of abstraction, functions as Token, whereas the language meaning, as the higher order of abstraction, functions as Value (Figure 12.1). Sometimes it is the language (Value) – the "meaning" or higher order of abstraction that the reader/viewer is familiar with and can use as the "Identifier" to identify the image. For example, suppose we have an image of a Minke whale with a caption, "The Minke whale is the current target of Japanese whalers". It may be that the reader/viewer has heard of the Minke as one among a variety of whales, but has never previously seen a picture of a Minke whale. S/he then uses the language as Identifier to *gloss* the image. On the other hand, suppose we have an image of the Indian Myna bird with the caption, "Indian Myna bird displaces native birds in urban habitats". In this case the reader/viewer may be familiar with the bird visually but not previously have heard it referred to verbally. In this case s/he uses the image as the Identifier to *visualize* the more abstract name of the bird. So, either the language or the image can be the point of departure to identify the other. If the language is the point of departure, it is the Identifier and it *glosses* the image. If the image is the point of departure, it *visualizes* the language.

Images identifying language: visualizing language elements

Drawing on our outline of *relational grammatical identification* above, we are proposing three types of intermodal identification: intensive, possessive and circumstantial, which are discussed in this section from the perspective of images visualizing language elements. The three types are illustrated by reference to Figure 12.2 showing the life cycle of a cicada (the labels for scenes 1–6 have been superimposed by Unsworth and Cléirigh).

In intermodal *intensive* identification the image visualizes the **qualities** (shape, colour, texture) of the identified participant. In Figure 12.2, Scene 5, the (unverbalized) qualities (shape, colour, texture) of the *fully grown nymph* are shown in the image. While both the image and the language refer to the same phenomenon the image elaborates qualities due to the inherent *epistemological commitment* (Bezemer and Kress, 2008) of the visual mode.

In intermodal *possessive* identification the image visualizes additional participant(s) not explicit in the language element(s). The image visualizes the (unverbalized) additional **things** (parts) that compose the identified participant. In Figure 12.2, Scene 6, the (unverbalized) things (parts) that compose *adult cicada* are shown.

In intermodal *circumstantial* identification the image visualizes language element **locations**. The image visualizes the (unverbalized) locations of the things (parts) that compose

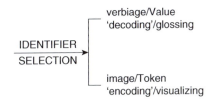

Figure 12.1 Image or language as identifier.

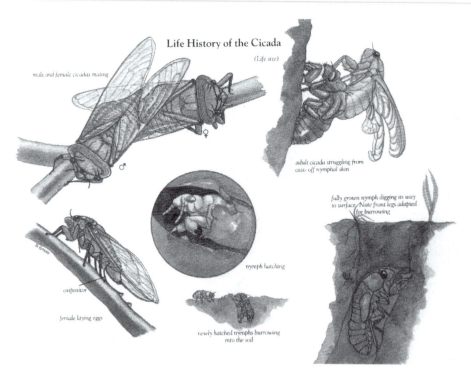

Figure 12.2 Life cycle of a cicada.
Source: Bird and Short, 1998: 29.

the identified participant. In Figure 12.2, Scene 2, the image visualizes the (unverbalized) location of the *ovipositor* (rear underside of the cicada's abdomen).

Images identifying language: visualizing language configurations

A language configuration refers to the semantic relation of process, participants and circumstances realized by the verb, noun groups and adverbial phrases. Intermodal circumstantial identification can occur when an image visualizes the **locations** of such language configurations. New circumstantial meanings, of Manner and Cause–Condition, can be encoded by this intermodal identification. That is, the image–language interaction constructs circumstantial meanings of Manner and Cause–Condition that are not constructed by either modality alone – consistent with Lemke's notion of *multiplying* meaning (1998a, 1998b).

- In the relation between the image and the language configuration the **locational** relation between image participants (i.e. their relative positions) can realize – visualize, show, demonstrate – the (unverbalized) **Manner: quality** of a language configuration. In Figure 12.2, Scene 1, the **Manner: quality** of *male and female cicadas mating* is shown as back-to-back, male-over-female.
- In the relation between the image and the language configuration the **locational** relation between image participants (i.e. their relative positions) can realize – visualize, show, demonstrate – the (unverbalized) **Causal–Conditional: result** or **consequence** of a language configuration. In Figure 12.3, Step 2 the **Cause: result** of *Wrap the bare end of one piece of wire tightly around one of the legs of the clothes peg* and *Do the same with the second wire on the*

other leg of the clothes peg are shown as uninsulated red wire around right peg leg and uninsulated blue wire around left peg leg.

- In the relation between the image and the language configuration, the **locational** relation between image participants (i.e. their relative positions) can realize – visualize, show, demonstrate – the (unverbalized) **Causal–Conditional: reason** or **condition** of a language configuration. (Illustrations not included due to lack of copyright approval, but see for example (McDonald, 2001: 170–171) where an image of a car-laden freeway leads to the billowing smoke stacks of an industrial city relates causally to the subtitle "Climatic Change: Global Warming".)

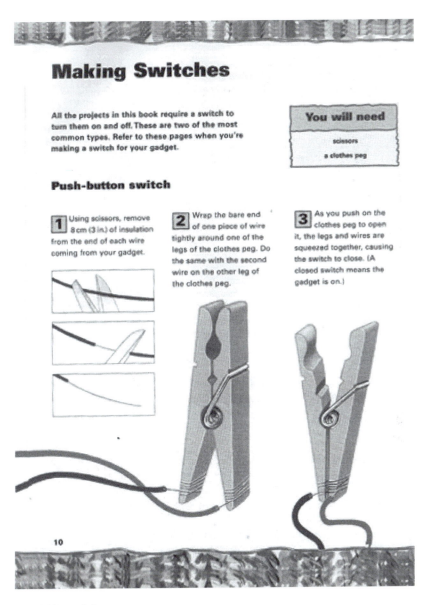

Figure 12.3 Making switches.
Source: Bartholomew, 2003: 10.

Language identifying image: glossing of the image

A language element can identify an image participant. In Figure 12.2, Scene 2, the participant element of the label *ovipositor* identifies (glosses) the located compositional participant (body part) in the image. A language configuration (participant(s) + process +/- circumstance(s)) can also identify (gloss) the spatial arrangement of image participants. In Figure 12.2, Scene 3, the **"doing"** configuration of the caption *nymph hatching* identifies (glosses) the locational relation between participants (nymph and broken egg) in the image.

Images and the "main" text

The images in Figure 12.2 appear on the right-hand side of a double-page spread in the children's information book with the main text occupying the left-hand side. Here we will consider the main text segment corresponding to scenes 1 and 2 in Figure 12.2. This segment is re-presented below, divided into clauses:

1. After mating
2. the female cicada lays her rows of eggs in bushes high in trees.
3. She makes slits in the twigs or branches with her strong, sharp ovipositor
4. and deposits the eggs into these slits.
5. It takes about six weeks for the eggs to hatch.

As we have indicated in discussing images and captions, the nature of the image–language relation is mutual identification. This is also the case for the relation between images and corresponding main text segments. In Figure 12.2, Scene 1 identifies (visualizes) the location of clause 1, and as previously noted, the manner in which the mating occurs. Clause 1 identifies (glosses) Scene 1, in that "mating" decodes the representational meaning of the spatial arrangement of the images of the two cicadas positioned rear-to-rear on a branch. Similarly Scene 2 visualizes clause 2 also indicating manner, and clause 2 glosses Scene 2. In clause 3 "makes slits" precedes what is depicted in Scene 2, but the participants in the language are visualized as is the manner (means) of making the slits (i.e. with the ovipositor). Scene 2 visualizes clause 4 also indicating manner and correspondingly clause 4 glosses the spatial arrangement of image participants in Scene 2. Of clause 5 only the participant "eggs" is visualized in Scene 2.

Intermodal identification and the reader

Intermodal identification accommodates the concept of functional specialization of image and language (Kress 1997b, 2000a, 2003a, 2003b) and the synergistic construction of meanings that cannot be derived from either mode separately. It is also a way of considering options available to readers in negotiating the meanings of multimodal texts. If an image appears in a text without any language, the image is only decoded (glossed) by language that can be generated by the reader. So if an image, or any part of an image, is unfamiliar to the reader – such as a cicada body part – it remains undecoded. A pedagogical function of language provided by the author is to supplement what can be provided by the reader for *decoding* (glossing) the image. If language appears without an image in a text, the language is only encoded by an image that can be visualized by the reader based on his/her prior experience of the language in relation to the actual phenomenon or some prior visual representation of it. So if any part of the language is unfamiliar to the reader – such as the word "ovipositor" – it remains unencoded visually. A pedagogical function of an image provided by the author, is to supplement what can be provided by the reader, for visually *encoding* the language. So, monomodal texts demand more of the visual or verbal experience of the reader than do bimodal texts. The more exotic/technical/abstract the field, the more important the intermodal identification pedagogically.

Image–language relations in reading comprehension

The increased extent and significance of images and image–language relations in a wide range of textual material in recent years is reflected in reading comprehension pedagogy requirements in government-mandated school syllabus documents in Australia and the United Kingdom. However, group reading comprehension tests used by governments and education authorities as indicators of student literacy standards and teaching effectiveness, in general, rarely conceptualize reading comprehension as involving images now such an integral part of most curriculum area reading materials and of reading materials more generally. In Australia, mandatory group reading comprehension tests for year three and year five children in government schools, previously conducted by the states, have been replaced by national tests in 2008. A number of the state tests did seek to assess children's meaning-making from the integrative use of images and language in their colour stimulus booklets. Preliminary results from a nationally funded study[1] investigating the role of image–language relations in children's reading comprehension suggest that the nature of these relations may influence the difficulty children experience in comprehending such texts (Unsworth and Chan, 2008).

Figure 12.4 is an extract from the stimulus booklet for the 2005 Basic Skills Test for year five students in New South Wales schools. The question below is one of those based on this extract:

Order these steps to show how a Greek water clock works. Write a number from 1 to 4 in each box to show the order.

☐ water drips into a container
☐ a float rises in the rising water
☐ cogs moving up turn a clock hand
☐ the float makes cogs move upwards

Only 56 per cent of the total year five cohort of Students in NSW scored the correct answer. Given that the nature and functioning of a Greek water clock is likely to be unfamiliar to most year five students, an examination of the image–language relations from the perspective of mutual identification can reveal potential obstacles to their reading comprehension.

In terms of the language elements identifying or glossing the image participants, this clearly occurs with the image figure as a whole ("a water clock (clepshydra)"; "A Greek Water Clock") and with some of the image figures as component parts ("Cogs"; "Clock hand"; "Float"). However, many of the parts of the image are not glossed by the language (frame, funnel, pipe, reservoir, shaft, wheel) as this glossing is less relevant to understanding the movement of the clock hands, and inclusion of labels would clutter the image. The language, "Water supply" and "Overflow", although perhaps obvious to adult readers, sets up a potentially challenging intermodal misidentification for the inexperienced student reader. This language appears, falsely, to be glossing *parts* of the image, when it is actually the nominalized forms of the more congruent linguistic realization of events: "water flows in" and "excess water flows out" (and there is no "water supply" or "overflow" visualized in the image). In terms of language configurations identifying (glossing)

185

TELLING THE TIME USING WATER

Long ago in a country called Egypt the people used water to help them tell the time. They marked the inside of a pot at measured spaces and made a small hole near the bottom of the pot. Then they filled it with water. As the water dripped through the hole, the water level inside the pot dropped below the marks. This told them how much time had passed.

Water

Marks on the inside of the pot

Hole

Dripping water

An Egyptian water clock

The ancient Greeks also developed a water clock (clepsydra).

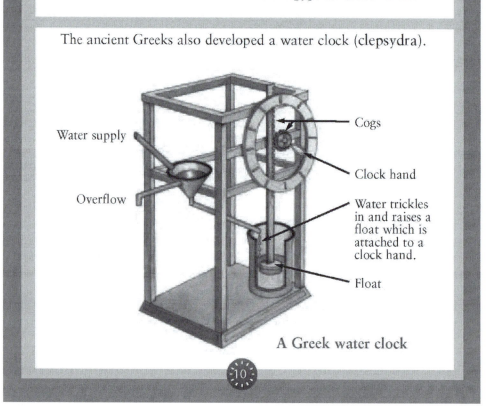

Water supply

Overflow

Cogs

Clock hand

Water trickles in and raises a float which is attached to a clock hand.

Float

A Greek water clock

10

Figure 12.4 A Greek water clock.

Source: Chapman, 1996.

the spatial arrangement of image participants as "doing" configurations, the language "Water trickles in…" effectively glosses the relevant part of the image, but it is semantically causally related to the second clause, "and raises a float"; however, this causal meaning is realized linguistically as simple addition – "and". This may well impede the understanding of the inexperienced reader since s/he has to unpack the reason–result relation.

If we now look at the text from the perspective of the image identifying (visualizing) the language elements, it is clear that through *intensive identifcation* the image visualizes the unverbalized qualities (shape, texture, quality) of the identified participant(s) – the clock and its labelled components – the "Cogs", "Clock hand" and "Float". Through *possessive identification* the image also identifies (visualizes) the unverbalized parts that compose the identified participant (frame, funnel, pipe, reservoir, shaft, wheel). In addition, through *circumstantial identification* the image visualizes the unverbalized locations of the image elements that compose the identified participant (the clock). But if we now examine the image identifying (visualizing) language configurations, focusing on the extended main caption text, the nature of further challenges for inexperienced readers becomes apparent, as explicated in Table 12.1.

There is a particular problem with the final clause in the language column in Table 12.1 ("which is attached to a clock hand") in that it does not adequately decode or gloss the image the children are presented with, which is likely to be very unfamiliar to the majority of them. Considering this and the nature of the other image–language relations described in this text, it is not surprising that only 56 per cent of ten-year-old children in year five at school were able to answer the sequencing question correctly. The informational material for teachers describing the test indicates that the question discussed here requires students to be able to "sequence steps by interpreting a diagram". The kind of intermodal analysis we have described "unpacks" into pedagogically useful information, what "interpreting" entails in terms of understanding image–language relations.

Table 12.1 Image visualizing language in the main caption text for the water clock

Language	Visualization in image
Water trickles in	This "doing" configuration is visualized by a vertical series of water drops positioned in an unlabelled reservoir and extending below an unlabelled pipe attached to the unlabelled funnel
and raises a float	This "doing" configuration is visualized only by a labelled figure above the water in the unlabelled reservoir. No raising of the float is visualized. Readers are required to be able to visualize it from their own experience
which is attached to a clock hand.	This "being" configuration is visualized by a series of connected parts: • float connected to (unlabelled) shaft • which has cogs which are connected to the cogs of an unlabelled wheel • which is connected to a clock hand (ambiguously positioned against or connected to an unlabelled wheel). Readers are required to fill in all the missing language that the image visualizes.

Conclusion

What is gained in our account is a more extravagant account of the synergistic construction of representational meaning. For example, in our intermodal intensive identification, the image visualizes the unverbalized qualities (shape, colour, texture) of the verbalized participant. So this takes into account the relationship between the language and aspects of visual representation in images that is not accounted for by an image–language relation of exposition, where "the image and the text are of the same level of generality" (Martinec and Salway, 2005: 350). The extravagant description of intersemiotic representation in our approach is apposite to pedagogic issues involved in children's negotiation of science texts. In such texts what is primarily at stake for the young readers is the effective negotiation of representational/ideational meanings that are frequently new and relatively complex to them. As we have shown in Table 12.1, if the text does not gloss unfamiliar image segments or unfamiliar language is not visualized in images, inexperienced readers in the field can face significant difficulty. While this has implications for multimodal text design for such learners, it also predicts where comprehension difficulties will be located, guiding the generation of test items, and pedagogically informing teachers about the need to gloss by "talking out" (Lemke, 1989; Unsworth, 2001) particular aspects of images with children and/or the need for "visualizing" particular text segments through supplementation with additional images or the provision of some other form of concrete illustration.

While we propose that intermodal identification is a very useful framework, it is certainly not sufficient. There are clearly other aspects of image–language relations (both in school science materials and beyond) that have not been addressed here. For example, *projection* is a part of the SFL system of logico-semantic relations. This system deals with the quoting or reporting of wording, or the quoting or reporting of thought. Speech or thought bubbles are noted as typical realizations in multimodal texts (Martinec and Salway, 2005; Matthiessen, 2007), and these certainly occur in science books and online science materials for children (Unsworth, 2006a). These are cases of images projecting texts, and Matthiessen suggests it is unlikely that text projects image, indicating that "this probably shades into elaboration" (Matthiessen, 2007: 35). However, there are examples in literary picturebooks for children where the main text projects an image (Unsworth, 2006b) and Martinec and Salway (2005) draw on Martin's (1994) suggestion that in the context of macrogenres, figures, tables, graphs and diagrams might involve the direct projection of ideas, bypassing wording, and reporting meaning directly. Clearly, there is much that remains to be done in theorizing the semiotics of image–language interaction, and in educational contexts in terms of the imperative to reconceptualize the nature of literacy and literacy pedagogy from a multimodal perspective, potentially much to be gained from advancing such theorizing.

Note

1 Unsworth, L., Barnes, G. and O'Donnell, K. *New dimensions of group literacy tests for schools: Multimodal reading comprehension in conventional and computer-based formats.* Australian Research Council funded project 2006–2008.

13

Power, social justice and multimodal pedagogies

Arlene Archer

Introduction

This chapter explores some of the links between multimodal pedagogies and social justice, looking at examples from South African educational contexts. The aim of doing this is to identify some of the challenges and opportunities of using multimodal approaches to pedagogy in local and global contexts of diversity. This will also be of interest in contexts where there are differentials in terms of access to economic and educational resources. The chapter focuses on the ways in which multimodal pedagogy can facilitate recognition of a range of student resources, whilst at the same time enabling access to dominant forms. This includes access to the discourses and knowledges of official curricula and formal methods of assessment, as well as creating dispositions towards meaning-making in individual and social worlds outside the classroom. Formal education often closes down access to a range of semiotic resources and multimodal pedagogies could potentially recover 'recognition' of these.

All teaching and learning is multimodal as it happens through speech, writing, gesture, image and space. These modes work together to create complex multilayered communicational ensembles which are produced in particular contexts of power. An explicitly multimodal approach to pedagogy goes beyond written and spoken language to value a range of modes, sometimes through formal assessment practices. This chapter demonstrates the ways in which multimodal pedagogies could open up spaces for reconceptualising which texts and which textual practices count and for whom, thus highlighting relations of power, social boundaries and inequality, political or commercial agendas.

Multimodal approaches in South Africa have tended to have a sharp focus on power differentials and issues of social justice (Archer, 2006; Kell, 2006; Stein, 2008; Stein and Newfield, 2006; Newfield, 2011; Thesen, 2001, 2007). Because resources like local languages and certain kinds of indigenous knowledge tended to be undervalued under the previous political dispensation, much of the research has been an attempt to make visible a range of students' resources which are often not noticed or valued in formal educational settings. In addition, African-appropriate pedagogy has been brought to bear on multimodality in our classrooms, as well as a focus on African representational and communication forms. Thus, a lot of the pedagogical interventions and research draw on indigenous languages, cultural forms and knowledges (Newfield and Maungedzo, 2006; Stein, 2008; Archer, 2008; Harrop-Allin, 2011). In South African educational contexts there is still differential access to education and sometimes poor access to resources such as teachers, textbooks and computers. The medium of instruction remains predominantly English, although this is not the first language of the majority of learners. Students have multiple language systems to draw on, and there is often a fluidity of movement between languages, varieties, genres and discourses. Also, given the

> political and economic load on the written English language … disenfranchised South Africans have long relied on other means and modes such as their bodies and voices to read and express complex meanings in a society where racial identity has signified so much.
>
> (Thesen and Van Pletzen, 2006: 19)

In order to make visible the resources that marginalized South Africans have developed, many researchers have shown the agency of students in designing texts.

Recognition of resources: agency, semiotic work and signs of learning

Multimodal pedagogies can inform a social justice and equity agenda because such pedagogies allow for 'broadening the base for representation' in classrooms (Stein and Newfield, 2006: 9). This approach to pedagogy has the potential to make classrooms more democratic and inclusive, enabling marginalized students' histories, identities, languages and discourses to be made visible. I would argue that 'recognition' of resources is an important feature of multimodal pedagogy employed in social justice. Recognition is about noticing resources in terms of some existing framework, making these visible and integrating them in terms of (e)valuation and application in a range of contexts. By resources, I mean both *students'* resources, including embodied resources such as dance and drama, and *semiotic* resources, such as colour and upcycled materials. The use of modes in classrooms is always 'the effect of the work of culture, history and power in shaping materials into resources for meaning-making' (Stein, 2008: 122). So, recognition of resources also entails recognition of how power is operating in various social practices.

Linked to 'recognition' is the notion of agency and design. Multimodal pedagogies can acknowledge 'learners as agentive, resourceful and creative meaning-makers who communicate using the communicative potential and multiple resources of their bodies and of their environment to interconnect' (Stein and Newfield, 2006: 8). In a multimodal approach to pedagogy and research there is a strong emphasis placed on student 'interest' and agency. In line with Halliday (1978), the position is that the semiotic resources available to a specific individual in a specific cultural, social and psychological history define semiotic 'potential'. How and why people choose to represent from a range of options points to the notion of design; the process of giving shape to the interests and purposes of the sign-maker for an assumed audience using the available semiotic resources (Bezemer and Kress, 2008: 174).

Recognition involves the teacher, the curriculum and the students as designers of meaning. People choose how to represent meaning from a range of possibilities which are shaped within a specific context. This may mean drawing on resources that were previously devalued and marginalized in an educational setting. The meaning-maker can choose to re-evaluate resources, assessing their appropriacy for immediate and changing contexts. Recognition develops self-reflexivity and the ability to understand the notion of semiotic choice, to select according to criteria, context and design. For instance, the choice of where to place a reference in academic writing has implications for authorial voice. Depending on the context, a reference placed at the beginning of a sentence, as in 'Smith (1991) argues that . . .' could foreground the cited author more than if the reference was placed in brackets following the statement, as in '. . . (Smith 1991)'. How people represent their meanings may be limited by the semiotic resources available and by students' competence in design. Even if choices are limited by context, these choices still communicate important information about students' identities and learning and therefore are important to recognize when developing curriculum and assessment practices.

A good example of work on recognition in South Africa is Harrop-Allin's (2011) examination of township children's musical games and their connection with music education. She looks at the differences between classroom and playground activities in Soweto primary schools, where some of the observed music lessons had no sound and consisted of writing facts about music. In contrast, on the playground, the children displayed a rich repertoire of games, music and dance. The children's hybrid music–dance practices reflect some of the rich cross-over styles characteristic of Soweto and other urban townships. They draw particularly on the local house dance music called 'kwaito' which is a blend of hip-hop and dance music with repetitive lyrics in Zulu, English or local township slang. Harrop-Allin argues that the games have implications for teaching and learning and explores the ways in which music teaching can develop the musicality already demonstrated in children's play. In this way, her research and pedagogical interventions recognize children's musical resources and utilize these in the classroom in order to connect with the children's lifeworlds.

However, if we understand recognition as simply noticing or theorizing resources, this runs the risk of institutionalizing situated practice. While it is educationally sound to validate local practices and resources, access to dominant practices has to be provided at the same time (Janks, 2000). Recognition needs to be coupled with integration, both in terms of evaluation and application. A transformative notion of recognition is needed; recognition with a particular direction, to achieve representational and communicative purpose. The transformative notion of recognition underlying Harrop-Allin's work means that children's music resources are seen, acknowledged, and also *developed* in richness and complexity. She achieves this through using and developing the games' narrative content, building on specific musical ideas and elements (such as melodies, clapping rhythms, dance formations, call and response forms) as well as encouraging the use of new musical resources, including self-made instruments. Here recognition is linked to development and 'transformed practice' (New London Group, 2000) where children's musical games are used to promote transformative, new learning. From this example, we can see that a multimodal approach to pedagogy stresses the making and production of meaning, rather than the acquisition of received knowledge or critique of received knowledge. Thus, fundamental to the notion of multimodality and a social justice agenda is the concept of transformation, that meaning-making does not so much involve use of a system, as the transformation of available resources.

Multimodal pedagogies and access

In pedagogy it is important to consider what is to be designed, and what social relations we want to design. Of particular interest in terms of social justice is the extent to which multimodal pedagogies can create unregulated spaces in the curriculum to enable a range of student resources to emerge, as well as the ways in which multimodal pedagogies can enable access to dominant forms. In a narrow sense, access is about trying to assist students to cope with the discourses and knowledges of official curricula and with formal methods of assessment. However, beyond curricula demands, access is also about the creation of dispositions towards meaning-making outside of the classroom. Access includes access to self-reflexivity, to a range of semiotic resources, to local practices in a global world, and to the knowledge structures and conventions of different disciplines. Formal education often closes down access to a range of resources, except the dominant ones. Recovering those semiotic resources means enabling access to power and to agency.

In exploring access, this chapter now looks at academic literacies and access to Higher Education in South Africa, including the use of new technologies. Researchers and practitioners in the field of 'academic literacies' have begun to look beyond language-focused pedagogies, to recognize the role of a range of modes in teaching and meaning-making. Thesen (2001), for example, examined utilizing multimodal texts in the first-year curriculum for access. She looked at a first-year course, 'Texts in Context', where the idea was to use visuals (disposable cameras and pictures of the university environment) to enable access for educationally disadvantaged students. She argues that multimodality in the Humanities requires students to engage with four 'layers' of language: the English language system, academic discourse, mode-specific language associated with the analysis of the visual and a metalanguage of critical analysis. These layers interact in highly complex ways and can, in fact, work against access, thus disadvantaging the very students that the multimodal curriculum was designed to empower. This study was important to enable educators and academic literacy practitioners to engage more critically with multimodal approaches to pedagogy. Thesen's later work (2007) continues to look at questions of power and access in Higher Education. She analyses the event of the lecture in Higher Education as a multimodal text and looks at the production of authority in lecture spaces in terms of the discourses circulating in South African society. Interestingly, she argues that lecture theatres provide important multimodal spaces for student learning and identity work to take place.

My own work explores aspects of multimodality and access to academic literacies in different disciplinary sites in Higher Education. This work re-looks at key concerns, concepts and approaches of an 'academic literacies' approach to teaching and research (predominantly focused on writing) using a multimodal perspective (Archer, 2006). I argue for the need to make conventionalized multimodal practices in Higher Education explicit in order to enable student access to these. Archer (2013), for instance, explores how voice may be realized in forms other than writing, and the implications of these multimodal forms for the academic literacies field. Earlier work looked at establishing a dialogue between less regulated spaces in the curriculum and the texts that emerge, and the more regulated genres of the curriculum so that students' representational resources can be utilized in innovative ways. An example of this was a Symbolic Object project in a first-year communication course in an engineering foundation programme for students from less advantaged educational backgrounds. In the project, students identified everyday objects that have symbolic meanings and examined these in a range of physical, cultural and communicational contexts. The focus of this pedagogical intervention was looking at how to use objects and symbolism in order to engage with questions of diversity and identity. Objects were seen as a way of eliciting student narratives and highlighting notions of change (Archer, 2007, 2008).

In thinking about student access, the relation between resources, recognition and new technologies cannot be ignored. Many educators and researchers in South Africa have explored these connections, particularly in response to the 'digital divide' (Castells, 1998). For instance, some have looked at ways of assisting students from under-resourced schools to integrate new technologies (e.g. Walton and Archer, 2004; Prinsloo and Walton, 2008) and have looked at the role of new technologies in teaching academic literacies, exploring how technological environments change the creation and distribution of knowledge (Huang and Archer, 2008; Walton and Pallitt, 2012). However, research in South Africa has also complexified the relationship to technologies of writing and computing, and looks at 'low tech' resources for meaning-making, such as posters and everyday objects or the 'lack' of technology – using a resource for a different means, a kind of 'resourcefulness'. This seems to be a global trend, however, and is not always only for economic reasons.

Using multimodal resources to access writing

For South Africa the link between the real recognition of resources and *writing* is important in terms of access. This applies to the public arena, school classrooms and Higher Education where writing as a resource tends to be valued over other modes. In the public arena, Cathy Kell (2006, 2009) looked at how the shift from speaking to writing to reading led to different degrees of empowerment in a particular context. She looked at how a group of families came together in a local savings club to access government subsidy aimed at supporting the building of houses. She tells the story of one participant, Noma, who articulated her problem with the housing by speaking about it as an individual problem at community meetings. Noma was then encouraged to write her story and more and more people began to read it. The story was referred to as 'powerful' and she was invited to tell her story at a provincial and then a national meeting. A month later, her house was rebuilt. Drawing on Kress and Van Leeuwen's (2001) strata of communicative practice, Kell refers to this trajectory as design, production and distribution. In her study, she describes the recontextualization of meaning-making as it traverses contexts and moves across modes. Noma's trajectory which involved writing a story about her problem house, shows that 'people can draw on many modes of meaning making, but that these are contingent and emergent, related to the extent of hybridity, novelty and redesign' (Kell, 2009: 90). The lack of breadth of written resources available in the wider community contributed to her story being viewed so powerfully. In this context, the spoken mode did not achieve Noma's aims, yet the written mode did.

Another example of the important link between multiple resources and writing is Newfield's work on the 'transmodal moment' in classrooms. According to Newfield, multimodal pedagogy has 'encouraged complex, creative and varied practices of text-making in classrooms that are counter-hegemonic at the same time as supportive of traditional language development goals' (Newfield, 2011: 31). Newfield and Maungedzo (2006) show how a multimodal approach to pedagogy which drew on African popular culture revitalized the poetry curriculum at a high school in Soweto. Shifting the curriculum focus from analysis, which is the mainstream approach to the teaching and learning of poetry in South Africa, to composition, enabled the students to 'modalize' poetry in different ways – as a spoken form, as performance, and even as embroidered cloth. Changing the audience meant the students could write poetry to friends, and, finally, even produce an alternative poetry anthology to the school anthology. It was the move from reading to writing using multimodal means that made this particular pedagogical intervention such a success. Here hegemonic language and pedagogic practices were challenged, whilst simultaneously providing access to dominant language practices.

One way of thinking about providing student access to writing that I have been exploring has been the use of multimodal texts to reflect on citation. Citation is a resource used in the design of meanings in socially shaped and regular ways. It is possible to cite in all modes, but the conventions differ and some modes are more legislated than others. Citation in visual and verbal modes involves appropriating a source into your argument, thus creating a 'new' composition. In music, citation is 'mixing'; in the fine arts, citation could be seen as 'collage'. Although all creativity is variation on a theme and seldom 'original', art can operate on a continuum from complex and nuanced intertextuality to derivative (akin to copying). In our globalized and technologized contexts, downloading images and music and accessing open sources has become the norm, raising questions around copyright and 'originality'. The use of sources in writing is perhaps more tightly policed and the conventions more firmly and widely known than in other modes and genres. In Archer (2013), I argue that it is useful to consider how these processes of textual construction work in order to become more explicit about the ways in which academic voice is constructed. This is important for enabling student access into academic discourse and the discourses of particular disciplines.

Teacher training and potential difficulties with multimodal pedagogies

I would like to discuss one instance which highlighted some of the possible difficulties associated with multimodal approaches to pedagogy. In a teacher training programme at a South African university, an exam question was set to ascertain how teachers would employ some of the ideas around multimodal pedagogies in the classroom. The exam question in the second-year curriculum studies course was based on my article on Symbolic Objects in *English in Education* (Archer, 2007). This article concludes by stating that the symbolic objects project 'can be adapted to the needs of a specific course and discipline in any context that engages in questions of identity, change, relativity of meaning, or material culture' (Archer, 2007: 16). The student teachers were asked how they thought they would apply some of these ideas to their own classrooms. The assumption underlying the Symbolic Object project is that 'culture' is dynamic, always contested, and any practice of culture involves some element of control, coercion or power. The project attempted to situate particular cultural practices within the broader systems of meaning and values that sustain them, and to highlight cultural practices as complex sets of meaning that are in tension with each other. Some of the student teachers did point to the changing meaning of objects across generations. Mostly they talked about how the meanings of an object had changed from the past. One student interestingly thought about the future: 'think of the next generation and what things will have a meaning in their lives or what symbolic objects will they have and why?' The reflection on change over time is a useful and interesting one, however, it still mostly pointed to a reified notion of culture. Rather than a notion of culture as change, there was a strong suggestion that 'cultural objects' are those that belong to 'tradition' and to the 'past'. This notion of culture as a traditional and separate 'thing' came up again and again. The following answer was typical of the type of answers given.

> I would introduce the project by introducing various types of symbols from various culture. I would break it up into four groups. The first English where I could show a symbol of a cross (for the Christian religion). The second Zulu is I could show a symbol of a cultural mask. The third is Jewish where I would show a symbol with the star of David. The fourth is Hindu and I would show their symbol as well. This would make learners recognise different symbols from different cultures.

Here one object signifies one 'culture' which is seen as having distinct boundaries, such as Jewish, Hindu, Zulu and English. The tragedy of this proposed classroom activity is that it lapses into a crude multiculturalism, which works against the idea of 'recognition' proposed here.

One of the main purposes of getting students to talk about objects of interest to them is to draw on their own resources in terms of 'situated practice' (New London Group, 2000). However, in many of these answers, relations of power in the classroom seem to remain the same with the teacher as authority. Often the answers suggest that the teacher provides the students with the objects, rather than elicits them from the students' lifeworlds.

> I would gather 5 different objects and display them in front of the class. I would then explain to them that we are learning about cultures and I would ask a different learner what each object symbolizes in their culture and why.

This does not seem conducive for students to talk freely and to debate contested meanings. There was also little sense of the volatile nature of this kind of classroom activity in the student teachers' answers, evidencing a lack of sensitivity in the envisioning and handling of the task. One teacher said, 'I will introduce it to learners by asking/talking about different cultures and religions there are. I will ask learners to state their religion/culture'. Here the potentially passionate subject matter becomes distilled into a bland multiculturalism which will not shift preconceptions or question stereotypes in any nuanced way.

Although there are many instances of ground-breaking pedagogical interventions and research projects that have resulted in social change, I mention the above to sound a cautionary note. If multimodal pedagogies are appropriated by the curriculum on a large scale, there could be losses, such as curriculum instrumentalism, where multimodality is seen as a way of inducting students into mainstream practices, including writing, instead of opening up interest in a range of resources and being open to possible transformation of established forms and practices as a result. It is clear that multimodal pedagogies understood as simply *including* a variety of text forms in the curriculum will not necessarily enable increased access to educational practices.

Designing a pedagogy for social justice

A multimodal approach to pedagogy is not about innovation only, nor is it about uncritically perpetuating the status quo. Rather, it is based on the premise that the tension between convention and a dynamic for constant change is the norm. In designing a pedagogy for social justice, a number of features are important.

Questioning boundaries between domains

Under the previous political dispensation in South Africa, there was a general ethos of boundary-making with an attempt to police a multitude of these boundaries. Local and global contexts are currently in a period of flux and transition where boundaries between practices are being debated, as are boundaries between academic disciplines and domains of knowledge. A curriculum which draws on and validates students' practices, resources and discourses is invaluable, as students interrogate their past situations and aspirations. Bernstein (1996) points out that power is maintained and relayed through the creation of boundaries between practices, and it is often in 'mixed' forms where power is played out. 'Breaking' or reinterpreting some standard generic conventions often signals an encounter of diverse knowledges and differently organized social worlds.

Exchanging cultural practices

Within multimodal pedagogies, it becomes possible to think of curriculum as a two-way exchange of resources rather than unidirectional transmission. The discourse and knowledge of the discipline are made available, whilst students' resources and are simultaneously utilized and validated. This enables a shift in power relations in the classroom from top-down imposition to negotiation and discussion. In a multimodal approach to pedagogy, projects are not simply springboards for students, but are a serious interrogation and utilization of students' representational resources. Also, discursive and generic conventions are brought into focus – to show what kinds of social situations produce them, and what the meanings of these social situations are.

Harnessing students' representational resources

I have argued that only resources which are visible can become available as elements in conscious design processes. In this way, different ways of thinking and practice in representation become available as resources for students and there is expansion of the repertoire of resources in order to create semiotically open classrooms. This includes multilingualism, indigenous and local cultural and semiotic practices.

Developing metalanguages of reflection

Recognition of resources is achieved through developing appropriate metalanguages. Metalanguages of 'reflective generalization that describe the form, content and function of the discourses of practice' (New London Group, 2000: 24) are important in achieving conscious awareness of the nature of the resources being used. A metalanguage constituted through combinations of primary and secondary discourses can provide other ways of knowing the world – with the 'productive diversity necessary for reconstruction and redesign' (Janks, 2000: 181). A metalanguage may feed into the language of the criteria for assessment purposes, especially when working in unfamiliar modes.

Creating less regulated curriculum spaces

A multimodal approach to pedagogy includes less regulated spaces in order to increase students' choices and allow scope for reflection. In these spaces, students can experiment with multimodal representation, draw on a range of discourses and employ humour or irony. They can draw on primary discourses as well as secondary discourses to create metalanguages to make sense of the curriculum.

Interrogating the relation between text and context in a social justice agenda

Theorizing the relation with context is crucial in thinking about power and social justice in a multimodal approach to pedagogy and research. South African researchers have grappled with theorizing the relationship between text and context, and tend not to see text as a cultural artefact, an object to be taken apart, interpreted and reassembled, but as an unfolding and contingent process. To go back to Kell's example, in looking at trajectories of texts, she looks at transduction (Kress, 2003b) in which a verbal performance was turned into a written story or a list became a set of building materials. It was not the semiotic modes themselves that determined such transformations, but the social conditions in which the texts were embedded. Noma's written story carried weight because of the context of lack of written resources in the wider community. Texts are always sites of struggle. The struggle for representation and which texts 'count' in the curriculum is important in culturally diverse societies where power relations are changing and boundaries between social practices blurring.

Final comments

This chapter has highlighted aspects of multimodal pedagogy and research in South Africa, in relation to power and social justice. I have shown how these pedagogical interventions and research around them is important in contexts like ours where there is still differential access to economic, educational and cultural resources. This chapter has argued that we need to see recognition in relation to access in the broadest sense and not access in the service of existing norms. It is clear that recognition of students' resources in multimodal pedagogies in South Africa has been more than just an 'improved teaching method'. Rather, it has been a revolutionary attempt to redress some of the inequities of our past and to engage with a context of diversity and democratic change with all the profound challenges, changes, contradictions and possibilities this implies. I have shown how through recognition of resources, multimodal pedagogies in this context have interrogated the relation between the local and the global, tradition and modernity. Central to democracy is the recognition of difference as well as commitment to dialogue across difference. A pedagogy for social justice values a conception of identity that lives with and through, not despite, difference, and views difference as productive.

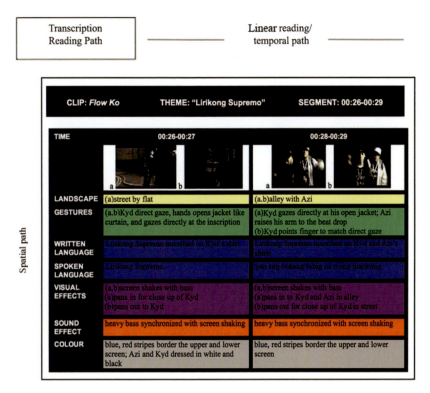

Plate 3.1 Multimodal transcription frame (Domingo, 2011, p. 224).

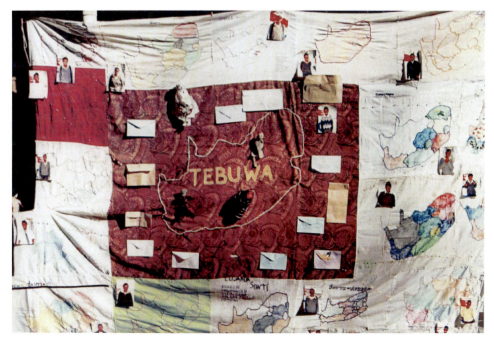

Plate 7.1 Thebuwa cloth with maps and poems (cloth, thread, paint, paper, doll-like figures, photographs, safety pins).

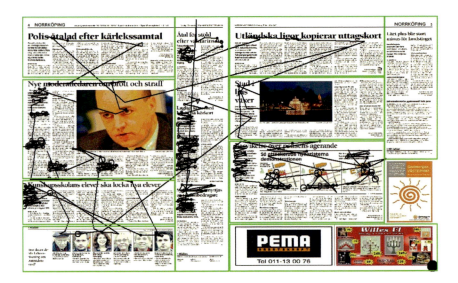

Plate 20.1 Reader's interaction with a newspaper spread. The circles indicate the position and duration of *fixations,* the lines connecting fixations represent *saccades*. The diameter of each fixation is proportional to its duration (the black dot in the bottom right corner represents one second). Fixations are stops or periods of time when the point of regard is relatively still. It is during fixations that we acquire useful information. Fixation duration is often used as a measure of how much cognitive effort is required for information processing. During saccades, the eyes move at a relatively rapid rate to reorient the point of regard from one spatial position to another. Saccades are very short, usually lasting from 20 to 40 ms. Our vision is suppressed and we are essentially blind during saccades.

Source: Holsanova, 2010.

Plate 20.2 A newspaper spread is read for one minute by two readers. (Continued opposite)

Source: Holsanova *et al.*, 2006.

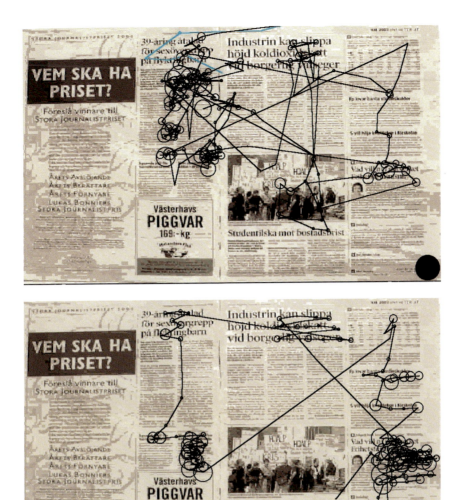

Plate 20.2 Continued.

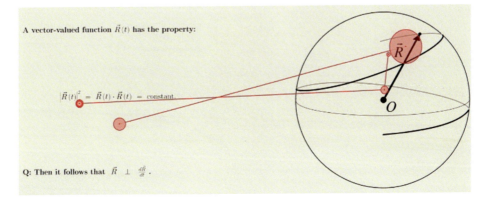

Plate 20.3 Mathematical problem-solving in vector calculus with illustration.

Source: Nyström and Ögren, 2012.

Plate 20.4 Reading two versions of information graphics: (a) separated graphics; (b) integrated graphics.

Source: Holsanova *et al.*, 2009.

The prometaphase begins with the **collapse of the nuclear membrane**. The structure of the chromosomes becomes visible: as they are condensed from pairs of chromatin fibres, they consist of two identical sister chromosomes attached to each other at the centromere.

The **fibres from the opposite poles of the mitotic spindle** now attach to the **centromeres**. As a result, each chromosome is now connected to both poles of the spindle. As the pairs of centrioles continue to move apart, the chromosomes are drawn into two directions at the same time.

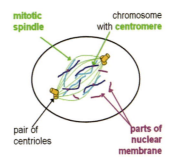

Plate 20.5 Example of color coding: keywords in the text and labels identifying parts of the illustration are of the same color.

Source: Folker *et al.*, 2005.

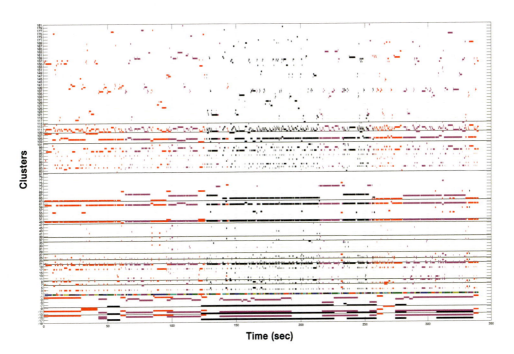

Plate 28.1 Time-stamped multimodal database.

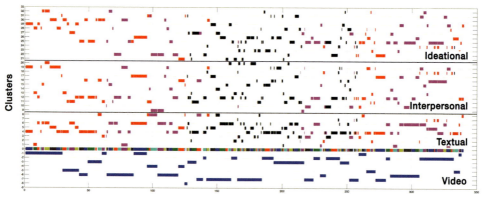

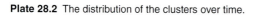

Plate 28.2 The distribution of the clusters over time.

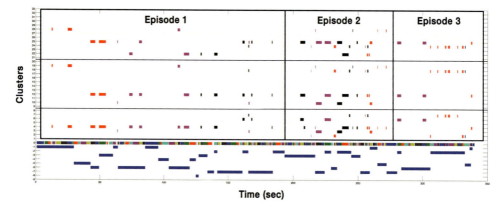

Plate 28.3 Most frequent cluster combinations-of-three.

(a)

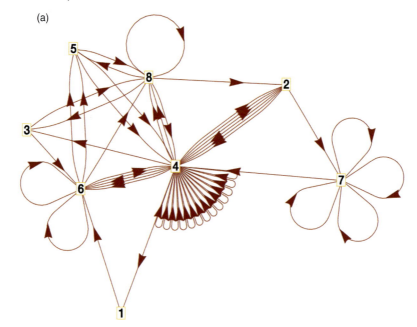

Plate 28.4 Network diagrams for textual metafunction: (a) Jon Scott; (b) Kevin Trenberth; (c) Myron Ebell. (Continued opposite)

(b)

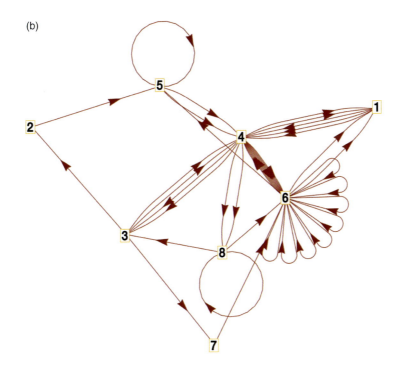

(c)

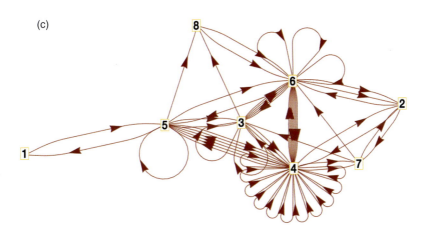

Plate 28.4 Continued.

Plate 33.1 The main home page; the *Culture* home page; the *Art & Design* home page; and a story page (left–right).

Plate 33.2 A montage of menus from the top of five home pages from the *Guardian*, 17 August 2012.

Part III

Multimodality across different theoretical perspectives

Introduction to Part III

The third part of the handbook examines multimodality beyond its roots in social semiotics, systemic functional grammar and discourse studies. As noted in Chapter 2, the multimodal character of communication, representation and interaction is acknowledged within many disciplines, and some of the ideas of multimodality are not new to some. Indeed, multimodal theory and research has drawn ideas, concepts and research tools from a wide range of disciplines including anthropology, sociology and art history.

The benefits and challenges of the relationship across a range of disciplines with multimodality is the focus of this part. The ten chapters included within it each explore how multimodality features within a specific theoretical approach to representation, communication and interaction. The approaches discussed are socio-interactional linguistics, visual studies, New Literacy Studies, multimodal corpora approaches, critical discourse analysis, semiotic paradigms, eye-tracking methods, socio-cultural studies, ethnomethodology and conversation analysis, and anthropology, each of which is briefly introduced below. It is important to be clear that these disciplines or approaches are not the only ones that have engaged productively with multimodality. These approaches have, however, foregrounded the need to look beyond language in order to understand how people communicate and interact and have the potential to contribute to the development of multimodal theory and research, including through the challenges they make to contemporary multimodal research.

In Chapter 14, Scollon and Scollon explore the connection between multimodality and socio-linguistics. Multimodality is differently construed in socio-linguistic work, which is based on the assumption that speech or writing are the primary carriers of meaning which other modes merely expand or exemplify. This is reflected in the fine-grained analysis of speech (lexis, intonation, rhythm and tone, hesitations and restarts), alongside more occasional discussion of, for instance, hand movements or shifts in the direction of gaze in talk (e.g. Erickson, 2004a). The methodological privileging of particular linguistic resources is also reflected in notions like 'non-verbal', 'paralinguistic' or 'context'. Nonetheless, multimodality has been central to much theorizing in social-linguistic traditions. Erving Goffman's notion of 'frame' (Goffman, 1974), for instance, suggests how people co-construct a 'definition of what goes on' in interactions using a range of different modes. Frames are established through beginnings and endings marked in a range of different modes of communication. Scollon and Scollon take the Natural History of the Interview (NHI) as an early example of interdisciplinary socio-linguistic research with a multimodal twist. They argue that while this study was innovative and significant for multimodality, it relied too much on language to provide the principles of analysis, a reliance that was supported by the belief that 'linguistics held the key which would unlock the structural, patterned truth of what had until then seemed to be highly elusive and subjective human experience'. Indeed, Scollon and Scollon cite the failure to recognize that this was not the case, as the 'fatal assumption' of the NHI project. That said, traces of the questions posed and some of the ideas raised in this early study can be seen in contemporary multimodal research.

How to describe image and to characterize seeing have been the basis of much philosophical and methodological discussion within art and visual studies. Visual studies is concerned with the central role of the visual in the cultural construction of social life and people's everyday experience of the world, socially, physically and psychologically. Studies of late twentieth-century culture have examined what has been termed a turn to the visual (Mirzoeff, 1999; Mitchell, 1995) in which the modern world is seen to have become a visual phenomenon. Visual studies connects with fundamental questions of 'reality', ideology and power, agency, as well as signification and the procedures and potentials for interpreting meaning.

Machin, in Chapter 15, explores how visual studies has engaged with some of the concerns that underlie multimodality at the same time as constructively challenging some of the basic premises of using a model of language and grammar to understand the visual. By engaging with these different perspectives the chapter hopes to clarify what a multimodal perspective can offer, and the benefits of engaging with the work of visual studies.

Multimodality has been taken up by many working within New Literacy Studies (NLS) and there is considerable connection between these two perspectives. NLS has been central in the theorization of the complexity of literacies as historically, socially and culturally situated practice (Street, 1998; Barton *et al.*, 2000). Key to this attempt to rethink literacy is the analytical focus of NLS on literacy events and literacy practices with texts in people's everyday lives, and the bid to document emergent literacies across different local contexts. This marks a shift in focus from the idea of literacy as an autonomous neutral set of skills or competencies that people acquire through schooling and can deploy universally to a view of literacies as local and situated. Within NLS there is increasing recognition of the complex interaction between local and global literacies and the need to be sensitive to how people's literacy practices traverse physical and virtual spaces (Pahl, 1999; Leander and Lovvorn, 2006; Alvermann *et al.*, 2001). The empirical description of new mediascapes is thus seen as essential to understanding how people negotiate social identity in relation to the economies and cultures of late modernity. The multimodal character of these representational and communicational landscapes is a major factor that brings NLS and multimodality together.

In Chapter 16, Street, Pahl and Rowsell address the different epistemological framings of New Literacy Studies and the multimodal tradition; one rooted in an ethnographic perspective and the other more focused on social semiotics and systemic function linguistics. They explore how New Literacy Studies can inform research from a multimodal perspective and vice versa. The chapter describes a number of research projects that combine these approaches and argues that 'Multimodality and New Literacy Studies, when brought together, serve to fill out a larger more nuanced picture of social positioning and group practices, texts, contexts, space, and time'.

As perhaps is already apparent through the chapters in Parts I and II of this handbook, multimodality tends to focus on small-scale qualitative research, indeed it often attends to single illustrative cases. In Chapter 17, John Bateman argues that 'as studies of multimodality progress, it is increasingly important to evaluate hypotheses and theories concerning multimodal meaning-making against data' and to move beyond illustrative cases to establish the degree to which the concepts of multimodality can explain uses of multimodality more generally. This chapter engages with how multimodal corpora can be used to critique and empirically validate multimodal concepts and to explore the potential boundaries of multimodal theory. In doing so, Bateman shows how the scale of multimodality as a method can be extended and the importance of empirically interrogating theory towards theoretical development and robustness.

Critical discourse analysis and multimodality have something of a shared history. In Chapter 18, Lilie Chouliaraki explores the potential of a framework that brings these two theoretical lenses together for the analysis of media discourse. Such a framework can, she argues, take into account how media texts are embedded in both technological artefacts and social relationships. Chouliaraki applies a multimodal discourse analysis onto media texts in order to study their visual and linguistic properties including camera/visual, graphic/pictorial or aural/linguistic. This framework enables the critical concerns on the ethical and political role of television and other media in the contemporary media landscape as a 'global village' to be addressed.

Hartmut Stöckl, in Chapter 19, argues that semiotics and multimodality are connected via conceptual and methodological origins and interests. He argues that, 'multimodality studies are in need of a semiotic underpinning' as they treat all signifying and communicative phenomena in the same way and that similarly, 'any semiotic venture presupposes a multimodal conception of signs, texts and communication from the start'. From this starting point the chapter outlines the points of departure and connection between semiotics and multimodality and the central concepts from semiotics that can travel into multimodal research.

How to apply eye-tracking methodology in multimodal research is the topic of Chapter 20, by Jana Holsanova. It gives an overview of different ways in which eye-tracking methodology can be used in research on multimodality. Various application areas associated with the use of eye-tracking methodology are summarized and the potentials and limitations of this methodology are listed. The chapter presents a new perspective that focuses on the reception of multimodality and emphasizes how multimodal messages are perceived by the users. The perspective is described in relation to three main production-oriented perspectives within multimodality: social semiotic multimodal analysis, a systemic functional approach and multimodal interactional analysis (each of which are introduced in Chapter 2). Holsanova argues and illustrates that eye-tracking measurements, in combination with verbal protocols, interviews, comprehension tests and questionnaires, are a suitable method for studying reception of multimodality. The chapter provides examples from eye-tracking studies focusing on the integration of various modes to demonstrate the use of these methods.

In Chapter 21, Ivarsson, Linderoth and Säljö analyse ideas of multimodality within the framework of a socio-cultural theory of mind and mediated action. According to this perspective, meaning-making through words, images, sounds and forms of mediation is not a 'private' affair of subjectively imposing values, knowledge or motives on one's 'own' perceptions. Nor is it a matter of unpacking or interpreting universal and culturally given meanings of an 'objective' world. Rather, meaning-making is seen as emerging from interpretative practices in social activities in which participants relate what they see and hear to the socio-historical resources, for instance by way of canons of representation, as well as to the situated resources they have available and which may be negotiated in the face-to-face interaction.

Luff, Heath and Pitsch demonstrate in Chapter 22 how workplace studies, an approach that draws on ethnomethodology and conversation analysis and ethnography to look beyond word. Modes of communication other than language are increasingly seen as relevant, given the concern of workplace studies with examining situated language and language use in interaction (Whalen *et al.*, 2002). Linguists working in conversation analysis and ethnomethodology in particular have focused on the role of gaze, gesture, drawing and texts alongside language in interaction (e.g. Goodwin, 2001, 2007; Heath *et al.*, 2002). For instance, Goodwin shows that when a speaker's gaze reaches his or her listener, they are expected to be oriented towards the speaker (Goodwin, 2001, 2007). If not, a pause or a restart follows. In this way, shifts in multimodal displays of orientation can suggest varying levels of engagement within different frames operating at the same time.

Luff, Heath and Pitsch show how ethnomethodological and conversation analysis focus on 'the situated character of practical action to address the ways in which particular actions and sequences of action contingently arise within the emergent or ongoing accomplishment of workplace activities'. Their analytical interest is primarily the contributions of others, of coparticipants, within the 'moment by moment, concerted and interactional accomplishment of particular actions and activities' and 'the practices and reasoning in and through which people produce particular actions and make sense of the actions of others'. They set out to discover and describe these practices, and explain how participants orient to and rely upon these practices. The forms of transcription and concepts for microanalysis within this approach have, as this chapter shows, much to offer a multimodal perspective.

Multimodality is intimately tied to the senses and perception, although the study of sense perception has traditionally fallen to psychologists. More recently this work has been a focus of anthropologists who have turned to look at the senses (Pink, 2006; Howes, 2003, 2005). Pink (2006) in *The Future of Visual Anthropology: Engaging the Senses* argues that visual anthropology has a new potential in a digital, visual time when the roles of image and writing and other senses give rise to new methodologies and practices within anthropology. In Chapter 23 on anthropology and multimodality, David Howes proposes a 'cross-cultural multi-modal theory of sense perception born out of the fusion of cognitive science and sensory anthropology'. The chapter draws on a series of case studies in the cultural life of the senses from Melanesia, and North and South America to illustrate the main tenets of his theoretical approach.

The ten chapters sketched above outline the potentials for combining a multimodal approach to research with other perspectives, as well as indicating some of the challenges in doing so. Opening up multimodal research to the ideas and scope of other perspectives may help in the further development of data transcription, research methods and analytical processes. More generally, the theoretical concepts that different perspectives work with may prove productive for multimodal research even if only in the new questions and challenges they raise for multimodality.

14

Multimodality and language

A retrospective and prospective view

Ron Scollon and Suzie Wong Scollon

Introduction

'Multimodality', a new term, has become a focus of academic and intellectual interest just within the past decade or so, while language has been at the center of such interests for millennia. The task of relating multimodality and language, then, is a task of relating this new and fresh but still largely amorphous perspective on human communication to a complex, ancient, richly developed, and historical one which is differently naturalized in different cultures. We look at this relationship within a retrospective view of just a few decades focused largely on research within a European–western sphere of activity. We focus on change in the past five decades, at the beginning of which students of nonverbal communication researched real-time conversation among humans as a form of social activism, resistance to political surveillance and oppression, driven by a structural model of language which gradually dissolved. The realization that other modes of communication did not function like language, which is sequential in contrast to spatially perceived images, forced a reinvention of multimodality. Logos, flashing light boxes and movement through the built environment require re-examination of foundational assumptions about the nature of language, communication, and the use of communicative modes to produce meaning. While language is no longer taken as an independent and prototypical model of all modes of communication, it continues to influence researchers in multimodality as a resource for ideas for the analysis of separate communication modes. Most striking is the understanding that no mode of communication operates in a monomodal fashion. New frameworks and perspectives are developing to conceptualize a new and complex set of relationships among all modes. Coupled with the new emphasis on concrete forms of human action, we suggest that a key area for developing analysis is the spatio-temporal integration of communicative modes across differing timescales.

Multimodality and language: merger and redistribution

'Multimodality' is a new term. 'Language' is a very old one. Multimodality has become a focus of academic and intellectual interest just within the past decade or so; language has been at or near the center of such interests for millennia. The task of relating multimodality and language, then, is a task of relating this new and fresh but still largely amorphous perspective on human communication to a complex perspective which is ancient, richly developed, and historical and one which is also differently naturalized in different cultures. Our brief discussion here is necessarily limited to looking at this relationship within a retrospective view of just a few decades focused largely on research within a European–western sphere of activity. Our prospective view is even more narrowly constrained.

First of all, multimodality is not simply a rephrasing of the field of study often called 'non-verbal communication' (NVC). Treating NVC separately from language has masked two important phenomena. First, language is itself often sharply divided as a subject of study between studies of written forms of language and studies of spoken forms of language, the so-called great divide between literacy and orality. Second, NVC studies rarely treat forms of communication which are not based on active real-time performance by humans. Such multimodal communicative phenomena as the design of objects, the built environment, works of art and graphics, film, video, or interactive media productions have fallen largely outside the purview of NVC. Furthermore, NVC has to date taken little interest in questions of the extra-verbal meanings of the design and material production of written communication such as typography, book design, color or materials used in printing, or the rapidly increased centrality of graphic design in the rise of advertising and other media productions.

Likewise, multimodality is not a rephrasing or even an extension of the vast historical array of language and linguistic fields of study. While it would be simplistic to say so, language and linguistic studies have largely been divided between studies of language as an abstract code and language as a tool for taking personal and social action in the world. Much of literary theory as well as formal linguistics is concerned with coming to understand language as a formal and logical system quite independently of any study of just how language is used. The contrasting line of research began, perhaps, with the rhetoric of Aristotle but continues in the present in the fields of rhetoric, pragmatics, socio–linguistics, or functional linguistics.

In the midst of these complex realignments of fields of study, however, language and language studies have played an important role first in the development of NVC and now, more recently, in the development of multimodality. In many areas both then and now, what is known about language – both codes and functions – has been taken as a kind of prototype of the newly developing knowledge of modes other than linguistic ones. Thus in semiotics much of the intellectual structure of the discipline is based on Saussurean models of language, especially his insistence on the arbitrary nature of the distinction between signifiers and the signified. Early studies of NVC took the hierarchical structuring of phonetics, phonemics, morphemics, and syntax which was foundational to structural linguistics as the prototype for the structuring of all modes. Hence we find terms such as 'proxemics' and 'kinesics', both based on 'phonemics' and its umbrella field of linguistics. The centrality of linguistics as the source of organizing metaphors continues as urban planners and geographers write of the narrative of places or take analytical positions which are described as discursive.

There are three general points which we will address in what follows. The first focuses on changes which have taken place since the groundbreaking studies of communication at mid-twentieth century. The organizing question is: What ever became of the very promising and widely comprehensive studies of pioneers such as Gregory Bateson, Ray Birdwhistell, Edward T. Hall, or Kenneth Pike?

The second point orients around the two meanings of 'modality', modality as mode of communication such as speech or writing or music, or modality as mood, the expression of shifting stances toward reality such as the distinction made in most languages between *realis* and *irrealis* modes. This is the difference between saying, 'It will be a nice day tomorrow', and 'It could be a nice day tomorrow'. Multimodality may be construed in either of these meanings and we will suggest, following Kress and Van Leeuwen (1996) that different stances toward reality are not similarly encoded in different modes.

Finally, the third point turns to suggestions about what kinds of studies might profitably develop in the near future as the study of multimodality and language matures as a field.

Five decades' change: from language and nonverbal communication to language and multimodality

Three foundational books captured the spirit of studies of language and nonverbal communication as of the 1950s, Kenneth Pike's *Language in Relation to a Unified Theory of the Structure of Human Behavior* (1954), Ruesch and Kees's *Nonverbal Communication: Notes on the Visual Perception of Human Relations* (1954 [1964]), and Edward T. Hall's *The Silent Language* (1959). Taken together these books evidence a rapid flowering of interest and collaboration during the 1950s across the fields of communication, linguistics, psychiatry, poetry and film. That interest was focused on coming to understand how language works pragmatically in relation to all other modes of human communicative behavior.

For our purposes what is most significant about these three quite different works is the centrality of language. For Pike it was language and the principles of linguistics which unified the study of all human behavior from the narrowest level of phonetic detail in speech up to the broadest levels of human events and, indeed, human life. Ruesch and Kees comment that their book represents a broad development of interest in "nonverbal forms of communication and with the verbal form largely in its pragmatic aspects" (1954 [1964]: 5). Like Pike, their concern was to develop a unified understanding of communication, not to separate nonverbal communication from linguistic communication as has become more common in the years since their pioneering work. Edward T. Hall's book indicates in the title that for him language provided the key structural/analogical means for understanding non-speech communication. While Hall's work did not come to public recognition until his 1959 book, Hall worked closely with his colleague, the linguist George L. Trager, at the US State Department's Foreign Service Institute in Washington, DC. In his autobiography (Hall 1992) he discusses the great importance of this collaboration in bringing linguistic principles of analysis to his work in areas of communication which had largely lain outside the purview of structural analysis. We note that Ray Birdwhistell joined Hall and Trager at the Foreign Service Institute during the year 1952.

Kendon and Sigman (1996) note that Birdwhistell, who coined the term 'kinesics' in his 1952 paper and which Edward T. Hall was to use later in his own publications, had argued that 'human body motion is culturally patterned and it can be analyzed using the same mode of approach that is used in analyzing the structure of spoken language' (Kendon and Sigman 1996: 231).

In a few words, even though there was a tremendous flowering of interest in the non-language aspects of communication, the leaders of these developments in communication, linguistics, psychiatry and other fields believed that linguistics held the key which would unlock the structural, patterned truth of what had until then seemed to be highly elusive and subjective human experience.

These three books were far from the only expressions of this new interest in language and nonverbal communication. They appeared against the background of a monumental extended study which involved some of the leading scholars in their separate fields: *The Natural History of the Interview (NHI)*. Leeds-Hurwitz (2005) gives a succinct summary:

NHI was begun at Stanford University's Center for Advanced Study in the Behavioral Sciences in 1955–1956 because the psychiatrist Frieda Fromm-Reichmann wanted to teach her students what she knew how to do particularly well but could not describe, how to use intuition to appropriately handle patients (Leeds-Hurwitz 1987, 1988). In addition to Fromm–Reichmann, the initial group included another psychiatrist (Henry W. Brosin), two linguists (Charles F. Hockett and Norman A. McQuown), and two cultural anthropologists (Alfred L. Kroeber and David M. Schneider).

(2005: 138)

The project was soon expanded to include Ray L. Birdwhistell and Gregory Bateson who at that time was at the Palo Alto Veteran's Hospital. Note that Bateson was the main source of existing filmed social interactional data, according to Leeds-Hurwitz. This was material he had filmed together with the poet and film-maker Weldon Kees while at Langley Porter Clinic in San Francisco. Perhaps the youngest researcher involved in their work at that time was Erving Goffman whose own work came to publication with *The Presentation of Self in Everyday Life* in 1959.

What is important about the *Natural History of the Interview* project for our purposes here are two things. First of all, the choice of the phrase 'natural history' to characterize this work connects studies of face-to-face communication to the long history in biology of the study of animal behavior *in situ*, especially studies of mammalian communication. This phrase 'natural history' comes into the work by the influence of Gregory Bateson (Leeds-Hurwitz 2005).

Perhaps even more important is that for this 'natural history' project the prototypical communication event chosen was a spoken interview. From the point of view of natural history of human communication the event analyzed might as easily have been a ball game, the cooking of a dinner, or a sequence of work in a factory. It is important, however, that the communicative event chosen was one in which spoken language holds the pivotal position. This is fully in keeping with the centrality of linguistic structural analysis that we have just seen in the other foundational projects of this time.

If we keep in mind Gregory Bateson's longstanding interest in locating human communication within the much broader perspective of mammalian communication, the focus of these comprehensive views of human communication was not on what was special to humans – grammar and the rest – but what was common among mammals – rhythm, physical size, facial expression, tail wiggling, hackles raising and the rest. And the question was: How does language fit into that? We shall return to this question below.

Interplay of academic and social climates

Perhaps it is easier to account for the centrality of language in this flowering of studies of non-linguistic forms of communication than it is to account for the development of these studies in the first place. As to the role of language, all of the main figures in this intellectual development acknowledge the stimulating role of what were then still relatively new discoveries of linguistic structure being promulgated by linguists beginning with Saussure in his lectures at Geneva (published posthumously in 1916), Sapir (1921) and Bloomfield (1933). It could be argued that these discoveries in linguistics were the leading discoveries in the social sciences during this period and it seems that everybody was anxious to see how they might be applied across the board to communication.

This does not really account, however, for the rapid development of an interest in non-linguistic forms of communication. Bateson brought his own background in biology. But perhaps more importantly, there is reason to think that it is not at all by accident that Edward T. Hall worked within the State Department in training a range of government personnel from diplomats to spies. The newly burgeoning Cold War was beginning to demand not only the ability to decipher and translate the languages of other nations but to be able to pass within them as essentially undetectable members. This nonverbal communication material was the stuff of passing as the member of a different social or cultural group, not simply knowing the language.

On the other hand, Ruesch and Kees suggest that a strong motive for them was resistance to political surveillance and oppression in their own country. In their book, Ruesch and Kees (1954 [1964]) position their work solidly as an activist, indeed anti-McCarthyist, project which they locate at a paradoxical point between enabling individual democratic freedom and enabling political and other forms of oppression. On the opening page they comment: 'Nightmarish dreams of the future depicted by Aldous Huxley in Brave New World and George Orwell in Nineteen Eighty-four seem to be almost upon us' (1954: 3).

They comment that specialists in mass communication from radio and television, advertising, and propaganda work toward a single end: 'capturing an audience and controlling its thought' (1954: 3). They go on to write,

> The trend of a number of approaches [in many different fields] has been toward an essential concern with nonverbal forms of communication and with the verbal form largely in its pragmatic aspects. Such a reaction against the overevaluation of the spoken and printed word, and against both commercialism and the relative exclusion of nonverbal elements, can in one sense be interpreted as a move toward safety. In a time of political or ideological crisis, there exists a tendency to censor words in the naïve belief that thought can be brought under absolute control. Although books can be burned, the use of certain words legally outlawed, and even the act of listening to particular broadcasts or speeches marked as a criminal offense, communication through silent action is more difficult to suppress. It has been widely noted how, under authoritarian regimes, human beings turn more and more toward the perception of the nonverbal, the evaluation of nonverbally codified things, and expression through gesture and action .... The present book was written in the midst of such contemporary trends in communication.
>
> (1954: 5)

This concern with social issues was widely shared among these researchers. Kendon and Sigman (1996) quote Birdwhistell's account of his own concern with social activism.

> For most of us one thing was clear ... one must be 'socially useful'. And we talked of the two pathways, on the one hand social work or labor organizing which would bring immediate proof of advocacy and social responsibility or, on the other, *social science*, whereby one could learn to save man by understanding him.
>
> (Birdwhistell 1980: 1; quoted in Kendon and Sigman 1996: 234)

While the history of studies of communication during that period of time remains to be written, for us it is more to the point of this chapter to ask: What happened to this body of work which extended across so many disciplines and in which so many figures who are now considered the founders of several fields participated? Why is multimodality now having to be reinvented?

In the first place, as Leeds-Hurwitz puts it, 'in its final form NHI is an unwieldy document, unpublishable due to a combination of its length and the complexity of the transcription forming the body of the material' (2005: 139).

The NHI project, like many others seeking to build a rapprochement between studies of language and studies of nonverbal communication/multimodality, came up against the heavy pressures of publication in a narrow modal range – academic publication as books and articles without the support of extended transcriptions and images. This, it is to be hoped, is currently being remedied to some extent with new media forms of presentation.

If we set aside questions of the social and political climates of the times and focus more directly on the stated relationship made between language and nonverbal communication, it becomes clear that two things happened to dissipate this early high level of energy and interest. In the first place the structural model of language itself was already in the process of dissolution through the work of post-structuralist, generative analysts. While Chomsky's (1957) *Syntactic Structures* did not in itself undermine confidence in the structural agenda, it did signal the rapidly developing critique among linguists and language scholars of the very models of language being used to drive the nonverbal communication project.

Simultaneous with this erosion of the structural-grammatical model of analysis was the developing understanding that other modes of communication simply did not function like language. As hard as they tried to locate them, scholars were not able in the end to discover a hierarchy of 'emes' from the lowest to the highest compositional levels. In a few words, the project failed because of the fatal assumption that all modes of communication were structurally analogous to language and would be patterned with analogous grammars. Insights which are now quite commonplace such as the understanding that language in both spoken and written forms unfolds its meanings in a linear sequence in contrast to images which are spatially perceived as unitary wholes were essentially fatal to the linguistic model of analysis that was being used as the basis for analysis. When the analysis extends to the built environment – rooms, plazas, or cities – it becomes clear that meanings in such semiotic spaces are produced in a highly complex process which combines both immediate and spatial visual or aural perceptions and linear and unfolding meanings as the person acts by moving through them (Lemke, 2002b).

In a world of logos, flashing light boxes, and texting, even linguistics is hard put to use conventional theories of language to account for these forms of pragmatic language use, much less provide the foundation for studies of meaning across all modes, whether these modes are treated in isolation or in their more normal configurations of combined modes. Although in the 1950s it had seemed the last word had been said about the relationship between language and nonverbal communication and all that remained was for the consequences to play out, the present interest in multimodality argues that it is again necessary to return to the foundational assumptions about the nature of language, of communication, and of the use of communicative modes to produce meaning.

Modes of expression and grammatical mood

While the older structural models of linguistics have largely failed to be productive in nonverbal communication and multimodality studies, languages remain rich sources of ideas for the study of multimodality as Kress and Van Leeuwen (1996, 2001) and others have amply demonstrated. This is particularly the case for functional linguistics or systemic functional grammar (Halliday, 1978, 1985). Here we would like to focus on just one aspect of linguistic coding that is important for studies of multimodality, the coding of modality or mood.

Note that there is the potential for confusion on this point. As the word 'modality' is used in the concept of 'multimodality', modality refers to the multiplicity of communicative modes such as, perhaps writing, speaking, gesture, attire, movement, or the design of objects and environments. The word 'modality' also refers, however, to a variety of stances which can be taken concerning the value of linguistic statements. The differences among the following statements are all differences in this form of modality or mood:

> I ate dinner. (Simple description of an action.)
> I should eat dinner. (Suggests a sense of obligation to the action.)
> I might eat dinner. (Suggests doubt about the possibility of the action.)
> I would eat dinner. (Suggests that conditions must be met before the action.)
> I can eat dinner. (Suggests the focus is on the ability to carry out the action.)
> I ought to eat dinner. (Suggests a moral obligation to the action.)

All languages have complex systems of modality to indicate the varying stances a speaker or writer might take toward the pragmatic force of a statement (Bybee and Fleishman, 1995; Chafe, 1995; Lemke, 1990a, 1995; Palmer, 2001). One of the primary distinctions is between what linguists call *realis* and *irrealis* modes. *Realis* is something 'real', 'definite', 'perceived by the person speaking'. *Irrealis* is 'imagined', 'unreal', 'indefinite', 'unknown' or 'unknowable'. This distinction is most often indicated by the use of a verb in the appropriate mode. Take the following two examples:

> *Realis*: I bought a book yesterday. (The speaker is claiming that the action is completed.)
> *Irrealis*: I might have bought a book yesterday. (The speaker gives us doubt about whether this action was actually carried out.)

The distinction between *realis* and *irrealis* does not need to be explicitly stated within the sentence, however. We can see this by comparing the following two conversational sequences:

Realis:

> A: I need to buy a book.
> B: There's a convenience store over there.
> A: I doubt they'll have the one I'm looking for.

Irrealis:

> A: I need to buy a book.
> B: There's a convenience store over there.
> A: Thanks, that should do the trick.

In the first vignette 'a book' means a definite, particular book. The person has a specific book in mind. In the second vignette 'a book' means just some book or perhaps any book. The person imagines that there is a book, but does not have any particular book in mind.

In language, modality is most often expressed explicitly with modal verbs, but the modal status may only be made explicit with further discussion.

It is probably fair to say that at this stage of the development of multimodality, the expression of modality is not as clearly coded into the modes as it is in the languages of the world. This is a question that might direct us toward studies of art or music history, ethnomusicology, graphic design and other fields which are likely to as yet be unfamiliar to researchers coming to multimodality from a background in language or linguistics.

Kress and Van Leeuwen (1996) have opened up this discussion of modality within multimodality with the concept of coding orientation in visual semiotics. We might summarize this issue by saying that all things being equal an image is felt to be more *realis* the closer it comes to normal human vision, the closer it comes to what one sees with the naked eye. For example, the so-called 'landscape' orientation of an image rectangle that is wider than it is high (about a 5:3 ratio) is the way we see the world under normal conditions. This landscape-oriented rectangle is used as the default orientation for cameras, movie and television screens, landscape painting, and many other forms of both moving and still images. The up-ended 'portrait' orientation is the 'realis' mode for pages of books and portraits.

Within the landscape framing of an image, color hues, densities, and intensities are also perceived to be *realis*. This is how the world looks to us. Kress and Van Leeuwen would call this a realistic coding orientation. It is the coding orientation which is preferred in home photography, travel imagery, or journalism where the desired stance is the depiction of reality. Images which depart from such a coding orientation (black-and-white photography, for example) express either an aesthetic of high art or a historical stage of the development of technology when color images, though desired, were not possible.

But this is not ever simply a matter of plain truth or reality. As Kress and Van Leeuwen point out, images used in the service of science achieve *realis* presentation to the extent they are abstracted from our commonsense view of the world. The coding orientation of science favors charts, sketches, drawings, or other forms of abstraction. The *realis* of travel photos becomes a kind of scientific *irrealis*.

In opening up multimodality research to examining 'grammatical' modality or coding orientation modality it is important to recall the lesson learned in the first wave of studies of nonverbal communication and language. Language and linguistic analysis may be an important source of concepts, but it is fatal to the research endeavor to simply transport linguistic analysis over into the analysis of other modes. The question of modality must necessarily be developed within each mode. This will often need to be done as an interdisciplinary project as multimodal analysts begin to probe into longstanding developments of modality in music, art, graphics design and other related fields.

Future directions in multimodality and language

Over the past century a complexly evolving network of studies has developed. We would like to suggest that both studies of language and multimodal research are now developing along somewhat convergent lines. What these have in common are three things: the focus on humans taking action through their use of communicative modes as resources; the consequent emphasis on concreteness in the human bodies and the resource materials out of which the multiple modes are constructed; and the physical sites in which and by which human meaning-making is accomplished.

This convergence is not simply a return to the first natural history studies of the NHI project but it does resonate well with that phase of development with one major difference. No longer is language taken to be the model by which these other phenomena are studied but, rather, language itself is taken to be equally grounded in human action with material means in specific earth-grounded sites of engagement. Human meaning-making is now understood to be accomplished in places and with materials which are predicated on rather different timescales (Lemke, 2000; Blommaert, 2005).

The sound waves of speech or music dissipate relatively much faster than the ink-formed letters of a hand-written note tacked to a message board. A gesture may be seen fleetingly in a glance or a photograph may hang framed on a wall for months or years. The placement of a sofa is more stable than the placement of the person seated on the sofa but the sofa is not as stable as the color of the paint used on the wall behind it. That paint is, again, less stable than the drywall material out of which the wall has been constructed. Each of these bodies or materials communicates within a distinct mode (human body placement, room furnishings, interior design, building construction) and each has a typical rhythm or time-scale within which it moves through the cycle from production through to dissolution or dissipation of its meaning.

This shift in focus from the structures of modes to their use as pragmatic resources in human action in the world entails a thoroughgoing reconceptualization of both theories and method-ologies. In the near run we suggest, following Lemke (2000) and Blommaert (2005), but also the geographers Crang and Thrift (2000), that it is urgent to bring to our thinking about both language and multimodality a careful spatial-temporal grounding.

Timescaling

Elsewhere we have put forward suggestions about how this might be done using the term 'geosemiotics' as a general term to cover the territory (Scollon and Scollon, 2003, 2004; but also R. Scollon, 2005a). Five fundamental timescale cycles might be identified based on human– geophysical measures of time:

- cardio-pulmonary timescale events lasting a fraction of a second
- metabolic timescale events centering on ingestion and digestion
- circadian timescale events occurring on 24-hour cycles
- lunar timescale events lasting a couple of weeks to a month
- solar timescale events lasting 3–4 months to 3–4 years

In addition to these timescales are, of course, the natural entropic timescales of the materials out of which modes are constructed. Entropy is the principle that nature tends to move struc-tures from order to disorder in isolated systems. An example is ice cubes in a glass of water which melt when heat dissipates the energy holding the ice molecules together. Thus entropic timescales have to do with decay or natural corrosion. Metal lasts longer than wood, wood lasts longer than sound waves in the air. Plastics, it seems, last longer than anything.

Cardio-pulmonary timescale events

Much of the work in social-interactional research is focused on a periodicity which is timed to the duration of breaths or heartbeats. Erickson (1980, 2004a) for example, has shown how missteps in the timing of speaker responses of durations briefer than a second can lead to mis-judgments of the speaker's overall linguistic competence. Auer et al. (1999) have shown that speaker turns as well as many other aspects of conversational interaction are timed to such heartbeat-sized intervals. And Goffman (1981) has commented that even momentary accidents such as occur when one stumbles on a piece of rough pavement open significant windows on how we present the self in public.

Metabolic timescale events

The periodicity established by human metabolic processes are perhaps more visible in their absence from studies of social interactions. There has been a tendency to study continuous stretches of communication which occur between coffee or toilet breaks. It is surprisingly rare in the literature to see more extended studies which bridge these metabolic events. But there is some evidence (R. Scollon, 2006; S. Scollon, 2006) that the nature of communicative events can be interestingly altered by the coffee and pastries that are eaten during such metabolic breaks.

Circadian timescale events

Once we move to the 24-hour circadian timescale it is more difficult to find studies of language or multimodality which make specific reference to this timescale or which theorize it as a significant aspect of the study. This should not be the case. Educators are fully aware of the importance of planning and scheduling at the day-by-day level. We also know in a practical sense that meeting organizers who are planning a meeting to run for several days must think rather carefully about where in such an extended agenda to place certain topics. Genres such as concluding resolutions cannot occur at the outset; general introductions of participants do not occur in closing such an event. There is much practical knowledge residing in protocol departments of government and businesses but so far very little work in multimodality has addressed this timescale of activity.

Lunar timescale events

Paydays, social security checks, utilities bills, or, in offices, reports and other documents, occur on a monthly cycle. It is common knowledge that one will encounter long lines at the post office or the bank on the one day of the month when welfare checks or social security checks are distributed. It has been reported that diets change depending on how close to the monthly pay day the meal comes. As is the case with circadian cycles, students of multimodality have paid relatively little attention so far to how communications which work on this level of periodicity integrate with cycles on both shorter and longer timescales.

Solar timescale events

Within the timescale of the year we do have some very suggestive studies. Barre Toelken (1969, 1987) notes Navajo prohibitions on telling winter stories in the summer, and a much more widely known set of annual cycles are concert and theater seasons. Both Erickson (2004b) and Wortham (2001) found in their studies of classroom education that the annual cycle of the school year was an important dimension in their analysis of teacher–student interactions on subject matter.

Conclusion

For nearly a century now there has been an evolving set of relationships between language and communication which is not language. Many different approaches have been used to seek an integration of these topics. We began by pointing out that multimodality is not a simple rephrasing of nonverbal communication. Language itself has been bifurcated in the European tradition beginning in Greece as literacy versus orality. Studies of NVC center on real-time performance, leaving out such multimodal phenomena as the design of objects, graphics, the built environment, film, video, books, color, texture and type.

Language has been treated abstractly as a code and functionally as a tool for taking action. What is known about language – both codes and functions – has been taken as a kind of prototype of the newly developing knowledge of modes other than linguistic ones. Researchers assumed for other modes the arbitrary nature of the sign, hierarchical structuring, and the centrality of linguistics as a source of organizing metaphors.

We traced the evolution of the study of communication over the past five decades from the groundbreaking studies of Bateson, Birdwhistle, Hall and Pike in which language was central across such disciplines as communication, linguistics, psychiatry, poetry and film. The focus was on how language works pragmatically in relation to all other modes of communication, and researchers believed that linguistics held the key. Even the natural history approach which treated human communication as a form of mammalian behavior observed *in situ* failed to integrate the role of language in the process but rather developed a cumbersome set of transcriptions.

In a complex interplay of academic and social climates, studies of nonverbal communication flourished. For one thing, the Cold War required for intelligence work an ability to pass or be indistinguishable from a member of a foreign group. For another, in America the McCarthy era required resistance to political surveillance and oppression which centered on censorship of words spoken or written. What happened to dampen the flurry of activity was, on the one hand, suppression of activist anthropologists and linguists like Melville Jacobs and Morris Swadesh and, on the other, the dissolution of the structural model of language through the work of post-structuralist, generative analysts. The contrast between the linear sequence of speech and writing and images spatially perceived as unitary wholes was too great.

In the present we would argue that language is no longer taken as an independent and prototypical model of all modes of communication. It does continue to be an influence on researchers in the field of multimodality, largely as a resource for ideas about how to begin to analyze separate communication modes. In examining 'grammatical' modality or coding orientation modality it is important to recall the lesson learned in the first wave of studies of nonverbal communication and language, that it is fatal to the research endeavor to simply transport linguistic analysis over into the analysis of other modes. The question of modality must necessarily be developed within each mode.

What is most striking about the present configuration of multimodality is the understanding that no mode of communication operates in a monomodal fashion, even if it is useful to abstract a mode from context for the purposes of close analysis.

Given the present conception of multimodality it seems clear that new frameworks and perspectives are developing to conceptualize this new and complex set of relationships among all modes. When this is coupled with the also new emphasis on concrete forms of human action, we suggest that a key area in which analysis is most likely to develop is in the spatio-temporal integration of communicative modes across differing timescales.

Further reading

Leeds-Hurwitz, W. (2005) 'The natural history approach: A Bateson legacy.' *Cybernetics and Human Knowing* 12(1–2): pp. 137–46.

Lemke, J. (2002) 'Travels in hypermodality.' *Visual Communication* 1(3): pp. 299–325.

Scollon, R. and S. W. Scollon (2003) *Discourses in Place: Language in the Material World*, London: Routledge.

Related topics

The perennial problem of the transformation of data to publishable form which inhibited earlier work in language and nonverbal communication is dealt with in Chapter 3 (Flewitt *et al.*).

The pivotal question of what, in fact, is a mode runs throughout research from the earliest studies of nonverbal communication to contemporary multimodal studies. This is taken up in Chapter 4 (Kress).

The early emphasis on the mammalian foundation of nonverbal communication is carried forward in the recognition in multimodal research on the materiality of meaning in Chapter 5 (Van Leeuwen).

Our suggested direction of development toward increasing study of communication within different timescales and across timescales is developed in Chapter 11 (Lemke).

15

Multimodality and theories of the visual

David Machin

Introduction

Much of the work within the area of multimodality has shown little engagement with broader theories of visual communication. Semiotics, over the past hundred years, particularly has produced extensive work based on similar claims to multimodality for there being a systematic way to analyse visual communication, treating it in much the same way as language as a system of signs. There are a number of criticisms, coming from within semiotics itself and from the field of visual studies, which have been made of such theories that apply to the variations of multimodality included in this volume. This chapter considers these criticisms for the purposes of using them as a resource to produce a more robust approach to multimodal analysis. The focus of the chapter is visual communication, although the points made apply equally to the study other communicative modes.

The rationale for systemic functional-based multimodality

The central issue raised throughout this chapter is: is it a reasonable or productive step to apply the model of systemic functional linguistics (SFL) to visual communication or any other communicative mode? Is it a necessarily a good move to try to explain one phenomenon by use of a framework developed to describe and understand another?

In linguistics one justification for the need to become multimodal in our analysis is that communication has itself become more multimodal (Kress and Van Leeuwen, 2001) leading to the demise of the authority of the written text. A purely linguistic, or monomodal, analysis will, therefore, miss much of how texts create meaning. But if we are indeed staring at the end of the domination of monomodal linguistic communication should we then be using models that were designed to study language to think about everything else? Would this new state of affairs not suggest rather that linguists should be looking outside of their own theoretical models rather than simply exporting their own? For several thousand years there has been debate about the nature of images, how they represent, and what they have in common with language, through Plato, Freud, Foucault, Goodman, and Habermas, not to mention a century of work in semiotics since

217

Charles Sanders Pierce. Should linguists not first consider this work and the problems that it has encountered, especially if these ideas have also frequently dealt with visual communication in terms of its similarity to, or difference from, language?

Outside of linguistics looking at other non-linguistic forms of communication has not been so unusual. Even the idea of calling the complex range of things that we can think of 'images' – photographs, abstract paintings, mirror images, the image we see through our eye, dreams, memories, verbal descriptions – a single *mode* of communication would in itself be considered problematic. Immediately we see from this list that 'reading images' is not a matter of researching such an identifiable thing as is 'language'.

In fact the call for analysis to be multimodal has been justifiably aimed particularly at linguists themselves to remind them of what might be missed in their analysis, when in fact few texts we now encounter are monomodal and as well as language include images, graphics and colours which all contribute to how they make meaning. But the problem of the justification for using a language-based model to describe communication in other modes remains.

There are three very attractive reasons why the multimodal approaches outlined in this volume might be promising both to linguists and to non-linguists. The first reason is that approaches to analysing visual communication, particularly in semiotics (Barthes, 1973) and iconology (Panofsky, 1972), have tended to deal only with *individual* visual signs. Clearly when we look at any part of an image, just as we look at a word in a sentence, we do not look at it alone or in isolation but as it appears as part of a composition, in what Kress and Van Leeuwen (1996) called 'visual syntax'. This will influence the meaning of that visual element. To give a simple example, a picture of a lion could be used to mean bravery on an emblem. But if that emblem also included a gun or a child the meaning would be changed in each case. Traditional semiotic approaches have had little to say as regards the way that visual elements combine. So it would be of value if we could explain how visual elements in compositions work together in a kind of visual syntax, as do words in sentences.

Second, these traditional forms of semiotic analysis created lists of iconographic uses of visual signs. So analysis could show what signs were chosen, but never provide any account of the system of available choices that lay behind these. Analysts could show how we could understand the historical origins of individual signs (Panofsky, 1972), but nevertheless the available repertoire remained as a list of unconnected signs. In *Reading Images*, Kress and Van Leeuwen were interested in exploring the idea that in visual communication communicators have access to a limited range of options and choices, as has been characterised in language by the system networks often generated in SFL, to describe available linguistic choices. So the multimodal approach could offer a degree of prediction in what visual semiotic resources are available for communication in concrete situations. Van Leeuwen (1996, 2005c, 2006) has specialised in making such semiotic inventories of available linguistic and visual choices.

Third, multimodality holds the promise of allowing us to think more precisely about the kinds of communicative functions images are able to fulfil. Writers such as O'Toole (1994) used this approach with the aim of providing a toolkit for the analysis of paintings, sculpture and architecture. He looked for the way that these forms of art used different features that worked together to realise the three functions of language described by Halliday (1978) to create mood of address, to communicate ideas and create coherence in the message. This held the promise of increasing our awareness of the way that artists communicate through these visual texts. The aim would be to replace terms such as 'evoke' and 'suggest' that we often use to discuss works of art with systematic and stable terms that allowed us to talk in concrete terms about how such a composition communicates. Others such as O'Halloran (2004) followed this approach to look at film and, more recently, Baldry and Thibault (2006) to look at new media.

These three reasons hold the promise of facilitating a more systematic way to analyse visual communication which has been largely dominated by more general open interpretation. All follow from the conviction that there exists a model for describing and understanding language that can be used to create a predictive toolkit for visual communication. In what follows I look at some of the questions that have been raised outside of multimodality about the way that we can view images as being like language and therefore where language is a good model to use for analysis. This kind of exercise is important in allowing multimodality to assess what it has so far demonstrated and to take firmer steps forward. There has been much excitement generated by this new pioneering approach but this chapter argues that time must now be taken to build carefully.

The problem of the icon for linguistic models of the visual

One of the major problems that has haunted traditional semiotic approaches from the start is the 'icon'. At the root of this problem is how much we can think of images as being like language or composed of abstract symbols that are like words.

Semiotics has always thought of itself as basically linguistic from the work of Charles Sanders Pierce at the end of the nineteenth century. In *Elements of Semiology* (1977c) Barthes wrote that images are the same as language: 'to perceive what a substance signifies is inevitably to fall back in the individuation of language; there is no meaning which is not designated, and the world of signifieds is none other than that of language' (1977c: 10–11).

The icon, however, challenges the claim to be able to describe the visual through linguistic terms. An icon is a sign that has some resemblance or reference to something in the world. So a photograph would be an icon; the figures of men and women that we see on toilet doors are icons; thick borders on a page are icons as they reference qualities of thick objects in the world and signify on this basis.

For Charles Sanders Pierce, who can be credited as the founder of what we call semiotics, a sign was something that 'stands for something for somebody in some respect or capacity' (Sebeok, 1994: 11). He saw three categories of sign: the index, the symbol and the icon. An example of an index would be, say, an animal footprint, which points to the nature of the creature. A symbol would be something that does not point to something, nor has resemblance and is therefore arbitrary. Examples are signs such as emblems, brands and of course, words (Langer, 1951). The icon in contrast represents through similarity. So a picture of a lion resembles and references a lion in the real world.

The problem is to do with whether the icon is a sign at all. And if they are not signs this raises the question of whether they work like language. Can we think of a photograph as a sign? Can we think of light and dark in a photograph or movie still, a saturated colour on a design, thick or thin borders on a page layout in the same way as signs in the same way we think about words? All these things reference the real world rather than symbolising them in the manner of words. For multimodality this has all sorts of implications for how we can break down images into elements, think about them in terms of communicative functions, and to know at which level to place them into systems of choices.

The icon is difficult as 'similarity' or 'resemblance' in itself is such a problematic concept. This creates problems for us being able to identify what are signs and what represents what. Put simply everything is similar to, or resembles, everything else in some respects. Humans are similar to each other in some respects and are also similar to animals. But are we signs for each other? Cars are similar to televisions but are they signs for each other? A painting of a person might represent the person, but does the person represent the painting? So resemblance is not enough for any sort of representation. Almost anything can stand for everything else (Goodman, 1976).

Of course icons can have natural connections with the world but at the same time be motivated, in other words symbolic. Arnheim (1969) has described such natural signs as 'part-time symbols'. We might see a photograph of a train coming towards us as a symbol of time looming upon us, but of course, we could just see it as a picture of a piece of railway equipment. Peirce (1931) himself described photographs as composites of iconic and indexical signs, but certainly not symbolic. Eco explains it that some icons

> refer to an established stylistic rule, while others appear to propose a new rule. In other cases the constitution of similitude, although ruled by operational conventions, seems to be more firmly linked to the basic mechanisms of perception than to explicit cultural habits.
>
> (1976: 216)

For Eco, therefore, these are certainly not like signs in language. There may indeed be patterns and conventions in visual representations but these are not symbolic and are based rather on habit and repetition in the manner of any cultural practice.

How then can we see semiotics as a science of signs if part of what it studies is not really like signs at all? Mitchell (1986) argues:

> The problem with the notion of sign is not just that it embraces too many sorts of things, but, more fundamentally, that the whole concept of 'sign' drawn from linguistics seems inappropriate to iconicity in general, and to pictoral symbols in particular.
>
> (p. 58)

In fact much of the changing terminology and new approaches to semiotics over the years have come up with new concepts that have always glossed over this fundamental problem.

If we go back to the origins of semiotics in the work of Saussure, the model used by Barthes and others, and the basis of what we know as linguistics, we get an immediate sense of how building systems with the icon is problematic. Saussure (1974) thought that signs only make sense as part of a formal, generalised abstract system. Meaning is structural and relational and certainly not referential as in the case of the icon. So the meaning of signs is relative and not due to any feature of the signifier. Signs do not make sense on their own but in relation to other signs. The problem for us is how would the icon fit in here?

The problem of the icon for multimodality

So what precise implication does this have for multimodality, for our three promises of what it can offer visual analysis? The problem is this: do images such as photographs or pictures and the things from the world such as light and dark, rain and sunshine, trees and animals, that we find in them work as signs in a way that allows us to not just create inventories of their meanings but to show how they combine? If they do resemble things in our everyday world can we think about them as conventional signs in the manner of language? In this case is there a way that such images can be incorporated into system networks and tables of communicative functions? How could a picture of a train be part of a system where meaning is structural and not relational?

In the foreword to Baldry and Thibault's *Multimodal Transcription* (2006), Lemke states that their aim for studying multimedia is to develop 'a systematic approach to understanding how combinations of words, images, and sounds, whether sitting on a page or flashing past in real time, make more meanings together than any one of them can make alone'.

This sounds exciting and is typical of Lemke's magnetic enthusiasm in the context of his own innovative contributions to the analysis of multimedia texts. But while it is one thing to consider the way that different elements make meaning, what we have covered so far suggests that it is quite a different step to assume that it is possible to identify all the different elements and treat them as of the same nature as the signs that make up language and then deal with them as one system.

Baldry and Thibault call their approach to the way that modes work together to create meaning their 'resource integration principle' (p. 4), which suggests that they believe that all elements can be treated as one system. Importantly, Baldry and Thibault do state that that 'different modalities adopt different organisational principles for creating meanings' (p. 4). But at no point do they develop why this might be the case, or spell out what this means. The danger here is that the problem of the icon and what images are is glossed and analysis moves swiftly on, just as in earlier semiotics.

Bal (1991) has been critical of the extent to which we can overlook the problem of the icon and simply break down images into individual signs. This language approach, she believes, means

> interpreting visual representation by placing its elements in a tradition that gives them a meaning other than their 'immediate' visual appearance suggests. A vase of flowers is not merely a vase of flowers; the little insects on the flowers, not merely insects. Instead they become signs. Those insects, for example, are the minuscule but undeniable symptoms of decay.
>
> (p. 177)

Bal's point could be one criticism of the approach taken by O'Toole (1994) in his groundbreaking *Language of Displayed Art*. In his analysis, elements become not what they are but are treated as symbols. Of Botticelli's painting *Primavera* O'Toole says 'the swirls of gauzy drapery highlight her womanly curves as well as conveying a sense of energy' (p. 17). Leaving aside the matter of interpretation for a moment this approach treats something that is like an everyday object, in this case a dress, as a symbol, in this case for energy. But does this look like a step forward in creating something like the systematic inventory that we earlier suggested that multimodality could provide? O'Toole also includes all manner of iconic characteristics as unproblematically incorporated into the system. He comments:

> At the rank of Figure the Representational function conveys to the viewer basic information about the character, social status, actions, and position of each individual... we 'read' people in everyday life: facial features and expression, stance, gesture, typical actions and clothing.
>
> (p. 15)

All of these are treated, like the dress, as symbols that can be assigned straightforward functions. In terms of the words of Eco, can we reasonably account for these cultural habits, these readings of everyday things such as posture, as symbols or even as signs, and can they all be contained within one 'integrated system'? In fact we might argue that the semiotic category of the 'representational function' that is part of the system is no different from the traditional semiotic iconographic analysis of individual elements but placing them within new terminology.

Baldry (2004) took up O'Toole's approach in a fascinating analysis of a car advert, where meaning is created multimodally. All aspects of film-making such as transitions, the participants, setting, soundtrack, noises, movement of participants, the way that new elements come into view as the camera pans, are all treated as signs. But how and at what level is never articulated. Therefore how this is like language, and whether or not the language-derived framework is therefore appropriate is not dealt with. In this kind of analysis there can be a sense that the subject of analysis disappears under the weight of analytical terminology.

In fact the way that visual communication references the real world or our experiences of it should be seem as a resource for analysis in itself. Van Leeuwen (2005c), drawing on Arheim (1969), has shown that much of the meaning potential in visual communication comes from metaphorical association. In his inventory of meanings for font shapes he demonstrated, for example, that heavier fonts can be seen as bolder, stronger and more stable than lighter slimmer fonts, although this can also suggest something overbearing and immovable as opposed to something more subtle. Here qualities of stronger and more stable things in the world are transferred to fonts and therefore to the things they describe. The meaning is transported from one domain to another. Van Leeuwen is able to make an inventory of typographic features including expansion, height, weight and curvature.

Kress and Van Leeuwen (2002) used the same principle in reference to qualities in the real world in their semiotic study of colour. In their analysis of colour they show how there are many features of colours that can create meaning on the basis of association. Saturated rather than diluted colours are associated with emotional intensity and excitement as opposed to moderation. Colour quality therefore references an emotional state by transference from one domain to another. Pure, rather than impure colours are associated with certainty as opposed to ambiguity. In these cases they are careful to describe and inventorise its features in a way that preserves their qualities and does not treat these as abstract signs. But in both these cases, typography and colour qualities, are these references to the real world like meaning-making through language? For Eco, as we have seen, certainly not.

Can we break images up into components?

If we are to directly follow a model from linguistics where we look for choices, systems and functions in images we would need to be able to identify some kinds of units for analysis: the signs themselves. In linguistic analysis identifying such choices is not difficult. For example, we can show that someone has chosen to use one particular verb over another. But is it quite so straightforward when we come to photographs or pictures?

Bal (1991) has argued that we do not read paintings or photographs by looking at individual elements that we perceive as arranged into a visual syntax. She argues that such reading is done discursively. What she means is that when we look at an image, any part, section or aspect of it may trigger off a particular interpretation. What we do not do, even when reading a written text, she argues, is assemble our comprehension of what is going on bit by bit as each word or clause comes to us or especially as each element of an image comes to us. So when we look at any visual composition any element can act, in Bal's terms, 'metonymically' (metonyms are where one part stands for the whole – 'I jumped on the bus' stands for my whole journey home), meaning that any one element can come to stand for an entire personal interpretation. Other elements may therefore be subordinated to, or incorporated within, this interpretation.

Bal's main criticism of iconographic reading of visual communication, which tries to identify all the relevant signs, is that it is a process that conflates interpretation and the sign itself.

Arguably we find O'Toole (1994) describing some of the features of Botticcelli's *Primavera* doing exactly what could be described as this kind of conflation. He explains how certain features of the painting have a modal function – how these elements engage the viewer:

> Modally the gaze is enhanced by the fact that it is at the centre of radiating arcs. Venus's head-dress, the arch of the trees behind her, and even the figures of Cupid above her and Flora to her left and the Grace to her right who seems to highlight the limits of her internal frame.
>
> (p. 8)

In his analysis the trees in this painting are not just trees but serve to suggest an arc. But for Bal this would be to confuse interpretation with the role of the icon.

In fact one criticism of O'Toole's work on the language of art is that while he claims to be offering a toolkit that would facilitate 'a language through which our perception of a work of art can be shared' (p. 4), he in fact relies on much contextual knowledge. While initially he places his work firmly against the kind of knowledge 'that can be read up in a library' (p. 4), his first step in analysis reveals the necessity to know all about Greek mythology, as we see from the quote above. The grace and charm he sees in the image seem more to do with his knowledge of the depicted characters. While analysing *Primavera* he says 'Many people think of the dance of the Three Graces as a painting in its own right' (p. 11). Here is evidence that the code is conflated with the interpretation based on extensive book knowledge. So to use his toolkit we would need to know who the Three Graces are and what people have written about them. In fact semioticians such as Panofsky (1972) emphasise the importance of tracing the history and politics of icons. Contextual and production knowledge are vital parts of our analyses. But we must be careful to distinguish where we rely on historical and contextual information and where our own system of analysis begins.

Bal (1991) has raised the problem of giving too much emphasis to particular iconographic signs at the expense of others that we know less about in our analyses. In her model, her 'synedochial principle', means that any element of an image is an iconographical sign for recognition (p. 188). But why we choose one over another as being of significance could be highly subjective. We could argue that this is one characteristic of O'Toole's analysis of *Primavera* that we saw above. The same could be said of Baldry's (2004) analysis of television adverts where the levels of analysis and therefore the chosen elements for iconographical reading can seem arbitrarily chosen.

Bal (1991) does see the possibility of readings based on indexical signification where we can think about a sign as working with a tradition as a whole which in turn operates by contiguity or influence (metonymy) (p. 180). So we might decode one element in a painting as a synecdoche for it – in other words what it means as a whole. So 'The image we *see* is subordinated to the meanings we *know*' (p. 181). The problem with this of course is that it means that images are polysemic (they have multiple meanings or interpretations) and would make a systematic inventory impossible.

Putting the kind of argument made by Bal in a different way, Dillon (2006) argues that because images do not have such definable parts any part of an image can set off a number of semiotic rules all at once or not at all. In a painting, such as *Primavera* or the photograph of the train, there is no way of being able to say what the elements are. It is this very flux of how visual elements can transform on examination that so fascinates writers in the field of visual studies such as James Elkins (1999, 2000). For Dillon (2006) grammar is rules for combining separate elements into connected units. Each element must be connected to others by one of the rules or else we have no sentence. In this sense it even becomes difficult to say something like images are made up of signs. But nor should we say that viewing images, as Stöckl (2004) suggests, are based on a 'simultaneous and holistic gestalt-perception' (p. 17), whereas language is naturally linear where the bits and chunks are presented to us in order. Mitchell (1986) and Elkins (1999) point out that we must not make the mistake of assuming that people will see any image as a whole. The attention and focus of viewers can be drawn to any part of an image that they might use to create meaning. Just as there are no components, nor is there any whole to speak of.

This leaves us with a problem. There are no individual parts so to speak of, nor is there a whole. So, from this perspective, how can we think about visual compositions as semiotic systems, or as being composed of semiotic systems?

This chapter argues nonetheless, that of course there are some visual codes. We have already mentioned some of them through colour and font shapes. Another example is in photographs where scenes are framed and therefore reference a point of view. We know that if we are positioned looking up at a subject then this tends to give them a position of power (although in films, issues of continuity sometimes reshape these codes). And we must have knowledge of these codes if we are to grasp their meaning. But as Dillon (2006) and Eco (1976) would argue these are unlike syntax. Meaning comes through reference to physical objects or to physical experiences of the world rather than being structural or relational, even though it is possible to place these into polarities that look like system networks (up–down, etc.). Pointing out the nature of these visual codes is a valuable analytical exercise as Jewitt and Oyama (2000) demonstrate, but it may be another thing to say that this is like language. Kress and Van Leeuwen have shown that it is possible to find and describe qualities in visual communication to an extent that gives some degree of predictability, in other words, rules without claiming that they are exactly like language.

Barthes (1977c), who in his later work was sceptical of finding a visual language, offers us a sense of the way that looking for codes at every level means that we can lose some of the way that images are used to legitimise. He illustrates this point through an advertisement for a brand of Italian pasta. In the image the pasta is placed in a string bag with fresh fruit along with a caption in Italian. Barthes analysed the advertisement at three levels. First, there is the linguistic message. To understand this you need to understand the code of the Italian language. Second, there is the denotational level of what the image depicts – fresh fruit – and third, the connotational level of what the image means, which is health, freshness, wholesomeness, etc. He says that the trick of the advert is to make it look as if the meaning is conveyed at the denotational level. In other words the process masks the conventional nature of the image. It would be a mistake, he believes, to try to lose the way that the denotational works by looking to break the image down into a system. And while the image is coded this means in the sense of being ideologically loaded with cultural associations, not in the sense of a code at the abstract symbolic level. This is in the manner where we saw that a bold thick typeface suggests strength by reference to thick heavy objects in the real world. Again this is coded but not in the abstract sense.

Barthes questions the idea of a language of images by asking if it is possible to conceive of an analogical code where a picture of an object that we know from the world could 'produce true systems of signs and not merely simple agglutinations of symbols'(…) 'since linguists refuse the status of language to all communication by analogy' (p. 32).

Post hoc analysis and the need to understand production factors

The problem of conflating interpretation and sign has been put another way by other critics, as 'post hoc analysis'. In other words we have an understanding of something and then construct our concepts round this. Forceville (1999) is of the view that much of the work of Kress and Van Leeuwen (1996) is based on contextual knowledge rather than through reading visual grammar, although he does choose some of the weaker parts of their toolkit in order to do so. For example, they read an image as being the visual realisation of the sentence 'The British stalked the Aborigines' because, he argues, they know things about the relationship between the British and the Aborigines, not through the codes within the image. They are able to identify volumes (the participants) and vectors (visual verbs) as they already know what is going on in the scene. Without this prior knowledge it would be much more difficult to attribute where the meaningful vectors were. Whether or not we might agree with such criticisms what is important here is to be sure that we are not conflating interpretation and the sign.

Bateman *et al.* (2004) have made the same criticism of Kress and Van Leeuwen's analysis of visual composition. They say 'it has not yet been established whether such an analysis is actually any more than a post hoc rationalisation of design decisions that occur on a page for quite other reasons' (2004: 67). In other words we must be careful that our concepts are not simply being imposed afterwards organised around our already existing understandings and need to impose our own frameworks. This is an important point if we wish multimodality to have predictability in the manner of linguistics.

In fact there has been much criticism of linguistic analyses of texts precisely for the reason that there is no attention given to context of production (Philo, 2007). In critical discourse analysis, often a target of such criticisms, it is notable that two of the best-known writers, Van Dijk (1993) and Fairclough (1995), both stress the need for contextual knowledge, yet this has not seriously been taken up by those working in this area and could be one major shortcoming of multimodal discourse analysis.

There is a further reason we should be concerned with production practice. Practitioners have manuals, for example, for film editing, for sound editing or for basic principles of graphic design. Such manuals, along with experience in the work place, have a huge influence over the nature of the texts that we analyse. Of course semiotic analysis should be able to reveal some of the conventions, some of the cultural habits, of which practitioners may not be consciously aware. But in the first place it would seem logical to find out what kinds of patterns are already described. In their excellent paper on colour, Kress and Van Leeuwen (2002) took the step of reviewing existing work on the meaning of colour, pointing out what was not yet known. While some multimodal work (see O'Halloran, 2004) acknowledges prior theoretical work, it is not necessarily clear in what ways this is limited and therefore how systemic functional approaches can take us one step further.

Conclusion

Mitchell, impatient with the inability of semiotics to produce a systematic framework for analysing visual communication, wrote that it is a 'burgeoning meta-language that proliferates endless networks of distinctions and semiotic "entities"' (p. 62). In other words it has a tendency to multiply the terms used and subsequently to turn the resulting interpretations into things. Mitchell cites Gerard Ginnette who talks of certain tendencies in academia towards the 'passion to name which is a mode of self expansion and self-justification: it operates by increasing the number of objects in one's purview' (1982: 53, cited 1986: 58). This chapter calls for care and to attend to the criticism it has raised to help avoid the same criticism being made of multimodality. In the 1970s, semioticians such as Umberto Eco

(1976) called for a semiotics that recognised the distinctiveness of the different types of signs. This is something that has not yet been taken up within multimodal approaches, although it has been acknowledged as needing attention (Kress and Van Leeuwen, 2001; Machin, 2007). So we must be cautious of what Mitchell has referred to as 'linguistic imperialism', where we simply blindly impose our models and methods onto new areas of study without being sensitive to the way that this may serve to conceal its very nature and of course where therefore it might reveal its nature. Most importantly it seems clear that we need to be aware of existing work on visual communication, discover where it has stumbled and where it has built, using the ideas we find as a resource to make a more robust multimodality.

Further reading

Bal, M. (1991) *Reading 'Rembrandt': Beyond the Word–Image Opposition*, Cambridge: Cambridge University Press.

Elkins, J. (2003) *Visual Studies: A Sceptical Introduction*, New York: Routledge.

Goodman, N. (1976) *Languages of Art*, Indianapolis, IN: Hackett.

Sebeok, T. (1979) *The Sign and Its Masters*, Austin, TX: University of Texas Press.

16

Multimodality and New Literacy Studies

Brian Street, Kate Pahl and Jennifer Rowsell

Introduction

We begin this chapter with an account of the epistemological framings of both multimodality and the New Literacy Studies, and outline the histories of each theoretical framework thus enabling each to be situated within their respective intellectual traditions. By doing this, we are able to identify where the intersections between the two fields lie and then describe research that sits within both traditions. The aim of the chapter is to provide the reader with an account of what research looks like that sits within the intersection of the New Literacy Studies and multimodality. The chapter begins with a historical analysis of the way in which the two intellectual fields have been constituted and then moves to a placing of specific research within those two fields. The chapter then outlines specific studies that work across the two fields, in the context of a more general mapping of the research space.

Research that merges New Literacy Studies with multimodality takes equal account of where, how, and by whom a text is made as it does of the physical features of a text as signifiers of contextual meanings. By understanding that literacy can be understood as ideological (Street, 1993) and that literacy is situated within a myriad of social practices, we argue below that the New Literacy Studies offers a locating standpoint for researchers. By equally locating multimodality as being about a focus on the material qualities of texts, we suggest that multimodality offers a way of showing how locating standpoints materialize in texts (Rowsell and Pahl, 2007).

Historical perspectives

The development and origins of multimodality, and the language of description it provides for non-linguistic phenomena is outlined in the introduction to this book. At the same time a parallel theoretical field was developing in the field of literacy. In 1983, Shirley Brice Heath published her seminal *Ways with Words* that outlined the literacy practices of three communities in the rural Carolinas: Trackton, Roadville and Maintown. Heath recorded how each of these different communities lived, spoke and wrote in different ways. Drawing on ethnographic research methods, she was able to record these ways of speaking and writing and identify that each community carried distinctive ways with words. However, in only one community, the middle-class residents of Maintown, did the children bring into the educational context literacy practices that were congruent with schooled literacy practices. Roadville children experienced different literacy practices in their homes, as did the Trackton children. Heath's work was published at about the same time as another key study by Brian Street of literacy practices in Iran, in which Street identified different literacy practices associated with different domains of practice. An understanding of the ideologically situated nature of literacy was born from Street's ethnographic work in Iran (Street, 1984, 1993). In his field-work in Iranian villages during the early 1970s (Street, 1984), what began to emerge as literacy practices were uses and meanings of literacy that were identifiable around three domains of social activity: *maktab* literacy practices, associated with the primary Qur'anic school; schooled literacy practices in the more secular and modernizing context of the State school; and commercial literacy practices associated with buying and selling fruit for transport to the city and the market. The practices in this third domain of social activity were quite different from either of the other sets of literacy practices. Characterizing them as literacy practices helped him to understand those differences, and he could then talk about whether there were certain identities associated with particular practices. In that context the identity associated with maktab literacy was derived from traditional authority in the village located in Qur'anic learning and with a social hierarchy dominated by men. Schooled literacy, on the other hand, was associated with new learning and with moderniza-tion, leading some village children to urban lives and jobs. Commercial literacy emerged in response to the economic activity of selling fruit to the nearby cities at a time of economic boom and involved writing notes, cheques, lists, names on crates and so on, to facilitate the purchase and sale of quanti-ties of fruit. The framework for understanding literacy that he was developing at this time, including the concept of 'literacy practices' (Street, 1984), aimed to provide an explanation for why commercial literacy was mainly undertaken by those who had been taught at the Qur'anic school rather than those from the modern State school, even though at first sight one might have expected the literacy skills of the latter to be more functionally oriented to commercial practices. Qur'anic literacy offered status and authority to carry on commercial practices, whilst those in the State school lacked a grounding in the local and everyday village life. In this village context, then, literacy, was not simply a set of functional skills, as much modern schooling and many literacy agencies represent it, but rather it was a set of social practices deeply associated with identity and social position. It was, he claimed, by approaching literacy as a social practice that the researcher found a way of making sense of vari-ations in the uses and meanings of literacy in such contexts rather than reliance on the barren notions of literacy skills, rates, levels that dominate contemporary discourse about literacy.

This approach by an English ethnographer linked with work in the US tradition of the eth-nography of communication which also identified ways in which everyday practice and ways of speaking and writing could be understood and interpreted, using ethnographic methodolo-gies (cf. Hymes, 1996; Hornberger, 1997, 2002). Gee likewise was examining the language practices of the African American children he studied, and argued for the need to situate eve-ryday language within wider contexts of social practice, as described in *Social Linguistics and Literacies* (1996). Gee used the term the 'New Literacy Studies' to describe the 'social turn' that had taken place in the 1980s and 1990s as researchers had documented literacy practices in community context, often using ethnography to aid an understanding of these practices.

Combined with an understanding of practice, this tradition focused strongly on context, a posi-tion articulated by Duranti and Goodwin (1992) in their edited collection, *Rethinking Context*. Scribner and Cole's *Psychology of Literacy* (1981) drew on their anthropological work with the Vai people in Liberia to further look at what counts as literacy in everyday settings and to consider ways in which an understanding of literacy is limited by a focus solely on 'schooled' literacy. Scribner and Cole asked researchers to focus on the social uses of literacy and the domains in which literacy was used. Street and Street likewise considered this in their paper on 'The schooling of literacy' which identified the notion of 'schooled' literacy practices as opposed to literacy practice undertaken as part of everyday life (Street and Street, 1991). Barton and Hamilton's 1998 study *Local Literacies* was a thorough, sustained project that explored and mapped literacy practices across the domains where they were used and using ethnographic methodology provided a rich textual account of these practices, focusing on one town, Lancaster. All these studies had a common focus on ethnography as a way in which repeated practices in everyday life could be accessed, understood and interpreted.

The role of ethnography

What united many of the researchers into literacy practices in everyday life was a focus on ethnography as a methodology. Street himself took from the British school of ethnography the interpretative methods that allowed him to observe and record literacy practices in Iran. Likewise Heath drew on the ethnography of communication, as developed by Hymes and others in the United States, in order to locate and trace literacy and language practices in three communities in the rural Carolinas (Heath, 1983). Researchers from the New Literacy Studies have drawn on the ethnographic fieldwork experiences of American anthropologists such as Hall (1999) and Wolcott (1994), Agar (1996), in particular described both 'etic' and 'emic' perspectives in ethnography and thereby opened up the possibility of taking account of both external views of literacy – the 'etic' – perspective and of the way literacy practices were interpreted and understood by people themselves in local context – the 'emic' perspective. Green and Bloome (1997) addressed the dilemma that this essentially anthropological approach raised for many working in the field of language and communication, that whilst adopting ethnographic approaches they did not necessarily want to become anthropologists themselves. Green and Bloome drew a distinction among three approaches to ethnography that enabled many to overcome this problem, referring to the notion of doing ethnography, adopting an ethnographic perspective and using ethnographic tools. They argued,

> that *doing ethnography* involves the framing, conceptualizing, conducting, interpreting, writing, and reporting associated with a broad, in-depth, and long-term study of a social or cultural group, meeting the criteria for doing ethnography as framed within a discipline or field, notably that of anthropology.
>
> (Green and Bloome, 1997: 183)

But they opened up other possibilities too:

> By adopting an *ethnographic perspective*, we mean that it is possible to take a more focused approach (i.e. do less than a comprehensive ethnography) to study particular aspects of everyday life and cultural practices of a social group. Central to an ethnographic perspective is the use of theories of culture and inquiry practices derived from anthropology or sociology to guide the research. The final distinction, *using ethnographic tools* refers to the use of methods and techniques usually associated with fieldwork. These methods may or may not be guided by cultural theories or questions about the social life of group members.
>
> (Green and Bloome, 1997: 183–84)

Heath and Street (2008) brought many of these threads together for those working in the field of language and literacy, invoking for instance the metaphor of 'juggling' to characterize the ways in which the ethnographer has to keep in play many levels of reality: 'We see learning ethnography as being a lot like learning to juggle. Both call for practice, close observation, and the challenge of having to manage more and more balls in the air' (p. 2). Wortham addressed work in the field of Linguistic Anthropology as it relates to education (Wortham, 2008) whilst Rampton and others have developed the notion of Linguistic Ethnography in the UK (Linguistic Ethnography Forum UK, 2005). This approach also informed the study of complementary schools by Blackledge and Creese (2010) in which researchers drew on ethnographic methods, notably linguistic ethnography to make sense of language and literacy practices in the community complementary schools in UK contexts that taught children home languages in out-of-school settings. Rosowsky (2008) likewise explored these practices from an ethnographic and embodied perspective. Further, in the United States, the work of David Bloome and colleagues provided a lens to making sense of literacy and language practices as they unfolded in the classroom, and, by seeing these as situated, were able to ground interpretative insights within understandings of wider social and cultural processes (Bloome, 2012: 8).

Following these leads, a wealth of research and publications have drawn upon ethnographic perspectives to describe literacy practices across different cultural contexts (Aikman, 1999; Doronilla, 1996; Heath, 1983; Hornberger, 1997, 2002; Kalman, 1999; King, 1994; Robinson-Pant, 1997; Wagner, 1993), contributing to both academic research and theory and to policy and practice. In the United States, critical literacy pedagogies were used to challenge hegemonic practices in public high schools (Blackburn and Clark, 2007; Kinloch, 2010; Morrell, 2008; Rogers *et al.*, 2009). This field, with its focus on practice through social activist and interrogation of texts in contexts, lent a developing weight to the need to operationalize the NLS in classroom settings. This field was also described by Larson and Marsh in a more accessible form for teachers in their book *Making Literacy Real* (2005).

Bringing the two traditions together

We can now begin to identify overlaps and ways in which both traditions – New Literacy Studies drawing upon ethnographic perspectives and multimodality. We identified that in late 1999, two traditions were developing. One, that of multimodality, placed text making within a tradition from social semiotics, and understood signs as being multimodal, imbued with intention and culturally shaped and constituted. The other, the New Literacy Studies, used ethnographic methodologies to look at ways of being and doing in communities and placed an understanding of literacy within a wider understanding of everyday life. What did these traditions have to say to each other?

In his inaugural lecture at King's College London, Brian Street made a bridge between these traditions. He described Kress and Van Leeuwen's work, *Reading Images* (1996) and signalled that their work could be taken as bringing together work from linguistic perspectives on semiosis and work from an ethnographic perspective, thus leading to an understanding of multimodality in social context (Street, 1998). His argument was that what is needed to understand contemporary texts, that often include both images and words in their presentation, is a combination of methods of analysis, an 'inter-disciplinary array of methods'. These might include a focus on literacy events and practices of the kind he had advocated in a 1988 paper on 'Literacy Practices and Literacy Myths'. Heath (1982: 50) had described a literacy event as 'any occasion in which a piece of writing is integral to the nature of the participants' interaction and interpretative processes'. The lens of literacy events was used by Moss, for instance, to look at children's reading in classrooms (Moss, 2003). Maybin characterizes the development of the notion of literacy practices that helped New Literacy Studies move into a more comparative phase:

Street has employed the phrase 'literacy practices' (Street, 1984: 1) as a more general abstract term focusing upon 'social practices and conceptions of reading and writing', although he later elaborated the term to take account both of 'events' in Heath's sense and of the 'social models of literacy that participants bring to bear upon those events and that give meaning to them' (Street, 1988). The concept of a literacy practice, like that of other social practices (Bourdieu, 1990), links individual agency in situated activities with broader social structures.

(Maybin, 2007: 4)

The distinction between events and practices was later taken up by Barton and Hamilton (1998) in *Local Literacies*, in which they described literacy events as 'activities where literacy has a role', and then literacy practices as 'regular repeated activities'. Literacy practices, then, can be understood according to Barton and Hamilton as a set of social practices; these are observable in events which are mediated by written texts (Barton and Hamilton, 1998), Street (2000) later added this commentary on the distinction:

... we bring to a literacy event concepts, social models regarding what the nature of the event is and that make it work and give it meaning. Literacy practices, then, refer to the broader cultural conception of particular ways of thinking about and doing reading and writing in cultural contexts. A key issue, at both a methodological and an empirical level, then, is how can we characterise the shift from observing literacy events to conceptualising literacy practices.

(Street, 2000: 1)

Given these important conceptual developments in New Literacy Studies, it is significant that we now find the terms being used in the field of multimodality; as Pahl has suggested: 'I extend the concept of literacy events and practices to the idea of multimodal events and practices as described by Lancaster to account for the way texts are multimodal' (2007: 81). This links with Street's insight in the 1998 paper that alongside literacy events and practices a wider range of semiotic systems are needed to make sense of everyday life. In the context of a discussion about the changing context of education, he argues that:

Employers realize this and in addition to the social characteristics they infer from observation and from references, they also implicitly or explicitly take into account awareness of the semiotic range required in their particular workplace and match that with the semiotic range indicated by applications.

(Street, 1998: 16)

Street, here signals that not to take account of multimodality would be problematic for schools as it would de-privilege children who are already drawing on a number of semiotic modes to make meaning. The curriculum of today, heavily focused in the United Kingdom and United States on a skills-based 'autonomous model involving a focus on print literacies', is rapidly being superseded by the reality of contemporary communication, embedded as it is now within screen-based technologies. This argument, for 'new literacies' was most forcefully put forward by Lankshear and Knobel in a series of books that critiqued contemporary curricula for their inability to cope with complex digital literacies emerging very rapidly (e.g. Lankshear and Knobel, 2003; see also Gowen, 1994, on workplace literacies).

Street's insight chimed with another, more globalized movement that had been developing under the guise of the 'Multiliteracies' curriculum in Australia and described in an important article written by a group called the New London Group in 1996. This group included Kress, Gee, Lo Bianco, Cope and Kalantizis, and others who focused on the curriculum of tomorrow in the context of the changing digital landscape and changing multiliteracies context, and the need to incorporate a multimodal perspective into the curriculum. This multiliteracies curriculum privileged the concept of design and focused on learning in schools needing to be organized around a much wider concept of communicative practice and representation that was currently presented to children in schools around the world (Cope and Kalantzis, 2000). This brings us to the final aspect that could be brought to bear on the intersection of multimodality and the New Literacy Studies, which is the concept of 'D/discourses', from Gee (1996, 1999). Gee identified that there were two types of discourses – 'language in use' which he saw as being 'little d' discourses and 'big D' Discourses which he identified as 'language plus other stuff', that is, 'forms of life which integrate words, acts, values, beliefs, attitudes and social identities as well as gestures, glances, body positions and clothes' (Gee, 1996: 127).

Studies that merged the insights of Kress, Street and Gee began to be published around the year 2000. Elizabeth Moje in her study of the literacy practices of 'gangsta' adolescents used a lens that included multimodality, and the work of Gee and Kress to examine the way these literacy practices sat within a much wider multimodal communicative landscape (Moje, 2000). She argued that,

> Specific to my research, for example, are the works of art, music, dress codes, makeup, tattoos, body movements gestures, and hand signs that gang-connected adolescents use to identify themselves and to claim power and space in and out of their gangs.
>
> (Moje, 2000: 656)

Street's (2005) edited volume *Literacies Across Educational Contexts* included a number of chapters on semiotic practices in and out of school, such as Bronwen Low's 'Sayin' it in a Different Way: Adolescent Literacies Through the Lens of Cultural Studies' set in a US context (Low, 2005) and Joanna Oldham's 'Literacy and Media in Secondary Schools in the United Kingdom' (Oldham, 2005). Pahl, in her study of three London homes, found that the children in the study used print literacy alongside drawing to represent their worlds. It became impossible to isolate literacy practices from the much wider range of semiosis that was presented to her within homes. A number of articles on children's home communicative practices (Pahl, 2001, 2002, 2004) outlined how these multimodal texts could be understood in relation to the social practices that were sedimented within them.

In addition, an understanding of the multimodal text as betraying traces of the practices that went into its making made an understanding of multimodal texts as linked to social practice more visible. For example, Rowsell (2000) drew on Gee's concept of D/discourses together with Kress's account of multimodality to look at publishing practices as instantiated within textbooks used by children in the context of the UK's National Literacy Strategy. Using a lens from Street of an ethnographic account of what went on when texts were used in practice, she was able to forge a link between Kress and Gee to understand how multimodal texts themselves instantiated Discourses of a particular kind. Rowsell's work described how D/discourses materialize in modalities in texts and reveal traces of ideas, values and concepts that inform how we take up the text (Rowsell, 2000, 2006). In an article on sedimentation of Discourses in textual modalities, Rowsell and Pahl maintain

> that conflation and intersection of Discourses become modalities in texts, which, alongside practices provide a formative picture of the meaning makers – not only their pathway into literacy but also how they make meaning in certain contexts and engage in practice.
>
> (Rowsell and Pahl, 2007: 392)

With a focus on how D/discourses could be instantiated within multimodal texts (Rowsell, 2000), and a focus on the literacy events and practices when children are interacting with multimodal texts (e.g. Moss, 2003), the two fields were coming together and were being actively used by researchers across the globe.

The relationship between NLS, as a theory focused on practice, and Bourdieu's theoretical framework has been articulated in a book by Grenfell *et al.* (2012) in which the authors acknowledge the importance of Bourdieu's theorising in order to situate NLS within a larger structural understanding of how power shapes the production of literacy practices. NLS conversely has a role to play in providing nuanced accounts, particularly drawing on linguistic ethnography within classroom settings, of how this plays out in the field.

The New Literacy Studies and multimodality – research studies

Instances of the synergy between the two fields will be now described in relation to how the intersections were formulated and mapped. An ethnographic lens gives multimodal analysis a social map. Like a map, ethnographies of contexts such as publishing companies or homes or prisons give us a deep sense of context and identities in contexts that serve as indexical tools in multimodal analysis.

The bringing together of the two fields was firstly achieved through a number of edited collections where researchers explored the intersection in their work. The first, *Multimodal Literacy* (Jewitt and Kress, 2003b) placed literacy within the wider field of multimodality, arguing that, 'The act of writing is itself a multimodal practice that draws on visual and actional modes, in particular resources of spatiality and directionality' (Jewitt and Kress, 2003b: 2). Some of the chapters in the book took an ethnographic perspective to understand the multimodal texts that were the subject of the research. In Moss's case, the lens of the New Literacy Studies was used to particularly powerful effect in that she draws on the concept of literacy events and the interactions around a text to analyse boys' responses to multimodal texts (2003b). Here, the fields are nearly brought together, but not quite; they remain clearly delineated within Moss's research, but usefully inform each other. Pahl (2003) used ethnography to understand multimodal texts without drawing explicitly on the New Literacy Studies, whereas Kenner places writing within a multimodal frame, and brings her understanding of writing as a social semiotic act to her analysis (Kenner, 2003). In this collection, then the focus was more on multimodality as an overall frame to understand text-making; only Moss's chapter signals a different field, that of literacy events as a tool for understanding.

Pahl and Rowsell's (2006) edited collection, *Travel Notes from the New Literacy Studies*, explicitly tried to link the two fields together. In their Foreword, Brian Street and Gunther Kress write of the New Literacy Studies and multimodality,

> while both approaches look at broadly the same field, from each of the two positions the field has a distinctive look: one that tries to understand what people acting together are doing, the other tries to understand about the tools with which these same people do what they are doing.
>
> (Kress and Street, 2006: ix)

Kress and Street identified a key point here, that while one focuses on practice (NLS) the other focuses on texts (multimodality). However, Pahl and Rowsell argued that seeing texts as traces of social practice and ethnography is essential to understanding the repeated practices that sediment into text-making (Rowsell and Pahl, 2007). In their introduction to *Travel Notes*, they argue that,

We need the multimodal in the New Literacy Studies in order to understand texts as material objects. Multimodality gives an analytic tool to understand artifacts such as children's drawings, and to recognize how literacy sits within a much wider communicational landscape.

(Pahl and Rowsell, 2006: 8)

However, they argue, the New Literacy Studies is important because, 'The New Literacy Studies ties the representation to social practice'(Pahl and Rowsell, 2006: 8). The volume showed the potential of using ethnography to inform multimodal analysis from digital environments (e.g. Marsh, 2006); to multimodality in the local (e.g. Stein and Slonimsky, 2006); to multimodality in corporations and the marketplace and in relation to power (e.g. Nichols, 2006; Janks, 2010; Nixon, 2011); and finally, multimodality in pedagogical environments (e.g. Flewitt, 2008; Millard, 2006). By focusing on the *contexts* for reading and writing and for multimodal communicative practices, ethnography enriches understandings of the multimodal text.

Pahl (2007) argued that by applying the lens of the New Literacy Studies to an analysis of multimodal texts, an understanding of the different domains of practice the child drew on when creating the multimodal text could be reached. This 'thickening' of domains of practice, sedimented within one text could be linked to notions of creativity and originality (Pahl, 2007). This analysis brought together both the New Literacy Studies and multimodality to look at one child's text. Street (2008) argued that it is possible to view multimodal texts as ideological, that is, as literacy practices are ideological and situated within power relations, multimodal texts could be understood as themselves imbued within the social contexts from which they were created, and subject to the same interrogations as literacy texts: he advocated therefore an 'ideological model' of multimodality (Street, 2008: 6). Muspratt *et al.* (1997) in Australia proposed a system of critical literacy to analyse text in relation to constraints and affordances of power relations. Likewise, multimodal texts could be subject to these same constraints. Kress and Van Leeuwen themselves hinted that a discussion of the constraints and affordances of multimodal texts was a wide open field for research in their 2001 book, *Multimodal Discourse*:

Is affordance more to do with the materiality of the medium in which the mode is constituted, or is it more a matter of the work of a particular culture with a medium over time, or is it a combination of both, sometimes more the one, sometimes more the other? It is a question which is in need of more exploration.

(Kress and Van Leeuwen, 2001: 125)

By seeing affordance as culturally shaped, the ideological nature of multimodality comes to the fore. Research on this needs to draw upon the ethnographic perspective outlined earlier with its focus on context and local meanings.

New Literacy Studies focuses especially on the notion of power and how literacy practices carry more or less power when we move across contexts. In Street's study (1984), those who had learned literacy in *maktab* schools had the authority and social capital to then apply their literacy skills to new commercial practices. Understanding the relationship between texts and power is inherent to a bringing together of the New Literacy Studies and multimodality. Finding traces of Discourses that are often rendered invisible gives texts and meaning-makers power (especially when Discourses are fundamental to identity and habits of mind). When doing ethnographic work in homes and communities, researchers have observed that children draw on local objects and terms in their creation of such texts. Uniting the local with the multimodal gives texts more salience in research contexts.

Ways of bringing the intersection into play: some data examples

In this section we suggest different ways in which researchers are currently using the New Literacy Studies and multimodality. We propose a typology that accounts for, and describes the different 'takes' on the intersection that we have found. We have found this useful to describe a rapidly changing research field. In Table 16.1 we make sense of these different intersections drawing on different researchers' work as merely examples, many more can be found in each type. Here we present clusters that are exemplified by research examples. Some researchers (Moss, 2003; Stein and Slominsky, 2006), focus on *reading as a situated social practice and literacy events and practices* within a multimodal landscape. Others (Ormerod and Ivanic, 2002; Kell, 2006) focus on texts, and then bring a New Literacy Studies-type approach to multimodal texts as being

Table 16.1 Typology to describe different research takes on the intersection between the New Literacy Studies and multimodality

Researcher	Field	Literacy tradition	Multimodality	Ethnography
Moss (2003)	Boys' engagement in non-fiction texts in the home and school	*Literacy events* focusing on reading and interaction around multimodal texts	Texts are understood as multimodal with a focus on events as well as practices	Ethnographies of reading
Stein and Slominsky (2006)	Literacy practices in households in South Africa	*Literacy events and literacy practices* within a multimodal context	Literacy events understood as multimodal	Ethnographic-style study of children's early literacy learning (CELL)
Ormerod and Ivanic (2002)	Children's project work in Junior school in the UK	*Texts* as focus of multimodal analysis	Sees literacy as embedded in wider semiotic landscape	Study looked at project work and home and school crossings
Kell (2006)	House-building practices amongst women in South Africa	*Texts* as focus of analysis – oral narrated texts within wider semiotic landscape	Text trajectories articulated as semiosis in a wider context	Ethnographic field work produced thick descriptions of context
Kenner (2000b, 2004)	Multilingual children's writing in urban homes	Multilingual literacies, focus on *text production in socio-cultural setting*	Sees writing as multimodal	Focus on wider community as context for multilingual literacies
Rowsell and Pahl (2007); Pahl and Rowsell (2010); Sheridan and Rowsell (2010); Rowsell (2013)	Material qualities of texts, focusing on artefactual literacies, sedimented identities in texts, modal learning	Material artefacts, texts, focus on *multimodal text production in material world*	Sees literacy as materially situated, uses multimodality as a lens for learning	Focus on material culture, process of meaning-making, collaboration

produced in social contexts. Some such as Kenner (2000b, 2004) who works in multilingual settings, consider texts to be multimodal and understand *literacy to be produced within a social context.* We also present a perspective uniting multimodality, ethnography and NLS with material cultural studies which we call 'artifactual literacies' (Pahl and Rowsell, 2010).

What could be added to this table is research drawing together the New Literacy Studies, ethnography and multimodality in the field of digital literacies (Alvermann, 2002; Androutsopoulos, 2006; Davies, 2006; Davies and Merchant, 2009; Gee, 2003, Lankshear and Knobel, 2003; Mackey, 2003; Marsh, 2006). It is important to highlight new work that looks at the intersection of cultural artefacts with the New Literacy Studies (e.g. Bartlett, 2005; Pahl and Rowsell, 2010, 2012) and space, place and the New Literacy Studies (e.g. Comber, 2007, 2010; Nixon, 2011). These emerging fields are being retheorized and focused on as a result both of the affordances and constraints of technological shifts but also a new interest from material cultural studies and cultural geography in the fields of literacy and communication. In their edited book *The Future of Literacy Studies* (2009) Mike Baynham and Mastin Prinsloo open up new directions within literacy studies. For example, Hull and Nelson (2009) point to a conceptualization of literacy that draws on a multimodal and aesthetically informed lens that recognizes the 'imaginative vigilance' that young meaning makers bring to text-making (Hull and Nelson, 2009: 221). This kind of thinking is a useful new direction for literacy studies in conjunction with multimodality.

Conclusion: socializing semiosis

The chapter has attempted to unite multimodality with New Literacy Studies. Although both approaches to literacy practice are epistemologically similar, they come at the study of literacy from different ends of the spectrum – one having its gaze fixed on texts and our use and production of texts, and the other fixed on practices, that is how texts are used in different spaces and contexts. Texts shape practice and are themselves in turn shaped by practice. The fields of multimodality and the New Literacy Studies deal with this dynamic and their merging is particularly necessary at this time, as new texts are introduced every day with more ways of mediating identities and more rhetorical and social networks than ever before.

Considering digital texts such as Facebook it is possible to see a merging of materiality and modal compositions through photographs and signage, with communities, cultural practices, and everyday life through rituals such as adding comments to your wall space. Using cultural practices like uploading images to complement text or using capital letters for emphasis in an email have become tacit and conventionalized, yet they represent concrete examples of merging semiosis with social practice. If both the multimodal and the sociocultural are part of sustained meaning-making then they need to be brought together to explain modern communication.

Just as it is impossible to separate the local from the global (Brandt and Clinton, 2002), so too it is impossible to separate semiotic representation from social practices and contexts in which texts are made. New fields drawing on NLS continue to open up. One issue that is emerging from literature is how complicated literacy is and the tendency to find a quick fix, grammar or framework to solve it (Leander and Boldt, 2013). One key direction is the spatializing of literacy research and practice (Leander and Sheehy, 2004). Soja's work (2010) has led to a focus on spatial literacies. Geographical approaches to literacy have led to new disciplinary boundaries being drawn (Edwards *et al.*, 2009). This critique of 'situated' literacies encompassed work on real and virtual classrooms and began a process, still ongoing, in which the links between offline and online spaces, and school and home began to be considered anew (Pahl and Rowsell 2012, Burnett *et al.* 2014). The spatial turn had a new direction in the focus on ecological literacies. Researchers such as Helen Nixon, Jennifer Rowsell and Sue Nichols began to deconstruct, using a mix of ecological theory and actor network theory, the way in which literacy is reified within commercial settings (Nichols, 2011; Nichols *et al.*, 2009, 2012; Nixon, 2011). By probing at the intersections between NLS and multimodality new fields can be mapped that look at space, time, identities, digital materializations, drawing on methodologies such as sensory ethnography (Pink, 2009). Broadening the scope of both NLS and multimodality to merge it with such fields as phenomenology, social geography and cultural studies has opened spaces for researchers to access the material and immaterial spaces of meaning-making (Mangen, 2010; Rowsell, 2013) These developments continue to create possibilities for research at this intersection as well as lively discussion of the limits of such approaches (Dicks *et al.*, 2011). The key point in the chapter is that all texts are made in social ways and there is a need for more dialogues of this kind between multimodal and New Literacy Studies scholars in order to better understand contemporary literacy.

Further reading

Grenfell, M,, Bloome, D,, Hardy, C., Pahl, K., Rowsell, J. and Street, B. (2012) *Language, Ethnography and Education: Bridging New Literacy Studies and Bourdieu*, New York: Routledge.
Jewitt, C. and Kress, G. (2003) *Multimodal Literacy*, London: Peter Lang.
Kress, G. (2010) *Multimodality: A Social Semiotic Approach to Contemporary Communication*, London: Routledge.
Pahl, K. and Rowsell, J. (2010) *Artifactual Literacies: Every Object Tells a Story*, New York: Teachers College Press.
Street, B.V. and Lefstein, A. (2007) *Literacy: An Advanced Resource Handbook*, London: Routledge.

Related topics

Multimodal data and transcription (Flewitt *et al.*, Chapter 3 this volume);
materiality (Van Leeuwen, Chapter 5 this volume);
multimodality and time (Lemke, Chapter 11 this volume);
culture and multimodality (Leander and Vasudevan, Chapter 10 this volume).

17

Using multimodal corpora for empirical research

John A. Bateman

Introduction: new methods, new challenges

As studies of multimodality progress, it is increasingly important to evaluate hypotheses and theories concerning multimodal meaning-making against data, i.e. actual artefacts and performances involving the deployment of semiotic resources drawn from and combining modalities of various kinds. Discussions of single illustrative cases play an important role in the initial stages of research and theory development, but as theories mature we need to establish the degree to which they can cover and explain uses of multimodality more generally. We need to be able to explore potential boundaries within which the theories might operate and locate gaps or inaccuracies in those theories' predictions. Until this is done, accounts remain 'working hypotheses' which may or may not be applicable in any particular case.

Consider, for example, the well-known proposal from socio-semiotics made by Kress and Van Leeuwen (2006) that the distribution of information spatially on a page can be characterised broadly in terms of an 'ideal'–'real' dimension running vertically and a 'given'–'new' dimension running horizontally. Although this has been adopted uncritically in many analyses, the empirical validation of the claim against data is still surprisingly thin. When examining, on the one hand, actual instances of short videos (Baldry and Thibault, 2006: 189–90) and online newspapers (Knox, 2007: 37–43) and, on the other, readers/viewers' physical perception of pages in terms of their eye-tracking behaviour (Holsanova *et al.*, 2006), the general applicability of Kress and Van Leeuwen's proposal appears questionable. This notwithstanding, the idea does sometimes suggest interesting and perhaps revealing analyses. The question then to be raised is just when, i.e. under what circumstances, might the proposal be applicable and when not. One method of exploring this is by applying the account *systematically* to a range of data selected so as to cover diverse cases of multimodal usage. Results might indicate that the proposal works well with particular kinds of page layouts, or in particular genres, or in artefacts from a particular historical period, or in particular media, but not in others. Or one might find that the account needs modifying to be reliably applicable at all. In each case, the account has been refined and made more powerful with respect to its ability to inform us about the workings of multimodal artefacts.

This is the essence of the idea underlying corpus-based approaches and their use for empirical research. Similar examples of hypotheses concerning the deployment of multi-modal resources can be made in almost all areas where multimodality is being explored and so it is to be expected that pursuing these issues empirically with respect to larger collections of data will contribute significantly to progress. In order to explore and validate theoretical hypotheses in this way, it is beneficial: (a) to refine the hypotheses to the point that they can be applied reliably to any actual instance of data, (b) to carry out analysis with respect to a systematically varying body of data, called a *corpus*, so as to see how well the hypotheses 'fit', and (c) subsequently to refine the hypotheses in the face of the results so as to improve their coverage of the data. Such hypotheses can be more or less complex in their own right – with the current state of the art in multimodality research there are far more questions than answers and so there is much to be explored, even with relatively simple hypotheses. At the same time, the sheer quantity of multimodal data available is exploding, with online media such as news reports, image banks, online communications and so on playing a major role. It is therefore easier than ever before to explore theoretical hypotheses concerning multimodality with respect to data. The technical means we have for *acquiring* multimodal data – for example, by the audiovisual recording of multimodal interactions in natural or controlled situations, perhaps even from multiple simultaneous perspectives, is also now well within reach of even the most modest research budgets, again making empirical corpus-based research into multimodal meaning-making a logical choice of method.

Carrying out corpus-based research on multimodality is, then, highly desirable at this time. However, the need to deal with 'multimodal data' itself raises substantial issues which need to be addressed in order to obtain the most benefit from corpus-based methods. A useful comparison can be drawn with the state of the art in language research, where corpus-based approaches already constitute a central methodological pillar. There the adoption of corpus-based methods was made possible by two advances: first, large quantities of recorded 'data' became readily available (i.e. texts in electronic form) and, second, effective tools for searching those data for patterns were developed. Both aspects need to be present for corpus analysis to be effective: insufficient quantities of data raise the danger that the patterns found are accidental and do not generalise, while a lack of facilities for searching larger-scale bodies of data means that researchers cannot get at the patterns, even if they are there.

When the data to be investigated involve multimodality these issues remain and raise further distinctive challenges of their own. As mentioned above, the availability of 'raw' (i.e. unprocessed) multimodal data can now often be taken for granted, but the tools for accessing such data and making it amenable to focused empirical research are in many areas just beginning to emerge. In the case of traditional text corpora, for example, it is often possible to take relatively simple approaches to viewing the results of corpus searches by presenting them 'directly' in the form of concordances and key word in context (KWIC) lists. This relies on patterns being discernible in the co-text of particular combinations of search items so that informal scanning of the results (i.e. actual reading through by the researcher) may suggest useful hypotheses. In the case of multimodal data, this quickly becomes less than ideal: simply replaying segments of the full, and often quite complex, multimodal artefact or activity matching some search criteria may suggest initial generalisations but is unlikely to take us very far in theory building. What is urgently required in the multimodal context are appropriate tools for *interacting with corpora* in order to reveal patterns that may by no means be accessible to simple observation.

This is therefore the main point of focus for the present chapter. Selected problems and challenges of employing corpus methods for multimodal materials as well as some of the tools and relevant practices of corpus design will be discussed, considering in particular how these need to be adapted and extended for effective multimodality research. The basic position taken will be to re-affirm the importance of adopting empirical, corpus-based approaches when exploring all aspects of multimodality, multimodal activities and multimodal artefacts, even though the complexity and diversity of multimodal communication renders the transferral of existing methods challenging. New corpus methods and research practices will need to be tailored specifically to support multimodal work by drawing on the state of the art in several areas where data-driven and corpus-based methods are being developed. As we shall see, particularly significant here is the steady growth that can now be observed in *cooperative work* bringing together approaches from the humanities, primarily linguistic and other communication studies based work, and computational techniques for the automatic processing of still images, moving images, sound, speech, body posture and much more; several such projects will be mentioned below.

Making data usable for multimodal corpus research

Definitions of the term 'multimodal corpora' share a certain looseness with the definition of 'multimodality' itself. A useful preliminary distinction is drawn by Allwood (2008) between sensory modalities and production modalities. Sensory modalities refer to physical perception according to the human sense organs, while production modalities are particular *ways of producing meaning* that may be apprehended by those senses – the very different production modalities of written language, gesture and pictures, for example, all share the sensory modality of sight, whereas the equally different production modalities of music and spoken language share the sensory modality of hearing. Allwood then takes a multimodal corpus to be any collection of machine-searchable data that combines modalities of either or both kinds. This leads to a primarily technological definition of multimodal corpora – i.e. sensory modalities operate by virtue of different physical substrates (light, sound waves, etc.) and so generally require different technological solutions for data capture, replay and search.

When probed more deeply, however, this view of modalities exhibits several problems. Much recent work in the philosophy and aesthetics of perception (e.g. Coessens, 2012) and its neuro-cognitive foundations (e.g. Clark, 2011; Seeley, 2012) places doubt on the sensory compartmentalisation that the simple identification of physical organs suggests. Similarly unclear is the situation with production modalities: for many artefacts and behaviours of interest within the field of multimodality, substantial issues remain concerning the identity and boundaries of the production modalities that may be involved (cf. Stöckl, 2004). The importance of deriving distinctions in this area by empirical investigation becomes particularly evident when philosophically and theoretically more adequate characterisations of the nature of the semiotic modes involved in multimodality are drawn upon. Kress (Chapter 4 this volume), for example, sees modes as being both socio-culturally generated in the practices of particular communities and formally constituted by their management of communicative needs. Neither of these aspects can be simply 'read off' from any artefact or behaviour: they need to be derived from analysis of actual instances of multimodal practices. The starting points for multimodal corpora should therefore always be *the artefacts or activities under empirical investigation* and not assumptions concerning modalities.

There will, moreover, always be a distance between the data being interrogated and the originary phenomenon that is the actual goal of study. Restrictions in corpus design will often need to be made on technical grounds and these must be carefully weighed with respect to their potential for revealing or hiding meaningful patterns. As an example, we can consider face-to-face interaction. Whereas face-to-face conversational interaction between two participants is (ontologically) an embodied, spatially situated three-dimensional temporally unfolding set of coordinated behaviours, data selected to make up a corpus of such interactions might consist of very different kinds of information. There may be a written transcription of what was said and by whom including written indications of intonation, or an audio recording of what was said, or a video recording with one fixed camera of what occurred, or two close-up video recordings, one for each participant, or a computer-regenerated three-dimensional representation of the activity with full motion-capture of the participants, and so on. Each kind of representation can be used for a multimodal corpus and might reveal significant properties of the activity under study. They are all nevertheless distinct from the original behaviour in a way that can often be overlooked with monomodal textual corpora. For multimodal corpora, in contrast, it will be common for a variety of levels of description to intervene between original behaviour or artefact and researchers interrogating that behaviour or artefact.

In some areas of multimodality more is known about the probable workings of the modes at issue than in others. When linguistic utterances are present, for example, assumptions concerning their phonological, lexical, morphological, syntactic and semantic organisation are well motivated and so naturally offer appropriate levels of description of *certain aspects* of the phenomenon under investigation. In other areas, such as gesture, there are also well developed proposals for characterising both the forms and functions of any gestures that might occur. In other areas still, however, such as document layout, accounts are in need of considerably more empirical research. What will become increasingly important in the future, therefore, is the ability of corpora to combine information with distinct theoretical statuses. Patterns can then be sought and hypotheses verified not primarily against data, but against *other levels of descriptions of data*. This is actually always the case, both by virtue of the nature of transcription (Ochs, 1979) and theory building in general; but it is worthwhile emphasising this particularly for multimodal research since it has important implications both for how corpora should be designed and for the kinds of tools that will be needed for using them. Bringing these considerations together, the definition of multimodal corpora taken here will be the following: multimodal corpora are collections of 'data' in which distinct semiotic modes are *presumed* (as a research hypothesis) to be at work. The data constituting a multimodal corpus are then 'recordings' of naturally occurring artefacts or activities hypothesised to manifest distinct modes – the issue of precisely which modes should not be prejudged (for further discussion of the identification of modes, see Bateman, 2011).

Once the target data have been fixed, they must then be *prepared* for corpus use. Bare data are generally insufficient for effective empirical research because it is difficult, or even impossible, to *interact* with the data in ways that are appropriate for framing and exploring research questions. This is the case even for monomodal text corpora (Garside *et al.*, 1997) but, for multimodal corpora, it presents a major problem. Consider a hypothetical case of researching whether dialogues in some body of films between same-gender and different-gender pairs of interactants are produced employing different camera angles: although straightforward to state, searching through a corpus of films to answer this question requires first that 'dialogues' be recognised, that participants in the dialogue be identified, that their gender be classified, that camera angles be classified and so on. Each of these is a difficult task, in some cases already going beyond what is currently technically possible on an automatic basis. The raw data become much more useful for research when *annotated* with categories directly supportive of further questioning. For example, in the present case, if the films in the corpus already had their participants 'tagged' whenever they appear, had the camera angles already labelled for each segment, had the genders of participants identified and the sequences where dialogue is occurring segmented, then the research question becomes straightforward to address with respect to the annotated data. Moreover, the annotations thus provided might be useful for an entire host of *other* research questions. This emphasises the value of cooperative work, which we will return to below – when annotations of data are made available to a broader research community, research can build on the categories that are already present and pursue more complex research questions without redoing the basic work of analysis.

This applies to all kinds of multimodal data. Consider a further hypothetical case exploring the combined use of hand gestures and falling/rising intonation in a certain kind of face-to-face interaction: again, if the data are already annotated with respect to intonation contours and, perhaps by a completely separate research group, with respect to classes of hand gestures, then the research question becomes readily addressable. If, on the other hand, each researcher had themselves first to identify and label all the intonation contours *and* identify and label all the hand gestures, then the simple research question becomes a major research effort. It is then highly desirable for annotations to be shared so that the value of data is multiplied and research can 'snowball' on the basis of growing bodies of annotated data. In short, the greater the extent of 'enrichment' of the material selected for a corpus, the more valuable for research that corpus becomes. Corpus annotation is consequently becoming increasingly sophisticated precisely in order to support such efforts (cf. McEnery and Wilson, 2001; Kingsbury *et al.*, 2002).

The need both to annotate data and to share such annotations subsequently on a broader scale is now commonly recognised, even though in the multimodal case there is still considerable uncertainty concerning just what kinds of data annotation might be useful; this issue is closely related to questions of data transcription in general (cf. Flewitt *et al.*, Chapter 3 this volume). Nevertheless, the challenges of making annotation shareable have now largely been met and solved by the development of the *Extensible Markup Language* (XML), the current recommendation of the World-Wide Web Consortium for capturing structured data of all kinds, multimodal data included.[1] As a consequence, XML is used as a representation and transfer format for data and associated annotations in virtually all of the more sophisticated approaches to multimodal corpora now being pursued and so we shall return to it in slightly more detail below.

The adoption of XML as a means for exchanging information has also led to the recent establishment of an international standard for linguistic annotation, called the *Linguistic Annotation Framework* (ISO, 2012). This standard does not itself specify the *contents* of any particular annotation scheme but instead offers guidelines within which annotation schemes can be developed for specific linguistic phenomena, including recommendations for both speech signals and video, making it highly relevant for multimodal corpus work in general; a characterisation of the scope of the framework and techniques employed is given in Ide and Romary (2004). Regardless of particular approach adopted, however, it is now clear that 'recorded' material constituting a multimodal corpus, perhaps drawing on a range of sensory modes, will need to be stored in a manner that supports multiple 'enrichment' according to various levels of annotation, i.e. description, as deemed useful for research. All multimodal corpora face this basic design challenge.

Types of multimodal data and corresponding tools

Different kinds of data raise different kinds of problems and so it is useful to characterise areas of modality with respect to their specific challenges, both for corpus-based approaches and corresponding tools. Some basic dimensions for organising the discussion can be distinguished on the basis of properties of the data to be covered. The broadest distinction relevant for discussions of multimodal corpora is that between *linear* and *non-linear* data. Linear data include material which is essentially organised to unfold along a single dimension of actualization. This dimension may either be in space, as in traditional written-text data, or in time, as in recordings of spoken language. Non-linear data include material where there is no single organising dimension that can be used for providing access. In the case of multimodality, this generally involves *spatially distributed* information and visual representations, such as that found on pages of documents, printed advertisements, paintings and so on, but can also include other kinds of *logical organisation*, as in the linking structure of websites, for example.

The distinction between linear and non-linear data is an essential one made at various times over the history of the study of media (cf. Lessing, 1853 [1766]; Kress, 2003b). Many discussions of multimodal corpora and tools in fact *only* consider linear data, paying little if any attention to non-linear data. Visual representations, such as photographs or images of paintings, are still more commonly *archived* than maintained in corpora, and a variety of classifications exist for the purposes of search and organisation. Typically, quite different communities are involved in the two cases – speech and interaction research on the one hand and press photography, art history, medical imaging and others on the other. Quite diverse frameworks have consequently emerged, some of which we will mention below. There is considerable potential here for consolidation, both of experiences and of frameworks.

In research explicitly aligned with corpus work, however, the single dimension of access found in linear data has offered a natural candidate for organising levels of annotation. The linear ordering provides a scaffold that can easily be enriched with further information. This is one of the main reasons why speech corpora, using *time-stamped* data, constitute by far the most developed type of multimodal corpora available today. Corpora for non-linear data are less developed and few tools specifically for corpus work have been developed with this area in mind. Unfortunately, tools built for linear data are often unusable for cases of strong non-linearity, although several attempts to add spatial information to time-based data are now underway. Explorations of the kinds of meanings involved in non-linear communicative artefacts, such as page-based media (including the web), as a consequence remain limited with respect to their empirical foundation – a situation in urgent need of change.

Those working with time-based media have long recognised that it is useful to set out the multiple levels of information involved as collections of tracks with temporal relationships indicated using spatial layout. The grouping of staves adopted in traditional Western musical notation is a system of this kind and similar techniques have been variously adapted for other time-based data, for example for the multimodal organisation of film according to simultaneous combination of music, gesture, movement and frame composition by the director Sergei Eisenstein in the 1920s and 1930s (cf. Eisenstein, 1961 [1938]: 265–66). Typically in such multimodal representations the tracks are represented visually in some form and co-temporality is indicated by either vertical or horizontal spatial alignment. The simplest form of notation for linearly unfolding multimodal data therefore consists of a series of textual renditions of visual or other features, possibly augmented by static images and colour codings of various kinds, although several alternative schemes of this kind exist (e.g. Norris, 2002).

The original motivation for such notations was to 'fix' transient phenomena in a readily inspectable form, such as in printed tables where the rows may indicate some selected analytic unit and the columns contain different facets of the information conveyed (cf., e.g.

Baldry and Thibault, 2006); such tables can then also be readily transferred to 'database tables' for large-scale online storage and retrieval. However, the predominantly 'written' orientation of scientific discourse and earlier technological difficulties in supporting researcher-guided access to non-written instances of language, such as naturally occurring spoken language, came to encourage a tendency whereby linguistic analysis is pursued with respect to transcripts rather than with respect to original data. Notation schemes of these kinds are then employed to transcribe (cf. Flewitt *et al.*, Chapter 3 this volume), or 're-present' their data in written form. Although this may function reasonably well for written text and spoken language corpora, it becomes increasingly impractical with multimodal analysis. The gap between transcription (still predominantly textual) and the material under analysis is simply too great to allow re-presentation. In the multimodal case there is almost always simply *too much occurring* to consider any re-presentation of the data as 'complete'. Attempting to achieve exhaustive 'transcription' then more often ends up as offering, in the words of Michael Halliday, "a running commentary" on the data rather than analysing it (Halliday, 1985: xvi–xvii). A considerable body of more informal multimodal 'analysis' consequently fails to go far beyond detailed (sometimes over-detailed) surface description – a critique made particularly clear in Forceville (2007: 1236).

In order to get beyond such re-descriptions, a different stance needs to be taken towards the information maintained. In particular, levels of annotation for multimodal corpora will be more useful when they 'code' particular selective aspects of the data under investigation rather than attempting to 'stand in' for those data. This argues for corpus designs and tools that actively support modularity of description for any levels of annotation being addressed, a property also provided by XML-based annotations as we shall see below.

Working with linearly organised data

Two of the most widely used and freely available tools for multimodal corpus analysis of linear data compatible with the above considerations are ELAN,[2] developed and maintained by the Max Planck Institute for Psycholinguistics in Nijmegen (Wittenburg *et al.*, 2006), and ANVIL,[3] developed by Michael Kipp while at the DFKI in Saarbrücken (Kipp, 2012). Both are XML-based and allow the enrichment of textual, audio and video data with arbitrary numbers of levels, also called tiers or tracks, of further annotation. In addition, and as increasingly common and also appropriate for multimodal work, the tracks displayed may include information whose descriptive and theoretical status is quite varied. For example, some tracks may be 'transcriptions' (i.e. transcodings of properties of the data to a textual form, as in phonetic representations); other tracks might encode analysis results or 'codings' (as in dialogue act assignment or rhetorical analysis); other tracks still may include annotation data produced manually within the tool, while others import analyses created either automatically by other software (as in syntactic analysis or speech signal data with fundamental frequency and intensity information) or manually with other more specialised tools. Such combinations of information will be increasingly required as research into more complex multimodal artefacts, behaviours and performances grows. Regardless of status, all information can be displayed together spatially aligned by virtue of the common timeframe of the medium. The tools themselves remain agnostic, however, concerning both what kinds of linguistic or other information may be added and what kinds of visualisations or analysis reports may be generated. As long as information is expressed in the required XML-compatible form, it may be imported and displayed in any of the ways that the tools provide.

Operations log, primary data and spatial annotations, annotation details

Selected time-based annotation tracks

Scroll bar and navigation

Figure 17.1 Example of working with ANVIL on gesture (screen image kindly provided by Michael Kipp).

An illustrative screen shot showing work with ANVIL is given in Figure 17.1; the general appearance of ELAN is similar. In the example shown we can see many of the features provided by time-based multimodal tools plus some more recent capabilities added within ANVIL for spatial annotation that we will return to below. In the top-half of the figure we find several information windows plus a video player, while in the lower-half of the figure we see the particular tracks selected for analysis. The current position in the video is marked by a vertical line intersecting the displayed tracks. Manual annotation is typically done by clicking within the graphically represented timeline of a specified track as a video is playing and selecting a particular classification category given by the annotation scheme defined for that track.

Several other tools of a more experimental nature are currently under development. In a broadly linguistic context, Baldry and colleagues (cf. Baldry, 2007) are working on a *Multimodal Corpus Authoring System*; Carter and Adolphs (2008) describe work with the *Digital Replay System* on two-party face-to-face interaction and gesture; and O'Halloran and colleagues (cf. O'Halloran *et al.*, 2012) present a prototype of an integrated environment containing an entire package of tools specifically targeting socio-semiotic multimodal analysis – one prime concern here is to explore visualisation and aural representations that may be more supportive of semiotic reflexion and 'meta-semiotic' discourse about signs and their analyses (O'Halloran, Chapter 28 this volume).

Tools are also emerging in many other areas to support empirically based multimodal research, for example in media studies where the investigation of audio-visual materials now similarly takes advantage of the technical advances made for working with such data. Recent examples of such systems include: the *Kivi* system, developed by Jan Müller at the Jacobs University Bremen for content-based manual annotation of TV news materials with a web-based interface (Müller, 2010); the *eMAEX* system, developed by Hermann Kappelhoff and colleagues (Kappelhoff and Bakels, 2011) at the Free University Berlin for the empirical investigation of narrative film's structuring of the affective responses of viewers; the *Lignes de temps* system[4] developed at the IRI research institute at the Pompidou Centre in Paris for film analysis and annotation; and the *Advene* (Annotate Digital Video, Exchange on the NEt) system of the LIRIS laboratory at University Claude Bernard in Lyon (Aubert and Prié, 2005) for cooperative web-based construction of 'hypervideos' from film data on the basis of given annotations.[5]

Each of these tools has some features that are particularly designed for its intended users; these generally draw on the different communities involved. *Lignes de temps*, for example, comes with a detailed classification scheme for the types of camera angles, camera movements, shot distances and so on as typically employed in film studies, O'Halloran's toolset employs a variety of descriptions from systemic-functional theory, and so on. The style in which results can be presented also varies according to intended use: *eMAEX* produces websites documenting a film scene-by-scene resembling a dynamic film protocol, while *Lignes de temps* produces on-demand recut versions of a film depending on the annotation tracks selected. It is therefore unlikely, and probably unnecessary, that a general tool for 'all purposes' be provided. More important is the capability mentioned above of *sharing* annotation data.

Despite their differences, the typical usage scenarios of current tools are all quite similar, however. An audio-visual artefact is segmented along several dimensions and the resulting segments are then categorised, often by hand, i.e. by groups of human annotators. Patterns are then sought in the resulting combinations of categories and their material realisation. In both the linguistic and media-based contexts, combining manual annotation with the results of automatic processing – such as speech processing for spoken language or shot and other technical feature detection in film and audio-visual data – will become increasingly important. Mature tools with extensive user-bases such as ANVIL and ELAN that support such capabilities consequently have much to offer in this respect, both for the annotation of data and for supporting subsequent searches for meaningful patterns.

Working with nonlinearly organised data

The tools mentioned until now as well as the kinds of annotations that they support are strongly linear. In the limited cases where information of a non-linear form has also been addressed, it has been usual to rely upon recognisable elements within a linearly unfolding audio-visual image for anchoring their non-linear aspects. For example, in the case of gesture it is often sufficient to identify the person whose gestures are being annotated and then information can follow relative to that person's arms, hands and other gesturally relevant body parts. The same holds for facial expression coding schemes. Even strongly spatial notions can often be treated in this way: for example, both proximity and gaze coding can be classified qualitatively according to relative distance or direction with respect to named protagonists. For many kinds of information relevant for studying the multimodality of dialogic interaction, therefore, the currently available tools can go a long way. For artefacts where time cannot be convincingly invoked as an organising dimension, however, other solutions must be explored – that is, whenever the form of multimodality being analysed involves data that make use, for example, of the two-dimensional area of the page or a three-dimensional volume within which 'communication' of some kind takes place, it is necessary to ensure that corresponding corpora record this aspect of the data in its own right.

Documents and other static page or 'canvas'-based artefacts are good examples of objects of multimodal analysis that do not make any convincing reference to temporal organisation. Annotating data of this kind consequently requires access to spatial properties of the information depicted instead of, or in addition to, temporal properties. In many cases, what is required is not the identification of properties that may be aligned with time-intervals but instead the identification of 'entities' within images, which may then receive various properties as annotations. These entities may belong either to what is represented or to the form of the images themselves, as in their layout organisation. A detailed proposal for annotating the latter is given in the layout structure and area model of the GeM framework described in Bateman (2008), where relations to other document description schemes, such as cascaded style sheets (CSS), XML formatting objects, and standards for hypermedia presentations (e.g. SMIL), are also discussed.

Other kinds of annotation schemes and tools for non-linear data have been developed within specific communities. For example, image-related functionalities are available for press photography, where meta-data about the topic and provenance of stored images are also maintained;[6] medical imaging, where substantial technical information may be associated with images of various kinds; computer-aided architectural design, where detailed 3D models of buildings and other structures need to be captured; Geographic Information Science (GIS), where multiple layer 'maps' describe geographic space at different levels of abstraction; and art history and digital humanities, where there is a growing awareness of the utility of allowing researchers to augment elements of artworks with descriptions and notes as well as permitting links to be drawn between visual elements from different artworks. Dedicated systems already involving substantial visual content of this latter kind include the *HyperImage* system developed by Martin Warnke and colleagues at the Leuphana University Lüneberg and an extended project building on this called *Meta-Image*, recently linked within the distributed digital image archive *prometheus* containing over 750,000 art images spread over 60 connected databases.[7] There is also an ongoing attempt in the *ImageNet* project[8] to provide visual examples for the linguistic entries (called synsets) of the Princeton WordNet (Miller *et al.*, 1990); ImageNet currently claims to have indexed over 14 million images for over 20,000 WordNet noun 'synsets' (Deng *et al.*, 2009). Relatively simple annotation tools for adding structured information to visual data are also becoming common – the photograph archive site *flickr*, for example, provides this as a basic functionality enabling particular people, locations or other objects within a photograph to receive user-specified descriptions for subsequent search.[9]

Closer to established corpus methods, several experimental tools under development now allow boxes and other shapes to be 'drawn' on top of a page or image being annotated without requiring temporal anchors; these include Baldry and colleagues' *Multimodal Web Browser and Analyser*[10] and O'Donnell's *UAM ImageTool*.[11] Moreover, some of the time-based tools mentioned above are also considering augmentation to include spatial information. For example, the *Kivi* tool allows particular spatial regions of the video data to be annotated for media-relevant categories, while ANVIL provides a scheme for adding markup and annotation of points within the video material displayed which can be grouped into polygons to demarcate regions (cf. Kipp, 2008) or show arrows and other line extents for annotating movement (as can be seen in the video pane in Figure 17.1). Similar functionality is provided by several other kinds of software systems, for example for marking areas-of-interest in eye-tracking experiments (Holsanova, Chapter 20 this volume). There is, however, much to be done for really usable corpus analysis tools for non-linear data to result. Here again there is a considerable need for consolidation of efforts across disciplines and approaches. Bateman (2008: 265–67) offers more discussion of the issues and some further examples of existing page-based corpora.

Annotation schemes for multimodal corpus work

Given the current significance of XML-based annotation for multimodal corpus work and the need mentioned above of ensuring that annotated data can be made available and shared within interested research communities, it is worthwhile setting out in slightly more detail how XML-based annotation functions. Two aspects are particularly important: the form of the annotation itself and the ways in which XML allows specific annotation schemes to be defined. Both are quite straightforward but nevertheless go far in providing a robust infrastructure for developing and maintaining substantial bodies of annotated data.

The first aspect, the form of the annotation, concerns how annotations and the data they are annotating are brought together. In early monomodal text-based corpora, it was common to add annotations directly into the data themselves. For example, part-of-speech information for lexical items might have been added to the relevant words in the corpus with forms such as 'can+N', 'can+V', 'can+MV' in order to disambiguate 'can' as a noun, a full verb or a modal verb respectively. This kind of solution has several drawbacks. First, it mixes data with information about the data; second, it makes the original data harder to see; third, there is no formal specification of just what kinds of additional information are allowed and in what form; and fourth, it becomes awkward to provide annotation information for *structural units* holding across the individual items in the data. Simple XML annotation provides a solution to the last problem by grouping elements together into specially indicated annotation units that can be embedded within other annotation units and which can themselves receive particular labels. An XML annotation unit is written within labelled opening and closing brackets; the label is referred to as a *tag*. The opening labelled bracket may include additional lists of attributes and values for those attributes written in the form Attribute = "Value". So we might, for example, write an XML-style annotation for 'can' as a singular noun as:

<N number = "singular">can</N>

The first pair of angled brackets identifies the type of the annotation ('N') and gives a value for its 'number' attribute; the second pair of angled brackets </N> matches the opening <N...> expression, thus marking the end of the enclosing annotation unit; the forward slash indicates that the annotation unit is being closed.

Still problematic with this simple style of annotation, however, is the fact that different kinds of information – for example, intonation, gesture, syntax, gaze and so on – often are not structurally aligned and so their boundaries may overlap. To deal with this issue, XML *stand-off annotation* (Thompson and McKelvie, 1997) is used rather than simple annotation. This technique works by leaving the original data untouched and placing all additional annotations in separate annotation files that are linked to the original data by means of *cross-references*. This then solves the first and second problem above also, since the original data is never altered: annotations simply 'point to' the relevant parts of the data that are intended to receive annotations. Each annotation file is then free to represent its own specific kind of information and there is no problem in having many, possibly even mutually inconsistent, annotations of the same data. This is particularly useful whenever mutually orthogonal or independent levels of abstraction are to be captured (e.g. syntactic structure, intonational phrasing, typography, layout, image contents, hyperlink structures, etc.) and whenever the form of the data does not allow insertion of extra textual material (as in video data). The Linguistic Annotation Framework (LAF) mentioned above works extensively with this style of annotation, as do most of the XML-based tools discussed. The 'regions' of data pointed to in LAF stand-off annotations may be of any dimensionality, which makes the scheme equally applicable to temporal intervals, to two-dimensional areas on a page or screen, to three-dimensional chunks of primary data and so on. Developments of this kind will strongly influence the development of future resources and tools for multimodal corpora and so represent an important step towards coordinating community efforts for larger scale empirical work. A detailed example of stand-off annotation is worked through in Bateman (2008: 260–64).

Neither the formal framework of XML nor a standard such as LAF addresses the further problem of knowing just which annotations – i.e. which tags, which attributes and which values – can be used: this is, however, equally important for sharing information effectively. XML addresses this concern by requiring that the tags, attributes, values and the embedding possibilities of specific annotation units within others all be explicitly defined in what is called an *XML schema*. In the multimodal corpus context, therefore, XML schemas provide a general representation within which the content of corpus annotation frameworks – i.e. the kind of additional 'mark-up' information referred to, in certain respects misleadingly, as 'grammars' in Baldry (2007: 180–81) – can be precisely specified and moreover, since XML-schemas are themselves instances of XML, be shared for cooperative work. Thus, for example, a schema for syntactic annotation might specify that there are tags corresponding to the major syntactic classes and indicate which elements may occur within others; similarly, a schema for facial expression annotation might specify the kinds of distinctions required in the Facial Action Coding System (Ekman and Friesen, 1978) and so on. Once an XML-schema has been defined, standard XML tools can then check whether any particular file or set of files written in terms of that schema uses its tags in the ways the schema allows. If this is not the case, then an error is flagged. Employing XML and XML schemas thus provides 'automatically' a basic quality control check on any data maintained. This is an increasingly vital and difficult task once the quantity of data grows and the, potentially quite complex, interlinking of different levels of annotation takes on a central role.

Decisions must still naturally be made concerning just what information is to be maintained in a multimodal corpus and, consequently, what particular XML-schemas should be defined. This is the principal locus of theoretical multimodal research since it is here that the development of multimodal theory and description really takes place. Specifying the developing state of theory in terms of XML annotation schemas is one way of progressively working towards improved coverage of data. Subsequently, as areas of multimodal analysis become more established and the resulting annotation frameworks gain stability, the schemes defined can be exchanged within their respective research communities and used across research teams to annotate data – thereby again multiplying the benefits of empirical research. A forerunner of such an effort was the very successful Text-Encoding Initiative of the 1990s, in which a standard annotation scheme was developed for text-based documents (TEI: Vanhoutte and van den Branden, 2010). The TEI provides a detailed XML-based scheme for documents and their parts (sections, subsections, paragraphs, etc.), which is now also serving as a basis for further annotation initiatives, some of which have already moved into multimodal document areas. One example here is the Comic Book Markup Language (CBML: Walsh, 2012), designed specifically for 'books' consisting predominantly of text–image–layout combinations functioning as sequential art.

However, for the reasons indicated above, annotation schemes for linearly organised data are by far the most common within the current state of the art in empirical multimodal corpus-based research. Annotation levels for many aspects of linguistic organisation are now freely available and can be used in all tools that support representations conformant with the XML standard. Communities working with ANVIL and ELAN have also produced a range of re-usable annotation schemes of specific relevance for multimodal corpus analysis; some of these are provided as examples downloaded with the systems when they are installed. One recent development of this kind is the definition of an international standard for annotating dialogue acts (ISO, 2011), already offered as an import/export functionality by ANVIL (Bunt *et al.*, 2012). Similar initiatives are being pursued for gesture and body posture. One result in this area is the Multimodal Utterance Representation Markup Language, MURML (Kranstedt *et al.*, 2002). It is certainly worthwhile, therefore, to consider the annotation schemes that are already available before undertaking corpus-based work on multimodality. Adapting or extending such schemes is often made straightforward by tools such as ANVIL or ELAN and, once defined, schemes can be distributed more broadly across relevant research communities. Preparing new schemes compatible with the XML standard is itself an excellent method of encouraging broader take-up of particular transcriptions, the development of corresponding tool support, and the availability of larger data sets.

A good example of a community-driven effort of this latter kind is the consolidation of experiences currently underway to provide an integrated collection of annotation schemes for the description of conversational 'behaviour' in general. The result of this initiative is the *Behavior Markup Language* (BML), a framework driven particularly by the need to model and generate embodied conversational behaviour for artificial agents. The BML architecture allows for an open-ended number of schemes, particularly gaze, gesture (adopting for example MURML), facial expression and speech. These are combined within a foundational layer of 'General Core Features' responsible for fine-grained synchronisation across behaviours.

Within BML, behaviours are seen as unfolding across a temporal profile consisting of a start phase, a 'ready' phase and a 'relax' phase; particular types of behaviours may have additional components, such as the 'stroke' of a hand gesture (i.e. the main meaning-bearing component, cf. Kendon, 1980). An example specification written in BML is then the following, taken from Kopp *et al.* (2006: 212):

```
<bml>
    <gesture id="g1" type="beat"/>
    <head type="nod" stroke="g1:stroke"/>
    <gaze target="object1" start="g1:ready" end="g1:relax"/>
</bml>
```

This describes (i) a hand *gesture*, labelled 'g1', characterised as providing a 'beat', (ii) a *head* movement categorised as a nod and synchronised with the main stroke of g1's gesture, and (iii) a *gaze* at a specified object across the interval defined by the ready and relax phases of the hand gesture. The italicised terms here and their respective attributes and values are all defined within the standardised BML XML-schema. It is worth noting that the BML annotation framework already addresses most of the issues noted by, for example, Carter and Adolphs (2008: 284) concerning accurate representations of highly interleaved and temporally overlapping communicative acts. Quite complex synchronised behaviours can be both described and automatically simulated using computational avatar realisation engines. Moreover, it is straightforward to use standard XML mechanisms for extracting particular combinations of features and values and for exporting these to statistical or other post-processing packages to look for reoccurring patterns.

There is a similar need for coding schemes capable of capturing the properties of non-linear data – but here the situation is much more fragmented. The development of annotation schemes for spatially organised data will need to leverage appropriately off rather different bodies of knowledge than are generally taken for linear multimodality. We saw one reason for this above in the very different communities concerned with non-linear data. There are consequently extensive categorisations of the distinct kinds of information representations that are employed in visual media – 2D graphs, animations, films, written text, photographs, drawings, comics, diagrams, flowcharts, maps, and many more. Some of these are already specified within standards, e.g. the extensive classification schemes developed for film and the moving image by the Motion Picture Expert Group (MPEG), or the many levels of detailed 2D and 3D object classifications provided for geographical and architectural information within computer-aided design. The question of precisely which *semiotic modes* might be involved is, however, not generally addressed. Most often these efforts are driven by the demand for tools for processing and distributing data within their respective communities and so, although very detailed, do not concern themselves with multimodality as a research topic. Nevertheless, having access to such fine-grained schemes worked out by experts in their respective domains is without question valuable input. Investigations of precisely how the described artefacts and behaviours function multimodally can then be taken up empirically adopting corpus-based methods.

Relations *between* all of these diverse elements also need to be defined and considered from an empirical perspective. Written text may play decisive roles for the interpretability of graphics, or spoken language for videos, diagrams may be animated, maps and three-dimensional architectural models may include diagrammatic representations (e.g. contour lines), and so on. There are therefore additional forms of semiotic organisation whose purpose is precisely to *combine* information offerings from other modes. Each of these different modal contributions potentially requires its own set of annotation schemes operating at various levels of analytic abstraction.

Conclusions: challenges and directions

For multimodal research, corpus-based approaches will need to move away from simple notions of a corpus as a 'collection of transcribed data' where the transcriptions more or less stand in for the phenomena to be studied. Instead multimodal corpora will increasingly become repositories of data seen from a variety of perspectives. This transition constitutes a major challenge for corpus-based multimodality research: theoretically motivated distinctions need to be brought to bear to organise material for analytic inspection but, in many areas, it is not yet known just what the distinctions necessary for explanatory accounts will be. Achieving productive states of balance between theoretical focus and empirical openness represents a considerable methodological challenge.

As a consequence, multimodal corpora will need to include levels of abstraction in their annotations ranging from low-level technical features (e.g. for spoken language: acoustic properties; for film: optical flow, colour balance, edge detection, cut detection, etc.), through transcriptions of selected perspectives on the data (e.g. for language: phonetics and intonation) and the results of experimental studies (e.g. for images or film: eye-tracking data), to more abstract analyses (e.g. for interaction: dialogue acts), to hypotheses of category attributions ready for empirical testing (e.g. for interaction: relations between dialogue acts and co-selections of gaze, gesture and intonation; or for documents: relations between rhetorical relations and distance and position relations between layout units, types of typographical realisations and eye-tracking predictions: cf. Hiippala, 2012). Supporting access to such combinations of information and the search for meaningful patterns is itself complex and new methods and techniques of visualisation will be crucial (cf. Caldwell and Zappavigna, 2011; Manovich, 2012; O'Halloran, Chapter 28 this volume).

An important step towards achieving results will be the adoption of standards by which community efforts can be multiplied and more powerful mechanisms for revealing patterns can be deployed. The modular design of distinct levels of XML annotation provides strong support for this, making it straightforward to progressively accumulate analyses and annotations with respect to common data sets. This consideration constitutes a compelling reason for changing from proprietary formats and corpus tools to more open, freely available and adaptable XML-based components that can be of use to a far broader research community. It is then worthwhile inquiring of any tool the extent to which it supports the import and export of XML-conformant data – regardless of whether one looks at the XML form oneself or not, providing data in this form makes it far more likely that the data is usable with other tools and can be exchanged. A common requirement, for example, is to move data from an XML format to databases for larger-scale storage (cf. Kipp, 2012) or to other processing software, such as sophisticated statistical packages and machine learning software for searching for patterns, or to visualisation tools.

Properly annotated data may then support the search for generalizations by allowing examination of potential *correlations* across the various levels of descriptions that corpora provide. Establishing such dependencies represents a crucial step towards understanding how multimodal meaning-making operates. Moreover, for larger-scale corpus work an increasing reliance on automatic analysis and visualisation methods in appropriate combination with manual approaches will be essential. Both ANVIL and the toolset described by O'Halloran and colleagues, for example, already provide views of data in terms of automatically generated transition diagrams showing the probability of transitions between various elements belonging to selected annotation categories (cf. Kipp, 2012; Podlasov *et al.*, 2012). Similarly, the use of machine-learning techniques or more sophisticated statistical procedures for revealing patterns is also on the increase (cf., e.g. for film: Cutting *et al.*, 2011). Thus, although searches for dependencies may still be supported by examining potential correlations on a case-by-case basis, as suggested in proposals for 'multimodal concordances' of the kind offered, for example, by Baldry (2007) or Carter and Adolphs (2008), or the web-based presentation of similarly classified film scenes generated by the eMAEX system (Kappelhoff and Bakels, 2011), augmenting such approaches with increasingly powerful automatic procedures for both data preparation and data analysis is the next step that must be taken.

Notes

All web links last accessed 8 September 2013.

1 http://www.w3.org/TR/xml/
2 http://www.lat-mpi.eu/tools/elan/
3 http://www.anvil-software.de/
4 http://www.iri.centrepompidou.fr/outils/lignes-de-temps/
5 http://liris.cnrs.fr/advene/index.html
6 As in, for example, the annotation schemes of the International Press Telecommunications Council, the Associated Press, etc. (e.g. NewsML: http://www.iptc.org/site/News_Exchange_Formats/).
7 http://www2.leuphana.de/meta-image/About Meta-Image.php
8 http://www.image-net.org/
9 Cf. http://www.flickr.com/photos/ha112/234233755/ for an example of this 'Add Note' feature.
10 http://mcaweb.unipv.it/
11 http://www.wagsoft.com/ImageTool/

18

Towards an analytics of mediation

Lilie Chouliaraki

In this chapter I discuss a framework for the analysis of media discourse – the 'analytics of mediation' – that takes into account the embeddedness of media texts both in technological artefacts and in social relationships and, hence, seeks to integrate the multi-modal with the critical analysis of discourse. On the methodological level, the analytics of mediation applies a multi-modal discourse analysis onto media texts in order to study their visual and linguistic properties: camera/visual; graphic/pictorial or aural/linguistic. On the social theory level, the analytics of mediation addresses critical concerns on the ethical and political role of television and other media in our 'global village'. Can television foster a cosmopolitan consciousness or does its 'fake proximity' alienate the spectator from the rest of the world? Can we talk about the media as agents of global citizenship or do the media lead to compassion fatigue – a Western denial of humanitarian problems? I illustrate such questions by drawing on one concrete example of television news.

Distant suffering in the media

One of the most important questions in social and political theory today is the question of how the Western world relates to distant suffering, to the powerless victims of famine, war or natural disaster. This is important because the capacity of the Western world to relate to distant suffering with a sense of care and act on it with a sense of social responsibility lies at the heart of contemporary conceptions of global citizenship and the cosmopolitan public (Barnett, 2003; Boltanski, 1999; Calhoun, 2001; Hannerz, 1996; Tomlinson, 1999).[1] Given that the Western world comes to know about distant suffering primarily through the spectacles of television or the Internet, the question of distant suffering is essentially a question about the ethical role of the media in public life today. Can the media cultivate a disposition of care for and engagement with the faraway 'other'? Can television create a global public with a sense of social responsibility towards distant sufferers?

These issues have always been on the agenda of public debate and of the social sciences. Nevertheless, we know little about the role of the media in shaping an ethical sensibility that extends beyond our own neighbourhood (Peters, 1999, 2005; Silverstone, 1999, 2005). On the one hand, as television news constantly bombards us with humanitarian emergencies, arguments about the compassion fatigue of the public abound (e.g. Tester, 2001). On the other hand, the Asian tsunami emergency has reinvigorated a sense of optimism about the role of television in making people sensitive towards distant suffering and active vis-à-vis far-away 'others'. Caught between the two positions, much theory on the media hovers unproductively between a positive view of the media as facilitating ethical action in public life today and a negative view of the media as undermining public action. This dilemmatic approach to the moral role of the media does not help us understand the question of ethics and public life in its full complexity. This is what I claim in the first section of the chapter, 'Mediation and public ethics: utopian and dystopian visions'.

In my view, the problem lies in the fact that questions about the relationship between media and public action are treated as 'grand' questions and are usually dealt with in 'grand' theory. They become the topic of philosophical argument on the existence of universal moral standards or they are the stake of political debates about the rise or decline of communitarian and cosmopolitan values. The perspective I propose here is different. I develop a methodology for the study of these 'grand' questions not through theoretical argument but through the analysis of particular examples of television news on suffering.

Drawing on Aristotle's advice that our enquiries into social life should be driven by the practical consideration of what 'is good or bad for man', I focus upon the ways in which particular news texts present the sufferer as a moral cause to the Western spectator.[2] This concrete engagement with values – what Aristotle call 'phronesis' (prudence) – grasps the question of ethics from the pragmatic perspective of praxis (Flyvbjerg, 2001, pp. 110–28; Ross, 1923/1995, pp. 31–49). This is the perspective that takes each particular case to be a unique enactment of ethical discourse that, even though it transcends the case, cannot exist outside the enactment of cases. In the phronetic spirit, then, the question of how the media shape the ethical dispositions of public life is recast in the form of a modest question: how does the news genre construe the misfortune of the distant sufferer? Is suffering presented as a case of action – whose action or to what effects? Or is suffering construed as of no concern to the spectator?

In the second section, 'The analytics of mediation', I present the theoretical premises of this methodology and propose an approach to media texts on suffering as regimes of pity, that is as semantic fields where emotions and dispositions to action vis-à-vis the suffering 'others' are made possible for the spectator.[3] I then proceed to discuss the two key dimensions of the analytics of mediation: 'multi-modality', which refers to two main meaning-making technologies of television, that is voice recording and moving image (in the section entitled 'Difference within the semiotic'), and 'multi-functionality', which refers to the work of these meaning-making technologies to simultaneously represent suffering in various degrees of proximity to the spectator and to orient the spectator towards certain options for action on the suffering (in the section 'Difference outside the semiotic').[4] Finally, in the section entitled 'The "analytics of mediation": an example', I provide a brief illustration of the analytics by referring to a specific example of mediation, namely the footage of the Iraq war.

The overall aim of this chapter is to present the analytics of mediation as a methodology that enables us to ask questions about how the news text is put together in language and image and how this text construes the spacetimes and the forms of agency in suffering in terms of a set of hierarchical regimes of pity. Hierarchical as these regimes may be, they are, nevertheless, neither fixed nor immobile. They have their own discursive conditions of possibility that can be reflexively revised and changed. The contribution of the analytics of mediation in the debate on public ethics, therefore, is that it practically demonstrates the contingency of these regimes of pity, their human-made nature, and so it offers us the language to revise them; in Aristotle's words, to make them 'good for man'.

Mediation and public ethics: utopian and dystopian visions

Here I take my point of departure in media and social theory, in order to discuss the two competing visions on the ethical role of television in social life that such theory presents us with, namely the dystopian or pessimistic and the utopian or optimistic one.[5] Both visions emphasize the fact that television creates a new connectivity between the spectator and the distant 'other'. Both visions also stress the role of the medium in 'manipulating' the spectator's sense of proximity to and, hence, her ability to connect with the spectacle of suffering. But the two visions differ in the ways they understand the impact that television has upon the quality of connectivity between the spectator and the sufferer. As a consequence, the two visions reach different conclusions as to the possibility of television to engage the spectator with the sufferer's misfortune, leaving social theory inconclusive as to the ethical role of the media in public life.

The dystopian vision

Kevin Robins' eloquent paradox, *intimate detachment*, echoes the pessimism of Adorno (Robins, 1994, p. 461). The pessimistic vision maintains that television appears to create proximity but in fact fosters distance. This narrative is deeply suspicious of technology because it entertains the illusion that audiences participate in public life when they are simply, in Adorno's words, *regressing in listening or watching* (1938/1982, p. 270). The reason is that the very technological form of the medium 'sanitizes' reality; that is to say, it cuts real life off from its raw sensations, depriving mediated suffering of its compelling physicality and shifting the fact of suffering into pixel fiction.

We can identify two versions of dystopia. The first version maintains that technology distorts the authenticity of the represented event and so we may call it the *intervention of technology* version of pessimism. Visual editing, soundtrack, repetition or fast tracking help the spectator create a sense of distance from the spectacle, whilst the zapping and switch off options strengthen the spectator's sense of control over what she watches (Miller, 1971, p. 183; Peters, 2001, p. 713; Tester, 2001, pp. 1–9). As a consequence, suffering becomes a thing to watch just as any other, and human pain turns into what Peters calls an *exercise in Pavlovian pity, as we are freshly torn by the day's allotment of collapsing buildings, fires, floods, and terror* (2005, p. 11).

The second version of dystopia maintains that it is the conditions of the home, where the spectator watches television, that interrupt her connectivity with the distant sufferer; we may call this the *domesticity of reception* argument. The second remove from the scene of suffering, therefore, occurs because the image of suffering, already fictionalized, is further contained within the spectator's domestic environment, be this the living room, the office or the local pub. Not only does this sever the reality of suffering from its own nexus of sensations but it also re-inserts suffering in another nexus of sensations: the spectator's own immediate physical states and moods. Because this nexus of sensations and feelings has existential priority over on-screen events, theorists claim, it is bound always to background the spectator's concern for the distant 'other' in favour of those who live 'at home' (Tomlinson, 1999, pp. 178–79).

The dystopian vision, in both its versions, clearly illustrates the paradox of technology. The capacity of technology to deliver immediacy is simultaneously the failure of technology to establish connectivity and this has dire consequences for contemporary ethical life, as the spectator lives in the illusion of a collective existence that is simply not there; she inhabits an inauthentic reality.[6]

The utopian vision

In the utopian vision, the immediacy of television's images and stories brings the world closer together. Part of the broad communitarian tradition of Durkheim and Merton, this narrative rests on the anthropological premise that the media work as symbols that generate authentic sociability. How so? In two respects.

In the *celebration of communitarianism* version of utopia, television introduces the spectator into a broad community of fellow-spectators simply by engaging her in the act of simultaneous viewing. This is a vision on the mass media as early as McLuhan's idea of the 'global village' (1964), but the argument is also present in current accounts of mediation, which claim that television establishes a spectatorial 'feeling in common' through the co-ordination of viewing action rather than through the message of communication itself (e.g. Castells, 1996; Mafessoli, 1996). Unlike the pessimistic thesis, where television erodes our sense of the real, here the dissemination of images has the positive effect of bringing spectators together, in new forms of sociality and emotional connectivity. What this view of mediation misses out, however, is an orientation towards the distant 'other', since the images that bring the sufferer close to our home do not act as testimony of the sufferer's pain but as a guarantee of the co-presence of spectators.

In the *democratization of responsibility* version of utopia, television's flow of messages from around the world increases the spectator's awareness of the existence of 'others' and, thereby, it also increases her concern for the misfortune of the distant sufferer. This kind of optimism takes its point of departure in the reflexive organization of the self in late modernity and begs the question of how the mediated experience of the spectator can translate into public-political consciousness (Giddens, 1990, 1991; Thompson, 1990, 1995). The constant flow of images and information on screen, the argument goes, inevitably opens up the local world of the spectator to the sight of the 'other' and, broadly, to non-local experiences, and enables the reflexive process by which the spectator comes to recognize non-local realities as a potential domain of her own effective action.[7] Despite its forceful rhetoric, however, this utopian version proposes no specific perspectives as to how such a new public life may be realized; the dream of moral reflexivity is asserted but the question of how we get there is essentially ignored (Chouliaraki, 2000, pp. 293–314).[8]

In summary, the paradox of technology haunts the utopian vision of mediation just as much as it haunts the dystopian one. Technology connects; but how and who connects with whom remain unaccounted for. Instead of closely studying the specific possibilities and limitations of technology to connect, media and social theory engages in an abstract, argumentative mode of theorizing that treats the role of technology in our culture in a dilemmatic, 'either – or' way and remains inadequate to address the issue of how mediation can cultivate a cosmopolitan ethics. Yet, if there is a lesson to be learned from the pessimistic account it is not so much that technology is to blame for failing to connect but that technological contact with the imagery of the 'other' does not necessarily link to ethical responsibility; nor does the act of simultaneous witnessing by definition cultivate democratic 'publics' (Barnett, 2003; Derrida, 1999; Silverstone, 2003).

In order to understand how mediation may shape the disposition of media publics as a mutual feeling of togetherness with fellow-spectators or as responsibility to the distant 'other', we need to keep separate the conceptual space between watching and acting. This is the space of mediation as a public-political space and it is to a discussion of the study of this space that I now turn.

The analytics of mediation

The key question is how we can study mediation as a process that sets up norms of public conduct and shapes the spectator as a citizen of the world. My own argument is that the potential of mediation to cultivate a cosmopolitan sensibility is neither de facto possible, as in the utopian vision, nor a priori impossible, as in the dystopian vision on mediation. The potential of mediation to shape a cosmopolitan sensibility has its own historical and social conditions of possibility. What we need to do in order to investigate these conditions of possibility, I propose, is to investigate empirically how television narrates concrete instances of human suffering (in this chapter, I take my examples from the genre of television news).

The term 'analytics', which Foucault borrows from Aristotle to distinguish his approach from a 'grand' theory of power, aims at describing how discourse manages to articulate certain values of human conduct as 'universal' at any historical moment and how, in so doing, it places human beings into certain relationships of power to one another (Flyvbjerg, 2001, pp. 131–38; Foucault, 1991). Media discourse on distant suffering, for instance, operates as a strategy of power in so far as it selectively offers the option of emotional and practical engagement with certain sufferers and leaves others outside the scope of such engagement, thereby reproducing hierarchies of place and human life. The object of study of the analytics of mediation, therefore, is the various genres across media (print, electronic and new) as regimes of meaning.

The term 'regime of meaning' refers to the bounded field of possible meaning relations that obey a certain regularity in the ways in which they combine and circulate and, as a consequence, in the forms of knowledge and identity they constitute in the medium where they appear. In the study of suffering, we speak of regimes of pity to refer to this array of semiotic practices that construe suffering as a meaningful spectacle with its own proposals of relating to the spectator.

We can perhaps better grasp the idea of a regime of pity through the example of the live footage of a major disaster. Visualizing the event through a street camera places the event in the temporality of emergency, of frantic and contingent activity, and endows it with the aesthetic quality of testimony, the first-hand knowledge of the eyewitness. This regime of pity offers a sense of close proximity to the scene of suffering and organizes the spectacle of suffering around action that may alleviate the sufferer's misfortune. This is different from the long shot of a city skyline. Here pity takes the form of aesthetic contemplation vis-à-vis the sublimity of the catastrophe and invites reflection over the event's causes and consequences. The long shot, as opposed to the 'involved' camera at street level, potentially entails an interest in historicity and analysis rather than actuality and activity. It is evident that the camera, with its different techniques of filming, is a key technology in shaping the regimes of pity on television.

Central, therefore, to the analytics of mediation is that distinction which refers to the role of technology in creating meaning about suffering – for example, the techniques of camera use and their various visual effects. This is the distinction between hypermediacy and immediacy, in Bolter and Grusin's terminology (2000). The analytics of mediation takes both hypermediacy and immediacy to be semiotic categories, that is to say categories that produce meaning in television by marking some form of difference.

On the one hand, there is the difference inherent in the medium of meaning making, in the technologies of verbal and visual recording that turn the screen into a material reality of images and narratives. This is hypermediacy. On the other hand, there is difference that lies outside the medium of meaning making and which is shown and enacted on screen in the asymmetrical relationship between, for example, the victims of earthquake in Islamabad and the UN forces that appear as benefactors who provide emergency aid. This is immediacy. In this sense, the analytics of mediation integrates the critical interest in the production of meaning on television, in 'difference within the semiotic', with the ethical function of television to shape specific dispositions of viewing and acting, in 'difference outside the semiotic'. The production of suffering as a television spectacle arises out of the interplay between these two dimensions of meaning making: the technologies of meaning production and the social relationships of viewing – or difference within the semiotic and difference outside the semiotic.

Difference within the semiotic: the multi-modality of mediation

Difference within the semiotic points to difference that lies inside the semiotic systems themselves. This point is well developed by Derrida. For Derrida, who pushed structuralist linguistics to its limit, the idea of difference is not a social category (difference among people) but a systemic category (difference within a sign system) that resides in the very organization of language.[9] Derrida's claim is that the sign, rather than being split in internal form (medium) and external content (representation), is seen as a *mark* that consists of both materialities:

> The possibility of repeating, and therefore of identifying, marks is implied *in every code*, making of it a communicable, transmittable, decipherable grid that is iterable for a third party, and thus for any user in general.
>
> (Derrida, 1982, p. 315)

By emphasizing that meaning operates as a 'mark in every code', Derrida tells us two things. First, following Saussure, the founder of structuralism, he tells us that not only language but also image is internally differentiated into form and content; that the image is itself a semiotic code. The implication of this claim is that the image now becomes an object of semiotic study in its own right. It is not a simulacrum or a signal, as theorists such as Baudrillard or Castells might wish it, but it has the potential to produce content and it has a grammar for the realization of meaning (Van Leeuwen, 2004, p. 17). This means that even when the content of television appears minimal, for example in 'raw' footage or 'pastiche' images, the screen still confronts the spectator with a meaningful message that is possible to systematize and to analyse.

At the same time, Derrida's understanding of meaning as consisting of both form and content – as a mark – pushes the point on visuality beyond the legacy of Saussure. Challenging the traditional superiority of language over the visual, Derrida insists that orality and visuality are two distinct but equally complex semiotic codes and that the relationship between them is fundamental in describing the process of meaning making (Howarth, 2002, pp. 36–42).[10] Meaning making combines marks that are both oral and visual – as the medium of television clearly shows. Meaning, then, comes about as a result not of a positivity, a fixed presence that these marks carry around, but as a result of the difference between the media of such marks, pictorial or spoken, and the content potential of these media – what they 'show' or 'say'. Meaning is always unfinished business because these marks constantly alter their relationship to other marks as they travel from context to context (Howarth, 2002,

p. 41). It is this capacity of the mark both to repeat itself, that is to change context, and to be identified, that is to be recognized as the same, the 'iterability' of the mark in Derrida's words, that lies at the heart of difference within the semiotic.

Let us take the example of a piece of news reporting on a boat accident in a remote province of India. How could this piece of news be represented on television? Depending on the journalistic resources available, this piece could be represented in at least two different ways. It could be represented through telephone link in the studio or through on-location footage of the rescue operation of the boat passengers. These are two possible inscriptions of the 'boat accident', a single content, on different media: on voice technology (telephone link) or on camera (moving image). It is obvious that the semiotic code upon which each medium inscribes the content of the event considerably alters the meaning of suffering in it. Listening to a brief verbal report is different from witnessing the scene of the rescuing of passengers. This difference bears, in turn, a tremendous effect upon the regime of pity that construes this instance of suffering. The brief verbal report renders the boat accident an instance of suffering without pity that makes no demand for response upon the spectator, but the intense visualization of rescue action renders the boat accident an instance of suffering with pity that incorporates the demand for action in the news story itself.

Iterability, in this context, helps us to understand the hypermediated dimension of mediation. It shows that the use of different media transforms the meanings of suffering, in ways that make it difficult to separate how these meanings both remain the same and become different. Wouldn't we react to the India news in its two diverse presentations by saying 'it's the same and yet it's not'?

Multi-modal analysis

Multi-modality is the study of the semiotic processes by which the hypermediated environment of television manages to create a coherent regime for the representation of suffering, a regime of pity, that construes the event of suffering as the spectator's immediate reality. The methodological principle of multi-modal analysis is that regimes of pity do not coincide with the specific image or language we watch on screen.

The image and language of suffering, rather, follow a systematic pattern of coappearance and combination, which organizes the potential for the representation of suffering under the generic conventions of the news broadcast. Because regimes of pity are patterns of co-appearance and combination rather than single pictures or sentences, they are best understood as analytical constructs that help us describe the semiotic choices by which the spectacle of suffering becomes meaningful to the spectator in the genre of the news. I take three aspects of the genre of the news to be relevant in the construal of regimes of pity: the 'mode of presentation' of the news text; the 'correspondence between verbal narrative and image' in the news text; and the 'aesthetic quality' of the news text.

Mode of news presentation

The mode of presentation of the news refers to the locations from which the news story is told and to the media that tell the story. Modes of presentation may include studio anchor, which secures the flow and continuity of the broadcast, usually accompanied by footage, archive or live. Whereas studio presentation may include the commentary of invited experts, footage may include oral testimony of witnesses from the scene of action. Choices over the mode of news presentation have an impact upon the ways through which the spectator comes to evaluate the news on suffering. Depending, for example, on how the visual presentation relates to anchor speech or to voiceover, each mode of news presentation offers the spectator a distinct approach to the reality of the event, a distinct form of narrative 'realism' (Ellis, 2000, pp. 193–200).

Narrative realism may evoke the tangible reality of facts based on the truth of what we see, on the power of visual perception. This is what we call 'perceptual' realism. Narrative realism may also bring about the reality of the heart, a reality evoked through strong feelings rather than facts, giving rise to a form of realism that we call 'categorical' realism. Finally, narrative realism can make use of the reality of doxa, a reality appealing to our deep-rooted certainties about what the world is or should be like. This is what we call 'ideological' realism. The realities both of the heart and of doxa are versions of 'psychological' realism, a way of knowing about reality that appeals to our emotional and moral sensibilities rather than to our quest for facts (Grodal, 2002, pp. 67–91).

News realism, it follows, is not about presenting the spectator with the single reality of suffering but is about presenting her with different realities about suffering different meanings through which suffering can be represented. When we analyse a piece of news, questions concerning the mode of presentation include:

- Is the news introduced in the studio? Is it supported by visual material? Is it reported on location?
- What sense of news realism is being evoked in the news?
- If the suffering is shown at all, is it shown in a manner that seeks to evoke a 'this-is-how-it-is' type of reality? Or does the emphasis fall more on a 'this-is how-we-feel-about-it' or 'this-is-how-sad–horrific–wrong' the suffering is? Does the emphasis of the narrative make an appeal to the spectator's sense of compassion, sense of righteousness or sense of justice? Alternatively, does it refrain from engaging the spectator in a sustained emotional relationship with the piece of news?

Verbal–visual correspondence

The sense of reality that each news text attempts to evoke for the spectator cannot simply be identified through the mode of presentation. In order to be able to describe precisely how types of realism emerge through the multi-modal combinations of the news text, we need to talk more specifically about the work that language and image perform in the news text. The verbal entails three modes of narrating the suffering, what I term below 'descriptions', 'narrations proper' and 'expositions',[11] whereas the image entails three modes of portraying suffering, the 'index', the 'icon' and the 'symbol'.[12] Let me focus, in turn, on each one of the two semiotic modes.

THE VISUAL

The impact of any news text is almost always a function of its visual referent.[13] It is the 'seeing it happen' that makes the strongest claim to the authenticity of suffering in television and 'burdens' the spectator with the moral role of the witness.

In this sense, the shift from no visual towards an increasingly intensive visualization of suffering is a shift towards an increasingly intensive involvement with the sufferer and thus an invitation for the spectator to remember and to repeat the sufferer's misfortune. For example, video images of human figures with their backs to the camera place us in the scene of suffering but they do not engage us with the sufferer. In contrast, a sequence of suffering children's close ups gazing at the camera invites us to urgently respond to their tragedy. The distinction between the former and the latter type of visualization is a distinction between news without pity that we hardly register as such and news with pity that make a demand upon us to speak up or do something about the misfortune (Chouliaraki, 2006a, pp. 70–76).

Because I discuss the visual–verbal correspondence of news texts below, the analytical questions about the visual that I am posing, at this point, do not address visual meaning in the news text as a whole but are only about the image layout on screen. Such questions include:

- What kind of visual representation does the suffering take in the news report? Is it graphic (map, diagram), photographic, archive film or live transmission?
- If graphic, is the representation static and minimal or dynamic and multiple (computerized, as for example, in Iraq war maps)?
- If there is written text, how does it interact with the image? Does the text add to the image (explicate, illustrate) or is it decorative, running simply in parallel to it?
- If video:
  - What point of view (above and afar or involved)?
  - What angle (direct/gaze level or oblique/profile or back filming)?
  - What framing (actors' position; distance from camera; relationship to the overall visual composition)?
  - What vectors of movement (between actors; towards the spectator; outside camera frame)?

THE VERBAL

If visualization tells us something about the degree of authenticity of a piece of news, it is the verbal mode that establishes the distinct sense of reality that the story evokes for the spectator. This is because words regulate the flow of edited images and create a meaningful story out of a usually unrelated flow of places and people. In ordering and organizing the spaces and temporalities of events, the verbal narrative of the news performs fundamental classificatory activities: it includes and excludes, foregrounds and backgrounds, justifies and legitimizes. It separates 'us' from 'them'.

Three narrative functions of the news are responsible for this classificatory work: descriptions, narrations or storytelling proper, and expositions. The hard facts of suffering are evoked mainly through descriptive narratives that tell us what we see and so they make the strongest claim to objectivity. For example, in the Indian boat accident news, a descriptive report sounds like this: Forty-four people drowned in the River Baytarani. In narration, the factual report of events is replaced by elements of fictional storytelling, such as a chronological plot (with moments of deliberate tension or suspense) as well as generic conventions of opening and/or closure: It was the end of an ordinary school day, when the boat transporting the children in the River Baytarani capsized; forty-four people drowned. The term exposition refers to the verbal narrative that incorporates a point of view within the news and, in so doing, explicitly articulates ethical judgement vis-à-vis the reported suffering: Forty-four people feared drowned in River Baytarani. Here, evaluation is contained, in a suppressed form, in the use of the affective/ impersonal process feared.

Although there is an obvious analytical value in differentiating among the three narrative types, we should be aware of the fact that, just as the semiotic modes of language and the visual are multi-functional, narratives, too, co-exist and complement one another; they are intertextual (Chatman, 1991, p. 30).

Concerning the role of the verbal mode in the news text questions may include:

- Is the news verbal text cast as a description of facts? Or does the text also entail elements of exposition, with value judgements and normative proposals about the suffering? Could the news report be a narration of events with emphasis on drama and suspense and with little consideration of the facts?
- If the report combines more than one narrative type, how do these relate to one another? Which one frames the rest? What role do the subserving narratives play in the development of the story?

The relationship between the verbal and the visual

Each type of realism – perceptual, categorical and ideological – brings together its own combination of linguistic narrative with image and, in so doing, it also establishes three distinct types of meaning relations in the news text. These are indexical, iconic and symbolic meanings. The realism of each news text depends, then, upon the distinct claim to the reality of suffering that each of the three types of meaning makes: the claim to the facticity of suffering, in perceptual realism, the claim to the emotion of suffering, in categorical realism, and the claim to justice around the cause of suffering, in ideological realism.

The claim to facticity is the claim of perceptual realism and builds upon an indexical relationship between the verbal and the visual. This means that perceptual realism relies heavily upon the image and uses descriptive language to tell us what we see on screen. Indexical meaning signifies precisely by employing language to establish some direct connection to the image and thereby to offer the spectator a 'window' to the outside world (Ellis, 2000, pp. 193–94; Messaris, 1997, pp. xvi–xvii; Nichols, 1991, p. 171). Although very little news text relies exclusively on indexicality – not even live footage that shows what is happening right now – all news texts inevitably entail an element of indexicality that grounds them to the world out there.

The claims to emotion and, more explicitly, to the ethics and politics of suffering inform psychological realism, in its two manifestations: categorical and ideological realism. Claims to emotion and to justice depart from the reliance on physical perception, that is to say on the link between what we see and what we hear. In the case of categorical realism, fact matters less and the welling up of the spectator's feelings towards the suffering matters most. In order to bring about emotions, categorical realism often relies on storytelling or narration proper, which frames the visual representation of suffering with dramatic urgency and sensationalism. This relationship between image and narration gives rise to iconic meaning, meaning that is related to its referent not through some direct or 'physical' connection but through similarity or family resemblance. Iconicity, then, does not attach itself to a concrete reality but, rather, represents an abstract reality by using image as the key-signifier of whichever generic condition it seeks to capture. In the typical 'famine in Africa' news stories, for example, images of emaciated children evoke the referent 'starvation' and function in a cumulative way to overwhelm the spectator with the reality of children's imminent death by famine.

Ideological realism works, similarly to categorical realism, through the association of the image with an abstraction. But, this time, abstraction does not take the form of a generic category such as famine. It takes the form of a specific ideological dilemma – for example, are we for or against humanity? – and urges the spectator to take a public stance vis-à-vis this dilemma. Here, the relationship between visual and verbal semiotic modes gives rise to symbolic meaning. Symbolic meaning is related to its referent neither by direct connection nor by family resemblance, but through discursive associations based on conventional knowledge and value, such as the doxa of 'us' as humane, 'them' as the savage. For example, in a news piece on a Nigerian woman convicted to death by stoning, the visual contrast between a close up shot of this young woman with her baby followed by a long shot of a crowd mobbing another woman in the streets evokes the cultural belief that Islam is an 'inhumane' culture.

In summary, each verbal–image combination makes a distinct claim to reality and thus activates a distinct emotional potential for the spectator. This analytical interest in the reality effects that the language and image of news texts bring about can be formulated in the following questions:

- What role does each mode, language and image, play in the news narrative? Do the verbal and the visual mode unfold in parallel worlds with a minimal relationship between them? Or is there a substantial referential relationship between the two?
- If there is direct reference between visual and verbal, does the verbal 'accompany' the visual in a strictly factual narrative of depicted events or does the verbal expand on the visuals?
- If the verbal expands upon the visual, what is the 'transfer effect' of language over the visual? What extra-pictorial meanings does the news narrative evoke, by means of an 'over-interpreting' voiceover? Alternatively, does the voiceover stop to allow for the power of the visual or of sound effects to come through? How does this type of verbal–visual combination impact upon the processes of news meaning making?

Aesthetic quality

The aesthetic quality of the news is a consequence of both its mode of presentation and of the relationship that the news text establishes between language and image. The aesthetic quality describes the overall semiotic effect of the news in terms of three historical tropes for the public staging of suffering, what Boltanski describes as 'topics of suffering' (1999). These historical topics for the representation of suffering are pamphleteering, philanthropy and sublimation. Pamphleteering is associated with the genre of political denunciation and aims to address the spectator's affective potential for anger vis-à-vis the evil-doer who inflicted the pain upon the sufferer. Philanthropy is associated with genres of Christian care and aims to activate the spectator's affective potential of tender-heartedness towards the benefactor who comforts the sufferer's pain. Finally, sublimation distances the spectator from the actuality of suffering and orients her towards a reflexive contemplation of the conditions of human misery.

The broadcast genre may endow the reported event with a single aesthetic quality, say philanthropic appeal towards famine victims, or it may select and combine elements of many topics. For example, the aesthetic quality of terror attack footage may draw simultaneously on tenderhearted philanthropy in the scenes of emergency aid, indignation against the perpetrators of evil in the public statements of eyewitnesses and political figures, and voyeuristic sentiments over the remains of buildings, trains or buses in a city centre. In so doing, the event invites the spectator to at once denounce the attacks, empathize with the victims and indulge in the sublimated contemplation of the aftermath of the attacks.

The aesthetic effect of the news, however, is not only related to the emotional potential for identification with the sufferer. It is also related to the ways in which a regime of pity produces the spectacle of suffering as authentic for the spectator. Against ideas that consider the news broadcast to be 'the' hard genre of factuality, we just saw that the news actually construes the factuality of the event it reports by employing one or another version of narrative realism. One of the aims of the analytics of mediation is to describe how each of these types of realism resolves the question of the reality of suffering, precisely by articulating aesthetic quality and a 'universal' public value. For example, the aesthetic quality of the Iraq war footage has been described as that of action films, drawing upon the spectator's cinematic experience. The political content of this aesthetics is minimal: it exhausts the spectator's response to the suffering in the consumption of the war as spectacle without reference to the causes and possible effects of this military conflict (Brooks *et al.*, 2003).

To conclude, the study of multi-modality in the news seeks to identify the process by which a concrete representation of suffering comes to articulate 'universal' public values – the values that connect the feelings of the individual spectator with the space of public action – with the urge to 'do something' about this sufferer. But which are these values? What are the options offered to the spectator to do something in the world out there? And how can the spectator be guided to endorse such values and articulate them as her own? In order to study the content of these public values, we must now turn to the study of the representations of proximity and agency in the news text; that is, to the ways in which the spectator – sufferer relationship takes on a specific ethical content on screen. This is the concern with mediation as difference outside the semiotic.

Difference outside the semiotic: the multi-functionality of mediation

Difference outside the semiotic points to a kind of difference that lies outside meaning-making systems, even though we can only encounter it through texts. Difference outside the semiotic lies in the asymmetries of power that traverse the social world and in the historical and political relations within or between social groups.[14] The concern with mediation as difference outside the semiotic, then, is a concern with the social relations of viewing that map out the world in terms of spectator zones and sufferer zones or in terms of spacetimes of safety and spacetimes of danger. Even though these are not clear-cut distinctions, there is a historically shaped topography of power, whereby it is the West that watches the rest of the world suffer (Bignell, 2000, pp. 139–65; see also Cohen, 2001).

By this token, the 'universal' values of the news broadcasts are the values of the West. Denunciation, empathy and aesthetic contemplation, what I have described just above as manifestations of the aesthetic quality of the news, are simultaneously historically and culturally specific dispositions of the public life of Western societies (Boltanski, 1999, pp. 3–54).

But even if difference outside the semiotic draws attention to the macro-picture of power, the empirical focus in the study of mediation is the local semiotic practice of the news broadcast. It is the concept of discourse that connects these two components of the analytics of mediation, the macro-perspective of power and the micro-perspective of the television text. The concept of discourse implies that the relationship between power and meaning is a relationship of mutual constitution. As Foucault has argued, every attempt to put something in meaning comes about from a position of power, because power connects and organizes the social positions from which meaning comes about (Chouliaraki & Fairclough, 1999; Howarth, 2002). Meaning, then, makes a claim to truth precisely from that power position which enunciates it. This is not 'the truth' but always a truth effect, a truth that seeks to re-constitute and re-establish power through meaning.

In this light, the power asymmetry that is embedded in the social relationships of television viewing may not in itself bring about the economic and political divisions of our world, but it certainly reflects them and consolidates them. Who watches and who suffers reflects the manner in which differences in economic resources, political regimes and in everyday life enter the global landscape of information. Similarly, who acts upon whose suffering reflects patterns of economic and political agency across global zones of influence and their historical divisions, North and South or East and West.

In the analytics of mediation, the relationship between singular practices of meaning making and the broader power relationships of meaning making is exemplified in the principle of the 'multi-functionality' of semiosis (Chouliaraki & Fairclough, 1999, pp. 139–55; Halliday, 1985/1995; Halliday & Hasan, 1989; Hasan, 1999). Multi-functionality assumes that every semiotic mode, language and visual creates meaning that fulfils more than one function at once. These functions are performed through the semiotic system itself and, in this sense, they are meta-functions of semiosis. But these functions are simultaneously social functions, because they serve two fundamental communicative needs of society.

The first is the social need to name and represent the world, the ideational metafunction of semiosis. The second is the social need to engage in interaction and relate to other people, the interpersonal meta-function of semiosis.[15] In so far as these two meta-functions concern themselves with the social effects of semiosis, that is with the representation of reality and with the orientation to the others, they appertain to mediation as difference outside the semiotic (Iedema, 2001a, pp. 191–93).

Critical discourse analysis

The analysis of mediation as difference outside the semiotic is critical discourse analysis (CDA). Critical discourse analysis is a method of analysis of the television text that treats the linguistic and visual choices on screen as subtle indicators of the power of television to mediate the world to the world. This is the power of television to classify the world into categories of 'us' and 'the other' and to orient the spectator towards this suffering 'other'.

In the analysis of *representations*, CDA looks into the construal of the scene of suffering within a specific spacetime that separates safety from danger. The category of space time refers to the place and the temporality of suffering. It tells us how close a specific instance of suffering is to the spectator and how urgent action on the suffering is. The analysis of spacetime then focuses on the axes of proximity/distance or urgency/finality.

In the analysis of *orientations*, CDA looks into the category of agency. Agency is about who acts upon whom in the scene of suffering. There are two dimensions of orientation that are relevant in establishing the social relationships of suffering. First, agency refers to how active the sufferer appears on screen and, second, it refers to how other actors present in the scene appear to engage with the sufferer. These two dimensions of agency come to shape how the spectator herself is invited to relate to the suffering, that is whether she is supposed simply to watch, to feel for or to act practically in relation to the 'others'' misfortune. Of course, those who live in poverty, destitution and war are by definition always 'others' for the safe spectator, yet there is a gradation in the 'othering' of sufferers in the news, ranging from those who deserve no pity to those whose misfortune we share as if it were our own. The study of agency, in this respect, focuses on the analytical axis of 'our own'/'other'.

This distinction between representation and orientation is necessary for analytical purposes; in practice, representations and orientations are not separate parts of the television text and we must look at once into both meta-functions in order to determine how they are brought together in each news sequence (Halliday, 1985/1995, p. 23).

Spacetime

The spacetime of suffering is the category that analyses how the spectator encounters the reality of the distant sufferer in different degrees of intensity and involvement. In this sense, spacetime is responsible for establishing a sense of immediacy for the scene of suffering and for regulating the moral distance between spectator and sufferer. But spatio-temporal immediacy is a fragile construction. This is so not only because most pieces of news come from far-away places, but mainly because issues like famine, war or death by stoning fall outside the spectator's lifeworld, outside her structure of experience. Yet, rather than lamenting the fact that the connectivity between spectator and sufferer is impossible to achieve, as some media pessimists do, we must accept the fragility of this relationship and acknowledge the difficulties of connecting.

According to Silverstone (2003, p. 770), the acknowledgement that mediation cannot completely connect us with the 'other' should lead us to problematize the act of mediation itself and the manner in which mediation construes places as proximal or distant. Just how effectively each piece of news articulates the spatial axis of proximity/distance or the temporal axis of urgency/finality in order to establish suffering as a reality for the spectator is the first of the two analytical priorities of the study of news of suffering.

Concerning *space*, the analytics of mediation asks questions such as:[16]

- Is space actively shaping action or is it only a background to action?
- Is space replaceable or unique?
- Is space internally differentiated or is it presented as a homogeneous entity?
- Are the spaces of danger and safety in any form of interaction with one another or are they strictly separated?

In order to respond to these questions on the representation of space, we focus on the following semiotic choices of the news:

1 *visual editing* (e.g. when footage from the Iraq war front is followed by sequences from anti-war demonstrations in European capitals);
2 *camera position* (e.g. filming from within the scene of action or from a location above and afar);
3 *graphic specification* (such as a map, the presence of written text or the split screen); or
4 *linguistic reference* (such as the use of adverbs of space; geographical references).

Concerning *time*, the analytics of mediation asks questions such as:

- Is the event taking place in the present or in the past?
- Is time open, with multiple possibilities or is it scripted in advance?
- How does the past impinge on the present?
- How does it impinge on possible futures?
- What has the greatest value: the past, present or future?
- Which future – distant or immediate?

In order to respond to these questions on the representation of time, we focus on the following semiotic choices of the news:

1 *visual intertextuality* (e.g. combining archive film, and hence a past reference, with on-location reports, thus shifting to right-now action); and
2 *linguistic reference* (the use of temporal adverbials such as *simultaneously, previously,* etc.; the use of tense, present or past; or the use of modality or imperatives) (Chilton, 2004; Fairclough, 2003a).

Depending on the broader multi-modal text in which these choices are embedded, the suffering may appear to be happening categorically in the right-here-right-now temporality or in the far-away-in-the-indefinite-past temporality. If emaciated children are placed in the timeframe of a fait accompli, in the past tense, there is little to do about them; if they are represented in terms of an ongoing temporality where coordinated action develops as we speak, famine becomes an emergency and acquires a radically different horizon of action.

Suffering, however, may also be represented with a higher degree of ambivalence. It may appear to be happening simultaneously here and there, in the past and right now. In the September 11 footage, for example, long shots over Manhattan in smoke establish a voyeuristic distance from the scene of action, but, paradoxically, they also establish a sense of proximity based on the temporality of reflection, on the chance they give to the spectator to ponder upon the circumstances and consequences of the terror attacks.

I would argue that the difference between categorical and ambivalent represen- tations of spacetime is a difference in the degree of spatio-temporal complexity, in which the suffering is shown to occur. Although Bakhtin says that all events have their own chronotopic universe, I prefer to reserve the term 'chronotopicity' for those events which involve more than one spacetime (Bakhtin, 1981, pp. 84–85, 243–58). We can talk, therefore, of the chronotope of a news event as that regime of multiple spaces (danger and safety) and temporalities (present, past or future) through which the event 'moves' back and forth and, in so doing, presents the spectator not with one single reality of suffering but with multiple realities relevant to the suffering. I define, therefore, the chronotope of suffering as that spacetime which increasingly expands to encompass four elements:

1   *concreteness*, which shows the minimal context of suffering as a physical space;
2   *multiplicity*, which moves the spectator through multiple physical contexts of suffering;
3   *specificity*, which shows the context of suffering as a singular space, by elaborating on its unique properties, or which individualizes the sufferer as a unique person with an array of attributes; and
4   *mobility*, which connects the contexts of safety and danger, suggesting a specific relationship of action between them.

The move from news defined by a minimum of these properties to news defined by increasing spatio-temporal complexity (chronotopes) is simultaneously a move from news with minimum potential for pity to news with maximum moral appeal and potential for engagement: the more complex the spacetime the less the 'othering' of the sufferer.

AGENCY

This is the analytical category that focuses on action upon suffering in terms of the agency of the sufferer herself and in terms of the system of other agents that operate in the scene of suffering. The type of action that these figures of pity play out on screen bears an effect on the spectator's own orientation to the sufferer. This is because the spectator of television news becomes an object of the moral regulation of mediation by being addressed primarily as a free subject, that is as someone who connects to television suffering through her own resources of emotion and capacities for action (Barnett, 2003; Rose, 1993, 1999).

Agency, however, is as fragile a category as proximity and equally difficult to achieve. This is because agency in television can only take the form of action at a distance and there are only two paradigms for conceptualizing public action at a distance in Western culture: the agora and the theatre. The first, the action of the agora, is contemplation and depends upon the spectator's objective deliberation and judgement upon suffering. The second, the action of the theatre, is identification and depends upon the spectator's participation in the psychological and emotional states of suffering.

The humane sufferer and the agora

In contemplation, which is the action of the agora, the spectator is expected to watch the sufferer's misfortune without bias and to judge it objectively. But the position of true impartiality is impossible. This is because, as long as there is a hierarchy of places of suffering that divides the world there will, inevitably, also be a hierarchy of the human lives that inhabit these places. It follows that the spectator is more likely to speak out about the suffering she is watching if the sufferer is construed as somebody like 'us' and, conversely, she is more likely to switch off if the sufferer fails to appear as one like 'us'. The agency of the spectator to engage in public speech about the suffering, then, depends upon the humanization of the sufferer.

In the analytics of mediation, humanization is a process of identity construction that endows the sufferer with the power to say or do something about her condition, even if this power is simply the power to evoke and receive the beneficiary action of others. The humane sufferer is the sufferer who acts. The difference, for example, between the September 11 sufferer and the sufferer in the Indian boat accident that I mentioned above is a difference in agency. The September 11 sufferer speaks; the Indian does not. The Indian sufferer, who is referred to as a number only, becomes an 'Other', with a capital 'O', in so far as her existence remains purely inactive (Cohen, 2001; Tester, 2001). Such a semiotic choice 'annihilates' the sufferer, in Silverstone's words; that is, it deprives the sufferer of her corporeal and psychological qualities and removes her from the existential order to which the spectator belongs.

The first group of questions concerning agency, then, have to do with the *sufferers' voice and humanness*:

- Is the sufferer given a voice, in language or in image?
- What kind of interiority is available to the sufferer? Is there a public–private boundary that gives her a certain 'depth' of consciousness?
- Does the sufferer co-exist or communicate with another or with other agents of suffering? What kind of ethical responsibility obliges these other agents in action?
- How does the sufferer connect with or communicate with the spectator? What kind of responsibility obliges the spectator in what type of action?

The humanization of the sufferer occurs either through the verbal mode or through the image. Concerning the *verbal mode*, the choice of the narrative type by which the news on suffering is reported plays an important role in the construal of the sufferer's identity as humane. Narration, or storytelling proper, for example, includes dramatic elements that may animate the figure of the sufferer as an actor and thus may humanize the sufferer to a greater extent than the factual description of an event. Similarly, the lexicalization of the sufferer and the choice of attributes to characterize the sufferer's condition are also instrumental in placing her within a hierarchy of active/humane or inactive/inhumane values.

Concerning the *visual mode*, a key choice is camera position and angle. It makes a difference to film the sufferer from afar and above in a group or to film her frontally gazing at the camera. The gaze, in this context, is appellative action and the camera choice to capture the sufferer's gaze is also a choice to give voice and to humanize the sufferer, whereas the choice to film her through long shots may alienate and dehumanize her. Images of African people filmed en masse in some Darfur safety camp, shadowy figures gazing over their water-swept land or emaciated children's body parts zoomed into focus, are just a few examples that show how visual 'Othering' contributes to sustaining powerful hierarchies of human life.

Another significant choice that regulates the humanization of the sufferer is visual juxta-position. Montage may link the scene of suffering to the zone of safety in various forms of connectivity. One form of connectivity may be the cause-and-effect relationship, which evokes the thought that 'what happened there may affect us here'. Another form of con-nectivity may set up a request-and-response relationship between safety and danger, eliciting the thought that 'if this is what is needed then this is how we should act'. Depending on the conceptual relationship established via visual juxtaposition, the sufferer may be placed beyond a zone of contact with the spectator, both spatially (too far out there to reach) and temporally (a figure of eternal misfortune without past or future), or alternatively she may be placed in an active relationship with the spectator.

The figures of suffering and the theatre

If, in contemplation, the agora model of action at a distance, the what to do vis-à-vis the sufferer, depends on the representation of the sufferer as properly humane, in the theatrical model of action at a distance, where the witnessing of suffering occurs mostly through emotions, the what to do takes a different twist. The witnessing of suffering is now mediated by the dynamics of social relationships that are already at play into the scene of suffering, the benefactor or the per-secutor. Agency in the theatre, then, depends on the orchestration of these two primary figures of action who connect the reality of distant suffering to the spectator's private feelings vis-à-vis the spectacle she is watching. We should not think of the benefactor and the persecutor only as 'real people' on the television screen, although this is very often the case. Rather, we should think of them as symbolic figures that focalize the affective potential of the spectator towards a par-ticular emotion. It is only when this private potential for feeling leads the spectator to identify with a cause, such as philanthropic care in the case of tender-heartedness or denunciation in the case of indignation, that the spectacle of distant suffering is able to constitute a group of spectators into a public – a collectivity with a will to act.

It is evident that the symbolic figures of the benefactor and the persecutor are taken here to be metonymic signs. They are, that is, carriers of meaning that use the private feelings evoked by the actors on suffering so as to articulate a public value of how to act towards the suffering. Whereas the tender-hearted impulse to protect or comfort the sufferer articulates the moral value of care for the 'other', the indignant impulse to denounce or even to attack the evil-doer articulates the moral demand for civil justice. In this respect, the task of the analytics of media-tion is to show how the figures of agency, benefactor and persecutor, literally incorporate the moral value associated with suffering in each particular piece of news and how they make it part of a persuasive theatre of action.

The second group of questions, then, has to do with the *presence of agents in suffering*:

- Is the scene of suffering populated by agents?
- If yes, who participates in the suffering and in what capacity?
- Does the text evoke or explicitly represent a benefactor – individual or collective – acting to alleviate suffering? Does it evoke a persecutor – individual or collective – inflicting the suffering?
- What is the overall dramaturgical composition of these figures? What potential for emotion and/or practical action does this composition induce?

In what way does the agency dimension of the analytics of mediation help us understand how television might cultivate a cosmopolitan sensibility? It indicates that neither too much emotion, the stuff of theatricality, nor too much impartial rationality, the stuff of the agora, is an adequate and sufficient condition for cosmopolitanism. Whereas the emotional bias risks overwhelming the spectator with sentimentalism and preventing the pursuit for an objective judgement of suffering, the bias in favour of impartial rationality risks removing the spectator from the drama of suffering and postponing altogether the urgent demand for action (Boltanski, 1999).

It is the task of the analytics of mediation to trace the concrete manifestations through which news broadcasts negotiate the tension between objectivity and tender-heartedness, between the generality of facts and the particularity of emotions as well as the subsequent effects that such negotiations have on the construal of the cosmopolitan disposition in each news item. As I have shown elsewhere, the cosmopolitan disposition seems to be emerging out of these multiple representations of the distant 'other', not as a full and positive presence but, rather, as a fleeting glimpse, as a temporary possibility (Chouliaraki, 2006a, pp. 192–97).

The 'analytics of mediation': an example

Let us now turn to a concrete example of the analytics at work. It comes from the Iraq war footage on the BBC, March–April 2003, and concerns the regular 'updates' of the Baghdad bombardments – some of the most visually arresting and emotionally compelling pieces of warfare on television.

In the analytics of mediation, the war footage is seen as a semiotic accomplishment, which combines camerawork and voiceover, or television's multi-modality, in order to establish a degree of proximity with the scene of suffering and to propose certain possibilities of action upon the suffering (Chouliaraki, 2005, 2006b).

The *mode of presentation* of the 'update' is moving image (the edited video of the previous night's footage) accompanied by voiceover, which comments on the image. On the *visual plane*, the point of view of the filming is from afar and above with a steady camera, probably from a terrace of the 'Palestine' hotel where foreign journalists stayed during the war. The camera captures Baghdad in its visual plenitude, allowing for the powerful audio-visual effects of the bombardment (blasts, explosions and fire) to fill up the screen. This pictorial composition conveys a strong sense of unrelenting action, with the harshness of repeated rattles and blasts turning the bombardment of the city into a spectacle of rare power and intensity.

The spectacular quality of the screen is framed by a *complex verbal narrative*, which combines narration with description and sporadic elements of exposition. Narration is the main narrative type of the voiceover, organizing the verbal text into a coherent whole and structuring the bombing activity in terms of the journalists' sense of time. This happens through the use of chronology: **by morning** *the buildings were* **still** *ablaze*, or **then** *we heard … we looked up … above us a buster … it swooped down … and it blasted.*[17] Narration is also organized around the journalists' own point of view, evident in the use of first-person plural in *we heard, we looked*. Chronology, the human perception of time, together with the use of the personal point of view, *we*, in perception verbs such as *hear* and *look*, construe the voiceover as a particular type of storytelling: the testimony of an eyewitness. Description uses language referentially to illustrate visual action, as in *the buildings were still ablaze and still under attack*, or *anti-missile flare spewing out of its wing*, both of which are followed by shots zooming in on a building on fire or on a plane releasing fire. In this manner, description invites the spectator to study the military action and its effects together with the eyewitness. Finally, exposition appears marginally and is dispersed across sentences: *a terrible deafening sound as though the earth was being ripped open . . . anti-missile flare spewing out of its wing . . . , let* *loose a ferocious barrage.* Such quasi–literary use of adjectives, together with the metaphors *spewing* and *let loose* and the simile *as though the earth*, seek to convey a sense of the horrific and the extraordinary that the sight of the bombardment impressed upon the eyewitness.

Concerning *spacetime*, the total visibility of the camera manages to keep the spectator resolutely outside the scene of action. She is an onlooker, who is watching from a safe distance. The quality of proximity of this detached perspective is cinematic, a witness position that turns the reality of the war into a spectacular panorama. Simultaneously, the temporality of the 'update', past tense about the detail of military action, reinforces the emotional distance of cinematic proximity. The scene of the bombardment is not a scene of suffering but a terrain for the study of the logistics of warfare.

Finally, concerning *agency*, the 'update' contains no visualization of human beings but only a panorama of military action. At the same time, the linguistic choices that verbalize the sufferer and the persecutor deprive these figures of any sense of humanness. The sufferer is mostly a collective entity or a non-living being and the persecutor is either diffused in the activity of air war or erased from the narrative. By cancelling the presence of the persecutor and the sufferer, the footage presents the bombardment of Baghdad, again, not as a scene of suffering but as a site of intense military action without agency.

As I have argued elsewhere, these features of the footage construe the bombardment of Baghdad in a 'sublime' regime of pity (Chouliaraki, 2005). The sublime is a specific regime of pity that constitutes distant suffering less through emotions towards the sufferer and primarily through aesthetic appreciation derived from the horror of suffering itself. Unlike many other reports on suffering, which portray human beings who appeal strongly to the spectator's emotion and action, the Iraqi sufferer enters this footage only on the condition that her very humanity is cancelled. And, with it, what is also cancelled is the potential for emotion and engagement with the sufferer that the spectator may have had the potential to feel.

Conclusion

In this chapter, I propose a methodology for the study of contemporary norms of public action that moves away from 'grand' theory and its dilemmatic approaches – approaches that either celebrate the role of the media in disseminating the values of global citizenship or disapprove of the media because they disempower the spectator and undermine the hope for a cosmopolitan sensibility.

Drawing on Aristotle's concept of phronetic research, I argue that the public values of, say, philanthropy or social justice always find their local enactment in particular practices of discourse. I therefore suggest that we begin our search for the possibility of a cosmopolitan disposition, that is to say the ethical disposition that connects the spectator with the distant sufferer, in the capacity of the discursive practices of television to produce proximity with the sufferer and offer to the spectator a sense of agency over the sufferer's misfortune.

The 'analytics of mediation' is the method I propose for the study of representations of suffering in television news – its regimes of pity. Capitalizing on Derrida's and Foucault's post-structuralist views of meaning and power, the analytics conceptualizes the process of mediation in semiotic terms, as textual difference, and takes the television text to be its object of study. The study of mediation as hypermediacy looks into the media technologies that produce meaning of suffering on screen – what I term difference within the semiotic – whereas the study of mediation as immediacy looks into the social relations of suffering that these meanings represent – what I term difference outside the semiotic.

It is these recurrent doubles of mediation between hypermediacy and immediacy or difference outside and within the semiotic that render possible the study of the television text as technology and meaning, as semiotic and social, as aesthetic and political.

Acknowledgement

This chapter was first published in *Critical Discourse Studies* (2006), Vol. 3, No. 2, pp. 153–78.

Notes

1 See Arendt (1973/1990), McGowan (1998), Villa (1999) and Peters (2005) for the historical argument that the discourse of 'universal' morality, a form of ethical practice informed by ideas of Christian care and civil responsibility, was first articulated into the public realm in the Europe of Enlightenment and today constitutes a powerful discourse of public ethics in the Western world.

2 Aristotle (1976, 1140a24–1140b12, 1144b33–1145a11). See also Walker (1998) for a situated and relational view that perceives ethics as practices of responsibility that encode and express values and modes of connecting to others. 'Morality', she argues, 'arises and goes on between people, recruiting human capacities for self awareness and others' awareness; for feeling and learning to feel particular things in response to what one is aware of; for expressing judgment and feeling in the responses appropriate to them' (1998, p. 5).

3 For the connection between pity and citizenship see Boltanski (1999, pp. 20–34) and Arendt (1973/1990, pp. 59–114); for the connection between private and public disposition see Peters (1999, pp. 214–25); and for the connection between the communication of the private self in the public sphere of television see Scannel (1991, pp. 1–9).

4 For semiotic analyses of suffering see Van Leeuwen and Jaworski (2002) on the Israeli–Palestinian conflict; Perlmutter and Wagner (2004) on the violent conflicts relating to the G8 Summit in Genoa; for the language of mourning in public and, specifically, media discourse see Butler (2003); for the language of mourning concerning the events of September 11 see Martin (2004); for the analysis of spacetimes see Chilton (2004). For discourse analysis of discourses of pity in the context of migration see Reisigl and Wodak (2000); and for discourse analysis of the language of involvement in news broadcasts see Wodak (1996, pp. 100–30).

5 As Peters reminds us, the core controversy in social and media theory reflects a deeper rivalry between Marx's conflictual view of society and Durkheim's consensual view of the social body (Peters, 1999, p. 223).

6 The most radical version of pessimism on the role of the media in social life is Baudrillard's thesis, where the media are considered to be responsible for the disappearance of the real into a *simulacrum*—a mirror image of reality that is nowadays the only authentic reality of the spectator, leaving no space for considering mediation as an ethical space (Baudrillard, 1988). For a philosophical response to the nihilism of Baudrillard's 'hyperreality' in the context of information technologies see Introna (2002, 2001). Taking a Levinasian position that asserts the condition of proximity as the sine qua non of an 'other' oriented ethics, Introna argues that, in the age of electronic mediation, ethical practice calls less for moral norms and codes and more for reclaiming or asserting face-to-face presence as a guarantee for sustaining responsibility towards the 'other'.

7 This optimistic account of the ethical force of mediation goes as far as considering the media to be changing democracy today towards a deliberative model. Deliberative democracy, as opposed to representative democracy, is a non-localized, non-dialogical model of democracy, which comes about when audiences use media information to form judgements about distant events and undertake public action in the local contexts of their everyday life. In the face of the crisis of representative forms of public participation through political parties and social movements, deliberative processes contain today the hope for new practices of politicization and collective action. See Thompson (1995, pp. 114–16) for examples of such possibilities; see also Alexander and Jakobs (1998, pp. 22–41) on American civil society.

8 Audiences, we are told, must turn their sense of responsibility *into a form of moral-practical reflection because this is the best – the only – option we have* (Thompson, 1995, p. 265).

9 For a criticism of this position, accusing Derrida of cutting the semiotic system off from social relations, see Butler (1997, pp. 150–51); see also Said (1978, p. 703).

10 Derrida's criticism of Saussure is a philosophical argument that explains the inferiority of writing in terms of the broader historical biases of Western thinking, which takes the form of the opposition between conceptuality/language and materiality/visuality. See also Shapiro (1993, pp. 6–12) for a criticism of the *linguistic reduction* perspective, which suggests that the verbal has a far greater range than the visual; and see Jay (1994, pp. 493–542) for a critique of the nineteenth- and twentieth-century suspicion of visual culture – what he calls the *antiocularcentric discourse*, particularly in French thought. Shapiro's and Jay's accounts on the antagonism between linguistic and vision-centred discourses reveal unresolved tensions in the debate.

11 Here I adapt Chatman's categories of three main text-types in communicative practice: *description, argument and narrative* (1991, p. 9).

12 For the use of Piercean semiotics in visual analysis and in media texts see Hall (1973/1980), Hodge and Kress (1988, pp. 19–20), Van Leeuwen (2001, pp. 92–118), and Schroeder (2002, pp. 111–16).

13 See Kress and Van Leeuwen (1996, 2001) and Van Leeuwen and Jewitt (2001) for the grammar of the visual; see also Van Leeuwen and Jaworski (2002) and Perlmutter and Wagner (2004, pp. 91–108). The Piercean typology corresponds to other classifications of meaning types, such as Panofsky's (see Van Leeuwen, 2001, pp. 100–17).

14 This is one of Foucault's basic claims (Foucault, 1970, 1972) and a major premise for the post-structuralist anchoring of discourse analysis in critical research; for discussions see Fraser (1997), Torfing (1998), Chouliaraki (2002) and Howarth (2002).

15 There is also the textual meta-function of semiosis, which looks inwards to the text itself and serves the social purpose of creating meaning that is recognized as coherent and intelligible; according to Jewitt and Oyama, the textual meta-function holds together *the individual bits of representation-interaction into coherent text wholes* (2001, p. 140). In so far as it concerns itself with the combination of language and image in coherent texts, the textual meta-function obviously appertains to the multi-modal analysis of television that I discussed above; it is part of mediation as difference within the semiotic.

16 These questions are adapted from Morson and Emerson's discussion on Bakhtin's concept of the *chronotope* (1990, pp. 366–75).

17 All examples are taken from a voiceover transcript of 8 April 2003.

19

Semiotic paradigms and multimodality

Hartmut Stöckl

Introduction – semiotics as a methodological 'must'

Multimodality and semiotics

Semiotics and multimodality are inseparable academic companions in many ways. Essentially, this is because semiotics is the conceptual and methodological precondition for multimodal research. Universalistic, highly generalized and frequently vague, semiotics aspires to study 'all forms of formation and exchange of meaning on the basis of phenomena, which have been coded as signs' (Johansen and Larsen, 2002: 3). Multimodality on the other hand describes the 'integrated use of different communicative resources' (Van Leeuwen, 2012: 549) and consequently looks at the common semiotic ground between the various modes and the principles governing their interaction. Plausibly then, multimodality studies are in need of a semiotic underpinning, which is hailed as a 'guiding rationale' – a pan-discipline, as it seems fit to treat all signifying and communicative phenomena in the same way (cf. Fix, 2001: 115). Vice versa, any semiotic venture presupposes a multimodal conception of signs, texts and communication from the start.

Both semiotics and multimodality research respond to a natural given in human communication, which Lotman (1990: 124–25) labelled 'semiosphere', i.e. 'the whole semiotic space of the culture in question'. This space is essentially a multimodal one and the cultural ecology of using signs is crucially determined by permanent and manifold mode-integration. It has been the relatively recent shifts in the tectonics of this space, i.e. non-verbal and para-verbal signs move into the centre of the semiosphere with functional repercussions on language, which have fuelled multimodality studies. At the same time multimodality research has formed a stronghold against the anti-semiotic, i.e. views that deny certain modes and media structure, representation and meaning (cf. Elkins, 1998: xii for images). Semiotics on the contrary has evolved to form a 'toolkit of analytical methods and concepts' (Chandler, 2007: 212), which is helpful to look beneath the surface of communicative artefacts and uncover their structural and functional regularities.

A semiotic research agenda

A glance into any of the various handbooks and textbooks on semiotics (e.g. Nöth, 1985; Sebeok, 1994; Martin and Ringham, 2000; Johansen and Larsen, 2002; Chandler, 2007) shows the unbounded and messy character of the field, which is exacerbated by the many ties semiotics traditionally keeps with linguistics, especially pragmatics, semantics, rhetoric and text linguistics. Semiotic paradigms, therefore, are to be understood here as eclectic sets of semiotic ideas, concepts and principles relevant to multimodal text analysis. References to schools of semiotics are only made in passing. As current multimodality studies are dominated by Sydney school social semiotics (Van Leeuwen, 2005a), which 'has adopted and adapted [...] from (primarily Jakobsonian) structuralism (with a Hallidayan twist)' (Chandler, 2007: 220), I will mainly build this chapter around traditional mainstream semiotics. Even though neatly pinpointing paradigms seems impossible, three large concerns of semiotics emerge (Larsen, 1998: 833; Pankow, 1995), which I will use to order and hold together my inevitably incomplete mix of concepts.

1   *Sign repertoires:* Which types of signs are there and how do they build codes? What are their strengths and weaknesses?
2   *Sign comprehension:* Which cognitive processes or mental patterns may be assumed to be in operation upon comprehending signs/texts in socially situated communication?
3   *Sign/text structure:* How do signs combine to form patterned texts (complex messages) in one mode and across modes? How do sign makers and text producers use their artefacts in communication?

This semiotic programme essentially entails studying multimodal artefacts in terms of the 'structure and function of all processes in which signs are involved' (Pankow, 1995: 469). Multimodality research may use semiotics in both theoretical and applied ways: it contributes to theory when it seeks to define 'mode', the distinctions between them and their differing 'reaches', but also when it generally models mode interrelations. Multimodal analysis applies semiotic theory when it looks at a particular communicative practice – 'it [social semiotics – H.S.] only comes into its own when it is applied to specific instances and specific problems' (Van Leeuwen, 2005a: 1).

In what follows I will explain major semiotic concepts and illustrate them on a prototypical multimodal print advertisement (cf. Figure 19.1), in some parts expanding the explanations to audio-visual text. My aim in doing so is to show the suitability of semiotic paradigms for proving two points essential to the thinking in multimodality research. First, various modes like language and picture differ semiotically and each possess their 'autochthonous semantics' (Holly, 2007: 392) or 'reaches' (Kress, Chapter 4 this volume), that is, their diverging potentials and deficits also called 'affordances' (Kress, 2010a: 84). Therefore, as Jewitt (Chapter 1 this volume) argues, 'not every mode is equally "usable" for a particular task'. Second, it seems that 'common semiotic principles operate in and across different modes' (Kress and Van Leeuwen, 2001: 2). This idea not only highlights the mode-independent, universal applicability of semiotic tools, but, more importantly, it emphasizes the inherently multimodal meaning-making through mode-integration and interaction. It is this tension between the semiotic commonalities and differences of modes, which has the potential to drive current multimodality research.

Basic points of departure

Multimodality – mode – medium

Both semiotics and multimodality research depart from the basic idea that humans make meaning by choosing signs of different types from distinct repertoires, arranging them according to social rules and practices in order to form textual objects or communicative events, which convey more or less determinate messages in situations and contexts shaped by place, time, medium and culture. Although central to multimodality research, the term 'mode' (cf. Kress, Chapter 4; Jewitt, Chapters 1 and 2 this volume) represents a rather heterogeneous concept as various notions converge in it. At least three elements seem to have been synthesized: first, modes can be seen as sets of certain types of signs along with their 'organizing principles' (Jewitt, Chapter 1 this volume), their 'grammars' or modal logics. This largely corresponds to the idea of codes – albeit conceived of as flexible and expandable in use. Where language has lexis, syntax and speech acts, pictures have visual shape, arrangement in space and perspective. Music commands such semiotic resources as tune, rhythm, tempo and orchestration, whereas noise (understood here as any naturally occurring and artificially produced sound phenomena which are not part of speech or music) relies on such code-relevant qualities as materials and movements used to make the noise and its origin or conventional sphere of use. Second, mode also refers to the channel of sensory perception through which we perceive signs. Here, we end up with such crude but binding distinctions between visual, auditive, tactile, olfactory and gustative signs. Clearly, modes like language or music cut across these distinctions as both signing systems can be realized scripted (writing, score) and acoustically articulated (speech, sound). Consequently, third, mode also essentially involves the notion of physical and technical medium as its 'material stuff' (Kress, Chapter 4 this volume) or 'the actions, materials and artefacts we use for communicative purpose (Van Leeuwen, 2005a: 285).

This integrated conception of 'mode' in many ways reflects the complexities of multimodal communication and the dynamics between system and use of signs, and between the semantic-cognitive and the material aspects of sign types. German media linguistics (Schneider and Stöckl, 2011: 22fff.) is terminologically more rigorous and therefore more restrictive in its use of mode. Here, in a first step, medium is confined to material and technology that helps to produce, transmit and store signs. As media enable modes and as each technical medium affects the structures, styles and contents of communication, media allow for and shape 'communicative forms' (Dürscheid, 2005). The technical medium 'i-Pad' allows for television, newspapers, books, radio, email – these would be its communicative forms, i.e. the procedures, techniques and social configurations of communicating as determined by the medium. It is only within the confines of the communicative forms that multimodal texts or artefacts and their genres are produced. These in turn are the sites for combining various types of signing modalities, i.e. modes. This layered model has the advantage of keeping modes apart from media. But it also highlights the step-by-step chain of influences from the medium onto the mode. Modes then are mainly seen as sign systems, which involve their coded structure and their sensory processing. Following this system of terminology, language cannot be a medium, but must be a mode, however one that can be realized or represented in the medial variants speech, writing and sign language. To generalize one can say that modes have 'mediality', i.e. representational forms and medial logics.

Types of multimodal text

If we consider possible types of multimodal text from the perspective of the modes involved, we may arrive at essentially three different prototypes: printed, audio and audiovisual (Stöckl, 2012: 20). The semiotic complexity, i.e. the number of modes involved and the potential for reciprocal integration, increases gradually from print to audiovisual text. So while printed text (writing, picture and typography) and audio text (speech, music, noise) only combine three modes each, audiovisual text may merge a maximum of modes, i.e. both medial variants of language, speech and writing, as well as the static and dynamic versions of picture and typography plus music and noise. It is interesting that the electronic, digital medium endows texts with hyper-textual, interactive and navigational qualities, yet essentially the medium does not alter the number and type of the modes possible. On the other hand, every type of multimodal text may be realized in different communicative forms: e.g. print as graffiti, poster, article, flag; audio as podcast, radio programme, music recording or political speech; and audiovisual as film, live performance, video or television. It is the communicative forms that determine the concrete use of the modes in the texts, their combination and patterning within the rules of the genre. What also deserves attention in an attempt to order the multimodal field is the difference in the status of the modes. While some are full-blown, archetypical and mainly independent like language and picture, others like typography or colour depend on them and are integrated into them. One can call the first type core modes and the latter peripheral or para-semiotic modes (Stöckl, 2004: 11–16).

Context – discourse – genre

After these somewhat general reflections on the semiotic logic of multimodal communication, the rest of the chapter will be devoted to the kind of back-up knowledge that sign structures in use rely on. My point here is that any working of a code is supported by a number of signposts that direct the recipient to the intended meaning potential. Similarly, these pointers also provide orientation for the text producer as a general frame of reference. The core concepts here are context, discourse and genre.

Adverts like the one in Figure 19.1 will – whatever signs they use to construct whatever message – have to function in a context of situation and culture (Halliday and Hasan, 1985: 5–9) predetermined and familiar to the communicators. The situation is characterized by cursory attention,

Figure 19.1 'A cavity ruins everything.' Colgate Toothpaste, Prolam Y&R, Santiago de Chile.

Source: Lürzer's Archiv 1/12: 41, 1.1201.

short processing time, potential resistance against commercial messages and a need, therefore, to be surprised, activated and impressed by the signs offered. Advertising makes ample and subtle references to those fragments of culture known to the targeted audience (i.e. weddings, figurative meanings of 'black' and 'white') – in fact adverts are highly culture-sensitive and will be misunderstood by those not familiar with the relevant knowledge. It is these contexts that support and shape any meaning made.

Following the principle of fusion (Cook, 2001: 108) adverts usually merge two domains of knowledge. One concerns the discourse of the product-type (i.e. toothpaste), the other discourse may come from any domain that is fit to transfer positive or argumentatively guiding qualities onto the product or the whole text (i.e. wedding ceremonies). The discourse of advertising – in the sense of socially constructed and shared knowledge about the world – makes use of whatever people in the culture and context can be expected to know and find cognitively stimulating in playful combination.

Finally, adverts – as any other texts – come in genres and realize larger text or discourse types (Renkema, 2004: 61–64). These are rules for putting together signs to form meaningful texts with a unified function. Adverts instantiate the persuasive or argumentative text-type – as its functions are well known, advertisers are free to offer a large variety of diverse messages. Whatever the sign structures are, the makers can trust they will be understood as a commercial brand message.

Sign types and semiotic structures

Semiotic key ideas

This section will be concerned with those fundamental concepts that relate to the workings of individual signs and the codes they come from. My aim here is to review selected semiotic theories with an eye to how they serve to explain the similarities and differences between the modes language, picture, music and noise. Of necessity, the choice of semiotic thinking presented here is restricted, yet it reflects key ideas in mainstream semiotics. F. de Saussure's thoughts explain the general structure of a code and how individual signs function within the overall system of a mode. C. W. Morris was concerned with how messages constructed using a code essentially operate on a semantic (meaning), syntactic (form) and pragmatic level (function). C. S. Peirce's notions of icon, index and symbol provide a crude but useful typology of signs that motivates essential differences in how signs come to make meaning. Finally, K. Bühler, R. Jakobson and M. A. K. Halliday are taken up as they provide ideas on the various functions signs pursue in communication.

Paradigmatic and syntagmatic sign relations

The most basic idea goes back to F. de Saussure's notion that the 'value' (Saussure, 1996), i.e. meaning of any one sign is determined by its relations to neighbouring signs in a semiotic system or repertoire. Such relationships, he posited, can be of two kinds: paradigmatic and syntagmatic (Chandler, 2007: 83–87). In a paradigm semantically and functionally related signs can be exchanged for one another. So, for instance, the words in the phrase 'this swift cheetah' could be replaced by 'that slow lion' – all words are related in meaning and in grammatical function (e.g. swift/slow – antonymic adjectives; cheetah/lion – taxonomically related nouns). A syntagm, that is, a phrase or sentence, combines signs which concord grammatically and semantically to express more complex meanings. So, for instance, 'The teacher criticizes the pupil' would be a well-formed syntagm, whereas 'The blue criticise stone' is not as it violates meaning and grammar. Syntagms, then, are horizontal combinations of signs, whereas paradigms are vertical sets of exchangeable signs. In our example (cf. Figure 19.1) the verbal text forms a simple sentence according to the rules of English: 'cavity' relates to 'hole' or 'gap' but in the advert's context also associates teeth and dental hygiene. In *A cavity ruins everything* semantic roles are assigned through grammar: *cavity* becomes an agent, and *everything* is the affected object linked to the noun through a material process. That language is strictly bound to the intricate workings of paradigmatic and syntagmatic relations of words in the system can count as one of its semiotic design features. If we compare this to the nature of pictures, we find that pictorial elements form configurations of visual gestalts (i.e. perceptible outer forms/shapes of objects and individuals) in a space, which are not essentially linear. What elements can go together is determined by the material forms/shapes of the signs, not so much by their meaning or issues of grammar. Paradigmatically it seems that (concrete) pictures are governed by the order of things in the worlds they depict or by the knowledge of them represented in communicators' minds. In the advert's image cross, dome, aisles, benches etc. form the complex sign of 'church'.

Semantics, syntax and pragmatics of sign systems

An equally basic idea is C. W. Morris's notion of sign systems functioning in three dimensions: semantics (meaning), syntax (form) and pragmatics (function) (Chandler, 2007: 196). We already saw that the syntactic potential of language and image crucially differ, yet both modes allow for a combination of single signs to more complex ones in order to flexibly express meaning. If we take a glance at music, it is obvious that here the syntactic combinability (in chords, tunes, rhythms, tempo etc.) is extreme, whereas a reliable semantics, i.e. signs representing concepts that relate to real or fictitious worlds, seems non-existent or weak. Noise, on the other hand, seems to have little or no syntax as noises do not really form phrases other than atmospheric clusters, e.g. big city or nature noises. The semantics of noise is restricted to its indexical function of pointing to objects, places, actions etc. In a radio commercial, for instance, footsteps on the floor indicate a person walking or approaching, an engine running signifies a car, and the crashing of the waves against the rocks suggests a place by the sea. In the absence of images, noises in audio texts can lend semiotic support to the telling of a verbal story. So what emerges in an inter-modal comparison is pronounced semantic and syntactic differences that are hard to ignore in any semiotic or multimodal theory. This is also borne out in the pragmatic domain. The sample advert shows that whereas language forms a clear transitive message of cause and effect, the picture represents a place/scenario in all its physical detail rife with contextual associations. Generally, language has its strengths in explaining, arguing and narrating; pictures are a potent means of depicting perceptual reality and evoking experience. Music, as used in a commercial for instance, works as a vague index to emotions, auras and movement (e.g. an ascending tune may point to an elated mood, a march may signal a festive and ceremonial situation, a fast-paced rhythm/tempo may indicate running/hurrying), whereas noise signposts places and actions in the worlds represented through language or picture (e.g. traffic noises may evoke the bustle of a cityscape).

Symbol, icon and index

On a very general level, these differing 'reaches' of the modes may be explained by reference to Peircean semiotic thinking. C. S. Peirce (Chandler, 2007: 36–38) distinguished three sign-types on the basis of the relation between the sign and the objects it depicts. Symbols arbitrarily relate to their objects – the semiotic form (i.e. the 'sign vehicle') does not motivate or explain the meaning made; therefore symbols are removed from perception/experience and count as abstract. Language is primarily symbolic in this sense; *Colgate Maximum Cavity Protection* would be a case in point. Icons establish a relation of similarity to the objects they depict – their shape resembles what they represent, they are close to perception.

Most pictures are predominantly iconic; the church and the people in it resemble our mental image of this fragment of reality. Indexes form a relation to the objects they refer to by way of logical or contiguous association. This means that the frequent co-occurrence of two phenomena (fire/smoke, fever/illness) allows one to stand for the other or makes one the 'symptom' of the other. In this sense a French *chanson* may signify Paris, a march represents a military ceremony or a pop-song may make you want to dance (music) – screeching tyres point to a braking car or a swoosh indicates people playing tennis (noise). In summary, while language is symbolic and pictures iconic, music and noise are indexical sign systems. These modal logics may not be binding as one sign can cut across the types (cf. 'Semiosis and meaning-making' below) and because signs entertain multimodal relations (cf. 'Linking modes' below), but this essential categorization of modes crucially constrains their meaning potential. None of these distinctions, however, infringes upon the generally conventional character of different signs and systems – Saussure, therefore, elegantly argued that signs are relatively motivated.

Semiotic functions

Taking language as a vantage point, some semioticians were concerned with the general functionality of semiotic modes. Bühler (1934/1990) started this train of thought by positing three language functions: the expressive – marking the identity, emotional state and intention of the sender, the referential – relating to fragments of real or fictitious worlds, and the appeal-function – impacting on the recipient. These functions mix and one or the other may dominate a textual message. The advert is strong in its referential and expressive functions as it presents a product and argues for it by dramatizing the effect of bad dental health. The text, surprisingly, has only indirect potential of appeal – a kind of fear of social stigma may be inferred from the signs presented. In an inter-semiotic comparison language is predominantly referential as are pictures, while music lacks exactly this function and has a strong expressive impact. Noise altogether shows a very limited capacity for reference, appeal and expression. These functional differences are borne out in the standard TV-commercial: here speech/writing and moving image are the main representational resources, whereas noise can work to support the referential and music is mainly oriented towards the expressive potential of the sender and the impact on the recipient.

Jakobson (1960) added another three language functions: the phatic – signs work to establish contact and open the channel; the poetic – signs attract attention to the form of the message and its structure; and the metalingual (meta-communicative) – signs comment on their own code. Ignoring the phatic, interestingly, it is the poetic and the meta-communicative functions, which are useful to pinpoint differences between modes. While language is fully poetic and meta-communicative, picture, music and noise do not have the resources to comment themselves explicitly. (In some ways sampling, juxtaposing and mixing musical pieces may have a loosely commenting effect.) The poetic, on the other hand, seems inherent in the workings of both music and picture as the shape and materiality of musical and pictorial signs and the ways in which they are configured are indispensable to their meaning. The potential message and communicative impact of pictures and music, therefore, seem to depend more strongly on their 'poetic' qualities, i.e. their structure and design. In the ad sample it is the overall white tint of the photograph in combination with the one person standing out in black, which enables the kind of meaning potential crucial for the multimodal link.

Finally, Hallidayan social semiotics (Halliday and Hasan, 1985: 16–23) claims three meta-functions to be valid for any sign repertoire aspiring to mode-status: the signing mode represents reality (ideational/representational), it mediates an interaction between sign user and recipient (interpersonal/interactional) and the mode forms textual patterns (textual/compositional). Although indeed applicable to all modes, again differences seem obvious. Music unaided is ideationally void or at least very weak, yet textually strong, whereas noise can hardly be said to configure in textual patterns on its own (if we ignore the option of sampling noises and putting them into a rhythmic texture of dubious semantic powers). Language and picture, on the other hand, seem to have their very own but full-blown resources to fulfil all three meta-functions. Again, the prototypical TV-commercial brings out these mode differences. As music is textually strong, it usually determines the rhythm to which the images are cut. Noise fits in only at those parts of the texture where it supports ideation. The representation of real or fictitious worlds mainly happens through a story or argument presented in language and pictures. Music and noise, however, may well contribute to the interactional potential of the commercial in that they dispose the recipient for the message.

Semiosis and meaning-making

Interactivity and fluidity of meaning-making

From today's vantage point, (early European and American) structuralist semiotics may seem rather static, as it is focused on general conceptions of the sign, its types and code structures. This section will highlight some more dynamic semiotic ideas, which help explain how meaning is construed by the recipient in a contextual and cognitive interaction with the semiotic structure of a text. It was Peirce's conception of 'semiosis' (Chandler, 2007: 29–33) as a communicative process of creating and actively mediating meaning through signs, which prepared the ground for post-structuralist and social semiotics. Peirce understood a sign not as a fixed bilateral unit but as mental and social action, a triadic cooperation between sign (material), object (referent) and its 'interpretant', i.e. the effect of a sign in the mind of the recipient interpreting a sign (Nöth, 1985: 38). Such a conception locates meaning in the conventions of a community and in the knowledge and thought of the sign-user. The idea of semiosis is crucial for explanations of the indirect and non-literal use of signs, connotative meaning and metaphor.

Multiple and non-literal meaning

The fluidity of meaning-making is first attested by the combination of symbolic, iconic and index-ical qualities in one sign system, therefore producing different readings. This is why Chandler (2007: 44f.) advocates speaking of modes of sign use, not of sign-types. The picture in the sample advert iconically represents a stereotypical wedding ceremony in a church. The black person against the uniformly white context indexically points to some salient irregularity or non-conformity. Finally, of course, the scene plays on the symbolic contrast of meaning between white (good, desirable teeth/situation) and black (bad, unacceptable teeth/situation). It is only through combining all these three readings that we arrive at the total meaning potential of the image.

Barthes (1996) provided a well-known explanation for how one sign or sign-complex can make various meanings simultaneously with his concept of 'connotation'. He argued that signifier and signified on the literal level (or first order of signification) can become the signifier on a connotative level (or second order of signification), to which a new signified – the signified of connotation – attaches. The graphic and acoustic shape (signifier) of the word *cavity* is tied to the signified 'empty space within a solid object' forming a linguistic sign on the first level. On a second level this sign acts as the signifier for the connotation 'medical/technical', which does not attach to the paradigmatically exchangeable 'hole'. In the context of dental health, of course, *cavity* also has the connotation of 'negative/undesirable/to be prevented'. The syntagmatic combination of *cavity* with *ruins* uses and underscores this particular connotation. Similarly, the white tint of the photographed scene is moti-vated by the culturally coded connotations of the colour white, such as 'pure/innocent/untainted/morally beyond reproach'. All these prove relevant to the multimodal meaning-making.

If the same or similar connotative meanings are persistently reused in the discourse of toothpaste advertising, they form what Barthes, following L. Hjelmslev, called the mythical or ideological order of signification (Chandler, 2007: 143–45). On this third level of meaning-making, patterns of con-notational use constitute the ideological narratives of a culture or a discourse. We are reminded here of A. Greimas' method of narrative semiotics, which also seeks to discover a 'deep structure' of norms values and attitudes in a social system through charting narrative structures (cf. Titscher et al., 2000: 126–29). The 'myth' inherent in most toothpaste advertising as instantiated in the sample text links good dental health to social acceptability and virtuous morals, to the effect that a neglect of dental hygiene is something to be feared. Finally, it needs pointing out that Peirce in principle saw this pro-liferation of meaning on various orders of signification as unlimited semiosis. In practice it will be limited by genre knowledge, as well as by the context and situation of a given text.

Metaphor, cooperativity and indirect meaning-making

Another way in which signs can make other than or more than the literal meaning is metaphor. Here, correlations in experience are used to link one conceptual domain to another. In the sample advert the severity of having dental cavities is understood in terms of the embarrassment and shock of a wedding spoilt by someone disturbing the ceremony. When, traditionally, meta-phor was explained as a property of linguistic signifiers, semiotically it is seen as a semantic transfer between signifieds on various levels (Chandler, 2007: 127). Cognitively, metaphor is rather viewed as a property and an essential operation of the human mind to build and structure concepts, irrespective of their semiotic representation. Many metaphors are multimodal (Forceville and Urios-Aparisi, 2009) and function across the modes as in the example. Their effect is to highlight some semantic aspects in the target domain, e.g. the social and ethical dimension of dental hygiene, and hide others, e.g. the mundane and routine of brushing teeth. In advertising discourse generally, metaphors do not only serve to explain the product, but they primarily make it less trivial and aesthetically more pleasing and interesting.

Finally, the interpretation of multimodal texts is also governed by the cooperative principle first formulated by H. P. Grice (1975). He argued that whatever is said in a communicative situation will be judged against standard expectations of relevance, quantity, quality (truth) and manner. If a speak-er's contribution or, semiotically, a string of signs seems to violate these maxims on the surface, recipients still assume cooperativity and will try to infer what is meant by recourse to shared knowl-edge and aspects of the context and situation. This willingness to cooperate in meaning-making by investing mental energy and doing semiotic work allows for the conventional indirectness of sign-use. In a multimodal text, interestingly, the signs from different modes act as mutual contexts to each other. Therefore, inferences from the signs offered in one mode can be made relying on signs offered in another mode. In the sample advert the scene depicted visually will not immediately be interpreted as relevant in the communicative situation of toothpaste advertising. However, knowing the verbal co-text (*A cavity ruins everything*) we understand the picture as representing an analogous example to explain how a small cause can have a great effect and, therefore, as relevant to the multimodal text. Vice versa, the semantic under-specification of the verbal claim (*A cavity ruins everything*) in terms of quantity (saying too little, i.e. just naming the product) and truth (exaggerating by using *everything*) is rectified by the visual co-text. It is this inherent reciprocity of multimodal meaning-making that will be the subject of the next section.

Linking modes

Multimodality as complementarity and transcription of modes

So far we have looked at selected semiotic notions and used them to point out essential similarities or differences between modes and to model how meaning is made across modes in the interpretation of multimodal texts. In this section the focus will be on those elements of semiotic theory that can explain the ways in which modes interact to form multimodal texts and create intermodal coherence. Generally, it is interesting to see that most terms used to describe the linking of modes emphasize their reciprocal inter-relation. The metaphor 'zip' (Holly, 2009), for instance, highlights how any two modes interlock to produce what Royce (1998) labels 'inter-semiotic complementarity'. 'Transcription' (Holly and Jäger, 2011: 153) foregrounds the cognitive activity of relating and translating meaning between modes that is needed on the part of producer/recipient to create and understand multimodal texts. It is also commonly accepted that multimodal linking operates between certain elements of the modes (e.g. words, phrase; pictorial elements; rhythm, tune), which connect semantically at 'edit points' (Van Leeuwen, 2005a: 184) in the structural design of the text.

Modelling multimodality on various levels of text description

Relations between modes may be described on a number of text levels. Using Morris' idea of any mode having a semantic, syntactic and pragmatic dimension, inter-modal relations can be analysed on the levels of meaning/content, form and function (Stöckl, 2009). More complex models – like Delin and Bateman (2002) – envisage five layers of structure: content, rhetoric, layout, navigation and language. Van Leeuwen (2005a: 179ff.) embracing both time- and space-based media suggests four types of inter-modal cohesion, which are best seen as mode-integrating principles: rhythm, composition, information linking and dialogue. This typology is mixed. First, it refers to the kinds of mode combinations: rhythm is a means to structure links between speech, music, noise and the moving image, whereas composition creates cohesive ties between writing and the static image. Second, the typology deals with levels of analysis: information linking is concerned with the semantic and logical relations between propositions. In summary, only a multilayered approach can do justice to the complexities of mode linking. For ease of demonstration and reasons of space, the following account will be restricted to the language–image link. However, comments will be made in passing about how the ideas presented relate to the other modes.

Information linking – semantics

For a combination of language (i.e. text) and image to create a coherent whole the content of both modes, their propositional meanings need to relate to one another in specific ways. Certainly, the most influential paradigm is the one started by Barthes (1977d). He proposed two major ideas. First, linguistic and iconic messages affect each other on both a denotational and a connotational level of meaning. Barthes states that denotatively language functions to 'fix the floating chain of signified' (Barthes, 1977d: 39), i.e. to decrease the inherent polysemy of the image. He calls this the 'denominative function', which serves to identify what is in the image (ibid.). Connotatively, language 'holds the connoted meanings from proliferating', it 'limits the projective power of the image' (ibid.) and has a 'repressive value' (Barthes, 1977d: 40). He called this function (ideological) 'interpretation'. Second, Barthes (1977d: 40f.) posited two principal ways in which language and image can relate to one another: 'anchorage' is a relation of informational redundancy and repetition between the two modes, whereas 'relay' envisages their essential informational difference or divergence and results in a complementary relation of content. Barthes also allowed for different orders/directions or dominances of text and image: whereas in 'anchorage' the picture is central and the text serves to interpret it, in 'illustration' the text is primary and is interpreted by the picture. It is probably fair to say that because these distinctions and theoretical foundations are so general and basic, they have found many followers but have also often been misconstrued as they are not hard-and-fast. On the other hand, it is easy to see how Barthes' ideas can be applied to other modes. Clearly, the linguistic messages in multimodal texts have similar, limiting functions with respect to the denotative and connotative meanings of music and noise. Language will mainly serve to disambiguate and to functionally determine sound meanings, which might relate to linguistic messages according to principles of information redundancy or complementarity.

In the sample advert, the dominance of the visual suggests a text–image relation of anchorage. Interestingly, however, on the denotative level the linguistic message does little to name pictorial elements (even though the figure in black can literally be a *cavity* in the white texture of the image). The text rather provides a context or knowledge frame, within which the picture is to be interpreted. The main semiotic inter-relation happens on the connotational level. Here the negative causality of the text is transferred onto the picture, which is why all the positive cultural signifieds of marriage are toned down and simply act as a catalyst for creating social embarrassment and fear. The smaller picture of the tube is a classic case of denotational anchorage, as *Colgate Maximum Cavity Protection* simply denotes/specifies the pictorial element.

Barthes' foundation was used and enhanced in Hallidayan social semiotics. Here the main idea was to compare the relation between text and image with the semantic relations between clauses in a complex sentence. This comparison is plausible because with both the conjunction of clauses as well as text-image links, relations between propositions or content are expressed. But in this way also the logic of language is projected onto the image, as we assume pictures function propositionally, something we can empirically not take for granted. Martinec and Salway (2005) propose a system for analysing semantic text–image relations that is both Barthes- and Halliday-inspired. The two main analytical dimensions are 'relative image–text status' and 'logico-semantic relation'. The status of text and image is equal, 'when a whole image is related to a whole text' (Martinec and Salway, 2005: 343) and unequal, when only parts of both relate to one another. This simple distinction may also be applied to modes other than language and image. Music in a commercial can have equal status if it plays throughout the film and relates to the moving images in their entirety. Noise rather tends to have unequal status, as isolated noises connect to only parts of the text or stand in for them. In the sample advert, the whole picture (in fact two) relates to the whole of the text – the parallelism between dental hygiene and wedding ceremonies can only work on the basis of this equal status. Equal status can occur in two types: either text and image are independent, i.e. 'the information they provide exists in parallel' (ibid.: 343), or text and image are complementary, i.e. they 'form part of a larger syntagm' (ibid.: 344). When applying this finer distinction to the sample, we face difficulties of interpretation as both cases could be argued. The processes expressed seem independent and conjoined: 'black figure ruins wedding by disturbing it' and *a cavity ruins everything*. However, in order to make sense of the conjoining one would need to integrate the information in a complementary fashion likening one to the other.

Logico-semantic relations are concerned with the ways in which information is related to one another in text and image. Following Hallidayan functional grammar, three main types are possible here. In 'elaboration' text and image essentially contain the same or similar information, one mode elaborates the content of the other. This would seem to be the case in the advert: the picture provides an 'exemplification' of the verbal claim, where *everything* is specified by the picture and the text remains general. In 'extension', one mode adds new information not present in the other, whereas in 'enhancement', information in one mode is supplemented with circumstantial information in the other. Again it is hard to see how these distinctions can be tidy if one considers the wealth of possible configurations between modes and the semantic tensions and functional overlaps that make mode-integration communicatively attractive. As both music and noise need to be seen as semantically deficient due to their indexical way of signifying (cf. above), it would seem to make little sense to subject intermodal links involving sound to the three logico-semantic types. If at all, music elaborates verbal and pictorial information, and noise may provide circumstantial information to text and image.

Formal mode integration – syntax

When the content-level of multimodal text analysis is mainly determined by the logic of language, the form-level is governed by criteria derived from the logic of pictorial space and composition. Formal analysis generally means to describe how text and image are distributed spatially and to conclude from this how they relate in perception and cognitive interaction. Following Kress and Van Leeuwen (1996: 183), three criteria may be used. First, 'framing' embraces all devices that create connections and disconnections between elements in a multimodal text. These may be verbal (types of phrases, punctuation) and visual (lines, text blocks, colour, size, shape). Framing orders the signs and syntagms of a semiotic product and, therefore, suggests plausible ways of reading. In the advert the white of the photo unites all elements of the church scenario. The coloured tube stands out from this and forms a separate frame, which also graphically integrates the writing. Both are related 'syntactically' as the white strip of toothpaste creates continuity and connection with the photograph. These observations support a close tie of language and image calculated to achieve complementarity. Second, a semantic emphasis may attach to those elements of a multimodal composition, which are visually salient through size, colour, contrast, placement etc. The black figure becomes salient against the white background and proves central for the intended analogy between dental health and wedding frame. Similarly, the tube as the advertised product achieves salience through colour, which indicates its importance for the genre. Third, specific 'information values' are associated with certain 'zones of the semiotic space' (Van Leeuwen, 2005a: 278). In the sample advert the horizontal dimension has been exploited to place the product on the right giving it the value of new information. Also, the tube is in the foreground and seemingly closer to the viewer, which affects its degree of importance. This kind of syntactic analysis would not be complete without pointing to the relative dominance of the image over the text. This is achieved through an integration of the writing into a pictorial element and through the small type-size of the verbal claim.

It is plausible to assume that music has its own devices of framing (mainly through pausing, changing tunes/harmonies/keys etc.) and salience (through volume, intensity, orchestration), whereas the main principle of integrating music with other modes must be rhythm. Noises as used in multimodal genres (film, commercials etc.) usually are distinct and neatly bounded sound phenomena – they can connect to language and image in many ways. Usually text and picture represent people, objects and places making the sounds or associated with them literally or symbolically (bells – church, wedding, solemnity). Generally, language and picture on the one hand and sound (music/noise) on the other can run parallel to one another, i.e. be simultaneous, or alternate in the texture of a multimodal artefact.

Functional mode integration – pragmatics

A functional analysis, finally, would look at the division of pragmatic labour between the modes. It would also sketch out the kind of semiotic work to be performed by the recipient. This level must be based on the other two and can attempt a general summary. For this a rhetorical framework proves useful, a tradition well rooted in semiotics (Doelker, 2007), and text linguistics (cf. Rhetorical Structure Theory – Mann and Thompson, 1988). The underlying idea here is to conceive of a text as 'a hierarchical organization of text segments' (Renkema, 2004: 111). In a multimodal text, such discourse segments may be constituted not only by units of sentences but also by visuals, music or noise. Any two segments are related to one another through semantic relations, which can be specified using the terminology of Rhetorical Structure Theory or the 'clause-relational' approach. What emerges from analyses of this kind is semantic maps or webs of a multimodal text, which model how major text parts are connected to one another in meaning and logic. So, for instance, the lead of a hard news story will present the main facts, whereas what follows serves as its 'elaboration'. Alternatively, infographics may function as a 'summary' of the events related in the article. The sad–solemn music played in a commercial may deliberately 'contrast' with the joyfulness of its verbal content. The babble and gurgling of a brook can be used as symbolic 'evidence' of a product's freshness. For our example, it is important to note that the main argument is not explicitly stated but follows a cause–effect logic: 'Because a cavity ruins everything, use Colgate …'. The claim is exemplified in the picture by offering an instance of something being ruined. Text and picture share the semiotic work: whereas language names the product and makes the claim, the image offers rich physical detail as a stimulus to the imagination and shows the product.

A critical endnote

My account of semiotic concepts and analytical frameworks in the previous four sections shows that multimodality research has taken and developed from semiotics a powerful heuristic hermeneutic. However many concepts we may add and however practical this interpretative toolkit may be, it cannot tie down meaning fully but only approximate it. These shortcomings of a semiotics focused on text structure may partly be offset by approaches that look at how producers deploy multimodal meanings in the artefacts they create and studies that uncover how recipients handle texts cognitively and socially. Multimodal analysis ultimately calls for a synthesis of production-centred, structural and reception-centred aspects of methodology.

Regarding the analytical categories and models presented here and those generally available it seems that some bias one mode over the other. Thus, for instance, a linguistic logic may be projected onto the picture or a pictorial logic onto language. If we seek to avoid the overgeneralization inherent in much semiotic theory, looking for common semiotic principles underlying all modes cannot be the only adequate approach in multimodal research. Instead, it would seem that a dual-step method is recommendable: first capture the specific 'grammar' of a mode and then describe the ways in which various modes connect and interlock formally, semantically and pragmatically. Whereas in the first step semiotics appears helpful to recognize similarities and differences between modes, in the second step text theory and rhetoric may prove useful to model inter-modal coherence. Finally, whatever method is used, it ought to be sensitive to the constraints and determining forces of genre on multimodal patterns. Also, any method ought to acknowledge the descriptive limitations resulting from terminological distinctions that inevitably turn out to be cruder than the complexities of communicative reality.

20

Reception of multimodality[1]

Applying eye-tracking methodology in multimodal research

Jana Holsanova

Introduction

The chapter presents a new perspective that concerns the reception of multimodality and emphasizes how multimodal messages are perceived by the users. This perspective is described in relation to three main production-oriented perspectives: social semiotic multimodal analysis, a systemic functional approach and multimodal interactional analysis. It is argued that eye-tracking measurements, in combination with verbal protocols, interviews, comprehension tests and questionnaires, are a suitable method for studying reception of multimodality. The chapter gives an overview of different ways in which eye-tracking methodology can be used in research on multimodality. Various application areas associated with the use of eye-tracking methodology are summarized. Potentials and limitations of this methodology are listed. The chapter provides examples from eye-tracking studies focusing on the integration of various modes.

Why a reception perspective?

The aim of most producers and designers is to create an aesthetically appealing, effective and user-friendly multimodal text design that makes it easy for the user to find, process and understand information. In other words, a functional text design should help users to accomplish their personal goals – get informed, perform an action, solve a problem, make a decision or learn something (Holsanova and Nord, 2011). However, design is not only a *product* of the design process, an organized arrangement of one or more elements that has been created in order to serve a certain purpose. It can also be conceived of as a starting point for *interpretation processes* (Bucher, 2007) since it invites the user to a certain interaction.

Thus, multimodality can be studied from both a *production* and a *reception* perspective (Holsanova, 1999, 2010; Bucher, 2011). Whereas the production aspect focuses on how information in multimodal messages is presented by the sign-maker or designer, the reception aspect emphasizes how multimodal messages are perceived by the users.

However, although the composition of multimodal documents and its potential for meaning-making have been discussed in the social semiotic tradition (Kress and van Leeuwen, 1996), as well as in the rhetorical tradition (Bateman, 2008; Schriver, 1997), the actual reception of the messages by actual users in a particular context of use has not been studied empirically. There is still little knowledge about how users actually are affected and interact with text design, how they read complex texts, what attracts their attention and what does not and how they integrate information from the language, images, sounds, and animations. Few studies on the reception of multimodality have been conducted so far (cf. Holsanova *et al.*, 2006; Holsanova, 2012).

The reception perspective is, however, important since it is not self-evident that all users can automatically integrate text and pictures. As Hannus and Hyönä (1999) showed, high-ability pupils were significantly better at integrating text and images in biology textbooks than low-ability pupils. Nor should it be taken for granted that users and learners will extract the information from a visualization that was intended by the designer or instructor (Scheiter *et al.*, 2008). Although it is argued that students learn better from pictures and words than from pictures alone (Mayer, 2009), all graphics are not equally effective, as Sung and Mayer (2012) have shown. Finally, it is not self-evident that illustrations always help users to comprehend the text. Nyström and Ögren (2012), in their eye-tracking study, found no overall performance benefit of illustrated mathematical problem-solving even though illustrations were clearly visually attended. Thus, there is a need for empirical research on users' interaction with multimodal messages. Eye movement measurement – in combination with other methods – is a suitable method for research on the reception of multimodality. By using eye-tracking methodology, we can follow the reading and scanning process in detail. We can trace exactly what is looked at, where, when and how often. The gaze reveals the chosen entry points, reading paths and the connections made between text and images.

Example: interaction with printed and digital media

In order to show how eye-tracking methodology can be used in research on multimodality we will have a look at one example that concerns readers' interaction with printed and digital media (Holsanova, 2010). Modern media messages are visually *fragmented* since they are built up of various visual elements and units and lack the flow of continuity (Holsanova and Nord, 2010). This tendency has also been described as atomization of news texts (Knox, 2007) or as modularization of the text design (Bucher, 2000). Media messages are also *multimodal* in the sense that they contain various modes: delimited parts of written text (articles, headlines, briefs, lists of items, fact boxes), static and dynamic pictures and graphics (photos, drawings, diagrams, graphs, maps, films, video clips, animations, typographic and layout elements) and auditive parts (speech files, sound, music, etc.). Moreover, media messages are *multisequential* since they offer various entry points and reading paths. Thus, there is no obvious linear order in which these messages should be perceived. All these characteristics influence the way media messages are attended to, processed and understood by the readers. The following questions arise: How do readers choose entry points and reading paths and navigate in the media? How do readers create coherence in the fragmented message? How do they integrate information coming from different sources (text, photos, graphs, etc.) in the process of meaning-making?

Plate 20.1 shows a typical example of how readers interact with a newspaper spread. The reading starts with early and very brief glances at the headlines and images (under one second), followed by some reading in selected articles. Note that no article is read in full. Some articles are read in portions, with successive start-ups. Also, reading depth varies. A couple of articles on the right are totally ignored, some parts of the articles, such as briefs, are read quite carefully. Readers may leave an article in the middle of a brief, jump to the end of another (previously attended) article or to a headline on a different page, and then return to the first article in order to read the last three sentences. Advertisements are attended to by very few readers, while newspaper notices are read in depth. Readers scan the spread in their search for entry points. When they find an interesting entry, they stop scanning and start reading. As soon as they feel finished, they continue scanning until they find the next interesting entry point. There is usually no general scanning phase before the actual reading. Rather, scanning and reading alternate continuously.

Many believe that images of various types are attended to in the same manner. However, when analyzing gaze behavior data from newspaper and net paper reading we find a lot of differences (Holsanova et al., 2008; Holsanova, 2010). Information graphics attract much more attention than maps, drawings or photos do (Holmqvist and Wartenberg, 2005; Holsanova et al., 2013). Press photos, for example, are fixated early on the spread for a very short time (mostly to identify objects or people) whereas information graphics are read later on the spread and get much more attention. For example, in Plate 20.1 the reader briefly glanced at the photo of Fredrik Reinfeldt – probably recognizing and categorizing him as the Swedish prime minister – and went on reading. In contrast, the reader devoted a large amount of time to information graphics on the right since he expected to get valuable explanations of a complex phenomena.

The example in Plate 20.1 also illustrates that readers do not process and interpret everything on the spread holistically, at one glance, as many believe. Although we are, for example, able to get the "gist" of a scene very early in the viewing process, we have to fixate parts of the scene, one by one, in order to examine the details. Reading and scanning are sequential processes where the focus of attention moves from one place to another, and where much of the spread is not seen. Human attention has limited capacity and does not allow us to actively read and process information in multiple places simultaneously. To perceive, read and cognitively process information in detail, it is necessary to direct the gaze to relevant pieces of information – letters, words, parts of the image – so that they fall onto a high-resolution area of the eye, the fovea.

In general, the above example illustrates the potential of empirical studies where hypotheses and assumptions about users' interaction can be tested against authentic user behavior (Holsanova, 2010). This concerns, for example, the myth that everything can be read at once, producers' assumptions about the placement of advertisement, designers' predictions about the inspection of photos versus information graphics and deep reading of articles, hypotheses and predictions coming from various theories concerning the role of saliency, composition, as well as suggestions for how to improve and redesign multimodal messages.

Eye movement measurements

As we have seen above, eye movements give us insight into the allocation of visual attention in terms of which elements (letters, words, parts of images) are fixated, for how long, in what order and how often (Holsanova, 2008). The direction of eye movements and the direction of attention are interconnected (Schneider and Deubel, 1995; Theeuwes et al., 1998) and eye fixations have been considered a boundary between perception and cognition, since they overtly indicate that information was acquired (Just and Carpenter, 1980). Eye movements "provide an unobtrusive, sensitive, real-time behavioral index of ongoing visual and cognitive processing" (Henderson and Ferreira, 2004: 18). In other words, eye movements offer us a "window on the mind" (Holsanova, 2001, 2008).

Where we look in a scene is partly determined by the scene constraints and driven by low-level image features, such as luminance, contrast, edge density, color and motion (Itti and Koch, 2000). But our way of perceiving objects in a scene is also triggered by high-level cognitive factors, such as our expectations, interests, intentions, task, goal and previous knowledge. "Visual perception […] is not a passive recording of stimulus material but an active concern of the mind" (Arnheim, 1969: 37). The influence and interaction between bottom-up and top-down factors is the subject of a current debate in the field (Nyström and Holmqvist, 2008; Foulsham and Underwood, 2008; Harding and Bloj, 2010).

Ecology or control?

Eye-tracking methodology allows for both explorative and experimental studies (for more detail see Holmqvist *et al.*, 2011). By conducting explorative studies, researchers can trace the interaction in the situational context where it usually occurs, providing ecological validity. On the other hand, they cannot obtain definite conclusions about the effects that caused the behavior. More conclusive results can be achieved when researchers test concrete predictions or assumptions derived from the theory against users' interaction with the material (Holsanova *et al.*, 2006), compare concrete producers'/designers' expectations with authentic users' behavior (Wartenberg and Holmqvist, 2005), or test alternative presentations that have been designed on the basis of theory-driven hypotheses (Holsanova *et al.*, 2009). In experimental studies, researchers use operationalizations, testable predictions and control for one aspect at a time (by ruling out all other aspects). For example, in carefully designed controlled experiments it is possible to investigate in a systematic way the role of individual differences and expertise, the role of the task or instruction and the role of bottom-up and top-down processes for the reception of multimodal messages (Holsanova, 2012). Experimental studies offer more conclusive answers about what caused the effect observed in the behavior. On the other hand, they often have less ecological validity. An alternative is to create a balance between ecological validity and experimental control. This can be achieved by using authentic materials with embedded experimental conditions (design alternatives), by using a realistic scenario, and by letting the user interact freely in a non-restrictive setting (Holsanova *et al.*, 2009). This means that we get relatively strong results while we are able at the same time to generalize to natural situations of use.

Application areas

Apart from traditional areas of reading research (Rayner, 1998), visual search (Viviani, 1990) and scene perception (Henderson, 2007), eye-tracking methodology has so far been applied in the context of multimodal research in the following areas:

- *Printed and digital media*, in particular how readers interact with newspapers, net papers and reading tablets, and how they browse the web (Bucher and Schumacher, 2006; Küpper, 1989; Garcia and Stark, 1991; Hansen, 1994; Widman and Polansky, 1990; Holsanova and Holmqvist, 2004; Holmqvist and Wartenberg, 2005; Holsanova *et al.*, 2006, 2008; Holmqvist *et al.*, 2003). However, there are still relatively few eye-tracking studies that investigate readers' interaction with various media in a systematic way.
- *Visual communication and advertisement*, in particular how users integrate text, pictures and graphics (Holmqvist *et al.*, 2003; Holsanova *et al.*, 2006, 2009, Holsanova, 2010), how they read cartoons (Carroll *et al.*, 1992), how they perceive advertisements and how much visual attention they devote to text and images both in printed media (Lundqvist and Holmqvist, 2001; Radach *et al.*, 2003; Rayner *et al.*, 2001, 2008) and online (Sandberg *et al.*, 2011; Simola, 2011; Gidlöf *et al.*, 2012; Holmberg, forthcoming). Apart from that, d'Ydewalle and De Bruyckner (2007) studied visual behavior of children and adults watching subtitled

television programs and Morrow *et al.*, (2012) investigated how older adults comprehend and learn from multimodal health materials and focused on the role of pre-existing knowledge for processing of such multimodal messages. There is a huge potential and a great need for empirical studies in this application area.

- *Design and education*, in particular how users and learners attend to information from multi-representational sources such as text, images, animations and textbook layout and whether they succeed in finding relevant parts of text and pictures and can integrate them. For example, Hegarty and Just have shown what role diagrams play in comprehension of scientific text (Hegarty and Just, 1993) and how students switch between related parts of text and diagrams (Hegarty and Just, 1993). Hannus and Hyönä (1999) investigated how 10-year-old elementary school children integrate text and images in biology textbooks. Eitel *et al.* (2011) studied how brief initial inspection of a picture may foster comprehension of text. Another issue concerns the way learners perceive and comprehend instruction materials that include cues (Folker *et al.*, 2005) or that are redesigned according to principles derived from multimedia learning theory (Holsanova *et al.*, 2009; Schmidt-Weigand *et al.*, 2010; Cierniak *et al.*, 2009; Johnson and Mayer, 2012). There is a growing body of empirical studies investigating perception and integration of text, images and graphics in this application area.
- *Communication and multimodal interaction*, in particular situations when communicative partners use speech, gestures, body language, facial expressions, and drawing (Holsanova *et al.*, 2008), as well as a field of user interaction with multimodal systems. Few studies have been conducted so far (but see Qvarfort, 2004; Gullberg and Holmqvist, 1999; Bucher and Niemann, 2012; Sandgren *et al.*, 2012; Richardson and Dale, 2005). These areas deserve to be focused on more extensively in future research.
- *Problem solving*, in particular how learners integrate text, illustrations and diagrams, how they mentally animate and visualize problems. Only a few studies have used eye-tracking methodology to examine comprehension and problem-solving from pictures and text (Hegarty, 1992; Hegarty and Just, 1993; Hannus and Hyönä, 1999; Freksa and Bertel, 2007; Nyström and Ögren, 2012).
- *Decision making*, in particular the issue of how eye movements unfold over the course of the decision process in a natural environment (including attentional shifts towards the chosen object) and whether it is possible to identify functional stages in the decision process (Russo and Leclerc, 1994; Gidlöf *et al.*, 2013). In this application area, there is a growing concern to take eye-movement research from the laboratory into the "real world" so that findings can be better generalized to natural situations.

Potentials of eye-tracking methodology

Eye-tracking methodology can be used in various ways in research on multimodality. First, it can be used as a processual measure providing a detailed account of the underlying perceptual and cognitive processes (Scheiter and Van Gog, 2009). We can infer what attracts users' attention and what does not, what items have been attended to, in what order, for how long and how carefully. Frequent transitions between parts of text and images are indicative of comparison or integration. Second, eye-tracking data can serve as a cue for another process measure, for example for users' verbal reports about the ongoing activity (Van Gog *et al.*, 2005). Third, based on the knowledge of how users processed certain materials, eye-tracking data may help us to improve the design of multimedia materials and multimodal messages. Fourth, showing dynamic visualizations of eye movement data can be used as a pedagogical tool, as a basis for discussion and comparison of chosen problem-solving strategies and may thus enhance learners' metacognition (Jarodzka *et al.*,

2010; Holsanova *et al.*, 2012). Fifth, since it has been suggested that is possible to guide novices' attention based on expert eye movements, eye-tracking data (in particular dynamic scanpaths) may serve as an instruction for other users (Van Gog *et al.*, 2009). Sixth, eye-tracking methodology can help us to reveal stages of decision-making processes (Gidlöf *et al.*, 2013). Finally, there are approaches in development where eye movement data is used for on-line diagnostics and support.

Limitations of eye-tracking methodology

While eye movement analysis reveals what parts of the message have been attended to, when, how often and in what order, it does not tell us *why* these parts of the message have been fixated and focused on. Furthermore, there is a vagueness in the interpretation of eye movement measures: long fixation may indicate that the focused information was interesting for the reader, but it may also indicate that it was confusing or problematic for the reader and thus difficult to process. Similarly, so-called integrative saccades, i.e. oscillation between semantically related parts of text and images (Holsanova *et al.*, 2009), may be interpreted as attempts to integrate text and images, as a successful integration of both, or as problems with the integration. Another potential limitation is the vagueness in linking eye movement data to concepts. Eye tracking provides data concerning perceptual and cognitive processes through the allocation of visual attention but it does not tell us about recipients' understanding of the messages. We cannot conclude from the eye movement protocol alone what aspects and properties of the image element have been focused on, or at what level of abstraction. Visual fixation does not reveal which concept was associated with it, or what the viewer had in mind. We still need some kind of referential framework in order to infer the ideas and thoughts to which these fixations correspond. Finally, we cannot identify the focus of audio attention with an eye tracker.

Triangulation of methods

To overcome these limitations, a method triangulation is necessary as a complement to eye-tracking measurements (Holsanova, 2012). For instance, thanks to the combination of eye movement data and verbal protocols, the process of stepwise categorization, interpretation and reconceptualization of image elements and the image as a whole could be investigated (Holsanova, 2001, 2008, 2011). By combining eye-tracking protocols, verbal protocols, interviews, comprehension tests and questionnaires, we get more insights into the rationality behind the behavior, comprehension and interpretation of the material, attitudes, habits, preferences and problems concerning the interaction with multimodal messages in various media (Holsanova and Holmqvist, 2004, Holsanova *et al.*, 2006). With the help of cued retrospective reporting based on records of eye movements we can obtain a more comprehensive picture of the learning or task performance processes (Van Gog *et al.*, 2005a, 2005b; Holsanova and Holmberg, 2011). By combining iconology, eye-tracking and psychophysiological reaction measurements we can trace three processes: visual perception and attention, meaning attribution and emotional reactions to mass-mediated visuals (Müller *et al.*, 2012). In sum, integrated methods are preferable when studying reception aspects of visual communication and multimodality.

Production and reception perspectives on multimodality

In the following, we will come back to the distinction between production and reception perspective on multimodality. Cognitive studies applying eye-tracking methodology will be related to the three main streams of multimodality research, characterized by Carey Jewitt (Chapter 2 this volume), and illustrated by a few examples.

We can argue that the social semiotic multimodal analysis, the systemic functional approach (multimodal discourse analysis) and the multimodal interactional analysis are mainly production-oriented. The *production* view of multimodality emphasizes the interplay of various modes of representation and their contribution to the content of the message, what is called intersemiosis (O'Halloran *et al.*, 2012). This view is stimulus-oriented and concerns the sign-makers' choices of modes (language, images, gestures, body language, sounds, music) in order to achieve a certain effect. Seen from this perspective, producers and designers relate to their audiences – they form and adjust their messages either to a present recipient (in the case of face-to-face interaction) or form their messages according to how an imaginary or hypothetical recipient would perceive the material (e.g. in the case of printed media messages).

Reception of multimodality is closely connected to recipients' ability to select, attend to, and process information. Such empirical studies are therefore recipient-oriented, based on the users' ability to link information from different sources, to filter, select, sort information, as well as the ability to focus attention and to ignore (parts of) the message. In the end, it is the recipients who ultimately choose among the available information: what they want to explore, mentally process and interpret, in what order and how deeply (Holsanova, 2010).

Let us first compare the *social semiotic* approach to multimodality and the reception perspective in cognitively oriented eye-tracking studies. Whereas the social semiotic approach emphasizes the way meaning potentials are selected and orchestrated to make meaning in particular contexts, the interest of the cognitive research lies in how the selected meaning potentials and their orchestration have been perceived and interpreted by the recipients. Furthermore, whereas a text represents a window on its maker in the social semiotic approach (Jewitt, this volume), eye movement data serve as a window on the mind of the user, revealing perceptual and cognitive processes underlying users' interaction with the multimodal messages.

Let us illustrate the relation of the semiotic and cognitive approaches (and their possible fruitful combination) with one study. From the cognitive perspective, the following questions arise: Do newspaper pages have inherent reading paths? Are the entry points and reading paths suggested by the designer identical with the actual entry points and reading paths that the readers or users actually choose?

In order to answer these questions, Holsanova *et al.* (2006) extracted general assumptions about reading paths from Kress and Van Leeuwen's (1996) theoretical model of the meaning of composition in newspaper layout and compared these assumptions with actual reading behavior on newspaper spreads by means of eye-tracking methodology. Some assumptions about entry points and reading paths on a newspaper spread could be confirmed (i.e. readers followed elements linked by *framing* devices, readers generally looked for graphically *salient* elements such as headlines and photos). Some of the assumptions, however, could not be confirmed. For instance, readers did not scan the semiotic space before taking a closer look at certain units, and advertisements did not attract readers' attention despite salience in color and font size. By using their expectations and genre knowledge, readers have already learned to ignore advertisements (see Plate 20.2). This shows that users take an active part in the interpretation process (according to their goals and expectations) and are not merely affected by unconscious bottom-up processes. In perceptual and cognitive terms, this can be seen as a competition between *salience* and *relevance*.

Let us continue with the *systemic functional approach* (multimodal discourse analysis). While the emphasis of this approach lies on intersemiosis, i.e. on the question of how individual modes contribute to the meaning of the message, the main issue in the cognitive approach is how users choose and integrate modes when perceiving the message.

293

Within the systemic functional approach, several important issues have been addressed, including the question of how mathematical symbolism is integrated with images (O'Halloran, 2005), how text and images in school books relate and interact (Unsworth and Cléirigh, Chapter 12 this volume), and the question of whether meaning is built up as a series of functional units (Baldry, 2004). There are examples of eye-tracking studies that investigate these issues from a recipient's perspective. A recent study by Nyström and Ögren (2012) analyzed how mathematical symbols and images are perceived, conceptualized and comprehended by the learners. Another study presented in Holmqvist and Holmberg (2011) showed how mathematical formulas are used in mathematical problem-solving by students with backgrounds in humanities and technology. The perception of intermodal relations in textbooks has also recently been addressed (see below).

Theoretical accounts of how meaning is built up, in particular whether it follows a rank scale (Baldry, 2004), i.e. a hierarchical organization of elements, and whether it has a constituent structure (O'Toole, 1994), have been tested empirically and traced in the behavior of the recipients. Boeriis and Holsanova (2012) combine semiotic and cognitive approaches and present a new methodology for deriving the dynamics of visual segmentation in relation to the underlying cognitive processes. By means of eye-tracking methodology and verbal protocols, the authors show that visual segmentation – as suggested by the social semiotic approach – can be traced in the behavior of individual viewers who perceive images and create meaning. In particular, visual zooming is seen as perceptually, cognitively, grammatically and analytically relevant.

Last but not least, there is a future possibility to include eye-tracking data in multimodal analysis software that contains a grammar for language, image, audio resources, and their inter-semiotic relations (O'Halloran et al., 2012). These data would then show which information source was attended to and processed, how various modes were integrated and which meaning potentials were currently in the focus of recipients' attention.

Let us finally relate empirical eye-tracking studies to the *multimodal interactional analysis*. The emphasis in the latter perspective is on how a variety of modes are brought into social interaction. Researchers explore the way people employ gestures, gaze, posture, movement, space and objects in the context of their situated interaction and co-construction of meaning. From a cognitive perspective, one could ask: Which of the modes is attended to by the partner/recipient? How does the partner link and integrate the attended modes in order to create meaning? How does the alignment of speech, gaze, gestures, etc. of the partners influence joint attention and comprehension?

Eye-tracking studies in this area of research are still very rare, but there are some examples of studies that partially address these issues. Gullberg and Holmqvist (1999) studied gestures occurring during speech and showed that listeners' visual attention is affected by speakers' gaze behavior: When speakers look at their own gestures, listeners tend to fixate them as well. Sandgren et al. (2012) investigated gaze behavior in child dialogues, in particular the timing of gazes in referential communication tasks requiring description of faces. The result was that turn shifts, requests for clarification and back channeling significantly predicted that the executors would gaze at the face of the task director. The authors conclude that the significantly higher association of gaze behavior with requests for previously unmentioned information indicates that gaze may be used to emphasize the verbal content. Bucher and Niemann (2012) studied the reception of PowerPoint presentations and investigated how meaning is constituted by different modes. Due to the co-presence of the different modes, the audience has to choose and integrate the information coming from various sources. The authors used eye-tracking methodology, knowledge tests and interviews to explore the dynamics of attention allocation in relation to comprehension and integration of various modes. In particular, they focused on performed referring actions – pointing, gestures, referring utterances – that link the verbal and the visual parts. Finally, Richardson and Dale (2005) investigated the coupling between a speaker's and a listener's eye movements. First, some participants talked about a television show while viewing pictures of actors on a screen. Later, other participants listened to these monologues while viewing the same screen. The results of a cross-recurrence analysis showed that a listener's eye movements most closely matched a speaker's eye movements. The authors conclude that just as eye movements reflect the mental state of an individual, the coupling between a speaker's and a listener's eye movements reflects the success of their communication.

Reception perspective: design principles and attentional guidance

In most complex materials, there are no explicit cues about relations and links between text and illustration to instruct the reader. When the eyes reach a certain point in the text, it is the reader who has to discover these semantic relations and referential links between the text, images and graphics.

The question then arises, how complex materials should be designed in order to guide and support the users and make it cognitively easier for them to integrate information from different sources. In the area of multimedia learning theory, cognitive load theory and instruction design, researchers have formulated principles reducing cognitive load, promoting text-image integration and supporting efficient learning (Chandler and Sweller, 1991; Sweller and Chandler, 1994; Mayer, 2001, 2005). Apart from design principles, there are other means that help readers to orient and navigate in the material, such as the rhetorical organization of the material, meta-textual, paratextual and graphical means. Also, various other cues can be added in order to guide users' attention to the relevant parts of text and graphics (see below).

We will have a closer look at three design principles (multimedia principle, spatial contiguity principle, and signaling principle) and some other means of attentional guidance. The *multimedia principle* states that students learn better from pictures and words than from pictures alone (Mayer, 2009), but all graphics are not equally effective. In an eye-tracking study conducted by Sung and Mayer (2012), a short online lesson was presented for students. The presentation contained instructive graphics (directly relevant to the instructional goal), seductive graphics (highly interesting but not directly relevant), decorative graphics (neutral but not directly relevant), or no graphics. Students who received any kind of graphic reported significantly higher satisfaction than the no graphics group. However, on a recall post-test, students who received instructive graphics performed significantly better than the other three groups. The authors conclude that adding relevant graphics to words helps learning but adding irrelevant graphics does not.

Nyström and Ögren (2012) investigated how the illustrations are utilized during mathematical problem-solving and whether they are beneficial to comprehension. They collected eye movement data and performance scores (true or false answers) from students who solved eight problems in vector calculus (see Plate 20.3). Twenty students solved illustrated problems, whereas another sixteen students solved the same problems, but without the illustrations. The results showed no overall performance benefit for illustrated problems even though they were clearly visually attended. However, students were more likely to answer that the question was true given an illustrated problem. Nyström and Ögren (2012) suggest that illustrations persuade students that an answer is true, irrespective of whether or not it actually is. Similar effects have been reported by McCabe and Caster (2008), namely that articles accompanied by brain images received higher credibility.

In connection with the persuasive effect of pictures, let us mention so-called "seductive details" in multimodal presentations. Moreno and Mayer state:

> Previous studies examining how students learn scientific explanations from text and illustrations found that adding extraneous sentences or illustrations, which are called *seductive*

details, resulted in poorer retention and transfer performance, even when the added material was intended to be interesting or entertaining.

(Moreno and Mayer, 2000: 118)

They point out the role of coherence for learning from instructional texts. Engebretsen, on the other hand, discusses the concepts of cohesion and tension in multimodal rhetoric and argues that all texts need both cohesion and tension in order to be understandable and engaging.

Tension is the inversion of cohesion, and is based on formal and semantic contrast, distance and discontinuity. While cohesion builds the textual platform for comprehension, tension forces the reader to react, engage, draw conclusions – in other words, actively interact with the text, which is also a central condition of a fruitful learning process.

(Engebretsen, 2012: 2)

It remains to be shown how this interesting issue can be operationalized and tested from a reception perspective.

The *spatial contiguity principle* states that "people learn more deeply from a multimedia message when corresponding words and pictures are presented near rather than far from each other on the page or screen" (Mayer, 2005: 183). Similar suggestions have also been made in the rhetorical tradition. Schriver (1997), for example, recommends semantically grouping related information into reader-oriented functional units called "rhetorical clusters" (e.g. verbal instruction with illustration). The design with verbal and visual information placed physically close to each other has been tested empirically with the help of eye-tracking methodology (Van Gog and Scheiter, 2010). Let us mention two studies in more detail.

Holsanova *et al.* (2009) studied the effects of the spatial contiguity principle in a naturalistic study of reading information graphics. A pair of information graphics (separated vs. integrated format) have been designed and embedded into a newspaper prototype. They contained the same text, the same illustrations, but had a different overall layout. Two authentic-looking newspapers were used consisting of 15 spreads with built-in information graphics that were subject to manipulation. Informants read one of the newspapers at their own pace. The data clearly show that different spatial layouts have a significant effect on readers' eye movement behavior. As we can see in Plate 20.4(a), in the separated format, readers do not switch between text and graphics. Instead, they treat them separately as two different units, and almost no integration occurs. In contrast, the *integrated* format with shorter physical distance between text and graphics facilitates integration (Plate 20.4(b)). It makes it easier for the reader to find the correspondences between referents in the text and in the illustration, and to mentally integrate information from the two different sources. The authors conclude that an *integrated format* with spatial contiguity between text and illustrations prolongs reading and facilitates text–graphics integration.

Johnson and Mayer (2012) investigated the perception of multimedia presentation, either as an integrated presentation where text was presented near its corresponding area of the diagram, and included additional labels identifying each part, or as a separated presentation where the text was presented below the diagrams, or as a legend below the diagrams. The result was that the readers of the integrated presentations made significantly more eye movements from text to diagram than the readers of separated format. When the learning outcome was measured, the integrated groups significantly outperformed the separated groups. The authors conclude that spatial contiguity encourages more attempts to integrate text and pictures and enables more successful integration of both.

Finally, the *signaling principle* states that "people learn more deeply from a multimedia message when cues are added that highlight the organization of the essential material" (Mayer, 2005: 183). Several signaling techniques can be used to guide the learner's attention, such as providing headings, lists of the main steps and a spoken emphasis on keywords. Further, Holsanova *et al.* (2009) showed that a coherent, conceptually pre-processed spatial format can guide the readers and contribute to easier processing of the materials. Last but not least, users' attention can be guided by textual reference to the illustration, use of labels, highlighting of keywords, graphical means such as arrows, pointers and speech bubbles, or by color coding (De Koning *et al.*, 2007; Folker *et al.*, 2005; Jeung *et al.*, 1997; Kalyuga *et al.*, 1999; Mautone and Mayer, 2007). Let us have a look at one example.

Folker *et al.* (2005) used color coding to make references between text and illustration more explicit (Plate 20.5). Twenty students read a textbook passage describing mitotic cell division. In the color-coding condition, keywords in the text and labels identifying parts of the illustration were of the same color. Participants in this group were significantly faster in processing the material than participants who had no explicit references between text and illustration.

Conclusions

From the above examples it follows that users and learners need to be supported in extracting the relevant information from the visualization and guided as to how best to deploy their perceptual and cognitive resources (Scheiter *et al.*, 2008). This support can be provided either by guiding learners' attention towards its relevant aspects or by teachers' instruction that similar information is conveyed in both text and illustrations and that comprehension is improved when a text segment and its accompanying illustration are studied together (Hannus and Hyönä, 1999). This would in turn improve students' competencies in dealing with visualizations and integration of text and images.

To sum up, there is a need for empirical studies of users' interaction with complex multimodal messages. The focus of cognitive research concerning the reception of multimodality lies on users' active role in the interaction with multimodal messages. This strand investigates general and individual patterns in the reception of multimodality, particularly factors influencing the perception and interpretation process, such as users' interests, attitudes, goals and motives, prior knowledge, experience, individual preferences, emotions and expertise. The perception and interpretation of multimodal messages are seen as an interactive meeting between the users, the multimodal message and the situation context (Holsanova, 2010). The meaning is thus not universal but co-created by the individual recipients who attend to and integrate various modes of representation from the messages (Holsanova 2013 in press). To conclude, the reception of multimodality is a valuable perspective that deserves more scholarly attention in future research, preferably using an interdisciplinary framework and integrated methods.

Acknowledgments

I would like to thank the Eye Tracking Group at Lund Humanities Lab for their comments on previous versions of the manuscript. The work has been supported by the Linnaeus Center for Thinking in Time: Cognition, Communication and Learning (CCL) at Lund University, funded by the Swedish Research Council (grant no. 349-2007-8695).

Note

1 It should be noted that the terminology varies across disciplines. Whereas 'multimodality' primarily concerns sensory modalities (vision, hearing, touch, smell and taste) and focuses on the integration of information across the sense modalities (so-called crossmodal interaction) in the psychological tradition, it denotes culturally shared set of resources for meaning-making in the social semiotic tradition (Kress, Chapter 4 this volume). Researchers in the social semiotic tradition use the terms *semiotic resources* or *modal resources* for space, color, gesture, gaze, body posture and movements, sound, voice and music, image, mathematical symbolism, written and spoken language, etc. Thus, 'mode' in this tradition includes both sensory information and format of representation. Within educational psychology and instructional design, scholars use the term *multiple representations* for diagrams, graphs, formulas, symbols, words, gestures, videos, models, pictures and sounds (Ainsworth, 1999; Schnotz and Bannert, 2003), they study *multimedia learning* (Mayer, 2001, 2005) and speak about *multi-representational sources* (Scheiter and van Gog, 2009). Finally, in HCI, research on *multimodal interfaces* includes interaction via speech, pen, touch, manual gestures, gaze, head and body movements (Oviatt, 1999).

Further reading

Hannus, M. and Hyönä, J. (1999) 'Utilization of illustrations during learning of science textbook passages among low- and high-ability children.' *Contemporary Educational Psychology* 24(2): pp. 95–123.

Holsanova, J., ed. (2012) Methodologies for Multimodal Research. Special Issue of *Visual Communication* 11(3), Sage.

Holsanova, J. and Nord, A. (2010) 'Multimodal design: Media structures media principles and users meaning-making in printed and digital media.' In Bucher, H-J., Gloning, T. and Lehnen, K. eds. *Neue Medie – neue Formate: Ausdifferenzierung und Konvergenz in der Medienkommunikation*, Frankfurt: Campus: pp. 81–103.

Holsanova, J., Rahm, H. and Holmqvist, K. (2006) 'Entry points and reading paths on newspaper spreads: Comparing a semiotic analysis with eye-tracking measurements.' *Visual Communication* 5: pp. 65–93.

Scheiter, K. and Van Gog, T. (2009) 'Using eye tracking in applied research to study and stimulate the processing of information from multi-representational sources.' *Applied Cognitive Psychology* 23: pp. 1209–14. Published online 23 December 2008 at http://www.interscience.wiley.com, doi: 10.1002/acp.1524.

Van Gog, T. and Scheiter, K. (2010) 'Eye tracking as a tool to study and enhance multimedia learning.' *Learning and Instruction* 20: pp. 95–99. doi:10.1016/j.learninstruc.2009.02.009.

21

Representations in practices

A socio-cultural approach to multimodality in reasoning

Jonas Ivarsson, Jonas Linderoth and Roger Säljö

Introduction

In human history, representations play a significant role for the development of knowledge, skills and identities and for all the various kinds of social practices that go into community building and social life in general. As Luria (1981) and many others have pointed out, people do not just live *in* the world, we can also communicate *about* it (cf. Cole, 1996: 120). A necessary prerequisite for being able to communicate about the world is that we have access to symbolic representations by means of which we can represent, categorize, configure and comment upon our experiences. Such resources allow us to distance ourselves from the world, and at the same time we become able to perspectivize what we see and hear *as* something, as instances of something we are already familiar with, or as novelties with some interesting, previously un-noticed, qualities. In other words, representations serve as resources for communicating and meaning-making, and they are essential to all human practices including perception, remembering and thinking and other psychological activities. What we refer to as cognition are activities of meaning-making made possible largely through the use of representations.

In the socio-cultural tradition (Wertsch, 1985, 2007; Vygotsky, 1986), the idea of mediation and mediated action is fundamental. The concept of mediation was originally introduced by Vygotsky to argue against the simplistic notion of human behaviour as simple responses to stimuli in the outside world. The idea of stimulus–response connections as the core of human learning and development was the basic assumption of the Pavlovian reflexology (and, in the West, of Watsonian behaviourism) which dominated psychology from the 1920s and during the decades to follow. To Vygotsky this kind of reductionism was a significant element of what led him to talk about the crisis in psychology and the failure of psychological research to contribute to the understanding of the interrelationships between culture, individual activities and what he referred to as "higher psychological processes" (Vygotsky, 1978) (i.e., learning, remembering, aesthetic experience and voluntary forms of behaviour). If we want to understand such genuinely human phenomena, psychological investigations must focus on the interaction between the child and significant others in the socio-cultural environment; mental processes are social in origin and they are mediated through interaction.

Mediation implies that humans, unlike other living creatures, think and act in "a roundabout way" (Vygotsky, 1994: 61), that is, by means of cultural artefacts that have evolved over time – symbolic representations (including linguistic tools) and artefacts. We think and act in social practices by means of concepts such as triangle, centimetre and democracy. In a similar vein, we use physical artefacts such as kitchen utensils, telephones and a range of other prosthetic devices in our daily activities. This distinction between artefacts and intellectual tools (the latter Vygotsky referred to as psychological tools, cf. Kozulin, 2003), by the way, is not to be taken as a categorical difference between a material and a non-material, ideational world (Cole, 1996). On the contrary, we use the alphabet (an intellectual or symbolic tool) and paper and pencil (artefacts) to write, and nowadays many of us use a global postioning system (GPS) navigator loaded with maps and symbols to take us from A to B in an unfamiliar environment. *Re*-presentation is achieved by combining symbolic tools and physical resources. On closer inspection, mediation always, at some stage, relies on materiality.

The tools for mediating the world that we encounter have their origin in society and in human activities; they emerge through practices that extend over time. All readers of this text know how to use expressions such as per cent, circle and virtuality in an intelligible manner in conversations. Through socialization, we appropriate the symbolic tools that are functional for meaning-making in social interaction. We may not understand them fully or know their origin and development (i.e. their socio-genesis), but we know how to use them "for all practical purposes" as ethnomethodologists put it. It is by appropriating such cultural resources that human beings are socialized into communities inhabiting, and continuously developing, symbolic universes, modes of expression, inscriptions and material artefacts. "As children are drawn into cultures, 'what is to hand', becomes more and more that which the culture values and therefore makes readily available" as Kress (1997a: 13) puts it.

Multimodality, language and activity: a socio-cultural interpretation

In the context of the emphasis on considering issues of multimodality in human communication expressed by many scholars (Jewitt, 2005; Kress, 2003b; Kress and Van Leeuwen, 1996/2006), there is a reaction against the dominant role that language and discourse play in studies of meaning-making and, perhaps, in studies of cultural practices in general. This critique is fuelled by the current developments in digital technology, where other modes of mediating events and communicating emerge as prominent in many contexts: "we make signs from lots of different 'stuff'" and not just through language, as Kress (1997: 13) puts it. In the socio-cultural tradition there is a strong emphasis on the decisive role that language (spoken and written) plays as a symbolic resource. Thus, there is an apparent contradiction between the "multimodal programme" and the sociocultural tradition in the attempts to study meaning-making and cultural production and reproduction.

We would, however, like to preface the presentation of some examples from our own work on issues of multimodality by commenting on these differences. From a socio-cultural perspective, the significance of other forms of mediation is readily accepted. Some of the earliest forms of symbolic expressions that we know in history are artefacts such as rock paintings, engravings on tools and ornamental jewellery to be carried in ceremonies, i.e. resources for communicating that were not directly based on linguistic mediation (although we would argue that, most likely, meaning-making practices involving conceptual mediation and analysis must have played a role when they were produced; but this is another matter). In fact, it is not until late in history that signs that are connected to linguistic (and numeric) systems appear, or, in other words, that inscriptions began to emulate speech. Put differently, in the socio-genesis of symbol systems and signs, images preceded representations of linguistic units such as words, sentences and phonemes; people represented what they saw or imagined (Lewis-Williams, 2002) long before they began writing words and well before they began to deconstruct words into smaller elements (Olson, 1994).

It is also obvious that other forms of meaning-making are significant in human development. Drawings, pictures and other symbolic tools are not second-order representations to language, but rather important elements of the human repertoire for meaning-making and for the building up of a social memory relevant for specific practices. One obvious example of this is the development of the techniques of making charts and maps to be used in navigation. The particular manner in which we now mediate the world through such artefacts has a long history which includes the development of projection techniques, the design of conceptual constructions (such as latitude and longitude) and even political deliberations and considerations (such as, for instance, no longer making Jerusalem the centre of the world map) (cf. Williams, 1992).

There is, however, some sense in which verbal language holds a special position in the sociocultural interpretation of mediation. Indeed, Vygotsky's famous dictum of language as "the tool of tools" testifies directly to this central role ascribed to linguistic mediation. Through the origin of this perspective in developmental psychology, a fundamental question is that of the connection between the biological, social and cultural dimensions of human development. The problem can be understood as a matter of how a biological creature such as a newborn child appropriates the cultural tools of his immediate and, eventually, more distant environment, to become a full-fledged participant in social interaction, equipped with a range of interactional and semiotic skills. In these processes of socialization, or (to put it more bluntly) in this process of humanization, language plays a fundamental role. In the words of the evolutionary psychologist Merlin Donald (2001), culture "hijacks" the human brain largely by infiltrating it with cultural categories and ways of understanding the world, and the most important mechanism by means of which this is achieved is language. In endless communicative encounters, we learn to structure and categorize what we hear and see by means of linguistic resources, and learning and development result in an increasing linguistic and symbolic control of our experiences (Rommetveit, 1985). In mundane, everyday conversations and interactional practices we re-present the world and re-call our past experiences and make them relevant to our present concerns.

Thus, with respect to the issues of what constitutes a mode, and in what ways modes differ, we would like to suggest a view where speech, writing, images, graphs and other symbolic resources are seen as elements of human repertoires for externalizing and objectifying experiences and for communicating about them (Säljö, 2005). These forms of mediation are interrelated, and they interact in complex ways in almost all kinds of social practices. Thus, our perceptions of a painting are shaped by discursively mediated ideas and conventions. We understand why the works of Picasso or the impressionists are interesting and innovative, since we know something about how they challenged contemporary traditions of painting. In a similar vein, our readings of a map of the world are informed by conventions and canons of representation (Wartofsky, 1979, 1983) for how one makes a projection of the world in two dimensions that have evolved over centuries. In more specialized activities in society, nurses and physicians learn how to read X-ray images and images from PET-scanners by being taught by more experienced colleagues what there is to "see" in what is represented. This learning is embedded in visual and discursive practices, where the two modes build on, and presuppose, each other in a successive shaping of the abilities of the novice to single out what is relevant to attend to (Ivarsson and Säljö, 2005).

301

Illuminating contemporary studies of such shaping of visual perception have been carried out by Goodwin (1994, 1997, 2001) in the context of doing science. What Goodwin shows in one study is how archaeologists engage in a particular kind of "seeing" when looking at objects and artefacts when excavating. In a different study, he illustrates how indicators in scientific measurements rely on users' ability to identify quite subtle variations in what there is to "see" when looking at a specially prepared piece of string serving as a test of chemical reactions in water. In the latter case, Goodwin (1997) demonstrates how perception has to be shaped in order for a less experienced member of an exploration team to see something as a particular kind of black, and to distinguish the relevant kind of blackness from other kinds of black. This shaping of vision in which one learns to discriminate between "black" and what is referred to by the experienced members of the team as "jet black" takes place through situated practices where language plays a crucial role as a mediating tool when observing artefacts.

In a totally different setting, these intimate interrelationships between speech, writing and images as resources for communication in human practices have been documented in the fascinating work by the archeologist and art historian Schmandt-Besserat (2007). What Schmandt-Besserat shows in her studies of the socio-genesis of literacy in the ancient Near East is how "writing shaped art" (p. 15) in the sense that pictures and images on pottery, glyptic art and on wall and floor paintings changed in character and composition as literacy spread as a mode of communication. Basically this transformation implies a shift where "art benefited from the paradigm developed by writing to communicate information" (p. 25). Thus, in the "late fourth millennium B. C., pottery paintings left behind preliterate repetitious animal motifs and glyptic abandoned its circular topsy-turvy compositions in order to tell stories" (p. 102). While "preliterate painters tried hard to achieve the utmost stylization, those of the literate period aim to be as informative as possible" (p. 24), and they attempted to tell stories by means of images. A psychologically interesting consequence of this development is that "preliterate pottery compositions formed an over-all pattern meant to be apprehended as a whole, or *globally*", while "those of the literate period were to be viewed *analytically*" (p. 24), i.e. as portraying events, dramatic episodes and social relationships that emerged as the various elements of the composition were viewed in relationship to each other. At the technical level of producing images, this implies that elements such as the design of space, the location of characters and their size and relative position began to be used as indicators of importance, hierarchical relationships (size as an indicator of rank), status and so on in order to narrate events. Thus, in "the literate period, 'reading' images became akin to reading a text" (p. 25). Or, in other words, the linearity of text and narrative began to have implications for the manners in which images were organized.

What is interesting for our purposes in Schmandt-Besserat's in-depth account of the intricate and dynamic relationships between image-making and writing in this formative period of the development of resources of objectification of human experiences is how the two visual modes interact with each other and assume different, and often complementary, functions. Thus, not only did written narratives provide models for art, there were also consequences in the other direction. Inscriptions on art objects, such as names and other messages, could take on a life of their own when presented in the context of a stele or a statue. The inscriptions would do one kind of job (for instance preserving the name of the king or the deity for eternity), while the material artefact would provide other symbolic information regarding the status of the person, his wealth and other qualities (for instance through its size or the nature of the material used for making a statue). Thus, the different symbolic elements of a statue such as its size, the material used, the posture of the person or deity portrayed and the inscriptions all contributed to the meaning-making.

In the following we want to approach the issue of multimodality from a socio-cultural perspective by means of a few examples intended to illustrate the interdependencies between modes. The point of our examples is to argue for the value of studying representations when they are part of human practices in which meaning-making is contingent on what, in Kress' terms, "is to hand" through different modes. Thus our point of departure to some extent follows Wittgenstein's (1953) dictum of studying meaning-making not in the representations themselves (be they words, images or something else), but rather in how they are used in social practices within activities and how they interact (Mäkitalo and Säljö, 2009).

By means of three brief empirical cases, we will illustrate how discourse is integral to meaning-making in multimodal settings, i.e. the point is one of showing how language fulfils a bridging function when engaging in multimodal communication. The first two examples are taken from contexts of gaming, and the third one is from a particular kind of practice that is central to the training of architects at university. Our ambition is to show how concepts emerge in practices as situated responses to what is happening in a world of non-linguistic representations. We also want to argue that the emergence of such concepts may be followed by a process of canonization and institutionalization, which eventually may result in a situation where a particular way of speaking and structuring the world will be seen as a more or less stable element of a practice that will be shared by those engaged in it. Once these conceptual innovations have been sedimented and become part of the established practices of meaning-making, new members approaching the specific knowledge community need to master them in order to appear competent. This is the cumulative element of language as a tool for meaning-making.

Illustration 1: gaming and the invention of concepts

The first illustration of this dynamic interplay between modes comes from the practice of playing computer and video games. Such digital games are commonly described as examples of interactive media with a high degree of multimodality in the sense that they build on combinations of images, animations, texts and sound. However, at the same time such games, when viewed as practices that people engage in, can also be conceived as social environments temporarily inhabited by players who interact with and against each other in order to achieve some built-in goal. When studying such gaming as a practice that people engage in, it becomes evident that discursive activities play a crucial role for the players' ability to play and to co-ordinate their actions. For instance, gamers can be seen to invent concepts and categories that they need in order to talk about the problems at hand in this multimodal practice (Linderoth, 2004). In the first brief excerpt, two children, Elin and Bea, are playing an action game in a shared virtual world. They are sitting next to each other in front of a television set. The screen image is split in two halves so that each player can see the game world through their avatar's perspective. When we enter the discussion in Excerpt 1, the two children have had some problems finding each other in the game world.

Excerpt 1

1. *Elin*:   Are you still in the sand-path?
2.   *(Bea's avatar has just entered a tunnel with a floor made of sand)*
3. *Bea*:   Yes
4.   *(Elin's avatar approaches the entrance to the tunnel)*
5. *Elin*:   Bea stay there, I will come to the sand-path now, stay there.

From this event and throughout the entire game session, the children make use of their self-invented concept "sand-path" in order to find and keep track of each other. This expression becomes a mediating tool for co-ordinating their movements in the game. By using the "sand-path" as a landmark, they can find each other when they need. Later on in the game session, the children make up another concept.

Excerpt 2

1. *Elin*:   These guns are not good, they are useless, right?
2. *Bea*:   Yes
3. *Elin*:   Aren't they bad, they are so useless.
4. *Bea*:   Yes but not that spin-weapon, did you think that one was bad?
5. *Elin*:   No, no the spin-weapon is awesome.

Here the girls are commenting on the qualities of different game weapons and come up with the concept of a "spin-weapon" in order to refer to a certain kind of science-fiction weapon appearing in the game. Both these examples illustrate how gaming as a practice is highly conducive to, in fact sometimes forces, the players to create new concepts as mediating tools in order to accomplish a shared understanding that enables them to go on with what they are doing. Purposive action in the animated virtual world where co-operation is assumed to take place relies on co-ordination by means of language.

Illustration 2: backspawning and hillhugging

The two examples above show concepts or categorizations that are very local and with a low degree of complexity. They are used by the players to localize each other in this specific game and to co-ordinate further action in a fairly immediate sense and with instant feedback. But the development of such new concepts can of course be more complex and general, and they may point towards more generic sets of behaviours or courses of action that apply to a wider variety of games. Many non-gamers have probably experienced that gaming is embedded in a particular kind of "lingo", a social language of its own, to use Bakhtinian parlance (Bakhtin, 1986), and they may have heard gamers use terms and expressions that are incomprehensible to outsiders. From a socio-genetic perspective, this type of game discourse may have emerged from the type of game practices we observed Bea and Elin engage in. Through sustained interaction in online gaming environments, there is a setting in which local conceptual innovations may live on to become permanent parts of an established tool-kit of communicative resources. As an illustration, one can look at the discourse practices used in the context of a battle game such as *Enemy Territory Quake Wars*. In this online multiplayer game, terms such as "backspawning" and "hillhugging" can be heard in voice-chats and read in the game-chat. To backspawn implies to let your avatar reincarnate at a point in the game world that is further away from the frontline; something that in certain situations can be beneficial for your team. "Hillhugging" refers to a type of behaviour where a player hides in the outskirts of the game world and tries to snipe his opponents, even though there are other more important tasks to attend to for the team. Hillhugging, therefore, is not appreciated, and in the game you may hear and read expressions like "work as a team, no hillhugging here or you will be kicked out".

That concepts and categories emerge from local practices, and then become sedimented and canonized within a certain discursive activity is, following a socio-cultural perspective, not unique for gaming; rather, this is an illustration of how language develops in the context of new activities and in response to other modes of representation. Since gaming is a rather new practice, this process becomes visible. In terms of how to theorize multimodality, these examples illustrate how actions in the highly graphical game world are constantly mediated through discursive practices; when interacting, and in order for there to be a game, the players constantly verbalize what they see in order to co-ordinate their activities and achieve goals. At an abstract level, images, animations and talk may be conceived as different modalities, but when engaged in practices, the distinction becomes blurred; talk is a mediating tool for acting in the graphical world, but it does its work by profiting on what is available through other modes.

While our first two illustrations show a practice in which the participants themselves need to invent some of the terminology they use, our third and final illustration shows a more common pattern. Here the participants are expected to acquire skills and terminology that are already established parts of a social language, i.e. they take over ways of narrating, thinking and producing and using images that are constitutive elements of highly specialized institutional practices. The particular context we will use as an illustration is learning some of the skills that go into reasoning and working like an architect.

Illustration 3: seeing the cityscape and seeing by means of the concept of cityscape

In our third empirical illustration, two parties are intensely involved in discussing an image within the context of education of architects at university (Figure 21.1). The specific situation is the so-called critique[1] (also known as the "crit" or design review), which is an important

Figure 21.1 Architectural critique as a communicative practice.

element of the training of architects. In this institutionalized practice, the students present their finished projects to an audience of professors, peers and experienced practising architects called upon to participate. The projects are generally, as in the present case, reported as an assembly of images, texts, floor plans, sections, elevations and other projections, which are printed on a few A3 sheets and posted on a wall. The posters, then, function as the material ground from which the students will receive feedback and critique on their work from the members of the audience. Thus, this is a formative moment where the students document their learning, and where they have to defend their solutions to the various dilemmas that characterize architectural design.

In the example used here as an illustration, the students had to solve the task of designing a number of ateliers. These should be placed on a specific building site, a real place in the city of the university. Just before our empirical illustration begins, the student, Anna, has finished the presentation of her project. One of the teachers, Bill, begins his critique/commentary. He does so by focusing on one of her images. The image in question is a watercolour painting made by Anna (Figure 21.2), but what is important to remember here is that we, as researchers, are not interested in interpreting the image as such. The work of interpretation, elicitation, discussion, evaluation or whatever we want to call it, is a practical concern for the participants we have studied; this is what *they* are expected to engage in. And it is by looking at *this work* (rather than the image as such) that we can begin to understand the role of the image in this specific practice of training of architects.

Through their commentary work, the teachers and the professional architects display a number of normative judgements and practical considerations in relation to both the educational and the occupational practice of architecture. In this commentary, one important move made by Bill is to introduce the terms/concepts of cityscape and landscape, respectively. By looking at the particular manner in which the notion of cityscape is elaborated and positioned, in relation to the image made by the student, we can begin to understand what makes this a case of architectural education.

Figure 21.2 The student image discussed.

Bill: Then this image. It's actually rather thinly sown with images of this kind because in my opinion this is an image that, perhaps not primarily talks about what does my house look like. But instead what does my atelier look like in the cityscape, in the landscape. You know how does it look when I stand and hang around here somewhere (*pointing to where the man stands*), right? And gaze towards Queen's Bridge. Then you will see, that is, you hint at how your buildings interplay with the jetty and, further out one sees the sea, Queen's Bridge which frames it all. So this is an on-the-spot account of the landscape, in which the building is a part, and I think it is a great image that tells about one of your most important thoughts, I believe, when it comes to the placing of the buildings. Isn't that correct?

(*Short pause. Bill, smilingly, makes a gesture inviting Anna to respond*)

Anna: ★it could be★ (*laughs*)

Bill informs his students that his reading of the image is structured by the concept of cityscape, but he also shows, in and through his commentary, how such a reading should be performed. In his comment, the importance of showing the exact look and feel of the suggested building is downplayed in favour of other aspects. What is subsequently exhibited as relevant noticings concern how the proposed buildings relate to some of the major landmarks in the scene, such as the bridge and the more distant sea. The relation between the buildings and their foundation, in this case a jetty, is also mentioned, and it is talked about as an "interplay", which is hinted at in the image.

In Bill's reading, this image is indicative of interesting thoughts on how to best place the buildings on the assigned building site. The placing of buildings is a most central and practical consideration that architects have to deal with. This is a multidimensional task that among other things includes an important rhetorical element. The issue is not just about how to place the buildings, but, equally importantly, the suggested placement must be argued for in relation to clients, municipal officials and other stakeholders, who will decide on projects on the basis of this type of presentations. What Bill sees in, or rather by way of, this image is something that is not present in the image itself. Although the jetty represented in the image is part of the building site, there was also a large piece of land that could be used by the students for placing the buildings. For Bill then, who has access to this information, the deliberate choice not to place the buildings on land is thus visible in the talked-about rendition. In other words, what is "seen" is something that is not in the image, but which still is a highly relevant element in how the problem has been solved by Anna.

Furthermore, the way the image is composed is simultaneously seen and commented upon as a constitutive part of the argumentation for this choice. As a professional architect, Bill is in a position to recognize qualities of a project without having them described for him. Those qualities are, in and by themselves, seen as motives for why a student has followed a certain design path. In this particular situation, which is part of a learning context, the unique qualities of the proposed ateliers are perceived and explicitly verbalized by the teacher. But the *verbalization* here is a pedagogical move, aimed at the larger audience of students present as he speaks. The 'crit' is a public event, where one of the pedagogical goals is to provide demonstrations of architecturally relevant ways of looking at (student) projects. What is demonstrated in this example are central elements of the skilled vision in relation to cityscapes. Bill's comment is recast as a question at the end; nevertheless, his remarks about the student's thoughts about placement should not primarily be seen as a genuine question about the presentation. Rather, his extended comment is intended as a model of how one should act and reason as a professional architect.

In other words, his commentary is occasioned by the fact that he is acting in a specific context where he can demonstrate to all those present important features of how to analyse images and how to provide solutions to architectural problems.

It is clear that the discussion that takes place in this example builds upon the image that has been produced by the student. The image as such holds a large potential when it comes to possible ways it could be made relevant in the interaction; in fact, the meaning potentials (Rommetveit, 1974) of this image are countless and relative to what activity it is part of. Given a context of arts education, it could for instance be discussed in terms of *technique* (perspective), *choice of material* (pigment behaviour), *aesthetics* (colour balance, temperature) and so forth. But, and this is important for our argumentation in this context, these notions are *not* brought up by the teachers; not in the short excerpt that we have shown, and not in the subsequent interaction.

It is in the selection and display of what counts as relevant ways of talking and thinking about the representations that the training of a specific profession is manifested. In our case, this socialization is in part built upon the practice where professional architects respond to representations already produced by students and when they tell them what those objects *are*, not in any essential sense, but in the *eyes* of the profession. Whether or not the notions of "cityscape", "placing" or "interplay" were consciously present with the student as the image was produced is made less important. It is the pedagogical practice of meaning-making in relation to the students' products in the particular instructional format that is of prime concern. What is exploited in this particular piece of interaction is a potential of showing how architects reason when they design, and the audience is not just the student who is responsible, but, rather, all those present in the room. The image becomes a vehicle for making architectural reasoning publicly visible. Thus, a particular social language is invoked and sustained as a relevant way of analysing images in the specific practice that is intended to convey insights into how one thinks and makes images in the context of architectural design.

Conclusions: images, language and social practices

The point of our discussion has been to argue for the interconnectedness between representational tools. Images, pictures and other visual tools form part of the human repertoire for sense-making, and they are embedded in discursive practices both when produced and when read. In order to make a drawing of an object, one has to have a certain conceptual control over how a three-dimensional object can be reproduced in two dimensions. In the evolution of human symbolic representations, achieving this kind of control was one of the dramatic steps towards using images as tools for representing reality, as has been argued by Lewis-Williams (2002) in his analysis of the differences between, for instance, body-painting and the production of symbolic images: the "notion that an image is a scale model of something else (say, a horse) requires a different set of mental events and conventions" (p. 181) than those that went into earlier, pre-historic forms of aesthetic expression, for instance in body-painting. In a similar vein, interacting with new images often requires conceptual adaptation and innovation as we tried to explain on a small scale with the excerpts from the young girls playing computer and video games. Engagement in pictures and animations may very well provoke linguistic innovation and *vice versa*.

A second point that we have argued for is that meaning-making is always relative to social practices. What is a relevant way of perceiving an image cannot be decided on, unless one considers the practice of which it is a part. All representations have meaning potentials, but what aspect of those potentials that are exploited is a situated affair. As we have tried to show with our brief example from the specific context of the training of architects, the images produced are subjected to highly specialized forms of analysis that are intended to communicate to students features of what Goodwin (1994) refers to as professional vision; institutionalized ways of "seeing", reasoning and producing images.

As Goodwin argues in his seminal paper, we see through the conceptual world of language, and this also goes for the perception of images. Even though images have some unique properties for meaning-making, for instance in terms of spatially organizing information, they are not appropriated in the same sense as are concepts and terms. Once a concept is appropriated, it becomes a tool for seeing and for extending our agency in a certain practice. From this point of view it will be less productive to separate images and objects, or even man-made items and natural objects. Be it a tree, a house or a painting, once our mind is "hijacked" by a certain discursive practice or social language, we will perceive the world through cultural lenses. But a fruitful angle from which to study the development of our capacities for communicating through different modalities is to take one's point of departure in practices rather than in qualities inherent to words, narratives, images or other representations. Wittgenstein (1953) advised philosophers not to analyse language when "it goes on holiday", as is so characteristic of traditional analytical philosophy when asking essentialist questions of "what is X?". Rather, we should investigate how language is used in interaction by people in situated activities. We believe that to understand human development and learning in the context of the developments brought about by digital media, a similar attitude has its merits; it is in social practices where people make use of increasingly diversified cultural tools that we can begin to explore what cognitive and aesthetic socialization is all about in contemporary society. Words, narratives, images and other representations may be distinct as cultural entities, but in meaning-making in practice they are always contingent on each other.

So, what does a socio-cultural approach have to offer research on multimodality and multimodal practices, and where are the shortcomings? The basic unit of analysis in sociocultural research is the notion of mediated action. This implies that the link between people and cultural tools is always part of the inquiry; people always act by using making use external resources. Such a perspective, thus, is an alternative to more essentialist approaches which analyse language, images or any other form of representation as disconnected from other resources for meaning-making. The other element of this equation is the emphasis on the situated nature of human action and communication; activities are always embedded in activity systems. The same image, for instance a drawing of house as in the case of the training of architects, can be part of many different activities, and people orient to it accordingly. If the analyses are carried out properly, situated understandings of the uses of cultural resources will emerge. An important component of such an approach is that it attempts to retain the integrity of human activities as they unfold in an increasingly complex and diversified society.

It is in our view important to conceive of the socio-cultural tradition as a perspective or an approach to research on communication and multimodality. Thus, it is not a single theory in any strong sense. Rather it invites consideration of how people engage in mediated activities and how they learn to interact and represent the world by means of the resources that they are accustomed to. The insights provided thus offer a complementary picture of what human development and learning are all about, and in this account the mastery of different modes for representing the world is one the most exciting features of individual and collective development in contemporary society.

Acknowledgement

The research reported here has been funded by the Swedish Research Council and the Knowledge (KK) Foundation. The authors are members of The Linnaeus Centre for Research on Learning, Interaction and Mediated Communication in Contemporary Society (LinCS). The chapter was written while the third author was a Finland Distinguished Professor at the Centre for Learning Research, University of Turku.

Note

1 In Swedish the term used in the training is "kritik", which is equivalent to critique in English. However, the intention of this kind of instructional format is not to criticize in any negative sense, but rather to provide expert commentary on the work done by the students.

Further reading

Daniels, H., Cole, M. and Wertsch, J. eds. (2007) *The Cambridge Companion to Vygotsky*, New York: Cambridge University Press.

Gee, J. P. (2003) *What Video Games Have to Teach Us About Learning and Literacy*, New York: PalgraveMacMillan.

Goodwin, C. (1997) 'The blackness of black: Color categories as situated practice.' In L. B. Resnick, R. Säljö, C. Pontecorvo and B. Burge, eds. *Discourse, Tools, and Reasoning. Essays on Situated Cognition*, New York: Springer: pp. 111–40.

Stevens, R. and Hall, R. (1998) 'Disciplined perception: Learning to see in technoscience.' In M. Lampert and M. L. Blunk, eds. *Talking Mathematics in School: Studies of Teaching and Learning*, Cambridge: Cambridge University Press: pp. 107–49.

Wells, G. (1999) *Dialogic Inquiry. Towards a Sociocultural Practice and Theory of Education*, Cambridge: Cambridge University Press.

22

Indefinite precision

Artefacts and interaction in design

Paul Luff, Christian Heath and Karola Pitsch

Introduction

In recent years we have witnessed the emergence of a substantial corpus of research concerned with the interplay of talk, visible conduct and the use of material and digital artefacts in complex organisational environments. These studies are naturalistic; they use field studies, frequently augmented by audio-visual recordings, to undertake fine-grained analysis of action and interaction in the workplace. They include studies of control rooms, for example in rapid urban transport, air traffic control and the emergency services, of health care, from general practice through to operating theatres and of financial institutions, and of news rooms, construction sites, law firms and architectural practices (e.g. Goodwin and Goodwin, 1996; Harper *et al.*, 1989; Heath *et al.*, 1994; Heath and Luff, 1992, 2000; Luff *et al.*, 2000; Suchman, 2000; Whalen, 1995). They have come to be known as 'workplace studies' and are *par excellence* 'multimodal' analyses of everyday organisational activities, revealing the ways in which those activities are contingently accomplished through social interaction.

These workplace studies have a curious provenance. They draw upon various analytic traditions within the social sciences, and yet their substantive and to some extent analytic concerns arise in part in the light of emerging debates within cognitive science and by those engaged in the design of new technologies. The plan-based cognitive models of system use found in artificial intelligence and human–computer interaction (see, for example, Card *et al.*, 1983) have been subject to sustained criticism particularly for their disregard of the situated character of human conduct and the socially organised practices and procedures that underpin the use of technologies in mundane activities (see, for example, Suchman, 1987; Winograd and Flores, 1986). These programmatic debates reflect a growing recognition that we know little of the ways in which people use tools and technologies in their everyday practical activities, be they complex digital systems or mundane objects such as pen and paper. In turn, the shortcomings of academic research resonate with the liturgy of problems that arise when seemingly well-designed technologies are deployed in organisational environments and not infrequently disrupt, even undermine the very activities that they were developed to support. These debates and problems have been accompanied by rapidly developing technologies, and the emergence of systems that were not simply concerned with supporting individual tasks and activities but with enabling cooperation and collaboration in the rapid globalisation of organisations and institutions, innovations. This in part led to a new field study known as Computer Supported Cooperative Work (CSCW). These developments correspond to a growing recognition within the social sciences that with the primacy attributed to speech and talk, the visible and the material features of social action and interaction have remained substantively and analytically *underdeveloped.*

In this chapter we wish to exemplify a particular approach to 'multimodal' analysis; an approach that addresses the fine-grained social and interactional accomplishment of everyday activities. We explore the ways in which seemingly simple or mundane technologies, in this case pen and paper, are critical for the organisation and accomplishment of activities. The setting is a leading international design practice, and the activity, of which we consider a very small part, finds the participants attempting to develop ideas for the structure of a new museum space. The thrust of this chapter, however, is not so much to consider the practical accomplishment of creative work (Cuff, 1992; Murphy, 2004, 2005), but rather to begin to show the richness and complexity of mundane interaction and to perhaps question the usefulness of the term, 'multimodality', a term that implies distinctive modes and channels in understanding social action and its situated accomplishment.

Background: methodological considerations

Despite the diverse range of analytic orientations that inform workplace studies, including for example activity theory, distributed cognition and symbolic interactionism, there are a number of common commitments that reflect a more general concern with the practical accomplishment of organisational activities. These commitments include prioritising the situated character of organisational action and its contingent accomplishment, a concern with rich or 'thick' ethnographic description, to coin Geertz's (1973) phrase, and a focus on practice and practical reasoning, and the socially organised production of workplace activities.

Our own approach, an approach that is reflected in a range of workplace studies (consider, for example, Goodwin, 1994, 1995; Goodwin and Goodwin, 1996; Mondada, 2003; Streeck and Kallmeyer, 2001; Whalen and Vinkhuyzen, 2000; Whalen *et al.*, 2002) draws on ethnomethodology and conversation analysis and adopts a particular take on the more general commitments that inform this broad range of ethnography. In the first place, our concern with the situated character of practical action addresses the ways in which particular actions and sequences of action contingently arise within the emergent or ongoing accomplishment of workplace activities. The principal contingency in this regard is the contributions of others, of co-participants, and our studies are concerned with the moment-by-moment, concerted and interactional accomplishment of particular actions and activities, even for example a single turn at talk or the passing of an artefact. Second, in addressing the practices that participants rely upon in the accomplishment of workplace activities, the concern is not simply with the tacit or the seen but unnoticed, but with the practices and reasoning in and through which people produce particular actions and make sense of the actions of others. The term 'methods', for example in 'ethnomethodology', is used to draw together the double-edged reflexive self- constituting character of human practice. Third, analysis is concerned with discovering and describing these practices, in particular explicating with regard to the ways in which participants themselves orient to and rely upon these practices in concerted accomplishment of the activity. In this regard, the action-by-action sequential character of interaction provides not just a topic for enquiry but a resource in enabling analysts to demonstrate, by virtue of the ways in which an action's production is oriented to by others, that participants themselves are orienting to and relying upon particular practices and procedures.

In the light of these commitments, video, or audio-visual recordings of 'naturally occurring' activities, become a critical methodological resource, enabling analysis of action and interaction that would otherwise remain inaccessible. Unlike conventional field work and observational data, video recordings provide the resources through which activities and events, as they are accomplished in ordinary everyday settings, can be subject to repeated and detailed scrutiny using slow motion and other facilities. Moreover, the data can be shown to and shared with others not only to enable collaborative observation and analysis, but to provide others with the opportunity to assess and comment upon insights and observations with regard to the materials on which they are primarily based. In workplace studies that often explore highly complex organisational environments, video recording is augmented by field observation and in some cases, interviews and discussions with the participants themselves; the field work provides the resources to enable researchers to access and understand particular activities and events and to become familiar with the procedures, regulations and materials that inform the practical accomplishment of actions in the setting.

It is worthwhile mentioning one further issue. Workplace studies evolved in part in the light of a growing interest in digital technologies and the ways in which they feature in organisational activities and interaction. In this regard, they have made an important contribution to our understanding of system use and to the ways in which design and development of technology might prioritise the endogenous and contingent demands of workplace activities. Ironically perhaps, this burgeoning corpus of ethnographic research powerfully reveals the significance of mundane artefacts to organisational activities, even activities that are produced in highly complex and in some cases sophisticated technological environments. So for example, studies of air traffic control demonstrated the importance and resilience of paper flight strips, despite successive attempts to replace these bits of paper with sophisticated digital representations of aircraft; such studies reveal how coordination and collaboration in air traffic control rests upon the particular characteristics of the strips and practices that inform their use (Harper *et al.*, 1989). Or for example, in studies of operating theatres, where surgery relies upon a range of highly sophisticated equipment, the participants' ability to unobtrusively position, exchange and manipulate simple tools such as knives, pliers and spatulas, forms a critical resource in the collaborative and concerted accomplishment of a complex activity (see, for example, Sanchez Svensson *et al.*, 2007). It is interesting to note that there is a growing interest in computer science and engineering in taking mundane artefacts seriously, and in attempting to embed and embody digital resources within ordinary everyday tools and technologies; an ambition that is driven in part by the discoveries of ethnography and workplace studies (see, for example, Brown and Duguid, 1994; Henderson, 1999; Luff *et al.*, 1992; Sellen and Harper, 2002; Weiser, 1991).

Determining a proposal

The design practice in our study includes architects, interior designers and graphic designers and traditionally specialises in the development of museum and gallery spaces. Alongside more general field work, we recorded design meetings often using two cameras to enable access both to the participants as well as various tools and artefacts, both digital and material. Paper and pen proved particularly important in this regard; many of the meetings involved the use of paper plans as well as sketches, with the designers discussing aspects of the drawings, annotating various documents and creating various designs. Like other design meetings, in particular those that arise in the early stages of a project (see, for example, Büscher *et al.*, 1999), the participants develop, discuss and debate thoughts and ideas and attempt to determine and give sense to proposals that may be imprecise and unclear. In turn, these meetings enable the participants to

313

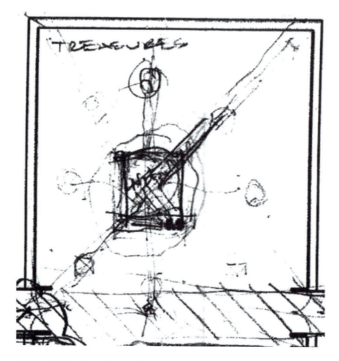

Figure 22.1 The initial sketch for the ship models room made on the paper plan, with the 'hub' in the centre; other cases are shown as feint circles around the hub and the case for the treasure model above it, labelled 'TREASURE' (sketch is made as if viewed from above).

'come to an understanding', both in terms of the ideas they have about the matters at hand and of an agreement or plan that provides the foundation to the next phase and the discussion it engenders. In other words, the participants attempt to render visible, imaginable, intelligible matters that may be tentative and vague whilst, through their very discussion, these ideas are developed and in some cases instantiated in one form or another.

Consider the following fragment. It is drawn from the early stages of developing a design for a gallery that will display an important collection of model ships. It has been decided that the models will be displayed in a number of cases of different sizes, with a large case in the centre containing one of the most important pieces in the collection, 'the treasure model'. The surrounding cases will be linked to the central display by rails or ramps. Figure 22.1 shows a detail that Steve and Ken, the two designers in the fragment, have drawn of the space on the large plan of the museum.

We join the action as Ken raises the issue as to the height and scale of the ramps that will connect the different cabinets (Figure 22.2).

Fragment 1[1]

> *Ken:* So I don't know what support – I don't think (0.2) we (.) just need to get a size of this; because then (.) yeah; if this is coming to a (0.5).This model has obviously got to come down, and be: at (0.7) that level (0.2)
>
> *Steve:* Yeah (.) °yeah° (0.2)
>
> *Ken:* Isn't it (.) so whether that's going away and then it sort of ramps up and then goes (0.2) and (wh(en) on some whether we ha:ng graphics and other objects out of (.) between these two: (—) sort of parallel rails...

Ken not only poses the problem of height and scale, but delineates the considerations that bear on the solution ('This model has obviously got to come <u>down</u>, and be: at (0.7) <u>that</u> level) and hints towards a resolution and the ways in which it will enable other objects and graphics to be displayed (<u>ha:ng</u> graphics and other objects out of (.) bet<u>ween</u> these two: (—) sort of parallel rails…). Steve's initial response to the constraints that bear upon the problem (yeah (.) °yeah°) provide Ken with the resources for proposing a solution to the problem; a solution that he assumes is intelligible to Steve. The talk alone, however, does not provide either Steve or the reader with the resources to have a sense of the proposal that Ken is developing and leaves a number of key elements ambiguous. For example, which models and cases he is referring to clarification and more importantly perhaps, what constitutes 'come down' and 'this level' with respect to the plan and the layout of the space remains unexplicated. Moreover, Ken's development of the proposals and their potential consequences for other objects and graphics remains similarly vague and imprecise.

The exposition of the constraints and proposals, their precision and relevance with regard to the design at hand and the emerging solution, rest upon the ways in which Ken inscribes the plan whilst he talks. As he says 'we (.) just need to get a size of this' he sketches around three of the walls of the room on the plan with the pencil he holds his right hand. When he says 'yeah: if <u>this</u> is coming' Ken brings his pencil down onto the small sketch of the case for the treasure model shown in Figure 22.1, angled so that Steve, who continues to look at the plan, can see its point. Ken presses the pencil harder into the sketch as he says 'this'. Moments later as he says '<u>this</u>' in '<u>this</u> model' Ken again points to the sketch of the treasure model with his pencil.

Once Ken has identified the treasure model he then makes his proposal for its height. Whilst still pointing to the sketch of the case with his right hand he raises his left hand to eye level. This secures a shift of alignment of Steve from the page to Ken's hand. Ken then gestures a downward arc with his left hand, suggesting the proposed shape of the ramp and

Ken   Steve

Ken: we (.) just
need to get a <u>size</u> of
this [...]

if this is coming to
a [...]

This model has   and be: at (0.7) <u>that</u>
obviously has   level
obviously got to
come <u>down</u>

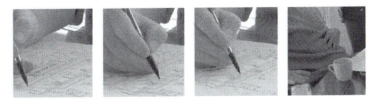

Figure 22.2 Fragment 1 images.

then whilst he says 'that' in 'be: at (0.7) that level' Ken taps the desk with his right hand. This gesture proposes that the height of the case for the treasure model be about the same as the height of the actual desk at which Ken and Steve are sitting. Steve seems to agree with this, and Ken then goes on to provide some further suggestions that might be a consequence of this decision.

The suggestion for the height of the treasure model can only be made sense of in the light of Ken's previous conduct. Though his fine-grained coordination of talk, inscription and gesture serves to reveal and determine the issue at hand – the size and scale of the room and the objects within it, and the details of a suggestion to address this issue – the relative heights of two of the cases: the large one in the centre and the one for the treasure model. They serve progressively to help define a problem, commence the discussion of a potential solution and allow Ken to go on to raise further consequences of this solution for the design. Ken's conduct also successively secures Steve's participation and alignment, first to the sketch on the paper page, then to Ken himself (as he says 'this model has obviously got to come down') and then to the desk (as Ken taps it). Despite appearing vague qualities of the inscription and gestures, they give a sense and precision to the constraints and the proposal, and serve to form an mutually intelligible foundation to the further development of the proposal.

Righting a proposal

In this regard, as Ken completes his proposal for the ramps, Steve begins to draw a case at the bottom of the same plan (see Figure 22.3). The drawing contrasts with the sketch. It is a more precise rendition of the arrangement and not simply indeterminately overlaid on a section of the plan. As he draws this, Steve suggests 'this (0.3) line almost could could star-, could start within the case'.

Fragment 2

> *Steve:* this euhm- (1.0) this (0.3)
> *Ken:* yeah yeah=yeah=yeah yeah
> *Steve:* line almost could could star- could start within the case; and then- I mean "obviously: (.) there'd be (.) (up) here? (0.1)

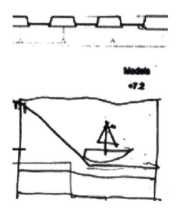

Figure 22.3 Steve's drawing of a case positioned just below the plan (side elevation).

Ken: so is this the case? (0.2)
Steve: yeah. (0.1)
Ken: yeah, that's what I'm saying< >exactly this pla:(te) that-
Steve: (one)
Ken: that- all the models to do wi:th: (0.7)
Steve: and then- again, that runs in here. (0.3)
→*Ken:*   all the models that are to do- this is inside, (sorry) which one- which model is
   this? this is (—) your: (0.6) treasure model? (0.2)
Steve: yeah>yeah>yeah (0.1) (0.1)
Ken: ah yea sorry, yeah?=
Steve: =so you have got loads, you've got loads in here
Ken: =yeah

After confirming which case they are talking about, Ken seem to agree ('yeah, that's what I'm saying<>exactly…') and twice to make a proposal of his own ('all the models that are to do-'), but this proposal is curtailed. It appears that Ken has misunderstood which model Steve has been drawing. Ken then goes on to repair his own misunderstanding (arrowed). This misunderstanding about which case Steve has been drawing arises despite Ken earlier asking 'so is this the case?' and getting an affirmative response from Steve ('yeah'). Indeed, when he gets Steve's affirmation Ken begins to draw on Steve's sketch, marking out a line under the boat that Steve has drawn and moving his pencil back and forth along this line.

Ken's recognition of his misunderstanding and his subsequent self-repair arises in the light of what Steve continues to do on the page. As Ken begins the gist of his new proposal ('this pla:(te) that- that- all the models to do wi:th:'), Steve starts to draw a long line a little further to the left of his existing sketch. He then goes on to complete the drawing of a larger box, making in apparent that he is now drawing the large case in the centre of the room, the one that will contain the collection of models (and presumably the one Ken is about to discuss).

Steve's drawing of the large box is accompanied by various perturbations in Ken's talk: as he completes his first long line, Ken utters 'that- that-'; and as Steve draws a line parallel to this, Ken's utters an extended 'wi:th'. These perturbations seem to be related to Steve's conduct on the page. Even before Steve continues his own proposal ('and then- again, that runs in here') Ken abandons his own sketching.

Steve's drawing helps clarify what the designers have been and are discussing. As well as providing a representation of the current proposals, they seem to be extended in a way that is sensitive to a possible misunderstanding by Ken. Rather than making the misunderstanding explicit, Steve allows Ken to discover the problem for himself and repair it, which Ken does. This seems to be a delicate way of dealing with a potential misunderstanding as well as allowing it to be managed without too much discussion about features of the drawings on the page or previous proposals that have been mentioned.

The two designers go on to discuss how they might use the ramps – both to hang models from them and to place models upon them – and also how the models could be lined up along the ramps to provide some coherence to the design. These discussions are also accompanied by sketches, made to the drawing of the new large case on the left (see Figure 22.5).

Through their conduct with their pens and pencils the designers discuss very specific details of the sketches they have drawn. The material activity over and on the page, particularly how they point, gesture and manipulate their pens, is therefore critical to how they discuss features of the design and also how each makes sense of the actions of their colleagues. It is difficult, however,

Ken: so is this the case? [....] exactly this pla:(te) that- that- all the models to do wi:th:

Figure 22.4 Fragment 2 images.

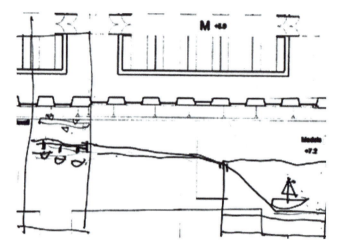

Figure 22.5 The extended drawing showing the 'treasure model'.

to delineate in the talk or the various gestures they make, specific details of the design they are suggesting. Even what would seem to be quite important features, like how many cases there will be, how many ramps will link the cases and the relative or absolute size of most of the cases, are left vague. The vagueness of the suggestions may in part be due to a lack of clarity in the brief at the time and their discussions being at the early stages of the design process. The ambivalence and ambiguity about what is being suggested might also help a colleague to put forward an alternative or even propose a contradictory idea. The openness of the proposals, whether they are spoken, drawn or made through hand gestures might provide for a certain defeasibility or open texture, allowing suggestions to be easily refined, clarified or transformed. Nevertheless, design concepts, 'ideas', have to be made visible to colleagues in some way. Sketches accompanied by talk, where the actual details of a proposal are left implicit, provide a means of doing this without an explicit commitment to a particular solution.

Although we have considered only a moment of the work of designers, we can begin to see how ideas, and proposals, are occasioned by, emerge within, and are articulated through, interaction. These ideas are progressively developed, clarified and transformed within the interaction. The contingent contributions of the participants are instantiated in one way or another within a set of modified plans and proposals and 'working agreement' as to how they will be applied within the practicalities of the project. In the case at hand, these seemingly vague formulations

Figure 22.6 The computer-aided design produced as a consequence of these discussions. This is a rendered drawing of the proposed exhibition space for the ship models, showing a large case with many models in it, linked to other cases all around it, including one for the 'treasure model' on the left.

imagined, exposed and discussed during these brief moments of interaction, are instantiated in ways that both reflect the preserve the original ideas, yet adjust or transform certain features that address both practical and aesthetic constraints within the overall plan. So for example when later presented to the design team the cases were of different heights and dimensions, with the treasure model case lower than the larger case (being below waist height); there were parallel links, or ramps, between the different cases (that emerged from within the cases) with a number of models hung from these ramps (Figure 22.6).

Modes of action

Over the last three or four decades we have witnessed a 'linguistic turn' in the social sciences and a wide-ranging recognition of the importance of language, discourse and talk to the accomplishment of social action and activities. These developments are to be welcomed, not least for the ways in which they draw attention to the fine details of conduct, practice and action and point to the ways in which organisations and institutions are founded upon, and sustained through, the practical accomplishment of everyday activities. The provenance of the term 'multimodal' and in particular its widespread application in the social sciences remains unclear; however, one suspects putting to one side its engineering connotations, that it arises in the light of a growing commitment to taking the visual, the material, even the tactile, seriously, and directing attention to the variety of means through which social action is accomplished. As a way of drawing attention to, or revitalising interest in, visible, material and other forms of action, the term 'multimodal' provides perhaps a useful contrast to the 'linguistic', but it may prove an unfortunate way of characterising communication and serve to impoverish analytic developments. The idea of multimodes for example inadvertently perhaps suggests separate or distinct channels, not unlike an earlier distinction 'verbal and nonverbal', and implies 'modes of communication' with the risk of neglecting social action and the accomplishment of 'situated' practical activities.

If we consider the fragments that we have briefly discussed in this chapter we can begin perhaps to see issues that might arise in the use of the term 'multimodal'. The actions of the participants, for example the way in which Ken develops and delivers a proposal, is accomplished through talk, gesture and sketching on the plan. The sense of the talk, and the determination of both the constraints and proposal derives from the co-participant's ability to both hear what it is being said and for example to see its inscribed manifestation in the sketch. The sketch reflexively constitutes the 'this' and 'that' of the talk, just as the talk enables the sketch to be seen as a way of addressing and resolving the 'problem' at hand. Similarly, the gesture provides the resources to gain determinate sense of how the ramps might appear and where they would be positioned. It would seem difficult and perhaps analytically unrewarding to attempt to delineate the distinct communicative contribution of the different modes, and indeed it may be misleading to believe that the co-participant himself is engaged in assembling the emerging action by virtue of combining the different modes.

The activity in which the participants are engaged, even within the first fragment, involves a number of actions in which for example Ken exposes the constraints that bear upon the position of the ramp and receiving some of alignment or agreement from Steve (with 'yeah (.) yeah'), proposes a sense of what they might look like and how they could be used. The production of the activity, and the ways in which it is accomplished, encourage and depend upon particular forms of co-participation from Steve. In the first case, for example, placing the pencil on the paper and beginning to sketch has Steve seeing, within the course of its articulation, just what Ken is referring to. As Ken develops the proposal, he produces a number of gestures that encourage the recipient to turn from the plans and witness the visible conduct of the speaker, the gestures providing an impression of the shape and position of the ramp. In turning towards Ken, Steve enables the activity to be produced in a particular way and thereby gain its sense and intelligibility. The production of the activity therefore is an interactional, concerted accomplishment; the ways in which it is accomplished and the sense of the display it provides is dependent upon the speaker's ability to continuously establish particular forms of co-participation from Steve. The activity's production is sensitive, and is shaped with regard to the contingent and emerging conduct of the co-participant; it involves the necessary interplay of the visual, vocal and material, and it may not necessarily be analytically fruitful or even viable to separate the relevance or contribution of these 'different modes' to the embodied, interactional accomplishment of the participants' actions.

Despite the long-standing commitment within the social sciences to qualitative research, the qualities of action, in contrast to their typicality or membership of a particular class of actions, is surprisingly disregarded. In this regard, design and design work provide lucid demonstration of the ways in which participants themselves orient to the qualities of particular actions both in their production and intelligibility. So for instance, it is been noted how in the fragments, the participants produce a representation of the proposed arrangement of connected cabinets in two rather different ways, the second version transforming and formalising a version of the first that establishes a common idea of what they are talking about. The initial sketch, coupled with the accompanying talk and gesture, delineates a possibility, embodied in part by virtue of the way in which it is lightly and vaguely drawn over the relevant section of the printed plan, whereas the distinct drawing, produced by the co-participants, renders a distinct and now potentially shared version of the 'solution'. The qualities of the two drawings, their relative preciseness, location, authorship and sequential evolution, renders two seemingly similar actions, qualitatively distinct, and significantly different in terms of their consequentiality for the final design of the display. In order for the designers to develop concepts and ideas that can be discussed these need to be made explicit but not too precisely. It should be possible for others to transform a suggestion, to propose an alternative or even ignore it. Sketches, gestures to vague objects, and transient references to unexplicated objects facilitate the accomplishment of creative discussions. The qualities of how activities are produced are critical to how they can been seen and recognised to meet the demands and commitments of the work in an organisational setting.

When considering the materials gathered in the design practice it becomes apparent, once again, how critical quite mundane artefacts are in supporting work in organisations. The paper plans facilitate collaboration. The paper plans offer stable resources around which two or more designers can sit to discuss emerging, developing and partially formed ideas. They can be annotated in a range of ways with a wide variety of marks with differing qualities. Recently, with the emergence of new technologies there has been a growing interest in the properties of the mundane objects to support everyday activities; of particular interest have been the capabilities or 'affordances' of paper. Drawing upon studies of the use of different kinds of paper artefacts in a variety of workplaces, researchers have revealed the importance of particular material properties of paper, for example, its mobility, portability and visibility (e.g. Sellen and Harper, 2002). However, what seems critical is how paper can support collaboration, especially how it can facilitate the production and development of activities in interaction (Luff et al., 1998). In architectural and design practices, for example, participants produce and make sense of each others' actions and activities by orienting to the moment-to-moment activities of the colleagues on and around the paper page. Such advantages seem to account for the resilience of paper in the workplace and suggest that rather than trying to replace paper with computer systems, or even design systems that simulate or mimic the properties of paper in some way, it may be more appropriate to develop innovative technologies that allow people to interweave their uses of paper and digital resources (Luff et al., 2006).

The focus on the affordances of paper, however, should not lead us to consider the properties of the artefact in isolation. In the case at hand, the pens and pencils designers hold and use when they are discussing their designs are essential for the production of creative work: not just to mark and annotate plans and sketchs, to but, in concert with talk and other visual conduct, they serve to reveal aspects of the size and shape of the proposals and in other ways animate the ideas under discussion. The ways they are held, how they can be used to point and gesture at the paper document, and the different kinds of mark that can be made when they are used to draw or write, provide resources not just to refer to objects on the page but to suggest the qualities of different concepts and ideas. These material actions can only be made sense of within interaction, inextricably bound to the talk and visual conduct of the participants.

Detailed studies of workplace interaction might also offer a distinctive contribution to studies of design practice. In disciplines as diverse as psychology, sociology and computer science, studies of design have been drawn upon to cast light on the nature of creativity and creative work. Although there has traditionally been a focus on the kinds of personalities and cognitive styles of creative individuals, recently there has been a growing interest in the ιcollaborative practices of professionals, and how communities of practice emerge (cf. Candy and Edmonds, 1999; Fischer, 2001, 2004). Studies of design have suggested that creative designs are accomplished collaboratively, through the ways designers assemble different kinds of materials to support innovation (Büscher *et al.*, 1999) and how 'shared languages' are developed to reflect on proposals, propose alternatives and exchange creative ideas (Mamykina *et al.*, 2002). Although there are ways in which these practices are particular to specific kinds of design practice and perhaps certain features that may be generic for different types of creative work, they are produced through interaction and the use of rather mundane objects. Communities of practice (Lave and Wenger, 1991) and communities of interest are maintained and sustained through interaction. It seems critical to understand the details of how these are accomplished by participants, through the sequential production and recognition, from moment to moment, of talk, visual conduct and the use of artefacts.

Naturalistic studies of activities in everyday settings can reveal how even apparently individual activities such as writing or drawing on a piece of paper are achieved through collaboration are critical to how everyday work is accomplished. Indeed, recent innovations in high-quality digital cameras and displays can help in delineating just how finely talk, gestures and material conduct are coordinated. Such materials, when analysed in detail, also bring into question efforts to discriminate the contribution of different modes of action. Even when what emerges from such analyses is still how little we understand about the ways gestures, talk and visual conduct are interrelated, it seems critical when trying to study complex concerted action not to fracture these from their interactional context.

Note

1 In these fragments the length of pauses or silences (in tenths of a second) are given in brackets as in '(0.2)', when a word or part of a word is emphasised it is underlined, and when a sound is stretched or elongated it is extended by a number of colons (the number of colons capturing the length of the sound, again in tenths of a second), as in 'ha:ng'. When there is no interval between adjacent utterances, the utterances are linked together with 'equals' signs. When part of an utterance is delivered at a pace quicker than the surrounding talk, it is indicated by being enclosed between '<'signs.

Further reading

Goodwin, C. (1981) *Conversational Organisation: Interaction Between Speakers and Hearers*, London: Academic Press.

Heath, C. C. and P. K. Luff (2000) *Technology in Action*, Cambridge: Cambridge University Press.

Luff, P., Hindmarsh, J. and Heath, C. (2000) *Workplace Studies: Recovering Work Practice and Informing System Design*, Cambridge: Cambridge University Press.

ten Have, P. (1999) *Doing Conversational Analysis: A Practical Guide*, London: Sage.

23

Anthropology and multimodality

The conjugation of the senses

David Howes

Introduction

The study of sense perception has traditionally fallen within the domain of psychology, where it is pursued on a sense-by-sense basis – i.e. one-sense-at-a-time. Recent research in sensory anthropology and cognitive neuroscience has shown this serial approach to be misguided. Sensory anthropologists have demonstrated that the senses are interactive, and the mode of interaction differs according to the sensory model of the society under study. Cognitive neuroscientists have shown how the processing of information in one sensory modality is often influenced by concurrent activity in other modalities. The first section of this chapter proposes a cross-cultural multimodal theory of sense perception born out of thinking the implications of the above-mentioned research in cognitive neuroscience and sensory anthropology together. The second section illustrates this theory through an analysis of the multisensory faculty psychology of the Desana Indians of Colombia. The third section presents an overview of some current directions and trends in multimodal research in anthropology.

Towards a cross-cultural multimodal theory of sense perception

It is commonly assumed that each sense has its proper sphere (e.g. sight is concerned with colour, hearing with sound, and taste with flavour). This modular conception of the sensorium is enshrined in the plethora of current picture books on "The Five Senses" which teach children how to individuate and use their sensory faculties. The specialization of the senses continues in adulthood and becomes institutionalized through such practices as going to an art gallery to see paintings or a concert hall to listen to music, a garden to smell the flowers or a restaurant to savour various dishes, and perhaps a gym to exercise. This compartmentalization of the sensorium is further reflected in the analytic orientation of most current research in the psychology of perception with its sense-by-sense (or "one sensory modality at a time") approach to the study of perceptual processes.

In recent years, however, a more interactive, relational approach to the understanding of how the senses function has begun to take shape as a result of the growing body of evidence which points to the "multisensory organization" or "integration" of the brain. As Calvert *et al.* write in

323

their introduction to *The Handbook of Multisensory Processes* (the most authoritative work in this new field):

> even those experiences that at first may appear to be modality-specific are most likely to have been influenced by activity in other sensory modalities, despite our lack of awareness of such interactions ...[To] fully appreciate the processes underlying much of sensory perception, we must understand not only how information from each sensory modality is transduced and decoded along the pathways primarily devoted to that sense, but also how this information is *modulated* by what is going on in the other sensory pathways.
>
> (2004: xi–xii, emphasis mine)

Examples of such modulation include the well-documented fact that, in noisy surroundings, speakers can be understood more easily if they can be seen as well as heard. Another more interesting example would be the illusion known as the "freezing phenomenon": when test subjects are shown a rapidly changing visual display, an abrupt sound may "freeze" the display with which the sound is synchronized, so that the display appears brighter or to last longer (Vroomen and de Gelder, 2004).

Many of the studies in the *Handbook of Multisensory Processes* use neuroimaging techniques to identify the multiple sites of multimodal processing in the brain. These sites include many regions long thought to be modality-specific or "primary sensory" areas as distinct from the so-called higher-order, "associative" areas traditionally assumed to be responsible for the formation of unified percepts out of the diversity of inputs. In addition to demonstrating the functional interdependence of the modalities, a number of these studies point to their functional equivalence or adaptability. For example, it is now clear that sensory-specific areas can be "recruited" or "remapped" by other sensory-specific areas in conditions of sensory deprivation, like blindness or deafness. Thus, visual cortex in blind individuals has been found to show activation in auditory tasks while auditory cortex in deaf individuals can be activated by visual tasks.

> Of note, the quality of sensation associated with activating the visual cortex in congenitally blind individuals, or the auditory cortex in congenitally deaf individuals, appears to derive from the nature of inputs. That is, visual inputs are perceived as visual even when auditory cortex is activated [in the case of the blind, while the reverse holds true in the case of the deaf] .... Furthermore, even in normal, nondeprived humans, there is evidence for extensive multisensory interactions whereby primary sensory areas of the cortex can be activated in a task-specific manner by stimuli of other modalities .... Common to these findings is the principle that inputs recruit pathways, cortical areas, and networks within and between areas that process the information, and the sensoriperceptual modality associated with the input is driven by the nature of the input rather than by the cortical area activated per se.
>
> (Sur, 2004: 690)

Such evidence of adaptive processing, or "cross-modal plasticity", poses a serious challenge to the conventional model of the sensorium as consisting of five structurally and functionally distinct modalities. In light of this challenge, some researchers have proposed that the phenomenon of synaesthesia (i.e. the union or crossing of the senses, e.g. hearing colours, tasting shapes) might provide a more productive model for conceptualizing perceptual processes than the conventional sense-by-sense approach that has dominated research on the senses and sensations to date.

The condition of synaesthesia is typically understood to be quite rare. Estimates of its incidence vary from 1 in 200 to 1 in 2,000 people (Ramachandran *et al.*, 2004: 868). The most commonly documented form is colour–grapheme synaesthesia in which written words or letters are perceived as having particular colours. There is some question as to whether subjects are not simply speaking in metaphor when they say "e" evokes the colour white, or "I" the colour crimson, and so on. The "metaphor explanation" of synaesthetic perception is, however, rejected by Ramachandran *et al.* in their chapter on "Synesthesia, Cross-Activation, and the Foundations of Neuroepistemology". Their objection rests on methodological grounds: "Since very little is known about the neural basis of metaphor, saying that 'synaesthesia is just metaphor' helps to explain neither synaesthesia nor metaphor" and merely compounds the mystery (Ramachandran *et al.*, 2004: 868). The authors go on to describe the experimental procedures they have devised to determine whether an alleged synaesthete's experiences are "truly perceptual" or merely conceptual (an important distinction when it comes to selecting test subjects since only those in whom the effect can be shown to be involuntary are considered desirable), and then offer a physiological explanation for the effect having to do with the "cross-activation of brain maps". Such cross-activation may come about by two different mechanisms, namely: "(1) cross-wiring between adjacent [brain] areas, either through an excess of anatomical connections or defective pruning, or (2) excess activity in back-projections between successive stages in the hierarchy (caused by defective pruning or by disinhibition)" (2004: 872).

In the case of colour–grapheme synaesthesia, the brain areas corresponding to graphemes and colours are situated right next to each other in the fusiform gyrus, and the potential for excess cross-activation or "hyperconnectivity" as a result of some genetic mutation in those individuals who naturally experience this effect is therefore strongly indicated. Ramachandran *et al.* conclude that

> far from being a mere curiosity, synaesthesia deserves to be brought into mainstream neuroscience and cognitive psychology. Indeed, [precisely because the neural basis of synaesthesia is beginning to be understood] it may provide a crucial insight into some of the most elusive questions about the mind, such as the neural substrate (and evolution) of metaphor, language and thought itself.
>
> (2004: 881)

There is much to be said for Ramachandran *et al.*'s "bottom-up" approach to the study of perceptual processes, but I find the physiological reductionism of their position unduly restrictive from my own perspective as a cultural anthropologist, and I think an equally valid case could be made for a "top-down" approach. Such an approach would start by examining the cultural organization of the sensorium and descend via the psychological to the physiological level of brain organization. In point of fact, due to the selective focus of their discipline – neuropsychology – Ramachandran *et al.* never ascend in what they call "the hierarchy" as far as the cultural level. This oversight constitutes a serious lacuna, for as cultural psychiatrist Laurence Kirmayer observes concerning the hierarchical systems view of neural organization (which Ramachandran *et al.* presumably share):

> Contemporary cognitive neuroscience understands mind and experience as phenomena that emerge from neural networks at a certain level of complexity and organization. There is increasing recognition that this organization is not confined to the brain but also includes loops through the body and the environment, most crucially, through a

social world that is culturally constructed. On this view, 'mind' is located not in the brain but in the relationship of brain and body to the world.

(Kirmayer, in press)

Ideally, Kirmayer states, "we want to be able to trace the causal links up and down this hierarchy in a seamless way".

Following Kirmayer's lead, let us imagine what a "Cross-Cultural Handbook of Multi-sensory Processes" would look like. Instead of presuming sensory processes to be confined to the brain, it would start with the investigation of the culturally patterned "loops" through the environment – that is, with the study of how culture mediates the relationship of brain and body to the world. Thus, a top-down approach to the study of synaesthetic perception would begin by drawing up an inventory of the range of cultural practices and technologies that generate different sensory combinations across different cultures and historical periods. For example, it is a good empirical question whether the incidence of colour–grapheme synaesthesia would be as high in an aural–oral society as it is in a visual–literate one, such as contemporary Western society. [1] In the latter, words and letters are experienced as quiescent marks on paper or a computer screen, which renders them available for colour-coding. In the former, words (being experienced aurally) might not tend to be seen so readily as they would be felt or smelled as well as heard. In my own ethnographic research in Papua New Guinea, I found evidence of audio-olfactory synaesthesia. In many Melanesian languages, such as Kilivila (the language of the Trobriand Islands), one speaks of "hearing a smell", and this association is carried over in Melanesian Pidgin, "mi harim smel". The reason for this is that most communication takes place face-to-face (i.e. within olfactory range of the other) and odoriferous substances (e.g. anointing the body with oil, chewing ginger) are used to augment the power of a person's presence and words (Howes, 2003: 73–77). In many African languages, like that of the Dogon of Mali, people also speak of "hearing a smell". According to Dogon conceptions, sound and odour coalesce because they have vibration as their common origin (Calame-Griaule, 1986: 39, 48).

These findings of audio-olfactory synaesthesia, familiar to scholars of sensory anthropology, would likely come as a surprise to most scholars of neuropsychology. For example, Stevenson and Boakes claim that: "Odors display taste properties but do not elicit auditory or visual sensations" (2004: 73).[2] On the contrary, in Mali as in Melanesia, auditory and olfactory sensations do modulate each other. Thus, what Stevenson and Boakes take to be a physiological given actually rests on certain culturally contingent (i.e. peculiarly Western) assumptions about the divisions of the sensorium and/or potential for cross-sensory activation. This example underscores the need for more conversation between the disciplines of neuropsychology and anthropology if contemporary cognitive neuroscience is to achieve a comprehensive understanding of the multiple possible forms of conversation and cross-activation between the senses. To put the matter another way, starting with cross-cultural examples such as these, which are *practical* (i.e. supported by cultural practices which form part of the "loop" through which all sensations must pass) as well as metaphorical, neuro-scientists could well be inspired to discover all sorts of heretofore unsuspected cross-linkages between the senses *wherever they may be localized in the brain.* [3]

Multimodal faculty psychology of the Desana Indians

A good case with which to open such a conversation, because of the way it leads into a more culturally informed appreciation of the phenomenon of synaesthesia, is that of the Desana, a

Tukano-speaking people of the Colombian rainforest.[4] For the Desana, all sensory phenomena are interconnected, a perception heightened by their ritual ingestion of hallucinogenic plants. According to their understanding of the nature of the cosmos, the Sun gives life to our world by infusing it with "colour energies". Each of these colour energies embodies a different set of values and potentialities. Red, for example, exemplifies the power of female fertility. Everything in the world contains a combination of these colour energies, which may be visible, as in the colours of flowers, or invisible, as in the rainbow of chromatic energies said to animate human beings. (Only the shaman is able to perceive the latter with the aid of the hallucinogenic vine and his special rock crystals.)

These life-giving colours form a primary set of sensory energies for the Desana. Secondary sets consist of such phenomena as temperatures, odours and flavours. Odours are believed to result from a combination of colour and temperature; flavour, in turn, arises from odour.

The Desana understanding and use of these sensory phenomena or qualia is complex and extensive. As regards odour, the Desana are extremely attentive to the odours in their environment, calling themselves "wira", which means, "people who smell". They hold that each individual has a "signature" odour. This underlying odour can be altered by changes in emotional states, by lifecycle changes such as pregnancy, or by changes in diet. Tribes or extended kin groups are said to share a similar characteristic odour which permeates the area they inhabit. Even when this living space shows no sign of human habitation, the tribal scent is said to still be present. In fact, when travelling through their rainforest environment, the Desana will continually sniff the air in order to detect the scent of the peoples inhabiting the region, as well as the odours of different Amazonian animals and plants. As the Desana move through the environment they say that they lay down what they call "wind threads", or scent trails, which can, in turn, be discerned by other people and animals.

Odours for the Desana are not simply indicators of presence, however, or of emotional state or dietary preference. Like colours, odours are believed to embody key values. One particular odour associated by the Desana with a range of items including deer and palm trees, for example, conveys the notion of male fertility. The odours of certain kinds of ants and worms, by contrast, are associated with feminine forces. Such perceived olfactory similarities make possible a variety of ritual substitutions. During certain ceremonies, for example, ants or worms may symbolize women, whose odour they share. They also necessitate an utmost attention to olfactory interrelations, as it is considered highly dangerous to combine odours (or colours) embodying contrasting forces indiscriminately. This is particularly emphasized in Desana cuisine in which great care is taken to blend food odours harmoniously, not in order to create pleasing dishes, but so as to preserve the proper order of the cosmos.

Desana artefacts, in turn, also contain multimodal meanings. The values associated with a Desana basket, for example, are manifested not only through its colours and patterns, but also through its texture, its odour and even through the flavour of the particular vines of which it was made (Howes, 2007). This, by the way, serves as a good illustration of how much sensory and aesthetic meaning may be suppressed when a multisensory artefact is turned into a purely visual display in a Western museum (see Classen and Howes, 2006).

The intensely multisensory nature of the Desana cosmic model means that every floral aroma, every bird song, every flutter of a butterfly suggests a particular cosmic value to the Desana and may be grouped together with other similar values in order to create a sensorial classificatory system which cut across species' boundaries. The synaesthetic nature of the Desana cosmos means that one sensory phenomenon readily suggests another phenomenon in a different perceptual field, if not a whole train of sensations. An odour will bring to mind a colour; a colour, an odour, along, perhaps, with a temperature and a vibration. A particular design or arrangement of colours used in Desana art, for example, will evoke odours, flavours and other sensations customarily linked with those patterns and arouse a host of related cosmological values. A good example of this is the synaesthetic associations the Desana make with a certain kind of flute. The sound of the flute is said to be yellow in colour, hot in temperature and masculine in odour. The vibrations it produces are said to remind people of correct child-rearing practices. I would emphasize that these synaesthetic, multimodal associations are culturally shared and not simply the idiosyncratic perceptions of some rare, genetically predisposed individual (as the condition of synaesthesia is understood in cognitive neuroscience). This form of synaesthesia transcends the domain of the neuropsychologist and involves those "loops" through the body, the environment, and the social world discussed earlier. That is, it is supported by the technology of ingesting hallucinogens, but also embodied in Desana material culture (e.g. basketry, musical instuments), ritual culture (e.g. healing practices), and so forth.

What is more, the Desana have their own brain science. The right hemisphere of the brain, Desana say, is concerned with practical and biological matters. This hemisphere is known as "existence-first". The left hemisphere has as its sphere divine, abstract ideals and is called "abstract-first". The right hemisphere perceives different sensory phenomena, the left translates them into underlying moral values. In another image, the brain is conceptualized as a buzzing beehive, with each hexagonal compartment containing honey of a different colour, flavour or texture and relating to a different area of human life. As with the synaesthetic associations they reflect, such cerebral models are not the domain of specialized individuals, but are generally shared among the Desana.

As regards art, its primary role among the Desana is to employ iconic images in diverse sensory fields in order to assist individuals to be "in tune" with the vibrating energies of the cosmos and the values these represent. Art, in fact, is a means of transcending the everyday realm of practical affairs and uniting oneself with the abstract ideals of the divine realm. The more sensory channels are involved in the process, the more complete the transcendence.

The Desana case nicely illustrates what David Le Breton (2006) has called "the conjugation of the senses", or *modulation* of perception. The senses cannot fruitfully be studied in isolation from one another, only in interaction – a truth which has also lately come to be recognized in neuropsychological circles, as exemplified by *The Handbook of Multisensory Processes*. At the same time, the Desana case challenges the physiological reductionism and individualism of cognitive neuroscience (e.g. Ramachandran *et al.*'s insistence that synaesthesia is a congenital condition, not a cultural code), and therefore points to the need for further dialogue. Conjugation, modulation, cultural mediation, the sociability of sensations – these are all critical issues for cognitive neuroscientists to start exploring in concert with anthropologists in order to arrive at a comprehensive understanding of how the sensorium functions.

Multimodality in anthropology

Anthropologists are, I think, privileged when it comes to studying multimodality because of their work conditions. As they typically come from Western, urban backgrounds, they cannot help but have their senses awakened by the new sounds, smells and savours of the non-Western societies in which they usually undertake their fieldwork. (Sociologists, customarily working within the more familiar sensory landscape of their own society, do not undergo a similar jolting of their senses.) Furthermore, anthropologists usually conduct research with small-scale groups, and rely on the methodology of "participant-observation" to gather their material. This approach requires a profound physical as well as intellectual integration into the culture under study.

Nevertheless, it is only within the last 20 years or so that anthropologists have come to reflect critically on the implications of multimodality for the conduct of their research. Why this long delay given that anthropologists have been interested in issues of sense perception, such as colour classification, since the beginning of the discipline? I suggest that much of the delay may be attributed to the enduring influence of the conventional Western hierarchized, compartmentalized model of the sensorium, which dates back to the Ancient Greeks (Vinge, 1975), and which has long been used to shore-up different ideological positions (Jones, 2006). For example, the interest in the study of perceptual processes on the part of the early anthropologists of the late nineteenth century went hand-in-hand with a firm belief that the "primitive" nature of indigenous peoples would be manifested by heightened attention to and acuity in the "primitive" senses of smell, taste and touch (relative to Europeans). Much of the sensory data which was collected during this period was hence explicitly or implicitly used to support the association of the "lower" races with the "lower" senses and the "higher" races with the "higher" senses (sight and hearing or the linguistic faculty). This integration of a social hierarchy with a sensory hierarchy can be found in the work of the nineteenth century natural historian Lorenz, who characterized Africans as "skin-men", Australians as "tongue-men", Native Americans as "nose-men", Asians as "ear-men", and Europeans as "eye-men" (Classen, 1997: 405). No attempt whatsoever was made to inquire into the meaning which the senses hold for the people themselves. The focus was exclusively on taking the measure of the senses and relating these findings to the (presumed) localization of different sensory functions in different regions of the brain (Howes, 2003: 3–6; Dias, 2004).

Increasing criticism and disavowal of racial stereotypes from the 1920s on led anthropologists to turn their attention away from the study of sensory practices and proclivities which were so closely tied to racist ideologies. At this time furthermore, many anthropologists preferred to concentrate on abstracting and analysing the social ideals and systems of the cultures they studied. This could be called the "God's eye view" syndrome. As for the sensory traits of culture, these were often disdained as mere packaging – more suitable for a tourist brochure than a scholarly work. In so far as anthropologists did study the sensuous expressions of a culture, it was only under the guise of existing Western categories, such as music (for the ears), or the visual arts (for the eyes), or food (but food studies had mostly to do with nutrition and little to do with taste).

An initial sensory awakening occurred in the 1950s. Inspired by Ruth Benedict's *Patterns of Culture* (1934), various anthropologists started exploring the "patterning" of sense experience across cultures. The guiding idea was expressed as follows:

just as linguistics requires a special ear ... [so cultural analysis requires a special honing of all the senses, since people] not only hear and speak and communicate through words, but also use all their senses in ways that are equally systematic ... to taste and smell and to pattern their capacities to taste and smell, so that the traditional cuisine of a people can be as distinctive and as organized as a language.

(Mead and Métraux, 1953: 16)

This approach yielded some highly perspicacious accounts of the alternate perceptual styles of non-Western peoples and cultures, but it was sidelined by the "textual turn" of the 1970s, when it became fashionable to treat cultures as "texts" which could be "read" by a knowledgeable anthropologist. This embrace of "the model of the text" impeded the development of a multimodal sensory anthropology by promoting a purely visual and literary model of culture – as well as one alien to the traditionally non-literate cultures often studied by anthropologists (see Howes, 2003: 17–28).

For anthropologists to come to their senses, therefore, three things were required. First, that the study of the role of the senses across cultures be disassociated from traditional hierarchies which linked the so-called lower senses to supposedly lower races. Second, that the central role of the senses as mediators and shapers of social knowledge and values be recognized. Third, that sensory practices and values be situated within a society's particular "sensory model" or way of understanding the world through the senses (instead of being filtered through "the model of the text" and other such categories of the Western imagination, such as "music", or "the visual arts" or "cuisine".)

These conditions came to fruition in the last two decades of the twentieth century when anthropologists finally began to take stock of the sensuous expressions of a culture *in their own right*, and started elaborating a relational, multimodal approach to the study of how the senses function. Part of the impetus for this revolution came from the critique of "visualism", or "God's eye view" syndrome mentioned earlier, but it was above all born out of experience in the field. For example, Paul Stoller experienced a sort of acoustic epiphany in the course of his apprenticeship as a sorcerer among the Songhay of Niger, which led him to revalorize the power of hearing (dubbed "the second sense" in the conventional Western hierarchy of the senses). He relates how a Songhay sorcerer once told him: "You *must* learn how to hear, or you will learn little about our ways" (Stoller, 1984: 560). Stoller's awakening to the significance of hearing among the Songhay led him to reflect on the importance of exploring the roles of different sensory *modes* of perception and not just focusing on the objects of perception. He writes in terms of sound that:

> Most anthropologists use the sound of language or music as a means to gather information with which they 'construct' the culture of the Other. We take the sound of language for granted. The Other, however, may consider language ... as an embodiment of [the power of] sound ....
>
> (Stoller, 1984: 569)

Other ethnographers, such as Susan Rasmussen (1999) and Vishvajit Pandya (1993), literally followed their noses to discover the centrality of olfactory codes among the Tuareg of Niger and the Ongee of the Andaman Islands, respectively.[5] Rasmussen writes that:

> Social and ritual uses of scent in Tuareg culture reveal that aroma has referents transcending its physical qualities. Smelling is not simply a pleasurable or painful chemical experience, which may trigger memories and alter moods or behaviors; it is also a symbolic and moral phenomenon.
>
> (Rasmussen, 1999: 69)

Rasmussen recounts how she had gone to Niger to study the role of music and songs in Tuareg spirit possession, but then found this research focus to be too narrow because Tuareg communicate with the spirits by means of incense as well. Only by overcoming her native tendency (as an American) "toward the compartmentalization of visual and oral from elements of taste and smell" was she able to make any headway (1999: 58). The instruction she received from her informants in how to prepare and drink tea the Tuareg way proved crucial in this regard.

Tuareg tea-drinking consists of three rounds: the first glass should be strong, the second sweet, and the third spiced. (For each round, while host and guests converse, the tea is mixed, boiled for a considerable length of time so that it "ripens", and strained three times.) The first glass is functional (for fortifying and sharpening the wits), while the last two are aesthetic, "but in all three glasses, there is sociability: one is supposed to be engaged in enjoyable conversation stimulated not only by the taste, but also by scent" (1999: 59). The mixing of the ingredients, and of the senses, thus both models and modulates the interaction between the participants. Amusingly, and quite tellingly, Rasmussen records that:

> When I sent some tea spices and condiments home to the United States, the difference in cultural associations became clear when my American relatives indicated they used them as potpourri sachet, rather than as condiments in tea or food.
>
> (1999: 59)

Judith Farquhar had her tastebuds jolted in the course of her study of the pharmacoepia of traditional Chinese medicine. In *Appetites*, she frankly admits that most of the herbal concoctions she was invited to sample "tasted simply horrid", that her palate never did become educated enough to discriminate Chinese medicine's Five Flavours, and that the idea of flavours as possessing medical efficacy seemed nonsensical to her, at least at first:

> the fact that drugs in the classic decoction form have flavor, that is, both an experiential quality and a classificatory function in a system of pharmaceutical effects raises the question of what the efficacy of a "flavour" is. Isn't it rather odd, at least for those of us steeped in the subject-object divide of Euro-American common sense, to think of a personal experience such as flavor acting directly on a biological condition?
>
> (Farquhar, 2002: 64)

In China, where food *is* medicine, specific combinations of flavours *do* have power in themselves. The taste is not incidental, not just a side-effect. What seems ephermeral is actually essential. Grasping this point proved vital to Farquhar's subsequent analysis of the experiential dimensions of Chinese medicine:

> This experiential side to Chinese medicine encourages a personal micropolitics, as patients [in collaboration with their physicians] seek to govern themselves and their immediate environment using techniques that fuse thinking and feeling, forming habits that make sense to their own senses.
>
> (2002: 66)

Like Chinese food, the complex flavours of Indian food are good to taste, but even better to theorize. This is because taste (*rasa*) is highly elaborated on multiple levels in the sensory model of Hindu India: for example, the Sanskrit gustatory vocabulary consists of a good six terms; Ayurvedic medical theory recognizes a range of "post-digestive tastes" (which are not the same as aftertastes); emotional states are classified as tastes (rather than what English-speakers call "feelings"); dietary differences determine an individual's rank in the caste system (with its progressive vegetarianism); and the order of the universe is held to depend on regular gustatory exchanges between humans and gods (Pinard, 1991). Indian anthropologists have coined a number of theoretical concepts to help interpret the role of

331

gustatory codes in Hindu thought and practice, concepts such as "gastrosemantics" (Khare, 2005), "rasaesthetics" (Schechner, 2001), and "gastropolitics" (Appadurai, 1981), and these concepts have contributed substantially to the sensualization of anthropological theory.[6]

Last, but no longer least, the domain of touch (and kinesthesia) has been opened to anthropological investigation. Consider Robert Kauffman's discovery, while undertaking a study of African music, that certain musical instruments were valued more for the ways in which they engaged the sense of touch than for the sounds they produced. Kauffman was alerted to the tactile aspects of African music only by the disconcerting fact that certain musical performances were scarcely audible, even to the performer. The *mbira*, a musical mouth bow, for instance, produces intense vibrations within the mouth but only very soft external sounds. Kauffman concluded that the concept of music as exclusively auditory in nature "has been one of the principal stumbling blocks in Western attempts to understand African music" (1979: 252).

Kauffman's findings regarding music are complemented by the late Cynthia Jean Cohen Bull's fascinating comparative study of the sensory underpinnings of select western and non-western dance styles, including Ghanaian dance. Bull begins by contrasting classical ballet and contact improv, which privilege different senses (vision and touch respectively) and thereby foster radically different subjectivities.[7] She goes on to explore the complex interplay between hearing and moving in Ghanaian dance, where no one just listens or watches (everybody moves), and the best dancers are able to respond to the multiple rhythms of the music through moving their hips to one beat, their heads to another, their shoulders to a third, and so on, all simultaneously. Ghanaians value flexibility within clear formal structures and they give expression to this value with every move they make in the dance.[8]

Conclusion

This chapter has touched upon some of the ways in which an anthropological (or cross-cultural) perspective on multimodality reveals a wide array of alternate modes of conjugating (discriminating and combining) the senses in cultural practice. The first lesson of the anthropology of the senses is that the senses operate *in relation to* each other in a continuous interplay of impressions and values. Cultivating the requisite cross-sensory awareness to grasp this interplay in a given cultural context is no easy task due to the deepset Western tendency to compartmentalize and hierarchize the senses. Different cultures divide up the sensorium differently, and also differ in the degree to which they elaborate different sensory fields (e.g. taste in the Indian context compared to sight in a Western context). The only constant is that there is little constancy to the multiple ways in which the senses can be combined (e.g. the privileging of audio-olfactory communication in Melanesian contexts compared to the elaboration of audio-visual communication, such as film and television, in a Western context). Tracing these permutations can be a source of many insights into "the multiple modes of human interconnection" (Finnegan, 2002), and is destined to radically reconfigure our understanding of the possibilities of human communication.

There are many potentially fruitful directions for research on multimodality in anthropology beginning with the basic question: "How many senses are there?" This question attracts different answers across cultures. Another key question is: "How many different sensory combinations might there be?" Further questions include: "What are the implications for cognition of a culture privileging one modality over another?" and: "How is the expression of such intermodal phenomena as synaesthesia affected by the way the senses are ordered in a given society?" The answers to these questions should be of interest to neuroscientists as well as anthropologists. As indicated previously, dialogue between these disciplines is vital if science is to arrive at a comprehensive understanding of how the sensorium functions. Thus far that understanding has been much too beholden to brain physiology (i.e. dominated by the discourse of neuroscience) and not sufficiently attuned to how "culture tunes our neurons" (Sacks in Howes, 2004: 22). Fortunately, this situation is changing thanks to the recent emergence of the interdisciplinary field of "sensory studies" where numerous humanities and social science disciplines have converged (see http://www.sensorystudies.org). Through the dialogue amongst these disciplines (e.g. history, sociology, anthropology) a more cultural (less purely psychophysical) understanding of how the senses work has begun to take shape. Neuroscientists will want to join in that conversation if they do not wish to be left behind.

In addition to acquiring knowledge about multimodality through the practice of anthropology, multimodality can come to the service of anthropology. This is particularly true with respect to the communication of anthropological knowledge. Traditionally, anthropologists have relied on texts and/or films to convey their findings. Both these media have serious limitations due to their intrinsic sensory biases: visual in the case of the text, audiovisual in the case of film. These biases can be mitigated through developing a disciplined conscious awareness of them (Howes, 2003: 10-17) though the challenge of conveying that awareness to the reader or viewer remains. An alternative solution, which has emerged thanks to the recent sensorial turn in museum studies (Classen and Howes, 2006), involves experimenting with the design of ethnographic and other exhibitions to bring the experiential, sensuous dimensions of our encounter with objects to the fore (Dudley, 2010) This move has entailed liberating museum pieces from their glass cases and allowing them (or their replicas) to be handled or smelled, or even tasted – as they were in the early days of the museum, it turns out (Classen, 2007; Candlin, 2010; Leahy, 2012).

Besides the new emphasis on encountering objects, or "experiencing the properties of things" (Dudley, 2012), the sensorial turn in museology has inspired researchers to use digital and other media to construct whole environments that simulate particular cultural contexts, like *Displace v. 1.0*, which was shown at the 2011 American Anthropological Association meetings.[9] Inspired by the example of the Desana sensory order, the Displace set enabled six visitors at a time to have their senses rearranged, and sensations transposed back and forth across modalities, during a 45-minute period. The shifting patterns of coloured light, sound, vibration, scent, taste, temperature and motion opened a crack in the conventional Western sensorium for those who experienced it, and enabled them to dwell, if only briefly, in a parallel sensory world. In this way, the burgeoning interest in multimodality is driving a revolution in the very content as well as presentation of knowledge.

Acknowledgements

Part of the research on which this chapter is based was made possible by a grant from the Conseil de Recherches en Sciences Humaines et Sociales du Canada.

Notes

1 Or even earlier periods of Western culture. For example, a form of audio-grapheme synaesthesia has been described for the Renaissance: "In a person's handwriting, Erasmus claimed, he could hear that person's very voice" (Smith, 2004: 28). See further Woolf (1986).

2 An example of odours displaying taste properties would be the classification of a given scent, such as vanilla, as sweet (see Stevenson and Boakes, 2004).

3 That is, proximity of brain areas would no longer be the determinative criterion (*pace* Ramachandran *et al.*), as indeed it is not given all the evidence of cross-modal activation, feed-forward and back- projection processes that has begun to emerge.

4 This account of the Desana sensory order is woven together from the analyses presented in Classen (1993), Classen *et al.* (1994), and Howes (2003), all of which in turn refer back to the brilliant ethnography of Gerardo Reichel-Dolmatoff (see especially Reichel-Dolmatoff, 1978, 1981).

5 Among the Ongee, the categories of the person, time and space are all mediated by the sense of smell (Pandya, 1993; Classen, 1993) instead of being visualized, as in the West.

6 Schechner's "Rasesthetics" is particularly noteworthy. He compares the very different ways in which theatrical experience is theorized gustatorially and viscerally in the Indian tradition descending from the *Natayashastra* and visually or intellectually in the Western tradition which stems from the *Poetics* of Aristotle. His analysis does, however, suffer from a certain essentialism (Mason, 2006), and could be more relational in my estimation.

7 In terms of subjectivities, Bull suggests that the ballet world is suffused with an ethos of competitive individualism, and she relates this to the visual objectification of the body. Contact improv is concerned with feelings rather than appearances, and cultivates a deep interiority accordingly.

8 In a related vein, Geurts (2002) records that among the Anlo-Ewe of Ghana, being able to stand upright and move on two legs is considered the hallmark of humanity, and the Anlo-Ewe language contains over fifty terms for different "kinaesthetic styles". Each of these ways of walking is held to say something about a person's moral character: for example, one may stride like a lion (*kadzakadza*) or zigzag as if drunk (*lugulugu*). Significantly, Anlo-Ewe people hold that loss of hearing is "the most grave impairment of sensory perception because with this loss would come a disruption to their sense of balance" (Geurts, 2002: 50). This led Geurts to treat the intertwined senses of hearing and balance as the keystone of the Anlo-Ewe sensory model.

9 For a complete documentation of the Displace experience see the Exhibition section of the Centre for Sensory Studies website (http://www.centreforsensorystudies.org). For a related experiment in promoting cross-modal and multimodal learning see the work of Art Beyond Sight (http://www.artbeyondsight.org/).

Further reading

Classen, C. (1997) 'Foundations for an anthropology of the senses.' *International Social Science Journal* 153: 401–12. (The classic review essay which defined the field of sensory anthropology.)

Finnegan, R. (2002) *Communicating: The Multiple Modes of Human Interconnection*, London: Routledge. (The most comprehensive overview of the anthropological literature on the senses as channels of communication.)

Howes, D. (2003) *Sensual Relations: Engaging the Senses in Culture and Social Theory*, Ann Arbor: University of Michigan Press. (An overview of the role of the senses in anthropological theory and a comparative study of the sensory orders of two Melanesian societies.)

Laplantine, F. (2005) *Le social et le sensible: introduction à une anthropologie modale*, Paris: Téraèdre. (A profound reflection on the social life of the senses and the varieties of sensory experience across cultures.)

Sutton, D. (2001) *Remembrances of Repasts*, Oxford: Berg. (A groundbreaking study of multimodality in the preparation and consumption of food in Greek culture.)

Part IV

Multimodal case studies

Introduction to Part IV

This final part concludes the handbook with a demonstration of how the theoretical concepts, methodological tools, and key factors described in the previous chapters can be applied. The ten chapters included in this part also indicate the scope of multimodal analysis and the types of research questions that it can be used to address, across a variety of contexts, phenomena and texts through a set of multimodal case studies.

A range of modes including space, gesture, gaze, body posture and movement, kineikonic mode, colour, sound, voice and music, image and written and spoken language, and three-dimensional objects are examined in the chapters. Each chapter foregrounds a specific mode within a multimodal ensemble, provides a brief introduction to the key literature on this mode, and through instances of multimodal analysis describes its semiotic resources, material affordances, and organizing principles. Each mode is examined in a specific context of use and how it features in and is shaped by people's social interaction – furniture designers, surgeons, tourists or school students – is explored.

Modes are always a part of a multimodal ensemble and, as these chapters show, the relationship between modes is key to the realization of meaning. The intention of analytically foregrounding a mode within this ensemble is to extend the understanding and descriptive language with respect to each mode and thus to better understand how these modes might work together.

The chapters demonstrate different uses of the term mode and associated concepts discussed throughout the handbook including the 'logics' of modes, semiotic resource, sign and mode, modal choice, genre and discourse. Given the strongly situated nature of communication the purpose of these chapters is not set out a universal inventory for a mode. That would not be possible or useful. Rather, the purpose of these illustrative multimodal case studies is to show that what is considered a mode and the types of interaction between modes is inextricably shaped and construed by social, cultural and historical factors.

Material products and three-dimensional objects can be understood as a set of semiotic resources, or a mode. Multimodal research has investigated the semiotic potentials of multimodal artefacts and their use in a variety of settings. In the context of the school science classroom, for instance, multimodal research has been conducted on students' use of science equipment in experiments (Franks and Jewitt, 2001), as has the use of models by teachers in their classroom demonstrations (Kress *et al.*, 2001). These studies have shown how the semiotic resources of three-dimensional objects can be seen as the material residue of social action – the traces of designed rhetorical work; designs which when activated in use do not determine, but play a part in shaping forms of interaction through the potentials and constraints that they offer. Another example of a multimodal study of artefacts is the work of Pahl and Pollard (2008) in their study of British families of Pakistani origin and migration, in which they worked with multimodal artefacts to explore families' narratives of migration and identity.

Björkvall, in Chapter 24, describes the dimensions of tables as products and three-dimensional objects. Tables are approached as material objects that are pertinent for a wide array of social and practical activities. The relation between practical function and symbolic meaning potential is brought to the fore when analysing such objects. He argues that the shapes and materials of tables have practical functionality and that they are at the same time symbolic: a robust round table made of pine wood may have a different meaning potential to that of a square table made of plastic. A number of semiotic resources of tables are discussed in the chapter including shape, size, finish, colour and so on. Through analytical examples, the chapter shows how a number of functional values are realized by differences in the size and elevation of the tabletop, as well as interpersonal aspects of tables. The examples in the chapter are drawn from IKEA tables of different types. The chapter provides a set of dimensions that could be applied to other objects or which could be elaborated and adapted as appropriate.

Considerable work has been conducted on gaze and gesture within interactional studies, conversation analysis and socio-linguistics, much of which has been informed by the seminal work of Charles Goodwin (2001, 2007a), David McNeill (2000, 2005a) and Adam Kendon (1990, 2004a). Gaze and gesture are central to multimodal research, the majority of which includes the analysis and discussion of both these modes. Multimodal research that foregrounds gaze and gesture has also been undertaken, and here I just briefly mention three examples. For example, Bezemer (2008) analysed gaze and gesture as key modes in students' displays of orientation in the classroom. He examined how gaze and gesture in the silent but active participation of a recently immigrated student in a secondary classroom in England demonstrated her understanding of the changing contextual grounds for meaning-making in the classroom. The function of gaze in a young child's interpretation of symbolic forms was the focus Lancaster's study of early literacy (2001). In a study of entry points and reading paths on newspaper spreads, Holsanova *et al.* (2006) investigated newspaper-reading from a multimodal perspective with eye-tracking data which found three main categories of readers: editorial readers, overview readers and focused readers.

In Chapter 25, Bezemer argues that much of the work on gesture to date has focused on its use in conversations. Extending that work he looks at the use of gesture in the professional activities of health-care professionals in operating theatres, taking surgical activity as an exemplar of all kinds of 'operations' in everyday and professional life. This enables an exploration of gesture in an environment where speech is 'the occasional accompaniment of gesture, rather than focusing on an environment in which gesture is the occasional accompaniment of speech, as scholars of gesture … have often done'. By moving beyond the conversation as a context for studying gesture Bezemer foregrounds the different semiotic potentialities of gesture as a mode. He draws on examples taken from audio- and video-recordings of operations from an ethnographic study of a surgical department in a hospital. Focusing on a small selection of clips from these recordings he develops a semiotic account of gesture.

Staying with gesture, Jaworski and Thurlow focus on gaze and gesture in Chapter 26 in the context of tourists' social interaction with and construction of place and identities to suggest that the tourist performance can be viewed as a form of multimodal discourse. The chapter argues strongly for a multisensory approach to tourism that attends to the multimodal and mediated practices of seeing and the interplay between the physical environment of the tourist site and tourist behaviour. The chapter analyses the displays of tourists' nonverbal, kinesic behaviour, to suggest that gesture and movement are socially regulated forms of mediated action that emerge at the intersection of mediational means, social actors and the socio-cultural environment. The chapter offers an account of how identity and mode are linked, and from a methodological standpoint it shows how one might use video and visual data effectively for multimodal analysis.

Multimodality theory offers new ways to think about the combination of sign-systems to be found in such cultural forms as narrative film, television, animation, moving-image art installations and machinima. In Chapter 27, Burn proposes a multimodal theory of the moving image, named the kineikonic mode: kineikonic results from a combination of the Greek words for 'to move' (*kinein*) and 'image' (*eikon*) (Burn and Parker, 2003) and emphasizes the interplay of all the modes which contribute to the moving image. The kineikonic attends to a grammar of the moving image at the level of the individual frame as well as the shot. Through the chapter Burn outlines his approach to the kineikonic mode and develops two analytical frameworks. The first, what he terms the *metamodal* relationship between the orchestrating modes of filming and editing and the contributory modes. The notion of the *metamodal* serves to emphasize the nesting of modes within modes in moving image texts. Second, the notion of the *kineikonic chronotope* – adapted from Bakhtin's metaphor of space–time relations in literature (Gibbons, 2010) is useful for the purpose of analysis, as it distinguishes between the spatial and temporal axis of the moving image. This allows for the distinction between the spatial axis of the single frame and an analysis of visual modes (e.g. visual design of characters and sets and functions of shot-grammar) and the temporal axis of the moving sequence (e.g. movement of bodies, music, sound and speech, as well as the movement of the camera and frame, etc.). The kineikonic framework and concepts are explored through two contrasting illustrative examples: one from a narrative film produced in 1948, and one from a machinima film made by 11-year-olds in 2013.

The semantic patterns arising from the integration of language, images and audio resources in multimodal texts are the focus of Chapter 28, what O'Halloran refers to as *multimodal analytics*. This task presents considerable theoretical and practical challenges that are addressed in the chapter. O'Halloran argues that the complexity of the analytical task requires suitable tools and techniques to capture and interpret the multimodal analysis that support linguistic, visual and aural choices and their interactions analysis in order to discern semantic patterns in multimodal texts. The chapter reports on research which aims to address these issues through a *multimodal digital semiotics* approach involving the development of interactive software with functionalities and facilities for systematic multimodal analysis of text, images and videos. The chapter provides a detailed account of the social semiotic approach underlying the design of the software and the mathematical and visualization techniques which are applied to the multimodal data and illustrates the resulting patterns and trends which are interpreted in relation to the situational and cultural context of the video recording.

Keeping attention on moving image, film and video for a third chapter, Van Leeuwen shifts attention to the role of colour as a code, mode, and modality in Chapter 29. The chapter argues that semiotic practices can only be properly understood in their social context, and, more particularly, in the context of the normative discourses which regulate or influence them. It does so with reference to the semiotics of colour. By focusing on colour in film and video, Van Leeuwen shows that contemporary semiotic practices are intricately interwoven with technological developments, and change as technology changes. He argues that contemporary digital technology has 'not only codified the modalities developed in the era of film and video, but also enabled the digital colouring and recolouring of parts of images' and that 'normative power has moved from art design to software design' as a result. He goes on to argue that this shift foregrounds the need to consider the affordances and constraints of semiotic software in understanding semiotic practices and the normative discourses which regulate and influence them to better understand how colour and other semiotic resources are used in digital environments.

The next chapter turns to the mode of sound and music. Van Leeuwen's *Speech, Music, Sound* (1999) is a study of sound and music from a multimodal perspective. The book draws on phonetic, linguistic, pragmatic, semiotic, and musicological sources, to suggest and illustrate a multimodal social semiotic approach to the communicative roles of sound. This includes rhythm, melody, and timbre in music, speech, everyday soundscapes, and soundtracks. In Chapter 30, West offers an analysis of interaction as a combination of music, speech, and gesture (including gaze, body movement, positioning in the room, use of artefacts, etc.) within an educational setting. The analysis of music as a mode is focused on its specific educational functions and how it adds resources for meaning-making to speech and gesture. This chapter goes beyond the view of a 'pure' musical communication and expands the notion of music as aesthetic experiences and ways of aesthetic expression. Musical learning is seen as a dynamic process of transformative sign making where an expansion of the access to diverse semiotic resources increases the repertoire of representations within the field.

The mode of space, and spatiality, have been important features of urban sociology and geography studies, and more recently in studies on technology and globalization. Multimodal studies have focused on the analysis of space with respect to the city, and buildings, such as O'Toole's analysis of the Sydney Opera House (2004), museums and exhibitions (e.g. Ravelli, 2006), the analysis of rooms, for example Kress and Van Leeuwen's (2001) analysis of a child's bedroom as an indicator of gendered identity, and the design of office spaces (e.g. Van Leeuwen, 2005c), and virtual spaces. The communicative function of space is the focus of Stenglin's case study in Chapter 31 which focuses on the analysis of *Scumbag*, an exhibition by artist Ella Dreyfus at a Sydney gallery. She analyses the exhibition from a communicative social semiotic perspective and examines the shift from two- to three-dimensional modes. In particular the chapter considers the ways some choices evoke responses from visitors in an attempt to 'unpack' the materialization of the communicative functions in three-dimensional space.

Image has received considerable attention across the disciplines including within sociology (e.g. Hamilton, 2006), anthropology (e.g. Pink, 2006; Howes, Chapter 23 this volume) and visual studies (Machin, Chapter 15 this volume). Image provided the foundation for multimodality with landmark studies by Kress and Van Leeuwen (1996) and O'Toole (1994). Numerous studies have examined the role of images, for instance, in education (e.g. see Jewitt, 2008b, for a review of images in education), advertising, and news reporting (e.g. Chouliaraki, 2006, Chapter 18 this volume; Knox, Chapter 33 this volume) among many other topics. Writing too has been the subject of much multimodal investigation; key studies include Kress on children's writing (1997a, 2003b), Scollon and Scollon (2003) on writing, space and place, Unsworth (2001) on literacy, and Kenner (2004) on bilingual scripts and learners.

The use of the modal resources of writing and image is the focus of Mavers in Chapter 32. She focuses on the relationship between drawing and writing in children's multimodal mapping as one instance of image in the multimodal ensemble. She shows how analysing image in the multimodal ensemble demands attendance to the variety of ways in which signs have been made. It examines how the children distributed meanings between modes and shaped meanings within these modes as they represented their knowledge and experiences. The case study shows the benefits of examining different 'levels' of text – individual textual items, relationships between items and whole-text interrelationships – using social semiotic methods for the analysis of image in the multimodal ensemble.

The shift from page to screen provides the context for Chapter 33, in which Knox focuses on the modal resources of structure and layout using a case-study example of online newspapers. Knox argues that the importance of visual communication in writing is now, perhaps more than ever, in focus with the emergence of the Internet and in ways that raise questions for researching writing and reading, as well as the critical exploration of related social practices and power relations. The chapter looks at the role of website structure, page design and layout in the reporting of news in online newspapers. Knox develops a framework for the analysis of the layout of online newspaper home pages, drawing on a framework based on systemic functional multimodal discourse analysis. Through the application of this framework he illustrates that while language plays a central role in the discursive practice of online news reporting, a consideration of layout and web structure is crucial to a holistic picture of these complex digital texts.

Taken as a set, the ten chapters presented in this final part of the handbook demonstrate how a multimodal approach can help better understand representation and communication, including the place of writing and speech within this multimodal landscape. The chapters address the questions outlined in the introduction to this handbook; they show what is involved in multimodal research and what kinds of research questions this perspective might attend to. The question of how to analyse modes, the kind of data that it might be useful to collect within multimodal research is examined. Processes for the analysis of multimodal data are also explored, including the contextual data that might be required for interpretation, the transcription of multimodal data, and ways of interrogating the distribution of meaning across a multimodal ensemble. The case studies give a sense of both the benefits and the limitations of a multimodal approach.

In summary, these chapters show the theoretical concepts and methodological procedures of multimodality in action, and are the final contribution of this handbook to a 'research toolkit' for multimodal analysis.

24

Practical function and meaning

A case study of IKEA tables

Anders Björkvall

Introduction

Objects like tables are different from many other multimodal artefacts given the importance of their practical function. To a large extent, a table is defined by its ability to serve as a surface of varying elevation for human interaction and activities, and for carrying objects. In this way, communication is not the primary function of tables. However, that is not to say that tables are not semiotic. Tables are multimodal and semiotic artefacts, and it will be shown in this chapter that their size, shape, and material have meaning potentials that combine in different ways.

This chapter presents an analysis of the semiotics of tables. The chapter is based on a larger study of meanings and uses of free-standing (rather than wall-mounted) IKEA tables in Australia. IKEA tables are usually designed in Sweden, produced somewhere in the world, sold globally, and used and interpreted locally. This raises questions about the relation between global and more culture-specific meanings of IKEA tables, which will also be considered in the chapter.

Theoretical issues in research on practical objects

The practical function of practical objects in relation to their more symbolic meanings is a theoretical concern that has been treated in different ways in previous research. Krampen (1989, 1995) recognises two meaningful layers in everyday objects. The first and *denotative* layer is described as that of direct functional meanings, which distinguish one type of object from another. The second layer has to do with *connotative* meanings, which are defined as stylistic variations in, for example, the shape of objects with the same functional meaning (Krampen, 1989: 134). A teapot can have the denotative functional meaning of 'allowing for pouring tea into cups', but it can also connote 'tradition', 'artistry' or 'Englishness' depending on, among other things, its shape. Connotation is relevant for the discussion of more local meanings of IKEA tables but will be related more to cultures and sub-cultures than is the case in Krampen's research.

O'Toole (2011: 64), discussing buildings, another type of artefact with obvious practical uses, says that practical function can be viewed as a sort of representation in itself (original italics): 'the function of a building is, first and foremost, the *use* for which it has been designed' but at the same time buildings 'signify' their function as use'. Operating in a Hallidayan tradition, O'Toole classifies this functional meaning of buildings as *experiential*, based on our experiences of how the built world works.

Van Leeuwen (2005a), also discussing buildings but in relation to the extreme functionalist architecture of the 1920s and '30s, advocates a social semiotic approach in which the relation between practical function and symbolic meaning is described as interdependent:

> [B]uildings are always both symbolic and functional ... Yes, of course, housing serves the basic functions of shelter, warmth, comfort, stability, and so on, but these are themselves semiotic, as they are inevitably culturally inflected, differently understood and differently practised in different cultures and eras.
>
> (Van Leeuwen, 2005a: 72–73)

A similar view to that of Van Leeuwen is adopted in this study of tables. If we believe that the practical functions of tables stem from culturally motivated human needs, it seems a difficult task to separate the practical and the semiotic, although it may be possible to discuss certain aspects of tables as more symbolic than others.

Another crucial theoretical issue is that of the relation between the design of an object and its use. Cubitt (1988: 129), in a case study of objects in a pub, writes that

> it seems increasingly that the intention behind designed objects plays a smaller and smaller role in their use as they move further, spatially, culturally, and temporally, from their point of manufacture. It is in their use that they find their meaning.

If meaning only equals use, the epistemological value of a semiotic analysis of the design choices in tables could be questioned.

However, Riggins (1990: 344) takes a more moderate position and says that the physical qualities and intended use of an object always influence its meanings 'regardless of how much the context has been altered'. In this view, design is more important and, in a way, also has the potential to work more globally and interculturally. In any case, the relation between design and use has methodological implications for the semiotic analysis of practical objects.

Methodology

The methodology of this study is inspired by Van Leeuwen's (2005a: 3) description of semiotic analysis in terms of the documentation of *semiotic resources* and the investigation of how these resources are used in various contexts and how new uses of existing resources develop. This study is primarily concerned with the documentation of semiotic resources of tables and their uses in different contexts, leaving out new uses for the time being.

The concept of semiotic resources comes from social semiotics, originally formulated by Halliday (e.g. 1978), but more recently discussed in regard to three-dimensional objects in Van Leeuwen (2003) and Kress and Van Leeuwen (2006). In this study of tables, a semiotic resource is defined as an observable feature of the table that has been drawn into the social and cultural process of meaning-making. This definition does not exclude the possibility that the same

343

resource may have obvious practical functions as well. When a semiotic resource is put to use, it realises a *semiotic potential*, or *meaning potential*, defined as possible meanings in various contexts. Semiotic meaning potentials can be further divided to address the design/use dichotomy discussed above. The *theoretical semiotic potential* of an object has to do with its design, previous uses and functions, as well as potential uses and functions. The *actual semiotic potentials* are those that users of an object consider relevant for meaning-making based on their specific needs in given contexts and their knowledge of the uses of the resources (Van Leeuwen, 2005a: 4).

The first stage of this study, aimed at identifying and describing the semiotic resources of tables and their theoretical meaning potential, included visits to the IKEA store in Sydney, where IKEA tables were photographically documented. The table sections in the 2007 Swedish and Australian IKEA catalogues were studied in detail. This stage also included interviews with IKEA staff about, among other things, their professional views of differences between IKEA tables.

The second stage was aimed at describing the actual meaning potential of the tables. Inspired by Riggins' (1990: 358, 1994: 106–11) ethnographic approach to the study of the meanings of domestic objects, this part involved documentation of how six different IKEA tables were placed in six different homes in the Sydney metropolitan area and interviews with the owners of the tables. In other words, the meaning potentials of 'objects and artifacts-in-place' (Rowsell, 2011: 335–36) were analysed. This stage also included a focus group discussion involving six other participants: two with Swedish backgrounds, one with an American background, and three Australians. Among other things, the participants were shown photos of four IKEA tables and were asked to physically touch and test three other tables in the IKEA store. The discussion then addressed the uses and looks of the tables and the participants' attitudes toward the different tables.

Human–table interactivity

In the analysis of practical objects, it is often useful to first ask what the design of the object allows us to do with it. Even though tables are multifunctional and allow us to do various things with them, for example sit around them and work or place other objects on them, there are differences in the design of IKEA tables that are directly related to *human–table interactivity*. Fleming (1999: 45) discusses the history of the table as a process of increasingly specified functionality due to more specified human activities and needs. In particular, he speaks of tables as extensions of the human body for different purposes. In this perspective, the basic distinction between IKEA tables seems to be that between tables with space for human knees underneath the table and tables without such a space. Tables such as dining tables and desks that allow humans to be seated at them with their knees underneath the table allow for a more *intense* relation between humans and the table. The legs of the human body can almost be absorbed by the space underneath the table if the chair on which the person is seated is placed close enough to the top of the table.

Tables without such a space for human knees do not allow the human body to be absorbed by the table. Such tables, for example coffee tables, are usually lower with a much more restricted space underneath the table. Because of the physical distance between human bodies and such tables, the relation is better described as *restrained*. The distinction between intense and restrained tables also has its realisation in the IKEA catalogues and on IKEA websites: restrained tables such as coffee tables and side tables are presented in one section and intense tables such as dining tables and desks in other sections.

I suggest that the meaning potential of human–table interactivity can be presented as a number of possible choices in a *system network*, as in Figure 24.1. The network should be read from left to right with the sub-systems of *interpersonal relations* (including *involvement*, *hierarchy* and *social distance*) and *display* indicated in capitals. The square brackets in Figure 24.1 stand for either/or relations, e.g. the interactive meaning potential of a table is either 'intense' or 'restrained'. These meaning potentials are *realised* either by knee space under the table or by the lack of such a space, which is marked by the downward sloping, fully lined arrows in Figure 24.1. The curly bracket following interpersonal relations in the upper right-hand corner of Figure 24.1 indicates that the choices that follow can be made simultaneously.

If the basic functional categorisation of tables that IKEA catalogues and websites provide is matched with the documented uses of different tables in Australian homes, it is clear that both intense and restrained tables can function as mediators between humans sitting around a table or between humans and objects placed on tables. Intense dining and meeting tables, desks and computer tables can be placed on a scale between *human* or *object orientation* marked by double-edged dotted arrows in Figure 24.1. Restrained coffee, side, storage and pedestal tables have also been placed on such a scale in Figure 24.1. It should be noted that the italicised types of tables in Figure 24.1 have been placed on the continuous scales based on their functional description in IKEA catalogues and on their functions and uses in real homes rather than on specific distinctive features in their design.

Coffee tables illustrate the continuum between human and object orientation quite well. On the one hand, they are perceived as object-oriented, which was obvious from the interviews but also made explicit in the focus group discussion:

CHAIR OF FOCUS GROUP:	What do you do with a coffee table?
PARTICIPANT 1:	Oh, you just put books on it and
PARTICIPANT 2:	Yes, and magazines and if you fix a cup of tea
CHAIR:	You put books on it and what else?
PARTICIPANT 3:	Remote controls.

On the other hand, coffee tables seem to have a certain amount of human orientation. The square Lack table in Figure 24.2 carries the typical remote controls in this Sydney home, but given its shape and placement it also has some human orientation related to its ability to position people around it, although the power of this human orientation is not as strong as for an intense dining or meeting table.

Moving further to the right in the system network in Figure 24.1, tables have meaning potentials with regard to interpersonal relations between humans sitting around the table and to the display of other objects. Interpersonal meaning potentials are more relevant the more human-oriented a table is, but as no IKEA table is exclusively human-oriented, they all have interpersonal meaning potential to different degrees, and they can all display other objects.

Let us start with the meaning potential of display, connected to object orientation in the system network. All tables can carry other objects, but object-oriented tables like desks and computer and pedestal tables tend to do so more permanently than human-oriented tables like dining and meeting tables. The latter are often (more or less) cleared of objects when the dinner or the meeting is over. The displayed objects can be of *immediate use value*, like knives and forks, keyboards or remote controls (cf. Figure 24.2). These objects are *active objects* that require actions to complement them. The objects can also have *contemplation value*, like displayed flowers and photos. These are more *passive objects* that do not require physical actions (but often mental consideration) to complement them (Riggins, 1990: 353). Again, there is no either/or distinction

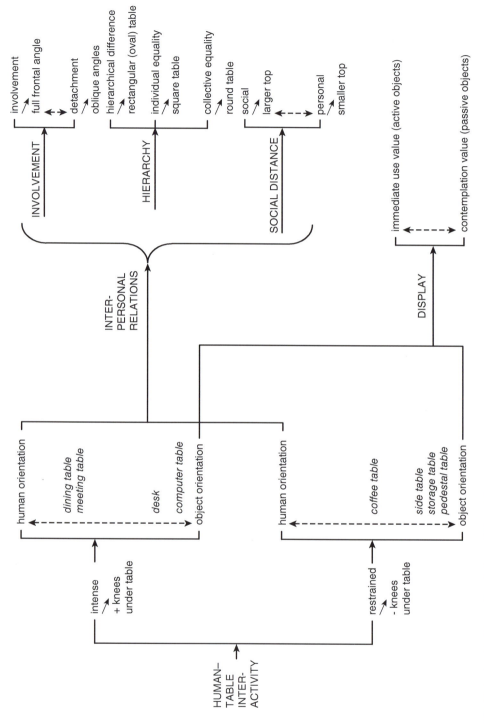

Figure 24.1 Human–table interactivity: system network.

Figure 24.2 The Lack table.

between the objects with immediate use value and those with contemplation value, which is marked by the double-edged dotted arrow in Figure 24.1.

The interpersonal meaning potentials have to do with a table's potential to structure face-to-face interaction between the people around it in a meaningful way. Human-oriented tables, which have this potential to a high degree, can be described as *social facilitators* that 'can give groups a different structure than what they would have without them' (Riggins, 1990: 351). The main interpersonal meaning potentials of tables have to do with involvement, hierarchy and social distance.

Involvement

In visual communication through images, involvement can be realised by the horizontal angles set up between the viewer of the image and what is depicted. The full-frontal angle is the angle of high involvement, and the higher the obliqueness of the angle is, the more what is depicted is *detached* from the viewer (Kress and Van Leeuwen, 2006: 133–40). The shape of table tops is by far the most important resource for meanings of involvement in tables.

The Björkudden rectangular table in Figure 24.3 allows people to face each other across the two long sides or two short sides from the full frontal angle of maximum involvement. This is also the case for a longer, oval table and a square table. The angles of higher obliqueness, and thus of relatively higher detachment, are created between people seated at the long sides and short sides, who thus have to turn their heads to face each other.

A round table does not distinguish between higher involvement and detachment in such an obvious way and allows for involvement between a larger number of people at the table. This is why the meaning potential of involvement/detachment is presented as scaled and not as an either/or relation in Figure 24.1.

Figure 24.3 The Björkudden table.

Hierarchy

In theories of film and image, hierarchical relations are often said to be realised by the vertical angles from which the viewer is positioned in relation to depicted persons (Kress and Van Leeuwen, 2006: 140). In tables, the vertical angle can have hierarchical meaning potential, but then it has more to do with the relative height of the chairs around the table than with specific features of the table. Just as with involvement, the shape of the table top is the major semiotic resource for meanings of hierarchy in tables.

For rectangular tables like the Björkudden table in Figure 24.3, the short ends have a long history of being reserved for the host and hostess or other important persons. The rectangular table is thus a table with the meaning potential of *hierarchical difference* (see Figure 24.1), which is also recognised by the owner of the Björkudden dining table in discussing a longer rectangular table in the IKEA catalogue. She does not speak explicitly about hierarchy but says that the interaction between people seated at the table is negatively affected by its formal character:

> I'm trying to steer away from the really long rectangular tables. [. . .] If you're sitting at that table you feel like it's going to be formal [. . .] Ehm, yeah, it's good for, maybe good for a meeting or something but. . .

Expressions like 'roundtable meeting' and 'roundtable discussion', on the other hand, highlight the specific interpersonal potential of the round table, where the singling out of one or two positions around the table is minimised by the shape of the table top: there are no separated sides. The round table has the meaning potential of *collective equality*.

The square table, like the rectangular table, separates the different sides from each other, but because the sides are of equal length all the sides have the same hierarchical status. In other words, the square table creates an individual separateness between the sides because of the distinct division between them, but because of their equal length there is no ranking of the sides. Thus, the square table has the hierarchical meaning potential of *individual equality*.

Social distance

The main semiotic resource for social distance between people is the size of the table top. The semiotic principle is quite simple: the larger the table top, the longer the physical and symbolic distance between the people surrounding the table (cf. Figure 24.1). Basically, everybody seated at a dining or meeting table of standard height (73–75 cm) shows most of the upper half of their body to other people around the table. The physical distance between people facing each other is often close enough for them to touch each other if they extend their arms, but it all depends on the size of the table top. In other words, a common social distance set by intense human-oriented tables is what Hall (1969: 113–14) calls *personal distance–far phase*. This is the distance humans usually keep for conversations of a more personal nature. The distance between people seated at large tables, like that between the two heads of the Grimle table in Figure 24.4, may be longer than four feet, resulting in what Hall (1969: 114–16) calls a *social*, more formal distance.

However, most tables set up much closer distances between people sitting next to each other. They are usually placed within the realm of *personal distance–close phase* (Hall, 1969: 113), which might be uncomfortable for people who do not have an intimate social relationship. Again, the angles between people have some importance, in this case to reduce the intimateness of the

Figure 24.4 The Grimle table.

close physical distance between partners at a table. The oblique detachment angle between partners at a table somewhat reduces the social distance-related implications of sitting next to each other. The angle of detachment makes it possible to actually sit through a dinner, or an evening at a long bar, without looking at or speaking to one's partner at the table, whereas it is more difficult not to socially engage with people in the high involvement setting, even though the physical distance may be longer.

The different meanings of table materials

Some features of tables seem to have more culture-specific meaning potentials than the interactive ones presented in Figure 24.1, with the human body as the basic point of reference. These meaning potentials have to do with the materials of the table and can be described as the more connotative meanings of tables, if connotation is understood as meaning potentials of semiotic resources with similar practical functions that are agreed upon within certain cultures or subcultures but not necessarily across them.

Judging from the interviews and the focus group, Australian IKEA customers recognise two styles of tables: 'modern' and 'country'. Modern tables are light, dark brown or black wooden tables, glass tables, and white tables. Country tables are made of solid wood, medium brown in colour, often antique-stained and, according to the interviews with staff at IKEA, country-style tables have been the best-selling IKEA tables for a long time, but modern tables have recently gained in popularity. There is a tradition of robust wooden tables in Australia. For instance, Avery (2007: 78) discusses how Australians in the late nineteenth century started to produce their own solid-timber furniture on a larger scale when the quality of English furniture exported to Australia was questioned due to, among other things, lifting veneers in the humid Australian climate. This solid-wood tradition was also reflected in the focus group, when one of the Australians said that 'there is something Australian about some of the furniture [*from IKEA*], [. . .] there is some colonial stuff, some Australian, colonial [. . .] a bit of timber'.

The owner of the Björkudden table in Figure 24.3, a 24-year-old Australian student, would never consider buying a dining table that was not made of solid wood. The light colour of her Björkudden table is the result of a compromise with her flatmate, who wanted a more modern-style table. The lighter wood had more modern connotations to both of them. The owner would otherwise have bought an antique-stained wooden table to get a traditional country-style table. That colour, and the solidity of the wood, has the meaning of 'family values' to her. In the focus group and in the other interviews, people with Australian backgrounds tended to describe such tables as representing 'family values' and being 'genuine' and 'sturdy'.

This meaning potential of antique-stained wood may be contrasted with the views of a participant who had just moved to Australia from Indonesia. He described the wooden tables at IKEA as too 'common' (in Australia) and 'boring'. Instead he preferred tables, like the Grimle table in Figure 24.4, that are more obviously industrially produced: '[*Grimle*] seems like [. . .] a product [. . .] that has been created by certain machinery [. . .] I don't think that common people can, can create it'.

The Grimle table is described as modern by all the participants in the study. However, the white melamine plastic-covered table top and the steel legs seemed to have other meaning potentials as well, and these varied between the participants with Australian and American backgrounds and those with Swedish or (various) Asian backgrounds. The two Swedes in the

Figure 24.5 The Laver table.

focus group described the Grimle table as a good-looking 'formal' dining table, reminding them of other Scandinavian modernist classics. To the participants with Australian or American back-grounds, the material of the table had the opposite meaning of 'informal'. Especially the steel legs were not considered solid enough for the table to be 'formal'. In the case of the Grimle table, it was obvious that the different cultural backgrounds of the participants and attached value systems for furniture materials were partially oppositional (cf. Björkvall and Karlsson, 2011 for a discourse approach to materiality and artefacts).

Glass, and frosted glass in particular, is a final example of a table material with more culture-specific meaning potential. When asked about the prototypical buyer of the Laver table in Figure 24.5, two of the three IKEA staff members interviewed answered that it would be a young person with an Asian background. The people in the study with various Asian back-grounds tended to like the tables with frosted glass, and the owner of the Laver table, who had lived in Indonesia for most of his life, said that glass is 'tidy', 'clean' and 'more luxury' than wood. He was also used to glass tables from his home in Indonesia, and from his Chinese family history. This 'luxury' was not at all recognised by the participants in the focus group, who called glass tables, among other things, 'ugly'.

Summary and discussion

The analysis has shown that the main semiotic resources for meanings of human–table interactivity are the design of the base of the table (knee space or not) and the shape and size of the table top. These are all more-or-less related to the table as an extension of the human body and, given the similar constitution of human bodies all over the world, we have reason to believe that their human-table interactive meaning potentials are somewhat global.

It is, however, important to note that this result is based on a study of IKEA tables and the findings of this study may not applicable to all other types of tables. One such table is the Japanese low table, used for dining. Initially the design of this table may be considered a restrained table, which is not the case for dining tables from IKEA (cf. Figure 24.1). However, the Japanese table is usually combined with low chairs or just floor pillows. This lowers the position of human bodies in relation to the table, creating a more intense relation between humans and the table, similar to that of the intense IKEA dining tables. Added to this, the elevation of the dining activity will be lower at the Japanese table, a fact that most certainly has a historically grounded meaning potential. This would require further research in order to be explored.

For the more connotative and arguably more culture-specific meaning potentials of tables, the main semiotic resource is the material, including its colour and solidity. Even though such meaning potentials are partly experientially based, having to do with people's physical experience of how other objects made of similar materials look and feel (Kress and Van Leeuwen, 2001: 74–78), they are probably also related to, for example, dining traditions in different cultures and historical uses and meanings of table materials. The association between solid antique-stained wood and 'family values' in Australia is an example of the importance of local traditions in meaning making of this type. The meaning potential of 'luxury' and 'tidiness' of frosted glass expressed by participants with various Asian backgrounds and the contrastive meaning potentials of, among other things, 'formal' and 'informal' for white steel-legged tables proved to be other more culture-specific meanings of table materials.

The theoretical discussion about the design vs. use of practical objects (e.g. Cubitt, 1988; Riggins, 1990) had methodological implications for this case study: the semiotic analysis of more theoretical meaning potentials of the design of the tables was combined with research methods focusing on uses and actual meaning potentials (photographic documentation, interviews and focus groups). One methodological point is that the meaning potentials of table materials could hardly have been identified without the more ethnographically oriented studies. The semiotic description of human–table interactivity, summarised in Figure 24.1, has also benefited from the interviews with real users of tables and the professionals that sell them.

The results of the study raise a number of questions for further research. One involves the more general implications of, for example, intense as opposed to restrained human–table interactivity. Is this a semiotic principle that is valid for other pieces of furniture and, if so, what social and cognitive implications does this have? It would also be interesting to further study how the interpersonal meaning potentials of tables are realised in different contexts. For example, the meaning potential of collective equality of a round table, or that of hierarchical difference of a rectangular table, is probably less recognised in an informal kitchen setting than in a more professional setting in a conference room. As mentioned, the global–local dimension of meanings of tables can clearly be further explored, and the tentative claim made here about the more global nature of human–table interactive meaning potentials could be challenged through further studies of meanings of practical objects in more or less local cultures and sub-cultures.

Finally, the theoretical question of practical functions in relation to meaning potentials can be reconsidered. In the case of tables, we can perhaps say that the human–table interactive meaning potentials presented in Figure 24.1 are somewhat more related to practical function than the more connotative meanings of table materials, but it is a matter of degree. The practical seems to always be somewhat semiotic in human artefacts.

Further reading

Csikszentmihalyi, M. and Rochberg-Halton, E. (1981) *The Meaning of Things: Domestic Symbols and the Self*, Cambridge: Cambridge University Press. (A classic study of the meanings of domestic objects and the personal histories surrounding them.)

Krampen, M. (1995) 'Semiotics of objects revisited.' In Sebeok, T. A. and Umiker-Sebeok, J. eds. *Advances in Visual Semiotics: The Semiotic Web 1992–1993*, Berlin: Mouton de Gruyter. (Summarises Krampen's work on the semiotics of everyday objects drawing on James Gibson's theory of affordance.)

Pahl, K. and Rowsell, J. (2010) *Artifactual Literacies: Every Object Tells a Story*, New York: Teachers College Press. (Addresses the question of meanings of artefacts from the perspective of literacy, learning and identity.)

Riggins, S. H. (1990) 'The power of things: the role of domestic objects in the presentation of self.' In Riggins, S. H. ed. *Beyond Goffman: Studies on Communication, Institution, and Social Interaction*, Berlin and New York: Mouton de Gruyter. (Presents an ethnographical approach to the semiotic study of domestic objects and provides a useful categorisation of such objects, partly based on that of Erving Goffman.)

Van Leeuwen, T. (2003) 'A multimodal perspective on composition.' Ivn Ensink, T. ed. *Framing and Perspectivising in Discourse*, Philadelphia: John Benjamins. (Contains a discussion of the compositional meaning potentials of three-dimensional objects.)

25

The use of gesture in operations

Jeff Bezemer

Introduction

Gesture has received ample scholarly attention, some of it dating back to Classical Antiquity. Most of this work is focused on the use of gesture in conversations. For instance, some of the most widely cited contemporary scholars of gesture, including Adam Kendon and David McNeill, have looked extensively at gestures produced in storytelling in informal settings. In this chapter, I look at the use of gesture in the professional activities of health-care professionals in operating theatres. While this may seem a somewhat atypical context for studying gesture, and indeed in some ways it is, I will describe surgical activity as an exemplar of all kinds of 'operations' in everyday and professional life (playing football, assembling IKEA furniture, repairing a car, etc.). In the words of Goffman, these are all examples of interactive engagements 'in which talk, when it figures at all, does so either as a desultory, muted side-involvement or as an irregular, intermittent adjunct to the coordination of the doings in progress' (1983: 7). Thus I explore gesture in an environment where speech is the occasional accompaniment of gesture, rather than focusing on an environment in which gesture is the occasional accompaniment of speech, as scholars of gesture – not including those studying sign language – have often done. By moving beyond the conversation as a context for studying gesture I bring to the fore different semiotic potentialities of this mode. In so doing I highlight the need to investigate multimodality across different types of settings, social activity and interactional configurations.

I draw my examples from an ethnographic study of a surgical department in a London hospital where we collected audio- and video-recordings of 20 operations. The examples describe different forms of professional activity, including 'operations' and conversations. In prior work we have used these recordings – alongside field notes and interviews with staff – to address questions about work, learning and communication. In this chapter I discuss a small selection of clips from these recordings and develop a semiotic account of gesture. Detailed methodological accounts of the ways in which I transcribed and analysed the clips can be found elsewhere (Bezemer et al., 2011). Ethical approval was granted by the Research Ethics Committee

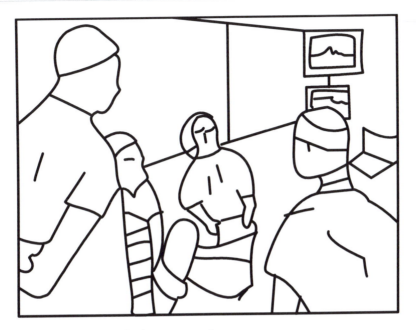

Figure 25.1 An anaesthetic team having a conversation.

of the National Health Service. All staff in theatre and all patients involved have given us informed consent to collect and use the data.

I will start the chapter by comparing my context for studying gesture – professional activity in the operating theatre – with the conversational context more typical of gesture studies, drawing out the differences in terms of people's bodily orientation and availability and use of resources for making gestures. In the following two sections I present three detailed examples of the use of gesture in operations and analyse the semiotic potential of gesture, respectively.

Gesture in two types of social activity

As a first orientation to the role of gesture in different kinds of social activity compare two snapshots of gatherings in an operating theatre during an operation. Figure 25.1 is a gathering of an anaesthetic team. From right to left, you can see a consultant anaesthetist, an anaesthetic registrar and an anaesthetic fellow seated at the head end of the patient, and a medical student standing on the left, respectively. Figure 25.2 is a gathering of a surgical team. Here you can see the medical student in the background; to his right are a researcher, a scrub nurse, a consultant surgeon, a surgical registrar (a senior doctor) and a senior house officer (a junior doctor), respectively. I treat these two snapshots as illustrations of two different kinds of social activity: the anaesthetic team is engaged in a conversation, and the surgical team in what Goffman (1981) called a 'coordinated task activity' and what I will call an 'operation', in the sense of 'concerted, joint action'. I do not want to suggest that anaesthetists converse more than surgeons; had I taken snapshots an hour earlier then we

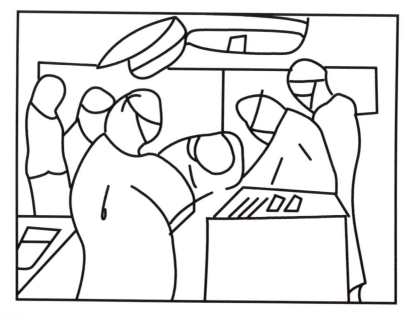

Figure 25.2 A surgical team doing an operation.

would have seen anaesthetists engaged in an 'operation' to put the patient to sleep and surgeons engaged in a conversation – for instance about the history of the patient. People can and do also shift between the two during a gathering, and engage in a conversation and an operation at the same time, as we shall see in Example 1.

I make the distinction between a conversation and an operation on the basis of observations in two interrelated areas: the bodily orientations of the team members and the availability and use of gestural resources.

Bodily orientation

The fronts of the members of the anaesthetic team all face the same centre point, enabling them to make their bodily actions visible and audible to others. The three doctors are seated on stools, having arranged themselves triangularly, and the medical student stands just outside that triangle, displaying a more peripheral participation in this activity. All team members maintain a certain interpersonal distance (Hall, 1969), and their gaze patterns suggest that the consultant is exercising his right to speak: the other three members gaze at his *face*. The surgical team have arranged their bodies differently. Their bodily comportment and gaze patterns are oriented to the *hands* of the surgeon who is making an incision in the abdomen of the patient. If in this context someone speaks, others do not always look into the speaker's eyes, defying gaze patterns of people in informal conversations (Goodwin 1981). Indeed they often don't talk at all, as in the moment that the snapshot in Figure 25.2 was taken. While not immediately visible in this snapshot, participants in these operations also often defy conventions for interpersonal distance in conversations (in the UK), standing shoulder-to-shoulder, or head-to-head.

As in the anaesthetic gathering, the surgeons' bodily arrangements mark divisions in the group: the operating surgeon stands on one side, his entire *upper body* tilted over the operating table so as to obtain a good view of the operative field. His assistants stand on the other side, *heads* (and shoulder) slightly tilted, so that their view of the operative field is not as good as that of the operating surgeon. The scrub nurse stands just outside this huddle, so that her view of the operative field is even more constrained. Her peripheral position also means that she may not be able to hear what the surgeon and his assistants say. Thus in the conversation participants orient their bodies to the face of the speaker, while in the operation participants orient their bodies to the hands of the gesture articulator.

Gestural resources

The snapshot of the anaesthetic team illustrates that in conversations the semiotic resource that is most readily to hand is one's own body. Conversations are often held while the participants remain in more or less the same position. For instance, sitting down and standing up often marks the beginning and end of a conversation. These circumstances shape the kinds of gestures people make and the functions they serve. Indeed, the gestures made by the members of the anaesthetic team depicted in Figure 25.1 as they are having a conversation are very similar to the ones described in detail by Adam Kendon (2004a) and others. For instance, they use gesture for 'representational' purposes, using their hands as 'models' for objects or actions, or as specifiers of the shape or size of a named object. For instance, the consultant might demonstrate how to intubate a patient, using one hand to act as a model of a patient's trachea and another to act as a model of the tube and of the action used to insert it. Or they might point at the top screen of the anaesthetic machine while talking about the patient's heart rate. In contrast, in the operation, participants usually (though not necessarily) manipulate objects (in our case, the patient's body), often using specially designed instruments. They also often move about, reconfiguring their bodies. Thus they have a wider range of resources available to make gestures with: their bare hands, the instruments they hold (which then become prosthetics, or extensions of their body), and the object they work on, and they can use these resources in different bodily positions.

The two examples show that the semiotic status of gesture varies according to the social activity that its users take part in: in 'operations' – which in my definition includes a football match and a car repair as much as a surgical operation – gesture is (almost) in constant operation and in focus; in conversations, speech is.

Gesture in surgical operations

In this section I present three examples of the use of gesture in surgical operations. The examples are taken from 'open' and 'laparoscopic' operations. In open operations the abdomen is opened up. In laparoscopic operations surgeons gain access to the abdomen through small incisions through which they insert a camera and other instruments. The difference between these two surgical procedures has implications for use of gesture. In open operations gestures can be made with bare hands or with instruments, but not all participants co-present have an equal view of these gestures. For instance, as noted above, in the *open* procedure depicted in Figure 25.2 the first assistant has a better view over the surgeon's actions than the second assistant, who has a better view than the scrub nurse. In contrast,

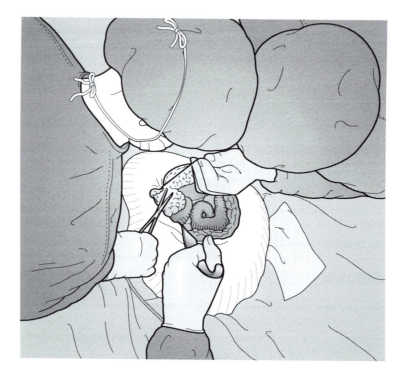

Figure 25.3 Example 1: consultant surgeon holds a stitch up.

in *laparoscopic* operations, the operating space and the gestures made within it are visible on screens that everyone present in the operating theatre can see. Yet only those holding laparoscopic instruments that are inserted in the patient's body are captured on camera. In the following section I will explore some of the implications of that difference for the communication between surgeons.

Example 1 (Figure 25.3) is taken from an open operation. A patient has been opened up. The surgeon has just tied a knot and is now holding the stitch between the thumb and index finger of his left hand, bringing the stitch under tension. The second assistant, who holds scissors in her right hand, is about to cut it. The first assistant holds a big retractor in his left hand. The surgeon is talking to the first assistant about some organizational issue in the hospital. Here the act of holding the stitch tight is interpreted by the second assistant as a request to cut it; and judging from the subsequent actions of the surgeon that is what the surgeon aimed to communicate with this gesture. It is a gesture which is accompanied by speech, but the two are semantically unrelated; they are part of two different activities: a conversation and an operation.

Example 2 (Figure 25.4) is taken from a laparoscopic procedure. A surgeon makes a sweeping movement with a closed grasper behind what is taken to be the *cystic duct*. This structure has been rendered visible through dissection; at the start of the operation it was still hidden behind layers of different kinds of tissue. Before removing the gall bladder, surgeons staple and cut the cystic duct. Surgical guidelines warn of the danger of mistaking the *common bile duct* for the *cystic duct*. Accidentally stapling and cutting the common bile duct causes significant complications. Therefore, surgeons are taught to ensure that they correctly

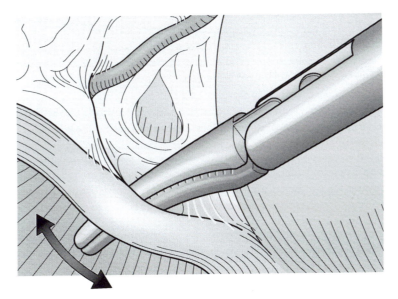

Figure 25.4 Example 2: consultant surgeon makes sweeping movement along the cystic duct.

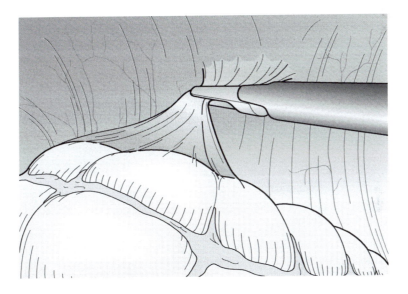

Figure 25.5 Example 3: surgical registrar holds tissue up.

identify the cystic duct before they staple and cut it by obtaining the 'critical view'. This is done by freeing up all structures connected to the gall bladder (imagine a bunch of entangled electric wires covered in mud: before cutting any of them you would want to clear the mud and separate the wires so as to correctly identify which wire is which). The surgeons I observed often made (a variety of) the sweeping movement visualized in Figure 25.4 before they proceeded to staple and cut. By making that sweeping movement operating surgeons communicated to other surgeons co-present – including trainees – that they believed they had obtained a critical view, and, by implication, that the structure touched by the grasper was indeed the cystic duct and that it was therefore safe to staple it and cut it. In most cases this gesture would be accompanied by an utterance such as, 'Are you happy?', prompting others to acknowledge their reading of the patient's anatomy.

Example 3 (Figure 25.5) is also taken from a laparoscopic procedure. A surgical registrar is separating tissue that connects parts of the colon to the abdominal wall. For that he uses a grasping instrument which is connected to the diathermy machine, a device that he can activate with a foot pedal. Upon activation an electric current runs through the instrument to cauterize and separate tissue. The figure shows the point where the registrar has grasped a bit of tissue and lifted it up. The consultant surgeon who is supervising this registrar then says, 'Yeah, that looks fine'. The registrar then separates the tissue. Thus the sequence of actions performed by the registrar is not only a preparation for a cut, it also communicates to the supervising surgeon where he is intending to cut. What's more, he waits for the surgeon to 'ratify' his proposal before he acts on it. That is, the registrar intends to communicate something as he holds the tissue up, and that gesture is not accompanied by speech.

All these gestures are performed and responded to frequently, by surgeons as well as by surgical trainees: they are part of a repertoire of surgical gestures that newcomers develop as they increase their participation in surgical activity. Some of these gestures are probably used across different hospitals and cultures (for instance, Example 1); others may be more typical of surgical practice in the UK, of the surgical department in the hospital where we did our research (Example 2), or even of certain surgeons (Example 3). Indeed, it may be useful to think of gestural variation as linguistic variation, with different, socially and culturally shaped gestural varieties. Developing such a repertoire, that is, learning to make meaning with, i.e., produce and read, gestures in these contexts, is an essential part of becoming a recognized member of a professional community.

The semiotic potential of gesture

I will now draw out some insights in the semiotic potential of gesture using the three examples of gesture in operations.

Gesture–speech relations

The examples illustrate two different semiotic relations between gesture and speech. All three examples are 'pointing gestures' in that someone displays and draws attention to or 'highlights' a particular point or area in a visible space. Pointing gestures have been well-documented, showing that speakers often point at objects or actions around them to identify the referent of a deictic element in their speech (see, e.g. Jaworski and Thurlow, Chapter 26 this volume). Examples from the operating theatre show that an object can also be identified *independent of* speech. For instance, in Example 1, the surgeon draws attention to the stitch without speaking about the stitch. In Example 3, the registrar draws attention to a specific area of tissue without speaking about it. Example 2 shows that if gestures at the operating table *are* accompanied by speech, the two modes might do different kinds of semiotic work. In this example, gesture (a sweeping movement) is used to construct the object pointed at as the cystic duct, while speech ('Are you happy?') is used to prompt acknowledgement from other surgeons co-present that it is indeed the cystic duct and thus safe to clip and cut. In other words, in this example gesture and speech are in a 'reciprocal' relationship (Kendon, 2004a: 174).

Affordances of gesture

Why do the surgeons in the examples not always use speech to direct attention to whatever it is they want the other to attend to? What choice do they actually have? For instance, the surgeon in Example 1 one could have said, 'can you cut the stitch please'. Yet a description of *precisely where* he wants the assistant to cut the stitch would at best be an imprecise gloss of the gesture he makes. By adjusting the point at which he holds the stitch between thumb and index finger he can direct the assistant to the point where he wants her to cut. The surgeon in Example 2 could have said, 'Are you happy for me to clip the cystic duct now?' Yet to specify what structure he treats as the cystic duct *in this patient* he would still need to make a pointing gesture. Similarly, in Example 3, the registrar could have said, 'Are you happy for me to cut this?' Yet to specify what 'this' refers to he would still need to make a pointing gesture. Indeed the referent of this gesture has no specific anatomical name at all (such as 'cystic duct'); it is just 'tissue'. Thus in the operation, pointing gestures appear to be the most 'apt' (see Kress, Chapter 4, this volume) means of identifying points of attention. Some of these points of attention can be described, but never without losing some of the specificity of the pointing gesture.

Different instruments have distinctly different affordances. For instance, the laparoscopic grasper held by the registrar in Example 3 is more 'apt' for pointing than the camera held by the consultant. The consultant can use the camera to direct the registrar's attention, yet he cannot use the camera to point at a specific position within that frame. To do that he needs access to an instrument such as the grasper held by the registrar. He could also point outside of the patient's abdomen, with a grasper at the screen, but that is still not as precise – and is tricky as the sterile grasper must not touch the non-sterile screen.

Distribution of gestural resources

When instruments with different affordances are distributed among the participants of an operation then the distribution creates differences in the meaning-making potential of participants. As noted above, in Example 3, the registrar has control over a grasper that he can use to point precisely, whereas the consultant can only use the camera to point, which is relatively imprecise. This often results in the participant with access to the more apt resource acting 'on behalf of' the other. For instance, at some point in the operation from which Example 3 was taken the registrar had difficulty interpreting the consultant's descriptions of where he wanted the registrar to cut ('I would go superficial to that', 'I kind of meant that other bit down there'). The registrar then clarified this by grasping a bit of tissue and saying, 'this bit here?', to which the consultant responded affirmatively ('that bit there, yeah'). Quite simply, when two people with different resources at their disposal come together and one reaches the limits of what can be done with his or her resources the person with access to better suited resources can help out, making proposals which the other can accept or reject. Such forms of collaboration are also common outside the operating theatre. For instance, differences in linguistic repertoires may result in one person suggesting words or phrases for the other ('Do you mean . . . ?'). Yet in the surgical example it was the limits of speech per se that the consultant was up against, not the limits of his language skills.

Forms of gesture

The examples also highlight the range of different forms that 'pointing' gestures can take. In studies of conversations 'pointing' often refers to pointing 'in the air', with the object pointed at located at some distance from the person pointing. Occasionally surgeons do also point 'in the air', without touching the referent. For instance, in laparoscopic operations, operating surgeons sometimes indicate where they want the camera holder to move the camera to by pointing in that direction. Yet in most cases when surgeons draw attention to an area there is no distance between the gesture articulator and the referent. The three examples illustrate different ways in which they achieve that. In some cases they *manipulate* the referent (a gentle stroke in Example 2), in other cases they *freeze a manipulation of* the referent (holding thread and tissue up in Examples 1 and 3, respectively). In other examples not described here I noticed how a surgeon used his fingers to draw attention to a bit of tissue which he wanted the assistant to cut. He 'wrapped' the tissue around the index finger of his right hand, and used the index finger and thumb of his left hand to *frame* (and freeze) the relevant tissue at the tip of his right index finger. These examples show that 'pointing from a distance' is only one of many different forms of gesture used to draw and display attention: a stroke, or a freeze, can do similar semiotic work.

Gesture in unfolding interaction

In all three examples the gesture of one person is followed by another action, performed by another person. In other words, the gestures are embedded in sequences of actions. Gestures can prompt or be prompted by other gestures (in Example 1, the holding of the stitch is followed by the cut of the stitch), or they can prompt or be prompted by a spoken utterance (in Example 3, the holding up of the tissue is followed by a ratification of the proposed next move). Mondada (2011) calls such sequences 'paired actions'; indeed they are organized in the same way that, say, an 'adjacency pair' of a question and an answer is: one action, such as a gesture, can project a course of action. Thus gestures can operate in pairs through which people can achieve complex tasks in the absence of speech. Mondada (2011) gives examples of a consultant surgeon and assistant organizing a task around such paired gestures, using speech only when the consultant does not want his gesture to prompt the response that is otherwise expected. That resonates with Goffman's observation that in coordinating action speech is 'especially critical when something doesn't go as indicated as expected' (Goffman 1983: 4).

Remaking gestures

People often reconstruct objects and actions they observed in a different time and space, where the resources of the original site are not available. Earlier I mentioned the example of the anaesthetist giving a demonstration in the corner of the operating theatre using his hands. With his gestures the anaesthetist could reconstruct what he had done a hour before in the anaesthetic room as he was intubating the patient, yet without the instruments he had available then. Similarly, the surgeons who were operating as the anaesthetist was having a conversation may well have remade some of the gestures they made during the operation when they were holding a debriefing in in the coffee room some time later, when their instruments were no longer to hand. These examples show that gestures can be remade as gestures. Gestures can also be remade as speech. For instance, the anaesthetist once told a trainee to hold the syringe 'like a dart'.

As gestures are remade, whether in gesture or speech or image or another mode, meaning changes (see Newfield, Chapter 7, this volume, for a discussion of these processes of 'transformation' and 'transduction'). For instance, none of the visualizations or descriptions in this chapter capture the four-dimensionality of gesture (it unfolds in time and in three-dimensional space). That has implications for making gesture visible for educational and research purposes: 'insiders' may demonstrate or describe gestures in a classroom, textbook or handbook, yet only when participating in the original site of production – in my case, the operating theatre – can one see gesture 'in full glory'.

Conclusion

In my account of gesture I have moved beyond the common separation often made between actions performed 'for the purposes of expression' and those made 'in the service of some practical aim' (Kendon, 2004a: 15). In my analysis of surgical examples I have suggested that these functions can go hand-in-hand: as people collaborate, for instance to cut a thread, they attach meaning to the manual actions they perform. In such contexts of concerted action embodied actions are never 'merely' actions. They are always also made for others, in the anticipation that they are read by others. That is, they are meaningful actions; indeed *gestures*.

Embodied actions may be meaningful, they are interpreted differently by different people. Gesture articulators take that into account. For instance, the gestures made for someone who is new to the activity being undertaken may be different from the gestures made for the experienced collaborator. The ability to read the gestures of others in a way that facilitates smooth accomplishment of the operation is often seen as a marker of expertise and membership of the community of practice that is responsible for the operation.

Moving beyond conversations I have portrayed gesture as a mode that is central to much of what people do in their everyday lives, namely engaging in joint operations; and as a mode that has vast semiotic potential, more than what studies of conversations have already shown. Looking at the placement of gesture in multimodal ensembles I have suggested that gesture can operate independent of other modes such as speech or be reciprocally related to them. Looking at the affordances of gesture I have shown that gesture has distinctly different potentialities and constraints, for instance to draw attention to objects. I have also pointed at the wide range of different forms of gesture, including direct manipulations of objects; noted that the distribution of gestural resources with different affordances requires participants to do collaborative semiotic work, such as pointing on behalf of the other; and showed that gestures are embedded in sequences of action that unfold in time; that is, that a gesture can prompt, change, sustain or close a course of action. Lastly, I have suggested that gestures are remade in different contexts using different gestural resources.

Above all I hope to have shown that we can gain important insights in the semiotic potential of gesture if we move beyond the conversation as a context for studying gesture. Only when we continue to extend the range of different contexts for investigating multimodality can we develop apt theories of meaning-making.

Acknowledgements

The chapter draws on research funded by the Economic and Social Research Council ('Digital Technologies in the Operating Theatre', RES 576-25-0027) and the London Deanery ('Mapping Educational Activity in the Operating Theatre', Simulation and Technology-Enhanced Learning Initiative). The research was conducted in collaboration with Gunther Kress, Alexandra Cope, Ged Murtagh and Roger Kneebone.

26

Gesture and movement in tourist spaces

Adam Jaworski and Crispin Thurlow

Tourist performance as discourse

What do tourists do in tourist destinations? How do they fill in the time allocated to visiting a new place – typically for the first and most likely for the last time? According to John Urry's (2002) powerful metaphor, the consumption of tourist destinations is a matter of the *tourist gaze* organizing the relationship between the individual and the object of the gaze. A vast body of work in critical tourism, sociology and anthropology has theorized the behaviour of tourists and hosts as *performance*, largely drawing on Erving Goffman's (1959) dramaturgic metaphor of social life. No matter how well signposted or tightly organized the tourist gaze may be in a particular destination, the tourist performance is always contingent, subject to re-enactments in different conditions, and unpredictable uptake.

In this chapter, we consider tourist performance as a form of multimodal discourse, as fundamentally – and, at times, solely – semiotic in nature. Three observations follow. First, the touristic experience is an intensely *mediatized* discourse; always pre-figured and largely determined through the discursive practices (i.e. representations and interactions) of other tourists, travel writers, and the travel industry. By the time tourists find themselves at their target destination, for the most part, they have a clear idea about what to expect and, more than likely, what to do. Second, tourist performance is always *embodied* action. Touristic 'ways of seeing' are seldom (just) about vision. It is for this reason precisely that a more multisensory approach to tourism which, specifically, attends to the multimodal and mediated practices of seeing and the interplay between the physical environment of the tourist site and tourist behaviour, is worthwhile. Third, tourist performance is always *mediated* action. Each and every communicative act, whether verbal or nonverbal, is bounded and reflexively configured by other semiotic structures of the environment (Goodwin, 2001). These include the layout of the space, built environment, various fixed and non-fixed physical objects, signage, other people present in the shared space, the socio-cultural norms of conduct, and any practices associated with the communicative frame (Goffman, 1974) which is believed to be taking place. We are concerned here with tourism behaviour as a form of *mediated action* (Scollon, 2001) understood in the sense of Pierre Bourdieu's (1990) *habitus*, i.e. a system of internalized, durable and transposable dispositions which generates similar practices and perceptions in agents belonging to the same class, and which can be adjusted to specific situations. These are enskilled historical bodies of tourists re-enacting their performances sedimented over decades of their predecessors' visits to specific destinations (cf. Blommaert, 2013). However, the *agents* are more loosely defined here as a global, imagined community of practice, or to use Ron Scollon's (2001) term, the 'nexus of practice'.

By focusing on the displays of tourists' nonverbal, kinesic behaviour in a specific site, we suggest that gesture and movement are socially regulated forms of mediated action emerging from the intersection of mediational means (discourses in place), social actors (historical bodies), and the sociocultural environment (participation frameworks) (Scollon and Scollon, 2004).

Introducing gesture and movement

In nonverbal communication studies, all body movement is subsumed under the umbrella term of *kinesics*, which involves gestures, non-gestural movements of the extremities, walking, body posture, stillness, head and trunk movements (e.g. body lean), and facial expressions including the direction of the gaze. Conventionally, nonverbal communication distinguishes between kinesic codes (e.g. gesture, movement, gaze) and contact codes (e.g. interpersonal space, spatial arrangement, touch). As we mean to show here, the two are less easily separated in practice, either formally or functionally. Gesture and movement are heavily implicated in the production of space, just as they are clearly shaped by the material and social organization of space.

The two types of gestures which will concern us here are (1) *deictic* or *pointing* gestures, and (2) *representational* or *ideational gestures*, also known as *gesticulations*, *illustrators*, or *mimes*. (Other types of gestures which do not concern us here include fully conventionalized *symbolic* or *emblematic* gestures, and *motor* gestures, also referred to as *batons* or *beats*; see Krauss *et al.*, 2000 for an overview.)

Deictic gestures may indicate persons, objects, directions, or locations, or may 'point to' nonexistent or imaginary referents. They are usually associated with, but are certainly not limited to, the use of the extended index finger with the rest of the fingers closed. The meaning of pointing gestures is closely related to their physical environment, or 'gesture space' (Haviland, 2000), and may occur with or without speech.

Representational gestures can co-occur, alternate with or replace speech and are generally associated with overcoming a lack in vocabulary or other linguistic means of expression, for example, due to a large distance between the interactants, noisy environment, etc. These gestures are not fully conventionalized yet they appear to form a continuum of *iconic* to *metaphoric* gestures. The former stand in direct pictographic relationship to their referents (e.g. the speaker may accompany the mention of a mountain range with the hand gesture tracing an imaginary hill top), while the latter may exhibit images of abstract concepts or convey the speaker's relation to the object, e.g. as if the speaker were holding an object displaying it to the listeners without indicating the shape of the object (McNeill, 2005b).

Goodwin (2003a: 229) argues that the distinction between iconic gestures and deictic gestures is untenable as '[p]ointing gestures can trace the shape of what is being pointed at, and thus superimpose an iconic display on a deictic point within the performance of a single gesture.' Instead, Goodwin (2003b) proposes a different taxonomy of gestures: *iconic*, *symbiotic* and *transformative*. Iconic gestures are illustrative of the action but performed outside of the environment of the action; symbiotic gestures are performed and made meaningful in relation to a particular environmental structure. 'The term Symbiotic is meant to capture the way in which a whole that is both different from, and greater than its parts, is constructed through the mutual inter-dependence of unlike elements' (Goodwin, 2003b: 20). Transformative gestures act upon what they are representing, physically altering the environment performing the act of *inscription*.

With particular but not exclusive reference to tourism, we view gesture, posture and body movement as banal, momentary enactments of *discourses* (i.e. ways of representing), *styles* (i.e. ways of being), and *genres* (i.e. ways of inter/acting) (Fairclough, 2003b). To some extent, these stylistic, discursive and generic meanings are akin, respectively, to the *ideational*, *interpersonal* and *textual* 'metafunctions' of Michael Halliday (1994).

In this way, we mean to go a little further than conventional analyses (or interpretations) of, for example, pointing, although we certainly share the basic understanding that these types of signalling behaviours are always situated and communicatively significant (e.g. Goodwin, 2003a; Kendon, 2004b). Rather than attending to gesture, posture and body movement as little more than 'context for talk', however, we want to think about their identificational, representational and inter/actional meanings *sui generis*. We want also to consider their ideological implications. To summarize:

a   *Representational meanings*: Gestures, postures and body movements realize particular versions or knowledges of the world; for example, tourism discourse consistently maintains mythol-ogies of intercultural exchange, of discovery, of (safe) adventures, of play, etc.

b   *Identificational meanings*: Gestures, postures and body movements performatively establish visitors' identities as *tourists*; in other words, tourists do 'being tourists' by taking up the kinds of practices they have seen and learned from past experiences and from mediatized representations, for example TV shows, postcards, holiday snapshots, guidebooks, and online photo albums (Thurlow and Jaworski, 2010); in doing so, tourists also style themselves into an imagined 'community of practice' of tourists.

c   *Inter/actional meanings*: Gestures, posture and body movement are intersubjective and made meaningful only in interaction with other people and the physical environment; they thus re-inscribe the *generic* nature of the texts (i.e. the tourist destination) in a succession of communicative acts involving verbal and nonverbal interactions, transition from place to place, shifting gaze, and so on. The realization of different stages in the consumption of a tourist space is constituted multimodally and is subject to cultural and historical variation. Finally, genres understood as sequences of communicative actions are embedded in social practices and need to be understood in terms of what they do to, for and between people including enacting and reproducing relations of power between Self and Other as well as other objects in space (Van Leeuwen, 2005a).

These meaning categories are separated here for analytical convenience; in practice, all three are dialetically inter-connected. Thus, the identities of tourists, the representations of tourist truths and the interactional organization of tourist sites work together – they *mediate* each other – in produc-ing the habitus (Bourdieu, 1990) of tourism as an individual and collective disposition to gaze and (inter-)act in certain ways. In doing so, we suggest, these micro-level practices also reproduce the ideologies and relations of power which structure tourism more broadly. As such, seemingly innocuous acts like pointing at, posing in front of, or ambling through a tourist site enact the neocolonial agenda which underpins even the most 'eco-friendly', 'sustainable' or 'alternative' kinds of tourism. Ultimately, the practices of tourism – whether verbal or nonverbal – re-inscribe an ideology of conquest, of control and of possession (Thurlow and Jaworski, 2010). To this end, gesture, posture and body movement are ideal semiotic resources.

367

Gesture and movement at the Piazza del Duomo di Pisa

Here we examine the role of gesture and movement in the specific setting of a landmark tourist site: La Piazza del Duomo di Pisa (the Cathedral Square) also known as Il Campo dei Miracoli (The Field of Miracles). In particular, we want to make the Leaning Tower of Pisa our primary object of study – or, more correctly, tourist performance in, around and on top of it.

The Piazza del Duomo ('Piazza' from hereon) is a roughly rectangular, walled enclosure containing several architectural monuments: the Duomo (the Cathedral of St. Mary of the Assumption), and Battistero (the Baptistery), the Campanile, or the freestanding bell tower, better known as the Leaning Tower of Pisa ('Tower' from hereon), The Camposanto (the walled cemetery) and two museums: the Cathedral Museum and the Museum of the Sinopie. The southern wall is lined with a tightly packed row of souvenir stalls. The low–rise buildings in the north-east corner contain the ticket office, souvenir shop, tourist information and locker room (for the oversize bags not allowed to be taken by tourists climbing the Tower). Most of the building-free area of the Piazza is covered by lawns cross-cut by roads and pavements running alongside, around and between the buildings.

Most tourists appear to enter the site through its western gate (Porta di Santa Maria) due to its proximity of car parks. On a sunny day in peak season (as the day when the data for this chapter were collected), the area around and within the Piazza is very crowded. Tourists walking in both directions between the car park and the gate pass numerous souvenir stalls, cafes and restaurants.

Our data consist of approximately three hours of tourist video footage shot by Adam on 5 July 2003 as a participant–tourist observer. The length of the video-recording corresponds roughly to half the time spent at the site which did not include visiting any other monuments other than climbing the Tower. In only one instance do we make reference to the verbal communication which accompanies the nonverbal behaviour under discussion. Our focus here is on the practices of gesture, posture and body movement situated in their broader context of use which surely include language but is also made meaningful through interaction with modalities other than language. (In this regard, we are struck by the subtitle of Adam Kendon's (2004a) excellent book *Gesture: Visible Action as Utterance*, which renders the nonverbal in terms of the linguistic.) Thus, for mainly analytic convenience, our attention here is directed more towards the spatial and representational 'contexts' of these nonverbal actions.

In order to demonstrate how these communicative functions are nonverbally realized – or embodied – we turn to four dominant kinesic resources found in our data. Presented here as indicative stills taken from the video footage.

Pointing

It is hard not to notice how much of the pointing behaviour in our data is a male performance. We find a gestural outlining of (and pointing to) the Duomo initiated by a woman but then taken up more fully by her male companion (see Figure 26.1a). We have one other noticeable, albeit brief, point in another extract (not shown); for the most part, however, touristic, 'landscape' pointing appears to be male-dominated (see Figures 26.1b–d, 26.4a, b). This projection of the body into space – a literal and figurative occupation of space – expresses a masculinist notion of space as knowable, as something to be traced (i.e. discovered, marked out and measured) and, ultimately, to be possessed (see Nash, 1996).

a   b

c   d

Figure 26.1 Examples of tourists' pointing behaviour.

Another performance of knowledge – this time more explicitly co-produced – where a visitor and guard locate some target object (or site) from on top of the Tower appears in Figure 26.1c. These gestures epitomize the kind of deictic pointing which occupies much of the literature (e.g. Kendon; McNeill; Clark), projecting a spatialized vector from the *origo* (or point-of-orgin actor) to a perceived target and in relation to an addressee. Clark (2003) notes that directing-to (or point-ing) vectors may be established by an arm, a head nod, a finger tap, the torso, a gaze, the voice, or some 'artificial device' such as a laser-pointer. We find two different 'pointing' forms. The boy on top of the Tower cups his hands and calls out to people on the ground below and then waves to them (see Figure 26.1d). Although not as clearly deictic as the quintessential single-finger point, these gestures are 'indicative signals' (Clark, 2003) which direct the attention of witnesses on the tower to the targeted 'objects' below. The spatial connection is drawn, in this case, by the gestures and the vocalization. Clearly, however, this act of hailing is also one which draws attention – or is intended to draw attention – to Self.

Clark (2003: 247) characterizes indexical gestures like pointing (also placing – see next sec-tion) as acts of 'social engineering' which draw the attention of addressees to some distant or absent 'object of indication' (McNeill, 2003). But, it seems, these acts are as much about the actor as they are about the object. Pointing – in whatever form – entails the 'structuring of space in terms of spatial locations' (ibid.: 293) but always in relation to the origo. It is a pin-pointing of Self in place as much as it is a pin-pointing of a particular place. As such, the boy's hailing of either known or presumably even unknown people below is a kind of 'interpellation' (Althusser, 1971) by which the subject both locates and produces himself. 'Look at me! Here I am! Up here! On top of the Leaning Tower of Pisa'.

Regardless of the form of the pointing, we suggest that this same principle applies. These momentary embodiments of space are material engagements with the material environment.

Posture, placing and posing

Many gestures and body movements in interaction are ignored, disattended (Goffman, 1974) or treated as irrelevant by participants. In order to make some of their gestures meaningful or communicative, participants may contextualize them in special ways, for example, by placing them explicitly in the field of vision of other participants (Goodwin, 2003b). This is perhaps most clear in the case of tourists' posing for snapshots.

As a form of posture (body orientation), this photographic posing constitutes a particular kind of placement action akin to the kind of gestural 'placing-for' described by Clark (2003). Like pointing, it too functions as an indicative signalling which focuses the viewer/audience's attention on the target object. It is not uncommon, for example, for other tourists to shift their attention to the sight beyond the fellow tourist who is so obviously posing.

Any act of indicating Other (whether the object or person of a point of placement), is equally an act of indicating and locating Self. Attention is drawn both to the object of the point, for example, but also to the origin of the point – the pointer. By the same token, if I place something on the table in front of you, I mean for you to attend to both the object and to me.

There is an 'iconic' image of the Leaning Tower of Pisa which circulates widely and, it seems, is familiar to almost all (Western) tourists; it's the snapshot of someone positioned in relation to the Tower in such a way as to create the scalar and perspectival illusion of either holding/pushing it up or kicking/pushing it down (cf. Thurlow and Jaworski, 2010). It is this highly ritualized, context-dependent practice (Goodwin's 'symbiotic' gesture) which we find being played out in our data (see Figure 26.2) where we find dozens of visitors marking their identities as tourists through the explicit performance of this knowledge.

a   b

Figure 26.2 Examples of tourists' posture, placing and posing.

In many respects, it is possible to think of these personalized poses with the Tower as a kind of bodily graffiti in which individual tourists look to 'tag' the Tower, to leave their mark. While the physical location of Self in the place is momentary, the representational (i.e. photographic) inscription is enduring and, through its constant repetition, it becomes substantial. The fleeting symbiotic gesture of the tourist remains frozen in its photographic representation and recontextualized as transformative. These are not just tourist performances, but also performative re-enactments of the spectacle itself.

The conceit of holding up or kicking over the tower enacts a particular sense of mastery and ownership – perhaps even a degree of disrespect. Some of the more reflexive, apparently playful variations of the theme express this even more powerfully; for example, a visitor appearing to tower over the Tower; a visitor appearing to hold the Tower in their hand, or a single finger appearing to topple the Tower. Whatever their intent, these 'conventionalized poses of the spectacle' (Scollon, 1998a: 107) are integral to the styling of the tourist identity (i.e. it's the thing to do in Pisa), the generic organization or staging [sic] of the Tower/Piazza, and, indeed, the discursive production of tourism as playful appropriation. These poses are quintessential embodiments in a nexus of practice which is predicated on symbolic consumption – of images and sights – and the conspicuous performance of this consumption.

In this regard, we find a moment in which a child is being bodily manoeuvred and sculpted by an adult (her mother?) in order to strike the 'Pisa Pose' (Figure 26.2b). Thus the schooling in the ways of the tourist is revealed – a habitual socialization into the imagined community of practice. The habitus is being corporeally rehearsed and enskilled.

Body movement and positioning

Another common mode for symbolically marking Self and for demarcating space is body movement and, in particular, the positioning of the body in relation to a built environment. In this case, two of the most striking – and quintessentially tourist – examples are found. In the first instance, tourists go to the effort of climbing the Tower (Figure 26.3a); in the second instance, we find rows of visitors seated on the steps at the foot of the Tower – many of whom are also gazing up at the Tower (Figure 26.3b).

a   b

Figure 26.3 Symbolically marking Self and demarcating space: (a) the effort of climbing the Tower; (b) rows of visitors seated on the steps at the foot of the Tower – many of whom are also gazing up at it.

371

Following Van Leeuwen (2005c), the Campo and the Tower in particular can be considered multimodal texts which facilitate a number of staged, goal-oriented processes. The overall goal of these texts may not be as clear as that of other text types (e.g. advertisements whose overall aim is to persuade the reader to buy a product), although the Opera della Primaziale Pisana, which runs and oversees the monuments of the Campo dei Miracoli, makes clear on its website that visitors should have 'a day of entertainment and culture'. For various local agents, such as souvenir stall-holders, municipal authorities and the Opera itself, the over-riding goal of maintaining the site is more than likely economic.

The different buildings and attractions in the Campo act as specific 'stages' of the tourist's 'reading path'. In other words, walking alongside their chosen path, the tourist engages in a series of communicative moves (stages) afforded by the site. Practically all the stages are optional, as one can arguably glimpse the sight of the Campo with all its buildings from Porta di Santa Maria (St. Mary's Gate) on the West side of the Campo. However, in order to enact the various possible 'gazes', the tourist may choose to spend a considerable amount of time at the site, although it is likely to be confined to one day.

And the ascent, the scaling, of the Tower is as much a social/symbolic act as it is a physical/material one. Indeed, whether it is going up the Tower (Figure 26.3a) or sitting down gazing up at the Tower (Figure 26.3b), these are quintessentially *territorial* behaviours which not only constitute the space (or territory) itself but also rehearse claims to space in a series of repetitive practices (e.g. like a dog turning in its basket or urinating against a tree). This marking and demarcating of space works to produce a sense of ownership of, or control over, the space. The tourist site is thus consumed, along with local people, their languages, their cultural traditions, and so on.

Sitting idly on the steps across from the base of the Tower (Figure 26.3b) may have none of the physical exertion or anticipation of climbing it, but this is no less an embodied act of significance. Indeed, this is a key moment in the staging of any tourist site – a kind of post- (or pre-) coital moment of calm after the conquest. 'There! I've done it!' So too is this an equally constructive moment: sitting and gazing up at the Tower, witnessing the performances of other tourists, produce the spectacle. These can also serve as an object-directed points or signalling gestures. In one instance, for example, we find one tourist who, when passing behind those seen sitting on the steps in Figure 26.3b, turns to follow their gaze. This apparently passive act of taking in the site is once again also an act of taking it, of possessing it for oneself.

Prosthetic embodiments

In Figure 26.4, we see how each of these nonverbal forms (i.e. pointing, posing and positioning) and each of the principle communicative functions (i.e. identificational, representational and inter/actional) are embodied technologically – or prosthetically – by means of the camera and video camera. In these cases, embodiment is itself mediated by technology. Of course, it would not be unreasonable to regard language and communication themselves as technologies – as culturally created enhancements of basic human capacities and of the 'natural' environment.

What our data confirm is how the tourist gaze is an embodied activity and not merely an act of production or reception. As Crang (1997: 365) puts it, '[a]ttention to practices suggests images, sights, activities are all linked through the embodied motion of the observer to create "proprioception" – an active, embodied engagement with the world through vision'. And viewing – itself an action – is always coupled with doing. In the first, a male visitor at the foot of the Tower

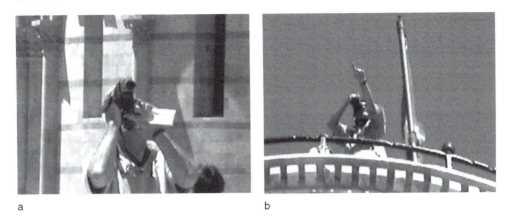

a   b

Figure 26.4 Prosthetic embodiments: (a) mapping and capturing the Tower by filming; (b) simultaneously photographing and pointing.

carefully maps and captures the Tower by filming up and down with his camera, before panning slowly across the Piazza (Figure 26.4a). This non-cinematic, uncreative tracing of the building is an instrumental landscaping.

In Figure 26.4b, the man on top of the Tower simultaneously photographs and points. Apprehension here is perceptual, gestural and technological accomplishment. Where the point initiates the apprehension of the unknown (to us) target, the click of the camera shutter completes the act. 'Gotcha!'

In both cases, the camera/video camera function as extensions of the body (McLuhan, 1974) enabling a kind of double location of Self: first, as a prosthetic pointing gesture (which others will often follow) and, second, as a representation (or record) of the space and one's place in it. This representational locating of Self can be explicit (i.e. when posed in front of the camera) or implied (i.e. when taking the image).

Conclusion: tracing space, locating self

It is received wisdom nowadays that space is as much a social construction as it is a physical phenomenon. Spaces are culturally and communicatively constituted, and the meanings of spaces are established by the way they are represented (e.g. written and talked about) and by the nature of social inter/actions that take place within them. As such, space is always in the process of becoming, of being *spatialized*. For Henri Lefebvre (1991), space can thus be thought of as being realized in three dimensions: *conceived* space which corresponds to mental or represented images of space; *perceived* space which corresponds to the material or physical space itself; and *lived* space which emerges through the intersection/ interaction of both conceived and perceived space (cf. Jaworski and Thurlow, 2010).

It is just such a lived space that tourists help create through their visits to the Leaning Tower of Pisa – a building which is as much a production of the tourist imagination as it is a lop-sided construction of stone and marble. In this case, the figurative tracing of the Tower by means of gesture, posture and body movement is heavily implicated in the making of the place itself. However historically and culturally situated the Tower may be, it is equally – if not more so – made meaningful through the stylistic, discursive and generic practices of tourism.

Just as others have argued that it is through our ways of seeing the world that we become viewing subjects (see Crang, 1997), it is through our bodies that we become doing subjects. In both cases, our viewing and our doing also produce us as knowing subjects and with a sense of the world as knowable. As Mike Crang (1997: 362) puts it, 'the world is apprehended as picturable, it is "enworlded" by being framed'.

In terms of multimodal analysis, we have focused on gesture and movement in tourist spaces as part of the complex interplay of various semiotic resources such as written and spoken language, built environment, layout, mediatizing texts of the tourist industry, and social actors' own ritualized performances in creating a sense (identity) of place and tourists' identity as 'tourists'. We have examined kinesic displays as forms of situated, embodied practice (Goodwin, 2001) and demonstrated how the referential and deictic gestures, and other movements of tourists are symbiotic and, once recontextualized on photographs, transformative (Goodwin, 2003b), for their meaning can only be fully understood against the backdrop of the physical environment in which they occur. The frozen poses in Figure 26.2 would be completely meaningless without the knowledge that from a different angle they would give the impression of tourists 'propping up' the Tower. And once seen in the photographs, the gestures indeed transform the Campanile into the Leaning Tower of Pisa, the tourist playground and accessory. In this sense, it is the textual function (in the sense of Halliday, 1994) of gesture and movement that is foregrounded in our data. For example, walking up and down the stairs of the Tower is made meaningful only because these *are* the stairs of the Leaning Tower of Pisa. People climbing up the stairs in a single file and circling the observation deck do so largely to trace the outline of the monument with their feet as it is in this act of embodied action that the performative act of consumption, control and appropriation takes place. Likewise, various acts of pointing documented here do not only fulfil their referential (ideational) function, but primarily the interpersonal function of placing Self in space and the textual function of tracing space.

Further reading

Edensor, T. (2001) 'Performing tourism, staging tourism: (Re)producing tourist space and practice.' *Tourist Studies* 1: 59–81.

Kita, S. ed. (2003) *Pointing: Where Language, Culture, and Cognition Meet*, Mahwah, NJ: Lawrence Erlbaum.

Low, S. and Lawrence-Zúñiga, D. eds. (2003) *The Anthropology of Space and Place*, Oxford: Blackwell.

Thurlow, C. and Jaworski, A. (2010) *Tourism Discourse: The Language of Global Mobility*, Basingstoke: Palgrave Macmillan.

27

The kineikonic mode

Towards a multimodal approach to moving-image media

Andrew Burn

Multimodality theory can offer new ways to think about the combination of sign-systems to be found in such cultural forms as narrative film, television, animation, moving-image art installations and machinima. This chapter will examine two examples: one from a narrative film produced in 1948, and one from a machinima film made by eleven-year-olds in 2013.

Multimodality and the moving image: a historical note

The moving image is not, of course, newly multimodal. The phenomenon of multimodality has been there from the beginning, and the earliest theorists and practitioners of moving-image art explored it, though they did not use the word multimodality. The montage theory of Eisenstein (1968), for example, theorised the relationships between filming, editing, dramatic movement, music and sound.

One version of the history of film shows its growth out of theatre, producing an art form which is multimodal in the sense of an accretion of more or less settled cultural forms, each new instance containing echoes (to use an auditory metaphor) or layers (to use a spatial one) of earlier moments. Theatre was already multimodal: its signifying systems integrate spoken language, dramatised action, gesture and facial expression, lighting, symbolic objects, representations of architecture. These modes can also be seen as orchestrated by two kinds of *framing* device, one spatial, the other temporal. The spatial device is the stage, in its many forms, and especially that facet which opens towards the audience, realised in classical theatre as the proscenium arch, and culturally cognate with all kinds of viewing aperture which frame the viewed object on the one hand, and the viewer's gaze on the other. The temporal device is the system of breaks, classically scenes and acts, which indicate shifts in time and location, theme, narrative component. Dramatic scripts contain finer framing structures: the turntaking of dramatic dialogue; the shifts of time and place indicated in stage directions; the framing of modes of address such as the soliloquy and aside.

The idea of frame here, while it has common-sense meanings, and is obviously appropriate to the discussion of the moving image in a literal sense, is also an important multimodal principle which operates across all semiotic modes. Van Leeuwen (2005a) proposes principles governing the function of frames: the segmentation and separating functions frames carry out; and the degrees of permeability which may apply. In film, the cinematic frame might dissolve, for example, in a film projected on a building; the temporal frame of a filmic sequence might be blurred by a dissolve transition; a spatial frame may be overlaid in a super-imposed image.

The young medium of film adopted and adapted the modes of theatre, then: both what I will call *contributory modes* (movement, lighting, costume, objects, sets and so on), and what I will call *orchestrating modes* (the overarching framing systems in space and time). The latter were, effectively, filming and editing. The camera provided spatial framing, as had the prosce-nium arch; but transformed the fixed location of the audience, allowing proximity and angle to the enacted events to become mobile, rather than fixed points in the auditorium. The practice of editing – cutting and rejoining sections of film – also replicated some aspects of theatrical scene and act breaks, indicating temporal and locational shifts, but added new ones. Camera and editing combined were able, for example, to introduce mobile points of view in a dramatised conversation, so that the audience could see one speaker from the point of view of the other, and then reverse this view with the change of speaker. This shot–reverse-shot structure, and the conventions of continuity editing in general, have become so normalised in film and television that we barely notice them.

However, the early history of film also contains the very different work of George Meliès, who used the properties of filming and editing to produce fantastic illusions. While these films were organised as fantastic dramas in certain ways, they also drew on practices in modern art: the layering of images in collage, the subversive juxtaposition of apparently unrelated images in sur-realism, the challenge to perspectival naturalism which had become the norm of art since the Renaissance. Here, multimodality is a question of how filming and editing frame the materials and signifying systems of the visual arts, both spatially and temporally. Meliès' work can be seen as an ancestor of the compositing work of the digital age: the layering of images for which Goffman's (1974) notion of laminated frames is peculiarly apt. The descendants of such work might be seen as the 'poetry' of the moving image: hyper-real or anti-naturalistic animation; video installations in galleries; the lyrical moving images of music video; the quotidian aesthetic of television advertising; the poetic punctuation of television interstitial idents; the mash-up formats of online video culture.

Towards a theory of the kineikonic

The moving image is often seen as a matter of filming and editing – what Metz (1974a) deline-ated as the proper substance of cinematic 'language', identified at the level of the shot, rather than the image. Indeed, Metz's cinematic grammar has served as the foundation for one version of a mutimodal approach to film (Bateman and Schmidt, 2011). The theory of the kineikonic takes a different approach. Burn and Parker (2003a, b) proposed a multimodal theory of the moving image, named 'the kineikonic mode', a portmanteau of the Greek words for 'to move' (*kinein*) and 'image' (*eikon*). The emphasis here was on the interplay of all the modes which contribute to the moving image: what Metz saw as the implications of the word 'film' (as opposed to 'cin-ema'), which 'designates the message in its plurality and codical heterogeneity' (1974b: 58). The kineikonic also attends to a grammar of the moving image at the level of the individual frame as well as the shot. In this theory, then, the related modes of filming and editing are seen as the *orchestrating modes* of whatever the moving image contains; and their orchestration occurs in both spatial and temporal dimensions. The logic of the spatial appears to dominate if the individual frame is selected; the logic of the temporal appears to dominate if the editing track or timeline is the focus. The nature of the moving image, or at least its orchestrating modes, is the relation between the two. All other modes are included in the analysis in principle, and are identified as *contributory modes*.

The approach to the kineikonic mode offered in this chapter develop two more analytical frameworks: the *metamodal* relation between the orchestrating modes (filming and editing) and the contributory modes, and the *kineikonic chronotope*, adapted from Bakhtin's metaphor of space–time relations in literature (Gibbons, 2010). These are not intended to represent a complete theory of the kineikonic, or a complete analytical apparatus, but rather an extension of the theory so far proposed. The conclusion will sketch the more obvious areas which remain to be developed.

The metamodal kineikonic

Metamodal emphasises the nesting of modes within modes in moving-image texts. The prefix 'meta-' is used to indicate 'beyondness' and 'adjacency' – cultural forms and modes within, beyond and next to each other.

The orchestrating modes, *filming and editing*, are the medium-specific meta-modes of the kineikonic. Filming produces spatial framing, angle, proximity and camera movement and provisional duration; editing produces temporal framing, and the orchestration of other contributory modes, especially sound and graphics.

The contributory modes have been attended to in various ways in the history of film theory. For example, Roland Barthes, in his seminal work *Mythologies* (1957/1972), looks at a very specific aspect of Mankiewicz's 1953 film of *Julius Caesar*: at the meaning of beads of sweat on the brow of Marlon Brando, who plays Mark Anthony. This reminds us that the great signifying systems of language, painting and music are not the only contributors to meaning: that a make-up artist dashing in to squeeze a drop of glycerine on Brando's forehead is part of the complex of contributory modes.

Figure 27.1 is a diagrammatic representation of the orchestrating modes and the contributory modes. This diagram is partial (many other contributory modes are possible), and indicates only commonly found modes in narrative film. The contributory modes are shown below the orchestrating modes. Each breaks down into more specific signifying systems. Language, for example, breaks into lexis and grammar, speech and writing; each of these categories further decomposes into specific resources, so that speech can be analysed syntactically, lexically, metrically, phonologically, and in terms of features such as tone and tonicity (Halliday, 1985). The diagram suggests similar progressive levels of granularity for the other modes.

One approach to the contributory modes, then, is decomposition, asking what the specialist role is of a particular resource in the wider context of the moving-image text.

However, the distinctive insight offered by a multimodal approach is to see how the modes work together, looking across and between modes, asking how they connect to make meanings. There are many ways to think about these processes. To use a musical metaphor, the combination of modes can be thought of as a fugue: the modes working as voices which build a theme, the relationship between them structured as a form of counterpoint. This polyphonic structure allows for the modes to develop their own contours, contribute their own colouring, yet contribute to an overall coherence. The fugue metaphor also suggests sequential structures, such as exposition, statement of theme, coda and so on, which apply well to the temporal aspects of the kineikonic.

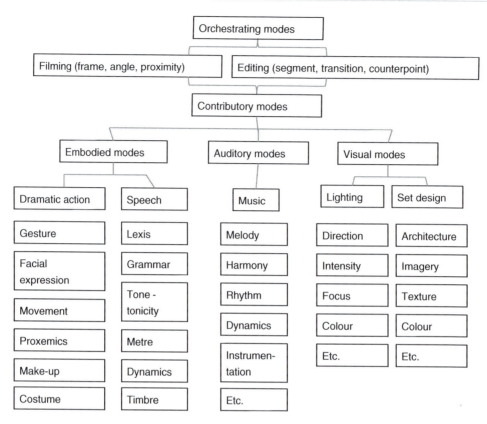

Figure 27.1 The metamodal kineikonic.

A sample analysis: metamodal relations in *Hamlet*

This example is taken from Laurence Olivier's film of *Hamlet* (1948). In the scene considered here, in Shakespeare's text, Ophelia is recounting to her father Polonius how Hamlet, apparently succumbing to madness, has visited her in her chamber. In the film, what is an offstage event in the play is transformed into a flashback, or *analepsis* (Genette, 1980), with the speech as accompanying voiceover. Figure 27.2 tabulates the main contributory modes in play (speech, music, action), and the orchestrating modes (filming and editing). The emphasis in this quite simple chart is on noting the modes and reading across them. No attempt is made to systematically represent space–time relations. The music column incorporates sections of William Walton's autograph score for this scene.

Olivier was criticised for subordinating the high art of theatre to the popular form of cinema; but also for the opposite: producing cinema that was too 'stagy'. The effort to combine the forms can be seen in two decisions in this scene.

On the one hand, the scene is an example of Olivier's determination to fragment sequences of verse and drama as little as possible by cutting; it contains one of many very long shots in the film, which privilege dramatic continuity (in the same space and time) over cinematic continuity (constructed by editing shots to create the illusion of continuous space and time).

On the other hand, the orchestrating modes are used to provide a bracketing effect, enclosing the cinematic flashback sequence. Hamlet is introduced as a ghostly superimposed figure (segment 4), suggesting both an other-worldly quality and that he is a product of her imagination

SPEECH		MUSIC	ACTION	FILMING	EDITING
1. As I was sowing in my Closet		Musical passage begins: D minor; low notes on 1st violin	Sewing; raises head	Medium C/U; central framing	First shot of the sequence fades from black
2.		1st violin passage continues	Eyes move to L	Zoom to C/U	First shot
3.		1st violin passage continues		Lighting dim to diffuse low-key	First shot
4. Lord *Hamlet* with his doublet all unlac'd,		Insistent repeated phrases	Head turn to L; Hamlet stands	Superimposed shot backlit; main shot still low-key-lit	Superimposition of long-shot of Hamlet; Fast dissolve to next shot
5. Pale as his shirt,		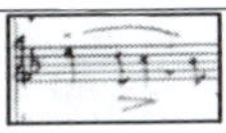 Sustained top E followed by descrescendo	Hamlet walks forward	Wider two-shot (C/U and LS); key light raised; back and fill lights raised	Second shot continues into long take
6. And with a looke so pitious in purport,		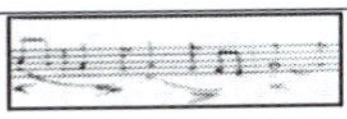 Falling cadence with crescendo and decrescendo	Hamlet comes close to Ophelia; she turns away from camera; raises hand to mouth	Camera moves up (low angle)	Long take
7. As if he had been loosed out of hell, To speake of horrors:		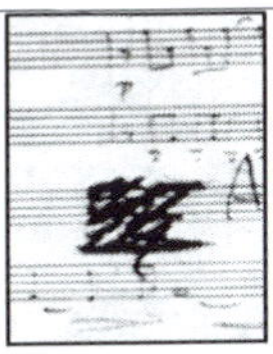 Harp enters			Long take
8. he comes before me.		 Violin cadenza			Long take
9. He tooke me by the wrist, and held me hard;		 Second cadenza	He seizes her right hand with his.	Frame maintains low angle medium shot.	Long take

[...]

| 10. And to the last Bended Their light | 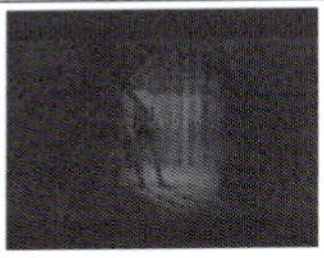 | Violin phrases lengthen; die away. | Hamlet walks backward; pauses in doorway | Camera tracks slowly towards Hamlet, excluding Ophelia from shot; lights dim to a spot on Hamlet. | Long shot dissolves into a superimposed image of Hamlet. |
| 11. On me. | 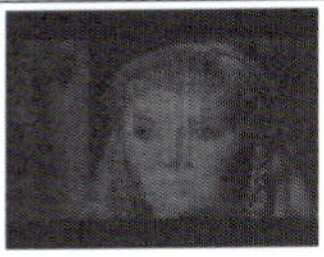 | Violin rising passage; harp chord on "me". | Ophelia looks at camera; then turns head to right, raising hand to face. | Close-up of Ophelia. | Long shot of Hamlet dissolves into close-up of Ophelia. |

Figure 27.2 Metamodal analysis of a scene from Olivier's *Hamlet*.

or memory. This shot then dissolves into the two-shot in which he walks towards her, a more naturalistic co-location of the characters in the same space (segment 5). At the end of the sequence, the lighting reduces to a tight spot on Hamlet (segment 10), and the shot dissolves again into a close-up of Ophelia's face, effectively superimposed on the figure of Hamlet in the distance (segment 11). The orchestrating modes, then, frame the social relations between the two: Hamlet is imagined or recalled by Ophelia (her face in closeup; his figure in long shot); Hamlet then dominates Ophelia, towering over her in the frame; Hamlet's distress is stretched over an extended period of time in order to intensify it; the psychic bond between the two is temporally and spatially framed by the two dissolve transitions.

However, the introduction of the superimposed shot disrupts the apparent naturalism. Cook argues that this film is firmly located in the mainstream 'continuity' style of Western cinema, whose controlling aim is to efface the markers of fragmented space and time to produce the illusion of spatio-temporal continuity (Cook, 2011). The superimposition in this scene, however, disrupts this a little, briefly disorienting the viewer: is Hamlet in her mind, or in her chamber? And, in relation to constructions of cultural value in film aesthetics, is this a formulaic popular piece or an example of radical montage? The uncertainty testifies to the confusion felt at the time about how to view this piece of popular Shakespeare; but also indicates the fragility of such reductive cultural valuations.

How do the contributory modes function within these frames? Here only speech and dramatic action are used as examples.

The speech is a first-person narrative in which a series of actions are attributed to Hamlet. The first ('he comes before me') is delayed by three adjectival phrases denoting madness. The second action ('He took me by the wrist, and held me hard') is amplified in the dramatic action by a series of movements of the arm and head in which Hamlet gazes at Ophelia, his distraction and distress indicated by these movements, by his facial expressions, and by the parting of his lips in the sigh which the speech denotes. The speech is also able to locate the events in a past tense, rather than the dramatic present. The bracketing of the scene between the two dissolve transitions has a similar effect: dissolves in film often signify a change in time or place.

So part of the intermodal relationship is a direct correspondence between the modes of dramatic action and speech: two voices in unison. The two modes also, however, perform their own distinctive kinds of semiotic work, suggesting the contrapuntal relation of the fugue. The simile in segment 7 is a good example of what language can do: the visual scene is unable to produce the specific effect of a comparison to hell. On the other hand, the dramatic action is obliged to make decisions about exactly how 'He took me by the wrist and held me hard'. He pulls her to her feet, and clasps her close in a kind of embrace, a move which serves to extend or amplify the meaning of the words. Between them, the language and action are constructing a polyphonic representation of the relationship between the characters. In the wider context of the play, questions of love, sex and power are raised in the unfolding of this relationship, and conveyed through speech, action, gesture and architectural imagery. The 'Get thee to a nunnery' scene, for example, sees the distressed Ophelia thrown weeping to the floor at the foot of a flight of stairs by Hamlet; some commentators have suggested that the repeated visual trope of staircases in the film recalls an event of sexual abuse suffered by Olivier as a boy (Cook, 2011).

The speech–action counterpoint also produces the temporal character of the sequence. A number of lengthy pauses in the speech are synchronised with the, slow pace of the accompanying gestures. Despite Olivier's claims about the importance of the verse, cinematic duration is privileged over the continuous flow of the verse. Lines are also cut, broken and recombined, partially dismantling the iambic pentameter. These transformations suggest a tension between a characteristically sparser use of speech in cinema, appealing to a popular audience, and the desire to preserve and venerate the dramatic text, the elevation of Shakesepeare which Shaw caustically labelled 'bardolatry' (1901/2000). These tensions between modes require a modification of the fugue metaphor, which would be unlikely to exhibit such tensions. It would be misleading to suggest that the multimodality of film guarantees a perfect union of the arts, a cinematic version of Wagner's *Gesamtkunstwerk*. Rather, we might expect to see tensions, leakages, and incoherences in film, whose chief characteristic might be semiotic and stylistic promiscuity rather than perfectly controlled harmony.

The interplay between the modes, then, elaborates the detail of narrative representations of sexuality and madness. We can add, briefly, that modes also conduct what Van Leeuwen (2005a) terms 'semiotic import', analogous to Barthes' principle of connotation. Here, the imported meanings struggle for coherence, in particular the tension in this scene between signifiers of Nordic austerity in set and costume, and of mock-oriental exoticism in Walton's score (Scott, 1998). Added to the tension between the Shakespearean dramatic tradition on the one hand and the style of popular cinema on the other, this suggests the cultural conflicts such a project could not hope to avoid, and which still exist in negotiations between the Shakespeare heritage industry and attempts to transform the plays for new audiences.

The kineikonic chronotype

Early work on the kineikonic mode suggested, for the purpose of analysis, a distinction between the spatial axis of the moving image and the temporal axis (Burn and Parker, 2003a, b). The former was associated with the 'synchronic syntagm' – effectively the single frame. This allows for an analysis of visual modes, such as the visual design of characters and sets, and certain functions of shot-grammar, such as the locating function of the establishing shot. The temporal axis was associated with the 'diachronic syntagm' – the moving sequence, such as movement of bodies, objects and landscapes; music, sound and speech; the movement of the camera and frame; and the succession of interstitial 'transitions' such as fades, wipes and dissolves. While this distinction may seem overly formalistic, even antagonistic to the very nature of the *moving* image, two justifications can be grounded in Barthes' (1978) analysis of the cinematic still, which argues that the still allows a resistance of the tyranny of narrative time, and relates to cultural practices such as the publication of stills in the *Cahiers du Cinéma*. We might say, then, that an analytical distinction between still and moving elements allows a critical perspective; but also that it relates to actual cultural practices in which stills represent aspects of (even the whole) film: posters, publicity photos, images in film magazines, on merchandise; and of course the illustrative use of stills in academic and educational discourse (Burn, 1999).

Two qualifications remain. The analytical separation of synchronic and diachronic syntagm is only the first step. The next is to consider how they relate to each other – how the logics of space (the disposition of bodies and objects in space; the relation of space to perception and point of view) are related to the logics of time (movement, rhythm, tempo, direction, tense, order, duration).

Finally, Gibbons (2010) valuably extends the notion of the chronotope to cover ways in which moving-image texts develop over space and time as a dialogic chain, moving through different spaces and times of production, of exhibition, and of transformation and dissemination, including the spatio-temporal contexts of online display. This contextual extension of the chronotope suggests a progressive move from discursive contexts and resources, through processes of textual design, to communicative contexts of dissemination and exhibition; and finally to contexts of interpretation, appropriation, transformation, and the practices of mash-up and remix cultures (Jenkins, 1992; Willett, 2009).

The kineikonic chronotype: making 'machinima'

This example is drawn from a project in which a group of 30 eleven-year-olds made a machinima film. Machinima is perhaps most recent cultural form in the world of animation. 'Machinima' is a portmanteau word combining machine and cinema, and is defined by Kelland *et al.* as 'the art of making animated films within a realtime 3-D environment' (2005: 10). In the example used in this chapter, the students used a proprietary 3-D animation software, building characters and sets, and composing them into a film narrative devised by the group.[1]

The process can be seen as a practical example of multimodality in action. Having devised the script, the children worked in specialist groups on character design, set design, music composition and recording, and performance and recording of the vocal track. Modes in use included, then, visual design, vocal acting, music, spoken improvisation and writing.

The students designing characters, for example, had to determine how to represent attributes of age, ethnicity, gender and narrative function. The software makes this possible by providing menus for clothing, face type and shape, age markers, ethnicity markers (skin colour, hair), makeup and 'distinguishing features such as scars and tattoos'.

The two girls designing the teenage protagonist Jeff chose straight brown hair and a pale complexion, because he was a geek 'who might play World of Warcraft, I imagine always geeky boys playing that'. Both girls had played The Sims, and described the kind of subversive practices enjoyed by players, such as building families and making them over-eat, or using the 'Die by Flies' cheat. They also described how creating Sims families resembled designing characters in Moviestorm:

> M: I played one Sims game and it's when you're a vet, and it's not like this but it's the same sort of basis, like you've got a character and you dress them up and you make them do stuff and make them go places.

Here, then, the design emphasis is on the synchronic syntagm: the spatial characteristics of the character and set. The image is built up in a series of layers: the image elements in the software, like those in Photoshop, are digital filters providing interchangeable options which can be freely experimented with, switched on and off, subjected to scalar enlargement or contraction, and so on. Though these forms of lamination seem distinctive of the digital era, they can also be seen in a longer cinematic tradition of layered composition in the filmic frame, the best early example being Mèlies, as we have seen.

Similarly, while these children are focusing on the spatial aspects of the textual chronotope, we can see traces of the extended dialogic chain within which their work sits. Earlier practices are hinted at: the images carries echoes of cultural types salient to the children (teenage girls, geeks and gamers).

Having made the assets, the children move to making the film itself. Here, then, they insert the spatial assets (sets and characters) into the moving sequence, using the software's virtual cameras to frame images and movement, and the timeline to construct the temporal sequence. The relations of the textual chronotope are built up, through semiotic decisions based on what they want to say, and how they have experienced such things articulated in their own experience of the moving image.

Martha and Rosa are editing the scene in which two characters, Jeff and Dr T, have arrived at Cleopatra's palace, and have to convince her guard to let them in. They describe what they need to add to make the script into a film:

RESEARCHER: What do you need to do to turn this [script] into a film?
M: Well, you need to add in, like, gestures, and, and we've –
R: And dialogue.
AB: What kind of gestures?
R: [*Smacks one fist into the other*] When they ask him if they can go in, and he says 'why?'.

They have not yet designed camera angles (this is done at a later stage with the Moviestorm software, after basic moves have been plotted). But they are asked how they would film a conversation:

AB: If you were filming two people talking, how would you do it?
R: You'd put the camera there, and one of them would be there, and one would be there [*indicating side-by-side with hands*].
AB: What's your other option?
R: You could put the camera on the person talking . . .
M: And then switch it round.

This bears out earlier research suggesting that children of this age may not spontaneously consider the shot–reverse-shot structure despite their familiarity with it (Burn and Durran, 2007). Here, then, they suggest a two-shot for a conversation, and gradually move towards the idea of shot–reverse-shot in response to questions. They are, however, quite confident about the idea of shot distance and its function of emphasis, and also describe kinds of camera movement. They also describe the function of low- and high-angle shots to signify power, although these have not been explicitly taught at this stage. When asked how these ideas could apply to their scene, they suggest that Cleopatra and the guard might be filmed from a low angle. Once they moved on to insert camera angles, they did exactly this (Figure 27.3).

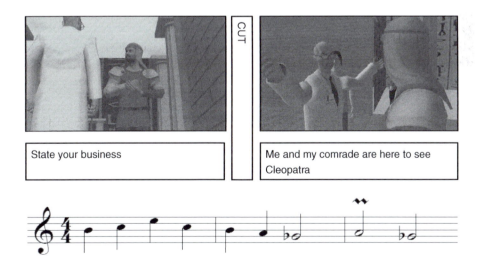

Figure 27.3 Shot–reverse-shot (low camera angle), speech and music.

Here, then, the textual chronotope develops through a series of understandings about the social meanings of the image they are creating. They can imagine the characters as figures in social space; and if the analogy for them is their own experience of bodies in social space, then co-location of two bodies in conversation is an obvious representational strategy. However, as they consider mobile point-of-view for future spectators, the temporal alternation of shot–reverse-shot becomes a more appropriate option. Here, then, two quite different temporal structures are imagined in relation to the disposition of (virtual) bodies in space, to the spatial frame of the (virtual) camera, and to the temporal frame of the timeline.

The contributory mode of speech adds a complementary temporality, framed in time with the edit – the gap between the two lines of dialogue align with the cut in the visual frame. Meanwhile, the social actions of the speech, indicating power (a command) and compliance (an information offer) align with the shot angles and gesture repertoires (fist in the palm; open arms), functioning as what Kendon (2004a) calls *utterance uses*, as distinct from gestures expressive of affect only. Here, the embodied modes of gesture and speech, usually produced simultaneously by an actor, are separately designed, the choice of gestures following the meanings of the pre-recorded speech. In effect they are realised within the editing as part of the orchestration function.

The contributory mode of music adds a different temporality – a sequence of three phrases which run across the cut. This sequence was designed by the Music group to connote an 'Egyptian' flavour, carried by the modal structure (Aeolian mode) and the mordant ornamentation on the penultimate note. Like Walton's score for the Ophelia scene above, this sequence signifies 'oriental' via pastiche, in a complementary relation to the imagery of hieroglyphs and Egyptian costumes provided by the set and character designers.

In general, then, the function of the kineikonic chronotope in this example can be summarised in three ways:

- The design of the contributory modes (character, set, music, speech) precedes the design of the orchestrating modes, and includes forms of lamination (of images), looping, iteration, remix and improvisation (music), and intentional construction of affective charge (speech).
- The design of the orchestrating modes constructs the synchronic syntagm (adjusting the virtual camera to choose distance and angle), followed by the diachronic syntagm (plotting the movements of characters, gestures, facial expressions; segmenting the shots). These decisions display particular social interests: affiliation to particular tropes in popular cinema (combat scenes, aliens, time travel and video-gaming protagonists); changing awareness of the social relation between their own preoccupations and those of possible future audiences.
- The wider chronotope reaches back to earlier experiences both of film and game, and of film-making projects in primary school; and forwards to later moments in the dialogic chain: exhibitions of the films in the local cinema and on YouTube. In interviews, the children imagined different meanings their film might hold for different audiences: peers, parents and undifferentiated global audiences.

Conclusion: future possibilities

Future work on the analytical possibilities of the kineikonic mode are suggested by researchers who have begun work with this approach.

Burn and Parker (2003a, b) have explored how the Hallidayan metafunctions operate in relation to the kineikonic mode. We have also looked at the material medium of animation in relation to Kress and Van Leeuwen's (1996) account of technologies of inscription (Burn and Parker, 1999).

Gibbons has developed, as noted above, the idea of the chronotope in relation to the kineikonic; and this model, perhaps alongside Kress and Van Leeuwen's semiotic strata, can be taken further. It is particularly important in its ability to encompass the wider socio-cultural contexts of moving-image production (Gibbons, 2010; Curwood and Gibbons, 2009).

Hurr has explored ways of documenting, tabulating and notating the kineikonic text, in relation to art-installation in gallery space. Her work shows how very fine-grained transcriptions can capture the wide range of contributory modes, and the framing functions of the orchestrating modes (Hurr, 2012).

Cannon has applied the analytical structure of the kineikonic to moving-image work by young people in a project with the Cinémathèque Française, exploring how the metaphor of the 'multimodal mixing-desk' can apply to digital production practices and associated literacies (Cannon, 2011).

However, as specific analytical protocols are developed, it might also be expected that the value of this general approach will be debated. From the point of view of the discipline of Film Studies, it might be objected that a fully elaborated field of film semiotics already exists, particularly in the tradition of Metz (e.g. Stam, 1992).

There are a number of answers to the question 'why do we need a multimodal theory of the moving image?' One is that Film Studies has arguably over-emphasised filming and editing, at the expense of the other semiotic modes; or else it has studied these other modes in isolation, as in specialist work on sound, music or lighting. Another argument is that film, in the age of 'new media', is no longer a self-contained multimodal form, if it ever was. Indeed, part of the argument of the kineikonic approach is that the moving image has never possessed the kind of formal purity some cineastes would like to assert; rather, it has always been a promiscuous medium, and the cultural frames surrounding it have always been permeable. Now, however, its frames are themselves newly enframed by the display and commentariat of YouTube, by the trailers and interactive design interfaces of film-on-demand, by the very different generic frames of computer games, and by the mobile transformations of smart-phones. Multimodality offers a way to read across these phenomena of contemporary communication: to pay full attention to the century-old grammar of the moving image while integrating this analysis coherently with an analysis of other frames, laminates and contexts. Most importantly, perhaps, it offers a way to read across from text to context, from producers of moving images to those who used to be known as audiences, but who increasingly actively remake moving-image texts for themselves. The contexts here include recreational 'work', professional work, and education, broadly conceived. In this latter context, where much of my own work has been situated, the kineikonic mode can be seen as the basis of a specific set of practices for which the word 'literacy' has often been a shorthand metaphor, whether in practice, research or policy (Burn and Durran, 2007; Jewitt and Kress, 2003a). Future work in this domain might find a better metaphor; but the wider social implication is that the expressive, communicative and artistic practices confined to elite groups in the time of Olivier are now accessible to eleven-year-olds. The kineikonic mode has become a common language; though, like all language, it is learned through an often uneven distribution of labour across domestic and educational sites, and the pedagogic processes involved, whatever their level of visibility, need to be differently provided for at all levels of education.

Note

1 The project was funded by First Light, and was a partnership between the Institute of Education, the University of Leeds, the British Film Institute, and Moviestorm Ltd.

28

Multimodal analytics

Software and visualization techniques for analyzing and interpreting multimodal data

Kay L. O'Halloran, Marissa K. L. E and Sabine Tan

Introduction

Multimodal analytics, the study of semantic patterns arising from the integration of language, images and audio resources in multimodal texts, presents considerable challenges which are both theoretical and practical in nature. First, frameworks for modeling the semantic contributions of the different resources and the meaning arising from the interaction of choices in multimodal phenomena are required. Such frameworks also need to account for resemiotization of multi-modal phenomena to investigate social practices over space and time (Iedema, 2001, 2003). In this respect, the social semiotic approach (Halliday, 1978; Halliday and Matthiessen, 2004) developed by Kress and Van Leeuwen (2006 [1996]) and O'Toole (2011 [1994]) has provided a powerful theoretical platform for investigating multimodal phenomena (e.g. see this volume).

Second, the complexity of the analytical task is daunting without suitable tools and techniques to capture and interpret the multimodal analysis. That is, linguistic, visual and aural choices and their interactions need to be stored, retrieved and analyzed in order to discern semantic patterns in multimodal texts. Existing approaches have included the use of tables and/or spreadsheets and multimodal annotation software tools (e.g. see Rohlfing *et al.*, 2006). However, manual coding is labour-intensive and the available software applications have some major drawbacks; that is, either the applications are not designed for sustained systemic analysis or the tools are designed for the analysis of one modality only (e.g. language, image or audio).

Lastly, the systematic analysis of linguistic, visual and aural resources results in multi-dimensional data structures which are particularly intricate for dynamic media such as videos and interactive digital media. The interaction of semiotic choices at different levels of analysis, coupled with the hybridity of digital genres, leads to such complexity that even a close multimodal analysis of a limited number of multimodal texts becomes a formidable task. For this reason, most approaches in multimodal studies to date have been 'top down' where generalized principles are illustrated via selected examples, or 'bottom up' approaches where theoretical frameworks are developed and exemplified through multimodal analysis (see O'Halloran, 2011; O'Halloran and Smith, 2013a). In reality, most research efforts combine these two approaches, but few studies are based on empirical evidence (Bateman, 2008).

In this chapter, we report on a research program in the Multimodal Analysis Lab[1] in the Interactive & Digital Media Institute at the National University of Singapore which aims to address these issues through a *multimodal digital semiotics* approach involving the development of interactive software with functionalities and facilities for systematic multimodal analysis of text, images and videos. The multimodal analysis is stored in an integrated database with view to modeling and visualizing the multimodal data to discern semantic patterns and trends. As the multimodal analysis software[2] is described in detail elsewhere (e.g. O'Halloran *et al.*, 2012; Podlasov *et al.*, 2012; also see O'Halloran *et al.*, 2010, 2011; Smith *et al.*, 2011), we focus on the social semiotic approach underlying the design of the software and the mathematical and visualization techniques which are applied to the multimodal data. In what follows, we describe the social semiotic approach, the associated methodology, the video selected for analysis, the mathematical and visualization techniques applied to multimodal data produced from the analysis, and the resulting patterns and trends which are interpreted in relation to the situational and cultural context of the video recording. The concluding section is concerned with the future of multimodal analytics, which may be broadly characterized as a multimodal digital humanities approach (e.g. Svensson, 2010; Berry, 2012).

Social semiotics and the metafunctional principle

Social semiotics is concerned with "the way people use semiotic 'resources' both to produce communicative artifacts and events and to interpret them …" (Van Leeuwen, 2005a: xi). The concept of 'semiotic resource' is central to the major approaches adopted in multimodal studies (e.g. Jewitt, 2009, Chapter 2 this volume). The term originates from Halliday's interpretation of language "not a set of rules, but as a *resource* [for making meaning]'" (Halliday, 1978: 192).

Halliday's (1978; Halliday and Matthiessen, 2004) 'metafunctional principle' provides a platform for theorizing how semiotic resources interact to create meaning. The metafunctional principle derives from Halliday's Systemic Functional Theory, which is based on the premise that the organization of semiotic resources (i.e. the 'grammatics') reflects the social functions which the resources are required to play (e.g. Halliday, 1978; Halliday and Matthiessen, 2004; Kress and Van Leeuwen, 2006 [1996]; Martin, 1992; Martin and Rose, 2007; O'Toole, 2011 [1994]). More specifically, language and other resources (i.e. visual, auditory, kinesthetic and spatial resources) are conceptualized as inter-related semantic systems that realize three metafunctions:

- *ideational* metafunction for representing experience and logical relations;
- *interpersonal* metafunction for enacting social relations (e.g. role relations, attitudes and modality or truth value); and
- *textual* metafunction for organizing the message.

The metafunctional principle provides an underlying basis for investigating the grammatics of semiotic resources and the ways in which semiotic choices interact to fulfill particular objectives in multimodal discourse – namely to engage and orientate readers to particular views of the world which are understood in relation to the situation and cultural context of the communicative act itself. In this way, Systemic Functional Theory provides a comprehensive conceptual framework for analyzing informational content (configurations of agents, participants, processes and circumstances), the social relations which are established (power, status and emotion), the

387

orientation to the ideas which are presented (modality and truth value), and the ways in which the choices are organized to achieve specific purposes (e.g. points of departure, given and new information). In the next section, we describe how the social semiotic approach has been integrated in the multimodal analysis software to analyze and interpret multimodal semantic patterns in videos, films and other dynamic media.

Multimodal analytics methodology

The complexity of multimodal analysis, involving language, image and audio resources, requires a range of software functionalities for the annotation, analysis, search and retrieval of semiotic choices. The software developed at the Multimodal Analysis Lab at the Interactive and Digital Media Institute provides a set of such functionalities for a multimodal analyst (see O'Halloran *et al.*, 2012): that is, media files can be imported, multimodal systems can be defined (according to metafunction), and annotations with time-stamped and spatial co-ordinates can be coded in strips and overlays respectively according to the pre-defined annotation systems. The resulting annotation units contain systemic choices for linguistic, visual and audio resources with time intervals and/or spatial co-ordinates. The annotations are stored in a database for later retrieval and analysis using mathematical and visualizations techniques. The ability to precisely encode the temporal and spatial relations of semiotic choices and store them in a database for retrieval and analysis is critical for advancing our understanding of how semiotic choices integrate to create meaning in both static and dynamic media.

In what follows, we illustrate how the multimodal software can be used to analyze multimodal texts, in this case, a televised news interview about climate science. Research into the communication of information about climate science in the public domain has focused on the pivotal role the news media plays in influencing how members of the public perceive and react to both scientific knowledge and the scientific community that advances and communicates this knowledge (Boykoff and Boykoff, 2004; Boykoff, 2011; Carvalho, 2007). In this case, we undertake a multimodal analysis of a televised news debate with an interviewer, a climate scientist and a climate denialist and then apply mathematical and visualization techniques to investigate the characteristics of the interview and the semantic patterns for each speaker which, as we shall see, are significantly different.

Televised news debate

We analyze a segment of an episode from "Happening Now", a Fox News Corporation breaking-news program aired on 25 November 2009[3] which is concerned with the climate science debate. In the segment, the interviewer and co-anchor, Jon Scott, interviews Dr Kevin E. Trenberth, a Distinguished Senior Scientist in the Climate Analysis Section at the National Center for Atmospheric Research in Colorado, and Mr Myron Ebell, Director of Energy and Global Warming Policy at the Competitive Enterprise Institute in Washington DC. The interview took place in the wake of the email controversy involving the hacking of a server at the Climatic Research Unit at the University of East Anglia on 20 November 2009, where climate scientists' personal emails and files were made available to the public on the internet. The controversy involved extensive media coverage where questions were raised about scientists' manipulation of climate data, as illustrated in the video segment under analysis.

The multimodal analysis of the Fox News interview includes Kress and Van Leeuwen's (2006 [1996]) frameworks for gaze (labeled as "contact", p. 149), interactive meaning (p. 149) and conceptual representational meaning (p. 105). In addition, Halliday's major linguistic systems for textual, interpersonal and ideational meaning (Halliday and Matthiessen, 2004) are used to analyze the linguistic choices in the spoken discourse. Using facilities in the multimodal analysis software, the system choices for language (for words, word groups and clauses), and images and video for the three speakers were time-stamped to record the exact time interval in which the semiotic choices were made during the televised debate.

k-Means clustering technique for multimodal data

Multimodal analysis produces information of high dimensionality and the inherent complexity of the data structures (i.e. for semiotic resource, metafunction, system, system choice, time interval and spatial co-ordinates) pose significant difficulties for the analyst. For example, the time-stamped multimodal data for the Fox News interview (155 clauses with 198 types of linguistic, image and video annotations) is displayed in Plate 28.1. The red, pink and black annotations correspond to linguistic, image and video choices for Jon Scott, the interviewer, Kevin Trenberth, the climate scientist and Myron Ebell, the climate denialist respectively, organized according to time interval on the *x*-axis and metafunction/system/system choice on the *y*-axis.

In order for such a complex data structure to be processed computationally and visualized in a manner helpful to the analyst, some form of dimensionality reduction has to be implemented to discern multimodal semantic patterns. The techniques which have been previously used include singular value decomposition and recurrence diagrams (E *et al.*, 2012) and temporal interval logic (O'Halloran *et al.*, 2013). In this case, we use *k*-means clustering (MacQueen, 1967) for grouping the data into clusters where each annotation unit (i.e. resource type, metafunction, system choice and time interval) belongs to the cluster with the nearest mean value, based on binary values of "0" for absence and "1" for presence of the system choice within a specified time frame, in this case for each clause. The *k*-centers (or mean) are determined from the data collection itself by an unsupervised iterative algorithm that aims to minimize the overall distance of every data point to its nearest cluster center (or mean). In this way, the multimodal data is divided into *k* clusters according to the resource type (language, image and video), metafunction (textual, interpersonal and ideational) and system choice based on iterative techniques which calculate the best value for *k*.

The cluster distributions for Jon Scott, Kevin Trenberth and Myron Ebell (red, pink and black respectively) are displayed in Plate 28.2 according to time on the *x*-axis and cluster number on the *y*-axis, where clusters 1–8 belong to the textual systems, clusters 9–20 belong to the interpersonal systems and clusters 21–32 belong to the ideational systems for language, and clusters (−8)–(−1) belong to the interpersonal and ideational systems for images and video.

The most repeated cluster combinations-of-three were calculated to find semantic patterns in the discourse and the most significant cluster combinations for the three speakers. Plate 28.3 shows the distribution of the most frequent cluster combinations-of-three over time, where three distinct episodes, Episodes 1–3, are identified in the news interview. As we may see from Plate 28.3, the discernable patterns in the distribution of cluster combinations for Jon Scott, Kevin Trenberth and Myron Ebell in Episode 1 appear to develop into a somewhat frenzied 'exchange' in Episode 2, with more frequent occurrences of cluster combinations within a shorter timeframe. Following this, the range of cluster combinations for Jon Scott and Kevin Trenberth is reduced in Episode 3, and contributions from Myron Ebell are noticeably absent. The three episodes are examined in more detail below.

In the first episode, Jon Scott is engaged in a question–answer type interaction where he and Kevin Trenberth are not competing for speaking time, but rather questions are asked and responses are made. Myron Ebell's cluster combinations in Episode 1 follow Kevin Trenberth's contributions. Episode 1 reflects a less tense part of the news debate interview, compared to Episode 2 where, if we refer back to the Fox News interview, we see that Kevin Trenberth is attempting to address Myron Ebell's arguments against him and his climate science colleagues. However, Myron Ebell seems to dominate the discourse in Episode 2, as indicated by the presence of extended black cluster formations which both precede and follow Kevin Trenberth's contributions. In Episode 3, Jon Scott, as interviewer, tries to bring the news debate interview to a close by acknowledging his guests. However, Kevin Trenberth interjects with new information and Jon Scott only gets as far as uttering his guests' names before he is interrupted. Thus, there is a repetition of cluster combinations which are "nil choices" because the clauses labeled with this cluster combination-of-three are minor clauses (e.g. minimal responses) which do not carry textual, interpersonal or ideational meaning.

From the cluster visualizations, we can observe patterns in the dynamics of the text that can be further investigated and verified through reference back to the text itself. The interview is clearly divided into three distinct parts, with a middle part dominated by Myron Ebell which is quite different from the rest. In addition, the examination of cluster combinations for each episode has shown unique characteristics, providing tangible preliminary evidence for the development of stages in the interview which may be particular to that register and genre.

Network visualizations of *k*-means clusters

In what follows, we illustrate how network visualizations of *k*-means clustering can be used to interpret how multimodal resources are utilized, in this case by the three speakers in the news interview. Network diagrams consist of (a) nodes which represent the clusters of systemic choices and (b) edges (i.e. connecting lines) which display transitions from one cluster to another, as indicated by arrows. The network visualizations provide an overview of the speakers' use of semiotic resources as the text unfolds in terms of the frequency and directional transitions between clusters of systemic selections. Such patterns, besides giving an indication of speaker profile, also contribute towards profiling texts and genres because such multimodal semantic patterns are indicative of patterns at a register level.

In what follows, we explore how the three speakers in the Fox News video utilize different resources according to textual, interpersonal and ideational metafunctions for language in order to organize their contributions to the interview, enact social relations, and construct their version of events surrounding the email hacking incident respectively. In each case, we provide a brief description of the system and the associated cluster formation and discuss the implications of these formations in the network diagrams. Only the network diagrams for textual meaning are provided, due to space constraints. The findings are discussed in relation to semiotic choices from the image and video systems.

Textual meaning

The system of Theme (Halliday and Matthiessen, 2004: 64–105) captures how the speakers organize their message in terms of conjunctions and cohesive devices (i.e. textual elements), interpersonal elements (e.g. continuatives like "yeah" and "now" and Finite elements like "do" in "do you think?") and the point of departure for the message with regard to ideational meaning (i.e. the topic). Simple clauses contain a topic, while multiple themes have textual and/or

Table 28.1 Clusters for textual metafunction

Cluster no.	Topic theme	Theme count	Textual metafunction
1	Marked	Multiple	Conjunctive Structural Theme, Topic Theme or Topic WH-Theme, Rheme
2	None	None	–
3	Unmarked	Simple	Topic TH-Theme, Rheme
4	Unmarked	Simple	Topic Theme, Rheme
5	Unmarked	Multiple	Continuatives, Interpersonal Finite Theme, Rheme
6	Unmarked	Multiple	Conjunctive Structural Theme, Topic Theme, Rheme
7	No choices		
8	Unmarked	Multiple	Interpersonal Finite Theme, Rheme

interpersonal components, in addition to the topic. The remainder of the clause which follows the topic is classified as the Rheme. In the Fox News video, the system choices for Theme formed eight clusters, as displayed in Table 28.1.

The network diagrams for the textual metafunction for Jon Scott, Kevin Trenberth and Myron Ebell are displayed in Plate 28.4(a)–(c) respectively, showing the cluster formations which reflect their respective manner of organizing their discourse, while also showing clusters which are outliers (i.e. atypical) for each speaker. In the following discussion, we focus on the most frequent clusters of choices (i.e. nodes) as indicated by the number of transitions (i.e. edges or connecting lines) associated with the cluster.

The network visualizations in Plate 28.4 display both similarities and differences between the speakers. Jon Scott, Kevin Trenberth and Myron Ebell select simple constructions most often, as displayed by the frequency of Cluster 4 (i.e. unmarked, simple textual organization). However, both Kevin Trenberth and Myron Ebell choose to logically connect their responses more often (e.g. "so," "if," and "and") as displayed by Cluster 6 (i.e. unmarked, complex textual organization with structural conjunctions), unlike Jon Scott whose role is to guide the discourse and ask questions, as displayed by Cluster 8 (i.e. unmarked, complex textual organization with Finite element for interrogative clauses).

Myron Ebell's use of textual resources is accompanied by conversational continuatives (e.g. "uh," "yeah," "now," and "look"), as displayed in Cluster 5 (i.e. unmarked, complex textual organization with continuatives). This stylistic characteristic forms part of Myron Ebell's repertoire in this interview, resulting in a relatively informal conversational style, which permits him to engage with the audience, even as he makes ungrounded assertions about scientists being part of a gang to deceive the general public.

On the other hand, Kevin Trenberth favours more sophisticated forms of textual organization, choosing marked constructions most often as displayed by Cluster 1 (i.e. marked, complex textual organization with a topic which differs from the expected point of departure), which is not surprising, given his academic background. Various examples for Kevin Trenberth (e.g. "and in my case," and "indeed, {on} personal emails") reveal that he foregrounds certain information to construct his responses in relation to the accusations being leveled against climate scientists. The network diagrams thus reveal differences in the ways in which the three speakers organize their discourse according to their different agendas, which are further explored below in relation to interpersonal and ideational meaning.

Interpersonal meaning

Interpersonal meaning is concerned with how interactants establish and manage the social relations which structure the interaction. For example, interpersonal meaning resources are used to construe social roles between interactants and to establish the speaker's own position in relation to polarity, truth-value and probability. The Mood system (Halliday and Matthiessen, 2004: 106–67) describes the basic system choices for interpersonal meaning. The Mood selections in the Fox News interview formed four major clusters which are displayed in Table 28.2.

The network diagrams (not displayed here) reveal that interpersonal meaning is managed differently by the three speakers in the Fox News video. That is, while the three speakers select choices from Cluster 12 which are the expected choices when information is exchanged (i.e. positive polarity, present tense, congruent Mood, full declarative, and typical Mood elements, i.e. Subject, Finite, and Complement), it is how this cluster combines with other clusters of choices for interpersonal meaning that is significant here. As we shall see, the patterns of interpersonal meaning are quite different for the three speakers.

Jon Scott utilizes interpersonal choices from Cluster 10 which aim to moderate the impact of the information which he presents using Mood Adjuncts (e.g. "just") and, in some cases, modality (e.g. "I guess"), making his delivery of information less forceful. However, there is no attempt on the part of either Kevin Trenberth or Myron Ebell to moderate the interpersonal force of their communication. In fact, Mood Adjuncts and modality choices from Clusters 10 and 11 are used to intensify (e.g. "will," "should," "totally," and "really") and emphasize (e.g. "simply") the points being made. This indicates the different agendas of interviewers and interviewees. An interviewer's role is not to put forth an argument but to manage the discourse as it develops so that an audience's interest is sustained. On the other hand, interviewees have limited time and opportunity to present their point of view convincingly to the audience. As such,

Table 28.2 Major clusters for interpersonal metafunction

Cluster no.	Polarity	Tense	Modality orientation	Modality	Mood congruence	Mood	Speech function	Interpersonal metafunction
9	Positive	Present	Objective implicit	Modalization probability: high	Congruent	Declarative: full	Knowledge Response: Contradict	Subject Mood, Finite Mood, Complement Residue, Adjunct Mood
10	Positive	Present	–	–	Congruent	Declarative: full	–	Subject TH-Mood, Finite Mood, Complement Residue, Adjunct Mood
11	Positive	Present	Subjective implicit	Modulation inclination: median	Congruent	Declarative: full	–	Subject Mood, Finite Modal Mood, Predicator Residue
12	Positive	Present	–	–	Congruent	Declarative: full	–	Subject Mood, Finite Mood, Complement Residue

emphasis and intensification become important components in their arsenal of resources to manage interpersonal meanings.

The other interesting difference in the cluster formations for interpersonal resources is that only Kevin Trenberth's discourse contains choices from Cluster 9 which function as contradictory responses (i.e. Knowledge Response: Contradict). This cluster reflects a strong degree of modality in an antagonistic interaction where one party is likely in disagreement with the other. This is perhaps indicative of Kevin Trenberth's position as reactor and responder in this interview, rather than initiator and accuser, which is the role adopted by Myron Ebell who smiles as he engages with the audience directly through gaze while reinforcing his points about the actions of the climate scientists. The multimodal analysis of the Fox News from the perspective of the temporal relations between language, image and video system choices (O'Halloran et al., 2013-in press) reveals the significance of Myron Ebell's direct visual engagement with the audience, unlike Kevin Trenberth who appears at times to be disengaged. The analysis of the temporal relations between semiotic choices also verifies the significance of the speakers' choices for ideational meaning, which are explored below.

Ideational meaning

Ideational meaning resources are concerned with the actual content of the message that is transmitted between interactants, as described by the Transitivity system (Halliday and Matthiessen, 2004: 168–305). The approach adopted for understanding the content in this study is to examine the process types which are selected. Process types are crucial in our understanding of experience; of 'what is going on'. The process types and their associated clusters are displayed in Table 28.3. These process types are selected from network diagrams (not displayed here) based on their frequency of occurrence and their inter-relationships with other cluster types.

Table 28.3 Major clusters for process types

Jon Scott		Kevin Trenberth		Myron Ebell	
Cluster no.	Process type	Cluster no.	Process type	Cluster no.	Process type
				21	None
				23	Material: Actor + Range
				24	No Process
25	Attributive: Intensive	25	Attributive: Intensive	25	Attributive: Intensive
		26	Attributive: Possessive	26	Attributive: Possessive
		27	Identifying: Intensive		
28	Verbal			28	Verbal
29	Material: Actor + Goal	29	Material: Actor + Goal		
30	Attributive: Circumstantial				
				31	Mental: Cognition

While the three speakers in the Fox News interview employ different sets of process types, as displayed in Table 28.3, the 'Attributive: Intensive' process in Cluster 25, where an attribute is assigned to a participant or entity, is common to all three. This finding is expected since the news interview is concerned with a major controversy, rather than a mere recount of the event. However, Myron Ebell utilizes a wider range of process types, which is reflective of his agenda to describe, criticize and even vilify the climate scientists involved in the controversy during the extended, uninterrupted span of speaking time he is allowed to have.

On the other hand, Kevin Trenberth's utilization of process types centers mainly on the two relational process types; i.e. Attributive and Identifying. Such relational process types are used to establish relations between disparate sets of entities by assigning a characteristic (attribute) or identifying a value (*X* is *Y*). These relational process types are used to create views about the state or nature of the world, particularly when abstract concepts and ideas are defined and conceptualized. Since Kevin Trenberth is an academic and climate scientist, such constructions are common to his field of discourse. In this case, as we have seen, however, Myron Ebell is able to utilize a wider range of process types which are woven into his conversational style of discourse and direct visual engagement with the audience to reinforce his version of events.

Control of the discoursal space

The allocation of airtime is seen as a critical factor in determining the control of discoursal space (e.g. Clayman and Heritage, 2002). However, this case study offers evidence that this may not necessarily always be the case, because Myron Ebell appears to control the discourse, yet he has the least amount of speaking time, as displayed in Table 28.4. The effect observed in the Fox News interview is the product of Myron Ebell's strategic selection of semiotic resources that combine (almost effortlessly, it appears) to create and reinforce his views, as further discussed below.

Myron Ebell has the least amount of speaking time when compared to the others, yet he is the only speaker who is allowed to speak for an extended single period of time without effective interruption. This, coupled with his strategy of keeping to a single key point – the climate scientists are engaging in unprofessional, immoral conduct – and repeating it in various forms that are easily accessed by his audience, especially using specific examples in a conversational style, creates a focus which has been repeated by other mainstream media.

Kevin Trenberth is thus faced with a difficult task because he is placed in the position of reactor or responder rather than initiator, even though he had the first opportunity to express his views in this news interview. Moreover, his familiarity and facility with academic discourse sets him apart from a general audience which is more used to conversational styles

Table 28.4 Speaking time

	Total speaking time	*% over total speaking time*	*% over total video*
Jon Scott	01:55.5	35.71	34.69
Dr Trenberth	01:51.8	34.56	33.57
Myron Ebell	01:36.2	29.73	28.88

of exchange. Instead he calls the hacking "illegal," claims that there has been a "tremendous amount of cherry picking," expresses his pride in climate scientists' work and brushes aside the disunity among climate scientists to proclaim the credibility of climate science research. Unfortunately, Kevin Trenberth's claims appear weak in light of the intense criticism which has arisen in the media in relation to the email hacking controversy. This highlights another issue – the need for interactants, especially interviewees in a time-constrained environment, to understand the context surrounding any discourse; that is, how discourses are interpreted in relation to other discourses in the dialogic space. In this case, the combination of time-based annotations, clustering techniques and network diagrams moves beyond obvious measures like total duration of speaking time to examine what actually happens as multi-modal system choices combine over time.

In summary, it is clearly not facts and reputation that help to win over an audience in a news debate interview. This is apparent in how Dr Kevin Trenberth, even with his knowledge of climate change and his credibility as a Nobel prize-winning scientist, ends up desperately trying to regain ground towards the end of the Fox News interview. Perhaps, because of the visual nature of the television news debate interview, the *person* takes center stage, where credibility is not established through logical argument or one's reputation, but through a populist yardstick based on information that is easily accessed and repeated in a public domain by media that may prioritize one particular perspective over another as a result of its own agenda; that is, news reports that sell (Weingart *et al.*, 2000) and a visual accessibility that attracts attention and positive evaluation from viewers.

Conclusion

One of the key innovations of the integrative, inter-disciplinary approach presented here is that many of the qualitative aspects of meaning making in a text previously described by Halliday (1978), Halliday and Matthiessen (2004), Martin (1992) and others is associated with quantifiable aspects of the data structures (E *et al.*, 2012; O'Halloran *et al.*, 2012; O'Halloran *et al.*, 2013-in press). There are recognizable limitations with the present approach, however; for example, significant multimodal semiotic choices (e.g. see O'Halloran, 2011) may not be detected using mathematical techniques which involve dimensionality reduction and also the cumulative semantic effect of multimodal choices are not taken into account. However, these problems stem from preliminary attempts to integrate computational and mathematical techniques with non-discrete data derived from multi-dimensional, complex semiotic events. It is quite possible that new mathematical approaches need to be developed for the field of multi-modal analytics such that multimodal choices can be modeled to detect significant semantic patterns, including those of stability and instability.

Despite its challenges, the aims of multimodal analytics are to enable and equip analysts with adequate tools and approaches to cast a critical eye on "the discourses of many millions of multiliterate social agents" (O'Halloran and Smith, 2013) in an increasingly advanced digital age that promises to evolve further in directions yet unknown. These discourses are no longer restricted to traditional forms and genres, but have instead become closely intertwined with the affordances of technology, limited only by the imagination and creativity of users. As such, the implementation of computational and mathematical techniques to analyse multimodal communication, with view to identifying and tracking evolving semantic patterns, is a critical and significant step towards understanding the increasingly complex and dynamic semiotic world which we now inhabit.

Acknowledgments

This work was supported by the US Air Force Office of Scientific Research (AFOSR) through the Asian Office of Aerospace Research and Development (AOARD) under research grants FA2386-09-1-4008 and FA2386-10-1-4107. We thank Dr Vahan Hovhannisyan for applying the k-means clustering technique to the multimodal data and producing Plates 28.1–28.4.

Notes

1 For further information, see: http://multimodal-analysis-lab.org/
2 For information about multimodal analysis software, see: http://multimodal-analysis.com/
3 "Illegal Act": http://video.foxnews.com/v/3945521/illegal-act

29

Colour: code, mode, modality

The case of film and video

Theo Van Leeuwen

This chapter argues that semiotic practices can only be properly understood in their social context, and, more particularly, in the context of the normative discourses which regulate or influence them. It does so with reference to the semiotics of colour, as the semiotic uses of colour, and the normative discourses which regulate or influence them, have been particularly complex and diverse. The chapter then focuses on the uses of colour in film, video and contemporary digital media, arguing that considerations of technology should play a crucial role in understanding contemporary semiotic practices.

1

In the French structuralist semiotics of the 1960s, 'code' was a key concept. Semiotics was first and foremost about the 'laws that govern signs' (Saussure, 1974[1916]: 16), about *langue* as law – in French the term 'code' means 'law'. Social semiotics, on the other hand, has followed Halliday (e.g. 1978: 192) in replacing the idea of 'code' with the idea of 'resource'. Instead of complying with rules, sign producers were viewed as making choices from semiotic resources based on their 'interest' (Kress and Van Leeuwen, 2006: 12). In *Reading Images* (ibid.: 12), we took the comparatively unconstrained semiotic production of children as a model for sign production generally. Rules became 'conventions and constraints which are socially imposed on our making of signs' and which 'attempt to limit and constrain the semiotic scope' of the combinations of signifiers and signifieds sign-makers produce.

Three things must be remembered here. First of all, semiosis is socially constrained to different degrees. Artistic practices, for instance, are less constrained than other semiotic practices, and the idea of creativity as a driving force for innovation, which now plays such a key role in business practices and consumer lifestyles, also pushes for the removal of constraints. But other contemporary semiotic practices are becoming more constrained, especially those involving forms, templates, scripts and 'interactive' computer programs. Today's children are confronted with this at an early age. Sitting in front of his computer, my six-year old grandson becomes a strong heavily muscled man trying to jump over a high bar. If he makes it, the gruelling obstacle run will continue, if not, he will get an electric shock and have to start the game again.

Although the game's art work suggests the possibility of unhindered passage underneath the bar or around the poles, this is 'technically' impossible. The rules of athletic high jumping are hard-wired into the game. My grandson's only choice is to become increasingly proficient at what the designers of the game have decided he should become proficient at. This is not to deny children creativity, only to say that, today, following rules forms a large part of their everyday reality, often well before starting school.

Second, 'rules' are of many different kinds (cf. Van Leeuwen, 2005a: 47–66). They include not just the law, or the codes of conduct of the workplace, the breaking of whose rules might cost you your freedom or your job. They also include the authority of the expert and the pervading influence of celebrities and other role models, forms of 'rule' to which most of us are constantly exposed through 'old' as well as 'new' media of communication, and the breaking of which may result in peer pressure to conform (the social pressure to acquire the latest mobile technology is an example). As 'rules' is perhaps not the best superordinate term for these different kinds of rule, I will from here on speak of 'normative discourses'.

Third, the idea that normative discourses 'constrain creativity' is a limited conception of social interaction which makes individual interest and subjectivity the central motif of semiotic thought and views the social as essentially negative and constraining, rather than as ultimately based on reciprocity and responsibility for others. Such a view can be argued at the broad level of philosophical discourse, as for instance in Levinas' critique of phenomenology (1969). Semioticians, however, have to argue it by studying semiotic practices as social practices shaped by the reciprocity of normative discourses (or, as it may be, by their relative lack), in their immediate dialogic instantiations as well in the broader social and cultural contexts where the normative discourses are created, maintained and changed by specific agents and agencies. The semiotics of colour is a rich domain for the empirical study of all these aspects, and hence for developing theoretical arguments of this kind.

2

Many colour codes (in everyday parlance the term 'code' continues to be used in this connection) have highly restricted domains of meaning and very specific contexts of application, and the same colour may mean quite different things in different colour codes of this kind. In the safety code designed by colour theorist Faber Birren (Lacy, 1996: 75), green identifies first aid equipment; red, hoses and valves. In the London Underground green identifies the District Line; red the Central Line. On Dutch milk bottles, green tops identify yoghurt; red, churned milk. Such codes fit the model of French structuralism (cf. e.g. Mounin, 1970: 157f. on the use of colour in traffic signs). They can be studied as neat 'systems'. But social semioticians should also study the processes of their creation, implementation and communication to the relevant publics, through studying the semiotic texts, artefacts and events that *surround* the colour code, and by means of ethnographic methods.

Two further things can be said about colour codes of this kind. First of all, the normative meanings of colour can only be understood in context – the context of application (e.g. travelling with the London Underground or shopping in a Dutch supermarket) as well as the context formed by the objects which red or green are the colours of. Colours do not come on their own. Their meanings cannot be separated from the objects they are the colours of. Even the colour field paintings of Rothko, Newman and Stella can only be experienced in conjunction with specific objects (paintings) and in specific contexts (art galleries), and they come with the normative interpretations created by critics like Clement Greenberg. All this is so, not just in the case of colour codes which identify objects like train lines or milk bottles, but also in the case of red as the colour of 'passion' or 'danger' or 'communism', or green as the colour of 'safe passage' or 'the natural environment'.

Second, the relation between the signifier and the signified may either be arbitrary or motivated. In the case of the London Underground or Dutch milk bottle tops, the colours have been arbitrarily designated. In the case of red as the colour of 'passion' or green as the colour of the 'natural environment' the relation between signifier and signified is clearly not arbitrary – the colour red has been, and continues to be, an apt choice for signifying 'passion' and the same applies to green as the colour of the 'natural environment'. It is therefore better to not say, as Saussure did, that all signification is arbitrary, or, as Kress did (1993) that all signification is motivated. Both types of relation can and do exist. However, if the broader social and cultural context is taken into account, it becomes evident that, in a given period or domain either arbitrariness or motivation may become the preferred and most highly valued mode of semiosis. Saussure's time saw the rise of modern bureaucracy with its predilection for arbitrarily assigned identification numbers and uniformity (it was also the time of Kafka!). Kress' time saw the ascent of the motivated symbolisms of corporate branding . In this broader sense, Saussure's choice for arbitrariness was, paradoxically, motivated.

3

Nevertheless, there are also 'colour codes' with a broader semantic reach and a wider field of application, for instance the colour codes which serve to cement unity between the members of an empire (imperial yellow in China), a political movement (the red of Communism), or a religion (the green of Islam) and which may be based on explicit normative discourses (e.g. Feng Shui in China). Such meanings, however, still depend on context. In the masks of Chinese Opera, for instance, yellow does not signify royalty and absolute power, but treachery and deceitfulness, and players with yellow masks are the adversaries of the red- or blue-faced protagonists.

In the West there are currently two broader systems of colour meaning, one based on experimental psychology, the other on the meaning and value systems of twentieth-century popular culture. Their influence on the training of design practitioners worldwide, and their circulation in global media has given both a global reach, so that in many places they exist alongside traditional colour meanings.

The psychological tradition began with Johann Wolfgang von Goethe's remarkable book *Theory of Colours* (1970 [1810]), which introduced the idea that people have individual colour preferences which are indicative of their personality and that colour can have direct effects: 'Experience teaches us that particular colours excite particular states of feeling' (ibid.: 305).

Goethe's ideas were picked up by romantic German painters who devised and used explicit colour codes for expressing character, though only in women, because they thought that the colour of male dress was determined by their profession (Gage 1999: 188–90) – black hair went with black, blue, white and violet to signify a 'proud and cool' yet 'cheerful and happy' personality; blonde hair went with blue, grey and crimson to signify 'solitariness, modesty, good-heartedness and calm', and so on (Gage, 1993: 207). By the end of the nineteenth century Goethe's ideas found their way into the new science of psychology, where experiments sought to confirm the meanings and effects of individual colours (e.g. blue as 'calming, depressing, peaceful, quiet, serious, nostalgic, melancholic, cool, calm and dreamy', cf. Gage, 1999: 192), and where tests were developed to establish people's personality traits on the basis of colour preferences. Their work acted as a normative discourse, validated by psychological expertise, and implemented by colour advisers to guide everyday practices of interior decoration, product design, fashion, and so on. Applied to personal life, these discourses focused on colour as signifying 'personality traits', as in this quote from a colour expert (Lacy, 1996: 29):

> A yellow entrance hall usually indicates a person who has ideas and a wide field of interests A home belonging to an academic would probably contain a distinctive shade of yellow as this colour is associate with the intellect, ideas and a searching mind .... A green entrance hall – say, a warm apple green – indicates a home in which children, family and pets are held in high importance ....A blue entrance hall indicates a place in which people have strong opinions – there could be a tendency to appear aloof as they can be absorbed too much in their own world.

Applied to public life, for instance to the interior decoration of hospitals, prisons, schools, restaurants, etc. – they focused on the effects of colour, as in this article from *The Independent* (February 2009):

> Scientists who monitored the performance of more than 600 people ... found that red stimulated a person's attentiveness whereas blue fertilized the imagination and inspired a more risk-taking attitude. The researchers ... suggest that the findings could be used for anything from designing the interior decoration or a school of university to the marketing or products and services.

In the following quote from fashion designer Ana Šekularac (quoted in Mora, 2009: 169), all these aspects resonate – colour preference ('favourite colours'), colour as expressing personality traits ('courage, energy, strength, and determination') and colour as effect ('red catches people's attention and evokes the strongest reaction of all colours'):

> I have two favourite colours: black and red .... Red catches people's attention and evokes the strongest reaction of all colours. Red carries a largely positive connotation, being associated with courage, energy, strength and determination, loyalty and honour.

The problem occurs when meanings of this kind are understood as a kind of universal dictionary of colour meanings which can be applied to any context. Such lists are now ubiquitous on the Internet. They should be taken with a grain of salt, not least because different versions often give quite different meanings for the same colours (cf. Van Leeuwen, 2010: 56–57).

4

Colour preferences and colour effects are generally thought of as something over which people have no conscious influence (though many psychologists are of course more subtle than that and recognize the role of culture). More recently designers as well as consumers increasingly understand colour on the basis of cultural references, rather than psychological discourses. Instead of 'a warm pink entrance hall indicates a home which is warm and loving' we may now have 'Blue Air technology melts retro Blue in this fresh breeze from the 60's classic cars' (Colour Marketing Group, quoted in Wyler, 2006: 25). Such a 'retro' style takes its meaning from associations people have with the period in question, in the same way as the meaning of 'floral', in the quote below (from fashion designer Davina Hawthorne, ibid.: 101) may derive from people's ideas about the kinds of people and contexts they associate with floral patterns:

> For my SS 2008 collection, the inspiration was a mix or armour, the floral and handcrafts. Recycled flowers were hand-painted with gold and then beaded and embroidered. The collection displays a multitude of colour changing subtly from layers upon layers of dirty blue, red and orange florals to intense bright gold.

Hawthorne here creates what, elsewhere (Van Leeuwen, 2005a: 40–42), I have called a 'composite of connotations'. Signs deriving from several different contexts are decontextualized and put together to create new, 'composite' meanings – armour being metallic and hard, flowers colourful and tender, handcraft indicating the human touch of the artisan – on the basis of 'interest', just as we described in *Reading Images* (2006: 12). Instead of a normative discourse, validated by scientific expertise, we now have the history of art and design (cf. e.g. Pastoureau's brilliant history of stripes and striped fabric, 2001) as an inexhaustible resource, an inexhaustible inventory of signifiers which can be given new life in new combinations. And commercial colour experts such as Kate Smith (2012) now move to providing rich information about the origins of colour names, about colour symbolism in different cultures and different contexts, and so on, rather than providing authoritative colour meanings such as that red means 'excitement', 'danger' and 'passion', green 'spring' and 'new birth', and so on.

This approach to sign production is not only used by designers, but also by consumers who may for example combine short stylishly coiffed dreadlocks (originally Rastafarian), jeans (originally working class), a stylish white shirt (originally 'white collar'), and Nike shoes (originally sport) to express the affiliations, attitudes and preferred activities that make up their lifestyle. Today's 'hipsters' create deliberately 'ungrammatical' outfits, often with clothes found in op shops, to express their stance against norms of conformity or gender, combining, for instance, heavily rimmed 1960s glasses (nerdy) with a white shirt and tie (conformity), earplugs (recent counterculture fashion), and tattoos.

5

The idea that colour is primarily about 'affect', meanwhile, continues to remain central. There can, of course, be no doubt that colour yields pleasure. It has done so throughout history, and it has therefore often been criticised as inimical to restraint and rationality, or as decadent or excessive. Pliny, who lived in the first century AD, criticized abundant colour and 'florid painting', and yearned for the more restricted palette of the earlier Greek art. The Renaissance rejected medieval pleasure in pure and abundant colour, favouring design and chiaroscuro over colour. Philosophers and art theorists would echo this until well in the nineteenth century as in Charles Blanc's then influential *Grammar of the Arts of Drawing* of 1879 (quoted in Riley, 1995: 6):

> The union of design and colour is necessary to beget painting just as the union of man and women to beget mankind, but design must maintain its preponderance over colour. Otherwise painting speeds to its ruin. It will fall through colour just as mankind fell through Eve.

More recently, philosophers like Kristeva and Derrida have celebrated colour as escaping the normative and as pure pleasure: 'It is through colour – colours – that the subject escapes its alienation within a code (representational, ideological, symbolic, and so forth) that it, as conscious subject accepts' (Kristeva, 1980: 221).

The problem with this point of view is that colour is always attached to coloured objects, and therefore conjoins its pleasures to the meanings and values which those objects may represent. Colour is multimodal, and, while always also affective, it can signify ideational, interpersonal, textual and aesthetic meanings (cf. Kress and Van Leeuwen, 2002). However, in certain periods or cultural contexts specific types of meanings may be more highly valued and produce more normative discourses (the discourse of colour as affect is also a normative discourse!). In the Middle Ages, normative colour discourses were preoccupied with the symbolic meanings of colour. Popes needed their masters of ceremony to act as colour experts, as in the case of Pope Alexander VI who wanted to dress in white when leading prayers for the victims of a flood, but was advised to wear violet instead, because white would express happiness and rejoicing, while violet would express mourning (Gage, 1999: 84). But at the same time, Medieval people loved strong, intense colours, in life as well as in art. Those who could afford it dressed in bright colours as illustrated by this twelfth-century quote from Chrétien de Troyes (Eco, 2002: 106):

> The lining was of white ermine, the finest and most beautiful you could see. The purple robe was cunningly worked with little crosses in various colours, violet and vermillion and turquoise, white and green, violet and yellow.

But the Renaissance introduced a 'monochrome' period, with black and white replacing colour in books, dress, and the environment, and colour becoming non-semiotic. Normative discourses such as the writings of Leonardo da Vinci now focused on the way colour could help artists in creating an illusion of reality, rather on the symbolic meaning potential of colour.

6

Two of the most important contemporary uses of colour are the expression of identity and the realization of textual structure.

The contemporary expression of identity, whether corporate or personal, has led to a return to colour as symbolic message. All aspects of corporate branding must express the corporation's values and ambitions. All aspects of personal style must at once express individuality and affiliation with others, in terms of values, attitudes and preferred activities, and this is realized, among other things by the colours of the clothes we wear, the car we drive, and the home we live in. For all this a rich array of normative discourses exists – in magazines, television makeover programmes, and on the Internet. And all involve choice, whether a choice of overall style (as in the 'modern' and 'country' styles offered, say, by IKEA, cf. Björkvall, Chapter 24 this volume) or through a 'composite of connotations' which may combine the 'period' and the 'modern', the 'office' and the 'home', the 'plain' and the 'colourful', and so on.

As for textuality, the structure of written texts is, today, often signalled, not by linguistic cohesion but by means of layout, colour and typography, so much so that without layout, colour and typography, many of these texts would be incomprehensible. Colour can segment text into various meaningful units by creating areas with distinct background colours, it can draw attention to particularly important elements of a text, and it can provide overall cohesion by virtue of its constancy across the whole of a text. The cohesive function of colour is often built into the software we use to create texts. Once a background colour is chosen for a PowerPoint presentation, for instance, it remains constant across all slides, thus creating a sense of unity while at the same time expressing identity, whether the identity of the speaker or an organization, or the identity of the genre of presentation. In website design, cascading style sheets are used to give sites an integrated 'uniform appearance' (Smith, 2005: 158), allowing a single external file to dictate the colour and typography of every page of the site. All of this applies, not just to colour in printed or electronic texts, but also to colour in combination with other modes. If in a building different colours are used for different departments, for instance, these colours provide departments with internal coherence as well as with distinct, individual identities in relation to other departments. The same is true for uniforms, graduation gowns, and so on.

7

The aesthetic dimension of colour should also be recognized. While Halliday recognized only the ideational function (in the case of colour, colour as realizing identificatory and symbolic 'codes' and connotations), the interpersonal function (in the case of colour, colour as expressing personality traits and having effects on others), and the textual function (in the case of colour, colour framing, salience and cohesion), Jakobson (1960) also recognized an aesthetic function, the 'poetic function', which, he argued, exists, not just in poetry, but also in everyday language:

> Why do you always say Joan and Margery, yet never Margery and Joan? Do you prefer Joan to her twin sister? 'Not at all, it just sounds smoother ... A girl used to talk about 'the horrible Harry', 'Why horrible?' 'Because I hate him'. 'But why not *dreadful, terrible, frightful, disgusting?*' 'I don't know but *horrible* fits him better'. Without realizing it, she clung to the poetic device of paronomasia.
>
> (Ibid.: 354)

Halliday rejected the 'poetic' function, along with several other functions Jakobson had posited. His arguments were linguistic: 'These functions are not distinguished in the linguistic system' (quoted in Parret, 1974: 95). But perhaps Jakobson *did* show that the poetic function has specific linguistic realizations: the 'prosodic' functions which 'flavour all our utterances, on their phonic, grammatical and lexical level' (ibid.) and the poetic system of rhyme, alliteration and metric structure. Colour, too, is 'prosodic', through colour accents, or by flavouring backgrounds, and colours too can rhyme or 'harmonize' in different ways, as is often seen in magazine advertisements, where the colours of sand and surf, or of the makeup and the seductive dress of a model may rhyme with those on the label of a bottle. Perhaps the replacement of linguistic cohesion by colour cohesion is driven by a renewed interest in aesthetics and in affect, necessary in a culture which requires strong affective investment in organizational cultures, consumer products, and so on.

In *Multimodal Discourse* (2001) Kress and I argued that a semiotic resource becomes a mode when it has developed the capacity to express ideational, interpersonal and textual meanings. In this sense colour clearly is a mode now. But it is a mode of a particular kind. First of all, like layout and typography, it is truly and necessarily multimodal, in that it can only exist in symbiosis with other modes. And second, because it can introduce (reintroduce?) aesthetics and affect in contexts where pure functionality has, for some time, held sway. This may worry some as an inappropriate amalgam of serious business and entertainment. But if it makes the serious more entertaining and entertainment more serious it can only be a gain.

8

Colour plays an important role in the theory of modality which Kress and I first unfolded in *Reading Images* (2006). We defined modality as a term for the signification of degrees of realism in visual representation, and further defined three kinds of realism, based on different criteria. Naturalism is based on perceptual criteria – the more what we see in an image looks like what we might have seen in reality, the higher its realism. This is the kind of realism that has strongly influenced the uses of colour since the Renaissance, when da Vinci discovered that distant objects become more blue, that shadows are affected by the colour of the surface in which they are cast, and so on, and today 'photorealism' is still a major objective in computer-generated image technology. Abstract realism is based on cognitive criteria – the more an image represents the generalized nature or abstract essence of what is represented, the higher its realism. This is the kind of realism in which the colour of grass is uniformly green instead of affected by subtle modulations of light and shade, or in which Van Gogh made the background of a portrait uniformly blue 'to give a mysterious effect' (Van Gogh, 1978: 6). Sensory realism is based on sensory criteria – the more an image almost physically, and synaesthetically affects us, by whetting our appetite, for instance, or sending a shiver down our spine, the higher its realism. Deleuze describes this kind of realism in the work of Francis Bacon: 'In Bacon's bullfights, for example, we hear the noise of the beast's hooves … and each time meat is represented, we touch it, smell it, eat it, weigh it' (2008: 30).

In each case, modality is signified by the degree to which the various means of visual representation are used – the degree of detail in the representation, the degree to which the background is represented, the degree to which depth is represented – and also four aspects of the representation of colour: the degree to which variations in darkness and lightness are represented, the degree of saturation of the colours, the degree of colour modulation (ranging from plain colour to subtle shaded and nuanced colour), and the degree of colour differentiation (ranging from monochrome to a maximally varied palette). In the case of naturalism, all of these are used to a high degree, but not to the maximum, which is reserved for visuals that are understood as 'more than real', aimed at sensory realism. In the case of abstract realism, the degree to which these means of representation are used diminishes. Scientific visuals, which aim at cognitive realism, are often simple line-drawings which do away with depth, colour, unnecessary detail, and so on, and art, too may reduce some of these parameters, though it may also, and at the same time, seek to be abstract and sensory, for instance by having colours which are strongly saturated but not strongly modulated, e.g. the plain colours of Matisse or Mondrian. All this is, however, strongly influenced by the capacities of the technologies used to represent fine-grained detail, tonal variation, high saturation, and so on. In the remainder of this chapter, I will apply this to the technologies of the moving image, film, television, and now computer-generated moving images.

9

Film was never meant to be black and white, and colour films existed well before what is usually regarded as the first full-colour feature film, Robert Mamoulian's *Becky Sharp* (1935). In the early days, films were hand-coloured, sometimes in as much as six colours. For *Voyage Across the Impossible* (1904), Georges Méliès had 200 employees, all women, colouring in the film, frame by frame. When films became longer and more copies had to be made, hand-colouring became impracticable, and other solutions had to be found, such as chemically tinting or toning films with a single colour during development. Sometimes different tints were used from shot to shot, as in a 1910 film about an arsonist setting fire to a factory: while he sneaked into the factory at night the image was blue, once he had set the building on fire, it turned red (Manvell, 1972: 29). The names of the tints were something like a dictionary of colour meanings – 'sunshine', 'purple haze', 'candle flame', 'inferno', 'nocturne', etc. (ibid.). Some early film processes produced convincing colours but were technically over-complicated, such as Pathécolor, which used up to six stencils to dye specific areas of each frame.

The breakthrough came in the mid-thirties when the Kodachrome and Technicolor processes were developed. Kodachrome film stock used three different layers of film, sandwiched together, with filters in between. The first layer was sensitive only to blue light. A yellow filter then prevented the blue light from reaching the other layers. The second layer was sensitive to blue and green only, but because blue had already been filtered out, it recorded only green light. A magenta filter then blocked out the green, so that only red light reached the third layer, which was panchromatic, sensitive to all three primary colours. In this way three versions of the image were created, one recording the blue, one the green, and one the red light. But all three were still black and white images. To get colour, dye-couplers were added to each layer for the relevant colours, and during development the colours would be chemically released and coupled to the exposed silver halide. Colour was added artificially, albeit always with the aim to reproduce the original colours, and as a result different film stocks represent colour differently.

In the Technicolor process, three separate negatives were recorded, one for each of the 'additive' primary colours, blue, green and red. Positive relief prints were then made from these negatives, dyed in the relevant colours, and transferred to a final single print. As the dyes were not added to the film stock during the manufacturing process, colour could, in principle, be varied from film to film, and this sometimes led to memorable colour experiments, as in John Huston's *Moby Dick* (1956) for which a more de-saturated, 'pastel' palette was developed (Manvell, 1972: 32). While Kodachrome stayed an amateur format, Technicolor was soon widely used in Disney animation films such as *Snow White and the Seven Dwarfs* (1938) and *Fantasia* (1940), in lavish musicals and in fantasy sequences such as those in *The Wizard of Oz* (1939).

The 1952 arrival of Eastman Colour Negative, which used dye-couplers and hence a much less complex printing process, gradually led to all films being printed in colour. European art films held out longest, and filmmakers like Bergman and Bresson were making black-and-white films until well in the 1960s – in the 1930s Rudolf Arnheim had argued that film can only be art in so far as it does not 'mechanically' reproduce reality: 'The reduction of actual colour values to a one-dimensional grey series … is a welcome divergence from nature which renders possible the making of significant and decorative pictures by means of light and shade' (Arnheim, 1967: 66).

The new medium of television could not handle the same tonal ranges and degrees of colour saturation as film and needed a more compressed tonal range and a less vibrant palette, favouring the blue and green rather than the red end of the spectrum. This became the norm for 'naturalistic' moving images, and it was left to the cinema to be 'more than real' and immerse the viewer in a more 'sensory' experience, especially in large, lavish productions using Technicolor, wide screen, and so on.

In short, before the arrival of computer-generated images, the three types of realism characterized different audiovisual media and genres – art film favoured the somewhat more abstract modality afforded by black and white; Eastman Colour Negative and colour television set the standard for everyday naturalistic modality; and Technicolor provided 'more than real' sensory modality (as did, in the amateur realm, Kodachrome, with its wide contrast range, highly saturated colours and vivid reds).

10

As black and white became the exception, art film started looking for other ways to achieve abstract modality, for instance through reduced colour differentiation. The French filmmaker Jean-Pierre Melville, particularly in his later films, which were based on the iconography of the American gangster film, sought to move that genre into the timeless realm of mythology and strip it of all surface realism and move it into the timeless realm of mythology:

> I don't want to situate my heroes in time; I don't want the action to be recognizable as something that happens in 1968 .... I am not interested in realism ....A film is first and foremost a dream, and it's absurd to copy life in an attempt to produce an exact re-creation of it.
>
> (Quoted in Thomson, 2005: 5)

This was to a large extent achieved by an art direction which avoided colour as much as possible:

> My dream is to make a colour film in black and white in which there is only one tiny detail to remind us that we really are watching a film in colour. I think we took a small step forward in a form of expression – cinema in colour – which has become dangerous. You can hardly work in black and white anymore. No producer would risk three or four hundred dollars when television is only interested in colour film.
>
> (Melville, quoted in Nogueira, 1971: 130)

A striking scene in Melville's *Le Samouraï* (1968) shows Alain Delon dressed in black trousers and a white T-shirt, in his apartment, which is uniformly white and grey. Even his pet bird, a female bullfinch, is black and white. The only colour comes from his skin and the red of the shotgun wound on his arm as he stoically bandages it.

The recent film version of the musical *Les Misérables* (Hooper, 2012) reduces colour in a similar way, and is largely dominated by greys and de-saturated browns, perhaps in part because it is a period piece, but also to move it away from documentary realism and yet express the squalor of nineteenth-century poverty. There are just a few colour accents: the gold in churches, the red of the revolutionary flag, the make-up of the prostitutes, the pale lilacs in the garden of Valjean and Cosette as Marius stands, lovelorn, at the gate.

Disney animation films traditionally reduce colour in another way. The characters have reduced modulation, but increased saturation, so that they are at once less than real and 'more than real', sensory. The background colours are more modulated, but at the same time reduced in tonal range, softer. And colours may be chosen for their symbolic meaning potential or their affective resonance, rather than naturalistically, as in expressionist paintings by artists like Nolde.

In films of this kind, colour derives from the art direction, or, in the case of animation films, the art work, rather than from the meaning potential of colour of the medium itself. Antonioni, in *The Red Desert* (1964) wanted to 'invent the colour relationships , and not limit myself to photographing only natural colours' (quoted in Chatman and Duncan, 2004: 91) and even had grass painted white and fruit painted grey to express the alienation from nature of his urban characters. Some ten years before *Star Wars* heralded the use of computer-generated imagery in the cinema, French filmmaker Alain Jessua had commented that 'in the cinema it is as if a painter has to paint his subject before painting his painting' and dreamt of working more directly with colour:

> In animation films the sky can be red and grass blue. That's what I would like to do, but it is unfortunately not possible at the moment. Colour has only just begun. Its passion at the moment is to imitate nature. I would like to be able to interpret reality directly on film. I would like to film the streets of Paris, changing reality with painting the pedestrians green, only by working in the lab.
>
> (Quoted in Gauthier, 1967: 68–69)

Meanwhile, the few black-and-white films which are still made today mostly use the medium to evoke an earlier era through reduced naturalistic modality, as in Spielberg's *Schindler's List* (1993) and George Clooney's *Good Night and Good Luck* (2005).

11

In his Introduction to Functional Grammar, Halliday (1985) distinguished between objective and subjective modality. Objective modality is expressed by a frame such as 'It is …' or 'There is …' followed by a modality term (e.g. 'It is possible that …', 'It is a fact that …'). Subjective modality is expressed by a cognitive mental process verb in the first person singular ('I believe that …', 'I guess that …', 'I know for sure that …'). Film also allows subjective modality (cf. Gabriel, 2011), by representing events as memories, or dreams, or hallucinations, rather than as 'reality'. Such subjective states are often expressed by changes in colour – black and white or sepia in the case of memories, and monochrome colour or increased contrast and grain in the case of dreams, for example.

Agnès Varda's *Jacquot de Nantes* (1991) is an affectionate and touching portrait of the film-maker Jacques Demy, Varda's husband and the maker of films such as *The Umbrellas of Cherbourg* (1964) which were inspired as much by his own life experience as by Hollywood musicals. The story of his early years in Nantes in the 1930s and 40s is told in black and white, but when Jacquot sees a play or a film (including Disney's *Snow-White and the Seven Dwarfs*) or a glamorous singer in a restaurant, the point-of-view shot is in glorious Technicolor, while the intent gaze of Jacquot remains in black and white. Thus the films and plays which will inspire his later films become 'more than real', deeply intense experiences. The images of Jacques Demy in 1990, already ill, and soon to die, are also in colour, but here the tonal range is reduced, and the colours are flatter and softer. Thus three modalities intertwine in the film: the 'less than real', modality of the distant past, the 'more than real', sensory reality of the world of film and theatre and music, and the naturalistic, documentary, almost 'home movie' modality of the shots of Jacques Demy in the present.

Dreams, too, must at once be 'less than real' and 'more than real', conveying the intensity of the dream experience. James Stewart's dream in *Vertigo* (Hitchcock, 1958) begins with a shot of the bouquet of flowers which he had seen Kim Novak buy, and which was also in the painting of Carlotta Valdez in the gallery scene. Soon the shot begins to alternate between naturalistic colour and a monochrome green, and then the bouquet changes from a photographic image into a cartoon style drawing with flat colours, against a uniformly black background. Next, the bouquet begins to disintegrate while the image alternates rhythmically between black and white and high colour differentiation and saturation. Next come shots we have seen earlier in the film, including the shot of Kim Novak in the cemetery. These again rhythmically alternate between naturalistic colour and vivid monochrome colours. Finally we see James Stewart's face, again with colour alternation, sucked into a kind of vortex abstractly represented by a deep blue background with receding lines.

Clearly, colour modalities are not only used to distinguish between different genres – art films, animation films, musicals, etc.) but also to distinguish between different levels and kinds of modality within films.

12

What Alain Jessua could only dream of in 1967, is now reality. Broadcast and cinema tools such as Pixar's RenderMan, or software combinations that are available to amateurs, such as Photoshop and Adobe AfterEffects can now increase 'photorealism' by adding tonal range, saturation, modulation, differentiation, luminosity, etc., or decrease it by flattening colour, changing from colour to black and white or monochrome, or reducing photographic images to cartoon-like outline drawings. There is no need to paint grass white or fruit grey, the colours of individual visual objects in a shot can now be digitally altered, 'in the lab'. There is no longer a categorical difference between photographic film and animations in which the sky can be red and the grass blue. Both work with the same means and can be 'composited' seamlessly. Images can even be 'aged' by fading the colours and adding lines and scratches, all with a few drags and clicks.

What once was the work of art directors and animation artists, drawing eclectically on a wide range of cultural resources, has now become a mode, a systematically organized 'language': 'We do have a language of vision now but it was created by corporate software developers' (Ellen Lupton, in Hunter, 2006: 135).

This new language, however, is still structured around the three kinds of realism we have discussed here – the abstract, 'less than real', modality which we see particularly in multimodal graphic design, including animations; the naturalism of everyday digital photography and video with which the internet is now awash; and the 'more than real', sensory photorealism of games and digitally enhanced blockbuster movies.

At the same time, a major step forward has now been achieved – the colours of people, places and things within any given image can now be digitally created or altered, something which had been impossible with film and video technology, thus allowing the symbolic use of colour, which previously had only been possible by means of art direction, and in animation films.

It is, however, in the 'sensory' realm that digital technology, for all its wonders, fails us. As I have argued elsewhere in detail (Van Leeuwen, 2010), the material, textural qualities of colour, such as transparency, translucency, lustre and texture have always been, and still are, as important as hue, value and saturation. Just as alphabetic writing pushed some of the expressive qualities of speech into the background, so digital technology deprives colour of the full range and full expression of all the qualities of material, tangible colour. As colour has become a mode, with its own well-codified rules of engagement, it has also become more abstract and less material.

13

By focusing on colour in film and video, this chapter has shown that contemporary semiotic practices are intricately interwoven with technological developments, and change as technology changes. In the era of film and video, colour could only be used for overall effects across whole scenes, and as a result was mainly used for signifying modalities – past versus present, dream versus reality, and so on. Expressing symbolic meanings through the colours of individual people, places or things within shots, an age-old use of colour, had to be achieved by the older technologies of dyeing and painting aspects of the to-be-filmed scene and through the semiotic work of makeup artists and costume and set designers, Today's digital technology has not only codified the modalities developed in the era of film and video, but also enabled the digital colouring and recolouring of parts of images. As a result, normative power has moved from art design to software design, and a consideration of the affordances and constraints of semiotic software, with their in-built structurings of semiotic resources, is, from now on, of fundamental importance in understanding semiotic practices and the normative discourses which regulate and influence them, not only in the case of colour, but also in the case of all other semiotic resources which have now been digitally reconfigured in the semiotic software that has become mainstream, and almost impossible to avoid, across the globe.

30

Music and designed sound

Tore West

Music accompanies many aspects of daily life, and affects us whether we are aware of it or not. We are surrounded by musical sound whether we go to a shopping mall or to a concert hall. Many choose to carry their own personal music players with them to be able to listen to their favourite music wherever they are. Smartphone applications controlled by bodily movement, surrounding sound and time of day, can add exciting or relaxing sound effects to daily activities. During the evolution of portable music players we have been accustomed to the possibilities of designing the soundtrack of everyday life.

In addition to music there are also other types of designed sound that affect most of our daily routines. Some might be musical in character while other would not fit into the common definition of music. This chapter will give some examples of how sound and music is designed as resources for meaning-making, and an example of how sound and music are analysed in a study of interaction in music education. Analysis of voice characteristics and the significance of tone of voice have already been discussed by Theo Van Leeuwen in Chapter 5 of this volume and for this reason I do not attend to it here.

An interest in integration of sensations from many fields where sounds play a part stands in contrast to the larger amount of studies where sound or fractions of sounds are examined in isolation. Separated from the context where they are produced or heard, sounds carry little meaning by themselves. The study of sound in wider contexts of communicative systems, such as speech, music, movies, video gaming, virtual worlds, or environment, necessitate records with broad representation of the system and analysis of relations to a wider social system. Such systemic analysis is theoretically and methodologically demanding. The development of video technology simplifies the recording of broader representations, however still limited by technology and coloured by methodological choices. Video recordings contain more information than our perception and cognition can handle analytically in real time. In the referred study, a multimodal transcription of video records made it possible to analyse the educational coherence of utterances in different modes and their potential for meaning-making. This revealed how messages transform over written symbols and spoken instruction, through actions of the teacher, into students' expressions that indicate meaning-making and learning.

Designed sound

Sound is surrounding us as noise, vibration, music and speech, but also as specific signals designed to warn or attract us. While the phonemes in spoken language have been subject to thorough study, the meanings of other sounds seem more elusive. These non-linguistic meanings of sounds are assigned by the context of other semiotic resources, and expressed in accordance to the traditions within which these have originated. Such systems of conventions can be very elaborate, like spoken language with its highly developed precision in expressions and interpretations. Music is a phenomenon that can be described as socially agreed upon systems of sounds that carry specific meanings, although less precise than spoken language. Between such systems of organised sound and what we perceive as racket and noise, there are more or less thought-out systems of sound that nonetheless are designed to carry meaning. Consider for instance the ring tones for mobile phones – a way to present yourself, similar to clothing and hairstyle – or the sound effects in radio shows and news broadcasts that indicate a change of subject and set a new mood. In interactions between humans and machines, sounds are typically used to confirm response from the machine; a clicking sound indicates that the machine has noticed a depressed button; a falling arpeggio signals a sent message.

Sound has an ability to bypass the linguistic system of awareness and stimulate emotions in ways that we are less verbally conscious of. This characterises sound as a system of signs perceived without being filtered out at more conscious levels of our perception and cognition. Reviews of the application of psychological emotion theories to sound design show, however, that very little is known about responses to designed sound, and that emotions also influence sound perception. Systems of sound are nevertheless an important bearer of information and meaning in most situations of our daily life. Indeed, the fact that we are not to any higher degree verbally aware of this is a factor that explains why we seldom pay attention to the impact of sound in our lives; it is also something that is used to manipulate our actions in more or less deliberate ways.

To build a strong business brand, companies work to integrate senses. The smell of a new car comes from a spray can and the crunch sound from cornflakes is developed in sound labs and trademarked together with the recipe and logo. Vehicle industries have specific divisions dealing with sound; one car manufacturer separates three kinds of sounds: irritating, informative and impressive sounds. The sound of the engine as well as that of a closing door is carefully designed to signal a sense of quality. Trademark protection has been provided for pictures, shapes and packaging, and even a colour. There are, however, very few sounds that have actually been registered as trademarks; a broadcasting company has managed to get a short melody of musical notes registered as a trademark and a few other jingles are also registered; the Metro-Goldwyn-Mayer media company has its growling lion sound registered. Harley-Davidson attempted to trademark its motorcycle exhaust sound claiming that customers bought the product just for the sound.

Even a very short piece of signature music can provide certain interpretations of a TV show, and motion pictures have brought about a novel world of audio based on specific sound stereotypes. In movies, sounds are used to connect sequences and to set the frame of mind to a certain mood, on its own or by discrepancies between image and sound. Music in films is used to provide continuity, cover up edits, facilitate changes of scenes, provide mood, entertain, give interludes, and to comment on the action. However, many sound objects in contemporary movies lack connection to any source in the film. They do not have a visible source in the image nor can they be identified through common knowledge about sounds and their sources. Such sounds evoke uncertainty and enhance suspense. The information deficit and ambiguity are suggested to evoke emotional reactions of fear and lack of power.

411

Unwanted and disturbing sounds can affect our well-being in many ways. Music is, however, often considered to have positive effects on people's health. Musical interventions are used to accomplish therapeutic goals concerning physical, emotional, cognitive, and social needs of individuals, and music therapy is an established healthcare profession. Listening to music improves blood oxygen capacity and has even been discussed in terms of doping in relation to the 2008 Olympics.

Music

In recording studios, the producer plays an important part in the making of music and sound effects of current media. Audio technicians in movies, broadcasting, music, and video gaming are designing the identity of productions. The producer decides what a recorded song will sound like by means of choosing and manipulating every sound that will accompany a song, as well as the singer's voice. Each instrument and sound is chosen to achieve a certain mood, and is positioned in the acoustic space allowing listeners to interpret a sound's identity in terms of distance or the type of space where it is produced or heard. With the possibilities brought by digital technology, each sound can be manipulated in ways that were not even thought of ten years or so ago. 'Vintage' amplifier and synthesizer sounds are re-created in digital environments, a singer can sing completely out of tune and still have each note corrected in the studio, and the laptop artist is a legitimate stage performer.

The boundaries between composing, orchestrating, arranging, producing, and performing have been blurred when all sounds can be digitally manipulated in a computer less expensive than most traditional music instruments. The idea of a sender and a receiver of a certain message become even more vague when the listener, in ways that the original producer has no control over, can manipulate sounds.

It has been shown in a growing number of studies that the choice of music has an impact on consumer behaviour. Classical and popular music have more positive effect on purchase intentions than easy listening and no music, and music can create a specific atmosphere to distinguish a restaurant from competitors. Absence of music seems to have negative effects on both atmosphere and spending behaviour.

Aural space, also known as auditory space or acoustic space, is a term used by soundscape designers to describe a lack of noticeable sound. Moments of aural space are used to redirect the attention of the listener, to build tension or to simply let the ear rest from sound. An interesting form of music in this context is the background music specifically designed to fill aural space in corporate situations, such as music played in elevators or while waiting on hold on the telephone. Such music is designed to make people calm in elevators, alert at work, or gently led to certain areas of department stores. Designed sound is also used to alter the impression of room size and to make you feel transferred to other surroundings.

An instance of specific musical meaning is the concept of leitmotif; the distinct musical themes associated with characters, places or ideas within a particular work of music. The theme is usually a short melody, a certain chord progression, or a rhythmic pattern, such as the opening theme of Beethoven's Fifth Symphony. Leitmotifs are used to tie together a work into a coherent whole, and relate the music to the libretto or story; they can also supplement or extend the plot. The concept is often associated with Wagner's extensive use of leitmotifs throughout his operas. Today, leitmotifs are very common in movie scores and video games.

In addition to how melodic, harmonic and rhythmic structures in music can carry meaning; certain qualities of sound are also frequently used to convey distinct messages. Culturally shaped conventions direct how the representational resources of sounds can be understood in specific contexts. Bad characters in operas are sung by baritones accompanied in the low register by the cellos, while the innocent maid is represented by a soprano voice accompanied by flutes and violins. Trumpets and drums are frequently used to signal power and military strength.

Even what is perceived as a single sound, whether it can be considered musical or not, has characteristics that change rapidly over its duration. Physical mediating characteristics of sound such as pitch, timbre, frequency spectrum, amplitude, onset, temporal envelope, formant-glide, micro-intonations are all important to the experience of even the shortest sounds. Recorded sounds are also subject to several sources of manipulation of various degrees of deliberation, such as room acoustics, microphone type and placement, dynamic compression, added reverberation, signal-to-noise ratio, or blending with ambient sounds, all of which possess narrative qualities.

The strength of the traditions in social institutions such as symphony orchestras and operas seem to have conserved the symbolic values assigned to instruments. Instruments not traditionally used in such large classical settings seem to change their symbolic values more rapidly; during the twentieth century the guitar moved in the broader public's eye from a pious accompaniment in religious settings to a symbol of sin in rock music.

Military music has, at least since the Ottoman military marching bands mentioned in the thirteenth century, been used both to give an impression of power and provide a steady beat for long marches on foot. The long tradition of these marching bands has had an influence on the western military music tradition as well as our classical music tradition from Mozart's time onwards. The strong Norwegian tradition of school bands even today retains the name *Janissary corps* from the ancient sultan's guard in the Ottoman standing army. Concert bands still have a structure built on drums and wind instruments reminiscent of that origin. The heavy metric beat associated with marching bands is also a significant component of modern popular music. Music played in clubs as well as in gyms that also have the purpose to encourage bodily movement consistently has a meter reminiscent of marching music. The heavy beats and shrill sound of the ancient military bands remain a noteworthy factor in warfare in our time, documented for example in the movie *Fahrenheit 9/11*, where US soldiers in Iraq were showed to listen to contemporary rock music with similar qualities to arouse their fighting spirits.

Music and sound in educational interaction

Music is still primarily discussed as an art form in terms of aesthetic objectification. The ways in which music is used in current media that forms the musical understanding of young people are rarely focused in the literature. Attempts have been made to describe how music is used to affect certain moods in movies, TV shows and commercials, or how it gently directs us to selected areas in shopping centres, as well as how specific melodic phrasings, rhythms and sounds mimic bodily movement and how these represent human emotional states. Such descriptions are, however, typically done from a perspective where music and sound are broken down into small components analysed in disconnection from their context.

The complex phenomena of sound and music as described above call for a complex analysis in order to understand how several components interact as resources for representation. One way to make such an analysis feasible is to clearly define an area of interest with specific claims for that particular field. That is, to define an area possible to analyse within realistic and practical limits rather than an exhaustive method with global claims to explain all kinds of sounds in all sorts of settings.

In a recent study of music education in Sweden, I worked with a colleague in an effort to analyse interaction in music education (Rostvall and West, 2005). Twelve hours of video records from 13 music lessons at upper secondary and tertiary levels including teacher training were transcribed and analysed in detail regarding processes of teaching and learning. The design of the study employs a close-up transcription of video recorded multimodal representations and an analysis of patterns of interaction. The main object was to increase the knowledge concerning how different interaction patterns during lessons affect the students' opportunities to learn, with a discussion and interpretation of the results of the analysis within a wider historical and sociological perspective. The overall analysis in the research program had a perspective where language, music and gesture were regarded as semiotic resources rhetorically orchestrated in the classroom, with a focus on how these modes of interaction interplay in the construction of knowledge. Learning was studied as a dynamic process of transformative sign making actively involving both teacher and students as suggested by Kress (2003b). The revealed patterns of interaction were similar to those found in our preceding studies of beginner levels of music.

Research design

The aim of the research design was to bring together understandings from four levels of scale: individual level, interpersonal level, institutional level, and societal level. Separate distinct theoretical perspectives were employed for analysis at the different levels of scale. The theories of cognitive schemata (Arbib, 1995) (networks of abstract mental structures through which individuals make meaning out of combinations of memories and sensory input) were used at the individual level; theories of face-to-face interaction (the reciprocal influence of individuals upon one another's actions) (Goffman, 1990) at the interpersonal level, and at the institutional level theories of institutions as social systems (relationships between social institutions and individuals understood as processes of social control of cognition) (Douglas, 1986) were applied. A framework of critical discourse analysis (a three-dimensional framework including the analysis of text, discourse practice and discourse reproduction and change) (Fairclough, 1995) placed the separate findings in society and history into an understanding at the societal level to relate discourse and action with cognition and society. The understandings generated from these theories were integrated into a broad-based comprehension of the complex field. The different theories and perspectives used at the different theoretical levels were regarded consistent and compatible since they all elucidate networks of experiences and actions in different ways that are not in conflict with each other (for a detailed account of the theoretical backing, see Rostvall and West, 2005).

The research design contained three stages of analysis. The first stage was descriptive with a written account of the video recorded actions. The second stage was more analytic; here the transcribed data were systematically broken down into small units that were systematically labelled. The third stage was where the results of the analysis were brought back to a new understanding in an interpretation or a synthesis.

Transcription

The complexity of a multimodal transcription was met by a graphic representation that placed utterances in separate modes in a table-like layout with colours representing different analytical coding (Figure 30.1; more examples available online at www.ualberta.ca/~iiqm/backissues/4_4/html/rostvall.htm; for more information on the transcription tool see West, 2007).

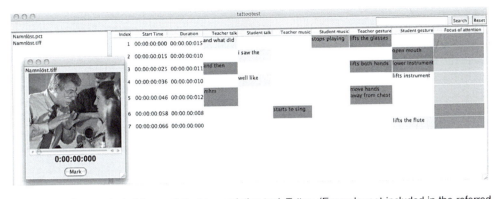

Figure 30.1 Screen shot of the analytical transcription tool, Tattoo. (Example; not included in the referred study.)

The separate modes were divided into communication units, or utterances, separated by changes in prosody, gestures or music (Green and Wallat, 1981). In the transcript, these units were represented in a table with a horizontal row of cells for every change in the interaction that could represent a new message. For example, a change in pace of the speech or a raised eyebrow would indicate a division between separate message units represented by a new row of cells in the table. Each new row thus represents a new communication unit, motivated by a modal change representing a potential change of the meaning-making. The transcript chart was also divided into vertical columns to represent time code, as well as musical activity, talk and gestures for teacher and students respectively. This design facilitated the analysis of coherence between messages and their potential for meaning-making across modalities, motivated by the need to analyse sound as part of a multimodal ensemble. We could follow how messages transformed from written music through spoken instruction, movements of the body and musical actions of the teacher, into musical and other expressions of the student.

From the multimodal perspective, music interplays with other resources for representation, and the semiotics of music is interdependent on other modes. Therefore, multimodality brings forward the need for analysis of music and sound as parts of a system of complex interactions with logics of other modes. A multimodal transcription made it possible to analyse the educational coherence of musical and spoken sound in relation to other utterances and their potential for meaning-making. It is assumed that coherence is vital to the students' possibilities to make sense of the teacher's instructions, and hence to transform the instruction into action. It also showed how messages transformed over written text and spoken instruction, through actions of the teacher, into students' expressions that indicated learning. In the transcript, this was represented in separate parallel columns with a cell structure containing descriptions of the observed actions.

Musical symbols were transformed over the teacher's actions as well as musical and spoken sounds, into students' actions and musical sounds. This dynamic process of transformative sign making actively involving both teacher and students gave an understanding of the learning opportunities during the lessons.

Analysis

The analysis was made of interaction as a combination of speech, gesture (including gaze, body movement, positioning in the room, use of artefacts etc.) and music within the specific educational setting. Musical communication was analysed with a focus on the specific educational functions and how it combines the resources for meaning-making to speech and gesture. In the observed lessons, the musical actions of the teacher was often of an instructive character with short sounds and musical utterances played or hummed firmly to comment on a student's mistakes, and to demonstrate how it should be played correctly. The teachers also led the students' playing more gently by playing or singing along with the student in an accompanying way, often combined with softer supportive gestures and a friendly face. The manner of playing, in combination with other communicative modes such as gaze and body posture, revealed that music was used in relation to the educational context in testing, instructional, analytical, accompanying, and expressive ways.

Observations of what the participants focused their actions upon revealed that the teacher focused their attention mainly on the printed music and the technical control of the instrument, while students' focus shifted between looking at and listening to the music, control over bodily movements and how to handle the instrument, the gestures of the teacher, as well as social and emotional aspects of the relation to the teacher.

This goes beyond the view of a 'pure' musical communication and expands the notion of music as aesthetic experiences and ways of aesthetic expression. Musical learning was seen as a dynamic process of transformative sign-making where an expansion of the access to diverse semiotic resources increases the repertoire of representations within the field.

Educational functions of music and sound were studied as a multimodal ensemble in conjunction with speech and gesture, in relation to a specific educational setting and learning outcome. This limited area of study is certainly a small fraction of what music and designed sound are in society, but still complex and time consuming enough to analyse considering that the analysis navigates in several layers of meaning at different levels of communication. One point of departure is that the analysis of separate modes, the transformations of messages through the different modes, and the coherence between modes have an effect on the potential for meaning-making.

A message often starts in one mode and then transform into another, from spoken language into gesture and music. Different modes bring different limitations and potentials, and the time-based logic of speech, gesture and music offer potentials for representations that differ from the space-based modes of image, artefacts and written symbols. Separate modes are not necessarily coherent when viewed independently; each mode holds specific semiotic resources, and the intertwined meanings of modes contribute to how instructions can be understood. Even with long experience from music education, it was seldom possible to understand each mode in the study separated from the others. Furthermore, the transcribed actions did not make sense if they were not combined; spoken language was often uttered in fragments of words and verbal sounds in restricted code referring to mutual experiences or musical conventions.

Much to our surprise, the music in our study seldom included melody, harmony, and rhythm together, usually common to definitions of music. Rather, it could be described as the sound of single notes next to each other without regard to pulse, meter, rhythm or melodic phrasing. Music during the lessons was predominantly dealt with as sight-reading exercises of separate notes or chords, where teachers commented upon students' mistakes in relation to the printed music. It seemed more important to correct single notes than working with more overarching musical structures such as melody or musical expression. As an example, a student repeated the same mistake playing one wrong note during several repetitions. The teacher asked the student to play again and again several times, without commenting on the wrong note. When the error continued he stopped the repetitions and started to ask the student the names of the notes in the printed score. After naming the notes correctly the student was asked to play once more, again repeating the same mistake. The teacher stopped and asked if the student found it difficult to read the music, to which the student responded 'no'. The teacher then went on to the next section of the song. The analysis of our transcription of this sequence showed that the student focused more on her fingers than the music, and that the situation could be seen as an example where the teacher and the student had different focus of attention, and when the student did not respond as expected, they did not understand each other's comments and actions and the situation remained unresolved.

Most of the time, teachers talked about the printed score as a complete representation, providing all the information for performing a piece of music. They did not consider the complex conventions of performance that the symbolic notation triggers in an experienced musician. Expressive aspects of musical performance were rarely discussed or performed. This resembled the reading of a text with focus on sounds of single letters without concern for words, phrases, accents, intonation, grammar, or coherence. Syllables rather than meaning were emphasised, that is, sound-form without relation to meaning-form.

The students' focus shifted between the printed music, complex motor control, auditory feedback, and the gestures of the teacher. This means that their focus of attention had to be divided between several semiotic resources, tangled in a multimodal course of interaction. One conclusion of this is that learning could be better supported with a more coherent educational design, where the students' attention is guided in one direction at the time to work against vague or ambiguous communication that divides the students' focus and makes them uncertain of what is expected from them.

After the descriptive stage, the records were analysed in relation to concepts constructed out of earlier work. This provided an analysis of how modes work in conjunction with method books and artefacts to support meaning-making in the context. With inspiration from sociolinguistics and after iterative analyses, five functions of the use of speech as well as of music use and gesture were distinguished, specific for the educational setting: testing/inquiring, instructional, analytical, accompanying, and expressive functions. The testing function consists of questions, investigating reason, or playing in a groping manner. Instructions aim to explain, value or claim how something should be with reference to the actions at hand. Analytical messages contain longer reasoning in several steps referring to each other, often to explain a causal relation. Accompanying indicates that participants lead and follow each other. Expressive functions are mainly trying to capture qualities that go beyond the semantic content of the words or beyond just playing the right notes from a score. Every message unit was coded with one of these functions, to search for emerging patterns.

At the third stage, the records were interpreted and discussed from the perspectives of interaction theory and institution theory. The music lessons were viewed as social encounters where actions create and re-create social orders, by means of the communication routines. The patterns of interaction were discussed in relation to opportunities for both teachers and students to learn and develop, and in relation to historic and societal aspects. This shed new light on the fact that many students drop out at an early stage of musical studies, something typically explained in terms of individual lack of talent. A significant factor could well be the traditional design of the tuition that excludes those that do not have other resources to make sense of the ways in which musical education is typically delivered. Apart from innate musical talent, an important factor for success in musical training seems to be a cultural heritage allowing relatives to fill in the gaps of the educational design. This opens the educational field to premeditated development.

A software tool with integrated transcription, coding and synchronized playback of video made it possible to view, transcribe and analyse the video records (West, 2007). The analysing transcription tool, Tattoo, was designed to aid the recognition of patterns by assigning separate

417

colours to represent different analytic codes. The presentation of results derived from the software tool support a grounded narrative of the actions and interaction as well as a discussion about how different patterns of interaction could affect learning possibilities. The tool is built around open standards to facilitate flexibility and collaborative development from shared ideas.

Conclusion

The understanding of music as a system of sounds with a long history of institutionally agreed upon potentials for representation motivates similar understandings of less developed sounding systems of signs. A multimodal investigation of music and other systems of meaning potentials mainly carried by sound, should take into consideration that such systems are the dynamic result of complex social interactions past and present. This means that the understanding of music and designed sound benefit from systemic analysis at several levels of scale, rather than the traditional view of sound as static codes with a fixed meaning potential.

A considerable component of the human auditory awareness is constantly occupied decoding meanings and intentions, while decoding and interpreting contextual sets of signs in the surrounding, and often to simultaneously transform all of this into complex reactions such as neuromuscular patterns of movement. This becomes apparent in the referred study, where students interpret sound, gestures and written signs to perform a response on their musical instrument valued in relation to implicit expectations.

An awareness of the complexity of such semiotic resources and motor processes supplements and challenges an understanding of successful music education as the result of specific musical talent. This poses new questions for tuition that could include more students in the conventions and practices of musical performance, as well as the understanding of other systems of sounds in our surroundings, in or out of schools.

Suggested reading

Altman, R. (1992) *Sound Theory/Sound Practice*, London: Routledge. (An exploration of how movie sound makes meaning, to expand the conception of movies as self-contained texts.)

Van Leeuwen, T. (1999) *Speech, Music, Sound*, London: Macmillan. (A multimodal exploration on the common grounds of speech, music and other sounds.)

31

Space and communication in exhibitions

Unravelling the nexus

Maree Stenglin

Introduction

Three-dimensional space is an omnipresent semiotic. It surrounds us from the moment of our conception in the womb and envelops all the activities of our daily lives. To this end it shelters and protects us while contextualising us as we work, sleep, eat, learn and carry out of the myriad of complex activities that constitute our lives. It also encompasses us as we enact our personal and social relationships, and temporally unfolds as we move through it. Even when we die it subsumes us: either through the burial of our bodies or the scattering of our ashes. It is therefore an all-enveloping semiotic.

Given the importance of space to all aspects of our lives, it is not surprising that a prolif-eration of cross-disciplinary work exists on this topic, the most relevant to this volume being canonical works concerned with the social dimensions of space. Works that explore social meanings are singled out as being important because they explore the social practices of communities such as the functioning of interpersonal relationships, their establishment and ever-changing nature. They also explore issues concerned with gender, class and culture. In doing so, they cross many disciplinary boundaries: anthropology, history, philosophy and social semiotics, as will now be discussed.

Overview of literature

Amongst the most renowned anthropologists to consider the social dimension of space is Edward Hall. Hall developed a theory of Proxemics (1966), which is concerned with cultural variation in human perceptions of space. One of Hall's landmark contributions concerns the way he classifies space along three dimensions: the intimate, the social and the public. 'Intimate' space refers to the 'bubble' of space around a person; 'social' spaces are those in which people engage in everyday social interactions with acquaintances and strangers, while 'public' spaces are those concerned with more impersonal interactions. Hall's work is particularly notable for the way his ideas have inspired other disciplines to explore the ways different communi-ties shape and use space.

Also concerned with social interaction is De Certeau's classic *The Practice of Everyday Life* (1984). This work is essentially concerned with the embodied unfolding of texts in time and space. In particular it explores spatial practices in cities such as walking and the way these can defy rigid social systems such as linear city grids strategically designed by planning bodies. Such 'tactics' are important as they create 'spaces' for the users and, in doing so, open up new possibilities and important potentials for social interaction.

Informed by Marxism and cross-disciplinary perspectives drawn from philosophy, history, sociology and anthropology, Lefebvre's work on *The Production of Space* (1991) also explores space within the context of the social sphere. Acknowledging that space has a mathematical dimension concerned with abstract geometry, Lefebvre explores the ways social space involves specific practices such as production, occupation and consumption (that is, movement and traversal through 'flow'). Lefebvre argues that space involves both a materiality and an element of abstraction. Its foundations lie in nature; superimposed on these foundations are multiple layers of spatiality embodying social relations with their complex and deep-seated contradictions and conflicts.

More recently the work of Tuan and Hoelscher (2001) has explored the more affectual dimensions of space. In particular, they have explored how people think and feel about space. Of specific concern are the ways people form attachments to places such as homes, neighbourhoods and abstractions such as nations. Also of interest to their research are the ways time can impact on feelings about space and place.

Social semioticians have also long been interested in understanding three-dimensional space. O'Toole (1994) first began by mapping the three communicative functions of space (representational, interactive and compositional) onto four different levels of organization – building, level, room and elements. Kress and Van Leeuwen (1996) began a tentative exploration of how textual meanings are organised in space, and later Van Leeuwen (1998, 2005a) began to systematically map choices for framing in three-dimensional (3D) space. In 2003 Scollon and Scollon developed geosemiotic theory consisting of three sub-systems: interaction order, visual semiotics and place semiotics. The following year two new tools for analysing interpersonal meanings in space emerged – Binding and Bonding (Stenglin, 2004). Stenglin's doctoral research also identified new tools for analysing space textually (Path-Venue and Prominence), and ideationally extended particulate structures to the analysis of 3D space.

Together these theoretical tools have enabled social semioticians to analyse a range of 3D spaces. White (1994), for instance, analysed the organization of the 'Shark' exhibition at the Australian Museum from the 'genre' perspective of the Sydney, School. Ravelli (2000) analysed the organization of space in the Olympic Store in the city of Sydney while Pang (2004), Martin and Stenglin (2007) and Stenglin (2007) have all analysed how multimodal meanings are made in museum exhibitions.

Informed by social semiotic theory, this chapter begins by introducing the three communicative functions which underpin all social semiotic approaches to space and then applies them to the analysis of one space, an exhibition called *Scumbag*.

The communicative functions of space

Social semioticians interested in the analysis of 3D space have all drawn on Halliday's metafunctional theory (1978). Halliday's theory suggests that the organisation of meaning occurs according to three communicative functions: the ideational, the interpersonal and the textual. The ideational function is concerned with the ways we construe our experience. In space, for instance, the *ideational function* is concerned with naming of different spaces and classifying them according to function, e.g. kitchen, bathroom and bedroom. Space also fulfils an *interpersonal function,* which is concerned with the relationship between a space and its occupant. Third, space fulfils a *textual function* through the organisation of a series of spaces into a meaningful whole.

As we begin to explore the three communicative functions of space, each metafunction will be exemplified through the analysis of *Scumbag*, an exhibition by award-winning Australian artist Ella Dreyfus. Displayed in April–May 2008 at Stills Gallery in Paddington, Sydney, *Scumbag* represents an important shift in the artist's practice: 'This exhibition marks a transition from the documentary and figurative style that has characterised my photographic practice to a new approach, which engages with the body in relation to objects, language and the inhabiting of space' (Dreyfus, 2008, Exhibition Catalogue). This shift from 2D to 3D media together with the artist's attempt to engage with several different semiotics makes it an ideal exhibition to analyse from a communicative social semiotic perspective beginning with the textual function, then moving on to explore the ideational and the interpersonal functions, respectively.

The textual function

Built spaces, like written and spoken texts, unfold in time. They also unfold in space. In systemic functional theory this is referred to as logogenesis. In accounting for the logogenesis of an exhibition, two types of tools are required. First, tools that describe the way three-dimensional spaces unfold *dynamically;* second, tools that enable *static* descriptions of three-dimensional spaces. Dynamic resources are required because buildings unfold through the dynamic unfolding of a user's pathway, while static tools are needed because a built space is a fixed and constructed entity.

The *dynamic* organisation of space can be analysed using the following resources, each of which is explained in the following section of the chapter:

- Path–Venue
- Prominence
- Information value (as developed by Kress and Van Leeuwen, 1990, 1996)

The *static* organisation of space can be analysed using two tools: framing (as developed by Kress and Van Leeuwen, 1990, 1996, 2006; Van Leeuwen, 2005a) and information value (Kress and Van Leeuwen, 2006) as we shall now see.

When analysing space dynamically, Path–Venue is an important tool as it enables us to consider a visitor's movement as it unfolds along a Path and Venue trajectory. The Path is the route which exhibitions scaffold for visitors. It consists of those space(s) designed to regulate 'people flow'. Its role is to channel, distribute and circulate occupants into a building or parts of a building. Paths are thus the built medium along which people move. In terms of their materialisation, Paths can be vertical or horizontal, linear or circular, stationary or moving.

Not only do Paths function to circulate, channel and distribute people, they are also designed to deposit them. The point at which people are deposited has been called the Venue. The term *venue* has been selected to denote this point because the actual word comes from Old French and literally means 'a coming'. Thus venues are the places visitors 'come to' or move towards as they stroll along the Paths but to attract the viewer's attention, we need to consider Path–Venue in tandem with Prominence.

Prominence is concerned with attracting viewers' attention in a space. Its function is to *draw* occupants out of one space and *lead them* into another. One of the central concerns of Prominence

421

is the 'drawing power' of a space: its potential for luring and enticing people to move towards the next space. As most buildings are made up of a series of spaces that unfold as people move through them, Prominence is a crucial element of most spatial designs, for if users are unable to 'see' how a building unfolds it is very difficult to move through it successfully.

Prominence may be created through visual elements that draw the occupant's gaze (e.g. vectors created in the flooring, arrows, colour contrasts, lighting), language (e.g. signage) as well as sounds (e.g. music). Prominence can even include smells such as the aroma of freshly ground and brewed coffee – a powerful lure for many tired museum visitors.

At the entrance to the Stills Gallery, we can identify a clear Path–Venue trajectory with strong Prominence (see Figure 31.1). Namely, as visitors enter the gallery and walk through the heavy glass doorway, there is one principal lure at the top of the stairs: a striking photograph of a pile of brightly coloured felt letters beckons to viewers. Saturated with vibrant colour and strongly down-lit, this photograph is undoubtedly the key choice for Prominence at the building's entrance. It creates a strong gaze vector that both lures visitors upstairs, and previews, in subtle ways, one field of the exhibition: the language of childhood. In the artist's own words the subject matter of the first photograph visitors see is innocuous: 'it's just a pile of letters' (personal communication, 23 April 2008).

In this way Prominence works with Path to channel visitors up and into the building and deposits them on top of the landing (the first Venue). As they move along the landing towards the actual exhibition (the main Venue), an empty white wall blocks their flow. The Path clearly divides here. Turning to the right, there are offices; turning to the left, visitors can see the actual felt letters from the photograph pinned to a nearby wall. However, the letters are no longer randomly thrown onto a pile. They have now been carefully arranged – into words and phrases – and pinned to a wall. Colourful, vibrant and alluring they function as another

Figure 31.1 The entrance to the Stills Gallery – a clear Path–Venue trajectory with strong Prominence. Ella Dreyfus, *Scumbag, Pile of Letters*, Stills Gallery, Sydney, 2008. Courtesy of the artist.

Figure 31.2 Prominence continues to lure visitors. Ella Dreyfus, *Scumbag*, Stills Gallery, Sydney, 2008. Courtesy of the artist.

strong choice for Prominence – one that entices the visitor further into the gallery while evoking childhood memories of fun, puns and playing language games (see Figure 31.2).

Furthermore, an important resource for analysing both dynamic and static textual meanings in three-dimensional space is information value. One aspect of information value is concerned with what is positioned as 'Given' and what is 'New' in space. As with images, left is associated with 'Given' and right with 'New' in western spaces (Kress and Van Leeuwen, 1996; Van Leeuwen, 2005a). This principle can be extended to three-dimensional displays. In particular, as a person moves through a series of interconnected spaces the logogenetic unfolding of choices for 'Given' and 'New' can be dynamically patterned in significant ways.

If we return to the spatial choices we have just discussed in relation to Path–Venue and Prominence, the 'Given' are the colourful fun-filled letters which then become the words of childhood displayed on the exhibition walls visitors approach. As they near the exhibition, however, two unexpected words become visible – 'horrific' and 'malicious'. Neither sits comfortably with the happy monosyllabic memories of childhood. Instead both point to a 'New' set of meanings with deeply negative associations – and in doing so, evoke the chill of apprehension.

At another important level, the left-to-right directionality of Given–New can operate in a space and give viewers a reading path to follow as their gaze moves from one wall to the next. When people enter *Scumbag*, for instance, many first notice that the words form phrases and that the phrases seamlessly flow from one wall into another (see Figure 31.3). One exhibition visitor uses a musical metaphor to describe this movement: 'the words segue and melt'.

This movement also gives the viewer a left-to-right reading path, a Given–New directionality. In fact following the walls around, we notice that the 'Given' (the felt phrases on

Figure 31.3 Showing the Given–New reading path. Ella Dreyfus, *Scumbag*, Stills Gallery, Sydney, 2008. Courtesy of the artist.

the first and second walls) give way to the 'New' – two walls filled with large, full–colour photographs depicting the felt words and phrases (Figures 31.4a and b). In the photographs, however, the words are not pinned to neutral white exhibition walls – they are displayed in the familiar, everyday spaces of home: kitchen, bedroom, bathroom, cupboard, pool and 'cubby' house (to see the colour photographs from the exhibition, readers can visit the artist's website at www.elladreyfus.com).

The everyday setting in the photographs provides the context for the words and phrases we have just decoded. In doing so, it gives voice to the taboo 'goings on' of domestic life: where home is neither refuge nor castle. Moreover, even those visitors who resist the left-to-right reading path find that when they turn, they, too, are confronted by photographic images evoking 'a house of horrors'.[1]

Furthermore the material framing of the main exhibition space strongly evokes meanings associated with domesticity. Framing, as originally conceptualised by Kress and Van Leeuwen (1990: 97–98, 1996: 183), refers to the strength of the (dis-)connection of elements in a visual composition. However, in their book *Multimodal Discourse*, Kress and Van Leeuwen refine framing, suggesting it is a common semiotic principle realized by different resources in different semiotic modes (2001: 3). This point is reiterated by Van Leeuwen in *Introducing Social Semiotics* (2005a: 14) together with a description of the resources that can be used to analyse framing in visual compositions and three-dimensional spaces. The framing resources identified by Van Leeuwen for analysing the framing of spaces in offices and schools are represented as a system network (2005a: 18).

Let us now apply this system network to the main exhibition space of *Scumbag*. First of all, the four walls combine to function as a solid, seemingly permanent partition that segregate the

Figure 31.4a Given–New: the new provides a context for the phrases. Ella Dreyfus, *Scumbag*, Stills Gallery, Sydney, 2008. Courtesy of the artist.

Figure 31.4b Photographic diptych. Ella Dreyfus, *Scumbag, Protect Myself*, 2008. Chromogenic print, 90 × 180cm. Courtesy of the artist.

exhibition from the other spaces in the gallery in the same way that the walls of our houses partition our private lives. Mitigating the partitioning of the main exhibition space are two openings: a window, rendered visually impermeable with a blind, and the entrance/exit that gives the space a small degree of permeability.

Such strong partitioning has an important interpersonal impact: it strongly segregates individuals, groups and activities. The late British sociologist, Basil Bernstein (1975), refers to this phenomenon as strong Classification and strong Framing. People living in strongly Classified and Framed houses find that the activities of domestic life are private, secluded and sealed from the gaze of neighbours and onlookers. In fact a safe, clean, protected home that provides both private and semi-public spaces for the activities of daily life is actually essential for human dignity. Sadly, however, the privacy afforded by the strong insulation of one domestic space from another can be, and is sometimes, abused. This is what the strong textual Framing of the exhibition space hints at too.

The ideational function

Let us turn to exploring the communicative functions of the exhibition from the point of view of ideational meaning. O'Toole (1994) has approached ideational meaning in built spaces by exploring the function(s) a space has been designed to fulfil. These include firstly, private/public; secondly, industrial, commercial, agricultural, governmental, educational, medical, cultural, religious, residential; and thirdly, domestic or utility (O'Toole, 1994: 86).

Using this framework, we can say that *Scumbag* has a public function. It is also educational and cultural; cultural as it is an art exhibition involving the display of mixed media – photographs and three-dimensional felt letters. Cultural also encompasses the fact that this exhibition pushes the boundaries of social norms, challenging viewers by deliberately disturbing the boundaries of what is publicly spoken about, and what tends to remain private, hidden and silent. Breaking the boundaries in a way that is both protected and secure also speaks to the core purpose of museums in western societies: to provide safe spaces for exploring unsafe ideas (Heumann Gurian, 2006).

A complementary perspective for thinking about ideational meanings is to think about field in relation to space (Stenglin, 2004). But the exploration of field is located later in the next section, the interpersonal function, because field couples with choices for Attitude to bond visitors into communities of affiliation.

The interpersonal function

The term interpersonal indicates that the meanings constructed by the ways we organise space extend well beyond the physical materiality of bricks and mortar. In fact, the spaces that we occupy in our daily lives, especially our homes, provide the setting for all our activities and impact significantly on the ways we behave and interact with other people. Interpersonally, one important aspect of the grammar of three-dimensional space is Binding and Bonding (Stenglin 2004, 2007, 2008, 2009; Martin and Stenglin, 2007). Binding is concerned with the relationship between space and an occupant while Bonding explores the patterns of interaction between the occupants of a space as well as theoretical resources for building solidarity and affiliation.

Binding organises the interpersonal relationships constructed between a space and its occupants into two main categories: security or insecurity. In particular, whether we feel secure or insecure inside a space appears to be strongly dependent on how firmly that space *closes in on* or *opens up around* us. Feelings of insecurity tend to be evoked if a space closes in around us too tightly evoking feelings of smothering (Too Bound). Spaces that make us feel Too Bound are elevators, dark caves and tunnels. At the other end of insecurity are spaces that do not enclose us tightly enough, either horizontally or vertically (Too Unbound). For instance in places like the Canadian Tundra a complete lack of vertical enclosure can evoke strong feelings of exposure and vulnerability (Too Unbound). The two spatial extremes of Binding discussed so far, feeling Too Bound and Too Unbound, tend to construct space in such a way that they establish relationships of insecurity with users. Although some users respond positively to these extremes, most occupants find they evoke strong feelings of insecurity.

The interpersonal organization of space can also evoke feelings of security. In particular, womb-like spaces that close around us firmly are an important choice for security (Bound). In making us feel Bound these spaces evoke a sense of comfort, snugness and safety. Spaces can also be designed to maintain their relationship of security with the occupant but feel more open (Unbound). This happens when ceilings and walls are receded or spatial boundaries are dematerialised through the use of glass walls. Such open spaces feel Unbound because they evoke a sense of freedom from enclosure and spatial restriction.

Finally, feeling Bound or 'at home' in a space means feeling secure, safe and protected. Linguistically, however, if the clause 'I feel at home' were to be analysed the phrase 'at home' would be coded as circumstance: location: place. This analysis captures the literal meaning but this phrase 'at home' also has a deeply metaphorical meaning; one that evokes a deep and abiding sense of sanctity and inner peace alongside personal wellbeing and strong feelings of security.

In the exhibition *Scumbag*, the spaces are tightly Framed (as discussed in the textual function). Such strong spatial Framing provides a firm sense of enclosure. It also means that the spaces are not scaled to monumental proportions that tower over the occupant. Rather they evoke the scale of the domestic spaces in which most of us grew up and with which we are familiar. The material scale of the space and the firmness of its enclosure thus evokes a sense of being 'at home'. It is therefore not surprising that one visitor's comment refers to it as a 'little house'. At a literal level, it feels like home.

Metaphorically, however, the Binding evoked by the space is one of insecurity. This insecurity seems to be evoked not by the organization of the space but rather its silence. Binding, for instance, has only been discussed in relation to vision but involves other semiotics such as tactility, odour and sound (Stenglin, 2004). The degree to which an occupant experiences a space as secure is also linked to the extent that sounds produced by the elements – rain, hail, wind – are audible in the space. During a hailstorm, for example, occupants of a space with a tin roof and no insulation would find the sounds amplified and may feel more vulnerable to the elements, that is, insecure.

Despite the enclosing walls and ceiling, the Binding experience of *Scumbag* is a silent one. The sounds of domestic life are missing. The main sound in the space is the echoic reverberation of visitor footsteps and the buzz of an air-conditioner. Metaphorically then, the silence of the space resounds with the physical and symbolic silence of the stories of domestic abuse that line the walls. In the words of one visitor, 'Something turns inside. Great to see the world of silence given some space' (visitors' comment book).

Profound silence marred by shame typifies a victim's response to abuse and such a visceral evocation is an important part of the meanings being made in this space. In the artist's own words, 'Pinned to walls in groups of phrases, where innermost thoughts are laid bare, they inscribe visually and linguistically, intimate aspects of identity that often remain shamefully and fearfully concealed "behind closed doors"' (Dreyfus, 2008, Exhibition Catalogue).

Alongside Binding, another important resource for exploring interpersonal meaning in three-dimensional space is Bonding. It is a multidimensional resource concerned with aligning people into groups with shared dispositions. There are at least three tools that materialise Bonding in the third dimension: icons, hybridisation and attitudinal alignment – the way a space aligns visitors into communities of rapport through the Yin–Yang coupling of field and Appraisal. Appraisal is a linguistic resource for analysing the feelings and values we negotiate with one another (White, 1997; 1998; Martin, 1997, 2000; Martin and White, 2005). However, word limits constrain the analysis here to a focus on Bonding through the coupling of field and Appraisal resources only.

427

Field can be defined as a set of activity sequences oriented to some global institutional purpose (Martin, 1992). When we apply the notion of field to the spaces of an exhibition, it means we can analyse a range of *activities* taking place. An activity orientation enables space to be classified in terms of 'doings' or processes. At one level, these activities refer to the act of viewing and experiencing an exhibition. So we can distinguish between the spaces for walking (the pathway – *stairs* and *corridor*), spaces for resting (the *seats*) and spaces for looking, listening, reading and musing (the main display space). In addition to identifying these activities, field is concerned with identifying the *objects* involved in these activities. In particular, these consist of hand-stitched *felt letters* and *words* as well as the *photographic images* displayed on two of the walls.

At a deeper level, we can apply field to an analysis of the actual content of the *Scumbag* exhibition. The words and phrases pinned to the first two walls are chilling. Reading from left-to-right we see the following:

> you never believe me
> its horrific
> i have no choice
> your malicious ways
> grow up
> immense pain
> mean and selfish
> despicable scumbag
> assume supremacy
> i exist
> total dismembering
> protect myself
> punishing silence
> i forgive you every day
> no visible wounds

At a global level, these are mostly words and phrases associated with the trauma of abuse.

> Verbal abuse: 'no visible wounds'
> Physical abuse: 'total dismembering'
> Passive aggressive abuse: 'punishing silence'

They also hint at hope, human rights and redemption.

> Survival: 'i exist'
> Forgiveness: 'i forgive you every day'

Each trauma, furthermore, evokes very strong feelings. So Appraisal theory is highly relevant to our exploration of Bonding, especially the system of Attitude, which is concerned with positive and negative evaluations of emotions, people and things. Attitude comprises three sub-systems of evaluation: Affect, Judgement and Appreciation. Affect is concerned with feelings and shared emotions. It aligns people around empathy. Judgement has to do with judging people's behaviour and aligns people around shared principles. Finally, shared Appreciation aligns people around joint tastes.

Significantly, all three systems unfold to negotiate affiliation in the interactions visitors have in the exhibition and the objects on display there. Initially, the brightly coloured and hand-stitched felt letters that are soft to touch functioned as a lure to the visitor. They led the visitor into the key exhibition space (through Prominence) while evoking positive feelings of Affect associated with warm memories of childhood play (happiness, security, satisfaction) within the spatial evocation of a 'home'. As the visitor approached the main space, however, negative feelings of propriety were quickly evoked by the display of the word 'malicious' alongside negative appreciations of reaction as 'horrific' became visible.

Thereafter the phrases pinned to the walls and the photographic images co-patterned to dynamically, and intensely, evoke feelings of negative Affect from the visitor (sorrow, unhappiness, disquiet). Alongside these, negative Judgements of propriety are evoked in relation to the perpetrators of the abuse alongside positive Judgements of the capacity, tenacity and resolve of the victims and survivors. Also strongly evoked are strong negative reactions of Appreciation intertwined with negative valuations of abuse. The cumulative effect of this co-patterning is an affectual charge that reverberates with pain and sadness but is alleviated by the hope of redemption and the tenacity of survival.

Underscoring these reverberations is the silence that has finally been broken within the safety of a public space. This experience no doubt gives victims a sense of collective belonging – they are no longer alone with their pain – they are now bonded into a community whose shared experience has been the experience of abuse, whether domestic or institutional or racial; verbal, physical, sexual or passive–aggressive. It is not surprising that many visitors to *Scumbag* were moved to tears and found the experience of the exhibition compelling – emotional, healing and cathartic (visitors' comment book).

Discussion

In reflecting on the multimodal analysis of the exhibition, this analysis has focused on the organization of 3D space. The multimodal nature of the exhibition suggests it would also be illuminating to analyse each of the other semiotic systems that are co-articulating in this exhibition. Of particular significance would be a visual image analysis of each photograph or diptych alongside a typographical analysis of the verbal text (Van Leeuwen, 2005b). The challenge would then be to synthesise the analysis of all three semiotics and map how choices for typography, visual images and space co-articulate.

Issues for further development

Building on the analysis in this chapter, several issues related to the three communicative functions of space warrant further development. First, *Scumbag* consists of one main display space. Most exhibitions, however, comprise several connected spaces that unfold temporally as visitors move through them. For the textual function to address this temporal unfolding, more dynamic modelling strategies need to be developed. The use of static 2D photographs are adequate in a single space but cannot capture the dynamic sense of traversal and flow that lies at the heart of the temporal unfolding of most built 3D spaces.

Other resources for the analysis of space that are useful to examine but which are not explored in this chapter include the ideational and interpersonal meanings of space. For instance, following Martin (1992), it is illuminating to apply two types of structure to the patterning of ideational meanings in space – serial and orbital (Stenglin, 2004; Martin and

Stenglin, 2007). Serial structures suit exhibitions whose content is chronologically organised because they segment 'texts' so that they unfold step by step, while orbital structures are organised around a nucleus with satellites. With respect to the interpersonal function, several key resources for materialising Bonding that can be usefully explored include the hybridisation of space, Bonding icons and choices for learning that align museum visitors into communities of belonging. In addition, interpersonal resources such as Kress and Van Leeuwen's resources for analysing power and social distance (2006) have proved useful for the multimodal analysis of institutional spaces (Ravelli and Stenglin, 2008). Given the field explored by the exhibition, resources for exploring how power and social distance are negotiated clearly have the potential to offer many powerful insights.

To summarise, this chapter has explored the organization of an exhibition from the social semiotic perspective of Halliday's communicative functions. In particular it has considered the ways some choices for textual, ideational and interpersonal meanings have co-patterned in *Scumbag* to evoke very powerful visceral responses from visitors. In doing so, it has been able to 'unpack' the materialisation of the communicative functions in 3D space. These tools can be used to inform two important challenges for the investigation of communication in museum and gallery exhibitions: the theoretical deconstruction of the ways meanings are organised alongside practical tools for informing the design of 3D spaces for display.

Note

1 Interestingly, one visitor (personal communication, May 2) read the walls against the grain of the 'left–right' directionality favouring instead, a top–bottom approach. If this approach is taken, the meanings become more fluid and less prescribed: 'you' – 'horrific' – 'malicious' – 'pain'. They also become more open-ended, positive or negative: 'I exist' – 'myself' – 'every day'.

Further reading

Martin, J. R. and Stenglin, M. (2007) 'Materialising reconciliation: Negotiating difference in a post-colonial exhibition.' In T. Royce and W. Bowcher eds. *New Directions in the Analysis of Multimodal Discourse*, Mahwah, NJ: Lawrence Erlbaum Associates: pp. 215–38. (An analysis of the ways an ideology of reconciliation is materialised in one exhibition by exploring Halliday's communicative functions.)

Ravelli, L. J. (2000) 'Beyond shopping: Constructing the Sydney Olympics in three-dimensional text.' *Text* 20(4): pp. 489–515. (A useful introduction to the three communicative functions of space in the context of retail and consumerism.)

Ravelli, L. R. and Stenglin, M. (2008) 'Feeling space: Interpersonal communication and spatial semiotics.' In E. Ventola and G. Antos eds. *Handbook of Applied Linguistics, Volume 2, Interpersonal Communication*, pp. 355–393. (A useful introduction to applying Kress and Van Leeuwen's interpersonal tools, in combination with Binding and Bonding, to the analysis of 3D space.)

Stenglin, M. (2009) 'Space odyssey: Towards a social semiotic model of 3D space.' *Visual Communication* 8 (1): pp. 425–47.

Van Leeuwen, T. (2005a) *Introducing Social Semiotics*, London: Routledge. (A good introduction to social semiotics as well as a detailed description of, and system network for analysing the textual 'Framing' of 3D spaces.)

32

Image in the multimodal ensemble

Children's drawing

Diane Mavers

Introduction

Image is diverse in terms of how it is made, by whom and for what purposes, as well as where it is displayed and how it is used. Produced by hand (e.g. fine art and woodcuts) and techno-logically mediated (e.g. photographs and animations), there are constancies and variations in what is represented and how across different media and genres. Methods of analysis span different disciplines and theoretical perspectives, for example cultural studies, visual anthropology, art history and sociology (e.g. Arnheim, 1969; Becker, 1981; Chaplin, 1994; Collier and Collier, 1986; Finnegan, 2002; Gombrich, 1982; Lister and Wells, 2001; Rose, 2001; Van Leeuwen and Jewitt, 2001). Where image is combined with writing, music, speech, and so on, meanings are distributed across modes. Choice of mode is significant for the meanings that can be made because modes have particular affordances – or potentialities and constraints – and this has epistemological significance (Kress, 2003b). Image as a component of multimodal ensembles on the page and the screen is a focus of wide-ranging study, including research interests such as discourse (e.g. Hodge and Kress, 1988; Kress, 2001; O'Halloran, 2005) transcription (e.g. Baldry and Thibault, 2006; Flewitt *et al.*, this volume; Norris, 2002), sites of display (e.g. Jewitt, 2008a; Jones, this volume; Scollon and Scollon, 2003), resources for learning (e.g. Archer, 2006; Bezemer and Kress, 2008) and use in the dynamism of communicational exchange (e.g. Goodwin, 2000; Leander and Wells-Rowe, 2006).

A social semiotic lens

Social semiotics is concerned with signs and sign-making. Making as against using signs is a theoretical principle that recognizes agency as individuals select the most apt resource for expressing particular meanings in accordance with their 'interest', and as shaped by and in response to the particular social context, and so is not arbitrary (Kress, 1993, 1997a). Social semiotic analysis examines how people make signs by combining form and meaning. The signifiers of graphic representation (its material forms) can be shown and described – but what about meaning? In his theorization of language as social semiotic Michael Halliday identifies three functional components or 'metafunctions'

431

that are always 'generated simultaneously and mapped onto one another' (Halliday, 1978: 112). The *ideational* refers to subject matter, such as our interpretation of the world and of being in the world; the *interpersonal* is concerned with social relations and hence roles, relationships and power; relevance to the 'context of situation' is the *textual* component (ibid.: 112–13). Beyond spoken and written language, the ideational, the interpersonal (or social) and the textual are always co-present in all modes of representation and communication (Hodge and Kress, 1988). Images such as photographs, paintings and drawings represent aspects of the world (e.g. people, places and events), take into account social relations (e.g. made for a political campaign, an art exhibition or schoolwork) and are actualized in ways that are cohesive and coherent (e.g. relations with writing and relevance to the social context). This tripartite co-presence of meaning regardless of mode provides a consistent framework for investigating signs and sign-making within and across modal realizations. Irrespective of what the image is, the configuration of the multimodal ensemble, or the age of the producer, text-making is a process of 'design' that entails selecting and combining resources from those made available socially and culturally in order to represent phenomena and to construct social relations (Kress and Van Leeuwen, 2001: 45–65).

Analysing children's drawing-foregrounded 'concept' maps from a multimodal social semiotic perspective

Children's drawings have been and are studied by psychologists investigating patterns of development (e.g. Cox, 1992; Golomb, 1974; Kellogg, 1969; Matthews, 1999) and by psychiatrists and counsellors exploring children's experience of trauma (e.g. Diem-Wille, 2001; Malchiodi, 1998). Located in the educational domain, other researchers are concerned with how children's drawings represent their conceptual knowledge, for example in science (e.g. Tunnicliffe and Reiss, 1999; Bowker, 2007). In research, as in education, great store is put by what children say and write, but there tends to be some apprehension about whether their drawings are a valid and reliable source of information. From a social semiotic perspective, it is not a case of whether writing or drawing is more 'truthful', but that their particular affordances enable certain expressions of meaning. Writing and drawing each 'do' some things well and some things less well. Social semiotic studies of children's writing and drawing as graphic multimodal ensembles in educational, home and community contexts investigate how they deploy the resources available to them and how this gives particular shapes to meaning (Bearne, 2003; Kenner, 2000a; Kress, 1997a; Mavers, 2003; Ormerod and Ivanic, 2000; Pahl, 2002; Stein, 2008; Zammit and Downes, 2002)

Map-making

This chapter focuses on drawing in children's 'concept' mapping produced for research purposes as one instance of image in the multimodal ensemble. As part of an evaluation of a child-only online environment, 35 children (18 boys and 17 girls) between the ages of 8 and 11 years from three schools distributed across England made maps. Both Novak and Gowin's (1984) concept maps and Buzan's (1993) mind maps are overviews of topics consisting of 'nodes' (individual textual items), linked by labelled lines, and organized hierarchically from top to bottom or radiating from a central theme respectively. What was distinctive about the mapping in this research was that drawing rather than writing was foregrounded and instructions with regard to layout were kept to a minimum. Provided with a black biro and a large sheet of white paper, the children were given 20 minutes to make maps entitled 'Being in GridClub'. The task was summarized as:

We want to understand what it's like being a member of GridClub.

- Who is part of GridClub and what kinds of things do they do?
- What do you do in GridClub and who do you meet?
- How do people work together in GridClub?

With eagerness to cooperate, the children represented facts, experiences and views in ways that could be readily understood. In the classroom, students often record what the teacher already knows. In this context, the children could not assume that what was well known to them was known at all by the research team. Framed by their prior experience of the evaluation process, map-making entailed making decisions about what might and might not be of interest, what would be foregrounded, what should be withheld, and so on. Produced on a different day and in different circumstances, there would likely be constancies and changes, just as in an interview. These texts are a distilled semiosis of club membership at a particular moment in time.

Methods of analysis

Extracting individual drawings for micro-examination directs analytical attention to the detail of their design. All images represent a selection. Produced mark by mark, it is neither possible nor necessary to represent everything that is observed, known, remembered or imagined. That which is selected represents the focus of the individual's immediate 'interest' (Kress, 1993). In picking out 'criterial features' (ibid.) – those attributes chosen for particular attention – objects, people, scenes and events are not shown in their entirety. Selections are not random or accidental. Rather they are highly principled, and this accounts for constancies and changes in what is drawn. For example, 53 different representations of the human nose were catalogued in drawings produced by 295 English children between the ages of 5 and 9 years (Paget, 1932). Variations represent shifts in what is being attended to, and this is shaped by what it is that is being drawn, for whom and for what purposes.

In many graphic texts produced by children, drawing and writing are co-present. Putting these modes into a relationship with one another entails making decisions about the deployment of resources and the distribution of meaning. Various approaches have been posited for conceptualizing the intermodal relationship between writing and image. The notions of 'anchorage, illustration and relay' (Barthes, 1977b), 'concurrence and complementarity' (Unsworth, 2006c) and 'expansion (elaboration, extension and enhancement), projection and complementarity' (Martinec and Salway, 2005) are concerned with the relative status of these modes as well as how they relate to one another in terms of form, function and meaning.

In graphic texts, certain resources become available for separating spatially items, and for putting them into a relationship with one another. This enables the text-maker to represent individual 'things', and conceptual connections or narrative links between them. Surrounding grouped images with white space or enclosing lines is a means of framing that connects what is within and separates this from what is beyond (Van Leeuwen, 2005a). This demarcates discrete textual items. Associations can be implied by positioning images in relatively close proximity or by superimposing one image with another. Arrangement, the addition of lines and directionality are other ways of creating intertextual relationships.

A graphic surface can be thought of as a material frame. What is chosen for representation within that frame defines what the graphic product is in all its semiotic plenitude. Across the full text, connections and disconnections are created by similarities in and differences between what is selected for representation and how entities are combined. Drawings of the same or

433

similar items in the same text may not be identical. In accordance with the changing interest of the sign-maker, there may be a 'shift in criterial detail' (Mavers, 2003), because what has been 'given' in one place does not require repetition, leaving room for the 'new' (Halliday, 1989: 55; Kress and Van Leeuwen, 2006: 179–85). The resources of layout, arrangement, comparative size, emphasis, colour, framing, etc. (Kress and Van Leeuwen, 2006: 179–85) provide means for foregrounding and for showing relationships across the text.

Analysing the maps

The analysis of these maps on the topic of 'Being in GridClub' was undertaken in response to the research questions: children's perceptions of who club members are, how they interact, and the activities in which they engage. Attendance to different 'units' of text was a way of examining the variety of ways in which the children made meaning: in individual nodes, in relationships between linked nodes and across the whole text. As these 'units' co-exist and co-function in multimodal texts, these analytical procedures were necessarily iterative and the analysis interlinked. In other words, in examining individual nodes, related nodes and the full text were bracketed but always framed the interpretation. Similarly, investigating a pathway of linked nodes demanded prior analysis of each individual node and its place as a thread of meaning in the full text. Initial cataloguing of content across the maps in a tally sheet classified according to emerging themes was a way of identifying systematically what had been represented, prior to extracting excerpts and full maps for micro-analysis. In what follows, examination of how children designed drawing and writing within discrete nodes, how they linked nodes and how they made meaning across the full map provides insights into how these methods were implemented and how they enabled response to the research questions.

The mapping was framed by scripted instructions and produced in the presence of the researchers. This provided certain contextual information. For example, whilst drawing dominates the space of the page, in the overall production of the maps there was constant switching between drawing and writing, suggesting ongoing decision-making in the process of design. Group interactions and reference to the setting simultaneous with processes of production provided insights into certain aspects of text-making (see also Holm Hopperstadt, 2008; Lancaster, 2007). For example, in one group, a poster on the wall gave rise to drawings of the frame surrounding the portal, which resembled the metallic strips and nuts and bolts of a construction kit, as at the bottom right of Rosie's map (Figure 32.1). Immediately after making their maps, in groups, the children were invited to talk about what they had done. Audio-recorded and transcribed verbatim, their accounts provided their interpretations and additional information. Furthermore, map-making was one research method amongst others. The project design also included observation of school clubs, group interviewing of club members, online and paper questionnaires, study of site materials (e.g. games), children's contributions and communicational exchange (e.g. special interest groups, web pages, e-messages, chat), as well as interviews with parents, teachers and site designers. These insights into the content, social practices and discourses of the club provided a context for interpreting the children's maps.

Nodes are shown as discrete items by their distancing with white space. Some of these are relatively brief. One of Michael's nodes depicts club members (Figure 32.2). His decision to draw two 'stick' figures – 'stick' figures made up 70 per cent of children's drawings of people across the 35 maps – might have been a consequence of the limited time given to complete the task. Omission of individuality suggests the homogeneous, the unspecified and the general. In this framed multimodal grouping, certain meanings made in drawing

Figure 32.1 Rosie's map (age 9).

Figure 32.2 A node from Michael's map (age 9).

and writing are congruent, whilst others are complementary. Numerosity is shared (the two drawn figures and the plural noun), as is humanity (drawn people and the label 'Pupils'). Conversely, his image shows similar size and omits gender, whilst his single-word label 'anchors' (Barthes, 1977b: 37) identity (as students). Dipika's group is also shorthand for quantity – she knew that club membership exceeded four (Figure 32.3). Similar sizing implies that membership of this club is available to people of broadly similar physical size,

435

Figure 32.3 A node from Dipika's map (age 8).

namely children. Her abutted writing 'Meeting other people that use gridclub' logs social encounters in the environment, and like the close positioning of her drawn figures, indicates the collectiveness of membership. Variations in appearance, such as different styles of hair, clothing and footwear attribute gender and distinctiveness, and indicate diversity of membership. Within and between the maps, these shifts between the named and the anonymous, the known and the unknown, the particularized and the generalized, represent the children's experiences and understandings of who members are. Where did this knowledge originate from? It was in part informed by joining a teacher-organized weekly school club, where children observed and advised one another, undertook activities collaboratively and shared the excitement of each other's experiences. Within the site, gender might be readily deduced through members' names appearing on websites, messages and postings, but such attributes as physical appearance were not. Olivia (age 10) articulated the complexities of knowing and not knowing people in an online community:

> [Y]ou Meet new friends even without meeting them which is a good way in meeting people and talking about things over the Internet (.) but if you don't really know them then you really don't know what they're like (.) but you do know what they're like as in what they like and what they do and things (.) but not as in what they look like and things.

In response to the task instructions, these nodes depict identity and social relations in the club. Elsewhere, combining person and object represents the activities in which members engage. What is being done is specified through a combination of bodily posture and the focus of attention. Orientation of Rosie's figure towards the computer with an arm extended towards the mouse mat represents involvement in a digital activity (Figure 32.4). The multimodal detail of the screen display to which the member's attention is directed consists of two figures oriented in the same direction. Two speech bubbles emanating from the mouth of the hatted figure contain the words 'come bake [*back*] here' and 'Im [*I'm*] a polis [*police*]'. Together, Rosie's drawing and writing identify character and suggest plot, namely a police officer chasing an offender. In the context of the map focus, exclusion of a label makes the assumption that this is sufficient to represent game-playing in the environment. She later explained that this club member is 'playing the cops and robbers game'. In subsequently describing her map, Rose specifically drew attention to the link to her game-playing node labelled 'Being in gridclub is FUN' (Figure 32.1). Capitalization,

Figure 32.4 A node from Rosie's map (age 9).

enlargement and near centrality of 'FUN' foregrounds a discourse that was a regular feature of interviews and shared by site designers, children, teachers and parents. Rosie commented: 'Grid-Club's good because all the games are fun but you can learn things from them as well'.

Rosie's map is by no means a random collection of ideas. Headed by the (given) map title, she identified four themes shown as separate, linked, linear threads, each of which emanate from the computer at the top left of her map: ideas/learning; fun/games; work/interesting; and communication/friends (Figure 32.1). Each is interpreted by its component parts (the discrete nodes) in relationship (connected to one another by labelled links). On the screen of the computer to the upper left of her page are displayed what we take to be two continents, and which Rosie later called a map (Figure 32.5). To the right, a drawing of a human head crowned with a glowing light bulb is a playful redesign of the dog with a light bulb on its head and the caption 'Start thinking' that launched the password-protected area of the club, something seen regularly by club members (and an idea taken up by others in the group). Directly connected by the 'vector' (Van Leeuwen, 2005a: 25) of a ruled line and the thrice-repeated word 'ideas' ('giving you ideas' on the link, 'Bright idea' inside the light bulb and 'I'm to [*too*] full of ideas' inside the brain), she indicates one of the benefits of belonging to the club. Like other map-makers, Rosie went beyond providing facts by also evaluating the environment. Situated in the context of ongoing research where interviewing, observation and questionnaires were described as ways of understanding children's perspectives, this is perhaps unsurprising. Speech and think bubbles in just over a quarter of the maps (e.g. 'I like learning because gridclub makes it fun' in the final node of this thread) may be a graphic means of making direct connection with the researchers in order to tell them what they think, as on previous occasions when the children had been invited to articulate their views in group interviews. The second and final nodes in this string are linked by the ruled labelled line 'I like learning'. Rosie described this linked theme as:

Figure 32.5 A linked theme from Rosie's map (age 9).

a computer with a map on because it gives you good ideas and it'll help you with your work in class and I've connected up 'I like learning' and there's a speech bubble and it says 'I like learning because GridClub makes it fun'.

In making a connection between a resource available in the environment and her evaluation of its benefits in terms of stimulating ideas and providing an enjoyable learning experience, Rosie shared in the discourse of 'edutainment' (Buckingham and Scanlon, 2001).

Over the course of the research, the children were observed engaging in a wide range of activities, were able to describe what they did in detail and said that they liked the choice offered by the environment. Across her map as a whole, Rosie represented a variety of resources offered by the club: an atlas (possibly from the encyclopaedia available on the site), a game (one of the many available) and communication (she said, 'I've done two pictures of computers and they've got writing on the screens and they're both saying "we are friends" because they're communicating with each other'). She also showed different ways of operating these resources: the mouse, present in the game playing and atlas nodes, is absent from the learning and communication nodes. In addition to making judgements in writing, laughing and smiling mouths – differentiated by the presence or absence of teeth according to Rosie – carry the affective and attitudinal, in that they represent members' pleasure and positive disposition. In all but one instance, Rosie drew club members in a profile orientation, indicating that they are preoccupied with activities on the computer. Like back-facing figures in other maps, this suggests that the business of the online club is what the figures are oriented towards, perhaps hinting at the privacy of this child-only world and the social exclusivity of the environment. By positioning the irises of the three single figures as a sideways glance, Rosie may be simultaneously registering the represented members' knowledge of being looked at and creating a polite response by recognizing the 'viewer'. This may imply a tension between communicating information as requested by the researchers and entry into the semi-private world of the club.

Some closing comments

Interpreting these maps was based on the theoretical assumption that children's meaning- making is principled. Framed by the affordances of drawing-foregrounded mapping, the children distributed meanings between modes, shaped meanings within them, and combined meanings across them as they represented their knowledge, experiences and views of what it meant to be a club member. They constructed a synthesized representation of what children do in the club, how they do it and why in a multimodally interdependent ensemble of drawing, writing, layout and linkage. Identifying different 'units' of text was an analytical method that enabled attendance to the parts and the whole: individual textual items, relationships between items and whole-text interrelationships.

Instances of image in the multimodal ensemble are generically particularized in terms of their 'content', 'style', how they are produced, how they are arranged graphically, and their social contextualization – compare, for example, the semiotic possibilities and limitations for shaping and distributing meaning in an academic scientific report (Lemke, 1998b: 102) or artworks and text panels in a photographic exhibition (Macken-Horarik, 2004: 487). This chapter has not attended to different kinds of image (e.g. paintings, photographs, film), or to the multimodality of image in relationship with modes beyond writing, such as in web pages and face-to-face interaction. Whatever the text and whatever the theoretical lens, examining image in the multimodal ensemble demands that seriousness is given to its design in relationship with other co-present modes.

Acknowledgements

These maps were gathered as part of an evaluation of GridClub (Manchester Metropolitan University), funded by the Department for Education and Skills (DfES) and managed by the British Educational and Communications Technology Agency (Becta). With thanks to Bridget Somekh (project director) and Cathy Lewin (co-researcher) who gathered the maps in two schools, to the schools for their support, and especially to the children.

Suggested reading

Kress, G. (1997a) *Before Writing: Rethinking the Paths to Literacy*, London: Routledge. (Social semiotic theory.)
Kress, G. and Van Leeuwen, T. (2006) *Reading Images: The Grammar of Visual Design*, 2nd edn, London: Routledge. (Social semiotic methods of analysis.)
Mavers, D. (2011) *Children's Drawing and Writing: The Remarkable in the Unremarkable*. New York: Routledge.

33

Online newspapers

Structure and layout

John S. Knox

Introduction

Newspapers are powerful social institutions, and play an important role in reporting and shaping public events, mediating information and influencing public opinion. Since the mid-1990s, newspapers have published on the world wide web along with other news-producing media institutions, including public broadcasters like the ABC in Australia and the BBC in the UK; news agencies like Reuters and Aljazeera; and news-reproducing aggregators like *google news* and *Fark*.

Visual communication has always been central to the discursive work of newspapers. Apart from the use of illustrations (which became widespread from the late nineteenth century) and then photographs, the layout of print newspapers has always been related to the mass-mediation of meaning between the institution and the readership (Barnhurst and Nerone, 2001; Machin and Niblock, 2006).

The importance of visual communication in writing is now, perhaps, more 'in focus' than ever before, and the emergence of the world wide web and of the 'new writing' (Van Leeuwen, 2008) raises questions for those who would research writing and reading, and also for those who would critically explore other social practices and power relations related to these two semiotic acts.

This chapter looks at the role of website structure and layout in the reporting of news in online newspapers, focusing on the *Guardian* online from 17 August 2012 as a case study. Language plays a central role in the discursive practice of online news reporting, but without a consideration of layout and web structure, any analysis of online newspaper discourse can only paint a partial picture.

Analysing newspaper layout

The visual communication of meaning in print newspapers through layout and page design has been studied from a number of perspectives (see Knox, 2009c, pp. 59–69). Most relevant to the approach taken here are studies by Evans (1976), Barnhurst and Nerone (2001), Kress and Van Leeuwen (1998) and Knox *et al.* (2010).

A former editor of the *Times*, Evans (1976) argues that newspaper design is communication, and provides classification schemes of front-page designs and other news pages, and the visual devices by which newspapers can communicate the relative importance of stories. Barnhurst and Nerone (2001) take an approach consistent with Evans, but explore the historical development of the design of print newspapers in the USA in the eighteenth, nineteenth and twentieth centuries, relating design practices and changes to social context. Kress and Van Leeuwen (1998) apply their 'grammar of visual design' to the layout of front pages, exploring in particular use of the top–bottom (Ideal–Real), left–right (Given–New) and centre–periphery (Centre–Margin) oppositions in newspaper page design. Building on the work of Kress and Van Leeuwen, Knox *et al.* (2010) explore the front-page design of two Thai newspapers which target different readerships, and the ways in which the respective designs are a construal of the relationship between the news institution, the news content and the readership of each newspaper.

In all these cases, layout is seen as a semiotic act, and there has been limited work on the design of online news that takes a similar perspective (see Knox, 2009c, pp. 74–86 for a review of other perspectives). Cooke (2003) employs grounded theory to look at changes in, and compare the layout of, webpages of online newspapers and other news websites. Bateman *et al.* (2007) argue that the layout of online newspaper home pages more closely resembles listings on a search engine than it does a print newspaper, and Bateman (2008) develops this work further in relation to other documents, setting out a model for the exploration of multimodal genres. Knox (2007) builds on the work of Kress and Van Leeuwen (1996) to develop a framework for the analysis of the layout of online newspaper home pages. Based on the analysis of children's news websites and other children's websites, Djonov (2007, 2008) sets out a framework for analysing website structure, and the links between different parts of the website. In the discussion that follows, the frameworks of Bateman (2008), Djonov (2007, 2008) and Knox (2007) are employed.

The three frameworks employed in this chapter are based on systemic functional multimodal discourse analysis (SF-MDA). They are *systemic* because they are based on a Saussurean view of meaning, where choices in communication are understood in relation to other choices that are *not* made (but could have been) in a given instance, and these choices are modelled as systems in SF-MDA. They are *functional* because structures used in communication are identified, described and classified according to their functions (see Knox, 2013).

Medium, production, consumption and newspapers

Print newspapers have sections (e.g. *News, Sport, World*), and these sections reflect the division of labour in the newsroom. In addition to reflecting institutional practices, the organisation of content in a newspaper is in large part determined by the medium, and what Bateman (2008) calls 'canvas constraints'. That is, the medium of print places limits on the number of stories that can appear on each page, due to the regulated, finite space of each page, and the practical constraints this sets (e.g. the quantity of ink the paper can absorb, the font size required to make reading practical).

In addition, the number of pages in a particular edition of a print newspaper, for example, is restricted by what Bateman calls production and consumption constraints. The institution of the newspaper has economic limits on how much paper and newsprint it can use on a given day. Costs of distribution are related to the physical size of the product, and social practices that have evolved over time mean that (typical) upper and lower time limits exist for readers' interaction with the newspaper on a given day (e.g. weekend editions of print newspapers are typically larger than weekday editions for this reason).

Bateman's argument is that a semiotic artefact (e.g. a print newspaper) and its established uses (e.g. typical newspaper reading practices in a culture) are related to the 'developed modes of expression' (or semiotic structure) typically associated with a genre. To illustrate, a print newspaper has a 'front page' (which has a certain cultural value and linguistic and visual conventions to go with it), headlines, photographs, comics and so forth due to the relations between the medium, the processes of production and consumption, and how these evolve over time in recurring patterns of meaningful social action. This is what Bateman refers to as *genre*.

Online newspapers are produced by the same institutions as print newspapers (though the practices in individual institutions differ, and the industry is in a state of flux – see Beckett, 2008; Paterson and Domingo, 2008). Often, the language of a given news report in a print and online edition of a newspaper is identical. But print and online newspapers are different artefacts in different media, with ramifications for the semiotic acts and relations they mediate.

The canvas constraints of online newspapers differ from those of print. The html webpage can extend almost indefinitely, and the website can likewise add sections and pages almost indefinitely. Also, pages viewed on screen give no physical indication of a reader's navigation – cues need to be 'built in' to the page design to allow readers to know 'where they are' in a text.[1]

Production constraints of online newspapers also differ in important ways from those of print. The cost of sending journalists and photojournalists to cover stories, and paying others to write 'opinion' pieces is the same regardless of where the reports are published. But the costs of producing the text and distributing it are considerably lower for an online newspaper. This means more content can be included, and therefore using material sourced from outside the news institution becomes much cheaper.

Consumption constraints for online newspapers also differ from print. Readers need a desktop or laptop computer, tablet, or mobile phone.[2] This device-based reading means that, in comparison with print-newspaper reading practices, readers of online newspapers typically read while engaged in other activities (e.g. working, 'chatting' with friends), and they may access online newspapers more often and for shorter periods than print newspapers (Barthelson, 2002).

As a result of these material and social differences in print and online newspapers, online newspapers have evolved in a way that is very different from print newspapers, and in a way that has been largely disregarded to this point in the literature.

Home pages and online newspaper structure

Print newspapers have a front page – widely recognised as the most important page in a newspaper. The front page is "the editorial face of the newspaper. From an infinite informational world, front page news carves out familiar group interests and identities in concentrated visual space" (Fishman and Marvin, 2003, p. 33).

Online newspapers have a home page, of which the same can be said. We can view the main home page of an online newspaper as the page that serves as the 'entry point' to the newspaper. In the semiotic structure of an online newspaper, home pages can be contrasted with story pages, as these two types of page (or classes of page) have a different functional structure. Home pages and story pages both typically have a banner (or Masthead) at the top of the page, a footer (or Signature) at the bottom, menus (or Navigation zones) and advertisements. Structurally though, they differ in that the main content area (or News zone) of a home page contains numerous stories in the form of *newsbites* (the short headline-plus-lead-plus-hyperlink stories found in online newspapers) and/or *newsbits* (the headline/hyperlink-only stories found in online newspapers) which are explicitly or implicitly categorised. In contrast, the main content area of a story page is typically dominated by a single news story (Knox, 2009c).

So-called 'section pages' are those pages that act as a home page for a section (e.g. *Sport, World News*) of an online newspaper. Not surprisingly (since they share the same function), home pages and section pages share a common structure. Systemically speaking, because they are the same structurally, home pages and section pages belong to the same class (and from this point on are both called 'home pages' in this chapter). Plate 33.1 shows four home pages and a single story page from the *Guardian* online, 17 August 2012. This plate illustrates that home pages can be identified, defined, and classified in opposition to story pages according to their functional structure (which is discussed further in the following section). The identification of these two classes of page is important for an understanding of the structure of online newspapers.

Website structure, as discussed in the literature on website design, has been described from two main perspectives according to Djonov (2005, 2007). The first, the segmental perspective, 'focuses on individual webpages instead of groups of webpages (hence "segmental") and determines the level of a webpage according to the number of clicks required to reach it from the [main] homepage' (Djonov, 2007, p. 149). In the second, the holistic perspective, 'the *horizontal dimension* of a website is determined by the number of sections the information is grouped into, whereas its *vertical dimension* is defined by the number of subdivisions (subsections, subsubsections, sub-subsections [*sic.*], etc.) within these sections' (Djonov, 2007, p. 150).

Taking an SF-MDA approach, Djonov builds on these two perspectives, and theorises website structure as a hierarchy of Themes. In SF-MDA, a Theme is an element that predicts what is to come in the remainder of a given structure.[3] Home pages and their hyperlinks 'aid users in predicting the type of information offered in the sections they lead to as well as the relationships that obtain between these sections' (Djonov, 2007, p. 152).

This approach to understanding website structure applies well to online newspapers, which have a recursive structure of sections, each of which has a home page with story pages, and optionally sub-sections, each of which has a home page with story pages, and optionally sub-sub-sections, each of which has a home page with story pages, and so on. That is, each (sub-)section of an online newspaper has its own home page, from which readers may follow hyperlinks to other home pages, or story pages.[4]

On 17 August, 2012, there were ten main news sections in the *Guardian*, namely: *News, London 2012, Sport, Comment, Culture, Business, Money, Life & Style, Travel* and *Environment*. Each section had its own home page.

Plate 33.2 shows a number of menus from the *Guardian* on this day. These menus are colour coded, and the headings and backgrounds on each page are coloured consistently with these menus, so that colour also functions as a navigation device for the reader and a classification device for content on home pages across the entire newspaper.

The top line in Plate 33.2 shows the menu at the top of the main home page which gives the main news section of the newspaper. The second line shows the menu of the *News* section,[5] the third line shows the menu at the top of the *London 2012* home page, and so on. The menus from the *Business, Money, Life & Style, Travel* and *Environment* home pages are not shown, but each has a similar number of items. The home pages in Plate 33.1 follow one hierarchy of Themes, from the main home page, to the home page of the *Culture* section, to the home page of the *Art & Design* sub-section (within the *Culture* section), to the home page of the *Art* sub-sub-section (within the *Art & Design* sub-section).

As the menus illustrate, all sections in the newspaper have their own sub-sections. Further, most of these sub-sections also have sub-sub-sections. Each section, sub-section, sub-sub-section (and so on) has its own home page. In total, the *Guardian* website has in the vicinity of 100 home pages.

Online newspapers differ in how many (sub-)sections and home pages they have, but this structural pattern is typical, if not universal in online newspapers. Using Bateman's terminology, this 'developed mode of expression' of online newspapers is related to canvas constraints (e.g. the need have an overt structure for readers to navigate multiple pages and sections viewed one-at-a-time on a single screen), production constraints (e.g. the division of labour in the newsroom), consumption constraints (e.g. the need for readers to be able to scan stories quickly, and to easily locate stories in their areas of interest), and to the ways in which the mass mediation of information from established newspaper institutions has evolved as they have moved from print to the world wide web.

Online newspaper readers read stories and story pages, but those story pages are mediated by at least one (and perhaps several) home pages in the reader's experience of the newspaper.[6] In terms of the number of stories an online newspaper reader encounters, by far the largest number of stories are the short newsbites and newsbits which dominate home pages.

Thus, online newspaper readers are home page readers, in a way that print newspaper readers are not 'front page readers'. The most important home page is the main home page of the newspaper, but given the pervasive role of home pages in the overall structure of online newspapers, a critical understanding of the design of home pages and the stories that appear on them is crucial for our understanding of online newspapers more broadly.

Analysing home pages

In SF-MDA, three main functions of communication are commonly recognised. The *ideational function* is the means by which experience, or a version of 'the way things are' is represented. The *interpersonal function* is the means by which the relations between the producer(s) of a text, the receiver(s) of a text and the content of a text are enacted. The *textual function* is the means by which ideational and inter-personal meanings are combined in a text in a way that makes it a coherent and cohesive whole.

In the discussion that follows, the structures by which each of these three functions are per-formed on online newspaper home pages are discussed.

The ideational function

The main home page of the *Guardian*, as shown in Plate 33.1, has three columns of news content. The left column of newsbites (which share essentially the same design, as discussed below – see also Figure 33.1) can be distinguished from the middle column of newsbites (which are dominated by an image with a superimposed headline). The third column of newsbites share the same design as the left column, but are grouped under headings (e.g. *Sport, Video Photography & Radio, Media*). The fourth, right-hand column consists of adver-tisements, menus and 'promotions' for *Guardian* content or other products/services provided by the institution, and is not news content.

This visual design of the news into three columns remains consistent as the reader scrolls down the page, with one important exception which is discussed below (under *The textual function*). The three columns act to classify the news, and provide a visual taxonomy of 'news' (left column), 'features' (middle column) and 'special' news (which is grouped into named cat-egories in the third column).

Online newspaper home pages vary in the extent to which they use visual taxonomies, and also the extent to which taxonomies are overt (with named categories and/or explicit devices such as borders and colour to frame different categories in the taxonomy). The visual taxonomy of news on the main home page of the *Guardian* as shown in Plate 33.1 is relatively overt, with clear, consistent columns framed by white spacing.

In comparison to the main home page, the *Culture* home page (second from left in Plate 33.1) makes a much greater use of horizontal sections. Columns are also employed as a categorisation device, but overall the use of headings and horizontal sections are much more important devices of categorisation on the *Culture* home page than they are on the main home page. The named categories (and sub-categories) of newsbites and newsbits on the *Culture* home page are:

a key generator of challenges and demands for multimodal theory and methods. Each of these issues and their consequences for multimodal research are briefly discussed here.

The social and cultural character of modes means that they are situated, fluid and changeable, rather than fixed and universal sets of resources and principles of use. In addition to creating inventories of modes and semiotic resources and analysing how these are used in a range of specific contexts, the purpose of several of the chapters in this handbook.

What a mode is, a question posed by Kress (Chapter 4), changes in relation to the social and cultural context and the expertise and knowledge of the person, and the resources of the environment. For instance, gesture in different contexts, in the surgical operating theatre (Bezemer, Chapter 25) or among tourists (Jarworski and Thurlow, Chapter 26), makes use of specific gestural resources and have significant similarities as well as differences in form and function. Digital technologies are an important aspect of context that can extend the range of resources for communication both by foregrounding particular modes and also by extending the resources of a mode or its organising principles in new ways. Application of multimodality to a range of digital technologies raises many interesting questions about modal resources. For example, can we now view digital filming and editing as modes in their own right? Given the increasingly central role of layout and layering in online environments can we talk of them as being modes?

Multimodality contributes to the discovery and development of new semiotic resources and new ways of using existing semiotic resources, as Van Leeuwen notes:

> Studying the semiotic potential of a given semiotic resource is studying how that resource has been, is, and can be used for purposes of communication, it is drawing up an inventory of past and present and maybe also future resources and their uses. By nature such inventories are never complete, because they tend to be made for specific purposes.
>
> (2005a: 17)

The discovery and development of new modal resources is linked to social change and society's need for new semiotic resources and new ways of using existing semiotic resources as the communicational landscape changes. Two factors central to this are the potentials of digital technology and the importing of semiotic resources in a global society. Digital synthesizers and other digital technologies, for example, have reshaped the possibilities of the 'human' voice to create new semiotic resources and contexts for the use of 'human' voices – in digital artefacts, public announcements, music and so on (Van Leeuwen, 2005a). This digital reshaping of voice has in turn impacted on the non-digital use of voice – for example providing different tonal or rhythmic uses of the non-digital voice not previously imagined. Similarly, digital technologies have been used to bring further knowledge of embodiment to bear on the development of human–technological interaction in general and extend the resources of movement in a range of contexts (Bayliss and McKinney, 2007; Wallis et al., 2010). For example, computer scientists working in robotics have collaborated with dancers to use embodiment in the field of performance with humans and robots in order to prototype and develop a robotic agent, designed to promote expressive interaction of the device and human dancers, in order to achieve 'performative merging' (Wallis et al., 2010). The digital has expanded and extended the resources of modes. Digitally enhanced aspects of the visual include digital visual effects (e.g. the visualizers that accompany audio players online, or performance software such as Isadora) and visual textural effects in software (e.g. PowerPoint) (Djonov and van Leeuwen, 2011).

The relationships across and between modes in multimodal texts and interaction are a central area of multimodal research, and multimodal research often investigates the relationship between a given context and the configuration of modes in a text or situated interactions – both to better understand the modal resources in use and to address substantive questions. The use of digital technologies can reshape the relationship between resources. A multimodal perspective can be used to analyse these configurations in the contemporary digital landscape. The ways in which contemporary digital texts are organized via textual features such as digital layering and hyperlinking and the impact of this on how people navigate multimodal digital texts has also been examined (e.g. Lemke, 2002b). Modal semiotic resources common to print based texts, such as textual linking, layering, layout, and the organization of time are also foregrounded and reconfigured in significant ways by digital technologies. Knox (Chapter 33), for example, has explored how online newspapers have reshaped newspaper layout, genres and the relationship of image, writing and video, and has mapped the 'wash-back' influence from online to print-based newspapers as well as reading pathways (Knox, 2007; Caple and Knox, 2012). Adami (2009) has examined the multimodal patterns of coherence and turn-taking on the social networking site YouTube.

Multimodal tools have the potential to identify and describe the reconfigurations of space, time and embodiment which digital technologies (e.g. mobile and GIS) make available, and address questions about how these technologies influence how people's interaction and experiences. As the design of digital technologies evolves so will modes as the digital serves to stretch and extend their material possibilities and semiotic resources in and through digital spaces.

This work is potentially useful when thinking about the take-up of designed resources (e.g. Jewitt, 2008a). Multimodality also has the potential to interrogate how spatiality and embodiment are configured and to draw attention to the new types of texts and/or interaction that are supported in emergent bodily interaction-based technologies. For instance, Wii games serve to reconfigure the relationships between players' physical bodies (and therefore social relationship), now with digital sensory feedback via wrist bands and body straps, virtual avatars, and the screen in ways that require physical digital mapping in interesting ways for what it means to collaborate and 'play together'. As this handbook illustrates, multimodality provides a set of resources to describe and interrogate these remappings, for example to get at the interaction across the 'physical' and the 'virtual' body. This type of digital remapping and extending of the physical is paramount in a range of digitally remediated contexts. The question of how screens and digital technologies remediate the role of the body is also relevant for understanding online multimodal interaction. Jones in his analysis of how people construct and consume multimodal displays of their selves in social networking environments (Chapter 9) examines how the different digital technologies available for producing and consuming displays affects the kinds of relationships that are possible between users of these sites and the kinds of social actions that these displays allow them to take.

A focus on mode, semiotic resources, materiality and modal affordance provides a descriptive language for examining interaction in these complex sites. For instance multimodal research in the surgical operating theatre shows the interactional impact of digital technologies being inserted into older established social environments (Bezemer et al., 2011). Surgeons undertaking key-hole surgery work in screen-based digital environments that, like the Wii, reorientate their gaze, body posture, team configurations, and require them to engage in physical–digital mapping. A multimodal approach also asks if the use of blended physical–digital tools of applications like those discussed here generate new forms of interaction and enable new action, physical, perceptual, and bodily experiences.

The iterative move between the designed affordances and constraints of digital technologies and what people can do with them is an ongoing design process and one which changes over time. No one can really know or predict what will happen with digital technologies and how they will unfold over the next decade or so. It is likely, however, that as the cost of digital complexity reduces we will see the mainstreaming of now elite and costly interactional forms – like eye tracking and gesture-based interaction; we will see new functionalities, new forms of interaction, new whole-body digital experiences. In short, the multimodal interaction potentials of digital technologies will increase and develop and in doing so extend communicative resources.

Multimodality moves beyond intuitive ideas about what a technology can do, to provide detailed analysis of the semiotic resources of digital technologies work, what they can and cannot do. It enables the construction of explicit understandings of a form of communication and thus makes it possible for these to be discussed, taught and evaluated. Multimodality can also help to design and implement new uses for semiotic innovations.

A core methodological strength of multimodality, evidenced by the chapters in this handbook, is that it can be applied to a broad range of texts, interactions, and contexts. That said, the particularities of these contexts place different demands on multimodal methodologies and it is certainly the case that digitally mediated representations, communication and interaction are a key generator of challenges for multimodal theory and methods. This includes challenges for data collection and management such as defining the unit of analysis and the how to conceive of this in the often blurry and unbounded landscape of the digital (e.g. the how to boundary a blog); how to transcribe digital data. The digital poses many challenges for multimodal methods such as, how to develop methods and theoretical concepts to capture the relationship between the text and the text in use; the naming of the yet un-named modal resources of the digital; processes of coding complex multimodal digital interactions; and how to analyse the multimodal character of digital texts in ways that move beyond atomising the text; methods for analysing time, space, embodiment. These are challenges that many of the researchers represented in this handbook are working on, including the MODE (the Multimodal Methods for Researching Digital Data and Environments project at MODE.ioe.ac.uk) team (directed by Jewitt with Bezemer, and including Price, Kress, Domingo, Flewitt, Burn, colleagues). These challenges that digital technologies throw up for multimodality is a focus for the future development of methods, concepts and analytical frameworks. This work will refine and extend the methodological repertoire of multimodality in ways that are of use beyond the realm of the digital.

Making new domains visible

Looking across the chapters in this handbook gives some indication of the degree to which multimodality is being taken up across a range of disciplinary fields and research sites (e.g. the classroom, the surgical operating theatre, touristic practice, the home). Multimodality draws attention to the 'non-linguistic' aspects and situates language (speech and writing) in a multimodal ensemble. This serves to make visible the representational and communicative practices of different sites, the types of texts that circulate across them and the practices that constitute them. In particular it helps to make explicit the modal resources and multimodal practices that are available in a site, the ways that these are used, and how participants articulate meaning and relationships through these. One role of multimodality is to make the invisible visible and to name processes that may have previously not been attended to: that is to seek out, interrogate and re-evaluate what may often be considered the mundane and marginalised aspects of communication. A future focus for multimodality is to extend into new domains, and their associated forms of representation, communication and interaction, that it can usefully make newly visible.

This handbook may serve as a useful guide to developing the three areas discussed in this concluding chapter and provide a starting point for addressing the question 'what next for multimodality?'.

Glossary

Active objects: Objects that require concrete physical action rather than mental consideration to complement them (Riggins 1990).

Activity system: This concept is central to the particular variant of a socio-cultural approach developed by A. N. Leontiev (but the idea is accepted by most scholars in this tradition). At an analytical level, a society can be thought of as divided into a number of activity systems (care, schooling, production, social services, etc.). Activity systems operate with different motives, and people's actions are therefore organized differently.

Actual semiotic potential: The meaning potential of a resource considered relevant by actual users in specific contexts (Van Leeuwen, 2005d). Depending on normative discourses, the social practice in which the resource is used and the specific needs of the user, this potential may to a larger or lesser degree coincide with the *theoretical semiotic potential* of the resource.

Affordance: A contested term, it originated in the work on cognitive perception of Gibson (1977) and was later taken up by Norman in relation to design (1988, 1990). Norman's view of affordance considers the material and social aspects of design. Modal affordance is used by Kress (1993) to refer to what it is possible to express and represent easily with a mode. From this perspective, affordance is used to refer to both the material *and* the cultural, and their connection.

Antonymy: The cohesive relation between elements of opposite meaning (e.g. good bad).

Appraisal theory: Concerned with evaluation – positive and negative – of emotions, people and things. In particular, the system of Attitude consists of three sub-systems: Affect, concerned with feelings and emotions; Judgement, which involves judging people's behaviour; and Appreciation, involving the appraisal of objects such as artworks.

Aural space (auditory space or acoustic space): This is a term used by soundscape designers to describe a lack of noticeable sound. Moments of aural space are used to redirect the attention of a listener, to build tension, or to simply let the ear rest from sound.

Avatar: A representation of oneself; in virtual worlds, the use of a digital depiction or symbol to mark one's identity.

Big 'D' Discourse: Situated speech that is shaped by saying–believing–doing–being–valuing–believing at particular times in particular places. The distinction was made by Gee to differentiate immediate strings of language from larger ways of being and doing. See also *little 'd' discourse*.

Binding: Concerned with the dialectic between affect and three-dimensional space. It is a scale that organizes spaces along a continuum from extreme openness to extreme closure. Extremes of binding evoke claustrophobic and agoraphobic responses, whereas median choices produce comfort zones of security and safety, or freedom and possibilities.

Bodily orientation/posture: This refers to the arrangements of people's bodies in relation to one another, objects and space, through the angle of their body, tilt, and spatial orientation of the body, and how this makes meaning (e.g. marking divisions in a group).

Bonding: A multidimensional resource concerned with the ways people negotiate affiliation around shared attitudes. In pedagogical and three-dimensional spaces like exhibitions, bonding is materialized by social interaction, learning activities, the hybridization of one space to serve multiple functions, bonding icons, and the (re-)alignment of visitors around shared attitudes.

Bonding icons: Social emblems of belonging. They include buildings (e.g. Sydney Opera House), leaders (e.g. Nelson Mandela), songs (e.g. national anthems) and symbols (e.g. flags). All bonding icons share two important characteristics: values get 'charged' into them and communities tend to either rally around them or reject them.

Chronotope: A term from Bakhtin, a typical pattern of narrative movement across settings (*topos*, space), including appropriate timings and pacings (*chronos*, time).

Cognition: In a socio-cultural perspective, thinking is seen as the ability of people to use intellectual tools that have emerged in culture. Thus, our understanding of the world is mediated by the fact that we have access to concepts, modes of reasoning and various forms of cultural expression (images, artefacts) which have developed over time.

Cognitive schemata theory: Describes networks of abstract structures through which individuals make interpretations, predictions and meaning out of combinations of memories and sensory input. Social schema theory describes how collective patterns of behaviour provide an external reality from which individuals acquire internal schemas. The metaphorical richness of texts can be interpreted in terms of schema theory where signs are looked upon as representations of schema assemblages.

Cohesive ties or cohesive links: Refers to meaningful non-structural relations between elements in a text, such as a pronoun referring to a noun or the repetition or synonymic/antonymic use of vocabulary, in foregoing or subsequent sentences.

Collective equality: One of the interactive meaning potentials of everyday objects. With regard to hierarchy, no single position in relation to the object is singled out by the design or layout of the object. For instance, in the case of tables, round tables have the meaning potential of 'collective equality'; the shape of the table top does not give prominence to one position around the table over another.

Connotational level: This is Roland Barthes' (1977b) second level of meaning of an image. Asking what an image connotes is to ask not just what is depicted but what ideas and values are communicated through what is represented, and through the way in which it is represented. While an image of a house may document a particular house at a particular time, at the connotational level it can communicate ideas such as belonging, wealth, safety, family or claustrophobia.

457

Connotative meaning of everyday objects: Stylistic variations in the shape or layout of objects with the same functional, denotative meaning (Krampen, 1989).

Contemplation value: Values or meaning potentials of passive objects, e.g. 'beauty' or 'calmness'.

Critical discourse analysis (CDA): A branch of linguistics that looks for the way that lexical and grammatical choices in language connote broader discourses. It asks what kind of world, social values, ideas and identities are being represented in the texts. The aim is to reveal what kinds of social relations of power are present in texts both explicitly and implicitly and therefore to show what kinds of inequalities and interests they seek to create or perpetuate.

Cross-modal plasticity: Recent advances in brain-imaging techniques have pointed to the functional equivalence or adaptability of the sensory-specific areas of the brain. For example, it is now clear that sensory-specific areas can be 'recruited' or 'remapped' by other sensory-specific areas in conditions of sensory deprivation, like blindness or deafness. Thus, visual cortex in blind individuals has been found to show activation in auditory tasks while auditory cortex in deaf individuals can be activated by visual tasks. This evidence of adaptive processing, or 'cross-modal plasticity', poses a serious challenge to the conventional model of the sensorium as consisting of five structurally and functionally distinct modalities.

Cross-sensory awareness: This is vital to the practice of *sensory ethnography*. It involves resisting the tendency to compartmentalize sense experience according to the conventional Western model of 'the five senses' and thinking across modalities instead. The enumeration, division and customary relations between sensory fields vary from one culture to the next.

Cultural studies: A field of scholarship that borrows disciplinary lenses from anthropology, sociology and critical theory in order to study cultural phenomena.

Deictic or pointing gestures: Movements of the body which indicate persons, objects, directions or locations, or may 'point to' non-existent or imaginary referents. They are usually associated with, but are certainly not limited to, the use of the extended index finger with the rest of the fingers closed. The meaning of pointing gestures is closely related to their physical environment, or 'gesture space' (Haviland, 2000), and may occur with or without speech.

Denotational level: Roland Barthes (1977b) described denotation as the first level of meaning of visual elements in an image. On this level images can be said to document. A photograph of a house simply depicts or documents that particular house at that particular moment. What this image means, such as 'home', 'suburbia' or 'wealth' is the second level of meaning. Of course no image has such 'innocent' or neutral meaning.

Denotative meaning of everyday objects: Direct functional meanings, which distinguish one type of object from another, e.g. a knife from a fork or a car from a bicycle (Krampen, 1989).

Design stratum: Refers to the category of media practices in which one uses semiotic resources, in all semiotic modes, to 'realize' discourses. A particular discourse can be realized in any number of ways. Also realized in design is the particular communication situation itself, 'which changes socially constructed knowledge into social (inter-)action' (Kress and Van Leeuwen, 2001: 5). See also *strata*.

Digital literacies: Literacy practices within digital contexts, using contemporary forms of communication such as text on screens, weblogs, text messaging, virtual worlds and gaming.

Discourse stratum: Refers to practices in which 'socially constructed knowledges of (some aspect of) reality' (Kress and Van Leeuwen, 2001: 4), function to organize social relations. Discourses, as constructions of reality, are ideologically laden and are available resources for people to work out particular designs. People often have many discourses available to them and select from among them. See also *strata*.

Distribution stratum: Refers to practices in the technical 're-coding' of semiotic products and events, for purposes of recording (e.g., tape recording, digital recording) and/or distribution (e.g., radio and television transmission, telephony). 'Recode' rather than 'record' is used to emphasize how distribution work is saturated with the production of meaning (Kress and Van Leeuwen, 2001: 21). See also *strata*.

Elaboration: A (logico-semantic) relation such that one element restates, specifies or clarifies the meaning of another.

Embodied action: All communicative action, whether spoken or textually represented, whether visual or auditory, is at the same time physically, spatially and bodily enacted (or accomplished). In the context of tourism and tourism studies, much has been made of the dominant role of vision (of 'sights') which tends to diminish the importance of the material, embodied experiences of tourists.

Embodiment: Refers to how media practices and social spaces are produced by the human body in its material form, and that the nature of the practices is in large part contingent on the forms, practices and plasticity of the human body. A person can also embody an identity or particular set of identities by the way one moves, interacts and communicates. Embodiment in this sense may be contrasted with represented bodies, such as avatars. However, it may also be argued that representations offer new forms of (virtual) embodiment.

Emic perspectives: Meanings and cultural practices interpreted and understood by people themselves in local contexts.

Enhancement: A (logico-semantic) relation such that one element qualifies the meaning of another (in terms of time, place, manner, cause, etc.).

Ethnographic research methods: Doing ethnography involves the framing, conceptualizing, conducting, interpreting, writing and reporting associated with a broad, in-depth and long-term study of a social or cultural group, meeting the criteria for doing ethnography as framed within a discipline or field, notably that of anthropology. Green and Bloome (1997) distinguish this from what they term an 'ethnographic perspective', by which they mean that it is possible to take a more focused approach (i.e. do less than a comprehensive ethnography) to study particular aspects of everyday life and cultural practices of a social group.

Etic perspectives: The interpretative framework used by the ethnographer to make sense of local 'emic' perspectives.

Extension: A (logico-semantic) relation such that one element adds to the meaning of another.

Eye-tracking: This methodology can be used to follow the reading and scanning process in detail. It can trace exactly what is looked at, where, when and how often. The gaze reveals the chosen entry points, reading paths and the connections made between text and images.

Fixations: This is a term used in eye-tracking methods to refer to stops or periods of time when the point of regard is relatively still. It is during fixations that researchers acquire useful information.

Fixation duration is often used as a measure of how much cognitive effort is required for information processing.

Frozen actions: A term coined by Norris to refer to actions that are somehow entailed in material objects, such as a half-full coffee cup which entails the action of drinking coffee or when investigating the layout of a room, we can identify the actions that have been taken or that are supposed to be taken, by the arrangement of the furniture.

Functional linguistics: Any work in linguistics which is primarily focused on deriving grammatical structures from the ways in which language is used as opposed to analysis of linguistic structure as language is abstracted from pragmatic usage. Many functional linguists trace their work to either or both the British linguist J. R. Firth and the early twentieth-century Prague school of linguists.

Functional specialization: Proposes that the resources of language are most apposite to the representation meanings such as those concerned with sequential relations and the making of categorical distinctions, while the resources of images are most apposite to the representation meanings such as those concerned with spatial relations and degree, quantity, gradation and continuous change.

Gaze: As in Urry's (2002) 'tourist gaze': a socially organized, systematized and regulated way of viewing and experiencing the world; follows, and is akin to, Foucault's (1973) earlier notions of discourse as institutionalized practice and knowledge production.

Genre: Configurations of semiotic choices unfolding as patterns of meaning in communicative objects and events which are particular to communities and cultures. Generic patterns can be seen as synoptic structures (e.g. orientation–complication–resolution–coda) or as dynamic phenomena which unfold or evolve over different place and time scales.

Genre theory: This differentiates between different types of texts on the basis of social purpose, staging (generic structure) and language features. In the past, genre theory has mainly been used to analyse spoken and written texts but it can also be applied to multimodal texts such as three-dimensional exhibitions.

Geosemiotic theory: Explores social meanings in the material placement of signs, in particular, how language and signs make meaning in relation to their physical placement in the world. It consists of three systems: interaction order, visual semiotics and place semiotics.

Grammatical mood: One of a set of distinctive verb forms that are used to signal modality in the sense of stance toward reality. Moods or modalities include conditional, imperative, indicative, injunctive, optative, potential, subjunctive.

Habitus: A term coined by Bourdieu (1990) to help explain the interplay of structural forces and individual agency in everyday life; habitus is the sum total of a person's socialized dispositions and ways of being; for the most part, individuals function largely unaware of the origins and/or sources of many of these dispositions and ways of being.

Higher-level action: An action with a starting and an ending point, which comprises many chains of lower actions. An example of a higher-level action is a conversation, which is made up of chains of utterances, chains of gesture units, chains of postural shifts, chains of gaze shifts, etc.

Hybridization: Involves the production of new cultural forms, identities, practices and spaces using multiple and diverse elements where the resultant artefact retains visible heterogeneity. For example, when an image and text are brought together in an advertisement, the result is a hybrid text in which both elements are present and whose functions are influenced by the other.

Hypertext: A medium of communication and expression in which elements within a segment of text are linked to other textual units which are not nearby, and may lie in other texts or files; the extension of such a medium to links among texts, images, videos, animations, etc.

Hyponymy: The cohesive relation between elements where one is a kind of another (e.g. spaniel dog).

Icon: One of the three basic categories of sign described by Charles Sanders Pierce, one of the pioneers in semiotics. Unlike words which are abstract and arbitrary, icons represent through similarity. For example, a picture of a house resembles a house in the real world. The figures of men and women that we see on toilet doors are icons. A photograph is an icon.

Iconic and metaphoric gestures: A continuum of body movements whereby the former stand in direct pictographic relationship to their referent (e.g. the speaker may accompany the mention of a building with the hand gesture tracing a rooftop), while the latter may exhibit images of abstract concepts or convey the speaker's relation to the object, e.g. as if the speaker were holding an object displaying it to the listeners without indicating the shape of the object.

Ideational concurrence: Refers to the similarity of the ideational meanings of two or more modalities, e.g. in writing and images, in the development of a text.

Ideational meaning: Meaning is concerned with the construal of experience and logical relations between meanings, such as temporal, causal and comparative relations.

Image dialogue: An exchange in which images become a dominant or singular modality for back-and-forth communication. Image exchange is thus taken up as a dialogic process, where one person offers an image in response to another's image, or in anticipation of another's image-based response.

Immediate use value: Values or meaning potentials of active objects such as 'to eat with' for a fork or 'to switch channels with' for a remote control.

Index: A sign that points to the nature of something, for example, an animal footprint points to the nature of the creature. The connection between the meaning and the sign is not arbitrary as in symbols but can therefore be to some extent observed as in smoke being an index of fire, a cough being the index of a cold, a finger pointing out a direction.

Indexical meaning: The kind of meaning relationship that depends on a material or causal connection between a sign and what it stands for, e.g. a footprint as a sign of a footstep.

Individual equality: One of the interactive meaning potentials of everyday objects that through their design create individuality and separateness between humans that surround them, but without the ranking of positions occupied by those humans. In the case of square tables, for instance, the different sides are separated from each other, but because of the equal length of the sides they all have the same hierarchical status, that of 'individual equality'.

Intellectual or symbolic tool: In the socio-cultural perspective, intellectual (or psychological or mental) tools are the means through which people think and communicate. Such tools (concepts, thought patterns, etc.) have emerged in culture over time, and are appropriated ('taken over') by children as they are socialized into cultural communities.

Interaction order: This is the first system of *geosemiotic theory*. It is concerned with social interactions that are structured. It involves objects (animate and inanimate) and actions (movement and gesture) as well as speech, language and discourses in place. The term was coined by Goffman to refer to the social relationships and situations which we create through language, interaction and behaviour, viz. the physical environment and other people in it. Different types of 'interaction orders' include the 'single' (a person alone in public), the 'with' (two or more people seen to be together), and the '*watch*' (one person or group creating a spectacle for another person or group to watch).

Interest: A term coined by Kress and refers to an individual's 'take' on the world at a particular moment in time as shaped by past experiences and in response to their interpretation of the immediate social context and representational need.

Intermodal identification: Refers to a relation between two modalities, e.g. writing and images, such that an element in one functions as the expression of an element in the other.

Intersemiotic (semantic) relationships: Meaning relations between the different semiotic systems such as writing and images that constitute a multimodal text.

Intertexts: Those other texts taken in some community to be of particular relevance to the interpretation of a given text.

Irrealis modes (moods): Constitute the main set of grammatical moods that indicate that a certain situation or action is not known to have happened as the speaker is talking. Common irrealis modes include optative, potential and subjunctive.

Kineikonic chronotope: A term adapted from Bakhtin's metaphor of space–time relations in literature to make the distinction between the spatial axis of the moving image and the temporal axis. That is, between the single frame (i.e. 'synchronic syntagm') and the moving sequence (i.e. 'diachronic syntagm'), such as movement of bodies, objects and landscapes; the movement of the camera and frame; and 'transitions' such as fades, wipes, or dissolves. This distinction allows for an analysis of spatial-static visual modes (e.g. the visual design of characters and sets) and the temporal modes.

Kineikonic mode: A term used in Burn's multimodal theory of the moving image. It is a combination of the Greek words for 'to move' (*kinein*) and 'image' (*eikon*). It works to emphasize the interplay of the modes that contribute to the moving image and its grammar: that is, the *contributing modes* (e.g. movement, lighting, costume, objects, sets and so on), and the *orchestrating modes* (the overarching framing systems in space and time – filming and editing).

Kinesics: The study of body language and movement from facial expressions and gestures to whole body movement.

Knowledge community: The concept of knowledge community emphasizes that knowledge develops around specific activities in society. Thus, it is not just individuals who learn and develop skills but so do collectives such as teams and organizations. A related term is community of practice, which also emphasizes the collective nature of knowing.

Leitmotifs: Short musical themes used to relate the music to the libretto or story of movies, operas or video games, and tie together a work into a coherent whole. They can also supplement or extend the plot. The concept is often associated with Wagner's extensive use of leitmotifs throughout his operas, where specific characters, things and situations were connected to certain musical themes.

Literacy practices: The broader cultural conception of particular ways of thinking about and doing reading and writing in cultural contexts. The knowledge, experience, feelings, values and capabilities that play a role in the reading and writing of texts including the models or conceptions of literacy held by those practising it.

Little 'd' discourse: Situated language practices that are connected stretches of language. It is a phrase that derives from the work of James Paul Gee. See also *big 'D' Discourse*.

Lower-level action: The smallest meaning unit of a communicative mode such as an utterance for spoken language, a gesture unit for gesture, a postural shift for posture, a gaze shift for gaze, and so on. Each lower-level action has a beginning and an ending point.

Machinima: This is perhaps most recent cultural form in the world of animation. 'Machinima' is a portmanteau word combining machine and cinema, and refers to the making animated films within a real-time 3-D environment (e.g. Second Life).

Mediated action: All communicative action is mediated in the sense that any 'message' is rendered meaningful partly or wholly by its context (e.g. the physical setting, participant relationship, tone or medium of a verbal message); all communication is therefore multimodal and systemic. Some messages are additionally *mediatized*. The notions of mediation and mediated action are central to a socio-cultural perspective. Mediated action implies that we think and act by means of the cultural and intellectual tools (concepts, discourses etc.) that have emerged in society. Concepts such as 'per cent', 'volt' and 'north' mediate the world for us in specific manners. Mediation also applies to physical tools such as hammers and rulers, which serve as resources for action in specific activities.

Mediatized discourse: While all language and communication is *mediated* some are also organized and produced in the institutional contexts of 'the media' (e.g. cinema, television, print media).

Meronymy: The cohesive relation between elements where one is a part of another (e.g. nose face).

Metafunction: The meaning potential – 'what can be meant' or 'what can be done' – with a particular set of modal (semiotic) resources. Michael Halliday (1985, 1994; Halliday and Matthiessen, 2004) proposes that four metafunctions are simultaneously realized in language; (a) experiential meaning: to construct experience of the world; (b) logical meaning: to make logical connections in that world; (c) interpersonal meaning: to enact social relations with that world; and (d) textual meaning: to create a semiotic world relevant to the phenomenal world being semioticized.

Metamodal relations: Burn uses this term in a multimodal theory of moving image to refer to the relationship between the orchestrating modes (filming and editing) and the contributory modes and to emphasize the nesting of modes within modes in moving image texts.

Mobile technologies: Digital artefacts – such as cameras, cell phones, and mp3 players – that are easily portable and that allow easy communication, documentation and text dissemination.

Modal complexity: An intricately interlinked mesh of numerous modes that allow for the construction of a higher-level action. The higher-level action of a dinnertime conversation, for example, is (co)constructed through the interlinked modes of spoken language, gesture, gaze, food, layout, and so on.

Modal configuration: The hierarchical relationships among modes that help construct a certain higher-level action. For example: in the construction of the higher-level action of a phone conversation, the object and the mode of object handling takes on the superordinate position, followed by the mode of spoken language.

Modal density: The modal intensity and/or complexity that makes up a higher-level action.

Modal intensity: The intensity or weight that a mode carries in the construction of a higher-level action. For example, the mode of spoken language takes on high modal intensity when social actors (co)construct the higher-level action of speaking on the phone.

Modal logics: The semiotic resources of each mode (or systems of semiotic resources) have come to be shaped through their different histories of usage. In turn, so has how people use modes to communicate. Each mode as it is realized in a particular social context comes to possess a specific logic and provides different communicational and representational potentials, referred to as modal logic.

Modality: There are two meanings in current use: (1) the mode of communication such as speech, writing or music (also sometimes called the medium of communication); (2) the linguistic expression of varying stances toward reality as indicated by words such as 'should', 'ought', 'may' (also sometimes called *grammatical mood*).

Mode: Within social semiotics, a mode – its organizing principles and resources – is understood as an outcome of the cultural shaping of a material. The resources come to display regularities through the ways in which people use them. In other words, in a specific context (time and place) modes are shaped by the daily social interaction of people.

Monomodal or monosemiotic: A communicative artefact or event is said to be monomodal when it is realized through a single communicative mode or semiotic resource (e.g. language, image or sound), for example, a written linguistic text or a photograph. Monosemiotic phenomena typically have one modality (i.e. visual, aural or somatic). Monomodal communication can be contrasted with *multimodal communication.*

Mood of address: Halliday (1985) was interested in the system in language for communicating mood. When we talk we communicate not only ideas, but about our relationship to those ideas as in when we make demands on people through the imperative mood. Halliday called this the 'interpersonal function' of language. In multimodality can ask how images also fulfil this function. For example, a bold and saturated colour can communicate emotional intensity.

Motor gestures (batons, beats): Always occur with speech and appear to be coordinated with the prosody of the speaker's voice.

Multilingual literacies: Literacy as manifested in many different languages, and many different script systems, realized in multiple locations and languages.

Multiliteracies: An approach to literacy learning based on an understanding of design and linguistic diversity.

Multimodal artefact: An object or a text in which more than one semiotic mode combine as resources for meaning-making.

Multimodal communication: Where there are degrees of combinations of different modes.

Multimodal ensemble: Refers to interrelationships between co-present modes. As the resources of different modes are combined, meanings are corresponding, complementary and dissonant as they harmonize in an integrated whole.

Multisemiotic: A communicative artefact or event which is constructed using more than semiotic resource (e.g. language, image and/or sound), for example a mathematics text consisting of language, mathematical images and mathematical symbolism. Multisemiotic texts may have one modality (visual, aural or somatic), for example, printed mathematics texts, which have a visual modality only, or multiple modalities (visual, aural and/or somatic), for example, classroom mathematics lessons.

New Literacy Studies: An approach to literacy learning as a social practice – shaped by context, texts and practices used to make meaning.

Nexus of practice: A term coined by Scollon (2001a) to describe an intersection of different, repeatable practices that are recognized as a specific genre of activity *and* the group of people engaging in that activity; the term is closely related to the notion of multimodality (Kress and Van Leeuwen, 2001). See also *mediated action*.

Orbital structures: Model experiential meaning. In orbital structures, there is one main element, a nucleus, and several dependent elements, the satellites. In three-dimensional spaces such as exhibitions a central element, e.g. a text panel, can function as the nucleus while the objects displayed around it (satellites) may elaborate its nuclear meanings.

Orders of indexicality: A term coined by Blommaert to refer to stratified, ordered patterns of indexical values attached to semiotic signs and creating specific expectations about meaning in particular social situations.

Organizational technologies: The organizations and institutions which shape semiotic products and events. Organizational technologies include universities, government bodies, corporations and research institutes which regulate and monitor products, collective goals and performances, actions and events. Organizational technologies impact on meaning-making and the nature of the *semiotic landscape*.

Parametric systems: Parametric systems organize semiotic resources as a set of parameters which all play a role in every instance, though to varying degrees. For example, all colours combine the parameters of hue (a value on the scale from red to blue), brightness (a value on the scale from light to dark), saturation (a value on the scale from the fullest expression of a colour to the most diluted, 'pastel' expression of the colour), as well as several other characteristics.

Passive objects: Objects that do not require physical action to complement them (Riggins, 1990), but often require mental consideration.

Path–Venue: Concerned with the channelling of people through three-dimensional space. Paths are the conduits along which people move. They can be vertical or horizontal, linear or circular, stationary or moving. The point at which people are deposited is the venue. Venues are thus places where people stop, stay and engage.

Performance: Termed after Goffman (1959), a metaphoric description of the everyday enactment, management and negotiation of social roles/identities; now also closely related to the notion of *performativity* (cf. Butler, 1990).

Performativity: A term coined by Bulter (1990) which accounts for the production of these identities as 'natural' through reiterative individual and cultural performances. (For example, in the context of tourism, performance is often used with specific reference to the staging of authentic cultural identities – and tourists' desire for encounters with an 'authentic' other.)

Phenomenology: A philosophical project which tries to reason from immediate experience and critique traditional categories imposed on experience (time, space, motion, person, etc.).

Place semiotics: Analyses the material locations in which human actions and social interactions take place. It includes both natural and built environments. There are three sub-systems of place semiotics: code preferences, inscription (fonts, physical materials, add-ons and extensions) and emplacement (decontextualized, situated or transgressive).

Platform events: A kind of '*watch*' in which the spectacle and the watchers are clearly separated by spatial configuration or features of the built environment (such as a raised stage) and in which the roles of spectacle and watcher are clearly differentiated. Examples include stage plays, beauty pageants and classrooms.

Polysemic: The ability of a sign, a visual element or feature to have multiple meanings or interpretations. What a painting or element in a painting, for example, means is therefore never fixed or singular but open. In Post Structuralism this meant that since there was always more than one interpretation of a sign we could never attempt to speak of its true meaning at all. Of course this creates problems for the very idea of truth and knowledge.

Pragmatics: The study of the social uses of language and paralinguistic means of communication including eye contact, gesture, conversational turn-taking. Pragmatics also includes the study of the force of an utterance in actual use as opposed to its potential meaning as an abstract code.

Production stratum: Refers to practices within the 'actual material articulation of the semiotic event or the actual material production of the semiotic artefact' (Kress and Van Leeuwen, 2001: 6). Production does not simply 'realize' designs in a straightforward, mechanical way (p. 66); rather, the specificities of material production, including the physical qualities and *affordances* of materials used (e.g., paint, clay, digital images, construction paper), shape new meanings. For instances, it is recognized that typographic form adds meaning to printed text, and that intonation and voice quality, similarly, add meaning to spoken text. See also *strata*.

Prominence: A tool concerned with 'people flow' in three-dimensional space. Analogous to Kress and Van Leeuwen's notion of salience, prominence is also concerned with attracting the viewer's attention but it aims to attract attention in order to draw people out of one space and lead them into another.

Prosthetic embodiments: A term used to describe the technological extension or enhancement of the capacities of the human body (e.g. the use of glasses, binoculars or cameras to extend sight). In practice, these technologies are no less a part of the body (cf. Haraway, 1991, on cyborg theory). See also *mediated action*.

Proxemics: The study of the uses of space, especially of the distances between speakers, to produce interpersonal meanings in language use.

Psychoanalytic theory: Theories of human motivation and behaviour which, following S. Freud, give prominence to the role of biological drives and unconscious desires in interaction with a conscious ego and its identity.

Rank: In systemic functional multimodality it is common, following O'Toole (1994), to approach analysis of an image or other media at specific levels or rank. These reduce from the work as a whole, to episode, figure and member. At each level the analyst considers how the elements or their combination realize the representational (ideas), modal (mood or attitude) and compositional functions. So a figure might realize the modal function through grace or stance.

Realis modes (moods): These constitute a category of grammatical moods which indicate that something is actually the case (or actually not the case); in other words, the state of which is known. The most common realis mood is the indicative mood, or declarative mood.

Register: In functional and discourse linguistics, a particular range of meanings that are typically at stake in some cultural activity or situation and found in its texts.

Remediation: The refashioning of established genres such as perspective paintings, photography, film and television in new digital media genres such as digital photography, computer games, and virtual reality. Remediation in new media brings to the forefront the significance of technology in the shaping of the *semiotic landscape*

Remixing: A form of *hybridization* in which cultural artefacts – such as music, art, lyrics – are manipulated and recombined in order to transform their original meaning. Recent examples include movie trailers that have been digitally remixed to convey new meanings: e.g., *The Shining* as a romantic comedy.

Representational gestures (gesticulations, etc.): Also referred to as 'ideational gestures', 'illustrators', or 'mimes'. They can co-occur, alternate with or replace speech and are generally associated with overcoming a lack in vocabulary or other linguistic means of expression, for example due to a large distance between the interactants, noisy environment, etc. These gestures are not fully conventionalized yet they appear to form a continuum of *iconic* to *metaphoric* gestures.

Representational meaning: Meaning is concerned with the construal of material or mental experience – the processes, participants and circumstances involved. Also known as experiential meaning.

Resemiotization or Resemioticization: A term coined by Iedema to refer to the phenomenon (or in the case of resemioticization, the process) in which a particular set of meanings is transformed from one semiotic system (and configuration of media and modes) to another as social processes unfold, as, for example, when an architect's drawing is transformed into a building, thus resulting in a change of meaning within and across contexts.

Reterritorialization: Refers to how social spaces are undergoing change and transformation in a world where the 'space of flows' (Castells, 2000) co-exists with place and boundary making. New territory construction involves not only the movement of old boundaries, or new divisions within bounded spaces, but also the way in which multiple social spaces are knit together, patched, cut up, laminated, and folded together.

Saccades: A term used in eye-tracking methodologies. During saccades the eyes move at a relatively rapid rate to reorient the point of regard from one spatial position to another. Saccades are very short, usually lasting from 20–40 milliseconds. Our vision is suppressed and we are essentially blind during saccades.

Scientific technologies: The tools and crafts most typically produced in science, applied mathematics and engineering. Scientific technologies include technical products and instruments produced in civil and electrical engineering, medicine, biotechnology, military research and nuclear research, for example, and data processing technologies such as computer hardware and software. Scientific technologies impact on meaning-making and the resulting nature of the *semiotic landscape*.

Semiosis: The act of meaning-making using *semiotic resources* (e.g. language, images, gesture, music and sound). The resulting patterns of meaning construct a social reality within its cultural context, relevant to a situation. The *semiotic landscape* consisting of communicative artefacts and events arising from semiosis is known as culture.

Semiotic landscape: Refers to the way *semiotic resources* are used in a specific historical and social–cultural setting. It includes the kinds of resources used, the degree to which they are used, the purposes for which they are used and the ways in which they are combined into multimodal texts or used separately. It also includes people's attitudes towards specific semiotic resources, and the way in which their use is learned and regulated.

Semiotic resources: The actions, materials and artefacts we use for communicative purposes – these can be physiological or technological – and the ways in which these resources can be organized. Theo Van Leeuwen (2005a: 285) states that 'Semiotic resources have a meaning potential, based on their past uses, and a set of affordances based on their possible uses, and these will be actualized in concrete social contexts where their use is subject to some form of semiotic regime'.

Semiotic system: Refers to the systematic way in which the use of *semiotic resources* is organized to convey meanings: writing, images, gestures and clothing are all semiotic systems.

Semiotic technologies: The technologies through which material objects are made, events take place, and the social and physical environment is controlled. Semiotic technologies consist of scientific and organizational technologies which impact on meaning-making and the nature of the *semiotic landscape*.

Semioticization of materiality: Materials and material qualities are semioticized when people begin to use them to convey meanings. This may be done in a number of ways. Explicit and more-or-less arbitrary codes could be developed, for instance colour codes linking specific colours to specific meanings. Meanings could also derive from cultural associations, e.g., in the case of colour, gold and 'royal purple', or from the metaphorical extension of a quality of the material, or an aspect of its articulation. For instance, literal irregularity in printed letter forms can come to mean 'rebelliousness', 'playfulness', 'lack of control' and so on, depending on the context.

Semiotics: This is broadly the study of signs. These can be road signs, the signs on toilet doors, words or the elements that make up an image. Ferdinand de Saussure has been credited with founding the systematic study of the importance of signs in social life over one hundred years ago. Other theorists such Charles Sanders Pierce and Roland Barthes have pioneered approaches to studying visual semiotics. Pierce was particularly interested in the range of different kinds of signs that can be found as compared to language that comprises abstract symbols. Semiotics has evolved to form a 'toolkit' to look beneath the surface of communicative artefacts and uncover their structural and functional regularities.

Sensory anthropology: This is 'primarily concerned with how the patterning of sense experience varies from one culture to the next in accordance with the meaning and emphasis attached to each of the modalities of perception. It is also concerned with tracing the influence such variations have on forms of social organization, conceptions of self and cosmos, the regulation of the emotions, and other domains of cultural expression' (Howes, 1991: 3).

Sensory ethnography: The practice of sensory anthropology. It involves the study of the social life of the senses in cultural context through the technique of 'participant sensation' (a variant of the conventional anthropological method of participant observation). Most essential to the successful pursuit of this science is the ability to bracket the assumptions of the Western psychology of perception and willingness to experiment with alternative ways of sensing.

Sensory fields: A field of sense is a culturally delimited domain of perception. Different cultures elaborate these domains to different degrees. In the West, for example, the power of vision has been extended technologically and metaphorically far beyond any of the other senses, while in so-called oral cultures hearing is often the dominant or master sense. However, rather than focus on dominance, it is best to attend to the ever-shifting relations between the senses to arrive at a full understanding of how the fields articulate.

Serial structures: Another way of modelling experiential meaning. Serial structures involve multiple nuclei, which are serially related. Thus the text/exhibition unfolds, step by step, with each step dependent on what immediately precedes it. This makes them a popular choice for temporally unfolding exhibitions such as recounts.

Sign activity: Any activity which people perform with signs.

Sign comprehension: Refers to the cognitive processes or mental patterns that may be assumed to be in operation upon comprehending signs/texts in socially situated communication.

Sign repertoires: Concerns which types of signs are present in a text and how they build codes as well as identifying their strengths and weaknesses.

Sign/text structure: Concerns how signs combine to form patterned texts (complex messages) in one mode and across modes, as well as how sign-makers and text-producers use their artefacts in communication.

Sign vehicle: The physical embodiment of a sign through which particular meanings or sets of meaning are transferred from one person to another.

Sites of display: Social occasions in which particular configurations of modes and media converge in a specific time and space in order to make particular social actions possible.

Socio-cultural approach: This approach to learning and development is grounded in the work of Lev S. Vygotsky (1896–1934) and his followers, in particular A. Luria (1902–1977) and A. N. Leontiev (1903–1979). Vygotsky was concerned with the cultural development of the child. He formulated his ideas in opposition to the dominant simplistic *stimulus–response* theories. Vygotsky argues that 'higher forms of psychological functioning' (thinking, memory, etc.) are social in origin, and children appropriate them through social interaction.

Socio-genesis: All cultural tools have a history. For instance, our current alphabetic script originates in other modes of writing (pictographs, logographic and syllabic writing). In a socio-cultural perspective, the history of transformations that cultural tools undergo in society is often interesting to study, since it gives insights into how abstract symbolic systems have emerged. The history may also add to our understanding of why they may be difficult to learn.

Socio-genetic perspective: This implies that one examines the origin and transformation of social practices and of the cultural tools used. For example, one might inquire into how the intellectual tools of systems of navigation and way-finding have developed through history, and how have the technologies have changed.

Socio-linguistics: The study of the effect of aspects of society on language or, conversely the study of the effects of the use of language on social organization either at local, interpersonal levels or more broadly. In some cases there is much overlap between work in socio-linguistics and in *pragmatics*.

Space (conceived, perceived, lived): In theorizing space as both a socially/culturally constructed as well as physical/material phenomenon, Lefebvre (1991) proposed that any experience of space ('lived' space) is a combination of its material properties ('perceived' space) and its symbolic representation ('conceived' space).

Stimulus–response connections: The idea of stimulus–response connections as the foundation of learning is the key element of behaviourism (and in Russia during Vygotsky's time, of reflexology). The original, basic assumption is that humans learn by being conditioned to respond to stimuli in novel manners; a natural response (salivation at the sight of food) is conditioned to appear as a conditioned response when the sound and food have been presented together for some time (classical conditioning).

Strata: Four 'layers' of media practices: *discourse* (a particular knowledge about some aspect of reality); *design* (the shaping of this knowledge into a particular kind of text or communicative event, for instance a story, or a report); *production* (the physical realization of the design, for instance the performance of a musical composition or the reading of a script); and *distribution* (the technical recoding of the message for purposes of storage and/or distribution, for instance, the broadcasting of a film). Different kinds of meaning are produced in and by each of these layers. They recognize how a vast array of media practices, on a continuum between the content and expression of communication, participate in the production of meaning. These strata of practices also recognize how semiotic meaning-making organizes and is organized by different social relations (Kress and Van Leeuwen, 2001).

Symbiotic and transformative gestures: Symbiotic gestures are performed and made meaningful in relation to a particular environmental structure; transformative gestures act upon what they are representing, physically altering the environment performing the act of 'inscription' (Goodwin, 2003b).

Symbol: A sign that has arbitrary meaning. Some signs (*icons*) can resemble things in the world – a picture of a house resembles a house in the real world. But symbols possess no such resemblance and are abstract. Their meaning must, therefore, be learned. Examples are words and numbers.

Symbolic notation: Any system that represents certain aspects of music through the use of written symbols. Musical notation is typically used as a guide with various symbols and signs of different logics, representing complex conventions of musical performance. Before the invention of modern recording techniques it was the only way to save and distribute musical works and is still regarded as the original documentation for many musical works.

Symbolic or emblematic gestures: Autonomous body movements independent of speech whose meaning has been conventionalized so that they may be easily interpreted within a discourse community, e.g. the 'thumbs up' gesture as an expression of approval in the English-speaking world.

Synaesthesia: The union or crossing of the senses such that the percipient experiences one sensation in terms of another, as in the case of hearing colours or tasting shapes. Synaesthesia is an artistic, cultural and even spiritual aspiration, quite apart from whatever might be said about it as a neurological oddity.

Synonymy: The cohesive relation between elements of similar meaning (e.g. couch divan).

System network: A taxonomic representation of the systematic, semiotic options that are possible within a semiotic or lexicogrammatical system or sub-system, e.g. the system of mood in English or the interactive meaning potential of an object or artefact, along with their realizations. The options should preferably be of the either/or type, usually indicated by square brackets. As described by Halliday (1994), for instance, a linguistic utterance may either be a 'demand for information' (question) or an 'offer of information' (statement). A 'demand for information', in turn may either be 'polar' (yes/no question) or not, and so on. In practical artefacts and objects some semiotic relations are better described as scaled, marked by double-edged dotted arrows, e.g. that between high involvement potential with, or detachment from, a person or an object.

Systemic functional analysis: A theoretical and practical approach to multimodal analysis based on Michael Halliday's (1985, 1994; Halliday and Mathiesson, 2004) systemic functional social semiotic theory, which views social reality and culture as patterns of meaning arising from semiotic choices. The systemic functional approach is functional and semantic in orientation, and it involves describing the meaning potential of semiotic resources as systems of meaning that are realized as paradigmatic features in multimodal objects and events.

Theoretical semiotic potential: The meaning of a semiotic resource made up by its previous and potential uses and functions (Van Leeuwen, 2005a). History, culture and social life constantly restrict, but also enable, the theoretical semiotic potentials of resources. See also *actual semiotic potential*.

Timescale events: Events that carry an inherent periodicity. For example, a breath, a cardiopulmonary timescale event which lasts a fraction of a second, or the day–night cycle of sleeping and waking which normally takes 24 hours.

Transduction: Kress's more recent formulations define transduction as a process of translation in which meaning-material is moved from one mode to another (Kress, 2010a; MODE, 2012). For example, writing might be remade as drawing, or speech as action – and this becomes increasingly complex when more than one mode is entailed.

Transformation: This is a foundational principle in social semiotics. It highlights the creative, agentive action of *sign-making*, which is based on the selection of apt, available resources to represent and communicate the sign-maker's interest. The term 'transformation' foregrounds the challenge by social semiotic theory to dominant theories of language as use of a 'stable (and largely autonomous) system of elements, categories and rules of combination'. Rather, the makers of messages 'stretch, change, adapt, and modify all of the elements used, all the time, and thereby change the whole set of representational resources with its internal relations' (Kress, 2000a:155).

Translocal or glocal: Refers to existing across time and space boundaries; for instance, identities travel (across multiple spaces and times) rather than remaining fixed in place.

Transmedia: A term widely used to name the phenomenon of the circulation and convergence of content across a range of media platforms (Jenkins, 2006a), while the term 'transmedia traversals' is used by Lemke (2007) to convey a sense of a 'dynamic semiotic cycle in which users interpret what is being displayed to them across many media'.

Transmedia franchise: Thematically unified collections of different media (books, films, games, websites, etc.), usually sharing common characters and real or fictional histories, but with different creators, often licensed by a claimant to intellectual properties rights in these characters and histories.

Transmodal: Used to categorize semiotic movement across modes as an external, material practice. This seems an apt term, since if multimodality refers to the existence and interaction of multiple modes as resources for meaning-making, 'transmodality' refers to a particular process, the shifting of modes – or 'multi-modes'.

Transmodal moment: This concept focuses attention on the multiple transformations that occur in processes of transduction – in materiality, genre, meaning, subjectivity and learning – as well as revealing the situatedness of transmodal semiotic action. That is, the examination of processes of transmodal translation in chains of semiosis. The move from one mode to the other has profound implications for meaning because of changes to what it is possible to mean. Given material variations and differences in the histories of social and cultural work, there can never be a 'perfect translation' from one mode to another. It is the task of the researcher to identify instances of transduction and to ask what is sustained, what is gained and what is lost.

Vectors: In mathematics and physics, vectors are used to indicate directions of force and velocity in the form of arrows. In much the same way, Arnheim (1969) argued that images may contain elements and shapes that serve to create vectors that for the viewer are used as cues for the relations between parts of the image. They are used by the eye as a guide for where to look. Kress and Van Leeuwen (1996) showed that vectors in images, such as a pointing finger, or direction of gaze, can be used to set up narrative structures.

Visual semiotics: This uses the grammar of visual design developed by Kress and Van Leeuwen combined with an analysis of how placing objects in space impacts on their meanings. Visual grammar tools include narrative/conceptual systems, interactive systems (contact, social distance, power, involvement) and modality, plus compositional principles (Given–New, salience, framing).

Visual studies: This is a highly interdisciplinary field combining approaches to the visual from art history, photography, media studies, critical theory, philosophy, documentary and cultural studies. Key writers in the field have been W.J.T. Mitchell, James Elkins and Mieke Bal who have written extensively on the nature of seeing and been involved in debates about the comparison of language and visual communication often through the journal *Critical Inquiry*.

Visual syntax: In linguistics 'syntax' refers to the rules governing the structure of sentences and therefore to the kinds of combinations and patterns that can be produced. 'Visual syntax' is an extension of the term in order to describe the rules governing the combining of visual elements and features in visual communication. The syntax is the relationship between these on the page.

'Watch': A configuration of social actors in which one social unit (person or group) provides a spectacle for another social unit (person or group) to watch.

Web 2.0 platforms: Refer to the evolution of software and digital infrastructure designed to promote and build on social capabilities of the internet. Examples include social networking sites, video sharing sites, wikis and blogs.

References

Adami, E. (2010) *Contemporary Patterns of Communication: The Case of Video-Interaction on YouTube*, London: LAP Lambert Academic Publishing.

Adolphs, S., Knight, D. and Carter, R. (2011) 'Capturing context for heterogenous corpus analysis: Some first steps.' *International Journal of Corpus Linguistics* 16(3): pp. 305–24.

Adorno, T. (1938/1982) 'On the fetish character in music and the regression of listening.' In Arato, A. and Gebhart, E. eds. *The Essential Frankfurt School Reader*, New York: Continuum.

Agar, M. (1996) *The Professional Stranger: An Informal Introduction to Ethnography*, 2nd edition, New York: Academic Press.

Aikman, S. (1999) *Intercultural Education and Literacy: An Ethnographic Study of Indigenous Knowledge and Learning in the Peruvian Amazon*, Amsterdam: Benjamins.

Ainsworth, S. (1999) 'A functional taxonomy of multiple representations.' *Computers and Education* 33: pp. 131–52.

—— (2008) 'The educational value of multiple representations when learning complex scientific concepts.' In Gilbert, J. K., Reiner, M. and Nakhlel, M. eds. *Visualization: Theory and Practice in Science Education*, New York: Springer: pp. 191–208.

Alač, M. and Hutchins, E. (2004) 'I see what you are saying: Action as cognition in fMRI brain mapping practice.' *Journal of Cognition and Culture* 4(3): pp. 629–61.

Albers, P. and Sanders, J. eds. (2010) *Literacies, the Arts and Multimodality*, Urbana, IL: National Council of Teachers of English.

Alexander, J. and Jakobs, R. (1998) 'Mass Communication, ritual and civil society.' In Liebes, T. and Curran, J. eds. *Media, Ritual and Identity*, London: Routledge.

Alibali, M. W., Flevares, L. and Goldin-Meadow, S. (1997) 'Assessing knowledge conveyed in gesture: Do teachers have the upper hand?' *Journal of Educational Psychology* 89: pp. 183–93.

Allwood, J. (2008) 'Multimodal corpora.' In Lüdeling, A. and Kytö, M. eds. *Corpus Linguistics: An International Handbook*, Vol. 1, Berlin: Mouton de Gruyter: pp. 207–25.

Althusser, L. (1971) *Lenin and Philosophy*, New York: Monthly Review Press.

Álvarez, I., Pérez, H. and Pérez-Carreño, F. eds. (2010) *Expression in the Performing Arts and the Study of Classroom Language and Literacy Events: A Microethnographic Approach*. Mahwah, NJ: Erlbaum.

Alvermann, D. E. ed. (2002) *Adolescents and Literacies in a Digital World*, New York: Peter Lang.

Alvermann, D. E., Hagood, M. C. and Williams, K. B. (2001) 'Images, language, and sound: Making meaning with popular culture texts.' *Reading online*. Available at www.readingonline.org/newliteracies/lit_index.asp?HREF=action/alvermann/indx.html (accessed 14 January 2009).

Andersson, R., Ferreira, F. and Henderson, J. M. (2011) 'I see what you're saying: The integration of complex speech and scenes during language comprehension.' *Acta Psychologica* 137: pp. 208–16.

Andrà, C., Arzarello, F., Ferrara, F., Holmqvist, K., Lindstrom, P., Robutti, O. and Sabena, C. (2009) 'How students read mathematical representations: An eye tracking study.' In *Proceedings of the 33rd Conference of the International Group for the Psychology of Mathematics Education*, Vol. 2: pp. 49–56.

Andrews, R. (2004) 'Where next in research on ICT and literacies.' *Literacy Learning: The Middle Years* 12(1): pp. 58–67.

Androutsopoulos, J. (2006) 'Sociolinguistics and computer-mediated communication.' *Journal of Sociolinguistics* 10(4): pp. 419–38.

Appadurai, A. (1981) 'Gastropolitics in Hindu South Asia.' *American Ethnologist* 8: pp. 494–511.

—— (1996) *Modernity at Large: Cultural Dimensions of Globalization*, Minneapolis, MN: University of Minnesota Press.

Arbib, M. A. (1995) 'Schema theory.' In Arbib, M. A. ed. *Brain Theory and Neural Networks*, Cambridge, MA: MIT Press: pp. 830–34.

Archer, A. (2006) 'A multimodal approach to academic "literacies": Problematising the visual/verbal divide.' *Language and Education* 20(6): pp. 449–62.

—— (2007) '"No goats in the mother city": Using symbolic objects to help students talk about diversity and change.' *English in Education* 41(1): pp. 7–20.

—— (2008) 'Cultural studies meets academic literacies: exploring students' resources through symbolic objects.' *Teaching in Higher Education* 13(4): pp. 383–94.

—— (2013) 'Voice as design: Exploring academic voice in multimodal texts in higher education.' In Pachler, N. and Boeck, M. eds. *Transformation of Representation: Essays in Honour of Gunther Kress*, London: Routledge (in press).

Arendt, H. (1973/1990) *On Revolution*, London: Penguin.

Aristotle (1941) 'De Interpretatione (On Interpretation).' Edghill, E. M., trans. In McKeon, R. ed. *The Basic Works of Aristotle*, New York: Random House.

—— (1976) *The Nicomachean Ethics*, Thompson, A. K., trans., Harmondsworth: Penguin.

Arnheim, R. (1967) *Film as Art*, Berkeley, Los Angeles: University of California Press.

—— (1969) *Visual Thinking*, Berkeley, Los Angeles: University of California Press.

Aubert, O. and Prié, Y. (2005) 'Advene: Active reading through hypervideo.' In *ACM Conference on Hypertext*: pp. 235–44. doi:10.1145/1083356 1083405.

Auer, P., Couper-Kühlen, E. and Müller, F. (1999) *Language in Time: The Rhythm and Tempo of Spoken Interaction*, Oxford: Oxford University Press.

Avery, T. (2007) 'Furniture design and colonialism: Negotiating relationships between Britain and Australia, 1880–1901.' *Home Cultures* 4(1): pp. 69–92.

Babbage, C. (1827) 'On the influence of signs in mathematical reasoning.' *Transactions of the Cambridge Philosophical Society, II*.

Bacall, L. (1979) *Lauren Bacall By Myself*, New York: Random House.

Bakhtin, M. M. (1981) 'Forms of time and of the chronotope in the novel.' In Holquist, M. ed. *The Dialogic Imagination: Four Essays by M. M. Bakhtin*, Austin, TX: University of Texas Press: pp. 84–258.

—— (1986) *Speech Genres and Other Late Essays*, Austin, TX: University of Texas Press.

Bal, M. (1991) *Reading 'Rembrandt': Beyond the Word–Image Opposition*, Cambridge: Cambridge University Press.

Baldry, A. (2004) 'Phase and transition, type and instance: Patterns in media texts as seen through a multimodal concordancer.' In O'Halloran, K. ed. *Multimodal Discourse Analysis: Systemic Functional Perspectives*, London: Continuum: pp. 83–108.

—— (2007) 'The role of multimodal concordances in multimodal corpus linguistics.' In Royce, T. D. and Bowcher, W. L. eds. *New Directions in the Analysis of Multimodal Discourse*, Mahwah, NJ: Lawrence Erlbaum Associates: pp. 173–94.

Baldry, A. and Thibault, P. (2006) *Multimodal Transcription and Text Analysis*, London: Equinox.

Baldry, A. and Montagna, E. eds. (in press) *Interdisciplinary Perspectives on Multimodality: Theory and Practice*, Campobasso: Palladino.

Banks, M. (2007) *Using Visual Data in Qualitative Research*, London: Sage.

Barnett, C. (2003) *Culture and Democracy: Media, Space and Representation*, Edinburgh: Edinburgh University Press.

Barnhurst, K. G. and Nerone, J. (2001) *The Form of News: A History*, New York: Guilford Press.

Barnouw, E. (1968) *The Golden Web: A History of Broadcasting in the United States 1933–1953*, New York: Oxford University Press.

Barthelson, M. (2002) 'Reading behaviour in online news reading.' Unpublished MA thesis, Lund University. Available online at http://www.sol.lu.se/humlab/eyetracking/Studentpapers/MariaBarthelson.pdf (accessed 6 October 2013).

Barthes, R. (1957/1972) *Mythologies*, Lavers, A. trans., New York: Hill & Wang.

—— (1973) *Mythologies*, London: Fontana.

—— (1977a) 'The grain of the voice.' In *Image, Music, Text*, Heath, S., trans., London: Fontana.

—— (1977b) *Image, Music, Text*, London: Fontana.

—— (1977c) *Elements of Semiology*, New York: Hill & Wang.

—— (1977d) 'The rhetoric of the image.' In *Image, Music, Text*, Heath, S., trans., London: Fontana.

—— (1978) 'The third meaning.' In *Image, Music, Text*, Heath, S., trans., New York: Hill & Wang.

—— (1996) 'Denotation and connotation.' In Cobley, P. ed. *The Communication Theory Reader*, London: Routledge: pp. 129–33.

Bartholomew, A. (2003) *Electric Gadgets and Gizmos*, Sydney: Scholastic.

Bartlett, L. (2005) 'Identity work and cultural artefacts in literacy learning and use: A sociocultural analysis.' *Language and Education* 19: pp. 1–9.

Barton, D. and Hamilton, M. (1998) *Local Literacies: Reading and Writing in One Community*, London: Routledge.

Barton, D., Hamilton, M. and Ivanic, R. (2000) *Situated Literacies*, London: Routledge.

Bateman, J. (2008) *Multimodality and Genre: A Foundation for the Systematic Analysis of Multimodal Documents*, New York: Palgrave-Macmillan.

—— (2011) 'The decomposability of semiotic modes.' In O'Halloran, K. L. and Smith, B. A. eds. *Multimodal Studies: Multiple Approaches and Domains*, Routledge Studies in Multimodality, London: Routledge: pp. 17–38.

Bateman, J. and Schmidt, K.-H. (2011) *Multimodal Film Analysis: How Films Mean*, London: Routledge.

Bateman, J., Delin, J. and Henschel, R. (2004) 'Multimodality and empiricism: Preparing for a corpus-based approach to the study of multimodal meaning-making.' In Ventola, E., Charles, C. and Kaltenbacher, M. eds. *Perspectives on Multimodality*, Amsterdam: John Benjamins.

—— (2007) 'Mapping the multimodal genres of traditional and electronic newspapers.' In Royce, T. D. and Bowcher, W. L. eds. *New Directions in the Analysis of Multimodal Discourse*, Mahwah, NJ: Lawrence Erlbaum Associates: pp. 147–72.

Bateson, G. (2000) *Steps to an Ecology of Mind: Collected Essays in Anthropology, Psychiatry, Evolution and Epistemology*, Chicago, IL: Chicago University Press.

Baudrillard, J. (1988) *Selected Writings*, Poster, M. ed., Cambridge: Polity Press.

Bauman, Z. (1998) *Globalization: The Human Consequences*, Oxford: Polity Press.

Bayliss, A. and McKinney, J. (2007) 'Emergent objects: Design and performance research cluster.' In Inns, T. ed. *Designing for the 21st Century: Interdisciplinary Questions and Insights*, Aldershot: Gower Publishing: pp. 150–65.

Baynham, M. and Prinsloo, M. eds. (2009) *The Future of Literacy Studies*, Basingstoke: Palgrave Macmillan.

Bearne, E. (2003) 'Playing with possibilities: Children's multidimensional texts.' In Bearne, E., Dombey H. and Grainger, T. eds. *Classroom Interactions in Literacy*, Maidenhead: Open University Press: pp. 129–43.

Bearne, E. and Kress, G. (2003) 'Editorial.' *Reading* 35(3): pp. 89–93.

Becker, H. S. (1981) *Exploring Society Photographically*, Evanston, IL: Northwestern University.

Beckett, C. (2008) *Supermedia: Saving Journalism so It Can Save the World*, Oxford: Wiley-Blackwell.

Belsey, C. (1980) *Critical Practice*, London: Routledge.

Benedict, R. (1934) *Patterns of Culture*, Boston, MA: Houghton Mifflin.

Benjamin, W. (1936) *The Work of Art in the Age of Mechanical Reproduction*. Available at http://www.marxists.org/reference/subject/philosophy/works/ge/benjamin.htm (accessed 10 October 2007).

Berg, M. (1997) 'Of forms, containers, and the electronic medical records: Some tools for a sociology of the formal.' *Science, Technology, and Human Values* 22: pp. 403–34.

Bernstein, B. (1975) *Class, Codes and Control: Towards a Theory of Educational Transmissions*, Vol. 3, London: Routledge.

—— (1996) *Pedagogy, Symbolic Control and Identity. Theory: Research, Critique*, London: Taylor & Francis.

Berry, D. M. (2012) 'Introduction: Understanding the digital humanities.' In Berry, D. M. ed. *Understanding Digital Humanities*: pp. 1–20. Basingstoke: Palgrave Macmillan.

Besnier, N. (1995) *Literacy, Emotion, and Authority: Reading and Writing on a Polynesian Atoll*, New York: Cambridge University Press.

Bezemer, J. (2008) Silent Communication in the Multilingual Classroom. Paper presented at AILA, Esen, 25–29 August.

Bezemer, J. and Kress, G. (2008) 'Writing in multimodal texts: A social semiotic account of designs for learning.' *Written Communication* 25(2): pp. 165–95.

Bezemer, J. and Mavers, D. (2011) 'Multimodal transcription as academic practice: A Social semiotic perspective.' *International Journal of Social Research Methodology* 14: pp. 191–206.

Bezemer, J., Murtagh, G., Cope, A., Kress, G. and Kneebone, R. (2011) '"Scissors, please": The practical accomplishment of surgical work in the operating theatre.' *Symbolic Interaction* 34(3): pp. 398–414.

Bignell, J. (2000) *Postmodern Media Culture*, Edinburgh: Edinburgh University Press.

Bird, B. and Short, J. (1998) *Insects*, Sydney: Scholastic.

Birdwhistell, R. (1952) *Introduction to Kinesics: An Annotation System for Analysis of Body Motion and Gesture*, mimeograph, Louisville, KY: University of Louisville.

—— (1980) 'Interview.' Unpublished manuscript.

Björkvall, A. and Karlsson, A.-M. (2011) 'The materiality of discourses and the semiotics of materials: A social perspective on the meaning potentials of written texts and furniture.' *Semiotica* 187(1/4): pp. 141–65.

Blackburn, M. and Clark, C. (2007) *Literacy Research for Political Action and Social Change*, New York: Peter Lang.

Blackledge, A. and Creese, A. (2010) *Multilingualism*, London: Continuum Press.

Blommaert, J. (2005) *Discourse: A Critical Introduction*, Cambridge: Cambridge University Press.

—— (2013) *Chronicles of Complexity: Ethnography, Superdiversity and Linguistic Landscapes*, Bristol: Multilingual Matters.

Bloome, D. (2012) 'Classroom ethnography.' In Grenfell, M., Bloome, D., Hardy, C., Pahl, K., Rowsell, J. and Street, B. eds. *Language, Ethnography and Education: Bridging New Literacy Studies and Bourdieu*, New York: Routledge: pp. 7–26.

Bloome, D., Carter, S., Christian, B., Otto, S. and Shuart-Faris, N. (2005) *Discourse Analysis and the Study of Classroom Language and Literacy Events: A Microethnographic Perspective*, Mahwah, NJ: Lawrence Erlbaum Associates.

Bloomfield, L. (1933) *Language*, New York: Holt.

Boeriis, M. and Holsanova, J. (2012) 'Tracking visual segmentation: Connecting semiotic and cognitive perspectives.' In Holsanova, J. ed. *Methodologies for Multimodal Research. Visual Communication* 11(3): Sage: pp. 259–81.

Boltanski, L. (1999) *Distant Suffering: Politics, Morality and the Media*, Cambridge: Cambridge University Press.

Bolter, J. (1998) 'Hypertext and the question of visual literacy.' In Reinking, D., McKenna, M., Labbo, L. and Kieffer, R. eds. *Handbook of Literacy and Technology: Transformations in a Post-typographic World*, Hillsdale, NJ: Erlbaum: pp. 3–14.

Bolter, J. D. and Grusin, R. (2000) *Remediation: Understanding New Media*, Cambridge, MA: MIT Press.

Bordwell, D. and Thompson, K. (2001) *Film Art: An Introduction* (6th edn), New York: McGraw-Hill.

Boulter, D. (1999) *Writing Space: The Computer, Hypertext, and the History of Writing*, Hillsdale, NJ: Erlbaum.

Bourdieu, P. (1977) *Outline of Theory of Practice*, Cambridge: Cambridge University Press.

—— (1990) *The Logic of Practice*, Nice, R., trans., Cambridge: Polity.

—— (1991) *Language and Symbolic Power*, Cambridge, MA: Harvard University Press.

Bourne, J. and Jewitt, C. (2003) 'Orchestrating debate: A multimodal approach to the study of the teaching of higher order literacy skills.' *Reading: Literacy and Language*, UKRA, July: pp. 64–72.

Bowker, R. (2007) 'Children's perceptions and learning about tropical rainforests: An analysis of their drawings.' *Environmental Education Research* 13(1): pp. 75–96.

Boykoff, M.T. (2011) *Who Speaks for the Climate? Making Sense of Media Reporting on Climate Change*, New York: Cambridge University Press.

Boykoff, M.T. and Boykoff, J. M. (2004) 'Balance as bias: Global warming and the US prestige press.' *Global Environmental Change* 14: pp. 125–36.

Brandt, D. and Clinton, K. (2002) 'The limits of the local: Expanding perspectives of literacy as a social practice.' *Journal of Literacy Research* 34(3): pp. 337–56.

Bremner, L. (2010) *Writing the City into Being: Essays on Johannesburg 1998–2008*, Johannesburg: Fourthwall Books.

Brooks, R., Lewis, J., Mosdell, N. and Threadgold, T. (2003) *The Media Coverage of the War in Iraq* [report commissioned for the BBC], Cardiff: Cardiff School of Journalism.

Brown, G., Maycock, B. and Burns, S. (2005) 'Your pictures is your bait: Use and meaning of cyberspace among gay men.' *The Journal of Sex Research* 42(1): pp. 63–73.

Brown, J. S. and Duguid, P. (1994) 'Borderline issues: social and material aspects of design.' *Human–Computer Interaction* 9: pp. 3–36.

Brown, R. W. and Hildum, D. C. (1956) 'Expectancy and the identification of syllables.' *Language* 32: pp. 411–19.

Bucher, H.-J. (2000) 'Formulieren oder Visualisieren? Multimodalität in der Medienkommunikation.' In Richter, G., Riecke, J. and Schuster, B-M. eds. *Raum, Zeit, Medium – Sprache und ihre Detemninanten*. Hessische Historische Kommission Darmstadt: pp. 661–91.

—— (2007) 'Textdesign und Multimodalität: Zur Semantik und Pragmatik medialer Gestaltungsformen.' In Roth, K. S. and Spitzmüller, J. eds. *Textdesign und Textwirkung in der massenmedialen Kommunikation*, Köln: UVK: pp. 35–64.

—— (2011) 'Multimodalität – eine Universalie des Medienwandels: Problemstellungen und Theorien der Multimodalitätsforschung.' In Bucher, H.-J. *et al.* eds. *Neue Medien – Neue Formate. Ausdifferenzierung und Konvergenz in der Medienkommunikation*, Frankfurt am Main: Campus: pp. 41–79.

Bucher, H. J. and Niemann, P. (2012) 'Visualising science: The reception of PowerPoint presentations.' In Holsanova, J. ed. *Methodologies for Multimodal Research. Visual Communication* 11(3): Sage: pp. 283–306.

Bucher, H.-J. and Schumacher, P. (2006) 'The relevance of attention for selecting news content: An eye-tracking study on attention patterns in the reception of print- and online media.' *Communications: The European Journal of Communications Research* 31(3): pp. 347–68.

Bucholtz, M. (2000) 'The politics of transcription.' *Journal of Pragmatics* 32: pp. 1439–65.

Buckingham, D. and Scanlon, M. (2001) 'Parental pedagogies: An analysis of British "edutainment" magazines for young children.' *Journal of Early Childhood Literacy* 1(3): 281–99.

Buckingham, D. and Willett, R. eds. (2009) *Video Cultures: Media Technology and Amateur Creativity*, Basingstoke: Palgrave Macmillan.

Bühler, K. (1934/1990) *Theory of Language: The Representational Function of Language*, Goodwin, D. F., trans., Amsterdam: Benjamins.

Bull, C. (1997) 'Sense, meaning and perception in three dance cultures.' In Desmond, J. ed. *Meaning in Motion: New Cultural Studies of Dance*, Durham, NC: Duke University Press.

Bunt, H., Kipp, M. and Petukhova, V. (2012) 'Using DiAML and ANVIL for multimodal dialogue annotation.' In *Proceedings of the Eighth International Conference on Language Resources and Evaluation (LREC 2012)*, European Language Resources Association: pp. 1301–08.

Burn, A. (1999) 'Grabbing the Werewolf: Digital freezeframes, the cinematic still and technologies of the social.' *Convergence* 3(4): pp. 80–101.

—— (2009) *Making New Media: Creative Production and Digital Literacies*, New York: Peter Lang.

Burn, A. and Parker, D. (2001) 'Making your mark: Digital inscription, animation, and a new visual semiotic.' *Education, Communication and Information* 1(2): pp. 155–79.

—— (2003a) *Analysing Media Texts*, London: Continuum.

—— (2003b) 'Tiger's big plan: Multimodality and moving image.' In Jewitt, C. and Kress, G. eds. *Multimodal Literacy*, Chapter 3, New York: Peter Lang.

Burn, A. and Dixon, H. (2005) 'English and the visual: from montage to manga.' *English Teaching: Practice and Critique* 4(1): pp. 1–5.

Burn, A. and Durran, J. (2007) *Media Literacy in Schools: Practice, Production and Progression*, London: Paul Chapman.

Burnett, C., Merchant, G., Pahl, K. and Rowsell, J. (accepted, 2014) 'The (im)materiality of literacy: The significance of subjectivity to new literacies research.' *Discourse: Studies in the Cultural Politics of Education*.

Büscher, M., Mogensen, P., Shapiro, D. and Wagner, I. (1999) 'The Manufaktur: Supporting work practice in (landscape) "architecture".' In Boedker, S., Kyng, M. and Schmidt, K. eds. *ECSCW '99*, Copenhagen: Kluwer: pp. 21–40.

Butler, J. (1990) *Gender Trouble: Feminism and the Subversion of Identity*, London: Routledge.

—— (1997) *Excitable Speech: A Politics of the Performative*, London: Routledge.

—— (2003) *Precarious Life: The Powers of Violence and Mourning*, London: Verso.

Buzan, T. (1993) *The Mind Map Book: Radiant Thinking – The Major Evolution in Human Thought*, London: BBC Books.

Bybee, J. and Fleishman, S. (1995) 'Modality in grammar and discourse: An introductory essay.' In Bybee, J. and Fleischman, S. eds. *Modality in Grammar and Discourse*, Amsterdam/Philadelphia: John Benjamins: pp. 1–14.

Cajori, F. A. (1952) *A History of Mathematical Notations: Volume II*, 3rd edition, Chicago, IL: Open Court Publishing Company.

—— (1974) *A History of Mathematical Notations: Volume I*, 2nd edition, Chicago, IL: Open Court Publishing Company.

Calame-Griaule, G. (1986) *Words and the Dogon World*, Philadelphia, PA: Institute for the Study of Human Issues.

Caldas-Coulthard, C. and Iedema, R. eds. (2007) *Identity Trouble: Critical Discourse and Contestations of Identification*, London: Macmillan/Palgrave.

Caldwell, D. and Zappavigna, M. (2011) 'Visualizing multimodal patterning.' In Dreyfus, S., Hood, S. and Stenglin, M. eds. *Semiotic Margins: Reclaiming Meaning*, London: Continuum: pp. 229–42.

Calhoun, C. (2001) 'Imagining solidarity: Cosmopolitanism, constitutional patriotism and the public sphere.' *Popular Culture* 14(1): pp. 147–72.

Calvert, G., Spence, C. and Stein, B. E. eds. (2004) *The Handbook of Multisensory Processes*, Cambridge, MA: MIT Press.

Campbell, S. J. (2007) 'GPS favored over Internet access on mobile device.' Available at http://www.geoconnexion.com/geo_news_article/GPS-favoured-over-Internet-access-on-mobile-device/2733 (accessed 1 August 2008).

Candlin, F. (2010) *Art, Museums and Touch*, Manchester: Manchester University Press.

Candy, L. and Edmonds, E. (1999) 'Introducing creativity to cognition.' In *3rd Conference on Creativity and Cognition*, Loughborough, UK: pp. 3–6.

Cannon, M. (2011) 'Fashioning and flow.' Unpublished MA dissertation, Institute of Education, University of London.

Caple, H. and Knox, J. (2012) 'Online news galleries, photojournalism and the photo essay'. *Visual Communication* 11(2): pp. 1–30.

Card, S. K., Moran, T. and Newell, A. (1983) *The Psychology of Human–Computer Interaction*, Hillsdale, NJ: Erlbaum.

Cardiff, D. (1981) 'The serious and the popular: Aspects of the evolution of style in the radio talk 1928–1939.' *Media Culture and Society* 2(1): pp. 29–47.

Carroll, P. J., Young, R. J. and Guertin, M. S. (1992) 'Visual analysis of cartoons: A view from the far side.' In Rayner, K. ed. *Eye Movements and Visual Cognition: Scene Perception and Reading*, New York: Springer: pp. 444–61.

Carter, R. and Adolphs, S. (2008) 'Linking the verbal and the visual: New directions for corpus linguistics.' *Language and Computers* 64: pp. 275–91.

Carvalho, A. (2007) 'Ideological cultures and media discourses on scientific knowledge: Re-reading news on climate change.' *Public Understanding of Science* 16(2): pp. 223–43.

Castells, M. (1996) *The Rise of the Network Society*, London: Blackwell.

—— (1998) *The Information Age. Economy, Society and Culture*, Vol. 2: *The Power of Identity*, Oxford: Blackwell.

—— (2000) *The Rise of the Network Society*, 2nd edition, Oxford: Blackwell.

—— (2001) *The Internet Galaxy*, Oxford: Oxford University Press.

Castells, M., Fernandez-Ardevol, M., Qiu, J. L. and Sey, A. (2007) *Mobile Communication and Society: A Global Perspective*, Cambridge, MA: MIT Press.

Chafe, W. (1995) 'The realis–irrealis distinction in Caddo, the northern Iroquoian languages and English.' In Bybee, J. and Fleischman, S. eds. *Modality in Grammar and Discourse*, Amsterdam/Philadelphia: John Benjamins: pp. 349–65.

Chandler, D. (2007) *Semiotics: The Basics*, London: Routledge.

Chandler, P. and Sweller, J. (1991) 'Cognitive load theory and the format of instruction.' *Cognition and Instruction* 8: pp. 293–332.

Chandler-Olcott, K. and Mahar, D. (2003) '"Tech-saviness" meets multiliteracies: Exploring adolescent girls' technology-related literacy practices.' *Reading Research Quarterly* 38(3): pp. 356–85.

Chaplin, E. (1994) *Sociology and Visual Representation*, New York: Routledge.

Chapman, H. (1996) *The Power of Water*, Sydney: Reed International Books Australia.

Chatman, S. (1991) *Coming to Terms: The Rhetoric of Narrative in Fiction and Film*, Ithaca, NY: Cornell University Press.

Chatman, S. and Duncan, P. (2004) *Michelangelo Antonioni: The Investigation*. Cologne: Taschen, p. 91.

Cherubini, M., Nüssli, M.-A. and Dillenbourg, P. (2008) 'Deixis and gaze in collaborative work at a distance (over a shared map): A computational model to detect misunderstandings.' *Proceedings ETRA*, Savannah, GA. New York: ACM: pp. 173–80.

Chilton, P. (2004) *Analyzing Political Discourse: Theory and Practice*, London: Routledge.

Chion, M. (1999) *The Voice in Cinema*, New York: Columbia University Press.

Chomsky, N. (1957) *Syntactic Structures*, The Hague: Mouton.

—— (1965) *Aspects of the Theory of Syntax*, Cambridge, MA: MIT Press.

Chouliaraki, L. (2000) 'Political discourse in the news: Democratising responsibility or aestheticising politics?' *Discourse and Society* 11(3): pp. 293–314.

—— (2002) 'The contingency of universality: Some thoughts on discourse and realism.' *Social Semiotics* 12(1): pp. 83–114.

—— (2005) 'Spectacular ethics: On the television footage of the Iraq war.' *Journal of Language and Politics* 4(1): pp. 143–59.

—— (2006a) *The Spectatorship of Suffering*, London: Sage.

—— (2006b) 'The aestheticisation of suffering on television.' *Visual Communication* 5(3): pp. 261–85.

—— (2012) *Self-Mediation: New Media, Citizenship and Civil Selves*, London: Routledge.

Chouliaraki, L. and Fairclough, N. (1999) *Discourse in Late Modernity*, Edinburgh: Edinburgh University Press.

Christie, F. and Martin, J. R. eds. (1997) *Genre and Institutions: Social Processes in the Workplace and School*, London: Continuum.

Cierniak, G., Scheiter, K. and Gerjets, P. (2009) 'Explaining the split-attention effect: Is the reduction of extraneous cognitive load accompanied by an increase in germane cognitive load?' *Computers in Human Behavior* 25(2): pp. 315–24.

Clark, A. (2011) 'Cross modal links and selective attention.' In MacPherson, F. ed. *The Senses: Classic and Contemporary Philosophical Perspectives*, Oxford: Oxford University Press: pp. 375–95.

Clark, H. H. (2003) 'Pointing and placing.' In Kita, S. ed. *Pointing: Where Language, Culture, and Cognition Meet*, Mahwah, NJ: Lawrence Erlbaum: pp. 243–68.

Classen, C. (1993) *Worlds of Sense: Exploring the Senses in History and Across Cultures*, London: Routledge.

—— (1997) 'Foundations for an anthropology of the senses.' *International Social Science Journal* 153: pp. 401–12.

—— (1998) *The Color of Angels: Cosmology, Gender and the Aesthetic Imagination*, London: Routledge.

—— (2007) 'Museum manners: The sensory life of the early museum', *Journal of Social History* 40: pp. 895–914.

Classen, C. and Howes, D. (2006) 'The museum as sensescape: Western sensibilities and indigenous artifacts.' In Edwards, E., Gosden C. and Phillips, R. eds. *Sensible Objects*, Oxford: Berg.

Classen, C., Howes, D. and Synnott, A. (1994) *Aroma: The Cultural History of Smell*, London: Routledge.

Clayman, S. and Heritage, J. (2002) *The News Interview: Journalists and Public Figures on the Air*, New York: Cambridge University Press.

Clifford, J. (1992) 'Traveling cultures.' In Grossberg, L., Nelson, C. and Treichler, P. A. eds. *Cultural Studies*, London: Routledge.

Clingman, S. (2011) 'William Kentridge's metonymic line: The art of transformation.' Paper presented at the University of the Witwatersrand, South Africa, 19 May.

Coessens, K. (2012) 'Sensory fluidity: Dialogues of imagination in art.' *Essays in Philosophy* 13(2): pp. 453–70. http://commons.pacificu.edu/cgi/viewcontent.cgi?article=1432&context=eip (Special Issue: *Aesthetics and the Senses*, C. Freeland, ed.)

Coffey, A., Holbrook, B. and Atkinson, P. (1996) 'Qualitative data analysis: Technologies and representations.' *Sociological Research Online* 1(1): http://www.socresonline.org.uk/socresonline/1/1/4. html.

Coffey, A., Dicks, B., Mason, B., Renold, E., Soyinka, B. and Williams, M. (2008) *Ethnography for the Digital Age*, http://www.cf.ac.uk/socsi/hyper/p02/index.html (accessed 16 July 2008).

Cohen, S. (2001) *States of Denial: Knowing About Atrocities and Suffering*, Cambridge: Polity.

Cole, M. (1996) *Cultural Psychology: A Once and Future Discipline*, Cambridge, MA: Belknap Press.

Collier, J. J. and Collier, M. (1986) *Visual Anthropology: Photography as a Research Method*, Albuquerque, NM: University of New Mexico Press.

Comber, B. (2007) 'Assembling dynamic repertoires of literate practices: Teaching that makes a difference.' In Marsh, J. and Bearne, E. eds. *Literacy and Social Inclusion: Closing the Gap*, London: Trentham Press: pp. 115–31.

—— (2010) 'Critical literacies in place: Teachers who work for just and sustainable communities.' In Lavia, J. and Moore, M. eds. *Cross-Cultural Perspectives in Policy and Practice: Decolonizing Community Contexts*, London: Routledge: pp. 46–57.

Cook, G. (2001) *The Discourse of Advertising*, London: Routledge.

Cook, P. (2011) *Cinematic Hamlet: The Films of Olivier, Zeffirelli, Branagh and Almereyda*. Athens, OH: Ohio University Press.

Cooke, L. (2003) 'Information acceleration and visual trends in print, television, and web news sources.' *Technical Communication Quarterly* 12(2): pp. 155–81.

Cope, B. and Kalantzis, M. eds. (2000) *Multiliteracies: Literacy Learning and the Design of Social Futures*, London: Routledge.

Cortada, J. W. (1987) *Historical Dictionary of Data Processing: Technology*, New York: Greenwood Press.

Coulthard, M. (1977) *An Introduction to Discourse Analysis*, London: Longman.

Cox, M. (1992) *Children's Drawings*, London: Penguin Books.

Crang, M. (1997) 'Picturing practices: Research through the tourist gaze.' *Progress in Human Geography* 21: pp. 359–73.

Crang, M. and Thrift, N. (2000) *Thinking Space*, London: Routledge.

Cruttenden, A. (1997) *Intonation*, Cambridge, MA: Cambridge University Press.

Crystal, D. (1969) *Prosodic Systems and Intonation in English*, Cambridge: Cambridge University Press.

Cubitt, S. (1988) 'Anxiety in public houses: Speculations on the semiotics of design consciousness.' *Journal of Design History* 1(2): pp. 127–39.

Cuff, D. (1992) *Architecture: The Story of Practice*, Cambridge, MA: MIT Press.

Cutting, J. E., Brunick, K. L. and DeLong, J. E. (2011) 'How act structure sculpts shot lengths and shot transitions in Hollywood film.' *Projections: The Journal for Movies and Mind* 5(1): pp. 1–16.

Cytowic, R. (2002) *Touching Tastes, Seeing Smells – and Shaking up Brain Science*, Dana Foundation. http://www.dana.org/news/cerebreum/detail.aspx?=2870 [Retrieved 2012/06/25].

d'Ydewalle, G. and De Bruycker, W. (2007) 'Eye movements of children and adults while reading television subtitles.' *European Psychologist* 12(3): pp. 196–205. doi: 10.1027/1016-904012.3.196.

Davies, J. (2006) 'Escaping to the borderlands: An exploration of the internet as a cultural space for teen-aged Wiccan girls.' In Pahl, K. and Rowsell, J. eds. *Travel Notes from the New Literacy Studies: Instances of Practice*, Clevedon, UK: Multilingual Matters: pp. 57–72.

Davies, J. and Merchant, G. (2009) *Web 2.0 for Schools: Learning and Social Participation,* New York: Peter Lang.

De Certeau, M. (1984) *The Practice of Everyday Life*, Rendell, S., trans., Berkley, CA: University of California Press.

De Koning, B. B., Tabbers, H. K., Rikers, R. M. J. P. and Paas, F. (2007) 'Attention cueing as a means to enhance learning from an animation.' *Applied Cognitive Psychology* 21: pp. 731–46.

Deleuze, G. (1983) *Cinema 1: The Movement-Image*, Tomlinsom, H. and Habberjam, B., trans., London: Athlone Press.

—— (1989) *Cinema 2: The Time-Image*, Tomlinsom, H. and Galeta, R., trans., London: Athlone Press.

—— (2008) *Francis Bacon: The Logic of Sensation*, Minneapolis: University of Minnesota Press.

Deleuze, G. and Guattari, F. (1988) *A Thousand Plateaus: Capitalism and Schizophrenia*, London: The Athlone Press.

Delin, J. and Bateman, J. (2002) 'Describing and critiquing multimodal documents.' *Document Design* 3: pp. 141–55.

Deng, J., Dong, W., Socher, R., Li, L.-J., Li, K. and Fei-Fei, L. (2009) 'ImageNet: A large-scale hierarchical image database.' In *Proceedings of IEEE Computer Vision and Pattern Recognition (CVPR)*: pp. 248–55.

Derrida, J. (1968) 'Différance.' In *Margins of Philosophy*, Chicago, IL: University of Chicago Press: pp. 1–27.

—— (1982) 'Structure, sign and play in the discourse of the human sciences.' In *Writing and Difference*, Chicago: Chicago University Press.

Descartes, R. (1683) *Geometria, anno 1673 Gallice Edita / Postea Cum Notis Fl. de Beaune in Latinam Linguam Versa / et Commentariis Illustrata Opera Francisci a Schooten: Volume 2*, 3rd edition, Amsterdam.

—— (1954 [1637]) *The Geometry of Rene Descartes, 1637*, Smith, D. E. and Latham, M. L., trans., New York: Dover.

Diamantopoulou, S. (2008) 'Engaging with children's graphic ensembles of an archaeological site: A multimodal social semiotic approach to learning.' *Journal of Language and Communication Studies* 41: pp. 81–105.

Dias, N. (2004) *La mesure des sens: les anthropologues et le corps humain au XIXᵉ siècle*, Paris: Flammarion.

Dicks, B., Mason, B., Coffey, A. and Atkinson, P. (2005) *Qualitative Research and Hypermedia: Ethnography for the Digital Age*, London: Sage.

Dicks, B., Soyianka, B. and Coffey, A. (2006) 'Multimodal ethnography.' *Qualitative Research* 6(1): pp. 77–96.

Dicks, B., Flewitt, R. B., Lancaster, L. and Pahl, K. (2011) 'Introduction to multimodality and ethnography: Working at the intersection.' *Qualitative Research* 11: p. 227.

Diem-Wille, G. (2001) 'A therapeutic perspective: The use of drawings in child psychoanalysis and social science.' In Van Leeuwen, T. and Jewitt, C. eds. *Handbook of Visual Analysis*, London: Sage: pp. 119–33.

Dillon, G. L. (2006) 'Writing with images: Introduction: image text multiples and other mixed modes.' At http://courses.washington.edu/hypertxt/cgi-bin/12.228.185.206/html/wordsimages/wordsimages.html.

Djonov, E. (2005) 'Analysing the organisation of information in websites: From hypermedia design to systemic functional hypermedia discourse analysis.' Unpublished PhD thesis, University of New South Wales. Available online at: http://handle.unsw.edu.au/19594/23915

—— (2007) 'Website hierarchy and the interaction between content organization, webpage and navigation design: A systemic functional hypermedia discourse analysis perspective.' *Information Design Journal* 15(2): pp. 144–62.

—— (2008) 'Children's website structure and navigation.' In Unsworth, L. ed. *Multimodal Semiotics: Functional Analysis in Contexts of Education*, London: Continuum: pp. 216–36.

Djonov, E. and Van Leeuwen, T. (2011) 'The semiotics of texture: from tactile to visual.' *Visual Communication* 10(4): pp. 541–64.

Doelker, C. (2007) 'Figuren der visuellen Rhetorik in werblichen Gesamttexten.' In Knape, J. ed. *Bildrhetorik*, Baden-Baden: Koerner: pp. 71–112.

Domingo, M. (2011) 'Analyzing layering in textual design: A multimodal approach for examining cultural, linguistic, and social migrations in digital video.' *International Journal of Social Research Methodology* 14(3): pp. 219–30.

Donald, M. (2001) *A Mind so Rare: The Evolution of Human Consciousness*, New York: Norton.

Doronilla, M. L. (1996) *Landscapes of Literacy: An Ethnographic Study of Functional Literacy in Marginal Philippine Communities*, Hamburg: UIE.

481

Douglas, M. (1986) *How Institutions Think*, New York: Syracuse University Press.

Dresang, E. (1999) *Radical Change: Books for Youth in a Digital Age*, New York: Wilson.

Dreyfus, E. (2008) *Scumbag*, Exhibition Catalogue, Paddington, Sydney: Stills Gallery.

Dudley, S. ed. (2010) *Museum Materialities*, London: Routledge.

—— (2012) *Museum Objects: Experiencing the Properties of Things*, London: Routledge.

Duranti, A. and Goodwin, C. eds. (1992) *Rethinking Context: Language as an Interactive Phenomenon*, Cambridge: Cambridge University Press.

Dürscheid, C. (2005) 'Medien, Kommunikationsformen, kommunikative Gattungen.' *Linguistik Online* 22(1). http://www.linguistik-online.de/22_05/duerscheid.html

E, Marissa K. L., O'Halloran, K. L. and Judd, K. (2012) 'Combining computational tools with systemic functional theory for discourse analysis.' In Norris, S. ed. *Multimodality in Practice: Investigating Theory-in-Practice Through Methodology*, Routledge Studies in Multimodality Book Series, London: Routledge: pp. 153–73.

Eco, U. (1976) *Theory of Semiotics*, London: Bloomington.

—— (2002) *History of Beauty*. New York, Rizzoli.

Economides, N. (1995) 'The economics of networks.' At http://www.stern.nyu.edu/networks/top.html (accessed 10 October 2007).

Edwards, R., Ivanic, R. and Mannion, G. (2009) 'The scrumpled geographies of literacies for learning.' *Discourse: Studies in the Cultural Politics of Education* 30(4): pp. 483–99.

Eggins, S. (2005) *An Introduction to Systemic Functional Linguistics*, 2nd edition, London: Continuum.

Eisenstein, E. L. (1979) *The Printing Press as an Agent of Change*, Cambridge: Cambridge University Press.

Eisenstein, S. (1961 [1938]) 'Montage.' In *Gesammelte Aufsätze I*, Zürich: Arche: pp. 229–80.

—— (1968) *The Film Sense*, Layda, J., trans., London: Faber & Faber.

Eitel, A., Scheiter, K. and Schüler, A. (2011) 'How brief initial inspection of a picture may foster comprehension of text.' In Carlson, L., Hölscher, C. and Shipley, T. F. eds. *Proceedings of the 33rd Annual Conference of the Cognitive Science Society*, Austin, TX: Cognitive Science Society: pp. 1358–64.

Ekman, P. and Friesen, W. V. (1978) *Facial Action Coding System: A Technique for the Measurement of Facial Movement*, Palo Alto: Consulting Psychologists Press.

Elkins, J. (1996) *The Object Stares Back: On the Nature of Seeing*, London, Harvester.

—— (1998) *On Pictures and the Words that Fail Them*, Cambridge: Cambridge University Press.

—— (1999) *The Domain of Images*, Ithaca, NY: Cornell University Press.

Ellis, J. (2000) *Seeing Things: Television in the Age of Uncertainty*, London: I. B. Tauris.

Engebretsen, M. (2012) 'Balancing cohesion and tension in multimodal rhetoric. An interdisciplinary approach to the study of semiotic complexity.' *Learning, Media and Technology*, doi:10.1080/174398842012655745.

Erickson, F. (1980) 'Timing and context in everyday discourse: Implications for the study of referential and social meaning.' *Sociolinguistic Working Paper* Number 67. Austin, TX: Southwest Educational Development Laboratory.

—— (2004a) *Talk and Social Theory: Ecologies of Speaking and Listening in Everyday Life*, Cambridge: Polity Press.

—— (2004b) 'Origins: A brief intellectual and technological history of the emergence of multimodal discourse analysis.' In LeVine, P. and Scollon, R. eds. *The Georgetown University Round Table on Linguistics 2002, Discourse and Technology: Multimodal Discourse Analysis*, Washington, DC: Georgetown University Press.

—— (2011) 'Uses of video in social research: A brief history.' *International Journal of Social Research Methodology* 14(3): pp. 179–89. doi: 10.1080/136455792011563615.

Evans, H. (1976) *Editing and Design: A Five-Volume Manual of English, Typography and Layout*, 2nd edn, Vol. 5, *Newspaper Design*, London: Heinemann.

Fairclough, N. (1995) *Critical Discourse Analysis: The Critical Study of Language*, London: Longman.

—— (2003a) *Doing Discourse Analysis: Textual Analysis for Social Scientists*, London: Routledge.

—— (2003b) *Analysing Discourse: Textual Analysis for Social Science*, London: Routledge.

Farquhar, J. (2002) *Appetites: Food and Sex in Postsocialist China*, Durham, NC: Duke University Press.

Finnegan, R. (2002) *Communicating: The Multiple Modes of Human Interconnection*, London: Routledge.

Firth, J. R. (1957) 'Modes of meaning.' In *Papers in Linguistics 1934–1951*, London: Oxford University Press.

Fischer, G. (2001) 'Communities of interest: Learning through the interaction of multiple knowledge system.' In *The 24th IRIS Conference*, Bergen, Norway: pp. 1–14.

—— (2004) 'Social creativity: Turning barriers into opportunities for collaborative design.' In *Proceedings of the 8th Conference on Participatory Design: Artful Integration: Interweaving Media, Materials and Practices*, Toronto, Ontario: pp. 152–61.

Fishman, J. M. and Marvin, C. (2003) 'Portrayals of violence and group difference in newspaper photographs: Nationalism and media.' *Journal of Communication* 53(1): pp. 32–44.

Fix, U. (2001) 'Zugänge zu Stil als semiotisch komplexer Einheit. Thesen, Erläuterungen und Beispiele.' In Jakobs, E.-M. and Rothkegel, A. eds. *Perspektiven auf Stil*, Tübingen: Niemeyer: pp. 113–26.

Fleming, J. A. (1999) 'The semiotics of furniture form: The French tradition 1620–1840.' *Journal of the Canadian Historical Association* 10: pp. 37–58.

Flewitt, R. S. (2005) 'Is every child's voice heard? Researching the different ways 3-year-old children communicate and make meaning at home and in a pre-school playgroup.' *Early Years* 25(3): pp. 207–22.

—— (2006) 'Using video to investigate preschool classroom interaction: Education research assumptions and methodological practices.' *Visual Communication* 5(1): pp. 25–50.

—— (2008) 'Multimodal literacies.' In Marsh, J. and Hallet, E. eds. *Desirable Literacies: Approaches to Language and Literacy in the Early Years*, London: Sage: pp. 122–39.

—— (2011) 'Bringing ethnography to a multimodal investigation of early literacy in a digital age.' *Qualitative Research* 11(3): pp. 293–310.

Flyvbjerg, B. (2001) *Making Social Science Matter*, Cambridge: Cambridge University Press.

Folker, S., Sichelschmidt, L. and Ritter, H. (2005) 'Processing and integrating multimodal material: The influence of color-coding.' In Bara, B. G., Barsalou, L. and Bucciarelli, M. eds. *Proceedings of the 27th Annual Conference of the Cognitive Science Society*, Mahwah, NJ: Erlbaum: pp. 690–95.

Forceville, C. (1999) 'Educating the eye? Kress and Van Leeuwen's *Reading Images: The Grammar of Visual Design* (1996).' Review article in *Language and Literature* 8(2): pp. 163–78.

—— (2007) 'Book Review: *Multimodal Transcription and Text Analysis: A Multimedia Toolkit and Coursebook* by Anthony Baldry and Paul J. Thibault.' *Journal of Pragmatics* 39(6): pp. 1235–38.

Forceville, C. J. and Urios-Aparisi, E. eds. (2009) *Multimodal Metaphor*, Berlin: Mouton de Gruyter.

Fortunati, L. (2005) 'The mobile phone between local and global.' In Nyiri, K. ed. *A Sense of Place: The Global and the Local in Mobile Communication*, Vienna: Passagen Verlag.

Foucault, M. (1970) *The Order of Things*, London: Tavistock.

—— (1972) *The Archaeology of Knowledge*, London: Tavistock.

—— (1973) *The Birth of the Clinic: An Archeology of Medical Perception*, Sheridan-Smith, A. M., trans., London: Tavistock.

—— (1991) 'Governmentality.' In Burchell, G., Gordon, C. and Miller, P. eds. *The Foucault Effect: Studies in the Governmentality of Culture*, London: Harvester Wheatsheaf: pp. 87–104.

Foulsham, T. and Underwood, G. (2008) 'What can saliency models predict about eye movements? Spatial and sequential aspects of fixations during encoding and recognition.' *Journal of Vision* 8(2): pp. 1–17. doi:10.1167/8.2.6.

Franks, A. and Jewitt, C. (2001) 'The meaning of action in the science classroom.' *British Education Research Journal* 27(2): pp. 201–18.

Fraser, N. (1997) *Justice Interruptus: Critical Reflections on the 'Postsocialist' Condition*, London: Routledge.

Freksa, C. and Bertel, S. (2007) 'Eye movements and smart technology.' *Computers in Biology and Medicine* 37: pp. 983–88.

Frith, S. (1988) *Music for Pleasure*, Cambridge: Polity.

Gabriel, G. (2011) 'Altered states, altered sounds: An investigation of how subjective states are signified in narrative fiction cinema.' PhD thesis, Cardiff University.

Gage, J. (1993) *Colour and Culture: Practice and Meaning from Antiquity to Abstraction*, London, Thames & Hudson.

—— (1999) *Colour and Meaning: Art, Science and Symbolism*, London, Thames & Hudson.

Galileo, G. (1638) *Discorsi e Dimostrazioni Matematiche, Intorno à Due Nuoue Scienze Altenenti*, Leida: appresso gli Elsevirii.

Garcia, M. R. and Stark, P. A. (1991) *Eyes on the News*, St. Petersburg, FL: The Poynter Institute.

Garside, R., Leech, G. and McEnery, A. eds. (1997) *Corpus Annotation: Linguistic Information From Computer Text Corpora*, London: Longman.

Gauthier, G. (1967) 'Entretien avec Alain Jessua.' *Image et Son* 206: pp. 68–71.

Gee, J. P. (1996) *Social Linguistics and Literacies: Ideology in Discourses*, London: Taylor & Francis.

—— (1999) *An Introduction to Discourse Analysis: Theory and Method*, London: Routledge.

—— (2001) 'Identity as an analytic lens for research in education.' In Secada, W. ed. *Review of Educational Research*, Vol. 25, Washington, DC: American Educational Research Association: pp. 99–126.

—— (2003, 2nd edn 2007) *What Video Games Have to Teach Us About Learning and Literacy*, New York: Palgrave.

Geertz, C. (1973) *The Interpretation of Cultures*, New York: Basic Books.

Genette, G. (1980) *Narrative Discourse*, Oxford: Blackwell.

Geurts, K. (2002) *Culture and the Senses: Bodily Ways of Knowing in an African Community*, Berkeley, CA: University of California Press.

Gibbons, D. (2010) 'Tracing the paths of moving artifacts in youth media production.' *English Teaching: Practice and Critique* 9(1): pp. 8–21.

Gibson, J. J. (1977) 'The theory of affordances.' In Shaw, R. E. and Bransford, J. eds. *Perceiving, Acting, and Knowing*, Hillsdale, NJ: Lawrence Erlbaum Associates.

—— (1986) *The Ecological Approach to Visual Perception*, Hillsdale, NJ: Lawrence Erlbaum Associates.

Giddens, A. (1990) *The Consequences of Modernity*, Cambridge: Polity Press.

—— (1991) *Modernity and Self-Identity*, Cambridge: Polity Press.

Gidlöf, K., Holmberg, N. and Sandberg, H. (2012) 'The use of eye-tracking and retrospective interviews to study teenagers' exposure to online advertising.' In Holsanova, J. ed. *Methodologies for Multimodal Research, Visual Communication* 11(3): pp. 329–45.

Gidlöf, K., Wallin, A., Dewhurst, R. and Holmqvist, K. (2013) 'Using eye-tracking to trace a cognitive process: Gaze behavior during decision making in a natural environment.' *Journal of Eye Movement Research* 6: pp. 1–14.

Gill, T. (2002) 'Visual and verbal playmates: An exploration of visual and verbal modalities in children's picture books.' Unpublished B.A. (Hons), University of Sydney.

Goethe, J. W. von (1970 [1810]) *Theory of Colours*, Cambridge, MA: MIT Press.

Goffman, E. (1959) *The Presentation of Self in Everyday Life*, New York: Doubleday.

—— (1963) *Behavior in Public Places: Notes on the Social Organization of Gatherings*, New York: Free Press.

—— (1974) *Frame Analysis: An Essay on the Organization of Experience*, New York: Harper & Row.

—— (1979) *Gender Advertisements*, New York: Harper Colophon.

—— (1981) *Forms of Talk*, Philadelphia: University of Pennsylvania Press.

—— (1983) 'The interaction order: American Sociological Association, 1982 Presidential Address.' *American Sociological Review* 48(1): pp. 1–17.

—— (1986) *Frame Analysis*, Boston, MA: Northeastern University Press.

—— (1990) *The Presentation of Self in Everyday Life*, London: Penguin.

Goldhaber, M. (1997) 'The attention economy and the net.' *First Monday*. At http://firstmonday.dk/issues/issue2_4/goldhaber/ (accessed 6 February 2002).

Golomb, C. (1974) *Young Children's Sculpture and Drawing: A Study in Representational Development*, Cambridge, MA: Harvard University Press.

—— (1999) 'Art and the young: The many faces of representation.' *Visual Arts Research* 25(1): pp. 27–50.

Gombrich, E. H. (1982) *The Image and the Eye: Further Studies in the Psychology of Pictorial Representation*, London: Phaidon Press.

Goodman, N. (1976) *Languages of Art*, Indianapolis, IL: Hackett.

Goodnow, J. (1977) *Children's Drawing*, London: Fontana Press.

Goodwin, C. (1981) *Conversational Organization: Interaction Between Speakers and Hearers*, New York: Academic Press.

—— (1994) 'Professional vision.' *American Anthropologist* 96: pp. 606–33.

—— (1995) 'Seeing in depth.' *Social Studies of Science* 25: pp. 237–74.

—— (1997) 'The blackness of black: Color categories as situated practice.' In Resnick, L. B., Säljö, R.,

Pontecorvo, C. and Burge, B. eds. *Discourse, Tools, and Reasoning: Essays on Situated Cognition*, New York: Springer: pp. 111–40.

—— (2000) 'Action and embodiment within situated human interaction.' *Journal of Pragmatics* 32: pp. 1489–522.

—— (2001) 'Practices of seeing visual analysis: An ethnomethodological approach.' In Van Leeuwen, T. and Jewitt, C. eds. *Handbook of Visual Analysis*, London: Sage: pp. 157–82.

—— (2002) 'Time in action.' *Current Anthropology* 43 (Supplemental special issue: Repertoires of time-keeping in anthropology): pp. S19–S35.

—— (2003a) 'Pointing as situated practice.' In Kita, S. ed. *Pointing: Where Language, Culture, and Cognition Meet*, Mahwah, NJ: Lawrence Erlbaum: pp. 217–41.

—— (2003b) 'The body in action.' In Coupland, J. and Gwyn, R. eds. *Discourse, the Body and Identity*, Basingstoke: Palgrave Macmillan: pp. 19–42.

—— (2006) 'A linguistic anthropologist's interest in archaeological practice.' In Edgeworth, M. ed. *Re-Encountering Archaeology: Ethnographies of Archaeological Practice: Cultural Encounters, Material Reflections*, Walnut Creek, CA: Alta Mira Press: pp. 45–55.

—— (2007a) 'Language, culture, social organization and the material word: Why a five field approach is necessary.' *Teaching Anthropology: SACC Notes* 13(2): pp. 5–9, 34.

—— (2007b) 'Participation, stance and affect in the organisation of activities.' *Discourse and Society* 18(1): pp. 53–73.

Goodwin, C. and Goodwin, M. H. (1996) 'Seeing as a situated activity: Formulating planes.' In Engeström, Y. and Middleton, D. eds. *Cognition and Communication at Work*, Cambridge: Cambridge University Press: pp. 61–95.

Goodwin, M. and Alim, H. (2010) '"Whatever (neck roll, eye roll, teeth suck)": The situated coproduction of social categories and identities through stancetaking and transmodal stylisation.' *Journal of Linguistic Anthropology* 20(1): pp. 79–194.

Goodwyn, A. (2000) 'An English teacher in the computer age.' In Goodwyn, A. ed. *English in the Digital Age*, London: Cassell: pp. 1–21.

Gowen, S. (1994) '"I'm no fool": Reconsidering American workers and their literacies.' In O'Connor, P. ed. *Thinking Work: Theoretical Perspectives on Workers' Literacies*, Vol. 1, Sydney, Australia: Adult Literacy and Basic Skills Action Coalition: pp. 123–35.

Gray, J. (2004) *Consciousness: Creeping Up on the Hard Problem*, Oxford: Oxford University Press.

Green, J. and Bloome, D. (1997) 'Ethnography and ethnographers of and in education: A situated perspective.' In Flood, J., Heath, S. and Lapp, D. eds. *A Handbook for Literacy Educators: Research on Teaching the Communicative and Visual Arts*, New York: Macmillan: pp. 1–12.

Green, J. L. and Wallat, C. eds. (1981) *Ethnography and Language in Educational Settings*, Norwood, NJ: Ablex.

Grenfell, M., Bloome, D., Hardy, C., Pahl, K., Rowsell, J. and Street, B. (2012) *Language, Ethnography and Education: Bridging New Literacy Studies and Bourdieu*, New York: Routledge.

Grice, H. P. (1975) 'Logic and conversation.' In Cole, P. and Morgan, J. L. eds. *Syntax and Semantics, Vol. 3: Speech Acts*, New York: Academic Press: pp. 41–58.

Grodal, T. (2002) 'The experience of realism in audiovisual representation.' In Jerslev, A. ed. *Realism and 'Reality' in Film and Media*, Copenhagen: Museum Tusculanum Press, University of Copenhagen: pp. 67–91.

Gullberg, M. and Holmqvist, K. (1999) 'Keeping an eye on gestures: Visual perception of gestures in face-to-face communication.' *Pragmatics and Cognition* 7(1): pp. 35–63.

Gumperz, J. (1982) *Language and Social Identity*, Cambridge: Cambridge University Press.

Guo, L. (2004) 'Multimodality in a biology textbook.' In O'Halloran, K. L. ed. *Multimodal Discourse Analysis*, London: Continuum: pp. 196–219.

Gupta, A. and Ferguson, J. (1992) 'Space, identity, and the politics of difference.' *Cultural Anthropology* 7: pp. 6–23.

Gustavson, L. (2008) 'Influencing pedagogy through the creative practices of youth.' In Hill, M. L. and Vasudevan, L. eds. *Media, Learning, and Sites of Possibility*, New York: Peter Lang.

Hall, C. (1999) 'Understanding educational process in an era of globalization: The view from anthropology and cultural studies.' In Lagemann, E. C. and Shulman, L. S. eds. *Issues in Educational Research*, San Francisco, CA: Condliffe Jossey-Bass: pp. 121–56.

Hall, E. T. (1959) *The Silent Language*, Garden City, NY: Doubleday.

—— (1964) 'Silent assumptions in social communication.' In Rioch, D. McK. and Weinstein, E. A. eds. *Disorders of Communication, Research Publications, Association for Research in Nervous and Mental Diseases* 42: pp. 41–55.

—— (1966) *The Hidden Dimension*, Garden City, NY: Doubleday.

—— (1969) *The Hidden Dimension: Man's Use of Space in Public and Private*, London: The Bodley Head.

—— (1992) *An Anthropology of Everyday Life: An Autobiography*, New York: Anchor Books.

Hall, S. (1973/1980) 'Encoding – decoding.' In Hall, S., Hobson, D. and Lowe, A. eds. *Culture, Media, Language*, London: Hutchinson: pp. 139–56.

Halliday, M. A. K. (1967–68) 'Transitivity and theme in English.' *Journal of Linguistics* Vols 3 and 4.

—— (1973) *Language in a Social Perspective: Explorations in the Functions of Language*, London: Edward Arnold.

—— (1978) *Language as Social Semiotic: The Social Interpretation of Language and Meaning*, London: Edward Arnold.

—— (1985/1995) *An Introduction to Functional Grammar*, London: Edward Arnold.

—— (1989) *Spoken and Written Language*, Oxford: Oxford University Press.

—— (1994) *An Introduction to Functional Grammar*, 2nd edition, London: Edward Arnold.

Halliday, M. A. K. and Hasan, R. (1976) *Cohesion in English*, London: Longman.

—— (1985) *Language, Context, and Text: Aspects of Language in a Social-semiotic Perspective*, Victoria: Deakan University Press.

—— (1989) *Language, Context and Text: Aspects of Language in a Social Semiotic Perspective*, Oxford: Oxford University Press.

Halliday, M. A. K. and Matthiessen, C. M. I. M. (1999) *Construing Experience Through Meaning: A Language Based Approach to Cognition*, London: Cassell.

—— (2004) *An Introduction to Functional Grammar*, 3rd edition, London: Arnold.

Hamilton, P. (2006) *Visual Research Methods*, London: Sage.

Hampel, R. (in press) 'Making meaning online: computer-mediated communication for language learning.' In Peti-Stantić, A. and Stanojević, M.-M. eds. *Language as Information. Proceedings from the CALS Conference 2012*. Frankfurt am Main: Peter Lang.

Hampel, R. and Hauck, M. (2006a) 'Computer-mediated language learning: Making meaning in multimodal virtual learning spaces.' *The JALT CALL Journal* 2(2): pp. 3–18.

—— (2006b) 'Transcribing interaction in audio and video conferencing environments.' Paper delivered at *Multimodal Workshop*, June 2006, The Open University, UK.

Hannerz, U. (1996) *Transnational Connections: Culture, People, Places*, London: Routledge.

Hannus, M. and Hyönä, J. (1999) 'Utilization of illustrations during learning of science textbook passages among low- and high-ability children.' *Contemporary Educational Psychology* 24(2): pp. 95–123.

Hansen, J. P. (1994) 'Analyse af Læsernes Informationsprioritering [Analysis of readers' information priorities].' *Kognitiv Systemgruppen Forskningscenter Risø*, Roskilde, July.

Haraway, D. (1991) *Simians, Cyborgs and Women: The Reinvention of Nature*, New York: Routledge.

Harding, G. and Bloj, M. (2010) 'Real and predicted influence of image manipulations on eye movements during scene recognition.' *Journal of Vision* 10(2): p. 8.

Harper, R., Hughes, J. and Shapiro, D. (1989) 'Harmonious working and CSCW: Computer technology and air traffic control.' In Bowers, J. and Benford, S. D. eds. *ECSCW '89*, Amsterdam: North-Holland: pp. 73–86.

Harrop-Allin, S. (2011) 'Playing with Barbie: Exploring South African township children's games as resources for pedagogy'. In *Learning, Teaching and Musical Identity: Voices across Cultures*, Bloomington, IN: University of Indiana Press: pp. 156–69.

Hasan, R. (1999) 'The disempowerment game: A critique of Bourdieu's view of language.' *Linguistics and Education* 10(4): pp. 25–87.

Haviland, J. (2000) 'Pointing, gesture spaces, and mental maps.' In McNeill, D. ed. *Gesture and Language*, Cambridge: Cambridge University Press: pp. 13–46.

Hayles, N. K. (1999) *How We Became Posthuman: Virtual Bodies in Cybernetics, Literature, and Informatics*, Chicago, IL: University of Chicago Press.

Heath, C. C. and Luff, P. (1992) 'Collaboration and control: Crisis management and multimedia technology in London underground line control rooms.' *CSCW Journal* 1: pp. 69–94.

—— (2000) *Technology in Action*, Cambridge: Cambridge University Press.

—— (2007) 'Gesture and institutional interaction: Figuring bids in auctions of fine art and antiques.' *Gesture* 7(2): pp. 215–40.

Heath, C. C., Jirotka, M., Luff, P. and Hindmarsh, J. (1994) 'Unpacking collaboration: The interactional organisation of trading in a city dealing room.' *CSCW* 3: pp. 147–65.

Heath, C., Luff, P., vom Lehn, D. Hindmarsh, J. and Cleverly, J. (2002) 'Crafting participation: Designing ecologies, configuring experience.' *Visual Communication* 1(1): pp. 9–33.

Heath, C., Hindmarsh, J. and Luff, P. (2010) *Video in Qualitative Research: Analyzing Social Interaction in Everyday Life*, London: Sage.

Heath, S. B. (1982) 'What no bedtime story means: Narrative skills at home and school.' *Language and Society* 11: pp. 49–76.

—— (1983) *Ways with Words: Language, Life and Work in Communities and Classrooms*, Cambridge: Cambridge University Press.

Heath, S. B. and Street, B. (2008) *On Ethnography: Approaches to Language and Literacy Research*, National Conference on Research in Language and Literacy: Teachers College Columbia.

Hegarty, M. (1992) 'Mental animation: Inferring motion from static displays of mechanical systems.' *Journal of Experimental Psychology: Learning, Memory and Cognition* 18: pp. 1084–102.

Hegarty, M. and Just, M. A. (1993) 'Constructing mental models of machines from text and diagrams.' *Journal of Memory and Language* 32(6): pp. 717–42.

Hegarty, M., Carpenter, P. A. and Just, M. A. (1991) 'Diagrams in the comprehension of scientific text.' In Barr, R., Kamil, M. L., Mosenthal, P. B. and Pearson, P. D. eds. *Handbook of Reading Research*, Vol. 2, New York: Longman: pp. 641–68.

Henderson, J. M. and Ferreira, F. (2004) 'Scene perception for psycholinguists.' In Henderson, J. M. and Ferreira, F. eds. *The Interface of Language, Vision, and Action: Eye Movements and the Visual World*, New York: Psychology Press: pp. 1–58.

Henderson, K. (1999) *On Line and Paper: Visual Representations, Visual Culture and Computer Graphics and Design Engineering*, Cambridge, MA: MIT Press.

Herman, L. (1952) *A Practical Manual for Screen Playwriting for Theatre and Television Films*, New York: New American Library.

Heumann Gurian, E. (2006) *Civilising the Museum: The Collected Writings of Elaine Heumann Gurian*, London: Routledge.

Hiippala, T. (2012) 'Reading paths and visual perception in multimodal research, psychology and brain sciences.' *Journal of Pragmatics,* doi:10.1016/j. pragma.201112.008.

Hodge, R. I.V. and Kress, G. R. (1974) 'Models and processes: towards a more usable linguistics.' *Journal of Literary Semantics* 1(3): pp. 5–22.

—— (1979/93) *Language as Ideology*, London: Routledge.

—— (1988) *Social Semiotics*, Cambridge: Polity Press.

Holland, D. and Lave, J. eds. (2001) *History in Person: Enduring Struggles, Contentious Practice, Intimate Identities*, Santa Fe, NM: School of American Research Press.

Holland, D. and Leander, K. M. (2004) 'Ethnographic studies of positioning and subjectivity: An introduction.' *Ethos: Journal of the Society for Psychological Anthropology* 32: pp. 127–39.

Holland, D., Lachicotte, J. R. W., Skinner, D. and Cain, C. (1998) *Identity and Agency in Cultural Worlds*, Cambridge, MA: Harvard University Press.

Holly, W. (2007) 'Audiovisuelle hermeneutik. Am beispiel des TV-Spots der kampagne "Du bist Deutschland".' In Hermanns, F. ed. *Linguistische Hermeneutik*, Tübingen: Niemeyer: pp. 389–428.

—— (2009) 'Der Wort-Bild-Reißverschluss. Über die performative Dynamik audiovisueller Transkriptivität.' In Linke, A. and Feilke, H. eds. *Oberfläche und Performanz: Untersuchungen zur Sprache als dynamischer Gestalt*, Tübingen: Niemeyer: pp. 389–406.

Holly, W. and Jäger, L. (2011) 'Transkriptionstheoretische medienanalyse. Vom Anders-lesbar-Machen durch intermediale Bezugnahmepraktiken.' In Schneider, J. G. and Stöckl, H. eds. *Medientheorien und Multimodalität*, Köln: Halem: pp. 151–68.

Holm Hopperstadt, M. (2008) 'How children make meaning through drawing and play.' *Visual Communication* 7(1): pp. 77–96.

Holmberg, N., Holmqvist, K. and Sandberg, H. (submitted) 'Children's visual attention to Internet adverts depends on individual level of oculomotor control.' *Media Psychology*.

Holmqvist, K. and Wartenberg, C. (2005) 'The role of local design factors for newspaper reading behaviour: An eye-tracking perspective.' *Lund University Cognitive Studies* 127. http://www.lucs.lu.se/LUCS/127/LUCS.127.pdf

Holmqvist, K., Holsanova, J., Barthelson, M. and Lundqvist, D. (2003) 'Reading or scanning? A study of newspaper and net paper reading.' In Hyönä, J. R. and Deubel, H. eds. *The Mind's Eye: Cognitive and Applied Aspects of Eye Movement Research*, Amsterdam: Elsevier Science: pp. 657–70.

Holmqvist, K., Nystrom, M., Andersson, R., Dewhurst, R., Jarodzka, H. and van de Weijer, J. (2011) *Eye Tracking: A Comprehensive Guide to Methods and Measures*, Oxford: Oxford University Press,

Holsanova, J. (1999) 'Olika perspektiv på språk, bild och deras samspel. Metodologiska reflexioner.' [Different perspectives on language, picture and their interplay. Methodological considerations.] In Haskå, I. and Sandqvist, C. eds. *Alla tiders språk*, Lundastudier i nordisk språkvetenskap A 55, Lund: Lund University Press: pp. 117–26.

—— (2001) 'Picture viewing and picture description: Two windows on the mind.' Doctoral dissertation. Lund University Cognitive Studies 83.

—— (2008) *Discourse, Vision and Cognition*, Human Cognitive Processing 23, Amsterdam, PA: John Benjamins Publishing Company.

—— (2010) *Myter och sanningar om läsning. Om samspelet mellan språk och bild i olika medier*, Norstedts: Stockholm.

—— (2011) 'How we focus attention in image viewing, image description, and during mental imagery.' In Sachs-Hombach, K. and Totzke, R. eds. *Bilder, Sehen, Denken*, Herbert von Halem Verlag: Köln: pp. 291–313.

—— (2012) 'New methods for studying visual communication and multimodal integration.' In Holsanova, J. ed. Methodologies for Multimodal Research, Special Issue of *Visual Communication* 11(3): pp. 251–57.

Holsanova, J. (2013 in press) 'In the eye of the beholder: Visual communication from a recipient perspective.' In Machin, D. ed. *Handbook of Visual Communication*. Berlin: De Gruyter.

Holsanova, J. and Holmqvist, K. (2004) 'Med blick pa nätnyheter. ögonrörelsestudier av läsning i nätbaserade tidningar (Looking at the net news. Eye tracking study of net paper reading).' In Holmberg, C.-G. and Svensson, J. eds. *Mediekulturer, Hybrider och Förvandlingar*, Stockholm: Carlsson förlag: pp. 216–48.

Holsanova, J. and Nord, A. (2010) 'Multimodal design: Media structures media principles and users meaning-making in printed and digital media.' In Bucher, H-J., Gloning, T. and Lehnen, K. eds. *Neue Medie – neue Formate: Ausdifferenzierung und Konvergenz in der Medienkommunikation*, Frankfurt, New York: Campus: pp. 81–103.

Holsanova, J. and Holmberg, N. (2011) 'Functional segmentation of task-solving process: Aligning eye movements and cued retrospective protocols.' Invited talk at the symposium Symposium Interacting with Electronic and Mobile Media: Oculomotor and Cognitive Effects (organizer: Pascal Wurtz), European Conference on Eye Movements, August, Marseille, France.

Holsanova, J., Rahm, H. and Holmqvist, K. (2006) 'Entry points and reading paths on newspaper spreads: Comparing a semiotic analysis with eye-tracking measurements.' *Visual Communication* 5: pp. 65–93.

Holsanova, J., Johansson, R. and Holmqvist, K. (2008) 'To tell and to show: The interplay of language and visualisations in communication.' In Gärdenfors, P. and Wallin, A. eds. *A Smorgasbord of Cognitive Science*, Nya Doxa: Nora: pp. 215–29.

Holsanova, J., Holmberg, N. and Holmqvist, K. (2009) 'Reading information graphics: The role of spatial contiguity and dual attentional guidance.' *Applied Cognitive Psychology* 23: pp. 1215–26. Published online December 2008 at http://www.interscience.wiley.com, doi: 10.1002/acp.1525

Holsanova, J. Holmberg, N. and Ek, J. (2012) 'Method for tracking reflected reading and multimodal learning of pupils with various abilities: Designs for learning.' In *Proceedings of the Designs for Learning Conference*, Copenhagen: pp. 92–94.

Holsanova, J., Sandberg, H., Holmberg, N. and Theobald, N. (2013) *How image content correlates with image perception*. Poster presented at the ECEM conference in Lund, August 2013.

Hornberger, N. (1997) 'Indigenous literacies in the Americas.' Introduction to *Indigenous Literacies in the Americas*, Berlin: Mouton de Gruyter: pp. 3–16.

—— ed. (2002) *The Continua of Biliteracy: A Framework for Educational Policy, Research and Practice in Multiple Settings*, Bristol: Multilingual Matters.

Howarth, D. (2002) *Discourse*, Milton Keynes: Open University Press.

Howes, D. (1991) 'Introduction.' In *The Varieties of Sensory Experience*, Toronto: University of Toronto Press: pp. 3–21.

—— (2003) *Sensual Relations: Engaging the Senses in Culture and Social Theory*, Ann Arbor: University of Michigan Press.

—— ed. (2004) *Empire of the Senses: The Sensual Culture Reader*, Oxford: Berg.

—— (2007) 'Sensory basket weaving 101.' In Alfoldy, S. ed. *NeoCrafts*, Halifax: Press of the Nova Scotia College of Art and Design.

Huang, C. and Archer, A. (2008) 'Discursive constructions of medical students' identities in informal course-based online discussions.' *Education as Change* 12(1): pp. 3–14.

Hull, G. and Nelson, M. (2005) 'Locating the semiotic power of multimodality.' *Written Communication* 22(2): pp. 1–38.

—— (2009) 'Literacy, media, and morality: Making the case for an aesthetic turn.' In Baynham, M. and Prinsloo, M. eds. *The Future of Literacy Studies*, Basingstoke: Palgrave Macmillan: pp. 199–228.

Hunter, L. (2006) 'Critical form as everyday practice: An interview with Ellen Lupton.' *Information Design Journal* 14(2): pp. 130–38.

Hurr, V. (2012) 'Documenting an encounter between art-film and multimodality informed by the production of digital moving images.' Working paper, at http://darecollaborativedotnet.files.wordpress.com/2012/11/v-hurr-film.pdf (accessed 22 March 2013).

Hymes, D. ed. (1996) *Ethnography, Linguistics, Narrative Inequality: Towards an Understanding of Voice*, London: Routledge.

Ide, N. and Romary, L. (2004) 'International standard for a linguistic annotation framework.' *Journal of Natural Language Engineering* 10(3–4): pp. 211–25. doi:10.1017/S135132490400350X. http://dx.doi.org/10.1017/S135132490400350X.

Iedema, R. (2001a) 'Analyzing film and television: A social semiotic account of hospital – An unhealthy business.' In van Leeuwen, T. and Jewitt, C. eds. *Handbook of Visual Analysis*, London: Sage: pp. 183–206.

—— (2001b) 'Resemiotization.' *Semiotica* 137, 1(4): pp. 23–39.

—— (2003) 'Multimodality, resemioticization: Extending the analysis of discourse as a multisemiotic practice.' *Visual Communication* 2(1): pp. 29–57.

Iedema, R., Feez, S. and White, P. R. R. (1994) 'Stage two: Media literacy – A report for the Write it Right Literacy in Industry Research Project Sydney: Disadvantaged Schools Program, N.S.W. Department of School Education.' In Special Issue: Gesture: Do Teachers Have the Upper Hand? *Journal of Educational Psychology* 89: pp. 183–93.

Ifrah, G. (2000) *The Universal History of Numbers: From Prehistory to the Invention of the Computer*, New York: John Wiley.

—— (2001) *The Universal History of Computing: From the Abacus to the Quantum Computer*, New York: John Wiley.

IKEA Catalogue 2007 (2006) Swedish and Australian (New South Wales, Queensland and Victoria) editions, Inter IKEA Systems BV. In Kress, G. and Van Leeuwen, T. *Reading Images: The Grammar of Visual Design*, London: Routledge.

Introna, L. (2001) 'Virtuality and morality: On (not) being disturbed by the other.' *Philosophy in the Contemporary World* 8(1), pp. 31–39.

—— (2002) 'On the impossibility of ethics in a mediated world.' *Information and Organisation* 12(2): pp. 71–84.

ISO. (2011) *International Standard ISO 24617–2. Language Resource Management – Semantic Annotation Framework (SemAF), Part 2: Dialogue Acts*, Geneva: International Organization for Standardization.

—— (2012) *International Standard ISO 24612. Language Resource Management – Linguistic Annotation Framework (LAF)*, Geneva: International Organization for Standardization, 1st edn: 2012-06-15: ISO 24612:2012(E).

Ito, M. (2003) 'Technologies of the childhood imagination: Media mixes, hypersociality, and recombinant cultural form.' In *Transitions to College: From Theory to Practice*. At http://edtransitions.ssrc.org/home.aspx (accessed 14 January 2009).

Ito, M., Okabe, D. and Matsuda, M. (2005) *Personal, Portable, Pedestrian: Mobile Phones in Japanese Life*, Cambridge, MA: MIT Press.

Itti, L. and Koch, C. (2000) 'A saliency-based search mechanism for overt and covert shifts of visual attention.' *Vision Research* 40: pp. 1489–506.

Ivarsson, J. and Säljö, R. (2005) 'Seeing through the screen: Human reasoning and the development of representational technologies.' In Gärdenfors, P. and Johansson, P. eds. *Cognition, Learning, and Communication Technology*, Hillsdale, NJ: Erlbaum: pp. 203–22.

Jacobson, M. J. and Azevedo, R. (2008) 'Advances in scaffolding learning with hypertext and hypermedia: A summary and critical analysis'. *Educational Technology Research Development* 56: pp. 93–100.

Jakobson, R. (1960) 'Closing statement: Linguistics and poetics.' In Sebeok, T. A. ed. *Style in Language*, Cambridge, MA: MIT Press.

Jakobson, R. and Halle, M. (1956) *Fundamentals of Language*, The Hague: Mouton de Gruyter.

Janks, H. (2000) 'Domination, access, diversity and design: A synthesis for Critical Literacy education.' *Educational Review* 52(2): pp. 175–86.

—— (2010) *Literacy and Power*, London: Routledge.

Jarodzka, H., Balslev, T., Holmqvist, K., Scheiter, K., Nyström, M., Gerjets, P. and Eika, B. (2010) 'Learning perceptual aspects of diagnosis in medicine via eye movement modeling examples on patient video cases.' In *Cognition in Flux: Proceedings of the 32nd Annual Meeting of the Cognitive Science Society*, Portland, OR: pp. 1703–08.

Jaworski, A. and Thurlow, C. (2010) 'Introducing semiotic landscapes.' In Jaworski, A. and Thurlow, C. eds. *Semiotic Landscapes: Language, Image, Space*, London: Continuum: pp. 1–40.

Jay, M. (1993) *Downcast Eyes: The Denigration of Vision in 20th Century Thought*, Berkeley, CA: University of California Press.

—— (2002) 'That visual turn: The advent of visual culture.' *Visual Culture* 1(1): pp. 87–92.

Jenkins, H. (1992) *Textual Poachers: Television Fans and Participatory Culture*, New York: Routledge.

—— (2006a) *Convergence Culture*, New York: NYU Press.

—— (2006b) *Confronting the Challenges of Participatory Culture: Media Education for the 21st Century*, Chicago, IL: MacArthur Foundation.

Jenks, C. (1995) *Visual Culture*, London: Routledge.

Jeung, H.-J., Chandler, P. and Sweller, J. (1997) 'The role of visual indicators in dual sensory mode instruction.' *Educational Psychology* 17: pp. 329–43.

Jewitt, C. (2002) 'The move from page to screen: The multimodal reshaping of school English.' *Visual Communication* 1(2): pp. 171–96.

—— (2005) 'Multimodal "reading" and "writing" on screen.' *Discourse: Studies in the Cultural Politics of Education* 26(3): pp. 315–32.

—— (2006) *Technology, Literacy and Learning: A Multimodal Approach*, London: Routledge.

—— (2008a) *Technology, Literacy and Learning: A Multimodal Approach* (paperback edition), London: Routledge.

—— (2008b) 'Multimodal classroom research.' *AERA Review of Research in Education* 32: pp. 241–67.

—— ed. (2009) *Handbook of Multimodal Analysis*, 1st edn, London: Routledge.

Jewitt, C. and Oyama, R. (2001) 'Visual meaning: A social semiotic approach.' In Van Leeuwen, T. and Jewitt, C. eds. *Handbook of Visual Analysis*, London: Sage: pp. 134–56.

Jewitt, C. and Kress, G. (2003a) 'A multimodal approach to research in education.' In Goodman, S., Lillis, T., Maybin, J. and Mercer, N. eds. *Language, Literacy and Education: A Reader*, Stoke on Trent: Trentham Books/Open University: pp. 277–92.

—— eds. (2003b) *Multimodal Literacy*, New York: Peter Lang.

Johansen, J. D. and Larsen, S. E. (2002) *Signs in Use: An Introduction to Semiotics*, London: Routledge.

Johnson, C. I. and Mayer, R. E. (2012) 'An eye movement analysis of the spatial contiguity effect in multimedia learning.' *Journal of Experimental Psychology: Applied* 18(2): pp. 178–91. doi:10.1037/a0026923.

Johnson, M. (1987) *The Body in the Mind: The Bodily Basis of Meaning, Imagination, and Reason*, Chicago, IL: University of Chicago Press.

Jones, C. (2005) *Eyesight Alone: Clement Greenberg's Modernism and the Bureaucratization of the Senses*, Chicago, IL: University of Chicago Press.

—— (2006) 'The mediated sensorium.' In Jones, C. A. ed. *Sensorium: Embodied Experience, Technology and Contemporary Art*, Cambridge, MA: MIT List Visual Arts Center and MIT Press: pp. 5–49.

Jones, R. (2000) 'Potato seeking rice: Language culture and identity in gay personal ads in Hong Kong.' *International Journal of the Sociology of Language* 143: pp. 33–61.

—— (2002) 'A walk in the park: Frames and positions in AIDS prevention outreach among gay men in China.' *Journal of Sociolinguistics* 6(3): pp. 575–88.

—— (2005) '"You show me yours, I'll show you mine": The negotiation of shifts from textual to visual modes in computer mediated interaction among gay men.' *Visual Communication* 4(1): pp. 69–92.

Jones, R. H. and Norris, S. (2005) 'Discourse as action/discourse in action.' In Norris, S. and Jones, R. H. eds. *Discourse in Action: Introducing Mediated Discourse Analysis*, London: Routledge.

Joseph, G. G. (1991) *The Crest of the Peacock: Non-European Roots of Mathematics*, London: I.B. Tauris.

Just, M. A. and Carpenter, P. A. (1980) 'A theory of reading: From eye fixations to comprehension.' *Psychological Review* 87: pp. 329–54.

Kalman, J. (1999) *Writing on the Plaza: Mediated Literacy Practices Among Scribes and Clients in Mexico City*, Cresskill, NJ: Hampton Press.

Kalyuga, S., Chandler, P. and Sweller, J. (1999) 'Managing split-attention and redundancy in multimedia instruction.' *Applied Cognitive Psychology* 13: pp. 351–71.

Kamil, M., Intrator, S. and Kim, H. (2000) 'The effects of other technologies on literacy and learning.' In Kamil, M., Mosenthal, P., Pearson, P. and Barr, R. eds. *Handbook of Reading Research*, Vol. 3, Mahwah, NJ: Erlbaum: pp. 771–88.

Kappelhoff, H. and Bakels, J.-H. (2011) 'Das Zuschauergefühl – Möglichkeiten qualitativer Medienanalyse.' *Zeitschrift für Medienwissenschaft* 5(2): pp. 78–95.

Kauffman, R. (1979) 'Tactility as an aesthetic consideration in African music.' In Blacking, J. and Kealiinohomoku, J. eds. *The Performing Arts: Music and Dance*, The Hague: Mouton.

Kell, C. (2006) 'Crossing the margins: Literacy, semiotics and the recontextualisation of meanings.' In Pahl, K. and Rowsell, J. eds. *Travel Notes from the New Literacy Studies: Instances of Practice*, Clevedon, UK: Multilingual Matters: pp. 147–72.

—— (2009) 'Literacy practices, text/s and meaning making across time and space.' In Baynham, M. and Prinsloo, M. eds. *The Future of Literacy Studies*, Basingstoke: Palgrave Macmillan.

Kelland, M., Morris, M. and Lloyd, D. (2005) *Machinima*, London: Course Technology PTR.

Kellogg, R. (1969) *Analyzing Children's Art*, Mountain View, CA: Mayfield.

Kendon, A. (1967) 'Some functions of gaze-direction in social interaction.' *Acta Psychologica* 26: pp. 22–63.

—— (1990) *Conducting Interaction: Patterns of Behaviour in Focused Encounters*, Cambridge: Cambridge University Press.

—— (2004a) *Gesture: Visible Action as Utterance*, Cambridge: Cambridge University Press.

—— (2004b) 'On pointing.' In *Gesture: Visible Action as Utterance*, Cambridge: Cambridge University Press: pp. 199–224.

Kendon, A. and Sigman, S. J. (1996) 'Ray L. Birdwhistell (1918–1994).' *Semiotica* 112(3/4): pp. 231–61.

Kenner, C. (2000a) 'Recipes, alphabets and I{heart}U: A four year old explores the visual potential of literacy.' *Early Years* 20(2): pp. 68–79.

—— (2000b) *Home Pages: Literacy Links for Bilingual Children*, Stoke on Trent: Trentham Books.

—— (2003) 'Embodied knowledges: Young children's engagement with the act of writing.' In Jewitt, C. and Kress, G. eds. *Multimodal Literacy*, New York: Peter Lang: pp. 88–106.

—— (2004) *Becoming Biliterate: Young Children Learning Different Writing Systems*, Stoke on Trent: Trentham Books.

Khare, R. S. (2005) 'Food with saints.' In Korsmeyer, C. ed. *The Taste Culture Reader: Experiencing Food and Drink*, Oxford: Berg.

King, L. (1994) *Roots of Identity: Language and Literacy in Mexico*, Stanford, CA: Stanford University Press.

Kingsbury, P., Palmer, M. and Marcus, M. (2002) 'Adding semantic annotation to the Penn TreeBank.' In *Proceedings of the Human Language Technology Conference (HLT 2002)*, San Diego: pp. 252–56. http// dl.acm.org/citation.cfm?id=1289207.

Kinloch, V. (2010) *Harlem on Our Minds: Place, Race and the Literacies of Urban Youth*, New York: Teachers College Press.

Kipp, M. (2008) 'Spatiotemporal coding in ANVIL.' In Calzolari, N., Choukri, K., Maegaard, B., Mariani, J., Odjik, J., Piperidis, S. and Tapias, D. eds. *Proceedings of the 6th International Conference on Language Resources and Evaluation (LREC 2008)*, Marrakech, Morocco: European Language Resources Association (ELRA).

—— (2012) 'Multimedia annotation, querying and analysis in ANVIL.' In Maybury, M. T. ed. *Multimedia Information Extraction*, Chap. 21: pp. 351–68. Hoboken, NJ: John Wiley and Sons. IEEE Computer Society.

Kirmayer, L. J. (in press) 'On the cultural mediation of pain.' In Coakley, S. and Shelemay, K. eds. *Pain and Its Transformations*, Cambridge, MA: Harvard University Press.

Knight, D., Evans, D., Carter, R. and Adolphs, S. (2008) 'Redrafting corpus development methodologies: Blueprints for 3rd generation "multimodal, multimedia" corpora.' Forthcoming.

Knox, J. S. (2007) 'Visual-verbal communication on online newspaper home pages.' *Visual Communication* 6(1): pp. 19–53.

—— (2009a) 'Punctuating the home page: Image as language in an online newspaper.' *Discourse and Communication* 3(2): pp. 145–72.

—— (2009b) 'Visual minimalism in hard news: Thumbnail faces on the smh online home page.' *Social Semiotics* 19(2): pp. 165–89.

—— (2009c) 'Multimodal discourse on online newspaper home pages: A social-semiotic perspective.' Unpublished PhD thesis, University of Sydney. Available online at: http://hdl.handle.net/2123/7696 (accessed 6 October 2013).

—— (2013) 'Multimodality and systemic functional analysis.' In Chapelle, C. A. ed. *The Encyclopedia of Applied Linguistics*, Oxford: Wiley Blackwell, pp. 4082–89.

Knox, J. S., Patpong, P. and Piriyasilpa, Y. (2010) 'ข่าวหน้าหนึ่ง (Khao naa nung): A multimodal analysis of Thai-language newspaper pages.' In Bednarek, M. and Martin, J. R. eds. *New Discourse on Language: Functional Perspectives on Multimodality, Identity, and Affiliation*, London: Continuum: pp. 80–110.

Kopp, S., Krenn, B., Marsella, S., Marshall, A. N., Pelachaud, C., Pirker, H., Thórisson, K. R. and Vilhjálmsson, H. (2006) 'Towards a common framework for multimodal generation: The Behavior Markup Language.' In Gratch, J., Young, M., Aylett, R., Ballin, D. and Olivier, P. eds. *Intelligent Virtual Agents*, Vol. 4133, Lecture Notes in Artificial Intelligence. Berlin and Heidelberg: Springer-Verlag. doi:10. 1007/11821830. Proceedings of the 6th International Conference, IVA 2006, Marina Del Rey, CA, USA, August 21–23: pp. 205–17.

Kostogriz, A. (2006) 'Putting "space" on the agenda of sociocultural research.' *Mind, Culture, and Activity* 13: pp. 176–90.

Kozulin, A. (2003) *Psychological Tools: A Sociocultural Approach to Education*, Cambridge, MA: Harvard University Press.

Kraidy, M. M. (1999) 'The global, the local, and the hybrid: A native ethnography of globalization.' *Critical Studies in Mass Communication* 16: pp. 454–67.

Krampen, M. (1989) 'Semiotics in architecture and industrial/product design.' *Design Issues* 5(2): pp. 124–40.

—— (1995) 'Semiotics of objects revisited.' In Sebeok, T. A. and Umiker-Sebeok, J. eds. *Advances in Visual Semiotics: The Semiotic Web 1992–1993*, Berlin: Mouton de Gruyter.

Kranstedt, A., Kopp, S. and Wachsmuth, I. (2002) 'MURML: A Multimodal Utterance Representation Markup Language for Conversational Agents.' Tech. Rep. 2002/05 SFB 360 Situated Artifical Communicators, Universität Bielefeld Bielefeld, Germany. http://www.sfb360.uni-bielefeld.de/reports/2002/2002-5.html (accessed 6 October 2013).

Krauss, R. M., Chen, Y. and Gottesman, R. F. (2000) 'Lexical gestures and lexical access: A process model.' In McNeill, D. ed. *Gesture and Language*, Cambridge: Cambridge University Press: pp. 261–83.

Kress, G. (1993) 'Against arbitrariness: The social production of the sign as a foundational issue in critical discourse analysis.' *Discourse and Society* 4(2): pp. 169–91.

—— (1997a) *Before Writing: Rethinking Paths to Literacy*, London: Routledge.

—— (1997b) 'Visual and verbal modes of representation in electronically mediated communication: The potentials of new forms of text.' In Snyder, I. ed. *Page to Screen: Taking Literacy into the Electronic Era*, Sydney: Allen and Unwin: pp. 53–79.

492

—— (2000a) 'Design and transformation: New theories of meaning.' In Cope, B. and Kalantzis, M. eds. *Multiliteracies: Learning Literacy and the Design of Social Futures*, Melbourne: Macmillan: pp. 153–61.

—— (2000b) 'Multimodality.' In Cope, B. and Kalantzis, M. eds. *Multiliteracies: Literacy Learning and the Design of Social Futures*, Melbourne: Macmillan: pp. 182–202.

—— (2001) 'Sociolinguistics and social semiotics.' In Cobley, P. ed. *Semiotics and Linguistics*, London: Routledge: pp. 66–82.

—— (2003a) 'Genres and the multimodal production of "scientificness".' In Jewitt, C. and Kress, G. eds. *Multimodal Literacy*, New York: Peter Lang: pp. 173–86.

—— (2003b) *Literacy in the New Media Age*, London: Routledge.

—— (2010a) *Multimodality: A Social Semiotic Approach to Contemporary Communication*, London: Routledge.

—— (2010b) '"Partnerships in research": Multimodality and ethnography.' *Qualitative Research* 11(3): pp. 239–60.

Kress, G. and Van Leeuwen, T. (1990) *Reading Images*, Geelong, Victoria: Deakin University Press.

—— (1996, 2nd edn 2006) *Reading Images: The Grammar of Visual Design*, London: RoutledgeFalmer.

—— (1996/2001) *Reading Images: The Grammar of Visual Design*, London: Arnold.

—— (1998) 'Front pages: (The critical) analysis of newspaper layout.' In Bell, A. and Garrett, P. eds. *Approaches to Media Discourse*, Oxford: Blackwell: pp. 186–219.

—— (2001) *Multimodal Discourse: The Modes and Media of Contemporary Communication*, London: Edward Arnold.

—— (2002) 'Colour as a semiotic mode: Notes for a grammar of colour.' *Visual Communication* 1(3): pp. 343–68.

Kress, G. and Street, B. V. (2006) 'Foreword.' In Pahl, K. and Rowsell, J. eds. *Travel Notes from the New Literacy Studies: Instances of Practice*, Clevedon, UK: Multilingual Matters: pp. vii–x.

Kress, G., Jewitt, C., Ogborn, J. and Tsatsarelis, C. (2001) *Multimodal Teaching and Learning: The Rhetorics of the Science Classroom*, London: Continuum.

Kress, G., Jewitt, C., Bourne, J., Franks, A., Hardcastle, J., Jones, K. and Reid, E. (2004) *English in Urban Classrooms: Multimodal Perspectives on Teaching and Learning*, London: RoutledgeFalmer.

Kristeva, J. (1980) *Desire in Language: A Semiotic Approach to Language and Art*, Oxford: Blackwell.

Kristeva, J. (1989) *Language: The Unknown – An Initiation into Linguistics*, New York, Columbia University Press.

Küpper, N. (1989) 'Blickaufzeichnung – Erforschung des Leseverhaltens beim Zeitungslesen.' *Deutscher Drücker* 31. http://calendardesign.de/leseforschung/Eyetrackstudy.pdf.

Lacy, M. L. (1996) *The Power of Colour to Heal the Environment*, London: Rainbow Bridge Publications.

Lakoff, G. and Johnson, M. (1980) *Metaphors We Live By*, Chicago, IL: University of Chicago Press.

Lamy, M.-N. and Hampel, R. (2007) *Online Communication for Language Learning and Teaching*, Basingstoke: Palgrave.

Lancaster, L. (2001) 'Staring at the page: The functions of gaze in a young child's interpretation of symbolic forms.' *Journal of Early Childhood Literacy* 1(2): pp. 131–52.

—— (2007) 'Representing the ways of the world: How children under three start to use syntax in graphic signs.' *Journal of Early Childhood Literacy* 7(2): pp. 123–54.

—— (2011) 'The dragon in the cave: Textual representations of fictional and every day events by children under three.' In Kümmerling-Meibauer, B. ed. *Children's Books from 0–3: Where Literacy Begins*, Amsterdam: John Benjamins.

Lancaster, L. and Roberts, M. (2007) 'It's a bear, it's a monkey jumping: Referential relationships in early mark-making.' Paper delivered at UKLA, July 2007, University of Swansea, UK.

Landow, G. ed. (1997) *Hypertext 2.0*, Baltimore, MD: Johns Hopkins University Press.

Langer, S. K. (1951) *Philosophy in a New Key: A Study in the Symbolism of Reason, Rite and Art*, New York: Mentor.

Lanham, R. (1994) 'The economics of attention.' In *Proceedings of 124th Annual Meeting*, Association of Research Libraries. At http://sunsite.berkeley.edu/ARL/Proceedings/124/ps2econ.html (accessed 13 September 2004).

—— (2001) 'What next for text?' *Education, Communication, and Information* 1(1): pp. 59–74.

Lankshear, C. and Knobel, M. (2002) 'Do we have your attention? New literacies, digital technologies and the education of adolescents.' In Alvermann, D. E. ed. *Adolescents and Literacies in a Digital World*, New York: Peter Lang: pp. 19–39.

—— (2003) *New Literacies: Changing Knowledge and Classroom Learning*, Buckingham, PA: Open University Press.

Larsen, S. E. (1998) 'Semiotics.' In Mey, J. L. ed. *Concise Encyclopedia of Pragmatics*, Amsterdam: Elsevier: pp. 833–46.

Larson, J. and Marsh, J. (2005) *Making Literacy Real: Theories and Practices for Learning and Teaching*, London: Sage.

Latour, B. (1987) *Science in Action*, Cambridge, MA: Harvard University Press.

—— (1999) *Pandora's Hope: Essays on the Reality of Science Studies*, Cambridge, MA: Harvard University Press.

Lave, J. and Wenger, E. (1991) *Situated Learning: Legitimate Peripheral Participation*, New York: Cambridge University Press.

Laver, J. (1979) *The Phonetic Description of Voice Quality*, Cambridge: Cambridge University Press.

Le Breton, D. (2006) 'La conjugaison des sens.' *Anthropologie et Sociétés* 30: pp. 11–18.

Leahy, H. R. (2012) *Museum Bodies: The Politics and Practices of Visiting and Viewing*, Farnham, Surrey: Ashgate Publishing.

Leander, K. and Sheehy, M. eds. (2004) *Spatializing Literacy Research and Practice*, New York: Peter Lang.

Leander, K. and Frank, A. (2006) 'The aesthetic production and distribution of image/subjects among online youth.' *E-Learning* 3: pp. 185–206.

Leander, K. and Lovvorn, J. (2006) 'Literacy networks: Following the circulation of texts, bodies, and objects in the schooling and online gaming of one youth.' *Cognition and Instruction* 24(3): pp. 291–340.

Leander, K. and Wells Rowe, D. (2006) 'Mapping literacy spaces in motion: A rhizomatic analysis of a classroom literacy performance.' *Reading Research Quarterly* 41(4): pp. 428–60.

Leander, K. and Boldt, G. (2013) 'Rereading "A Pedagogy of Multiliteracies": Bodies, texts and emergence.' *The Journal of Literacy Research* 45(1): pp. 22–46.

Leeds-Hurwitz, W. (1987) 'The social history of the natural history of an interview: A multidisciplinary investigation of social communication.' *Research on Language and Social Interaction* 20: pp. 1–51.

—— (2005) 'The natural history approach: A Bateson legacy.' *Cybernetics and Human Knowing* 12(1–2): pp. 137–46.

Lefebvre, H. (1991) *The Production of Space*, Nicholson-Smith, D., trans., Oxford: Blackwell Publishing.

Leibniz, G. (1849) *Mathematische Schriften: Band I*, Halle: Druck und Verlag von H. W. Schmidt.

—— (1859) *Mathematische Schriften: Band IV*, Halle: Druck und Verlag von H. W. Schmidt.

Leitner, G. (1980) 'BBC English and Deutsche Rundfunksprache: A comparative and historical analysis of language on the radio.' *International Journal of the Sociology of Language* 26: pp. 75–100.

Lemke, J. (1989) 'Making text talk.' *Theory into Practice* 28: pp. 136–41.

—— (1990a) 'Technical discourse and technocratic ideology.' In Halliday, M. A. K., Gibbons, J. and Nicholas, H. eds. *Learning, Keeping and Using Language: Selected Papers from the 8th AILA World Congress of Applied Linguistics, Sydney 1987*, Vol. II, Amsterdam: John Benjamins: pp. 435–60.

—— (1990b) *Talking Science: Language, Learning, and Values*, Norwood, NJ: Ablex.

—— (1995) *Textual Politics: Discourse and Social Dynamics*, London: Taylor & Francis.

—— (1998a) 'Metamedia literacy: Transforming meanings and media.' In Reinking, D., McKenna, M., Labbo, L. and Kieffer, R. eds. *Handbook of Literacy and Technology: Transformations in a Post-Typographic World*, Hillsdale, NJ: Erlbaum: pp. 283–302.

—— (1998b) 'Multiplying meaning: Visual and verbal semiotics in scientific text.' In Martin, J. R. and Veel, R. eds. *Reading Science: Critical and Functional Perspectives on Discourses of Science*, London: Routledge: pp. 87–113.

—— (1998c) 'Introduction: Language and other semiotic systems in education.' *Linguistics and Education* 10(3): pp. 245–46.

—— (2000) 'Across the scales of time: Artifacts, activities, and meanings in ecosocial systems.' *Mind, Culture, and Activity* 7(4): pp. 273–90.

—— (2002a) 'Opening up closure: Semiotics across scales.' In Chandler, J. L. R. and Van de Vijver, G. eds. *Closure: Emergent Organizations and Their Dynamics*, New York: Annals of the New York Academy of Sciences, Vol. 901: p. 100.

—— (2002b) 'Travels in hypermodality.' *Visual Communication* 1(3): pp. 299–325.

—— (2005) 'Place, pace, and meaning: Multimedia chronotopes.' In Norris, S. and Jones, R. eds. *Discourse in Action*, London: Routledge.

—— (2006) 'Towards critical multimedia literacy: Technology, research, and politics.' In McKenna, M., Labbo, L., Kieffer, R. and Reinking, D. eds. *Handbook of Literacy and Technology*, Vol. II, Mahwah, NJ: Erlbaum (LEA Publishing).

—— (2007) 'Transmedia traversals: Marketing meaning and identity.' In Baldry, A. and Montagna, E. eds. *Interdisciplinary Perspectives on Multimodality: Theory and Practice*, Proceedings of the Third International Conference on Multimodality, Campobasso: Palladino: pp. 576–96.

—— (2012) 'Multimedia and discourse analysis'. In Gee, J. P. and Handford, M. eds. *Routledge Handbook of Discourse Analysis*, London: Routledge: pp. 79–89.

—— (2013) 'Feeling and meaning in the social ecology of learning: Lessons from play and games.' In Baker, M., Andriessen J. and Järvelä, S. eds. *Affective Learning Together: The Socio-Emotional Turn in Collaborative Learning*, London: Routledge.

Lessing, G. E. (1853 [1766]) *Laocoon: An Essay on the Limits of Painting and Poetry*, Beasley, E. C., trans., London: Longman, Brown, Green, and Longmans *and others*.

Leu, D., Kinzer, C., Coiro, J. and Cammack, D. (2004) 'Toward a theory of new literacies emerging from the internet and other information and communication technologies.' In Ruddell, R. and Unrau, N. eds. *Theoretical Models and Processes of Reading*, Vol. 5, Newark, DE: International Reading Association: pp. 1570–613.

Levinas, E. (1969) *Totality and Infinity*, Pittsburgh, PA: Duquesne.

Lewis, C. and del Valle, A. (2008) 'Literacy and identity: Implications for research and practice.' In Christenbury, L. Bomer, R. and Smagorinsky, P. eds. *Handbook of Adolescent Literacy Research*, New York: Guilford Press: pp. 307–22.

Lewis-Williams, D. (2002) *The Mind in the Cave: Consciousness and the Origins of Art*, London: Thames & Hudson.

Liben, L. S. (2003) 'Thinking through maps.' In Gattis, M. ed. *Spatial Schemas and Abstract Thought*, Cambridge, MIT Press: pp. 45–77.

Lim Fei, V. (2004) 'Developing an integrative multi-semiotic model.' In O'Halloran, K. L. ed. *Multimodal Discourse Analysis*, London: Continuum: pp. 220–46.

Linderoth, J. (2004) *Datorspelandets mening: Bortom idén om den interaktiva illusionen* [The meaning of computer gaming. Beyond the idea of the interactive illusion], Göteborg: Acta Universitatis Gothoburgensis.

Linguistic Ethnography Forum UK. 'UK linguistic ethnography: A discussion paper.' At http://www.ling-ethnog.org.uk/documents/discussion_paper_jan_05.pdf.

Lister, M. and Wells, L. (2001) 'Seeing beyond belief: Cultural studies as an approach to analysing the visual.' In Van Leeuwen, T. and Jewitt, C. eds. *Handbook of Visual Analysis*, London: Sage: pp. 61–91.

Lomax, A. (1968) *Folk Song Style and Culture*, New Brunswick, NJ: Transaction Books.

Lomax, H. and Casey, N. (1998) 'Recording social life: Reflexivity and video methodology.' *Sociological Research Online* 3(2). Available at http://www.socresonline.org.uk/socresonline/3/2/1. html (accessed 16 July 2008).

Lotman, J. (1990) *Universe of the Mind: A Semiotic Theory of Culture*, Bloomington, IN: Indiana University Press.

Lou, J. (2005) 'Connecting the online and the offline: A preliminary study of display names in computer-mediated interactions.' Poster presented at *Language and Global Communication Conference*, July 7, at Cardiff University, Wales.

Low, B. (2005) '"Saying it in a different way": Adolescent literacies through the lens of cultural studies.' In Street, B. V. ed. *Literacies Across Educational Contexts*, Philadelphia, PA: Caslon: pp. 105–23.

LucasArts and Sony Online Entertainment (2003) Star Wars galaxies: An empire divided. Massively multiplayer online roleplaying game.

Luff, P., Heath, C. C. and Greatbatch, D. (1992) 'Tasks-in-interaction: Paper and screen based documentation in collaborative activity.' In Turner, J. and Kraut, R. eds. *CSCW '92*, Toronto: ACM Press: pp. 163–70.

Luff, P., Hindmarsh, J. and Heath, C. (2000) *Workplace Studies: Recovering Work Practice and Informing System Design*, Cambridge: Cambridge University Press.

Luff, P., Heath, C., Kuzuoka, H., Yamazaki, K. and Yamashita, J. (2006) 'Handling documents and discriminating objects in hybrid spaces.' In *CHI* 2006, Montreal: pp. 561–70.

Luff, P., Adams, G., Bock, W., Drazin, A., Frohlich, D., Heath, C. *et al.* (2007) 'Augmented paper: Developing relationships between digital content and paper.' In Streitz, N., Kamesis, A. and Mavrommati, I. eds. *The Disappearing Computer: Interaction Design, System Infrastructures and Applications for Smart Environments*, *LNCS* 4500, Heidelberg: Springer-Verlag: pp. 275–98.

Luke, A. and Carrington, V. (2002) 'Globalisation, literacy curriculum practice.' In Fisher, R., Lewis, M. and Brooks, G. eds. *Raising Standards in Literacy*, London: Routledge: pp. 231–50.

Luke, C. (2003) 'Pedagogy, connectivity, multimodality and interdisciplinarity.' *Reading Research Quarterly* 38(10): pp. 356–85.

Lundqvist, D. and Holmqvist, K. (2001) 'Bigger is better: How advertisement size affects reading, memory and attitude.' http://www.sol.lu.se/humlab/eyetracking/papers.htm (accessed 6 October 2013).

Luria, A. (1981) *Language and Cognition*, New York: Wiley.

Lürzer's Archiv/Lürzer's Int'l Archive: Advertising Worldwide. European Edition, Vol. 1/2012.

McCabe, D. P. and Caster, A. D. (2008) 'Seeing is believing: The effect of brain images on judgments of scientific reasoning.' *Cognition* 107: pp. 343–52.

McCloud, S. (1994) *Understanding Comics: The Invisible Art*, New York: Harper Collins.

McDonald, R. ed. (2001) *Encyclopedia of Discovery Earth*, Sydney: Weldon Owen.

McDowell, L. ed. (1997) *Undoing Place? A Geographical Reader*, New York: Arnold.

McEnery, T. and Wilson, A. (2001) *Corpus Linguistics*, 2nd edn, Edinburgh Textbooks in Empirical Linguistics, Edinburgh: Edinburgh University Press.

McGowan, J. (1998) *Hannah Arendt: An introduction*, Minneapolis: University of Minnesota Press.

Machin, D. (2007) *Introduction to Multimodal Analysis*, London: Hodder Arnold.

Machin, D. and Niblock, S. (2006) *News Production: Theory and Practice*, London: Routledge.

Macken-Horarik, M. (2003) 'A telling symbiosis in the discourse of hatred: Multimodal news texts about the "children overboard" affair.' *Australian Review of Applied Linguistics* 26(2): pp. 1–16.

—— (2004) 'Interacting with the multimodal text: reflections on image and verbiage in ArtExpress.' *Visual Communication* 3(1): pp. 5–26.

Mackey, M. (2003) 'Television and the teenage literate: Discourses of "Felicity".' *College English* 65(4): pp. 389–410.

McLuhan, M. (1964) *Understanding Media*, London: Routledge & Kegan Paul.

—— (1974) *Understanding Media: The Extensions of Man*, 2nd edition, Cambridge, MA: MIT Press.

McNeill, D. (1992) *Hand and Mind: What Gestures Reveal about Thought*, Chicago, IL: University of Chicago Press.

—— ed. (2000) *Language and Gesture*, Cambridge: Cambridge University Press.

—— (2003) 'Pointing and morality in Chicago.' In Kita, S. ed. *Pointing: Where Language, Culture, and Cognition Meet*, Mahwah, NJ: Lawrence Erlbaum: pp. 293–306.

—— (2005a) *Gesture and Thought*, Chicago, IL: University of Chicago Press.

—— (2005b) *Hand and Mind: What Gestures Reveal about Thought*, Chicago: The University of Chicago Press.

MacQueen, J. B. (1967) 'Some methods for classification and analysis of multivariate observations.' In Le Cam, L. M. and Neyman, J. eds. *Proceedings of 5th Berkeley Symposium on Mathematical Statistics and Probability*: pp. 281–97.

Maffesoli, M. (1996) *The Contemplation of the World: Figures of Community Style*, Minneapolis: University of Minnesota Press.

Mäkitalo, Å. and Säljö, R. (2009) 'Contextualizing social dilemmas in institutional practices: Negotiating objects of activity in labour market organizations.' In Sannino, A., Daniels, H. and Gutierrez, K. eds. *Learning and Expanding With Activity Theory*, New York: Cambridge University Press.

Mäkitalo, Å., Carlsson, C. and Säljö, R. (2009) 'The art and skill of engraving: Craftsmanship and the evolution of knowing and technologies.' In Oser, F., Renold, U., John, E. G., Winther, E. and Weber, S. eds. *VET Boost: Towards a Theory of Professional Competencies: Essays in Honor of Frank Achtenhagen*, Rotterdam: Sense: pp. 331–49.

Malchiodi, C. A. (1998) *Understanding Children's Drawings*, London: The Guilford Press.

Mamykina, L., Candy, L. and Edmonds, E. (2002) 'Collaborative creativity.' *Communications of the ACM* 45: pp. 3–6.

Mangen, A. (2010) 'Point and click: Theoretical and phenomenological reflections on the digitalization of early childhood education.' *Contemporary Issues in Early Childhood* 11(4): pp. 415–31.

Mann, W. C. and Thompson, S. A. (1988) 'Rhetorical structure theory: Toward a functional theory of text organization.' *Text* 8: pp. 243–81.

Manovich, L. (2005) 'Remixing and remixability.' At http://newmediafix. net/daily/?p=204 (accessed 14 May 2008).

—— (2012) 'How to compare one million images.' In Berry, D. M. ed. *Understanding Digital Humanities*, Basingstoke: Palgrave Macmillan: pp. 249–78.

Mantovani, F. (2001) 'Cyber-attraction: The emergence of computer-mediated communication in the development of interpersonal relationships.' In Anolli, L., Ciceri, R. and Riva, G. eds. *Say Not to Say: New Perspectives on Miscommunication*, Amsterdam: IOS Press: pp. 229–45.

Manvell, R. (1972) *The International Encyclopaedia of Film*, London: Rainbird Reference Books.

Marsh, J. ed. (2005) *Popular Culture, New Media and Digital Literacy in Early Childhood*, London: RoutledgeFalmer.

—— (2006) 'Global, local/public, private: Young children's engagement in digital literacy practices in the home.' In Pahl, K. and Rowsell, J. eds. *Travel Notes from the New Literacy Studies*, Clevedon, UK: Multilingual Matters: pp. 19–39.

Martin, B. and Ringham, F. (2000) *Dictionary of Semiotics*, London: Cassell.

Martin, J. R. (1992) *English Text: System and Structure*, Philadelphia, PA: John Benjamins.

—— (1993) 'Genre and literacy: Modelling context in educational linguistics.' *Annual Review of Applied Linguistics* 13: pp. 141–72.

—— (1994) 'Macro-genres: The ecology of the page.' *Network* 21: pp. 29–52.

—— (1997) 'Analysing genre: Functional parameters.' In Christie, F. and Martin, J. R. eds. *Genre and Institutions: Social Processes in the Workplace and School*, London: Continuum: pp. 3–39.

—— (2000) 'Beyond exchange: Appraisal systems in English.' In Hunston, S. and Thompson, G. eds. *Evaluation in Text: Authorial Stance and the Construction of Discourse*, Oxford: Oxford University Press: pp. 142–75.

—— (2004) Mourning: How we get aligned.' *Discourse and Society* 15(2–3): pp. 321–44.

Martin, J. R. and White, P. R. R. (2005) *The Language of Evaluation: Appraisal in English*, London: Palgrave.

Martin, J. R. and Rose, D. (2007) *Working with Discourse: Meaning Beyond the Clause*, 2nd edition, London: Continuum.

Martin, J. R. and Stenglin, M. (2007) 'Materialising reconciliation: Negotiating difference in a post-colonial exhibition.' In Royce, T. and Bowcher, W. eds. *New Directions in the Analysis of Multimodal Discourse*, Mahwah, NJ: Lawrence Erlbaum Associates: pp. 215–38.

Martinec, R. (2000) 'Types of processes in action.' *Semiotica* 130(3/4): pp. 243–68.

—— (2004) 'Gestures that co-concur with speech as a systematic resource: The realization of experiential meanings in indexes.' *Social Semiotics* 14(2): pp. 193–213.

Martinec, R. and Salway, A. (2005) 'A system for image–text relations in new (and old) media.' *Visual Communication* 4(3): pp. 337–71.

Martinec, R. and Van Leeuwen, T. (2008) *The Language of New Media Design*, London: Taylor & Francis.

Mason, D. (2006) 'Rasa, "rasaesthetics" and dramatic theory as performance packaging.' *Theatre Research International* 31(1): pp. 69–83.

Massey, D. (2005) *For Space*, Thousand Oaks, CA: Sage.

Matthews, J. (1999) *The Art of Childhood and Adolescence: The Construction of Meaning*, London: Falmer Press.

Matthiessen, C. (2007) 'The multimodal page: A systematic functional exploration.' In Royce, T. and Bowcher, W. eds. *New Directions in the Analysis of Multimodal Discourse*, Mahwah, NJ: Erlbaum: pp. 1–62.

Mautone, P. D. and Mayer, R. E. (2007) 'Cognitive aids for guiding graph comprehension.' *Journal of Educational Psychology* 99: 640–52.

Mavers, D. (2003) 'Communicating meanings through image composition, spatial arrangement and links in primary school student mind maps.' In Jewitt, C. and Kress, G. eds. *Multimodal Literacy*, New York: Peter Lang: pp. 19–33.

—— (2007) 'Semiotic resourcefulness: A young child's email exchange as design.' *Journal of Early Childhood Literacy* 7(2): pp. 153–74.

—— (2011) *Children's Drawing and Writing: The Remarkable in the Unremarkable*, New York: Routledge.

Mavrikis, M. and Geraniou, E. (2011) 'Using qualitative data analysis software to analyse students' computer-mediated interactions: The case of MiGen and Transana.' *International Journal of Social Research Methodology* 14(3): pp. 245–52.

Maybin, J. (2007) 'Literacy under and over the desk: Oppositions and heterogeneity.' *Language and Education* 21(6): pp. 515–30.

Mayer, R. E. (2001) *Multimedia Learning*, Cambridge: Cambridge University Press.

—— (2005) 'Principles for managing essential processing in multimedia learning: Coherence, signaling, redundancy, spatial contiguity and temporal contiguity principles.' In Mayer, R. ed. *Cambridge Handbook of Multimedia Learning*, New York: Cambridge University Press: pp. 183–200.

—— (2008) 'Multimedia literacy.' In Corio, J., Knobel, M., Lankshear, C. and Leu, D. eds. *Handbook of Research on New Literacies*, New York: Erlbaum: pp. 235–376.

Mead, M. and Métraux, R. (1953) 'Introduction.' In Mead, M. and Métraux, R. eds. *The Study of Culture at a Distance*, Chicago, IL: University of Chicago Press.

Merleau-Ponty, M. (1964) *Signs*, Evanston, IL: Northwestern University Press.

—— (2002) *Phenomenology of Perception*, London: Routledge.

Messaris, J. (1997) *Visual Persuasion*, London: Sage.

Metz, C. (1974a) *Film Language*, Chicago, IL: Chicago University Press.

—— (1974b) *Language and Cinema*, The Hague: Mouton & Co.

Millard, E. (2006) 'Transformative pedagogy: Teachers creating a literacy of fusion.' In Pahl, K. and Rowsell, J. eds. *Travel Notes From the New Literacy Studies: Instances of Practice*, Clevedon, UK: Multilingual Matters: pp. 234–53.

Miller, G. A., Beckwith, R., Fellbaum, C., Gross, D. and Miller, K. (1990) 'WordNet: An online lexical database.' *International Journal of Lexicography* 3(4): pp. 235–44.

Miller, J. (1971) *McLuhan*, London: Fontana.

Mirzoeff, N. (1999) *An Introduction to Visual Culture*, London: Routledge.

Mitchell, W. J. T. (1986) *Iconology: Image, Text, Ideology*, Chicago, IL: University of Chicago Press.

—— (1995) *Picture Theory: Essays on Verbal and Visual Representation*, Chicago, IL: University of Chicago Press.

—— (2002) 'Showing seeing: A critique of visual culture.' *Visual Culture* 1(2): pp. 165–81.

—— (2005a) 'There are no visual media.' *Visual Culture* 4(2): pp. 257–66.

—— (2005b) *What Do Pictures Want?* Chicago, IL: University of Chicago Press.

MODE (2012) *Glossary of Multimodal Terms*, http://www.multimodalglossary.wordpress.com (accessed 18 June 2012).

Moje, E. B. (2000) 'To be part of the story: The literacy practices of gangsta adolescents.' *Teachers College Record* 102(3): pp. 651–90.

Mondada, L. (2003) 'Working with video: How surgeons produce video records of their actions.' *Visual Studies* 18: pp. 58–73.

—— (2011) 'The organization of concurrent courses of action in surgical demonstrations.' In Streeck, J., Goodwin, C. and LeBaron, C. eds. *Embodied Interaction. Language and Body in the Material World*, Cambridge: Cambridge University Press.

Mora, C. (2009) *Colour in Fashion*, Singapore: Maomao Publications.

Moreno, R. and Mayer, R. E. (2000) 'A coherence effect in multimedia learning: The case for minimizing irrelevant sounds in the design of multimedia instructional messages.' *Journal of Educational Psychology* 92(1): pp. 117–25.

Morrell, E. (2008) *Critical Literacy and Urban Youth: Pedagogies of Access, Dissent and Liberation*, London: Routledge.

Morrow, D., D'Andrea, L., Stine-Morrow, E., Shake, M., Bertel, S., Chin, J., Kopren, K., Gao, X., Conner-Garcia, T., Graumlich, J. and Murray, M. (2012) 'Comprehension of multimedia health information among older adults with chronic illness.' In Holsanova, J. ed. Methodologies for Multimodal Research, Special Issue of *Visual communication* 11(3): pp. 347–62.

Morson, G. S. and Emerson, C. (1990) *Mikhail Bakhtin: Creation of a Prosaics*, Stanford, CA: Stanford University Press.

Moss, G. (2003) 'Putting the text back into practice: Junior-age non-fiction as objects of design.' In Jewitt, C. and Kress, G. eds. *Multimodal Literacy*, New York: Peter Lang: pp. 73–87.

Mounin, G. (1970) *Introduction à la sémiologie*, Paris: Éditions de Minuit.

Müller, J. (2010) *The Kivi Handbook*. Jacobs University, Bremen Bremen. http://keyvisuals.jacobs-university.de/kividemo/docs/handbook/html/. The Key Visuals Project.

Müller, M. G., Kappas, A. and Olk, B. (2012) 'Perceiving press photography: A new integrative model, combining iconology with psychophysiological and eye tracking methods.' In Holsanova, J. ed. Methodologies for Multimodal Research, Special Issue of *Visual Communication* 11(3): pp. 307–28.

Multimedia Toolkit and Coursebook with Associated Online Course, London: Equinox.

Murphy, K. M. (2004) 'Imagination as joint activity: The case of architectural interaction.' *Mind, Culture, and Activity* 11: pp. 267–78.

—— (2005) 'Collaborative imagining: The interactive use of gestures, talk, and graphic representation in architectural practice.' *Semiotica* 156: pp. 13–45.

Muspratt, S., Luke, A. and Freebody, P. (1997) *Constructing Critical Literacies*, Sydney: Allen and Unwin; and Cresskills, NJ: Hampton.

Nash, C. (1996) 'Reclaiming vision: Looking at landscape and the body.' *Gender, Place and Culture* 3: pp. 149–69.

National Research Council of the National Academies (2006) *Learning to Think Spatially: GIS as a Support System in the K-121 Curriculum*, Washington, DC: The National Academies Press.

New London Group (1996) 'A pedagogy of multiliteracies: Designing social futures.' *Harvard Educational Review* 66: pp. 60–92.

—— (2000) 'A pedagogy of multiliteracies: Designing social futures.' In Cope, B. and Kalantzis, M. eds. *Multiliteracies: Literacy Learning and the Design of Social Futures*, Melbourne: Macmillan: pp. 9–37.

Newfield, D. (2009) 'Transmodal semiosis in classrooms: Case studies from South Africa.' Unpublished PhD thesis, Institute of Education, University of London.

—— (2011) 'Multimodality, social justice and becoming a "really South African democracy".' In Hawkins, M. ed. *Social Justice Language Teacher Education*, Bristol: Multilingual Matters: pp. 23–48.

Newfield, D. and Maungedzo, R. (2005) *Thebuwa: Poems From Ndofaya*, Johannesburg: Denise Newfield Publishers.

—— (2006) 'Mobilising and modalising poetry in a Soweto classroom.' *English Studies in Africa* 49(1): pp. 71–94.

Newton, I. (1736) *The Method of Fluxions and Infinite Series; With Its Application to the Geometry of Curve-Lines; With Comments by John Colson*, London: Printed by Henry Woodfall and sold by John Nourse.

—— (1739) *Philosophiæ Naturalis Principia Mathematica: Tomus* 1 (Facsimile reprint of a 1739 edition by Barrillot and filii, Genevæ. ed.). Boston, MA: Adamant Media Corporation.

Nichols, B. (1991) *Representing Reality*, Bloomington: Indiana University Press.

Nichols, S. (2006) 'From boardroom to classroom: Tracing a globalised discourse on thinking through internet texts and teaching practice.' In Pahl, K. and Rowsell, J. eds. *Travel Notes From the New Literacy Studies: Instances of Practice*, Clevedon, UK: Multilingual Matters: pp. 173–94.

—— (2011) 'Young children's literacy in the activity space of the library: A geosemiotic investigation.' *Journal of Early Childhood Literacy* 30(2): pp. 164–89.

Nichols, S., Nixon, H. and Rowsell, J. (2009) 'Shaping the identities and practices in relation to early years literacy.' *Literacy* 43(2): pp. 65–74.

Nichols, S., Rowsell, J., Nixon, H. and Rainbird, S. (2012) *Resourcing Early Learners: New Players, New Spaces*, London: Routledge.

Nixon, H. (2011) 'From bricks to clicks: Hybrid commercial spaces in the landscape of early childhood literacy learning.' *Journal of Early Childhood Literacy* 11: pp. 114–40.

Nogueira, R. (1971) *Melville on Melville*, London: Vintage.

Norman, D. A. (1988) *The Psychology of Everyday Things*, New York: Basic Books. (The paperback version is Norman, 1990.)

—— (1990) *The Design of Everyday Things*, New York: Doubleday.

Norris, S. (2002) 'The implication of visual research for discourse analysis: Transcription beyond language.' *Visual Communication* 1(1): pp. 97–121.

—— (2004a) *Analyzing Multimodal Interaction: A Methodological Framework*, London: Routledge.

—— (2004b) 'Multimodal discourse analysis: A conceptual framework.' In Levine, P. and Scollon, R. eds. *Discourse and Technology: Multimodal Discourse Analysis*, Washington, DC: Georgetown University Press: pp. 101–15.

—— (2006) 'Multiparty interaction: A multimodal perspective on relevance.' *Discourse Studies* 8(3): pp. 401–21.

—— ed. (2012) *Multimodality in Practice: Investigating Theory-in-Practice Through Methodology*, Routledge Studies in Multimodality Book Series, London: Routledge.

Norris, S. and Jones, R. eds. (2005) *Discourse in Action: Introducing Mediated Discourse Analysis*, London: Routledge.

Nöth, W. (1985) *Handbuch der Semiotik*, Stuttgart: Metzler.

Novak, J. D. and Gowin, D. B. (1984) *Learning How to Learn*, Cambridge: Cambridge University Press.

Nyström, M. and Holmqvist, K. (2008) 'Semantic override of low-level features in image viewing – both initially and overall.' *Journal of Eye Movement Research* 2(2): pp. 1–11.

Nyström, M. and Ögren, M. (2012) 'How illustrations influence performance and eye movement behaviour when solving problems in vector calculus.' *Proceedings, LTHs 7:e Pedagogiska Inspirationskonferens* 30 August 2012.

O'Halloran, K. L. (1999) 'Towards a systemic functional analysis of multisemiotic mathematics texts.' *Semiotica* 124(1/2): pp. 1–29.

—— (2000) 'Classroom discourse in mathematics: A multisemiotic analysis.' *Linguistics and Education* 10(3): pp. 359–88.

—— (2003a) 'Implications of mathematics as a multisemiotic discourse.' In Anderson, M., Saenz-Ludlow, A., Zellweger, S. and Cifarelli, V. eds. *Educational Perspectives on Mathematics as Semiosis: From Thinking to Interpreting to Knowing*, Brooklyn, NY: Legas: pp. 185–214.

—— (2003b) 'Intersemiosis in mathematics and science: Grammatical metaphor and semiotic metaphor.' In Simon-Vandenbergen, A., Taverniers, M. M. and Ravelli, L. eds. *Grammatical Metaphor*, Amsterdam: John Benjamins: pp. 337–66.

—— (2004a) 'Visual semiosis in film.' In O'Halloran, K. ed. *Multimodal Discourse Analysis: Systemic Functional Perspectives*, London: Continuum: pp. 109–30.

—— ed. (2004b) *Multimodal Discourse Analysis*, London: Continuum.

—— (2005) *Mathematical Discourse: Language, Symbolism and Visual Images*, London: Continuum.

—— (2007) 'Systemic Functional Multimodal Discourse Analysis (SF-MDA) approach to mathematics, grammar and literacy.' In McCabe, A., O'Donnell, M. and Whittaker, R. eds. *Advances in Language and Education*, London: Continuum: pp. 75–100.

—— (2011) 'Multimodal discourse analysis.' In Hyland, K. and Paltridge, B. eds. *Companion to Discourse Analysis*, London: Continuum: pp. 120–37.

O'Halloran, K. and Smith, B. eds. (2011) *Multimodal Studies: Multiple Approaches and Domains*, Routledge Studies in Multimodality, London: Routledge.

—— (2013a) 'Multimodal text analysis.' In Chapelle, C. A. ed. *Encyclopedia of Applied Linguistics*, Hoboken, NJ: Wiley-Blackwell.

—— (2013b) 'Multimodality and technology.' In Chapelle, C. A. ed. *Encyclopedia of Applied Linguistics*, Hoboken, NJ: Wiley-Blackwell.

O'Halloran, K. L., Tan, S., Smith B. A. and Podlasov, A. (2010) 'Challenges in designing digital interfaces for the study of multimodal phenomena'. *Information Design Journal* 18(1): pp. 2–12.

—— (2011) 'Multimodal analysis within an interactive software environment: Critical discourse perspectives.' *Critical Discourse Studies* 8(2): pp. 109–25.

O'Halloran, K. L., Podlasov, A., Chua, A. and E, M. K. L. (2012) 'Interactive software for multimodal analysis.' In Holsanova, J. ed. Methodologies for Multimodal Research, *Visual Communication* 11(3): Sage: pp. 363–81. doi:10.1177/1470357212446414.

O'Halloran, K. L., E, M. K. L., Podlasov, A. and Tan, S. (2013) 'Multimodal digital semiotics: The interaction of language with other resources.' In Thompson, G. ed. *Text and Talk: Special Issue for Michael Halliday* 33(4–5): pp. 665–90.

O'Toole, M. (1994) *The Language of Displayed Art*, London: Leicester University Press.

—— (2004) 'Opera Ludentes: The Sydney Opera House at work and play.' In O'Halloran, K. L. ed. *Multimodal Discourse Analysis*, London: Continuum: pp. 11–27.

—— (2011 [1994]) *The Language of Displayed Art*, 2nd edn, London: Routledge.

Ochs, E. (1979) 'Transcription as theory.' In Ochs, E. and Schieffelin, B. eds. *Developmental Pragmatics*, New York: Academic Press: pp. 43–72.

Oldham, J. (2005) 'Literacy and media in secondary schools in the United Kingdom.' In Street, B. V. ed. *Literacies Across Educational Contexts*, Philadelphia, PA: Caslon: pp. 170–87.

Olson, D. (1994) *The World on Paper: The Conceptual and Cognitive Implications of Reading and Writing*, Cambridge: Cambridge University Press.

Onishi, N. (2008) 'Thumbs race as Japan's best sellers go cellular.' *The New York Times* January 20.

Ormerod, F. and Ivanic, R. (2000) 'Texts in practices: Interpreting the physical characteristics of children's project work.' In Barton, D., Hamilton, M. and Ivanic, R. eds. *Situated Literacies: Reading and Writing in Context*, London: Routledge: pp. 91–107.

—— (2002) 'Materiality in children's meaning-making practices.' *Visual Communication* 1(1): pp. 65–91.

Paget, G. W. (1932) 'Some drawings of men and women made by children of certain non-European races.' *Journal of the Royal Anthropological Institute of Great Britain and Ireland* 62: pp. 127–44.

Pahl, K. (1999) *Transformations: Children's Meaning Making in Nursery Education*, Stoke on Trent, UK: Trentham Books.

—— (2001) 'Texts as artefacts crossing sites: Map making at home and at school.' *Reading: Literacy and Language* 35(3): pp. 120–25.

—— (2002) 'Ephemera, mess and miscellaneous piles: Texts and practices in families.' *Journal of Early Childhood Literacy* 2(2): pp. 145–65.

—— (2003) 'Children's text making at home: Transforming meaning across modes.' In Jewitt, C. and Kress, G. eds. *Multimodal Literacy*, New York: Peter Lang: pp. 139–54.

—— (2004) 'Narratives, artifacts and cultural identities: An ethnographic study of communicative practices in homes.' *Linguistics and Education* 15(4): pp. 339–58.

—— (2007) 'Creativity in events and practices: A lens for understanding children's multimodal texts.' *Literacy* 41(2): pp. 86–92.

Pahl, K. and Pollard, A. eds. (2006) *Travel Notes From the New Literacy Studies: Instances of Practice*, Clevedon, UK: Multilingual Matters.

Pahl, K. and Rowsell, J. eds. (2006) 'Introduction.' In *Travel Notes From the New Literacy Studies: Instances of Practice*, Clevedon: Multilingual Matters: pp. 1–18.

Pahl, K. and Pollard, A. (2008) '"Bling – the Asians introduced that into the country": Gold and its value within a group of families of south Asian origin in Yorkshire.' *Visual Communication* 7(2): pp. 170–82.

Pahl, K. and Rowsell, J. (2010) *Artifactual Literacies: Every Object Tells a Story*, New York: Teachers College Press.

—— (2012) *Literacy and Education: Understanding The New Literacy Studies in the Classroom*, 2nd edition, London: Sage.

Palfreman, J. and Swade, D. (1991) *The Dream Machine: Exploring the Computer Age*, London: BBC Books.

Palmer, F. R. (2001) *Mood and Modality*, 2nd edition, Cambridge: Cambridge University Press.

Pandya, V. (1993) *Above the Forest: A Study of Andamanese Ethnoanemology, Cosmology, and the Power of Ritual*, Delhi: Oxford University Press.

Pang, A. (2004) 'Making history in "From Colony to Nation: A Multimodal Analysis of a Museum Exhibition in Singapore."' In O'Halloran, K. ed. *Multimodal Discourse Analysis*, London: Continuum: pp. 28–54.

Pankow, C. (1995) 'Semiotics.' In Verschueren, J. ed. *Handbook of Pragmatics*, Amsterdam: Benjamins: pp. 469–76.

Panofsky, E. (1972) *Studies in Iconography: Humanistic Themes in the Art of the Renaissance*, Oxford: Westview Press.

Parret, H. (1974) *Discussing Language*, The Hague: Mouton.

Pastoureau, M. (2001) *The Devil's Cloth: A History of Stripes and Striped Fabric*, New York: Columbia University Press.

Paterson, C. and Domingo, D. eds. (2008) *Making Online News: The Ethnography of New Media Production*, New York: Peter Lang: pp. 1–11.

Peirce, C. S. (1931) *Collected Papers of Charles Sanders Peirce*, Cambridge, MA: Belknap Press.

Pennycook, A. (2007) *Global Englishes and Transcultural Flows*, New York: Routledge.

—— (2010) *Language as a Local Practice*, Abingdon, Oxon: Routledge.

Perlmutter, D. and Wagner, G. (2004) 'The anatomy of a photojournalistic icon: Marginalisation of dissent in the selection and framing of "A Death in Genoa".' *Visual Communication* 3(1): pp. 91–108.

Peters, J. D. (1999) *Speaking into the Air: A History of the Idea of Communication*, Chicago: University of Chicago Press.

—— (2001) 'Witnessing.' *Media, Culture and Society* 23: pp. 707–23.

—— (2005) *Courting the Abyss: Freedom of Speech and the Liberal Tradition*, Chicago: University of Chicago Press.

Philo, G. (2007) 'Can discourse analysis successfully explain the content of media and journalistic practice?' *Journalism Studies*, 8(2): pp. 175–96.

Pike, K. (1954) *Language in Relation to a Unified Theory of the Structure of Human Behavior*, Glendate, CA: Summer Institute of Linguistics.

Pinard, S. (1991) 'A taste of India.' In Howes, D. ed. *The Varieties of Sensory Experience*, Toronto: University of Toronto Press.

Pink, S. (2006) *The Future of Visual Anthropology: Engaging the Senses*, Oxford: Routledge.

—— (2007) 'Walking with video.' *Visual Studies* 22(3): pp. 240–52.

—— (2009) *Doing Sensory Ethnography*, London: Sage.

—— (2011) 'Multimodality, multisensoriality and ethnographic knowing: social semiotics and the phenomenology of perception.' *Qualitative Research* 11(3): pp. 261–76.

Piper, H. and Stronach, I. (2008) *Don't Touch!*, London: Routledge.

Pirow, P. C. (1988) *Excellence in Information Systems: A Study of Information Systems Through the Ages*, Oxford: Woodacres.

Pittenger, C. and Danehy, J. J. (1960) *The First Five Minutes: A Sample of Microscopic Interview Analysis*, Ithaca, NY: Martineau.

Podlasov, A., Tan, S. and O'Halloran, K. L. (2012) 'Interactive state-transition diagrams for visualization of multimodal annotations.' *Intelligent Data Analysis: An International Journal* 16(4): pp. 683–702.

Prinsloo, M. and Walton, M. (2008) 'Situated responses to the digital literacies of electronic communication in marginal school settings.' In Pecora, N., Osei-Hwere, E. and Carlson, U. eds. *Yearbook 2008: African Media, African Children*, Göteborg: Nordicom, Göteborgs universitet.

Prosser, J. ed. (1998) *Image-Based Research: A Sourcebook for Qualitative Researchers*, London: RoutledgeFalmer.

Qvarfordt, P. (2004) 'Eyes on multimodal interaction.' *Linköping Studies in Science and Technology* No. 893, Department of Computer and Information Science, Linköping University.

Radach, R., Lemmer, S., Vorstius, C., Heller, D. and Radach, K. (2003) 'Eye movements in the processing of print advertisements.' In Hyonä, J., Radach, R. and Deubel, H. eds. *The Mind's Eye: Cognitive and Applied Aspects of Eye Movement Research*, Amsterdam: Elsevier Science: pp. 609–32.

Raessens, J. and Goldstein, J. eds. (2005) *Handbook of Computer Game Studies*, Cambridge, MA: MIT Press.

Ramachandran, V. S., Hubbard, E. M. and Butcher, P. A. (2004) 'Synesthsia, cross-activation, and the foundations of neuroepistemology.' In Calvert, G., Spence, C. and Stein, B. E. eds. *The Handbook of Multisensory Processes*, Cambridge, MA: MIT Press.

Rasmussen, S. (1995) *Spirit Possession and Personhood Among the Kel Ewey Yuareg*, Cambridge: Cambridge University Press.

—— (1999) 'Making better "scents" in anthropology: Aroma in Tuareg sociocultural systems and the shaping of ethnography.' *Anthropological Quarterly* 72(2): pp. 55–73.

Ravelli, L. J. (2000) 'Beyond shopping: Constructing the Sydney Olympics in three-dimensional text.' *Text* 20(4): pp. 489–515.

—— (2005) *Museum Texts: Museum Meanings*, London: Routledge.

—— (2006) *Museum Texts: Communication Frameworks*, London: Routledge.

Ravelli, L. R. and Stenglin, M. (2008) 'Feeling space: Interpersonal communication and spatial semiotics.' In Ventola, E. and Antos, G. eds. *Handbook of Applied Linguistics, Volume 2, Interpersonal Communication*, Berlin: Mouton de Gruyter: pp. 355–93.

Rayner, K. (1998) 'Eye movements in reading and information processing: 20 years of research.' *Psychological Bulletin* 124(3): pp. 372–422.

Rayner, K., Rotello, C. M., Stewart, A. J., Keir, J. and Duffy, S. A. (2001) 'Integrating text and pictorial information: Eye movements when looking at print advertisements.' *Journal of Experimental Psychology: Applied* 7: pp. 219–26.

Rayner, K., Miller, B. and Rotello, C. M. (2008) 'Eye movements when looking at print advertisements: The goal of the viewer matters.' *Applied Cognitive Psychology* 22(5): pp. 697–707.

Reichel-Dolmatoff, G. (1978) 'Desana animal categories, food restrictions, and the concept of color energies.' *Journal of Latin American Lore* 4(2): pp. 243–91.

Reisch, G. (1535) *Margarita Philosophica*, Basileae.

Reisigl, M. and Wodak, R. eds. (2000) *The Semiotics of Racism: Approaches in Critical Discourse Analysis*, Vienna: Passagen.

Reiss, M., Boulter, C. and Tunnicliffe, S. D. (2007) 'Seeing the natural world.' *Visual Communication* 6: pp. 99–114.

Renkema, J. (2004) *Discourse Studies*, Amsterdam: John Benjamins.

Richards, C. (2001) 'Hypermedia, internet communication, and the challenge of redefining literacy in the electronic age.' *Language Learning and Technology* 4(2): pp. 59–77.

Richardson, D. C. and Dale, R. (2005) 'Looking to understand: The coupling between speakers' and listeners' eye movements and its relationship to discourse comprehension.' *Cognitive Science* 29: pp. 39–54.

Riggins, S. H. (1990) 'The power of things: The role of domestic objects in the presentation of self.' In Riggins, S. H. ed. *Beyond Goffman: Studies on Communication, Institution, and Social Interaction*, Berlin: Mouton de Gruyter.

—— (1994) 'Fieldwork in the living room: An autoethnographic essay.' In Riggins, S. H. ed. *The Socialness of Things: Essays on the Socio-Semiotics of Objects*, Berlin: Walter de Gruyter.

Riley, C. A. (1995) *Colour Codes: Modern Theories of Colour in Philosophy, Painting and Architecture, Literature, Music and Psychology*, Lebanon, NH: University Press of New England.

Robins, K. (1994) 'Forces of consumption: From the symbolic to the psychotic.' *Media, Culture and Society* 16: pp. 449–68.

Robinson-Pant, A. (1997) *Why Eat Green Cucumbers at the Time of Dying?: The Link Between Women's Literacy and Development*, Hamburg: UNESCO.

Rogers, R., Mosley, M., Kramer, M. A. and the Literacy for Social Justice Teacher Research Group (2009) *Designing Socially Just Learning Communities*, London: Routledge.

Rohlfing, K., Loehr, D., Duncan, S., Brown, A., Franklin, A., Kimbarra, I. *et al.* (2006) 'Comparison of multi-modal annotation tools: Workshop report.' *Online-Zeitschrift zur Verbalen Interaktion, Ausgabe* 7: pp. 99–123.

Rommetveit, R. (1974) *On Message Structure*, London: Academic Press.

—— (1985) 'Language acquisition as increasing linguistic structuring of experience and symbolic behavior control.' In Wertsch, J. V. ed. *Culture, Communication, and Cognition: Vygotskian Perspectives*, Cambridge: Cambridge University Press: pp. 183–202.

Rose, G. (2001) *Visual Methodologies: An Introduction to the Interpretation of Visual Materials*, London: Sage.

Rose, N. (1993) 'Government, authority and expertise in advanced liberalism.' *Economy and Society* 22(3): pp. 283–99.

—— (1999) *Powers of Freedom: Reframing Political Thought*, London: Routledge.

Rosowsky, A. (2008) *Heavenly Readings: Liturgical Literacy in a Multilingual Context*, Bristol: Multilingual Matters.

REFERENCES

Ross, D. (1923/1995) *Aristotle*, London: Routledge.

Rostvall, A.-L. and West, T. (2005) 'Theoretical and methodological perspectives on designing video studies of interaction.' *International Journal of Qualitative Methods* 4(4): Article 6. At http://www. ualberta. ca/~iiqm/backissues/4_4/html/rostvall.htm (accessed 25 September 2006).

Roten, Y. D., Fivaz-Depeursinge, E., Stern, D. J., Darwish, J. and Corboz-Warnery, A. (2000) 'Body and gaze formations and the communicational alliance in couple-therapist triads.' *Psychotherapy Research* 10(1): pp. 30–46. At http://www.informaworld.com/smpp/title~content=t713663589~db=all~tab=i ssueslist~ branches=10 – v10 30–46.

Roth, W., Pozzer-Ardenghi, L. and Han, J. (2005) *Critical Graphicacy: Understanding Visual Representation Practices in School Science*, Dordrecht: Springer.

Rotman, B. (1987) *Signifying Nothing: The Semiotics of Zero*, London: Macmillan Press.

—— (1988) 'Towards a semiotics of mathematics.' *Semiotica* 72(1/2): pp. 1–35.

—— (2000) *Mathematics as Sign: Writing, Imagining, Counting*, Stanford, CA: Stanford University Press.

Rowsell, J. (2000) 'Publishing practices in printed education: British and Canadian perspectives on educational publishing.' PhD thesis, University of London.

—— (2006) 'Corporate crossings: Tracing textual crossings.' In Pahl, K. and Rowsell, J. eds. *Travel Notes From the New Literacy Studies: Instances of Practice*, Clevedon, UK: Multilingual Matters: pp. 195–218.

—— (2011) 'Carrying my family with me: Artifacts as emic perspectives.' *Qualitative Research* 11(3): pp. 331–46.

—— (2013) *Working With Multimodality: Learning in a Digital Age*, London: Routledge.

Rowsell, J. and Pahl, K. (2007) 'Sedimented identities in texts: Instances of practice.' *Reading Research Quarterly* 42(3): pp. 388–401.

Royce, A. (1984) *Movement and Meaning: Creativity and Interpretation in Ballet and Mime*, Bloomington: Indiana University Press.

Royce, T. (1998) 'Synergy on the page: Exploring intersemiotic complementarity in page-based multimodal text.' *Japan Association Systemic Functional Linguistics Occasional Papers* 1(1): pp. 25–50.

—— (2002) 'Multimodality in the TESOL classroom: Exploring visual-verbal synergy.' *TESOL Quarterly* 36(2): pp. 191–205.

—— (2007) 'Intersemiotic complementarity: A framework for multimodal discourse analysis.' In Royce, T. and Bowcher, W. eds. *New Directions in the Analysis of Multimodal Discourse*, Mahwah, NJ: Erlbaum: pp. 63–109.

Royce, T. and Bowcher, W. eds. (2007) *New Directions in the Analysis of Multimodal Discourse*, Mahwah, NJ: Erlbaum.

Ruesch, J. and Kees, W. (1954 [1964]) *Nonverbal Communication: Notes on the Visual Perception of Human Relations*, Berkeley, CA: University of California Press.

Russo, J. E. and Leclerc, F. (1994) 'An eye-fixation analysis of choice processes for consumer nondurables.' *Journal of Consumer Research* 21: pp. 274–90.

Sacks, H., Schegloff, E. A. and Jefferson, G. (1974) 'A simplest systematics for the organisation of turn-taking for conversation.' *Language* 50(4/1): pp. 696–735.

Sacks, O. (1989) *Seeing Voices*, New York: Vintage Books.

Said, E. (1978) *Orientalism*, New York: Vintage.

—— (1985) *Orientalism*, London: Penguin Books.

Säljö, R. (2005) *Lärande och kulturella redskap: Om lärprocesser och det kollektiva minnet* [Learning and cultural tools. On learning processes and the collective memory], Stockholm: Norstedts Akademiska Förlag.

Sanchez Svensson, M., Heath, C. C. and Luff, P. (2007) 'Instrumental action: The timely exchange of implements during surgical operations.' In *ECSCW* 2007, Limerick, Ireland: pp. 41–60.

Sandberg, H., Gidlöf, K. and Holmberg, N. (2011) 'Children's exposure to and perceptions of online advertising.' *International Journal of Communication* 5: pp. 21–50.

Sanders, J. (2010) 'Relationships between artistic and written composing: A qualitative study of fourth-grade students' composing experiences.' In Albers, P. and Sanders, J. eds. *Literacies, the Arts and Multimodality*, Urbana, IL: National Council of Teachers of English: pp. 110–35.

Sandgren, O. Andersson, R., van der Weijer, J., Hansson, K. and Sahlén, B. (2012) 'Timing of gazes in child dialogues: A time-course analysis of requests and back channelling in referential communication.' *International Journal of Language and Communication Disorders* 47: pp. 373–83.

Sapir, E. (1921) *Language*, New York: Harcourt, Brace.

Sassoon, R. and Gaur, A. (1997) *Signs, Symbols and Icons: Pre-History to the Computer Age*, Exeter: Intellect Books.

Saussure, F. de (1916 [1959]) *Course in General Linguistics*, New York: Philosophical Library.

—— (1964 [1916]) *Course in General Linguistics*, London: Peter Owen.

—— (1974) *Course in General Linguistics*, Baskin, W., trans., Glasgow: Collins.

—— (1996) 'Linguistic value.' In Cobley, P. ed. *The Communication Theory Reader*, London: Routledge: pp. 99–114.

Scannel, P. ed. (1991) *Broadcast Talk*, Oxford: Blackwell.

Schafer, R. M. (1977) *The Soundscape: Our Sonic Environment and the Tuning of the World*, Rochester, VT: Destiny Books.

Schechner, R. (2001) 'Rasaesthetics.' *The Drama Review* 45(3): pp. 27–50.

Schegloff, E. A. (2006) *Sequence Organization in Interaction: A Primer in Conversation Analysis*, Cambridge: Cambridge University Press.

Scheiter, K. and van Gog, T. (2009) 'Using eye tracking in applied research to study and stimulate the processing of information from multi-representational sources.' *Applied Cognitive Psychology* 23: pp. 1209–14. Published online 23 December 2008 at www.interscience.wiley.com, doi: 10.1002/acp.1524.

Scheiter, K., Wiebe, E. and Holsanova, J. (2008) 'Theoretical and methodological aspects of learning with visualizations.' In Zheng, R. ed. *Cognitive Effects of Multimedia Learning*, Hershey, PA: IGI Global.

Schiffrin, D. (1994) *Approaches to Discourse*, Oxford: Blackwell.

Schmandt-Besserat, D. (2007) *When Writing Met Art: From Symbol to Story*, Austin, TX: University of Texas Press.

Schmidt-Weigand, F., Kohnert, A. and Glowalla, U. (2010) 'Explaining the modality and contiguity effects: New insights from investigating students' viewing behaviour.' *Applied Cognitive Psychology* 24: pp. 226–37. doi:10.1002/acp.1554.

Schneider, J. G. and Stöckl, H. eds. (2011) *Medientheorien und Multimodalität: Ein TV-Werbespot – Sieben methodische Beschreibungsansätze*, Köln: Halem.

Schneider, W. X. and Deubel, H. (1995) 'Visual attention and saccadic eye movements: Evidence for obligatory and selective spatial coupling.' In Findlay, J. M., Kentridge, R. W. and Walker, R. eds. *Eye Movement Research: Mechanisms, Processes and Applications*, Amsterdam: Elsevier Science: pp. 317–24.

Schnotz, W. and Bannert, M. (2003) 'Construction and interference in learning from multiple representations.' *Learning and Instruction* 13: pp. 141–56.

Schriver, K. A. (1997) *Dynamics in Document Design: Creating Texts for Readers*, New York: John Wiley.

Schroeder, K. C. (2002) 'Discourses of fact.' In K. B. Jensen ed. *A Handbook of Media and Communication Research*, London: Routledge pp. 98–116.

Schüler, A., Scheiter, K. and Schmidt-Weigand, F. (2011) 'Boundary conditions and constraints of the modality effect.' [Special Issue.] *Zeitschrift für Pädagogische Psychologie* 25(4).

Schulten, S. (2001) *The Geographical Imagination in America, 1880–1950*, Chicago, IL: University of Chicago Press.

Scollon, R. (1998a) *Mediated Discourse as Social Interaction: A Study of News Discourse*, London: Longman.

—— (1998b) 'Reading as social interaction: The empirical grounding of reading.' *Semiotica* 118: pp. 281–94.

—— (2001a) *Mediated Discourse: The Nexus of Practice*, London: Routledge.

—— (2001b) 'Action and text: Towards an integrated understanding of the place of text in social (inter)action, mediated discourse analysis and the problem of social action.' In Wodak, R. and Meyer, M. eds. *Methods of Critical Discourse Analysis*, London: Sage: pp. 139–84.

—— (2005a) 'The rhythmic integration of action and discourse: Work, the body and the earth.' In Norris, S. and Jones, R. H. eds. *Discourse in Action: Introducing Mediated Discourse Analysis*, London: Routledge.

—— (2005b) *MDA website*. At: http://www.aptalaska.net/~ron/NEXAN/FOOD%2007/mda/watch.htm (accessed 14 September 2007).

—— (2006) 'Food and behavior: A Burkean motive analysis of a quasi-medical text.' *Text & Talk* 26(1): pp. 107–25.

Scollon, R. and Scollon, S. (2003) *Discourses in Place: Language in the Material World*, New York: Routledge.

—— (2004) *Nexus Analysis: Discourse and the Emerging Internet*, London: Routledge.

Scollon, S. (2003) 'Body idiom in platform events: Media representation and hegemony in the vicarious conversation.' *Social Semiotics* 13(1): pp. 89–102.

—— (2006) 'Change and conflict in definitions of obesity: A Burkean motive analysis.' *Sociolinguistics Symposium* 16, Limerick, Ireland, July 6–8.

Scott, D. (1998) 'Orientalism and musical style.' *The Musical Quarterly* 8(2): pp. 309–35.

Scribner, S. and Cole, M. (1981) *The Psychology of Literacy*, Cambridge, MA: Harvard University Press.

Sebeok, T. (1979) *The Sign and Its Masters*, Austin, TX: University of Texas Press.

—— (1994) *Signs: An Introduction to Semiotics*, Toronto: University of Toronto Press.

Seeley, W. P. (2012) 'Hearing how smooth it looks: Selective attention and crossmodal perception in the arts.' *Essays in Philosophy* 13(2): pp. 498–517. http://commons.pacificu.edu/cgi/viewcontent.cgi?article=1434&context=eip. Special Issue: *Aesthetics and the Senses*, Freeland, C. ed.

Sefton-Green, J. and Sinker, R. ed. (2000) *Evaluating Creativity: Making and Learning by Young People*, London: Routledge.

Sellen, A. and Harper, R. H. R. (2002) *The Myth of the Paperless Office*, Cambridge, MA: MIT Press.

Shapiro, G. (1993) 'In the shadows of philosophy. Nietzsche and the question of vision.' In Levin, D. H. ed. *Modernity and the Hegemony of Vision*, Berkeley, CA: University of California Press.

Shapiro, M. (1973) *Words and Pictures*, The Hague: Mouton.

Shaw, G. B. (1901/2000) *Three Plays for Puritans*, Harmondsworth: Penguin.

Shepherd, J. (1991) *Music as Social Text*, Cambridge: Polity Press.

Sheridan, M. P. and Rowsell, J. (2010) *Design Literacies: Learning and Innovation in a Digital Age*, London: Routledge.

Silverman, K. (1988) *The Acoustic Mirror*, Bloomington, IN: Indiana University Press.

Silverstone, R. (1999) *Why Study the Media?* London: Sage.

—— (2002) 'Complicity and collusion in the mediation of everyday life.' *New Literary History* 33(4): pp. 761–80.

—— (2003) 'Proper distance: Towards an ethics of cyberspace.' In Liestøl, G. *et al.* eds. *Digital Media Revisited: Theoretical and Conceptual Innovations in Digital Domains*, Cambridge, MA: MIT Press: pp. 469–90.

—— (2005) 'Mediation and communication.' In Calhoun, G. *et al.* eds. *The Sage Handbook of Sociological Analysis*, London: Sage: pp. 188–207.

Simola, J. (2011) *Investigating Online Reading with Eye Tracking and EEG* (Studies in Psychology), Helsinki: University of Helsinki Press.

Smith, B. A., Tan, S., Podlasov, A. and O'Halloran, K. L. (2011) 'Analysing multimodality in an interactive digital environment: Software as a meta-semiotic tool.' *Social Semiotics* 21(3): pp. 353–75.

Smith, B. R. (2004) 'Listening to the wild blue yonder: The challenges of acoustic ecology.' In Erlmann, V. ed. *Hearing Cultures: Essays on Sound, Listening and Modernity*, Oxford: Berg.

—— (2010) 'Employing eye-tracking technology in researching the effectiveness of recasts in CMC.' In Hult, F. M. ed. *Directions and Prospects for Educational Linguistics*, New York: Springer: pp. 79–97.

Smith, C. (2005) *Photoshop and Dreamweaver Integration: Creating High-Impact Web Pages*, New York: McGraw-Hill Osborne.

Smith, K. (2012) Sensational colour. http://www.sensationalcolor.com.color-messages-meanings/ (accessed 29 December 2012)

Smith, N. and Katz, C. (1993) 'Grounding metaphor: Toward a spatialized politics.' In Keith, M. and Pile, S. eds. *Place and the Politics of Identity*, New York: Routledge.

Soep, E. (2006) 'Youth media citizenship: Beyond "youth voice".' *Afterschool Matters* 5: pp. 1–11.

Soja, E. W. (1989) *Postmodern Geographies: The Reassertion of Space in Critical Social Theory*, London: Verso.

—— (2010) *Seeking Spatial Justice*. Minneapolis: University of Minnesota Press.

Stam, R. ed. (1992) *New Vocabularies in Film Semiotics*, London: Routledge.

Stein, P. (2003) 'The Olifantsvlei fresh stories project: Multimodality, creativity and fixing in the semiotic chain.' In Jewitt, C. and Kress, G. eds. *Multimodal Literacy*, New York: Peter Lang: pp. 123–38.

—— (2008) *Multimodal Pedagogies in Diverse Classrooms: Representation, Rights and Resources*, London: Routledge.

Stein, P. and Mamabolo, T. (2005) 'Pedagogy is not enough: Early literacy practices in a South African school.' In Street, B. ed. *Literacies Across Educational Contexts; Mediating, Learning and Teaching*, Philadelphia, PA: Caslon Press: pp. 25–42.

Stein, P. and Newfield, D. (2006) 'Multiliteracies and multimodality in English in education in Africa: Mapping the terrain.' *English Studies in Africa* 49(1): pp. 1–22.

Stein, P. and Slominsky, L. (2006) 'An eye on the text and an eye on the future: Multimodal literacy in three Johannesburg families.' In Pahl, K. and Rowsell, J. eds. *Travel Notes from the New Literacy Studies: Instances of Practice*, Clevedon, UK: Multilingual Matters: pp. 118–46.

Steinkuehler, C. A. and Williams, D. (2006) 'Where everybody knows your (screen) name: Online games as "third places".' *Journal of Computer-Mediated Communication* 11(4): At http://jcmc.indiana.edu/vol11/issue14/steinkuehler.html.

Stenglin, M. (2004) 'Packaging curiosities: Towards a grammar of three-dimensional space.' PhD thesis, University of Sydney.

—— (2007) 'Making art accessible: Opening up a whole new world.' *Visual Communication*, special edition, *Immersion* 6(2): pp. 202–13.

—— (2008) 'Binding: A resource for exploring interpersonal meaning in 3D space.' *Social Semiotics* 18(4): pp. 425–47.

—— (2009) 'Space odyssey: Towards a social semiotic model of 3D space.' *Visual Communication* 8(1): pp. 35–64.

Stevenson, R. and Boakes, R. (2004) 'Sweet and sour smells: Learned synesthesia between the senses of taste and smell.' In Calvert, G., Spence, C. and Stein, B. E. eds. *The Handbook of Multisensory Processes*, Cambridge, MA: MIT Press.

Stöckl, H. (2004) 'In between modes: Language and image in printed media.' In Ventola, E., Charles, C. and Kaltenbacher, M. eds. *Perspectives in Multimodality*, London: John Benjamins: pp. 9–30.

—— (2009) 'Beyond depicting: Language-image-links in the service of advertising.' *Arbeiten aus Anglistik und Amerikanistik* 34(1): pp. 3–28.

—— (2012) 'Medienlinguistik: Zu Status und Methodik eines (noch) emergenten Forschungsfeldes.' In Grösslinger, C., Held, G. and Stöckl, H. eds. *Pressetextsorten jenseits der News: Medienlinguistische Perspektiven auf journalistische Kreativität*, Frankfurt/Main: Lang: pp. 13–34.

Stoller, P. (1984) 'Sound in Songhay cultural experience.' *American Ethnologist* 11(3): pp. 559–70.

Streeck, J. and Kallmeyer, W. (2001) 'Interaction by inscription.' *Journal of Pragmatics* 33: pp. 465–90.

Streek, J. (1993) 'Gesture as communication I: Its coordination with gaze and speech.' *Communication Monographs* 60: pp. 275–99.

Street, B. V. (1984) *Literacy in Theory and Practice*, Cambridge: Cambridge University Press.

—— (1988) 'Literacy practices and literacy myths.' In Säljö, R. ed. *The Written Word: Studies in Literate Thought and Action*, Language and Communication Series Vol. 23, Heidelberg: Springer-Verlag: pp. 59–72.

—— ed. (1993) *Cross-Cultural Approaches to Literacy*, Cambridge: Cambridge University Press.

—— (1998) 'New literacies in theory and practice: What are the implications for language in education?' *Linguistics and Education* 10(1): pp. 1–24.

—— (2000) 'Literacy events and literacy practices: Theory and practice in the new literacy studies.' In Martin-Jones, M. and Jones, K. eds. *Multilingual Literacies: Reading and Writing Different Worlds*, Amsterdam/Philadelphia: John Benjamins: pp. 17–29.

—— ed. (2005) *Literacies Across Educational Contexts*, Philadelphia, PA: Caslon.

—— (2008) 'New literacies, new times: Developments in literacy studies.' In Street, B. V. and Hornberger, N. eds. *Encyclopedia of Language and Education*, Volume 2: Literacy, New York: Springer: pp. 3–14.

Street, B. V. and Street, J. (1991) 'The schooling of literacy.' In Barton, D. and Ivanic, R. eds. *Writing in the Community*, London: Sage: pp. 143–66.

Suchman, L. (1987) *Plans and Situated Actions: The Problem of Human–Machine Communication*, Cambridge: Cambridge University Press.

—— (2000) 'Making a case: "Knowledge" and "routine" work in document production.' In Luff, P., Hindmarsh, J. and Heath, C. C. eds. *Workplace Studies: Recovering Work Practice and Informing System Design*, Cambridge: Cambridge University Press: pp. 29–45.

Sung, E. and Mayer, R. E. (2012) 'When graphics improve liking but not learning from online lessons.' *Computers in Human Behavior* 28(5): pp. 1618–25. 10.1016/j.chb.2012.03.026.

Sur, M. (2004) 'Rewiring cortex: Cross-modal plasticity and its implications for cortical development and function.' In Calvert, G., Spence, C. and Stein, B. E. eds. *The Handbook of Multisensory Processes*, Cambridge, MA: MIT Press.

Sutton-Spence, R. and Woll, B. (1999) *The Linguistics of British Sign Language: An Introduction*, Cambridge: Cambridge University Press.

Svensson, P. (2010) 'The landscape of digital humanities.' *Digital Humanities Quarterly* 4(1): http://digital-humanities.org/dhq/vol/4/1/000080/000080.html.

Sweller, J. and Chandler, P. (1994) 'Why some material is difficult to learn.' *Cognition and Instruction* 12: pp. 185–233.

Swetz, F. J. (1987) *Capitalism and Arithmetic*, La Salle, IL: Open Court.

Tartaglia, N. (1537) *La Nova Scientia*, Venice.

Tester, K. (2001) *Compassion, Morality and the Media*, Milton Keynes, UK: Open University Press.

Theeuwes, J., Kramer, A. F., Hahn, S. and Irwin, D. E. (1998) 'Our eyes do not always go where we want them to go: Capture of the eyes by new objects.' *Psychological Science* 9: pp. 379–85.

Thesen, L. (2001) 'Modes, literacies and power: A university case study.' *Language and Education* 14(2 and 3): pp. 132–45.

—— (2007) 'Breaking the frame: Lectures, ritual and academic literacies.' *Journal of Applied Linguistics* 4(1): pp. 33–53.

Thesen, L. and Van Pletzen, E. eds. (2006) *Academic Literacy and the Languages of Change*, London: Continuum.

Thibault, P. J. (2000) 'The multimodal transcription of a television advertisement: Theory and practice.' In Baldry, A. ed. *Multimodality and Multimediality in the Distance Learning Age*, Campobasso: Palladino: pp. 311–86.

Thompson, H. S. and McKelvie, D. (1997) 'Hyperlink semantics for standoff markup of read-only documents.' In *Proceedings of SGML Europe '97: The Next Decade – Pushing the Envelope*: pp. 227–29.

Thompson, J. (1990) *Ideology and Modern Culture*, Cambridge: Polity Press.

—— (1995) *Media and Democracy*, Cambridge: Polity Press.

Thomson, D. (2005) *Death in White Gloves*. Notes accompanying DVD of *Le Samouraï*, The Criterion Collection, FILMEL-CICC-TCP.

Thurlow, C. and Jaworski, A. (2010) *Tourism Discourse: The Language of Global Mobility*, Basingstoke: Palgrave Macmillan.

Titscher, S., Meyer, M., Wodak, R. and Vetter, E. (2000) 'Narrative semiotics.' In Titscher, S., Meyer, M., Wodak, R. and Vetter, E. *Methods of Text and Discourse Analysis*, London: Sage: pp. 125–35.

Toelken, B. (1969) 'The "pretty languages" of yellowman: Genre, mode, and texture in Navajo coyote narratives.' *Genre* 2(3): pp. 211–35.

—— (1987) 'Life and death in the Navajo coyote tales.' In Swann, B. and Krupat, A. eds. *Recovering the Word: Essays on Native American Literature*, Berkeley, CA: University of California Press: pp. 388–401.

Tomasello, M. (2003) *Constructing a Language: A Usage-based Theory of Language Acquisition*, London: Harvard University Press.

Tomlinson, J. (1999) *Globalization and Culture*, London: Sage.

Torfing, J. (1998) *New Theories of Discourse: Laclau and Mouffe and Žižek*, London: Blackwell.

Translation Directory, 'Trans-modal translation.' http://www.translationdirectory.com/articles/article2184.php [Retrieved 2012/06/26].

Trask, R. L. (1993) *A Dictionary of Grammatical Terms in Linguistics*, London: Routledge.

Trudgill, P. (1974) *The Social Differentiation of English in Norwich*, Cambridge: Cambridge University Press.

Tuan, Y.-F. and Hoelscher, S. (2001) *Space and Place: the Perspective of Experience*, 2nd edition, Minneapolis, MN: University of Minnesota Press.

Tunnicliffe, S. D. and Reiss, M. J. (1999) 'Students' understandings about animal skeletons.' *International Journal of Science Education* 21(11): pp. 1187–200.

Turner, V. (1982) *From Ritual to Theatre: The Human Seriousness of Play*, New York: PAJ Publications.

Underwood, G., Humphrey, K. and Foulsham, T. (2008) 'Knowledge-based patterns of remembering: Eye movement scanpaths reflect domain experience.' *HCI and Usability for Education and Work*, LNCS 5298, Berlin: Springer: pp. 125–44.

Unsworth, L. (2001) *Teaching Multiliteracies Across the Curriculum: Changing Contexts of Text and Image in Classroom Practice*, Buckingham, UK: Open University Press.

—— (2006a) 'Image/text relations and intersemiosis: towards multimodal text description for multiliteracies education.' Paper presented at the 33rd International Systemic Functional Congress (PUCSP, São Paulo, Brazil).

—— (2006b) 'Multiliteracies and a metalanguage of image/text relations: Implications for teaching English as a first or additional language in the 21st century.' In *Tales Out of School: Identity and English Language Teaching: Special edition of TESOL in Context*, Series S(1): pp. 147–62.

—— (2006c) 'Towards a metalanguage for multiliteracies education: Describing the meaning-making resources of language–image interaction.' *English Teaching: Practice and Critique* 5(1): pp. 55–76.

—— (2008) *Multiliteracies and Metalanguage: Describing Image/Text Relations as a Resource for Negotiating Multimodal Texts.* In Leu, D., Corio, J., Knobel, M. and Lankshear, C. eds. *Handbook of Research on New Literacies*, Mahwah, NJ: Erlbaum: pp. 377–405.

Unsworth, L. and Chan, E. (2008) 'Assessing integrative reading of images and text in group reading comprehension tests.' *Curriculum Perspectives* 28(3): pp. 71–76.

Unsworth, L. and Cléirigh, C. (2009) 'Towards a relational grammar of image–verbiage synergy: Intermodal representations.' In Dreyfus, S., Hood, S. and Stenglin, M. eds. *Online Proceedings for Semiotic Margins Conference*, Sydney, December 2007. At http://www.asfla.org.au.

Unsworth, L., Thomas, A., Simpson, A. and Asha, J. (2005) *Children's Literature and Computer Based Teaching*, Maidenhead, UK: Open University Press.

Urry, J. (2002) *The Tourist Gaze*, 2nd edition, London: Sage.

Uttal, D. H. (2000) 'Seeing the big picture: Map use and the development of spatial cognition.' *Developmental Science* 3(3): pp. 247–86.

Van der Putten, J. (2010) 'Comparing results from constant comparison and computer software methods: A reflection about qualitative data analysis.' *Journal of Ethnographic and Qualitative Research* 5: pp. 99–112.

Van Dijk, T. A. ed. (1985) *Handbook of Discourse Analysis*, London: Academic Press.

—— (1993) 'Principles of critical discourse analysis.' *Discourse and Society* 4(2): pp. 249–83.

—— (2012) *Discourse in Society* website. At http://www.discourses.org (accessed 2 May 2012).

Van Gog, T. and Scheiter, K. (2010) 'Eye tracking as a tool to study and enhance multimedia learning.' *Learning and Instruction* 20: pp. 95–99. doi:10.1016/j.learninstruc.2009.02.009.

Van Gog, T., Paas, F. and Van Merriënboer, J. J. G. (2005a) 'Uncovering expertise-related differences in troubleshooting performance: Combining eye movement and concurrent verbal protocol data.' *Applied Cognitive Psychology* 19: pp. 205–21.

Van Gog, T., Paas, F., Van Merriënboer, J. J. G. and Witte, P. (2005b) 'Uncovering the problem-solving process: Cued retrospective reporting versus concurrent and retrospective reporting.' *Journal of Experimental Psychology: Applied* 11: pp. 237–44.

Van Gog, T., Jarodzka, H., Scheiter, K., Gerjets, P. and Paas, F. (2009) 'Attention guidance during example study via the model's eye movements.' *Computers in Human Behavior* 25: pp. 785–91.

Van Gogh, V. (1978) *The Complete Letters of Vincent van Gogh*, Boston: New York Graphic Society.

Van Leeuwen, T. (1985) 'Rhythmic structure of the film text.' In Van Dijk, T. A. ed. *Discourse and Communication: New Approaches to the Analysis of Mass Media Discourse and Communication*, Berlin: Walter de Gruyter: pp. 216–32.

—— (1996) 'The representation of social actors.' In Coulthard, C. R. and Coulthard, M. eds. *Texts and Practices*, Routledge: New York: pp. 32–70.

—— (1998) 'Textual space and point of view.' Paper presented to the Museums Australia State Conference, *Who Sees, Who Speaks – Voices and Points of View in Exhibitions*, Australian Museum, September 21.

—— (1999) *Speech, Music, Sound*, London: Macmillan.

—— (2001) 'Semiotics and iconography.' In Van Leeuwen, T. and Jewitt, C. eds. *The Handbook of Visual Analysis*, London: Sage: pp. 92–111.

—— (2003) 'A multimodal perspective on composition.' In Ensrink, T. ed. *Framing and Perspectivising in Discourse*, Philadelphia, PA: John Benjamins.

—— (2005a) *Introducing Social Semiotics*, London: Routledge.

—— (2005b) 'Typographic meaning.' *Visual Communication* 4(2): pp. 138–43.

—— (2005c) 'Multimodality, genre and design.' In Norris, S. and Jones, R. H. eds. *Discourse in Action: Introducing Mediated Discourse Analysis*, London: Routledge: pp. 73–94.

—— (2006) 'Towards a semiotics of typography.' *Information Design Journal* 14(2): pp. 139–55.

—— (2008) 'New forms of writing, new visual competencies.' *Visual Studies* 23(2): pp. 130–35.

—— (2010) *The Language of Colour: An introduction*, London: Routledge.

—— (2012) 'Multimodality and multimodal research.' In Margolis, E. and Pauwels, L. eds. *The Sage Handbook of Visual Research Methods*, London: Sage: pp. 549–69.

Van Leeuwen, T. and Jewitt, C. eds. (2001) *Handbook of Visual Analysis*, London: Sage.

Van Leeuwen, T. and Jaworski, A. (2002) 'The discourses of war photography: Photojournalistic representations of the Palestinian – Israeli war.' *Journal of Language and Politics* 1(2): pp. 255–76.

Vanhoutte, E. and van den Branden, R. (2010) 'Text encoding initiative (TEI).' In Bates, M. and Maack, M. N. eds. *Encyclopedia of Library and Information Sciences (ELIS) 3rd edn*, chap. 512, New York: Taylor & Francis: pp. 5172–81. doi:10.1081/E-ELIS3-120043748. http://www.tandfonline.com/doi/abs/10.1081/E-ELIS3-120043748.

Ventola, E., Charles, C. and Kaltenbacher, M. eds. (2004) *Perspectives on Multimodality*, Amsterdam: John Benjamins.

Villa, D. (1999) *Politics, Philosophy, Terror: Essays on the Thought of Hannah Arendt*, Princeton, NJ: Princeton University Press.

Vinge, L. (1975) *The Five Senses: Studies in a Literary Tradition*, Lund: Royal Society of Letters at Lund.

Virilio, P. (1994) *The Vision Machine*, Indianapolis, IN: Indiana University Press.

Viviani, P. (1990) 'Eye movements in visual search: Cognitive, perceptual and motor control aspects.' *Reviews of Oculomotor Research* 4: pp. 353–93.

Voithofer, R. J. (2005) 'Designing new media education research: The materiality of data, representation, and dissemination.' *Educational Researcher* 34(9): pp. 3–14.

Vroomen, J. and de Gelder, B. (2004) 'Perceptual effects of cross-modal stimulation: Ventriloquism and the freezing phenomenon.' In Calvert, G., Spence, C. and Stein, B. E. eds. *The Handbook of Multisensory Processes*, Cambridge, MA: MIT Press.

Vygotsky, L. S. (1978) *Mind in Society: The Development of Higher Psychological Processes*, Cambridge, MA: Harvard University Press.

—— (1986) *Thought and Language*, translated from Russian by A. Kozulin, Cambridge, MA: MIT Press.

—— (1994) 'The problem of the cultural development of the child.' In Van der Veer, R. and Valsiner, J. eds. *The Vygotsky Reader*, Oxford: Blackwell: pp. 57–72.

—— (2004 [1930]) 'Imagination and creativity in childhood'. *Journal of Russian and Eastern Psychology* 42(1): pp. 7–97.

Wagner, D. (1993) *Literacy, Culture and Development: Becoming Literate in Morocco*, Cambridge University Press: Cambridge.

Walker, U. M. (1998) *Moral Understandings: A Feminist Study of Ethics*, London: Routledge.

Wallis, M., Popat, S., McKinney, J., Bryden, J. and Hogg, D. (2010) 'Embodied conversations: Performance and the design of a robotic dancing partner.' *Design Studies* 31(2): pp. 99–117.

Walsh, J. A. (2012) 'Comic Book Markup Language: An introduction and rationale.' *Digital Humanities Quarterly* 6(1). http://digitalhumanities.org/dhq/vol/6/1/000117/000117.html.

Walton, M. and Archer, A. (2004) 'The Web and "information literacy": Scaffolding the use of Web sources in a project-based curriculum.' *British Journal of Educational Technology* 35(2): pp. 173–86.

Walton, M. and Pallitt, N. (2012) '"Grand Theft South Africa": Games, literacy and inequality in consumer childhoods.' *Language and Education* 26(4): pp. 347–61.

Wartenberg, C. and Holmqvist, K. (2005) 'Daily newspaper layout-designers' predictions of reader behaviour: A case study.' Lund University Cognitive Studies 126. http://www.lucs.lu.se/LUCS/126/LUCS.126.pdf.

Wartofsky, M. (1979) *Models: Representation and the Scientific Understanding*, Dordrecht: Reidel.

—— (1983) 'From genetic epistemology to historical epistemology.' In Lieben, L. S. ed. *Piaget and the Foundations of Knowledge*, Hillsdale, NJ: Erlbaum: pp. 1–17.

Weingart, P., Engels, A. and Pansegrau, O. (2000) 'Risks of communication: Discourses on climate change in science, politics and the mass media.' *Public Understanding of Science* 9: pp. 261–83.

Weiser, M. (1991) 'The computer for the 21st century.' *Scientific American* 265(3): pp. 94–104.

Wertsch, J.V. (1985) *Vygotsky and the Social Formation of Mind*, Cambridge, MA: Harvard University Press.

—— (1991) *Voices of the Mind: A Sociocultural Approach to Mediated Action*, Cambridge, MA: Harvard University Press.

—— (2007) 'Mediation.' In Daniels, H., Cole, M. and Wertsch, J. V. eds. *The Cambridge Companion to Vygotsky*, New York: Cambridge University Press: pp. 178–92.

West, S. (2004) *Portraiture*, Oxford: Oxford University Press.

West, T. (2007) 'Multi-layered analysis of teacher–student interactions.' *Pedagogies* 2(3): pp. 139–50.

Whalen, J. (1995) 'A technology of order production: Computer-aided dispatch in public safety communications.' In ten Have, P. and Psathas, G. eds. *Situated Order: Studies in the Social Organisation of Talk and Embodied Activities*, Washington, DC: University Press of America: pp. 187–230.

Whalen, J. and Vinkhuyzen, E. (2000) 'Expert systems in (inter)action: Diagnosing document machine problems over the telephone.' In Luff, P., Hindmarsh, J. and Heath, C. eds. *Workplace Studies: Recovering Work Practice and Informing System Design*, Cambridge: Cambridge University Press: pp. 92–140.

Whalen, J., Whalen, M. and Henderson, K. (2002) 'Improvisational choreography in a teleservice work.' *British Journal of Sociology* 53: pp. 239–59.

White, P. R. R. (1994) 'Images of the shark: "Jaws," gold fish or cuddly toy? An analysis of the Australian Museum's Shark exhibition from a communicative perspective.' Unpublished monograph, Department of Linguistics, Sydney University.

—— (1997) 'Death, disruption and the moral order: The narrative impulse in mass-media "hard news" reporting.' In Christie, F. and Martin, J. R. eds. *Genre and Institutions: Social Processes in the Workplace and School*, London: Cassell: pp. 101–33.

—— (1998) 'Telling media tales: The news story as rhetoric.' PhD thesis, University of Sydney.

Widman, L. and Polansky, S. H. (1990) *Annonsläsning: En ögonrörelseundersökning av DN-läsare* [Advertisement Reading: An Eyetracking Study of DN-readers]. Stockholm: Dagens Nyheter.

Willett, R. (2009) 'Parodic practices: Amateur spoofs on video-sharing sites.' In Buckingham, D. and Willett, R. eds. *Video Cultures: Media Technology and Amateur Creativity*, Basingstoke: Palgrave Macmillan: pp. 115–32.

Williams, J. E. D. (1992) *From Sails to Satellites: The Origin and Development of Navigational Science*, Oxford: Oxford University Press.

Williamson, J. (1978) *Decoding Advertisements: Ideology and Meaning in Advertising*, London: Marion Boyars.

Winograd, T. and Flores, F. (1986) *Understanding Computers and Cognition: A New Foundation For Design*, Norwood, NJ: Addison-Wesley.

Wittenburg, P., Brugman, H., Russel, A., Klassmann, A. and Sloetjes, H. (2006) 'ELAN: A professional framework for multimodality research.' In *Proceedings of LREC 2006, Fifth International Conference on Language Resources and Evaluation*: pp. 1556–59. http://www.lat-mpi.eu/papers/papers-2006/elan-paper-final.pdf.

Wittgenstein, L. (1953) *Philosophical Investigations*, Oxford: Blackwell.

Wodak, R. (1996) *Disorders of Discourse*, London: Longman.

Wolcott, H. F. (1994) *Transforming Qualitative Data: Description, Analysis and Interpretation*, London: Sage.

Woolf, D. R. (1986) 'Speech, text, and time: The sense of hearing and the sense of the past in renaissance England.' *Albion* 18(2): pp. 167–84.

Wortham, S. (2001) *Narrative in Action: A Strategy for Research and Analysis*, New York: Teachers College Press.

511

—— (2008) 'Linguistic anthropology of education.' *Annual Review of Anthropology* 37(3): pp. 1–15. At http://arjournals.annualreviews.org/doi/pdf/10.1146/annurev.anthro.36.081406.04401.

Wyatt-Smith, C. and Kimber, K. (2009) 'Working multimodally: Challenges for assessment.' *English Teaching: Practice and Critique* 8(3): pp. 70–90.

Wyler, S. (2006) 'Colour terms between elegance and beauty.' In Plümacher, M. and Holz, P. eds. *Speaking of Colors and Odors*, Amsterdam: John Benjamins: pp. 113–28.

Yeager, P. ed. (1996) *The Geography of Identity*, Ann Arbor, MI: University of Michigan Press.

Zammit, K. and Callow, J. (1998) 'Ideology and technology: A visual and textual analysis of two popular CD-ROM programs.' *Linguistics and Education* 10(1): pp. 89–105.

Zammit, K. and Downes, T. (2002) 'New learning environments and the multiliterate individual.' *Australian Journal of Language and Literacy* 25(2): pp. 25–36.

Index

Note: glossary terms are shown in **bold**.

9 781138 245198

An environmentally friendly book printed and bound in England by www.printondemand-worldwide.com

PEFC Certified

This product is
from sustainably
managed forests
and controlled
sources

PEFC™
PEFC/16-33-415

www.pefc.org

This book is made of chain-of-custody materials; FSC materials for the cover and PEFC materials for the text pag

Reprint of # - C8 - 246/174/31 - PB - Lamination Matt - Printed on 16-Jul-18 06:47